LEASEHOLD ENFRANCHISEMENT

AUSTRALIA AND NEW ZEALAND
The Law Book Company Ltd.
Sydney: Melbourne: Perth

CANADA AND U.S.A.
The Carswell Company Ltd.
Agincourt, Ontario

INDIA
N.M. Tripathi Private Ltd.
Bombay
and
Eastern Law House Private Ltd.
Calcutta and Delhi
M.P.P. House
Bangalore

ISRAEL
Steimatzky's Agency Ltd.
Jerusalem: Tel Aviv: Haifa

MALAYSIA: SINGAPORE: BRUNEI
Malayan Law Journal (Pte.) Ltd.
Singapore and Kuala Lumpur

PAKISTAN
Pakistan Law House
Karachi

LEASEHOLD ENFRANCHISEMENT

SECOND EDITION

By

N. T. HAGUE, Q.C.

M.A., LL.B.(CANTAB.)

of Lincoln's Inn, Barrister-at-Law

LONDON

SWEET & MAXWELL

1987

First Edition 1967
Second Edition 1987

Published by
Sweet & Maxwell Limited of
11 New Fetter Lane, London.
Computerset by Burgess & Son (Abingdon) Limited.
Printed and bound in Great Britain by
Butler & Tanner Limited, Frome, Somerset

British Library Cataloguing in Publication Data
Hague, N.T.
Leasehold enfranchisement.—2nd ed.
1. Leases—England
I. Title
344.2064'346 KD899

ISBN 0-421-28360-2

PREFACE

NEARLY 20 years have elapsed since the Leasehold Reform Act 1967 came into force and the first edition of this book was published. In the meantime, many points of law have been determined by the courts, and there have been numerous decisions of the Lands Tribunal and (since 1980) leasehold valuation tribunals on valuation matters arising under the Act. In addition, Parliament has amended the 1967 Act in several important respects, notably by extending the rateable value limits and making other amendments by section 118 of and Schedule 8 to the Housing Act 1974. I have ventured a good deal of criticism of the latter amendments (see paragraphs 1–15 *et seq.*), but they have had the welcome side-effect of keeping me in steady employment and I must not be thought ungrateful to the Parliament which saw fit to enact them. All these matters have been duly incorporated into the text, and I have also endeavoured to give guidance on other points which happen to have come my way or which appear likely to cause difficulty. The reader is, I hope, given due warning when an opinion expressed is my own and either unsupported by, or contrary to, authority.

The format of this book remains similar to that of the first edition, with one important difference. In the first edition, valuation matters received only the briefest of attention, amounting to no more than a few lines. Now, however, there is a full new Chapter 9 ("Valuation"), containing 53 pages, in which I have endeavoured to set out in some detail the relevant law and the valuation principles and practice which have evolved. Chapter 9 also contains some typical worked examples, which I hope will be of assistance to those concerned with the valuation aspects of claims under the Act. I have also added a new section on "Avoiding the Act" to Chapter 17, together with two new Chapters dealing with section 153 of the Law of Property Act 1925 and the Places of Worship (Enfranchisement) Act 1920 as amended.

My thanks are due to several professional colleagues who have kindly allowed me to pick their brains and draw on their knowledge and experience in this somewhat specialised area of the law; in particular, I should mention Mr. Simon Berry, of these chambers, and Mr. David Neuberger, Q.C. On the valuation side, over the years I have had the privilege of working closely with several able surveyors, who have instructed me as to the arts and techniques made necessary by the difficult valuation provisions of the Act; in particular, I should mention Mr. Michael Hopper F.R.I.C.S. and the members of Messrs. Gerald Eve & Co. Without that instruction Chapter 9 could not have been written; but I must emphasise that the statements and views expressed in that

Chapter are mine alone. My thanks are again due to my wife who has typed the major part of the text and footnotes. I am grateful to the publishers, who must frequently have despaired of ever receiving completed scripts, for their patience and assistance and for the preparation of the tables of cases and statutes. My thanks are also due to Mr. John Pugh-Smith of Gray's Inn, barrister, for preparation of the index.

The law is stated as at May 1, 1987.

NIGEL HAGUE

LINCOLN'S INN
May 8, 1987

CONTENTS

CONTENTS

TABLE OF CASES

TABLE OF STATUTES

[The references in **bold** type denote material set out in the appendices.]

TABLE OF STATUTORY INSTRUMENTS

[The references in **bold** type denote material set out in the appendices.]

Chapter 1

INTRODUCTION

THE term "leasehold enfranchisement" has for many years been used to describe the principle that leaseholders should be enabled to become freeholders, by the compulsory purchase of the fee simple of their holdings, together with any intervening leasehold interests. Prior to the Leasehold Reform Act 1967 there was no Act of a general nature[1] facilitating enfranchisement. **1–01**

1. Background

Early history

There is nothing at all new in the idea of leasehold enfranchisement, for it appears to have started as a serious political demand in about 1880. The subject was much debated before the Royal Commission on the Housing of the Working Classes, 1884–85, and in a special supplementary report,[2] ten of its fifteen members[3] concluded that "legislation favourable to the acquisition on equitable terms of the freehold interest on the part of the leaseholder would conduce greatly to the improvement of the dwellings of the people of this country." On the other hand, Lord Salisbury, in a dissenting report, thought that such legislation would do little, if anything, towards improving the housing of the poor, that it might entirely arrest the grant of building leases, and that "the supply of new houses for the working classes in suburban districts would be very materially checked." A short time previously, the first Bill to enable leaseholders to purchase their freeholds had been introduced into Parliament.[4] In 1886, a Select Committee on Town Holdings was appointed to inquire (among other matters) into "the expediency of giving the Leaseholders facilities for the Purchase of the Fee Simple of their Property." The Select Committee recommended[5] that there should be no general scheme of leasehold enfranchisement, but that local authorities should be given powers to compel enfranchisement in suitable areas. The recommendations neither of the Royal Commission nor the **1–02**

---

[1] s.153, Law of Property Act 1925 and the Places of Worship (Enfranchisement) Act 1920 are both very limited in scope: see para. 1–04.

[2] Reports from Commissioners, 1884–85, Vol. 30.

[3] Including Cardinal Manning.

[4] Leaseholders (Facilities of Purchase of Fee Simple) Bill 1884.

[5] Reports from Committees, 1889, Vol. 7.

Select Committee were ever implemented, and none of the numerous Leasehold Enfranchisement Bills subsequently introduced into Parliament ever reached the Statute Book.

The Jenkins Committee Report

1–03 In 1948, a Leasehold Committee was appointed to consider, *inter alia*, leasehold enfranchisement. In its Final Report[6] presented in June 1950, the majority of the Committee under the chairmanship of Jenkins L.J.[7] recommended against any measure of leasehold enfranchisement. But they did recommend that the protection of the Rent Acts should be given to long leaseholders at the expiry of their terms, a recommendation which was subsequently implemented by Part I of the Landlord and Tenant Act 1954. However, a minority of the Committee (Mr. A. L. Ungoed-Thomas, K.C.,[8] and Mr. C. L. Hale, M.P.) recommended that occupying ground lessees of dwelling-houses should have the right of leasehold enfranchisement by compulsory purchase of the fee simple and any intermediate reversions.[9] While Part I of the Leasehold Reform Act 1967 broadly followed the recommendations of the Minority Report, it differed from those recommendations in many respects, and in particular on the important question of the purchase price payable by the tenant for the landlord's interest.

Previous legislation

1–04 Prior to the Leasehold Reform Act 1967, there were only two statutes enabling a tenant to acquire the freehold of his holding. Both of these are of only minor importance.

(a) *Section 153, Law of Property Act 1925*

This section makes provision for the enlargement of the residues of very long terms into fee simple estates. It applies only where (i) the term originally created was for at least 300 years, of which no less than 200 years remain unexpired[10]; (ii) there is no rent of any money value payable[11]; and (iii) the lease is not liable to be determined by re-entry for

---

[6] (1950) Cmnd. 7982.

[7] The first chairman was Lord Uthwatt, who died in 1949, Jenkins L.J. (later Lord Jenkins of Ashley Gardens) being appointed in his place.

[8] Later Ungoed-Thomas J.

[9] The author, although of a different political persuasion to the minority, has always found the minority report wholly convincing, and considers it regrettable (and in the long run, disadvantageous to landlords) that its recommendations were not implemented.

[10] subs. (1).

[11] subss. (1)(*b*), (4).

breach of covenant.[12] The section is thus of limited application. It is set out in Appendix B and is discussed in detail in Chapter 18.

(b) *Places of Worship (Enfranchisement) Act 1920*

This Act gave a right of compulsory purchase of the freehold to the trustees of churches, chapels and other places of worship held on leases originally granted for terms of at least twenty-one years. The Act was extended by the Leasehold Reform Act 1967[13] to cover also any minister's house or caretaker's house used in connection with a place of worship. The Act, as amended by the 1967 Act and other legislation, is set out in Appendix B and is discussed in detail in Chapter 19.

The 1966 White Paper

Generally

The White Paper on Leasehold Reform in England and Wales,[14] which was published on February 18, 1966, set out the (Labour) Government's intention to introduce a Bill to enable a long leaseholder to acquire compulsorily either the freehold or a 50-year extension of his existing lease. The White Paper is based on the doubtful proposition that there is something basically unjust to tenants in the long leasehold system, and that it had conferred undue benefits on landlords.[15] Thus, the White Paper asserted that the system "has worked very unfairly against the occupying leaseholder,"[16] and that it was "quite indefensible, if justice is to be done as between freeholder and occupying leaseholder, that at the end of the term, the law should allow the ownership of the house to revert to the freeholder without his paying anything for it so that he gets not only the land but also the house, the improvements and everything the leaseholder and his predecessors have added to it."[17] 1–05

"Equity"

The White Paper is notable chiefly for the first appearance of a new so-called "principle" on which the compensation provisions of Part I of the Leasehold Reform Act 1967 (as originally enacted)[18] were based. The 1–06

[12] subs. (2)(i).
[13] s.40. There were other minor amendments.
[14] (1966) Cmnd. 2916.
[15] For an alternative and preferable justification for enfranchisement, see para. 1–08.
[16] Para. 1.
[17] *Ibid.*
[18] ss.9(1), 15(2).

principle is "that the land belongs in equity to the land owner and the house belongs in equity to the occupying leaseholder."[19] This involved a radical departure from the ordinary rule that whatever is attached to the soil becomes part of it ("*quicquid plantatur solo, solo cedit*").[20] Why the principle applies only to an occupying leaseholder, as opposed to *e.g.* one who has erected or improved a house but then sub-let, was not made clear.

The White Paper's use of the word "equity" in this context has attracted a good deal of well-merited criticism.[21] It is clear that the word is used strictly in a political "social justice" sense, and not in the lawyer's sense. Moreover, in the view of the author,[22] the White Paper's "principle" in fact operates contrary to normal concepts of social justice. It was no doubt intended to reflect the position at the grant of a normal 99-year building lease, under which the landlord reserved a "ground rent" and the builder erected a building, the latter making his profit by selling the lease with the building erected. At that point, however, the reversion was so remote that its value reflected only the ground rent it carried, and the question of who the building belonged to in "equity" was of no practical importance. But for many years prior to the White Paper, landlords and tenants had been dealing with long tenancies on the basis that the building as well as the land would revert to the landlord at the end of the tenancy. So many landlords had purchased and had their reversions valued (*e.g.* for estate duty purposes), and nearly all tenants had purchased their tenancies, on that basis. By 1967, many Victorian building leases were due to expire shortly. The application of the White Paper's "principle" in such cases deprived the landlord of a substantial part of the true value of his reversion and simply transferred it to the tenant, who made a windfall gain. Although the 1967 Act was passed primarily to meet the anxieties of ordinary householders in South Wales and other areas where the long leasehold system was widespread, it is notorious that the persons who in fact derived most benefit from the 1967 Act were relatively wealthy purchasers of short residues of long tenancies of houses in Belgravia, Chelsea, Kensington, Westminster and similar expensive areas of London, just under the £400 Greater London rateable value limit.

---

[19] Para. 4, cited by Lord Denning M.R. in *Official Custodian of Charities* v. *Goldridge* (1973) 26 P. & C.R. 191 at p. 204. See also para. 14.

[20] *Minshall* v. *Lloyd* (1837) 2 M. & W. 450 at p. 459; and see Megarry and Wade *The Law of Real Property* (5th ed.), p. 731.

[21] See *e.g.* Megarry and Wade, *supra*, p. 1127; the preface to Cheshire, *Modern Real Property* (10th ed.) ("the White Paper's analysis might not perhaps have amused Lord Nottingham"); and Cheshire and Burn, *Modern Law of Real Property* (13th ed.), p. 472.

[22] Who nevertheless supports the principle of enfranchisement for rather different reasons; see para. 1–08.

Flats and maisonettes

Only houses, and not flats and maisonettes, are affected by Part I of the Leasehold Reform Act 1967.[23] The White Paper gave the reason for this limitation as follows[24]: "The system of long leases for flats has arisen only in recent years. Different considerations of equity apply and there would be many practical difficulties in providing for enfranchisement of flats." As to what are "the different considerations of equity" referred to, the author has never heard any plausible suggestions and is unable to offer any satisfactory explanation. The arguments in the White Paper,[25] and also other justifications for enfranchisement,[26] seem clearly to apply with equal force to flats and maisonettes. The cynic's explanation would be that in the 1960s there was little political demand for enfranchisement of flats and maisonettes (a situation which is now changing). **1–07**

The practical difficulties referred to are technical conveyancing difficulties. "Flying freeholds or freeholds in the air give rise to peculiarly difficult conveyancing problems."[27] The main problems arise from the fact that the burden of a positive covenant does not run with the land.[28] As long ago as 1965 the Wilberforce Committee Report on Positive Covenants Affecting Land[29] made recommendations for dealing with these problems, in particular to enable flats to be sold freehold, but these recommendations have not been implemented. More recently, the Law Commission has proposed the assimilation of the law regarding positive and negative covenants into a single law of "land obligations,"[30] and has published a draft Land Obligations Bill for that purpose.[31] But "the history of this project is long and sad,"[32] and despite the Law Commission's stress on the urgency of the matter, it seems likely to be some time before the necessary legislation is enacted.

Furthermore, if flats and maisonettes are sold freehold, practical difficulties arise as to proper arrangements for the repair of the block in which they are situate, the maintenance of the common parts, the provision of common services and the general management of the block.

---

[23] s.2.
[24] Para. 8.
[25] See para. 1–05.
[26] See para. 1–08.
[27] *Gaidowski* v. *Gonville & Caius College, Cambridge* [1975] 1 W.L.R. 1066 *per* Ormrod L.J. at p. 1069H.
[28] Megarry and Wade, *supra*, at p. 761.
[29] (1965) Cmnd. 2719.
[30] 17th Report of Law Commission (1981–82) No. 119, para. 249.
[31] Report on Law of Positive and Negative Covenants (1984) Law Com. No. 127, Appendix A.
[32] 17th Report (1981–82) No. 119, para. 2.49. See also 11th Report (1975–6) No. 78, para. 17; 13th Report (1977–8) No. 92, para. 2.30; and 16th Report (1980–1) No. 113, para. 2.54; and (1972 B) 31 C.L.J. 157 (H.W.R. Wade).

The Law Commission in its report proposed the individual developers should be able to create their own schemes for freehold ownership within the framework of the draft Land Obligations Bill.[33] It is, however, doubtful if this would be satisfactory, particularly if the 1967 Act is to be extended to flats and maisonettes.[34] In practice, it is likely that legislation analagous to the New South Wales Strata Titles Act or the American "condominium" legislation will be necessary to ensure proper maintenance and management. In May 1986 the Lord Chancellor appointed a committee to consider these matters. Any extension of the 1967 Act to flats and maisonettes will almost certainly have to be delayed to await the outcome of the committee's deliberations.

The above conveyancing problems do not however apply as regards leases of any length. There are no technical legal obstacles to conferring on occupying leaseholders of flats and maisonettes rights to extended leases,[35] although practical management difficulties would be likely to arise in many instances.

Alternative justification for enfranchisement

1–08 As mentioned above, the author does not agree with the "moral entitlement" arguments of the White Paper. Nevertheless, the author does broadly agree with the statement in the White Paper that the long leasehold system "has worked very unfairly against the occupying leaseholder,"[36] and considers that enfranchisement at a proper price[37] was a justifiable (and indeed necessary) reform in the public interest, for rather different reasons. These stem from the inherently unsatisfactory nature of an occupying leaseholder's interest[38] during the last 50 or so years of his term. While there is an outstanding residue of more than that length, the fact that the lease will one day come to an end is usually of little practical consequence. The lease retains more or less its full value, and remains readily marketable. When there are less than 50 years to run, the lease[39] starts to become a depreciating asset, although the depreciation

[33] See (1984) Law Com. No. 127, paras. 7.1 *et seq* and 22.1 *et seq.*

[34] The defective drafting of many existing leasehold flat schemes does nothing to encourage the view that matters can safely be left to individual draftsmen.

[35] *Cf.* Housing Act 1985, ss.118(1)(*a*), 139(1)(*a*) and Sched. 7, Part III (grant of lease pursuant to the "right to buy" of a secure tenant).

[36] (1966) Cmnd. 2916, para. 1.

[37] See para. 1–10.

[38] His interest of a different kind to the purely investment interest of the freeholder (or a leaseholder who has sub-let). The property is his home, and therefore of a special importance to him quite apart from the money it represents.

[39] Which is usually the leaseholder's only capital interest of any substance.

does not become too serious until there are only 35 or so years left. From then on, however, the depreciation gathers increasing momentum, and becomes progressively more acute.[40]

When depreciation starts to have a serious impact on an occupying leaseholder his position becomes an unfortunate one. His home has become a depreciating asset, and the capital locked up in it starts being whittled away by the passage of time at an increasing rate. If he wishes to continue living there, the only practical and effective way he can preserve its full value is to acquire the freehold or the grant of a longer lease. If on the other hand he wishes to sell and move elsewhere, he has great difficulty in realising the proper value of his interest, partly because of the problems encountered by potential purchasers in obtaining mortgage facilities, but mainly because of the unsatisfactory nature of the shorter lease. Take, for instance, a 25-year term. It lacks the permanence to attract the ordinary house-purchaser, who would immediately land himself in the difficulties outlined above.[41]

For practical purposes, these factors render it essential for a leaseholder 1–09
to negotiate the purchase of the freehold, or the grant of a longer term, from his landlord. Here lies the crux of the matter, for (in the absence of legislation) the landlord holds all the cards in any such negotiation. He can refuse to sell or grant a new lease altogether, whether his reasons are good or bad. He can dictate any price and any terms he likes, generous, reasonable or extortionate. He can adopt a "take-it-or-leave-it" attitude, knowing full well that the tenant has no real option except to take it. The landlord is the only person from whom the leaseholder can obtain the freehold or a longer lease, and so has a completely monopolistic and unassailable negotiating position. There are few comparable situations where the bargaining powers are quite so unequal. Prior to the passing of the 1967 Act many landlords (particularly "family landlords") were in fact willing to sell reversions at a fair price or grant longer leases on reasonable terms, but "company landlords and some well-known public bodies more often operated strictly on commercial principles with little or no consideration of the interests of the lessees,"[42] and a few were totally unreasonable and unco-operative. The landlords who took an undue advantage of their bargaining position were in a minority, but it was their

[40] See *e.g.* the Table in Capital Gains Taxes Act 1979, Sched. 3, which provides for the value of leaseholds to be notionally written down for the purposes of calculating gains or losses in connection with capital gains tax.

[41] It is sometimes suggested that the purchaser can regard the purchase price as commuted rent in advance, but this is hardly realistic.

[42] The Law Society's view set out in a White Paper on residential leasehold property—Summary of Report by Professional Bodies (1962) Cmnd. 1789, p. 6.

activities which were largely responsible for the justified sense of grievance felt by some leaseholders.[43]

In the view of the author, this situation called for redress prior to 1967, and likewise calls for redress today as regards flats and other properties outside the 1967 Act, in order to put the parties into a more equal bargaining position. No solution other than enfranchisement, or the grant of a longer lease, appears practicable. In addition, the fact that the property will revert to the freeholder at the end of the term acts as a positive disincentive on the leaseholder to modernise and make improvements, or to effect repairs beyond what may be necessary to avoid a dilapidations claim, which is removed by enfranchisement or the grant of a new lease.

Objections to enfranchisement

Purchase price

1–10 The main and most frequently voiced objections to enfranchisement and to the Leasehold Reform Act 1967 centre on the purchase price to be paid by the tenant for the landlord's interest.[44] Thus one critic of the 1967 Act has stated that "its object was merely to enrich certain tenants at the expense of their landlords."[45] It has to be accepted that some proponents of enfranchisement regard it as being an essential ingredient, or at any rate an inevitable consequence, of enfranchisement, that the tenant is enabled to acquire the freehold at a lower price than its true value.[46] However, that is not really so, and the objection is less than fair to responsible advocates of enfranchisement. For it is really not an objection to enfranchisement as a principle, but to the financial terms upon which enfranchisement should be granted.

The view of the author is that, contrary to the assertions of the 1966 White Paper,[47] there was and is no real justification for enfranchisement at any price other than at the full market value of the landlord's interest, subject to two qualifications. First, by the time the 1967 Act came to be enacted, Part I of the Landlord and Tenant Act 1954 had been in operation for several years and had already affected the market value of

---

[43] In Cardiff, which was developed almost entirely on 99-year leases granted mainly in the later part of the 19th century and where there are consequently large numbers of leases with under 35 years to run, the terms quoted by different landlords showed wide differences, which itself caused "a lot of feeling."

[44] The objection to the 1967 Act is to the rent payable under s.15(2) during the 50-year extension of an extended lease, which effectively results in all value in the buildings being transferred without compensation to the tenant.

[45] H.W.R. Wade *Administrative Law* (5th ed.), p. 686.

[46] See *e.g.* Jenkins Committee Final Report (1950) Cmnd. 7982, paras. 62 and 89.

[47] 1966 Cmnd. 2916: see para. 1–06.

residential properties subject to long leases. The price ought to take the effect of the 1954 Act into account. Secondly, it would not be at all unfair for improvements wholly effected by the tenant and for which the landlord has given no consideration to be ignored. A purchase price calculated on this basis was recommended by the minority of the Jenkins Committee,[48] and in retrospect it is unfortunate that this recommendation was not implemented. Such a basis also appears to have been intended by Parliament for higher rateable value properties under section 9(1A) of the 1967 Act, introduced by section 118 of the Housing Act 1974. But the relevant provisions were badly drafted, and enabled their intention to be defeated.[49] The defects have now been partly remedied by section 23 of the Housing and Planning Act 1986.[49a]

Other objections

Certain other objections to the principle of enfranchisement should be noted: **1–11**

(a) *Sanctity of contract.* It is said that enfranchisement involves interference with existing contractual and property rights. This argument is a somewhat battered veteran, invariably deployed against any reform concerning contractual or property relationships. But there is no valid objection to interference by the legislature when such relationships have become out of balance. There are many justifiable examples, of which the Rent Acts, the Agricultural Holdings Act and the Landlord and Tenant Act 1954 are the most obvious in the landlord and tenant field.

(b) *Compulsory purchase.* It is said that enfranchisement involves the compulsory purchase by one individual of another's property.[50] It is difficult to see any objection to this provided proper compensation is paid. For in such circumstances the argument amounts to little more than saying that an individual has a right to invest in a particular kind of property, and few would subscribe to such a proposition. It is also said that compulsory purchase is only justified if the property is purchased by a public or local authority or by statutory undertakers and used for public purposes, and that a compulsory purchase by an individual for his own private purposes cannot be in the public interest.[51] This reasoning is fallacious, for the concept of public interest is not confined to actual uses

---

[48] (1950) Cmnd. 7982 Minority Report para. 111.

[49] See paras. 9–42 *et seq.*

[49a] See para. 9–43.

[50] This argument has been unsuccessfully deployed before the European Court of Human Rights at Strasbourg: see paras. 1–24 *et seq.*

[51] It is of interest that the majority of the Jenkins Committee, although recommending against leasehold enfranchisement (see para. 1–03), were not deterred by this objection from recommending that freeholders be entitled to acquire compulsorily the interests of intervening tenants: (1950) Cmnd. 7982, para. 114.

by the public or for public purposes. It may well be desirable in the public interest for property rights to be compulsorily adjusted in favour of individuals. Historical examples include the Inclosure Acts, which in effect provided for the extensive compulsory acquisition by individuals even of common lands, where not one but many individuals had rights. More modern examples include section 428 of the Companies Act 1985 (a 90 per cent. successful take-over bidder can acquire compulsorily the shares of the dissentient 10 per cent.) and section 191 Law of Property Act 1925, as amended by the Rentcharges Act 1977 (compulsory redemption of rentcharges).

(c) *Retrospective legislation.* It is said that enfranchisement involves retrospective legislation,[52] but this involves a fundamental misconception. Any existing state of affairs is the result of past actions, and so almost all legislation in the landlord and tenant field is thus in a wide sense "retrospective." However, legislation is only objectionable as retrospective legislation if it applies directly to past acts, and not if it relates only to the present state of affairs brought about by past acts.

(d) *Fragmentation of estates.* It is said that enfranchisement would lead to a damaging fragmentation of estates, and the loss of beneficial unified control. This argument has limited validity, because many estates were fragmented long before the 1967 Act was passed, and in others no attempt was made to enforce any amenity covenants for the benefit of the whole. So the argument is really one for exemption or modification in particular cases, which was partially met by section 19 of the 1967 Act.[53]

2. The Leasehold Reform Act 1967

Outline

1–12 Part I of the 1967 Act, which mainly[54] came into operation on January 1, 1968, gave effect to the proposals outlined in the 1966 White Paper.[55] The following is the basic framework of Part I.[56] A tenant of a leasehold house,[57] who is in occupation of the whole or part of the house as his only or main residence, is entitled to acquire either the freehold or a lease extended by 50 years, if all the following conditions are fulfilled:

[52] A similar argument was used by Conservative spokesmen to restrict the effect of the Leasehold Reform Act 1979 to future avoidance devices only: see para. 1–19. But the argument was conveniently ignored shortly afterwards on the enactment of the "right to buy" provisions of the Housing Act 1980 (now Part V Housing Act 1985).

[53] See Chap. 10.

[54] Certain transitional provisions contained in ss.34–36 came into force immediately the Act was passed on October 27, 1967: s.41(4).

[55] Leasehold Reform Act 1967 Commencement Order 1967 (S.I. No. 1836).

[56] Set out in s.1(1).

[57] But not a flat or maisonette: s.2(1).

(a) His tenancy is a "long tenancy," *i.e.* a tenancy granted for an original term of more than 21 years, or granted by way of extension of such a tenancy.[58]
(b) His tenancy is "at a low rent," *i.e.* at a rent of not more than two-thirds of the 1965 rateable value.[59]
(c) The rateable value of the property in question on March 23, 1965, was not more than £400 in Greater London or £200 elsewhere.[60] These limits have now been increased in relation to the rateable value on April 1, 1973.[61]
(d) At the date of the tenant's claim, he has been occupying the whole or part of the house as his only or main residence for the previous three (originally five) years or for at least three (originally five) years in the previous ten years.[62] A tenant may also count the occupation of a deceased tenant who was a member of his family and with whom he was residing towards the qualifying period of residence.[63]

A tenant who wishes to exercise his rights under the Act must serve a Notice of Leaseholder's Claim in a prescribed form.[64] If he wishes to acquire the freehold, this must be conveyed to him, and detailed provisions are made concerning the contents of the conveyance or transfer and the discharge of mortgages, rentcharges and other incumbrances affecting the landlord's interest.[65] The purchase price is the market value of the reversion, but if the lease has not already been extended under the Act, on the assumption that it was to be so extended.[66] If the tenant wishes to acquire an extended lease, he must be granted a term equal to the residue of his existing lease plus 50 years[67]; but during the 50-year extension the rent is increased to a revised modern ground rent of the site (without including anything for the value of the building on the site).[68]

Provision is made for cases where the landlord wishes to redevelop or occupy the house himself,[69] and for comprehensively managed estates[70];

---

[58] ss.1(1)(*a*), 3.
[59] ss.1(1)(*a*), 4; but see the proviso to s.4(1).
[60] ss.1(1)(*b*), (4).
[61] s.1(5)(6), added by Housing Act 1974, s.118.
[62] s.1(1)(*b*), (2), amended by the Housing Act 1980, Sched. 1, Part 1.
[63] s.7.
[64] s.5 and Sched. 3, para. 6.
[65] ss.8, 10–13.
[66] s.9(1), amended by the Housing Act 1969, s.82. A different basis of valuation applies if the 1973 rateable value exceeds £1,000 in Greater London or £500 elsewhere: see para. 9–15.
[67] s.14.
[68] s.15(2).
[69] ss.17, 18.
[70] s.19.

and there are special rules where the landlord is a local authority or other public body.[71] Contracting out is not permitted,[72] and there are further provisions regarding tenancies held in trust,[73] missing landlords,[74] ecclesiastical land,[75] Crown land[76] and other miscellaneous matters. With certain exceptions, the county court has jurisdiction in matters of dispute,[77] other than matters of valuation which are determined by leasehold valuation tribunals[78] (originally the Lands Tribunal).[79] Part I of the 1967 Act also included certain transitional provisions relating to tenants otherwise qualified whose leases expired after December 8, 1964.[80]

Part II of the 1967 Act

1-13 Part II of the 1967 Act made certain amendments to Part I of the Landlord and Tenant Act 1954 and the Rent Act 1965.[81] These amendments are outside the scope of this book and are not further discussed. Part II also amended[82] the Places of Worship (Enfranchisement) Act 1920, discussed in Chapter 19.

3. Subsequent Legislation

Section 82 of the Housing Act 1969

1-14 In two early cases before the Lands Tribunal,[83] it was ruled that the tenant himself must be considered a competitor in hypothetical open market stipulated by section 9(1) of the 1967 Act, so that the purchase price should reflect "the tenant's bid."[84] Section 82 of the Housing Act 1969 reversed that ruling by excluding "the tenant and members of his family residing in the house" from those "buying or seeking to buy."[85]

---

71 ss.28–30.
72 s.23.
73 s.6.
74 s.27.
75 s.31.
76 s.33.
77 s.20.
78 Housing Act 1980, s.141 and Sched. 22. An appeal lies to the Lands Tribunal.
79 s.22 of the 1967 Act.
80 ss.34, 35.
81 ss.38, 39 and Sched. 5.
82 ss.40 and Sched. 6.
83 *Custins* v. *Hearts of Oak Benefit Society* (1969) 209 E.G. 239 and *Haw* v. *Peek* (1969) 210 E.G. 347.
84 See further para. 9–17.
85 The amendment was not, however, carried through into the new s.9(1A) introduced by Housing Act 1974 s.118: *Norfolk* v. *Trinity College, Cambridge* (1976) 32 P. & C.R. 147, L.T: see para. 9–40.

Section 118 of and Schedule 8 to the Housing Act 1974

These provisions substantially amended the 1967 Act in four respects: 1–15
(1) by increasing the qualifying rateable value limits; (2) by extending the time-limits for applications under section 19 in respect of areas containing houses within the increased rateable value limits; (3) by altering the basis of valuation of the freehold in the case of houses within the increased rateable value limits; and (4) by providing machinery for a notional reduction in rateable value attributable to improvements made by the tenant or any previous tenant. Unfortunately, these provisions, particular (3) and (4), are badly drafted and give rise to the numerous and serious difficulties mentioned below.

The Parliamentary history whereby the above provisions came to be enacted can only be described as farcical, and reflects badly on the legislative process.[86] Briefly, what happened is as follows. On April 1, 1973, new rating valuation lists had come into force in which 1965 rateable values were increased on average by 150 per cent. The 1973 equivalents of the 1965 rateable values of the 1967 Act of £400 in Greater London and £200 elsewhere[87] were thus £1,000 and £500. The Bill, introduced by the then recently-elected Labour Government, which eventually became the Housing Act 1974 therefore contained an innocuous and non-controversial consequential clause[88] substituting the latter figures in cases of new or converted houses where "the appropriate day" (*i.e.* the day when the house first appeared in the valuation list)[89] fell on or after April 1, 1973. At the Committee stage in the Commons, the Conservative Opposition introduced[90] and, with the help of three rebel Government supporters, obtained the passing of an amendment raising the rateable value limits to £1,500 and £750, although only in respect of leases granted prior to March 23, 1965. The argument for limiting the raised limits to such leases was that it would otherwise be unfair to landlords who had granted long leases in the belief that they would be unaffected by the 1967 Act; but the argument is not really a tenable one.[91]

---

[86] The author has been greatly assisted in writing this account by a lucid summary prepared by the late Sir Noel Hutton, Q.C., formerly Chief Parliamentary Counsel, which begins: "No-one is going to believe the following story but it is as true as the writer can make it."

[87] s.1(1)(*a*).

[88] Reproducing a similar clause in the Housing and Planning Bill introduced by the previous Conservative Government.

[89] s.1(4); and see para. 2–17.

[90] To be fair, the Opposition may have been intending only to embarrass the Government by forcing it to reject an amendment giving rights to tenants against landlords.

[91] The argument is one used by Conservative spokesmen on enfranchisement matters, and is based on the objection to retrospective legislation. But it involves a misunderstanding of that objection. In particular, the argument overlooks the fact that, if valid, it applied to leases granted prior to March 23, 1965.

Moreover, in any event March 23, 1965, was clearly the wrong date,[92] and at the Report stage in the House of Lords it was replaced by a Government amendment[93] which followed the intention of the original amendment, but substituted February 18, 1966 (the date of the White Paper) for March 23, 1965. The amendment also clarified some alleged ambiguities in the original amendment.[94] The involvement of Parliamentary Counsel rendered the amendments clear from the purely drafting point of view, but the result remains illogical and unsatisfactory.

Meanwhile, in the interval between the Committee stages in the Commons and the Lords, the Conservative Opposition woke up to what it had done. The raising of the rateable value limits not merely gave richer tenants of larger houses the right to enfranchise, but also gave them very substantial windfalls (free of capital gains tax)[95] at the expense of their landlords. By this time, it had become politically difficult to do a "U-turn" and reduce the rateable value limits back to their original levels, so the Opposition announced at the Committee stage in the Lords (on July 15, 1974) that they proposed at the Report stage to introduce an amendment to increase the compensation for the freehold payable by this class of leaseholder up to the true value of the reversion.[96] That amendment was duly introduced at the Report stage nine days later (on July 24, 1974), having been received by the Government department with responsibility for the Bill only the previous afternoon.[97] Owing to a printers' strike, the Bill itself had not been reprinted since the Committee stage in the Commons, and there were no printed copies of the amendment. After a very short and perfunctory debate, in which the drafting and detailed effect of the clause were not considered at all, the Opposition pressed the clause to a division in which they were successful.[98] On the very same day, the amendment was considered by the Commons. There were no Hansard reports of the Committee and Report stages in the Lords, and photocopies of the amendments themselves had reached the vote office in the Commons only a few minutes before the proceedings began. The intention had been to get the Commons to agree the Lords' amendments that day, but this intention was frustrated when it was discovered that the Liberals had not been provided with notes on the

---

[92] The 1967 Act was not then even on the horizon.

[93] Hansard H.L., Vol. 353, col. 1728. The same Government amendment also introduced what is now Housing Act 1974, s.118(2), as to which see para. 10–02.

[94] The ambiguities were in fact unreal. Some landlords had misunderstood the original amendment and thought that the 1965 rateable value limits were to be raised to £1,500 and £750.

[95] The "only or main residence" exemption in the Finance Act 1965, s.25 (now s.101 of the Capital Gains Taxes Act 1979) is nearly always applicable.

[96] Hansard H.L., Vol. 353, col. 981.

[97] *Ibid.* col. 1763.

[98] *Ibid.* col. 1770.

amendments which had been furnished to the Conservatives.[99] But the next day (July 25, 1974) all the Lords' amendments were agreed to, without any real debate,[1] and the Bill received the Royal Assent a few days later.

The Parliamentary history of the provisions for a notional reduction of rateable value in respect of tenants' improvements[2] is little better than the foregoing. An amendment introducing similar provisions had been moved by a Conservative member[3] (who explained that the amendment was based on Part III of Schedule 5 to the Rent Act 1957) at the Committee stage in the Commons,[4] but it was opposed by the Government and defeated on a division. An almost identical amendment was introduced by the Conservative Opposition at the Report stage in the Lords.[5] The debate on the amendment was similarly short and the detailed machinery and effect of the amendment were never considered at all. Despite a warning from the Government spokesman that the amendment might be unsatisfactory, it was pressed to a division and passed.[6] The proceedings on the subsequent approval of the amendment by the Commons later the same day and the next day is the same as above. 1–16

Thus it was that section 118 of and Schedule 8 to the Housing Act 1974 came to be enacted. What became section 9(1A) and (1B) of the 1967 Act and Schedule 8 to the Housing Act 1974 were passed into law at an impossible speed, without the benefit of any drafting by Parliamentary Counsel, and without any opportunity for consideration and comment by Members of Parliament, let alone others. The results, not surprisingly, are deplorable, containing the anomalies and uncertainties mentioned below. Both section 9(1A) of the 1967 Act (even as subsequently amended by section 23 of the Housing and Planning Act 1986[6a]) and Schedule 8 to the Housing Act 1974 are, in the view of the author, a disgrace to the statute-book. The blame must be shared equally between the politicians concerned[7] and the draftsmen advising them, all of whom meddled irresponsibly in areas beyond their comprehension and skills.

---

[99] Hansard H.C., Vol. 877, col. 1737.

[1] *Ibid.*, col. 1949.

[2] Now to be found in Sched. 8 to the Housing Act 1974.

[3] Mr. Hugh Rossi, M.P. for Hornsey.

[4] Hansard H.C., Vol. 875, col. 1298.

[5] It had previously been moved but withdrawn at the Committee stage; Hansard H.L., Vol. 353, col. 978.

[6] *Ibid.* col. 1755.

[6a] See para. 1–21.

[7] There must be excepted from this criticism Baroness Young who conducted the Opposition case in the House of Lords, in a difficult situation not of her making, with notable distinction. She was, however, badly let down by her draftsmen.

Criticism of section 9(1A)

1–17 The following are some of the defects of section 9(1A):

(1) Much the most serious defect is that there is no parallel provision dealing with the rent payable during the 50-year extension of an extended lease. The draftsman wholly failed to understand and appreciate the necessary connection inherent in the 1967 Act between the freehold price and that rent.[8] The result is that a tenant who obtains an extended lease in fact obtains the major financial benefit conferred by the unamended 1967 Act; and formerly if he immediately thereafter claimed the freehold, he obtained the freehold at a considerably lower price than a tenant who simply claimed the freehold.[9]

(2) In some cases, a house with a rateable value within the 1965 rateable value limits has a rateable value of over £1,000 in Greater London or £500 elsewhere. In such a case, the freehold must be valued under section 9(1A), *i.e.* more unfavourably to the tenant than prior to the amendment, although it may be doubted if that was intended.[10]

(3) The valuation is to be made "on the assumption that the tenant has the right to remain in possession of the house and premises under the provisions of Part I of the Landlord and Tenant Act 1954." Some tenancies are in fact within the protection of Part II (and not Part I) of the 1954 Act.[11]

(4) The tenant's improvements which have to be disregarded include improvements made in pursuance of an obligation to the landlord (and may include even the house itself if constructed pursuant to a building lease).[12]

(5) The provisions regarding tenant's repairs are illogical, and lead to the absurd conclusion that a tenant who in breach of covenant allows his house to fall into disrepair pays less for his freehold than a tenant who maintains his house in proper repair.[13]

---

[8] During the passage of the Bill, the author was asked to draft an amendment so that the price payable for the freehold of houses above the £1,000/£500 rateable value limits would be the full market price. This the author did by an amendment to s.15(2) raising the rent during the 50-year extension to the full market rent. He was then upbraided for dealing *only* with the extended lease and not dealing *at all* with the freehold price—which illustrates the degree of understanding of those responsible.

[9] *Mosley* v. *Hickman* (1986) 278 E.G.728, C.A. affirming the Lands Tribunal (*sub. nom Hickman* v. *Phillimore Kensington Estate Trustees* (1985) 274 E.G. 1261). The effect of *Mosley* v. *Hickman* has now been reversed, subject to exceptions, by the Housing and Planning Act 1986, s.23: see para. 1–21.

[10] See para. 9–14.

[11] See para. 9–45.

[12] See para. 9–47, where another drafting defect is noted.

[13] See para. 9–46.

Criticism of Schedule 8 to the Housing Act 1974

The main defects are: 1–18

(1) The tenant's improvements which are within the Schedule include improvements made in pursuance of an obligation to the landlord (and may even include the house itself if constructed pursuant to a building lease).[14]

(2) The Schedule includes unduly strict time-limits which appear to serve no useful purpose, and are a trap for the unwary.[15]

(3) It is wholly unclear from what date a notional reduction in rateable value takes effect.[16]

(4) The Schedule fails to make it clear whether more than one claim to a notional reduction can be made, either in respect of the same or different improvements.[17]

(5) The Schedule fails to provide for a notional reduction in respect of tenant's improvements made after April 1, 1973 (which may result in the freehold being valued under section 9(1A) rather than section 9(1) of the 1967 Act).[18]

(6) The procedural provisions of the Schedule are unsatisfactory in failing (i) to require the landlord to serve a notice in reply to the tenant's notice claiming a notional reduction,[19] (ii) to require the tenant to deliver to the landlord a copy of his application to the Valuation Officer,[20] or (iii) to deal with sub-tenancies.

(7) There is no provision for an appeal from the Valuation Officer.

(8) As originally enacted, the Schedule declared that "the decision of the county court shall be final," a provision which caused considerable difficulty and litigation.[21] It was repealed by the Housing Act 1980,[22] but no consequential amendment was made to deal with the time-limits of the Schedule in the event of an appeal.

(9) As originally enacted Schedule 8 made no provision for payment

---

[14] See para. 2–26.
[15] See paras. 2–28 *et seq.*
[16] See paras. 2–36 *et seq.*
[17] See paras. 2–34 and 2–35.
[18] See para. 2–23.
[19] See para. 2–29.
[20] See para. 2–31.
[21] See *Pearlman* v. *Keepers and Governors of Harrow School* [1979] 1 Q.B. 56, C.A, overruled on the effect of this provision by *Re Racal Communications Ltd.* [1981] A.C. 374.
[22] Sched. 21, para. 8(*b*).

by the tenant of the landlord's costs,[23] but this omission has now been rectified.[24]

(10) As originally enacted, Schedule 8 included erroneous references to the wrong Act and a non-existent Schedule. These drafting errors have now been rectified.[25]

Leasehold Reform Act 1979

1–19 This curious little Act was introduced to counter the device for increasing the purchase price on enfranchisement held to be successful by the House of Lords in *Jones* v. *Wrotham Park Settled Estates*.[26] The Bill which became the Act was introduced by the Labour Government shortly prior to the dissolution of Parliament for the 1979 General Election. In its original form, the Bill would have benefited the applicant in the *Jones* case itself (as well as other tenants on the same estate affected by the device). However, the Conservative Opposition argued that it therefore involved retrospective legislation,[27] and only agreed to facilitate the Bill's quick passage if it applied only to future devices of the same kind.[28]

Housing Act 1980

1–20 This Act amended the 1967 Act in the following respects: (1) the five-year residential qualification period was reduced to three years, thus bringing it into line with the "right to buy" provisions of Part I of the Act[29]; (2) leasehold valuation tribunals were constituted and given full jurisdiction in valuation matters in place of the Lands Tribunal[30]; (3) certain "shared ownership tenancies" were excluded from the 1967 Act[31]; and (4) several further minor amendments were made.[32]

---

[23] Comparable to ss.8(4) and 14(2) of the 1967 Act, whereby the landlord's investigation, conveyancing and valuation costs arising out of a Notice of Leaseholder's Claim are payable by the tenant.

[24] Para. 4, Sched. 8, introduced by para. 8(*d*) of Sched. 21 to the Housing Act 1980.

[25] By para. 8(*a*), (*c*) and (*e*) of Sched. 21 to the Housing Act 1980.

[26] [1980] A.C. 74: see para. 11–22.

[27] The argument is a bad one, for if valid it would apply to the whole of Part I of the 1967 Act itself as well as any legislation affecting existing relationships between landlords and tenants. See further note 91, *supra*.

[28] Hansard H.C., Vol. 965, cols. 1271–4.

[29] Para. 1, Sched. 21. The residential qualification period under the right to buy provisions has now been reduced to two years by s.3 of the Housing and Building Control Act 1984, but there has been no further reduction in respect of the 1967 Act.

[30] s.142 and Sched. 22.

[31] s.140, now replaced by Sched. 4A to the 1967 Act, introduced by the Housing and Planning Act 1986, Sched. 4, para. 6: see para. 14–07.

[32] By Sched. 21. The most important were (i) (by para. 3) an amendment to the definition of "long tenancy", intended to combat an avoidance device: see para. 3–06; and (ii) (by para. 6) an amendment to the basis of fixing the price on enfranchisement of certain intermediate tenancies: see para. 11–17.

Housing and Planning Act 1986 1–21

Section 23 of this Act amended section 9(1A) of the 1967 Act[32a] so as to reverse the effect of the decision of the Court of Appeal in *Mosley* v. *Hickman.*[32b] However, the amendments were not retrospective and in particular do not apply to cases where the tenant had served a Notice of Leaseholder's Claim to an extended lease before March 4, 1986 (the date of the Court of Appeal's decision).[32c] The result of the amendment is illogical and unsatisfactory, because in cases where an extended lease has been granted the purchase price under section 9(1A) now bears no relationship to the market value of the landlord's interest.

The Act also introduced new provisions excluding certain "shared ownership tenancies" from the 1967 Act.[32d]

Other legislation

Further minor amendments to the 1967 Act have been made by several other Acts, in particular the Rentcharges Act 1977, the Rent Acts 1968 and 1977 and the Housing and Building Control Act 1984. All the amendments are taken into account in the text of the 1967 Act in Appendix A, and mentioned elsewhere in this book. 1–22

4. Construing the 1967 Act

The 1967 Act is an expropriatory Act, in the sense that it confers upon qualified tenants rights of compulsory acquisition. However, these rights are expressly described as being "on fair terms,"[33] and the Act is not confiscatory or penal.[34] It is frequently argued on behalf of landlords that the 1967 Act should therefore be construed strictly. It has been said that there is force in that argument, although "too much weight should not be given to it."[35] On the other hand, in a case in the House of Lords Lord Russell of Killowen delivering the leading speech attributed "minimal if any force to the point" and had "regard only to the statutory provisions."[36] 1–23

[32a] Introduced by the Housing Act 1974, s. 118: see paras. 1–15 and 9–39, *et seq.*

[32b] (1986) 278 E.G. 728: see para. 9–42.

[32c] subs (3): see para. 9–44.

[32d] s.18 and Sched. 4, adding a new Sched. 4A and other provisions to the 1967 Act.

[33] s.1(1). The words "on fair terms" do not add anything, and are apparently merely declaratory of the provisions of s.9 (purchase of freehold) and s.15 (grant of extended lease).

[34] *Metheun-Campbell* v. *Walters* [1979] Q.B. 525, *per* Goff L.J. at p. 529F and *per* Roskill L.J. at p. 541G.

[35] *Ibid. per* Goff L.J. at pp. 529G, 536F; and see *per* Buckley L.J. at p. 542F. See also *Pollock* v. *Brook-Shepherd* (1983) 45 P. & C.R. 357, *per* Lawton L.J. at pp. 359 and 362.

[36] *Jones* v. *Wrotham Park Settled Estates* [1980] A.C. 74 at p. 113E; and see *Manson* v. *Duke of Westminster* [1981] Q.B. 323, *per* Stephenson L.J. at p. 332F.

It is considered that the latter approach is the correct one. The principle that in doubtful cases a penal or expropriatory statute is to be construed so as to avoid the penalty or expropriation does not require that, if the statute has two possible meanings, it must necessarily be construed in that manner; it is a secondary last-resort canon of construction to be applied only "where after full inquiry and consideration one is left in real doubt."[37]

5. European Convention on Human Rights

Outline

1–24 The United Kingdom has ratified the Convention for the Protection of Human Rights and Fundamental Freedoms, of November 4, 1950 (generally known as the European Convention on Human Rights) together with its First Protocol. The first part of article 1 of the First Protocol provides: "Every natural or legal person is entitled to the peaceful enjoyment of his possessions. No one shall be deprived of his possessions except in the public interest and subject to the conditions provided for by law and by the general principles of international law." In 1979, the Grosvenor Estate,[38] doubtless stimulated by suggestions that the 1967 Act might contravene article 1 of the First Protocol,[39] complained by a petition[40] to the European Commission on Human Rights[41] that the 1967 Act enabled certain tenants to purchase the freeholds without the freeholder's consent and on terms that were unjust, in breach of article 1.

The Commission

1–25 In 1984, the Commission referred the case to the European Court of Human Rights at Strasbourg. The Commission in its report expressed its opinion that the 1967 Act does not contravene article 1.[42] The Commission considered that the applicants were indeed "deprived of their possessions" by the 1967 Act, but that such deprivation was "in the public interest." There is a strong presumption, although a rebuttable one, that what a national government does is in the public interest, and

[37] *R.* v. *Ottewell* [1970] A.C. 642, *per* Lord Reid at p. 649D, and see also *Farrell* v. *Alexander* [1977] A.C. 59 at pp. 75C, 89B and 94F.
[38] Which is (or was formerly) the freehold owner of a large number of enfranchisable properties in the Mayfair and Belgravia areas of London.
[39] See an article entitled "Even Freeholders May Have Human Rights" (H. Kidd) at (1979) 249 E.G. 31; also Megarry and Wade, *The Law of Real Property* (5th ed.), p. 1128, and Wade, *Administrative Law* (5th ed.), p. 686.
[40] Application no. 8793/79, *James* v. *United Kingdom.*
[41] Under article 25 of the Convention, all petitions are made first to the Commission.
[42] The Commission's report is summarised in the 81 L.S.Gaz. 2628.

the Commission and the court allow a fairly wide "margin of appreciation" in that respect. The Commission considered that the United Kingdom Parliament was entitled under the margin of appreciation to form the view (set out in the 1966 White Paper),[43] on reasonable grounds, that the long leasehold system generated injustice and that tenants under long leases had a "moral entitlement" to enfranchisement; and that the 1967 Act was "in the public interest" notwithstanding that the property was not acquired for public use. Whatever may be thought of the reasoning in the 1966 White Paper, that conclusion appeared to be clearly correct.

More questionable was the Commission's conclusion as to the compensation payable, particularly in respect of properties with 1973 rateable values of £1,000 or less in Greater London and £500 or less elsewhere. The Commission accepted that "the taking of property to implement social or other public policy without payment of compensation reasonably related to its value would normally constitute a disproportionate interference with the right to property" set out in article 1, but considered that it followed from Parliament's view that tenants enjoyed a moral entitlement to the freehold that the premium they would be required to pay for it would be modest, and that "only thus could the legitimate aim of legislation, the balancing of perceived injustice, be rectified effectively."

The European Court of Human Rights

The judgment of the European Court of Human Rights at Strasbourg was given on February 21, 1986.[44] The Court dismissed the application, for reasons similar to those in the Commission's opinion. Although the court accepted that the taking of property for no reason other than to confer a private benefit could not be in the public interest, it held that the compulsory transfer of property from one individual to another might constitute a legitimate means for promoting the public interest, so that the 1967 Act was not *ipso facto* an infringement of article 1. The "margin of appreciation" available to a legislature in implementing social and economic policies is a wide one, and the legislature's judgment as to the public interest had to be respected unless it was manifestly without reasonable foundation; and although there might be a difference of opinion whether long leaseholders had a "moral entitlement" to the freehold, that view was not outside the margin of appreciation. **1–26**

As to the level of compensation, the Court pointed out that article 1 did not guarantee the right to full compensation in all circumstances, and

[43] See para. 1–06.

[44] Shortly reported in *The Times*, February 22, 1986. The above account of the European Court's decision is based on that report.

held that legitimate objectives of public interest might justify less than full reimbursement of the market value. Given Parliament's view that "in equity the bricks and mortar belong to the leaseholder,"[45] and the wide discretion enjoyed by the legislature, the Court concluded that the valuation basis of the 1967 Act afforded a fairer balance between the interest of society and the landlord's right of property.

The Court also held that there was no violation of article 13 of the Convention, which guarantees all persons whose rights are enshrined in the Convention an effective remedy before a national authority. The court considered that article 13 did not go so far as to guarantee a remedy allowing a state's laws as such to be challenged.

[45] White Paper on Leasehold Reform in England and Wales (1966), Cmnd. 2916, para. 4: see paras. 1–05 *et seq.*

Chapter 2

PREMISES QUALIFYING

In order for a tenant to be able to exercise the rights conferred by the 1967 Act, he must be the tenant (holding under a long tenancy at a low rent)[1] of the whole[2] of a leasehold "house."[3] It is not sufficient that he is such a tenant of part only of a "house," unless (it appears) he is already the freeholder of the remaining parts.[4] His rights extend to the "house and premises."[5] In addition, the house and premises must be within certain rateable limits.[6] **2–01**

1. House

Definition

The basic definition of the expression "house" is contained in section 2(1) of the 1967 Act, which provides: **2–02**

> "For purposes of this Part of this Act, 'house' includes any building designed or adapted for living in and reasonable so called, notwithstanding that the building is not structurally detached, or was not or is not solely designed or adapted for living in, or is divided horizontally into flats or maisonettes; . . . "

Certain points arise on this definition[7] (which, despite the word "includes" appears to be exhaustive[8]).

"Building"

This denotes some kind of permanent erection. A cave, movable

---

[1] s. 1(1)(*a*); see Chap. 3.

[2] s. 1(1); and compare s. 1(2)(*a*).

[3] s. 1(1). But the property need not have been a "house" throughout the qualifying residential period: *Gaidowski* v. *Gonville and Caius College, Cambridge* [1975] 1 W.L.R. 1066, *per* Ormrod L.J. at p. 1070B.

[4] *Harper* v. *Harris* (1968) 112 S.J. 954, Wandsworth C.C.; and see *Peck* v. *Anicar Properties Ltd.* [1971] 1 All E.R. 517, *per* Lord Denning M.R. at p. 519c.

[5] s. 1(1).

[6] s. 1(1)(*a*), (5), (6); see paras. 2–16 *et seq.*

[7] The definition follows the definition of house as used in the Housing Act 1957 given by Lord Denning M.R. in *Ashbridge Investments Ltd.* v. *Minister of Housing and Local Government* [1965] 1 W.L.R. 1320 at p. 1324G.

[8] See *Tandon* v. *Trustees of Spurgeons Homes* [1982] A.C. 755, *per* Lord Roskill at p. 764G.

caravan[9] or boathouse would not be included; but a well-equipped beach-hut probably is.[10]

"Designed or adapted for living in"

The mere fact that the building is used for the purpose of a residence is not, of itself, sufficient. However, the building need not have been purpose-built as a residence; a converted mews stable,[11] coach-house, warehouse, barn, oast-house, shop, or similar building which has been sufficiently adapted qualifies. The degree of adaptation necessary is uncertain, but it is probably sufficient that it could be lived in as a permanent or semi-permanent residence. However, residence need not have been the sole purpose of the design or adaptation of the building, and a purpose-built combined shop and residence,[12] or a building sufficiently adapted for that purpose[13] qualifies (provided it is a house "reasonably so called").

"Reasonably so called"

2–03 This requirement was inserted in the definition of "house" in order to exclude certain buildings fulfilling the above two requirements of the definition. "... Otherwise it would apply to the Ritz Hotel or Rowton House[14] and a large purpose-built block of flats when quite obviously the Act was not intended to include such edifices"[15]; other examples are a large office block with a pent-house flat, and a factory with some small residential accommodation such as a caretaker's flat.[16] It seems probable that an immobile caravan or converted railway carriage is excluded for this reason, although each may be a house for other purposes.[17] Whether a building is a house reasonably so called depends on its character at the date of the Notice of Leaseholder's Claim.[18] The most important factor is usually the physical appearance of the building.[19] But other relevant matters which may be taken into account for this purpose are the history

[9] An immobile caravan connected to the main services might satisfy this requirement (*cf. Makins* v. *Elson* [1977] 1 W.L.R. 221), but is probably not a house "reasonably so called."

[10] *Cf. Spraggs* v. *Prentice* [1950] E.G.D. 519.

[11] *Millett* v. *Hanover Square Freeholds Ltd.* (1969) 119 New L.J. 296, Bloomsbury and Marylebone C.C. (Judge Mais).

[12] *Tandon* v. *Trustees of Spurgeons Homes, supra.*

[13] *Lake* v. *Bennett* [1970] 1 Q.B. 663, C.A.

[14] A working men's hostel: see *R* v. *Rent Tribunals for Bethnal Green and Paddington, ex p. Rowton Houses Ltd.*(1947) 149 E.G.329.

[15] *Lake* v. *Bennett, supra, per* Salmon L.J. at p. 672C, echoing Megarry, *The Rent Acts* (10th ed.), p.505.

[16] *Tandon* v. *Trustees of Spurgeons Homes, supra, per* Lord Fraser of Tullybelton at p. 762A.

[17] *Cf. Makins* v. *Elson, supra.*

[18] *Tandon, supra, per* Lord Roskill at p. 766A.

[19] *Tandon, supra, per* Lord Fraser of Tullybelton at p. 762B.

of the building, the terms of the lease, the proportions of the building respectively used for residential and non-residential purposes,[20] and its situation. "A building in a residential street is more likely to be reasonably called a house than the same building would be if it were in a busy street in the commercial area of the town."[21]

However, the test is not whether a building would ordinarily or correctly be called a house, but whether it can be reasonably described as such; and it is only "if nobody could reasonably call the building a house"[22] that a building otherwise within the definition is not a house. Thus, in one case concerning a combined shop and residence, it was said that "no doubt the building could reasonably be described as a shop with living accommodation above, but it would equally reasonably be described as a house, the ground floor of which has been made into a shop."[23] As appears, that case was concerned with a building which was built as a wholly residential house. However, it is now settled (after considerable judicial disagreement) that even a purpose-built shop with living accommodation above, situated in a terrace of similar properties, is normally a house "reasonably so called."[24] A house converted into an hotel[25] or boarding house clearly remains a house reasonably so called on the above test, as does a house converted into flats. But it is thought that purpose-built hotels and small blocks of flats are not "houses."[26] On the other hand, it is considered that a building built to look like a house but in fact containing two or more flats or maisonettes is a house reasonably so called, even if the flats or maisonettes are completely separate and have their own external doors.

Exclusion of flats and maisonettes

As mentioned above, a building may be a house even if it "is divided 2–04

[20] *Tandon, supra, per* Lord Roskill at p. 766A.

[21] *Tandon, supra, per* Lord Fraser of Tullybelton at p. 762E.

[22] *Tandon, supra,* at p. 767D, where Lord Roskill (with whom Lords Scarman and Bridge of Harwich agreed) also said that if the building is designed or adapted for use as a residence "only exceptional circumstances, which I find hard to envisage, would justify a judge in holding that it could not reasonably be called a house." This appears to be unduly wide, and there are several circumstances in which nobody would call the building a house: see nn. 14, 15, *supra.*

[23] *Lake* v. *Bennett, supra, per* Cross L.J. at p. 673.

[24] *Tandon, supra.* The House of Lords by a 3–2 majority reversed the 2–1 decision of the Court of Appeal (at [1982] Q.B. 41). Disregarding a covered yard (used for the purposes of the shop), the shop and residential areas were each 50 per cent. and including the yard the areas were 75 per cent. shop and 25 per cent. residential. 85 per cent. of the rental value was attributable to the shop. For a useful discussion, see [1982] Conv. 378 ("The House on 'House' ").

[25] *Cf. Epsom Grandstand Association Ltd.* v. *Clarke* (1919) 35 T.L.R. 525 and *Luganda* v. *Service Hotels Ltd.* [1969] 2 Ch. 209, both cited by Lord Denning M.R. in *Lake* v. *Bennett, supra,* at p. 670.

[26] Notwithstanding the dicta of Lord Roskill in the *Tandon* case referred to in n. 21, *supra.*

into flats or maisonettes"[27]; and it is provided that "where a building is divided horizontally, the flats or other units into which it is so divided are not separate 'houses,' though the building as a whole may be."[28] Whether or not such a building is in fact a house thus depends entirely on whether it is a house "reasonably so called."[29]

In the converse situation of the vertical division of a building, it is provided that "where a building is divided vertically, the building is not a house, though any of the units into which it is divided may be."[30] Thus each of a pair of normal semi-detached houses is a "house" on its own, as is each of the normal terrace (or "town") houses in the same terrace. As to the position where two or more of such houses have internal connections between them, see para. 2–07.

Exclusion of overlapping premises

2–05 It is also provided that references in the 1967 Act to a house "do not apply to a house which is not structurally detached and of which a material part lies above or below a part of the structure not comprised in the house."[31] This provision would have excluded flats and maisonettes if they had not already been excluded,[32] and its purpose is to deal with other premises where there is some overlapping or "overhang." The expression "structurally detached" in the above context means actual physical detachment from any other structure, and separation merely by party walls, ceilings or floors from the rest of the structure is not sufficient.[33]

If a house includes one or more rooms built on an archway over an entrance way not included in the tenancy, the matter is likely to depend on the exact physical structure of the archway and the precise wording of the parcels clause of the lease. If part of the archway is not included in the demise, or if there is a basement under the entrance way,[34] the house is probably outside the Act. However, if the whole of the archway itself was included in the demise,[35] and there is no basement beneath the entrance way, the house is within the Act.[36]

---

[27] s. 2(1).
[28] s. 2(1)(*a*).
[29] As to which see para. 2–03.
[30] s. 2(1)(*b*).
[31] s. 2(2).
[32] See para. 2–04.
[33] *Parsons* v. *Trustees of Henry Smith's Charity* [1974] 1 W.L.R. 435, H.L.
[34] As in *Phelps* v. *City of London Corporation* [1916] 2 Ch. 255.
[35] It appears that the prima facie rule that the external walls are included in a demise (see *Sturge* v. *Hackett* [1962] 1 W.L.R. 1257) applies equally to external horizontal surfaces: see *Graystone Property Investments Ltd.* v. *Margulies* (1984) 47 P. & C.R. 472, C.A. and *Cresswell* v. *Duke of Westminster* (1985) 275 E.G. 461, C.A.; but *cf.* *Cockburn* v. *Smith* [1924] 2 K.B. 119, particularly *per* Bankes L.J. at p. 128.
[36] *Cresswell* v. *Duke of Westminster, supra.*

Material part

2–06 Problems frequently arise as to what constitutes a "material" part of a house for this purpose. Suggested meanings of "material" are "important"[37] and "material to the tenant or to his enjoyment of the house"[38]; but the matter is "largely factual and one of common sense," to be decided by the judge, who may visit the premises.[39] As a general rule, eaves and drainpipes, cupboards, box rooms, water tanks, chimney breasts and the like are not sufficiently "material" to take the house outside the Act. So, too, a lavatory is probably not a "material part," unless it is the only lavatory in the house.[40] But the whole or any substantial part of any living room, bedroom, kitchen or bathroom usually constitutes a material part, as does an entrance hall, a cellar[41] or a built-in garage. A staircase is probably a material part, at any rate if it is the only or main staircase of the house.

Identification of "house"

2–07 It is sometimes difficult to determine the precise premises which constitute the relevant "house" within the provisions discussed above, particularly in cases where buildings have been altered since they were first erected. Such alterations may result in a change in the identity of the original premises, *e.g.* if two or more adjoining cottages are fully converted into a single residence which thereupon becomes the only relevant "house."[42] But merely connecting two detached houses by a covered way and using them together does not alter their identity and they remain separate "houses."[43] Furthermore, inserting a connecting doorway in the party wall between adjoining terrace houses does not, of

---

[37] *Parsons* v. *Trustees of Henry Smith's Charity* [1973] 1 W.L.R. 845, *per* Lord Denning M.R. at p. 849 H; but see *per* Stephenson L.J. at p. 853 (whose judgment is marred by a misunderstanding of s. 2(5)). The "overhang" in that case comprised approximately 10 per cent. of the total floor area and included a bathroom, a W.C., a substantial part of a dressing room and half of a small bathroom; it was considered that this was clearly a "material part," and the point was not argued in the House of Lords.

[38] *Ibid. per* Stephenson L.J. at p. 854 D.

[39] *Ibid.* [1974] 1 W.L.R. 435, H.L. *per* Lord Wilberforce at p. 440C.

[40] Held to be a material part in *Garbutt* v. *Trustees of Gunter Estate* (1981) West London C.C. (unreported).

[41] It is sometimes difficult to know if a cellar, accessible only or mainly from another house, has been included in a demise. Often it has been demised by virtue of s. 62(2), Law of Property Act 1925, although not expressly mentioned: *Grigsby* v. *Melville* [1974] 1 W.L.R. 80, C.A.

[42] *Gaidowski* v. *Gonville & Caius College, Cambridge* [1975] 1 W.L.R. 1066, *per* Ormrod L.J. at p. 1071 A; and see *Dixon* v. *Allgood* (1986) 281 E.G. 183, C.A., at p. 187.

[43] *Fowell* v. *Radford* (1969) 21 P. & C.R. 99, C.A.

itself, alter their separate identity,[44] even if the houses are used together and assessed as a single hereditament for rating purposes.[45]

It has been said that "one must look at three things to find out what is the 'house': (1) the lease itself; (2) the portion occupied as a residence; and (3) the physical condition of the structure."[46] Although this test has been applied in other cases,[47] it is an unsatisfactory one, and usually of little or no assistance. As to (1), what has to be considered is the property at the date of the Notice of Leaseholder's Claim,[48] and the lease, or (more commonly) the leases, of the property usually merely reflect its original physical condition. As to (2), although importance has sometimes been attached to this factor,[49] it is respectfully suggested that reliance on it is unsound. Whether a room forms part of a "house" should not depend on the use which the tenant happens to be making of it at the date of his Notice of Leaseholder's Claim; what is a house ought to be governed by the physical qualities of the building, not on the use made of it. Moreover, the definition of "house" expressly contemplates that it may not be "solely designed or adapted for living in,"[50] so it seems illogical to say that a room incorporated into a building is not part of the house because it is used for a non-residential purpose.

It is therefore suggested that item (3) of the above test, *i.e.* "the physical condition of the structure," is much the most important (and in many cases, the only) factor in determining what is the relevant "house." In the case of two adjoining houses much will depend on the number of interconnecting doors or passages, and the extent to which the houses remain capable of use as self-contained units, with separate kitchens, bathrooms, central heating systems, electrical circuits and the like. In one case where doorways were made between two adjoining houses at all four floor levels and the two houses occupied by one family, it was held that the two original houses had lost their original identity (notwithstanding that they retained separate front doors, kitchens and services) and

---

[44] *Peck* v. *Anicar Properties Ltd.* [1971] 1 All E.R. 517, C.A.; *Wolf* v. *Crutchley* [1971] 1 W.L.R. 99, C.A.

[45] *Wolf* v. *Crutchley, supra.*

[46] *Peck* v. *Anicar Properties Ltd., supra, per* Lord Denning M.R. at p. 519b. It is difficult to see how this test can properly be derived from the wording of the Act, and in particular Lord Denning's reliance on s. 1(1) seems unjustified. The actual decision in *Peck* appears an odd one, and is best explained by fact that the point had not been taken in the county court: see at pp. 518 and 519 ff. The House of Lords allowed the landlord's petition for leave to appeal, but the appeal was not pursued.

[47] *Wolf* v. *Crutchley, supra*; *Gaidowski, supra,* at p. 1073G.

[48] *Tandon* v. *Trustees of Spurgeons Homes* [1982] A.C. 755, *per* Lord Roskill at p. 766A.

[49] See *Wolf* v. *Crutchley, supra, per* Cairns L.J. at p. 104C and *Gaidowski, supra, per* Ormrod L.J. at p. 1071G and Sir Gordon Willmer at p. 1073H.

[50] s. 2(1).

together formed the relevant "house" for the purposes of the 1967 Act.[51] A similar conclusion was reached in a case where there were only two doorways between two adjoining houses, at ground floor and third floor levels, but the two original houses were run as a single private hotel with only one kitchen, one dining room and single water and central heating systems.[52]

2. "House and Premises"

Outline

The right to acquire the freehold or an extended lease conferred by the 1967 Act extends not to "the house" as defined above alone but to "the house and premises."[53] It is thus "the house and premises" which must be included in the parcels clause of the conveyance[54] or extended lease.[55] Furthermore, it is the rateable value of "the house and premises" which is relevant in considering whether the property falls within the rateable value limits[56] and if it does and the tenant has claimed the freehold, in determining the basis of ascertaining the purchase price.[57] 2–08

Meaning of "premises"

In order to be part of the "house and premises," the premises must be any "garage, outhouse, garden, yard and appurtenances" which fulfil both of the two qualifying conditions set out below.[58] 2–09

"Garage"

An internal garage, and usually also a garage directly accessible from the house itself, is part of the "house" itself so that this reference is probably limited to other separate or external garages. A garage has been said in another context to be a place for reasonable shelter and protection of a car[59]; its meaning in the context of the 1967 Act is probably wide enough to include also any carport or other erection used for that purpose,

---

[51] *Galbraith* v. *Church Commissioners for England* (1979) Westminster C.C., unreported (Judge Ruttle).
[52] *Norfolk Square (Northern Section) Ltd.* v. *Schmid* (1978) Bloomsbury & Marylebone C.C., unreported.
[53] s. 1(1).
[54] s. 8(1): see para. 6–16.
[55] s. 14(1): see para. 7–08.
[56] s. 1(1)(*b*), (5), (6): see paras. 2–21, 2–22.
[57] s. 9(1A): see para. 9–14.
[58] s. 2(3).
[59] *Barnett* v. *National Parcels Insurance Co. Ltd.* [1942] 1 All E.R. 221 (insurance against theft).

as well as a garage for housing bicycles, boats or the like. But a car-parking space is not included under this head (though it may be part of a "yard" or "appurtenance"). It is immaterial that the garage is one of a detached block.

"Outhouse"

This expression includes any building or erection ancillary to the house, such as a garden shed, greenhouse, summer house, boiler house, coalshed, outside lavatory, stable, kennel or the like. It is considered that it does not include a residential building, such as a gardener's cottage, which would constitute a "house" on its own.

"Garden"

A garden includes a rough garden and a vegetable garden, as well as a normal formal or pleasure garden.[60] It is considered to be immaterial that the garden may not adjoin the house, *e.g.* that it is the other side of a private or public road.[61] But a rough pasture, fenced off from the formal garden of the house, has been held not to be a garden.[62] An orchard is probably not a garden, although it may be an "appurtenance."[63]

"Yard"

A yard can be covered or uncovered. It is usually a surfaced area, but probably need not be.

"Appurtenances"

These are not confined to incorporeal hereditaments, but extend to driveways, passageways, forecourts and similar pieces of land, as well as a lake or part of a river or stream. The expression would also include most garages, outhouses, gardens and yards of the kind discussed above.[64] However, to constitute an appurtenance, any such premises must be within the curtilege of the house. It is not sufficient that it was included in the same lease as the house, or that it is advantageous or convenient or even (it appears) necessary for the full enjoyment of the house.[65] The premises and the house must together constitute an integral whole, and the test appears to be whether a conveyance of the house by its name

[60] *Methuen-Campbell* v. *Walters* [1979] 1 Q.B. 525, C.A., *per* Goff L.J. at p. 538.
[61] *Cf. Cargill* v. *Phillips* [1951] S.C. 67 (Rent Acts).
[62] *Methuen-Campbell* v. *Walters, supra.*
[63] *Trim* v. *Sturminster R.D.C.* [1938] 2 K.B. 508, *per* Slesser L.J. at pp. 515–6.
[64] *Methuen-Campbell* v. *Walters, supra*, following *Trim* v. *Sturminster R.D.C., supra.*
[65] *Methuen-Campbell* v. *Walters, supra*, particularly *per* Buckley L.J. at p. 543.

alone would pass the piece of land or premises.[66] A rough pasture fenced off from the formal garden of a house has been held not to be an appurtenance,[67] and it is considered that similarly neither the surrounding parkland[68] nor the tree-screening strip of land of a mansion house is an appurtenance.[69]

Qualifying conditions

The two qualifying conditions,[70] both of which must be satisfied if the garden, etc., is to be part of the house and premises, are that "at the relevant time," *i.e.* the date when the tenant serves his Notice of Leaseholder's Claim,[71] the premises must be as follows: 2–10

"Let to him with the house"

The tenant must at the date of his Notice of Leaseholder's Claim also be the tenant of the premises[72] from the landlord of his house, but that alone is not sufficient.[73] In order to be let "with" the house, the premises must, it is considered, have been let as part of the same transaction as the original lease or subsequently by way of addition to the original lease (*e.g.* by way of a supplemental lease[74] for the residue, or approximately the residue, of the original term) by the landlord for the time being to the tenant for the time being.[75] It does not suffice if the premises were originally let to the tenant of a different house,[76] nor if the letting was for a weekly or other short term. Despite a suggestion to the contrary,[77] it is considered that assistance can be obtained from cases on the comparable phrase "let together with" in section 26(1) of the Rent Act 1977.[78]

---

66 *Ibid.*

67 *Ibid.*

68 *Trustees of Bedford Estate* v. *Rock (V.O.)* (1983) 267 E.G. 449, L.T.

69 This may seem a fanciful point in view of the rateable value limits, but the author was concerned in a case in which the point arose, but not decided (the proceedings being settled).

70 s. 2(3).

71 s. 37(1)(*d*).

72 Not necessarily under a "long tenancy."

73 *Gaidowski* v. *Gonville & Caius College, Cambridge* [1975] 1 W.L.R. 1066, C.A.

74 Including a tenancy granted to satisfy a proprietory estoppel: *Ellis* v. *Duke of Westminster* (1982) West London C.C., unreported (Judge Thomas).

75 Such an addition is probably a sufficiently "reasonably close connection" (*per* Ormrod L.J. in the *Gaidowski* case, *supra*, at p. 1073A) or "connecting link" (*per* Sir Gordon Willmer at p. 1074D).

76 *Gaidowski* case, *supra.*

77 *Ibid. per* Ormrod L.J. at p. 1072 H.

78 See *Mann* v. *Merrill* [1945] 1 All E.R. 708, C.A. and Megarry on *The Rent Acts* (10th ed.) Vol. 1, p. 99.

"Occupied with and used for the purposes of the house or any part of it by him or by another occupant"

2–11 If the tenant has sub-let or assigned any premises (otherwise than to an occupant of the house) such premises are excluded from "the house and premises." The same consequence follows if such premises are used by him (or another occupant of the house) for the purpose of a business unconnected with his (or the other occupant's) occupation of the house.

A tenant whose "house and premises" are a few pounds over the rateable value limit can sometimes use this qualification requirement to bring his property under such limit. If he sells, underlets or licences (say) a garage to a third party, it will cease to be part of his "house and premises," and its rateable value (after any necessary apportionment) must be deducted in ascertaining the relevant rateable value.[79] It appears that even a short underletting or licence is sufficient, at any rate provided the third party occupier uses the garage and the transaction is not a sham. Although the landlord will probably be entitled to object to the severance and require the tenant to include the garage in his conveyance or extended lease,[80] this will not render it part of the "house and premises" again.

Other premises which may be included

2–12 In some cases it may be inconvenient for the landlord to have to retain "other premises[81] let with the house and premises," but not fulfilling the second condition above, "whether in consequence of an assignment of the term therein or a sub-letting or otherwise."[82] The landlord might, for instance, be left with a small part of garden which has been assigned or a garage which has been sub-let. In such a case, if at the date of service of the Notice of Leaseholder's Claim the landlord has an interest in the other premises he can, within two months thereafter, give written notice to the tenant objecting to the further severance of the house and premises.[83] The two month time-limit is absolute, and the landlord's right is lost unless it is complied with; moreover, the landlord's notice must be given with or before his Notice in Reply to Leaseholder's Claim, unless the right to object is thereby reserved.[84] If a landlord's notice is given, the other premises will also be included in the conveyance or extended lease if the

---

[79] See para. 2–20.
[80] Under s. 2(4): see para. 2–12.
[81] "Premises" in this context appears to mean premises which would otherwise be comprised in the house and premises, and does not include property of other kinds let with the house.
[82] s. 2(4).
[83] s. 2(4)(*a*).
[84] Sched. 3, para. 7(2). The prescribed form of Notice in Reply contains a paragraph covering the matter: see para. 20–089.

tenant agrees, or if the court is satisfied that it would be unreasonable to require the landlord to retain them without the house and premises.[85] But this does not mean that the other premises become part of the "house and premises" for other purposes, *e.g.* in determining where the same are within the rateable value limits, as is sometimes mistakenly thought.

If the tenant's interest no longer includes the other premises, he is nevertheless treated for the purposes of the 1967 Act as holding a tenancy of the other premises on identical terms, the actual tenant of the other premises being treated as a sub-tenant.[86] The tenant will thus have to purchase the freehold (or take an extended lease) of the other premises, and so become the landlord (or intermediate landlord) in respect of such premises.

Parts which may be excluded

Conversely, in some cases it may be inconvenient for the landlord to include in the conveyance or extended lease any part of the house and premises which lies above or below other premises. In such a case, if at the date of the service of the tenant's Notice of Leaseholder's Claim the landlord has an interest in the other premises, he can, within two months thereafter, give written notice to the tenant objecting to the further severance from those other premises of the part.[87] (Again, the two month limit is absolute, and the landlord's right is lost unless it is complied with; and the landlord's notice must be given with or before the landlord's Notice in Reply to Leaseholder's Claim unless the right to object is thereby reserved[88]). That part will then be excluded from the house and premises if the tenant so agrees, or the court is satisfied that any hardship or inconvenience likely to be caused to the tenant by the exclusion is outweighed by the difficulties involved in further severance and any hardship or inconvenience likely to result from it.[89] The court must take account of anything that can be done to mitigate the effects of the exclusion, including any undertaking offered by the landlord for that purpose.[90] 2–13

Minerals

Special provision is made with regard to underlying minerals com- 2–14

---

[85] s. 2(4)(*b*).
[86] s. 2(7).
[87] s. 2(5)(*a*).
[88] Sched. 3, para. 7(2). The prescribed form of Notice in Reply contains a paragraph covering the matter: see para. 20–089.
[89] s. 2(5)(*b*).
[90] *Ibid.*

prised in the tenancy.[91] These may always be excepted by the landlord, provided proper provision is made for the support of the house and premises as they have been enjoyed during the tenancy and in accordance with its terms.[92] This will normally involve the grant of a full right of support, and it is considered that no right to let down the surface can be reserved even if provision is made for full compensation. If he wishes to work the minerals, the landlord therefore will have to apply to the High Court under the Mines (Working Facilities and Support) Act 1966 for the grant of the necessary working facilities. In contrast to the other premises which may be excluded, there is no time limit within which the landlord must decide to except the minerals.[93] Moreover, it appears that he can decide to do so even after he has served his Notice in Reply, and although he has not reserved the right to do so in it; but a landlord is well advised to require the minerals to be excepted as soon as possible, and to make such requirement in his Notice in Reply. There is no exclusion of minerals if the landlord cannot be found and the tenant acquires the freehold under section 27.[94]

Conveyancing

2–15 If any part of the premises is excluded, the conveyance or extended lease probably operates as a surrender of the tenancy as regards that part, and its contents must be determined as if such surrender had taken place before the date of service of the Notice of Leaseholder's Claim.[95] Nevertheless, so that the landlord can show that the excluded part is no longer subject to the lease, it is advisable for there to be an express surrender of it, either in the conveyance[96] or extended lease, or else by a separate document.

3. Rateable Value

2–16 The 1967 Act applies only to properties within certain alternative rateable value limits, set out below.[97] It is thus necessary to ascertain the rateable value of "the house and premises" at the relevant dates for that purpose, and sometimes also for the purpose of determining the basis of valuation of the freehold.[98] Further, the rateable value on "the appropri-

[91] If not comprised in the tenancy, they will not form part of "the house and premises" anyway.
[92] s. 2(6). See Precedent No. 15, Appendix A.
[93] s. 2(6) does not require the landlord to "object" to the inclusion of the minerals.
[94] *Re Robertson's Application* [1969] 1 W.L.R. 109: see para. 17–22.
[95] s. 2(7).
[96] See Precedent No. 14, Appendix A.
[97] See paras. 2–21 and 22.
[98] See para. 9–14.

apportionment or aggregation must be made, even though the house and premises may subsequently have been separated or jointly rated. An apportionment can be made for the purpose of the 1967 Act of a property comprising two or more houses let under one lease to one tenant (even though no such apportionment can be made for the purposes of the Rent Acts on an application by the tenant).[19] Any question arising as to the proper apportionment[20] or aggregation of rateable values is decided[21] by the county court, whose decision is "final,"[22] *i.e.* there is no right of appeal of any kind.[23]

Alteration of rateable value

Most alterations in thm rateable value of a hereditament shown in the valuation list result from a proposal for an alteration made by a "person" (including a rating authority) "who is aggrieved" or by the valuation officer.[24] Any such alteration has retrospective effect from the first day of the rating year in which the proposal for the alteration is made, *i.e.* the previous April 1, but never from an earlier date.[25] It is therefore seldom that an alteration is relevant to the ascertainment of the rateable value on March 23, 1965. But many proposals for alteration of the 1973 valuation list were made before April 1, 1974 and it has been held (notwithstanding the inappropriate wording of the relevant statutory provisions[25a]) that any alteration made pursuant to such a proposal must be taken into account in ascertaining the rateable value on April 1, 1973.[25b] Unless an alteration is made pursuant to such a proposal, it is usually immaterial that the original entry in the valuation list was erroneous due to a mistake on the part of the valuation officer, or that the alteration has been made as a result of a change of use (*e.g.* from office to residential user), or that the 2–19

---

[19] *Parsons* v. *Trustees of Henry Smith's Charity* [1973] 1 W.L.R. 845, C.A. This point was left open when the case reached the House of Lords, *sub nom. Parsons* v. *Viscount Gage* [1974] 1 W.L.R. 435.

[20] As to the factors to be taken into account in making an apportionment, see *Bainbridge* v. *Longdon* [1925] 2 K.B. 26, D.C., approved in *Beck* v. *Newbold* [1952] 2 All. E.R. 412, *per* Somervell L.J. at p. 415.

[21] It is not necessary for the court to decide an exact apportionment if (as is usually the case) the effect of an apportionment is agreed between the parties: *cf. R.* v. *City of Westminster London Borough Council Rent Officer, ex p. Rendall* [1973] Q.B. 959, C.A.

[22] Rent Act 1977, s.25(2), applied by s.37(6) of the 1967 Act, as amended.

[23] *Field* v. *Gover* [1944] K.B. 200, C.A.

[24] General Rate Act 1967, s.69(1)(2).

[25] *Ibid.* s.79; *Rodwell* v. *Gwynne Trusts Ltd.* [1970] 1 W.L.R. 327, H.L.; *Duke of Westminster* v. *Rendall,* Dec. 4, 1986 (unreported), C.A.

[25a] Rent Act 1977 s.25(4), applied by s.37(6) of the 1967 Act as amended, in terms applies only where there is an alteration effective from not later than "the appropriate day".

[25b] *MacFarquhar* v. *Phillimore, supra*; the different reasons given by Dillon L.J. and Nicholls L.J. appear to be in conflict (although Lloyd L.J. agreed with both) and are unsatisfactory.

rating authority[26] has made a retrospective refund of rates.[27] However the valuation officer can direct an alteration in the valuation list without any proposal if the alteration is "necessary to correct any clerical or mathematical error,"[28] and such an alteration is fully retrospective.[29]

Exclusion of "premises"

2–20 The 1967 Act applies only if the combined rateable value[30] of "the house and premises"[31] is within certain alternative limits. As mentioned above, what is included in "premises" for this purpose is ascertained as at the date of service of the Notice of Leaseholder's Claim. If the relevant rateable value is only a little above one of the limits, a tenant may be able to obtain the benefit of the Act by temporarily sub-letting part of the premises, thus taking them outside the definition of house and premises.[32] (As to notional reductions in the rateable value, see paras. 2–23 *et seq*).

Rateable value limits

2–21 The alternative rateable value limits depend on the combined rateable value of the house and premises on "the appropriate day" (the meaning of which is discussed above) and on April 1, 1973 (the date on which new rating lists came into effect). The alternatives can be summarised as follows:

(i) **If the appropriate day was before April 1, 1973.** The 1967 Act applied originally only if the rateable value of the house and premises was not more than £200 if outside Greater London,[33] or not more than £400 if in Greater London.[34] Those limits continue to apply.[35] But even if the rateable value on the appropriate day exceeded those limits, and the tenancy was created on or before February 18, 1966,[36] as a result of amendments made in 1974 the 1967 Act nevertheless applies if the

---

[26] Under its powers in the General Rate Act 1967, s.9.
[27] *Rodwell* v. *Gwynne Trusts Ltd., supra.*
[28] This expression does not include an error in measurement: *John Hunter & Son (Transport) Ltd.* v. *Lanarkshire Assessor* [1963] R.A. 320.
[29] General Rate Act 1967, s.80(1).
[30] For definition of rateable value see para. 2–18.
[31] For definition see paras. 2–08 *et seq.*
[32] Such part will not then be occupied by the tenant and so be outside the definition in s.2(3): see para. 2–11.
[33] "Greater London" means the London Boroughs, the City of London and the Temples: see London Government Act 1963, s.2.
[34] s.1(1)(*a*).
[35] But the basis of valuation may have altered: see para. 9–14.
[36] The date on which the Government's White Paper setting out proposals for leasehold reform (Cmnd. 2916) was published.

rateable value of the house and premises on April 1, 1973 was not more than £750 if outside Greater London, or not more than £1500 if in Greater London.[37]

The restriction to the original rateable value limits as regards tenancies created after February 18, 1966, was introduced in order that such leases, created on the assumption that they would be outside the 1967 Act, should not subsequently be brought within the Act. On April 1, 1973 there was on average an increase in rateable values of about 150 per cent. and the limits of £500 and £1,000 were no more than the equivalent of the previous limits of £200 and £400. The restriction was enacted to meet an argument as to retrospective legislation, but is illogical and indefensible; there is no sensible distinction between such leases and leases granted prior to 1966 when no legislation at all was contemplated.[38] Note, however, that a tenancy is normally "created" for this purpose only at the date of its grant.[39] But if it was granted immediately upon the termination of an earlier tenancy, even though after February 18, 1966, it is treated as "created" at the commencement of the earlier tenancy, if under s.3(3) of the 1967 Act the two tenancies fall to be treated as a single tenancy.[40]

(ii) **If the appropriate day is on or after April 1, 1973.** In such cases rateable value on the appropriate day will necessarily be based on the 1973 valuation list. Provision is made for two alternatives: 2–22

(a) If the tenancy was created on or before February 18, 1966, the 1967 Act applies if the rateable value of the house and premises on the appropriate day was not more than £750 if outside Greater London, or not more than £1,500 if in Greater London.[41] (The limits correspond with those applicable where there was a pre-April 1, 1973 rateable value). Such cases are of their nature, obviously very rare, if indeed any exist at all.

(b) If the tenancy was created after February 18, 1966, the 1967 Act applies only if the rateable value of the house and premises on the appropriate day was not more than £500 if outside Greater London, or not more than £1,000 if in Greater London.[42] Again, the limits correspond with those applicable where there was a pre-April 1, 1973 rateable value.

---

37 s.(1)(6), added by the Housing Act 1974, s.118.
38 See further the author's comments at para. 1–15.
39 *Roberts* v. *Church Commissioners for England* [1972] 1 Q.B. 278, C.A.
40 *Bates* v. *Pierrepoint* (1978) 37 P. & C.R. 420, C.A.: see para. 3–10.
41 s.1(5)(*a*), added by the Housing Act 1974, s.118.
42 s.1(5)(*b*), added by the Housing Act 1974, s.118.

4. Notional Reduction in Rateable Value

Outline

2–23 If a tenant, or a predecessor of the tenant, has made improvements to his property, those improvements may have resulted in an increase in the rateable value of the property which takes it outside the rateable value limits[43] or which results in the freehold being valued on a basis more favourable to the landlord.[44] Provision is therefore made for the rateable value of the house and premises on April 1, 1973, (but not any other date) for the purposes of the 1967 Act as amended to "be adjusted to take into account any tenant's improvements in accordance with Schedule 8 to the Housing Act 1974."[45] The rateable value can be notionally reduced by an amount intended to correspond with the increase in the rateable value attributable to the improvements made by the tenant or a predecessor of the tenant.

It is not necessary for the tenant to be qualified to exercise the rights conferred by the 1967 Act in order to obtain a notional reduction in the rateable value. For example, a tenant can invoke the Schedule 8 procedure immediately he has acquired the tenancy, and before obtaining the three-year residential qualification; indeed, this is an advisable course to take, in order to ensure that a notional reduction has been obtained before he serves his Notice of Leaseholder's Claim.[46] Similarly, a company, which cannot exercise any rights under the 1967 Act,[47] can apply, *e.g.* in order to bring the property within the rateable value limits and thus enhance the value of its tenancy. Contrary to what appears to have been thought by the Court of Appeal in one case,[48] the procedures for obtaining a notional reduction in the rateable value and for claiming the freehold or an extended lease are totally separate and distinct, and there is no single "legislative machinery" or "procedure" in the Act.[49]

2–24 Unfortunately, Schedule 8 is badly drafted.[50] Its wording closely follows the wording of, and it is clearly based on, the provisions of Part III of Sched. 5 to the Rent Act 1957. Those provisions enabled a tenant of a "controlled tenancy" to obtain a notional reduction in rateable value in order that the dwelling-house in question should not be within the

---

[43] See paras. 2–21, 22.
[44] *i.e.* under s.9(1A) rather than s.9(1) of the Leasehold Reform Act 1967, as amended: see para. 9–14.
[45] s.118(3) of the Housing Act 1974; and see s.1(4A) of the 1967 Act as amended.
[46] But see paras. 2–36 *et seq.*
[47] s.37(5); *Duke of Westminster* v. *Oddy* (1984) 270 E.G. 945, C.A.
[48] *Pollock* v. *Brook Shepherd* (1983) 45 P. & C.R. 357; see para. 2–34.
[49] *Ibid, per* Lawton L.J. at p. 362.
[50] See paras. 1–16 and 1–18.

decontrol provisions of the 1957 Act and so remained subject to Rent Act control. It was clearly important that the question whether the tenancy was decontrolled should be settled as soon as practicable. So any application had to be made within six weeks after the 1957 Act came into force, and there were short and strict time-limits for each of the subsequent steps in the procedure. Rather different considerations apply as regards Schedule 8, under which an application can be made "at any time."[51] The adaptation of the 1957 Act provisions for the different purposes of the Housing Act 1974, Sched. 8, was ineptly done, and its wording has given rise to considerable litigation and many practical difficulties and uncertainties.[52]

The difficulties of Schedule 8 have been exacerbated by two cases in the Court of Appeal. It is respectfully suggested that part of the decision in the first case, *Pollock* v. *Brook-Shepherd*,[53] was based on an erroneous premise and decided *per incuriam*[54] and that certain dicta in the second case, *Duke of Westminster* v. *Oddy*[55] are erroneous and ought not to be followed.[56]

Qualifying improvements

Schedule 8 applies only to "improvements made by the execution of works amounting to structural alteration, extension or addition."[57] 2–25
Obvious examples are "the erection of a garage in the grounds,"[58] the building on of additional rooms and the full conversion of a house into self-contained flats.[59] "Structural" has been said to mean "something which involves the fabric of the house as opposed to the provision merely of a piece of equipment . . . it matters not whether the fabric in question is load-bearing or otherwise, if there is any substantial alteration, extension or addition to the fabric of the house."[60] Another definition of structural is "appertaining to the basic fabric and parts of the house as distinguished from its decorations and fittings."[61] The words "works amounting to" in

[51] See the original s.1(4A) of the 1967 Act introduced by the Housing Act 1974, s.118(4). A different s.1(4A) was substituted by the Housing Act 1980, Sched. 21, para. 2, but the original was ambiguously drafted in other respects, and it is clear that there is no time-limit by which the tenant must claim a notional reduction.

[52] See the author's strictures in para. 1–18.

[53] (1983) 45 P. & C.R. 357, discussed by the author at (1983) 266 E.G. 187.

[54] See para. 2–34.

[55] (1984) 270 E.G. 945.

[56] See para. 2–41.

[57] Housing Act 1974, Sched. 8, para. 1(2).

[58] The jejeune example mentioned in note 1 to the Form of Tenant's Notice set out in Schedule 8.

[59] See *Effra Investments Ltd.* v. *Stergios* (1982) 264 E.G. 449, L.V.T.

[60] *Pearlman* v. *Keepers and Governors of Harrow School* [1979] 1 Q.B. 56 *per* Geoffrey Lane L.J. at p. 72G.

[61] *Pickering* v. *Phillimore* (1976) West London C.C. (Judge White) unreported, cited with approval by Eveleigh L.J. in *Pearlman, supra,* at p. 79D.

the definition means that one must look at the final result of the works.[62] The installation of a full central heating system (gas-fired boiler providing domestic hot water and serving 20 radiators) involving substantial works to the fabric of a permanent nature has been held to be within the definition.[63]

It is considered that alterations the purpose of which is to alter the fabric (whether or not load-bearing) are within the definition. Examples are the removal of walls or the erection of new walls; the blocking up of old windows and doors or the provision of new ones; and the installation of a new staircase or a false ceiling. On the other hand, it is thought that alterations made for other purposes,[64] *e.g.* the installation of fittings and equipment (even if the installations are intended to be permanent), are not "structural" and are therefore outside the definition, unless they involve substantial interference with the fabric.[65] Examples of non-structural works are installations of sinks and cookers with the necessary plumbing,[66] fitted cupboards, bookshelves, a modern fireplace instead of old fire dogs,[67] a ventilator, additional radiators or a television aerial. Furthermore, it is thought that the replacement of old baths, basins, lavatories, boilers, water tanks, etc., and replumbing and rewiring, all fall within the category of repairs and renewals as opposed to improvements, and are outside the definition for that reason. But the question is one of fact and degree to be decided on the facts of each case; and the works involved in, *e.g.* the complete modernisation of a kitchen or the conversion of a bedroom into a new bathroom,[68] may involve sufficiently substantial interference with the fabric to be "works amounting to structural alteration, extension or addition" and so within the definition. However, works of this kind frequently have not in fact affected the rateable value,[69] and the question whether they are qualifying improvements is thus of no practical consequence.

2–26 It would have been sensible and fair to landlords if the qualifying improvements had been confined to improvements other than those which the tenant was contractually bound to make,[70] because the landlord

---

[62] *Pearlman, supra, per* Eveleigh L.J. at p. 79F.

[63] *Pearlman, supra,* distinguishing *Re Gaskell's S.E.* [1894] 1 Ch. 485 (decided under the Settled Land Acts 1882 to 1890).

[64] Consider *Bickmore* v. *Dimmer* [1903] 1 Ch. 158, C.A.

[65] As in *Pearlman, supra,* which must not be taken as authority that the installation of any central heating system is structural.

[66] *Cf. Monk* v. *Murphy* (1949) 153 E.G. 222, C.A. (Rent Acts).

[67] See *Pearlman, supra, per* Lord Denning M.R. at p. 67C.

[68] *Rendall* v. *Duke of Westminster* (1981) West London C.C., unreported, not dealt with on appeal at (1982) C.A.T. No. 203.

[69] As in *Rendall* v. *Duke of Westminster, supra*; see para. 2–32.

[70] As in, *e.g.* s.2(1)(*b*) of the Landlord and Tenant Act 1927 (compensation for tenant's improvements) and s.34(*c*) of the Landlord and Tenant Act 1954 (tenant's improvements ignored in fixing new rent of business premises).

has given consideration for the making of such improvements. But Schedule 8 significantly fails to do this, and it appears that a tenant can obtain a notional reduction even if he was contractually bound (*e.g.* by a covenant in his lease) to make the improvement. Frequently, however, the grant of the tenancy was made conditional upon the completion of improvements; in such a case there is no tenancy even in equity[71] until the improvements have been completed,[72] so the improvements were not made by the tenant or a predecessor of his.[73] An extreme example of this situation occurs in the common case of a building agreement, where the builder becomes entitled to the grant of a tenancy only upon the house being built. (However, even in the case of a true building lease, *i.e.* a lease containing a covenant to build a house, it is considered that the house itself is not an "improvement" within the Schedule,[74] which contemplates only alterations, extensions or additions to an existing house.)

Maker of improvements

The Schedule applies only "where the tenant, or any previous tenant, has made or contributed to the cost of an improvement. . . ."[75] The previous tenant must have been a tenant under the current tenancy[76] or a prior tenancy which under section 3(3) of the 1967 Act is treated as single composite tenancy with the current tenancy[77]; improvements made by a tenant under any other tenancy are not included. Moreover, it has been held, it is considered correctly, that the tenant or previous tenant must have been the tenant at the time when the improvements were made, and improvements made prior to the grant of the tenancy are not within Schedule 8.[78] It has also been held that a tenant who arranged for improvements to be done and was personally liable to the contractors to pay for them had "made" the improvements, even though they were in fact wholly paid for by another, so that the tenant had contributed nothing to the cost[79]: *sed quaere.*[80] 2–27

---

[71] *i.e.* under the principle of *Walsh* v. *Lonsdale* (1882) 21 Ch.D. 9, C.A.
[72] *Cornish* v. *Brook Green Laundry Ltd.* [1959] 1 Q.B. 394, C.A.; and see further para. 3–03.
[73] See para. 2–27.
[74] Sched. 8, para. 1(2).
[75] Sched. 8, para. 1(3).
[76] See paras. 2(2)(*c*), 3(1)(*b*) and 3(4).
[77] *Bates* v. *Pierrepoint* (1978) 37 P. & C.R. 420, C.A.; *Rendall* v. *Duke of Westminster, supra.*
[78] *Gage* v. *Duke of Westminster* (1984) West London C.C., unreported (Judge Harris Q.C.), applying *Trustees of Henry Smith's Charity* v. *Hemmings* (1983) 265 E.G. 383, C.A., decided on comparable words in the Rent Act 1977, s.70(3)(*b*).
[79] *Oddy* v. *Earl Grosvenor* (1980) Westminster C.C., unreported (Judge Ruttle).
[80] The tenant's claim to an extended lease failed on other grounds: see *Duke of Westminster* v. *Oddy* (1984) 270 E.G. 945, C.A.

Procedure

2–28 In order to obtain a notional reduction in the rateable value, the tenant must follow the procedure set out in Schedule 8, culminating in either an agreed notional reduction or a certificate issued by the valuation officer as to the amount of such reduction. Unless and until the tenant serves a Schedule 8 notice setting this procedure into operation, neither the court nor a leasehold valuation tribunal can take any account of chance that the tenant might obtain a notional reduction, however probable that may be, but must determine the matter before it solely on the basis of value shown in the valuation list in force on April 1, 1973.[81]

The Schedule 8 procedure can be conveniently divided into four steps, three of which must be taken by the tenant. As will appear, it is essential for the tenant to comply properly and promptly with the steps he is required to take, otherwise he may lose his right to any notional reduction of the rateable value. The four steps are as follows:

(1) *Schedule 8 notice*

2–29 **Form of notice.** The first step which the tenant must take is to serve on the landlord a Schedule 8 notice, *i.e.* a notice in "the prescribed form" of the first of the two forms set out at the end of the Schedule.[82] In this form, the tenant must complete the First Schedule by descriptions of the improvements he relies on and the Second Schedule by descriptions of the works involved in those improvements. He must also propose a figure to which the rateable value should be reduced. The form requires the landlord to agree to the notional reduction claimed and, if he does not do so, to state whether he agrees:

(a) that the improvements were made "by the execution of works amounting to structural alteration or extension of the premises or a structural addition thereto" (*i.e.* whether they are qualifying improvements discussed above[83]);
(b) that the works set out in the Second Schedule to the Notice were involved in the making of the improvements;
(c) that the tenant or a previous tenant under the tenancy made or contributed to the cost of the improvements; and
(d) the proportion of the cost so contributed.

The Schedule 8 notice should be properly completed, for the omission

[81] *Effra Investments Ltd.* v. *Stergios* (1982) 264 E.G. 449, L.V.T.; *Duke of Westminster* v. *Oddy, supra*, at p. 947, col. 1. As to the date from which a notional reduction takes effect, see paras. 2–36 *et seq.*
[82] Sched. 8, para. 1(1). Unusually, the form and its explanatory notes are part of the statute.
[83] See para. 2–24.

of any material particulars may possibly render a notice invalid. As much detail as possible (including copies of any specifications and plans) should be set out or incorporated in the Second Schedule; although the absence of such details will probably not invalidate the notice, it may put the tenant at risk as to the costs of court proceedings. Moreover, the tenant should include details of all the improvements on which he intends to rely, because he may not be entitled to serve a subsequent Schedule 8 notice.[84] Obtaining the necessary information and details, particularly in cases of improvements carried out by a predecessor in title, is frequently far from straight-forward. Sources of information which sometimes prove fruitful are the builders and/or architects concerned, and licences granted by the landlord and local authorities (who frequently retain copies of plans and specifications referred to in applications for planning permission or building regulation and similar approvals). The landlord himself often has helpful documentary information; but it is considered that this cannot be obtained by the tenant except by way of discovery after proceedings have been commenced.

Service of notice. A Schedule 8 notice can be served in any manner permitted for the service of other notices under the 1967 Act.[85] No express provision is made as regards sub-tenancies.[86] Although it may suffice to serve a Schedule 8 notice on "the reversioner," this is by no means clear,[87] and the only safe course is for a sub-tenant to serve all his landlords.

(2) *Application to the county court*

The procedure of Schedule 8 provides for an initial period of six weeks 2–30
during which the landlord and the tenant are supposed to agree the amount of the reduction.[88] If at the end of that six-week period there has been no such agreement and any of the other matters specified in the Schedule 8 notice have not been agreed, the tenant can apply to the county court to determine such matters.[89] The application must be made within a further six weeks from the expiration of the initial six-week period "or such longer time as the court may allow."[90] The application for the longer time can be made after the expiry of the further six weeks.[91]

---

[84] See para. 2–36.
[85] 1967 Act, s.22(5); see para. 5–06.
[86] Sched. 3, para. 8(1)(*a*) relates only to the service of a Notice of Leaseholder's Claim.
[87] Sched. 1, para. 1(1) deals only with matters arising from the service of a Notice of Leaseholder's Claim.
[88] Housing Act 1974, Sched. 8, para. 1(2).
[89] *Ibid.* para. 1(2). The court has no power to determine the *amount* of the notional reduction.
[90] *Ibid.* para. 1(3). It appears that such an application cannot be made until the first 6-week period has expired.
[91] *Arieli* v. *Duke of Westminster* (1983) 269 E.G. 535, C.A.

The court has an unfettered discretion on the application, and it is not necessary for the tenant to show any exceptional circumstances.[92] It is thought that the court will normally extend time unless the landlord would be unfairly prejudiced or there has been inordinate delay on the part of the tenant, and in particular will do so where the landlord himself has done little or nothing to progress the matter.[93] It appears to have been suggested in one case[94] that an extension will be less readily granted if the purpose of the proposed reduction is to bring the house and premises within the rateable value limits of the 1967 Act as amended (as opposed to altering the basis of valuation), but this seems unsound.

The usual procedural rules in the county court apply. Thus, in appropriate cases the tenant may be ordered to give full particulars of the improvements on which he relies and other matters on which he relies[95]; and both parties can be ordered to give discovery of any relevant documents. The relief granted by the court usually consists of a series of appropriate declarations. As originally enacted, Schedule 8 provided that any determination by the court of the matters in dispute should be "final and conclusive." After much litigation, it was eventually held that this precluded any form of appeal or judicial review[96]; but that provision has been repealed[97] and appeal lies to the Court of Appeal in the ordinary way.

(3) *Application to valuation officer*

2–31 Once all the matters relating to the improvements have either been agreed or determined by the court, Schedule 8 provides for a period of two weeks during which the parties are supposed to agree a notional reduction.[98] If no agreement is reached at the end of that two-week period, the tenant can apply to the valuation officer for a certificate of the notional reduction. The application must be made within the period of four weeks from the expiry of the two-week period.[99] There is no provision for extension of the four-week period, and a certificate issued pursuant to a late

[92] *Arieli* v. *Duke of Westminster, supra*; *Johnston* v. *Duke of Westminster* (1984) 272 E.G. 661 (wrongly entitled *Johnston* v. *Duke of Devonshire* in the report, probably to the relief of the Grosvenor Estate Trustees whose conduct attracted criticism from the Court of Appeal).

[93] *Johnston* v. *Duke of Westminster, supra*; and see *Re Stone* (1969) 114 S.J. 36, C.A. (analogous provisions of the Inheritance (Family Provision) Act 1966, s.5(1)).

[94] *Mayhew* v. *Governors of Harrow Road Trust* [1985] C.L.Y. 1913, Bloomsbury C.C. (Judge Wild): a harsh decision depending on its special facts.

[95] *Brewer* v. *Duke of Westminster* (1985) West London C.C., unreported (Judge Oddie).

[96] *Re Racal Communications Ltd.* [1981] A.C. 374, overruling *Pearlman* v. *Keepers and Governors of Harrow School* [1979] 1 Q.B. 56 on this point.

[97] By the Housing Act 1980, Sched. 21, para. 8(*c*).

[98] Para. 3(1).

[99] *Ibid.* (This paragraph is wrongly set out in the Queen's Printer's copy of the Housing Act 1974; the latter part governs the whole of para. 3(1), not merely sub-para. (*b*) thereof). It appears that an application cannot be validly made until the two-week period has expired.

application is a nullity[1]; and it has been held that a tenant who has missed the time-limit cannot serve a fresh Schedule 8 notice and consequently loses completely his right to a notional reduction.[2]

In the case of a determination by the county court, the above periods start from the date on which the judge makes the order, and not when the written order is finally issued by the court office.[3] Schedule 8 does not deal with the position arising in the event of an appeal.[4] It is considered that there is no suspension of time as a result of an appeal from the county court; and valuation officers have been advised, it is considered correctly, to accept any application based on a county court decision and not to delay the issue of a certificate, notwithstanding that the decision is under appeal. But if an improvement is determined to be a relevant improvement only by the Court of Appeal[5] or the House of Lords, there will have been no relevant determination and as regards that improvement time cannot start to run until then.

Form of application. The application by the tenant to the valuation officer must be in "the prescribed form," *i.e.* the second of the two forms set out at the end of Schedule 8 and must state the name and address of the landlord.[6] Unfortunately, there is no provision for a copy of the application to be shown to the landlord, either by the tenant or the valuation officer, before the latter issues his certificate. This can cause difficulty if the information set out in the tenant's application is erroneous or disputed, but this only becomes clear after the certificate has been issued by the valuation officer, who must send a copy to the landlord.[7] In order to avoid this difficulty, it is suggested that it is a good practice for the valuation officer to ask the landlord for any comments on the form of the application before the certificate is issued. It is considered that an error in the tenant's application does not render it a nullity, but that no reliance can be placed on a certificate issued in pursuance of it unless the certificate has been amended appropriately. 2–32

(4) *Certificate of the valuation officer*

In his certificate, the valuation officer must certify whether or not the 2–33

---

[1] *Pollock* v. *Brook-Shepherd* (1983) 45 P. & C.R. 357, C.A., affirming Judge Macnair (West London C.C.) on this point.

[2] *Pollock* v. *Brook-Shepherd, supra*, reversing Judge Macnair on this point. For a discussion and criticism, see para. 2–34.

[3] *Cf.* R.S.C., Ord. 59, r. 19(3)(*a*).

[4] Doubtless because, as originally enacted, an appeal was precluded: see para. 2–29. Parliament failed to pick up the point in the amendments made by the Housing Act 1980, Sched. 21.

[5] As happened in *Pearlman* v. *Keepers and Governors of Harrow School* [1979] Q.B. 56.

[6] Sched. 8, para. 3(1), (3).

[7] *Ibid.* para. 3(3).

improvements have affected the rateable value on April 1, 1973, of the hereditament of which the house and premises consist (or, as the case may be, in which they are wholly or partly comprised), and if so the amount by which the rateable value would have been less if the improvements had not been made.[8] The notional reduction is then that amount, reduced proportionately if only part of the cost was contributed by the tenant or a previous tenant.[9] If, when the tenant's application is made, there is pending a proposal for an alteration in the valuation list relating to the hereditament which would have effect from April 1, 1973,[10] or earlier, the valuation officer must not issue his certificate until the proposal is settled.[11] No provision is made for the valuation officer to hear or take account of any arguments or evidence of the parties as to the appropriate notional reduction in the rateable value, but there seems no reason why either party should not make representations in correspondence. No appeal lies to a local valuation court or elsewhere, and the valuation officer's certificate can only be challenged by proceedings for judicial review.[12]

The fact that a qualifying improvement has been made does not mean that it has affected the rateable value and so does not necessitate a notional reduction being certified. Many structural alterations, including some quite substantial ones, in practice have little or no effect on the rateable value. Much depends on the basis on which rateable values in the district were originally assessed for the purposes of the 1973 valuation list. If, for instance, a bathroom was then valued at the same rate per square foot as a bedroom, the conversion of a bedroom into a bathroom will not have affected the 1973 rateable value.[13] Another situation which sometimes arises is that the valuation officer's records show that the existence of the improvement was not known to him or his office at the time of the preparation of the 1973 list and therefore not then taken into account; in such cases, it necessarily follows that there should be no notional reduction.[14]

Service of subsequent Schedule 8 notice

2–34 There is no statutory provision which expressly prohibits the service of

---

[8] *Ibid.* para. 3(2).

[9] *Ibid.* para. 3(4).

[10] There can have been few such applications: see *Marks* v. *Phillimore* heard with *MacFarquhar* v. *Phillimore* (1986) 279 E.G. 549, C.A.

[11] *Ibid.* para. 3(5). It is very unlikely that there are now any such proposals still pending: see para. 2–19. The effect of para. 3(5) appears to have been misunderstood in *Duke of Westminster* v. *Oddy* (1984) 270 E.G. 945.

[12] Under R.S.C., Ord. 59. An unsuccessful challenge was made in *R.* v. *Valuation Officer for Westminster and District, ex p. Rendall* (1986) 278 E.G. 1090, C.A., affirming Taylor J., unreported.

[13] *R.* v. *Valuation Officer for Westminster and District, ex p. Rendall, supra.*

[14] *Ibid.* per Taylor J. (not mentioned in Court of Appeal).

more than one Schedule 8 notice. Nevertheless, it has been held by the Court of Appeal in *Pollock* v. *Brook-Shepherd*[15] that if a tenant's Schedule 8 notice is not effective by reason of his failure to observe one of the time-limits laid down by Schedule 8 mentioned above, he is not entitled to serve another Schedule 8 notice relying on the same improvements. It was said that the tenant "has no right to another chance to put right what was not done properly in the first place."[16] However, the Court of Appeal reached this unfortunate and Draconian conclusion as the consequence of an underlying assumption[17] that any notional reduction would affect the basis of valuation[18] of a freehold being acquired under a Notice of Leaseholder's Claim which had been served before the first Schedule 8 notice. As a result, it was said: 2–34

> "it must follow as a matter of necessary implication that there is no right to make a second application under Schedule 8, because if a second application was permitted it would completely destroy the purpose of inserting a mandatory timetable."[19]

If the underlying assumption is correct, this reasoning cannot be faulted. But if the underlying assumption is not correct, the foundation of the reasoning disappears. If, for instance, the notional reduction would take effect only from the date of the Schedule 8 notice, the mandatory timetable has a manifest purpose, and the implication made by the Court of Appeal could not be justified. For reasons which appear below,[20] the author considers that the underlying assumption is not in fact correct. Furthermore, the Court of Appeal also assumed, apparently as part of its reasoning, that the Notice of Leaseholder's Claim and the first Schedule 8 notice were both part of a single "legislative machinery" or "procedure,"[21] which is plainly not so.[22] It is accordingly submitted that *Pollock* v. *Brook-Shepherd* was decided *per incuriam* and ought not to be followed.

Even if *Pollock* v. *Brook-Shepherd* was correctly decided, it may well be that it only precludes a second Schedule 8 notice being served with the intention of affecting an existing Notice of Leaseholder's Claim. Thus it may be that a second Schedule 8 notice can be validly served if either no Notice of Leaseholder's Claim at all has been served or if it is intended only 2–35

[15] (1983) 45 P. & C.R. 357, discussed by the author at (1983) 266 E.G. 187.
[16] *Ibid. per* Lawton L.J. at p. 363.
[17] Agreed by both parties before the West London C.C. (Judge Macnair). On the facts of the case, the assumption was required by both parties, the tenant because he wished to rely on his prior Notice of Leaseholder's Claim, and the landlord in order to found his argument.
[18] *i.e.* whether the freehold should be valued under s.9(1) or s.9(1A): see para. 9–14.
[19] *Pollock* v. *Brook-Shepherd, supra, per* Griffiths L.J. at p. 363.
[20] See paras. 2–36 *et seq.*
[21] *Pollock* v. *Brook-Shepherd* (1983) 45 P. & C.R. 357, *per* Lawton L.J. at p. 362.
[22] See paras. 2–36 *et seq.*

to affect a subsequent Notice of Leaseholder's Claim served three years[23] after an existing Notice of Leaseholder's Claim has been withdrawn.[24] (*Pollock* v. *Brook-Shepherd* is not authority for the proposition that a tenant has only "one bite at the cherry" in any circumstances, as is sometimes mistakenly thought[25]). It is unclear whether *Pollock* v. *Brook-Shepherd* also precludes an assignee of the tenant from serving a second Schedule 8 notice. If it does, the question of whether or not the assignor or a predecessor in title of his has served an abortive Schedule 8 notice becomes a potentially important matter of title, which should be investigated on the purchase of a house held on a long tenancy at a low rent.

It is also unclear whether a tenant can serve a second Schedule 8 notice in reliance on improvements different from those specified in his first notice. This is frequently a point of practical importance. A tenant is often unaware that improvements were made by a predecessor-in-title; and even when he becomes aware, it can take a considerable amount of expensive and time-consuming research to ascertain the necessary details of the improvements, all of which is unnecessary if other improvements are sufficient to reduce the rateable value below the relevant critical figure.[26] Nevertheless, it has been held in the county court that a tenant must include all the improvements in a single Schedule 8 notice, and cannot serve a second one.[27] It is considered that this is not correct and involves an unwarranted extension of *Pollock* v. *Brook-Shepherd.* However, until the point has been properly considered by the Court of Appeal, tenants must be advised to make sure that they include all potentially qualifying improvements in a single Schedule 8 notice.

Date from which notional reduction takes effect

2–36 Schedule 8 fails to make it clear from what date a notional reduction which is agreed or certified by a valuation officer's certificate takes effect, *i.e.* the extent to which it operates retroactively.[28] This is frequently a matter of considerable practical importance. Suppose, for instance, that a tenant of a house and premises in Greater London with a rateable value on April 1, 1973, of £1,520[29] serves a Notice of Leaseholder's Claim to

---

[23] The tenant is barred from serving a further Notice of Leaseholder's Claim for three years: s.9(3).

[24] This appears to have been the view of Lawton L.J. in *Pollock* v. *Brook-Shepherd, supra*, at p. 363 ("the tenant might be able to go on again after three years").

[25] The P. & C.R. headnote is too wide.

[26] *i.e.* £1,000 or £1,500 in Greater London, £500 or £750 elsewhere: see ss.1(6) and 9(1A) of the 1967 Act as amended.

[27] *Newman* v. *Duke of Westminster* (1984) West London C.C., unreported (Judge Harris Q.C.).

[28] See para. 1–18.

[29] *i.e.* over the £1,500 limit in s.1(6): see para. 2–21.

acquire the freehold, a claim which on the face of it is clearly invalid. If he subsequently obtains a valuation officer's certificate of a £30 notional reduction, does that operate to validate his previously invalid claim, or does it only affect a fresh claim made subsequently? Similarly, suppose that a tenant of a house and premises with a rateable value on April 1, 1973, of £1,020 serves a Notice of Leaseholder's Claim to acquire the freehold. That claim is a valid one, but the purchase price will on the face of it be ascertained on the basis of valuation set out in section 9(1A) of the 1967 Act, and not under section 9(1).[30] If he likewise subsequently obtains a valuation officer's certificate of a £30 notional reduction, does that alter the basis of valuation (and thus alter an important term of the statutory contract created by the Notice of Leaseholder's Claim[31])? Or will it only affect a claim made subsequently?[32]

There appear to be the following five possible dates from which, on the true construction of Schedule 8, an agreed notional reduction or a valuation officer's certificate might take effect: 2–37

(1) *The date of agreement or certificate*

Prima facie, this date appears to be the obvious and logical one, for it enables the validity of a tenant's claim as regards rateable value, and/or the basis of valuation of the freehold, to be ascertained immediately the Notice of Leaseholder's Claim is served. As regards the validity of a claim, section 1(1) of the 1967 Act specifies the several conditions for eligibility to make a claim,[33] and the obtaining of any necessary notional reduction in the rateable value would appear to be essential in order to satisfy the rateable value condition.[34]

The main argument against this date is that it deprives the strict time-limits of Schedule 8 imposed on a tenant of any apparent purpose; for a tenant who delayed operating the machinery of Schedule 8 would thereby delay his service of a Notice of Leaseholder's Claim and so would be acting against his own interest. In addition, it could result in a tenant's claim being delayed and even defeated altogether by matters beyond his control (such as the hearing date of any court proceedings and the issue of

[30] ss.9(1A), 5(1) and 37(1)(*d*); and see *Effra Investments Ltd.* v. *Stergios* (1982) 264 E.G. 449, L.V.T.

[31] See s.5(1), and para. 5–08.

[32] In order to make such a claim, the tenant would have to withdraw his Notice and wait another three years: see s.9(3)(*b*).

[33] s.1(4A) expressly provides that the function of Schedule 8 is to enable a "tenant to have the rateable value of the house reduced for the purposes of this section."

[34] This is assumed in other parts of the 1967 Act. See *e.g.* s.5(1) ("where a tenant of a house has the right to acquire the freehold or an extended lease and gives notice of his desire to have it"), and Sched. 3 para. 6(*b*)(iv), as introduced by the Housing Act 1980, Sched. 21, but not yet in force.

the valuation officer's certificate) and/or by "determined resistance by the landlord."[35] For these reasons, the author agrees with the view expressed in *Duke of Westminster* v. *Oddy*[36] that this date is not the correct one.

(2) *The date of service of Schedule 8 notice*

2–38 The right to a notional reduction in the rateable value is conditional upon and arises from the service of a Schedule 8 notice, and, as in the case of a Notice of Leaseholder's Claim, one would expect that right to be effective as from (and not before) the date of service. Furthermore, the wording of para. 1(1) of Schedule 8 is consistent with, and affords some support for, the date of service being the correct date.[37] That date is also the most natural and convenient one, albeit that the tenant's right to a reduction and the amount of any reduction both remain to be determined. On this footing, a Notice of Leaseholder's Claim relying on a notional reduction in rateable value will be valid if served contemporaneously with or after the Schedule 8 notice; and the court or leasehold valuation tribunal would doubtless adjourn any proceedings in which the rateable value is in issue until the outcome of the Schedule 8 notice is known.

If the date of service of the Schedule 8 notice is the correct date, the time-limits in Schedule 8 have clear and obvious purpose of ensuring that the position under a contemporaneous or subsequent Notice of Leaseholder's Claim is ascertained as soon as possible.[38] In the view of the author, this date is the correct date. It was unfortunately altogether ignored as a possibility in *Duke of Westminster* v. *Oddy*.[39]

(3) *The date of service of a Notice of Leaseholder's Claim*

2–39 It has been judicially stated that a notional reduction operates with effect from the date of any prior Notice of Leaseholder's Claim.[40] In the view of the author, this is not correct, and it would require far clearer words to validate retrospectively a claim which was invalid (by reason of the rateable value limits), or to alter retrospectively one of the terms (the

---

[35] See *Duke of Westminster* v. *Oddy* (1984) 270 E.G. 945, *per* Eveleigh L.J. at p. 948; however, the reasoning is difficult to follow and there appears to be some confusion between the 1967 Act procedure and the Schedule 8 procedure.

[36] *Supra*, disagreeing with Judge McDonnell (Westminster C.C.) on this point: see further para. 2–41.

[37] Notwithstanding the absence from Schedule 8 of any express provision comparable to s.5(1).

[38] The existence of a claim to the freehold or an extended lease may of itself be prejudicial to the landlord: see *Pollock* v. *Brook-Shepherd*, *supra*, *per* Lawton L.J. at p. 359 (where, however, the prejudice is somewhat exaggerated).

[39] (1984) 270 E.G. 945, discussed at para. 2–41.

[40] Although there is no clear statement to that effect, this appears to be the result of *obiter dicta* in *Duke of Westminster* v. *Oddy*, *supra*.

basis of valuation of the freehold) of the statutory contract already made. The date also gives rise to difficult practical and legal problems. If it is the correct date, the result appears to be that a tenant can claim a retroactive notional reduction "at any time,"[41] however long, after claiming the freehold or an extended lease, *e.g.* during the course of any court or leasehold valuation tribunal hearing; in such a case, the court or tribunal would presumably be bound to grant an adjournment pending the outcome of the Schedule 8 notice.[42] And if a Schedule 8 notice is served after a court or tribunal decision, would that decision be treated as effectively reversed by subsequent events? See further para. 2–41.

(4) *April 1, 1973*

The argument in favour of April 1, 1973, is based on the fact that the notional reduction affects the rateable value on that date, the reduced rateable value being substituted for the purposes of the 1967 Act.[43] But it is plainly fallacious to conclude that this substitution is itself retroactive to that date.[44] "Parliament did not say that the adjusted figure shall be deemed to have been the rateable value on April 1, 1973."[45] Furthermore, the same comments as those in para. 2–39 apply. **2–40**

(5) *The date of hearing of court or tribunal proceedings in which the amount of the rateable value is relevant*

It is impossible to see how such an arbitrary and fortuitous date can be justified on the wording of Schedule 8.[46]

Duke of Westminster v. Oddy[47]

The first and main point decided by the Court of Appeal in this case related to the question whether the tenant occupied "in right of the tenancy,"[48] and determined the appeal in the landlord's favour. But Eveleigh L.J.[49] went on to express the view *obiter* that a notional **2–41**

---

[41] s.1(4A).
[42] Such an adjournment could cause considerable loss to the landlord which could not be compensated for in an order for costs.
[43] See note 2 to the prescribed form of notice set out in Schedule 8.
[44] The word "will" in note 2 to the prescribed form indicates the contrary.
[45] *Per* Judge McDonnell in *Duke of Westminster* v. *Oddy* (1984) 270 E.G. 945.
[46] The date appears to have formed the basis of an argument on behalf of the tenant in *Pollock* v. *Brook-Shepherd* (1983) 45 P. & C.R. 357, which argument was rejected by the Court of Appeal.
[47] (1984) 270 E.G. 945.
[48] See para. 4–02.
[49] Kerr L.J., the other member of a two-member Court of Appeal, simply agreed and did not give any reasons of his own.

reduction of rateable value would have been effective for the purposes of a Notice of Leaseholder's Claim served prior to the Schedule 8 notice.[50] However, Eveleigh L.J.'s reasoning is, with respect, difficult to follow and unconvincing. Unfortunately, the arguments on behalf of both tenant and landlord are not properly dealt with, and the landlord's alternative argument that the date of service of the Schedule 8 notice is the correct date was altogether ignored.[51]

Some brief comments on what appear to be the main points in the reasoning of Eveleigh L.J. may be ventured.

1. Eveleigh L.J. contrasted the wording of section 1(1)(*a*) with that of section 1(1)(*b*), pointing out that the reference to "the relevant time" is contained in the latter, and concluded that the rateable value condition, contained in section 1(1)(*a*) need not therefore be satisfied at "the relevant time" (the date of service of the Notice of Leaseholder's Claim).[52] But para. (*b*) of section 1(1) necessarily requires a fixed date for the calculation of the qualifying residential period, whereas para. (*a*) is concerned with current matters, and the contrast is of no real significance. Indeed, para. (*a*) contains the word "is," which suggests that all the conditions therein contained must then be satisfied in order for the tenant to make a valid claim. (Moreover, Eveleigh L.J.'s argument logically leads to the manifestly incorrect conclusions that the house need not be held on "a long tenancy at a low rent" when the tenant serves his Notice of Leaseholder's Claim and that he need not then be "occupying the house as his residence."[53])

2. Eveleigh L.J. considered section 5 to be neutral, and asserted that a Notice of Leaseholder's Claim "is a procedural step which the tenant must take if he is to call upon the court for assistance in enforcing his right to enfranchisement," or "an invitation to the landlord to treat,"[54] and that "its role is largely procedural."[55] These remarks overlook the critical function of a Notice of Leaseholder's Claim in forming a statutory contract and fixing the date by reference to which the purchase price is determined.

3. Eveleigh L.J. said that the landlord's argument amounted to saying that the tenant's Notice of Leaseholder's Claim was of no effect, drew attention to the provisions of the 1967 Act expressly rendering such a notice of no effect, and stated that "nowhere is it enacted that a notice is

---

[50] Disagreeing with the contrary view of Judge McDonnell in the county court.

[51] *Pollock* v. *Brook-Shepherd, supra*, was cited in argument, and an article by the author at (1983) 266 E.G. 187 referred to, but neither are mentioned in the judgment.

[52] *Duke of Westminster* v. *Oddy, supra*, at p. 946, col. 2 (the reference to "section 1(*a*)" is clearly a mistake for subs. (1)(*a*)).

[53] See paras. 3–14 and 4–03.

[54] *Duke of Westminster* v. *Oddy, supra*, at p. 947, col. 1.

[55] *Ibid.* at p. 947, col. 2.

of no effect if given before there has been an adjustment of rateable value."[56] But it could hardly be contended that such a notice was other than invalid and of no effect if one of the other conditions was not satisfied, but there is equally no specific provision in the 1967 Act expressly so stating; and clearly no such specific provision is to be expected, let alone required.

4. Eveleigh L.J. referred to the legal maxim "*id certum est quod certum reddi potest.*"[57] That overlooks the necessity of serving a Schedule 8 notice, and in any event entirely begs the question of the date from which the tenant becomes eligible to enjoy his statutory rights.

Whether subsequent notional reduction might affect the purchase price

The author has seen a suggestion that, although a notional reduction in rateable value does not operate retroactively for the purpose of determining the validity of a tenant's claim,[58] nevertheless it does operate retroactively for the purpose of determining the basis of ascertainment of the purchase price if the tenant otherwise has a valid claim to acquire the freehold.[59] The argument in favour of this suggestion is based on the wording of subss.(1A) and (1B) of section 9, and in particular the use of the word "is" in subs.(1B). This, it is said, shows that the rateable value is for valuation purposes treated as a matter of objective fact, of which the valuation officer's certificate is declaratory and constitutive. 2–42

The author does not agree with this suggestion. It is very unlikely that Parliament would have intended a notional reduction to be retroactive for one purpose but not the other, and the minor differences in wording between section 1(4A) and section 9(1B) are insufficient to force the court to such a surprising and illogical conclusion. In the author's view, the date from which a notional reduction takes effect must be the same, and the purpose for which the notional reduction is used cannot affect that question. However, this is a further matter which remains to be properly clarified by the courts.

---

[56] *Ibid.* at p. 947, col. 1.
[57] *Ibid.* at p. 947, col. 2.
[58] *i.e.* contrary to the dicta in *Duke of Westminster* v. *Oddy, supra*: see para. 2–41.
[59] *i.e.* whether under subs. (1) or (1A) of s.9: see subs. (1B) and para. 9–14.

CHAPTER 3

TENANCIES QUALIFYING

3–01 In order for a tenant to be entitled to exercise the rights given by the 1967 Act, his tenancy must have been a "long tenancy" and "at a low rent," both on the date when the tenant gives his Notice of Leaseholder's Claim[1] and also during the whole of his qualifying three years[2] period of residence.[3] (An exception to this rule was made by the transitional provisions of section 34 of the 1967 Act, but it is considered that these are now spent and are not further discussed.[4]) His tenancy must at those times have comprised the whole of the house,[5] unless, it appears, he is already the freeholder of the remaining part.[6] But the tenancy need not have comprised any part of the "premises".[7]

1. LONG TENANCY

"Tenancy"

3–02 The tenancy may be an immediate tenancy or a sub-tenancy[8], including a sub-tenancy created by the grant of a lease to a secure tenant in pursuance of the "right to buy" provisions of Part V of the Housing Act 1985,[9] and it may be a tenancy at law or in equity.[10] The most common example of a tenancy in equity is a specifically enforceable agreement for a lease taking effect as an equitable tenancy or sub-tenancy under the

---

[1] s. 1(1)(*a*), as amended.

[2] Originally five years, but reduced to three years by Sched. 21 to the Housing Act 1980, para. 1(1).

[3] s. 1(1)(*b*): see *Harris* v. *Plentex Ltd.* (1980) 40 P. & C.R. 483.

[4] A full discussion will be found in Chap. 16 of the 1st edition of this book (1967).

[5] For an example of a case where the tenant failed because his tenancy extended to part only of the house, see *Baron* v. *Phillips* (1978) 38 P. & C.R. 91, C.A.; see further para. 3–08.

[6] *Harper* v. *Harris* (1968) S.J. 954; and see *Peck* v. *Anicar Properties Ltd.* [1971] 1 All E.R. 517, *per* Lord Denning M.R. at p. 519c.

[7] s. 1(1).

[8] s. 5(2).

[9] Housing Act 1985, s.118(1)(*b*); see further para. 3–07.

[10] L.R.A. 1967, s. 37(1)(*f*).

principle of *Walsh* v. *Lonsdale*.[11] But none of a tenancy at will, a tenancy at sufferance[12] (which is not really a tenancy at all), a mortgage term still liable to be terminated by the exercise of any right of redemption or otherwise, or a portions or similar term created by way of trust under a settlement, constitutes a tenancy for the purposes of the 1967 Act.[13] However, a former mortgage term which is no longer subject to any right of redemption, *e.g.* because the term has been assigned by way of realisation of the security or because the right of redemption is statute-barred, has ceased to be a mortgage term and is a tenancy within the Act.[14]

Primary definition

The primary meaning of a "long tenancy" is a tenancy originally granted for a term certain exceeding 21 years.[15] A term cannot as a matter of law commence before the date of its grant[16] (although as a matter of contract between the parties, it may operate as regards payment of rent as from some earlier date).[17] For the purposes of the Act the term thus begins on the later of (i) the commencement date stated in the *habendum*, and (ii) the date of the grant, and ends on the day which is specified to be the last of that term. That a grant is in equity is immaterial,[18] and it is considered that if there was a specifically enforceable prior agreement for a lease, the term commences on the date when it first became specifically enforceable.[19] For this purpose, however, there must be a fully concluded and legally binding agreement. In many cases, there is no such agreement and the whole transaction remains in negotiation until the actual grant of the formal lease[20]; and (contrary to popular misconception) the agreement of the draft of the lease does not constitute a binding contract for a lease.[21] Furthermore, if the prior agreement is conditional upon some act or event occurring, the agreement is not specifically enforceable, and no equitable 3–03

[11] (1882) 21 Ch. D. 9, C.A. See Megarry and Wade, *The Law of Real Property* (5th ed.), pp. 640 *et seq.*

[12] *Hayes* v. *Poole Corporation* (1968) Poole C.C., unreported (Judge Pennant).

[13] s. 37(1)(*f*).

[14] *Re Fairview, Bromyard* [1974] 1 W.L.R. 579.

[15] s. 3(1). The word "certain" means only that a fixed maximum duration of the term must be specified: *Eton College* v. *Bard* [1983] Ch. 321, C.A.

[16] *Roberts* v. *Church Commissioners for England* [1972] 1 Q.B. 278, C.A., following *Shaw* v. *Kay* (1847) 1 Exch. 412, *Earl Cadogan* v. *Guinness* [1936] Ch. 515 and other cases.

[17] *Bradshaw* v. *Pawley* [1980] 1 W.L.R. 10.

[18] s. 37(1)(*f*).

[19] This point did not arise in *Roberts* v. *Church Commissioners for England, supra.*

[20] *Hollington Bros. Ltd.* v. *Rhodes* [1951] 2 T.L.R. 691 (omitted from the report at [1951] 2 All E.R. 578 n).

[21] *Phillips* v. *Edwards* (1864) 33 Beav. 440; *Hollington Bros. Ltd.* v. *Rhodes, supra*; and *Leveson* v. *Parfum Marcel Rochas (England) Ltd.* (1966) 200 E.G. 407 (where the authorities are conveniently considered).

tenancy arises until the condition is fulfilled.[22] Examples which frequently arise in practice are where there is a prior agreement for a lease, conditional either upon the tenant doing certain specified works, in which case the grant will have taken effect in equity only from the date of the completion of the works,[23] or upon the completion of the surrender of a prior tenancy, in which case the grant will have taken effect in equity only from the completion of the surrender.[24] Some agreements contain a clause expressly providing that in any event there is to be no tenancy (but only, *e.g.* a licence) until the actual grant of the formal lease, thus attempting to negative the principle of *Walsh* v. *Lonsdale*. It is considered that equity will nevertheless "deem to be done what ought to be done" and that a specifically enforceable agreement containing such a clause will nevertheless constitute an equitable tenancy.[25]

Provided that the term of the tenancy is over 21 years, it is immaterial that it may determine earlier (subject to the exception relating to tenancies terminable after a death or marriage, dealt with below).[26] Thus it is immaterial that the term may be terminated before the expiry of 21 years from its commencement by the action of one of the parties, *e.g.* under a landlord's "break" clause, or by a tenant's notice, or by re-entry and forfeiture for non-payment of rent or breach of covenant by the tenant, or by any other event,[27] *e.g.* if "the lease shall cease to be vested in a member of the Association."[28] But there must be a single term of over 21 years and a tenant cannot add together two or more consecutive terms of under 21 years even if he has been tenant continuously for over 21 years.[29] The test is that the tenant "must at some point of time be, or have been, in a position to say that, subject to options to determine, rights of re-entry and so forth, he is entitled to remain tenant for the next 21 years, whether at law or in equity."[30]

3-04 In the case of a tenancy granted to continue as a periodic tenancy after the expiration of a term of years certain, or to continue as a periodical tenancy if not terminated at the expiration of such term, there are deemed to be two separate tenancies: (a) one granted to expire at the earliest time (at or after the expiry of the term of years) at which the tenancy could (under its terms and apart from any enactment) have been brought to an end by notice to quit given by the landlord, and (b) the other granted to

---

[22] *Cornish* v. *Brook Green Dry Cleaners Ltd.* [1959] 1 Q.B. 394, C.A.
[23] *Ibid.*
[24] *Rendall* v. *Duke of Westminster* (1982) West London C.C., unreported.
[25] The point was argued, but not decided, in *Roberts* v. *Church Commissioners for England*, *supra*.
[26] But see para. 3-05.
[27] s. 3(1).
[28] *Eton College* v. *Bard* [1983] Ch. 321, C.A.
[29] *Roberts* v. *Church Commissioners for England*, *supra*.
[30] *Ibid. per* Russell L.J. at p. 284C.

commence at the expiration of the first.[31] If a tenancy is granted for a term of (say) 20½ years followed by a yearly tenancy, the critical factor will thus be whether under the provisions of the lease the landlord can, by serving a notice to quit in due time, prevent the yearly tenancy coming into effect at all. If he can, neither tenancy will be a "long tenancy."[32] If he cannot, the first tenancy will be for at least 21½ years and so be a long tenancy, and if the second tenancy is at a low rent the second tenancy will be deemed also to be a long tenancy.[33]

The tenancy must be a valid tenancy, granted by a person having power to do so, or at any rate binding on the landlord by estoppel[34] or otherwise at the date of the Notice of Leaseholder's Claim. A lease for 99 years, purportedly granted by a statutory corporation with no power to lease for a term exceeding 3 years, has been held not to create a long tenancy.[35]

Exception

Certain tenancies terminable after a death or remarriage, even though for a term exceeding 21 years, are excluded from the definition of "long tenancy." As originally enacted, a "tenancy granted so as to become terminable by notice after a death or marriage" was not treated as a long tenancy.[36] Such tenancies included a lease for life, converted by section 149(6) of the Law of Property Act 1925 into a 99-year term determinable on three months notice after a death or marriage. The purpose of the exception was to exclude from the 1967 Act any tenancy granted to a relative, servant or other person effectively for his or her life. However, the exception was used by some landlords as a device to avoid the 1967 Act in other cases, by including in a lease granted for a term of over 21 years a clause giving the tenant (but not the landlord) the right to determine the tenancy by notice after the death of H.R.H. the Prince of Wales (hence the common description "Prince of Wales clause").[37] Unless the rent reserved was a full rack rent (in which case the tenancy would not be "at a low rent" and outside the 1967 Act for that reason[38]) such a right was valueless and in practice would never be exercised. The efficacy of this device has not been tested, and it is arguable that it would not work **3–05**

---

[31] s. 37(4).

[32] s. 3(1).

[33] s. 3(2); see paras. 3–09 *et seq.*

[34] See Spencer Bower and Turner, *Estoppel by Representation* (1977) paras. 188 *et seq.* However, a lease granted *ultra vires* a statutory body is not binding on the grantor by estoppel: *Rhyl U.D.C.* v. *Rhyl Amusements Ltd.* [1959] 1 W.L.R. 465.

[35] *Gorman* v. *Porthleven Harbour and Dock Co.* (1970) Redruth C.C., unreported (Judge Chope).

[36] s. 3(1) proviso, now amended by the Housing Act 1980, Sched. 21, para. 3.

[37] An alternative death sometimes specified was that of the last survivor of the living issue of King George V.

[38] See paras. 3–13 *et seq.*

on the following alternative grounds[39]: (i) that in the context, only tenancies terminable by notice given by the landlord are within the exception,[40] and (ii) that the clause is rendered void by the anti-avoidance provisions of section 23 of the 1967 Act.[41]

3–06 By an ill-considered and badly drafted amendment,[42] the above exception has now been limited to tenancies which fulfil either of the following conditions:

(a) The tenancy was granted[43] before April 18, 1980[44] or in pursuance of a contract entered into before that date.[45] This important condition prevents previously existing Prince of Wales clauses being affected.[46]

(b) The notice terminating the tenancy is capable of being given at any time after the death or marriage of the tenant; the length of the notice is not more than three months; and the terms of the tenancy preclude its assignment (other than an assignment by way of exchange[47] of a secure tenancy[48] under the Housing Act 1985)[49] and also the subletting of the whole of the premises comprised in it.[50]

Any person granting a "lease for life" should take care to ensure that the latter restrictions are included in the tenancy. It is unclear how the first restriction will operate if (as is frequently the case) it is devised to grant a lease to two persons, *e.g.* husband and wife, for their joint lives

---

[39] These arguments are not affected by the fact that Parliament has now amended the proviso to s. 3(1) apparently on the assumption that the device works, because "the beliefs or assumptions of those who frame Acts of Parliament cannot make the law": *I.R.C.* v. *Dowdall O'Mahoney* [1952] A.C. 401, *per* Lord Radcliffe at p. 426. See also *Davies Jenkins Co. Ltd.* v. *Davies* [1968] A.C. 1097, *per* Lord Morris of Borth-y-Gest at p. 1121.

[40] It is considered that this argument is difficult to sustain, because the wording of the proviso to s. 3(1) is unambiguous. See *e.g. Mayor and St. Mellons R.D.C.* v. *Newport Corporation* [1952] A.C. 189 and *Stock* v. *Jones (Frank) (Tipton) Ltd.* [1978] 1 W.L.R. 231, H.L.

[41] See paras. 17–01 *et seq.* This is the stronger argument, which it is considered might well succeed, notwithstanding *Jones* v. *Wrotham Park Settled Estates* [1980] A.C. 74.

[42] By the Housing Act 1980, s. 141 and Sched. 21, para. 3.

[43] It is thought that s. 3(2) of the 1967 Act (considered in para. 3–09) is inapplicable for the purpose of ascertaining the date of grant, but the contrary is certainly arguable; *cf. Bates* v. *Pierrepoint* (1978) 37 P. & C.R. 420, C.A.

[44] The date when the amendment was introduced in the Bill which was enacted as the Housing Act 1980.

[45] Para. (a) of the proviso to s. 3(1) as amended.

[46] This involved a misunderstanding of what is meant by retrospective legislation: see paras. 1–15, note 91 and 1–19, note 27.

[47] *i.e.* under the Housing Act 1985, s.92.

[48] As defined by *ibid.* s.79.

[49] Housing (Consequential Provisions) Act 1985, Sched. 2, para. 12.

[50] Para. (6) of the proviso to s. 3(1), as amended. It is considered that these restrictions are unnecessarily narrow, and that Parliament could have achieved its purpose by simply restricting the operation of the proviso to notices given by a landlord. The restriction of the length of notice to three months is particularly pointless.

and for the life of the survivor. The safest course is to grant a lease to the younger for his or her life and at the same time grant an option (limited to take effect within 21 years[51]) to the elder to be granted a lease for his or her life after the death of the younger.

Other long tenancies

Four other types of tenancy, not within the above primary definition (and not continuation tenancies, dealt with below) are also included in the definition of a "long tenancy." These are: 3–07

(i) A tenancy with a covenant for perpetual renewal unless it is a tenancy by sub-demise from one which is not a long tenancy.[52] In the normal case such a tenancy is converted into a 2,000 year term.[53]

(ii) A tenancy for less than 21 years with a covenant for non-perpetual renewal, without payment of a premium, which has been once or more renewed so that the total of the terms granted exceeds 21 years.[54] An obvious way in which this provision can be avoided is by the grant of such a tenancy with options for renewal,[55] with provision for a small (but, to be safe, not merely nominal) premium to be paid on each renewal.

(iii) A tenancy of a house created by the grant of a lease to a "secure tenant" pursuant to the "right to buy" provisions of Part V of the Housing Act 1985, notwithstanding that the lease was granted for a term of 21 years or less.[56] Such a tenancy can, however, only be granted by way of a sub-tenancy where the landlord[57] itself has an interest sufficient to grant a term of over 21 years from the date of the secure tenant's notice, claiming to exercise the right to buy.[58] This exception is therefore of very limited application, arising only in cases where the lapse of time between such notice and the actual grant of the sub-tenancy has resulted in the term of the sub-tenancy being 21 years or less.

(iv) A tenancy of a house created by the grant of a "shared ownership" lease pursuant to section 143 of the Housing Act 1985, notwithstanding that the lease was granted for a term of 21 years or less.[59]

---

[51] See the Perpetuities and Accumulations Act 1964, s. 9(1).

[52] s. 3(1).

[53] Law of Property Act 1922, Sched. 15.

[54] s. 3(4). This subsection was included to cover some leases of this kind affecting properties in Abertillery, Gwent.

[55] Such options do not offend the rule against perpetuity: Perpetuities and Accumulations Act 1964, s. 9(1); nor are they invalidated by s. 149(3) of the Law of Property Act 1925: see *Weg Motors Ltd.* v. *Hales* [1962] Ch. 49, C.A.

[56] Housing Act 1985, s.174(*a*).

[57] *i.e.* a local authority or other public body subject to the "right to buy" provisions of Part V of the Housing Act 1985.

[58] *Ibid.* Sched. 5, para. 4.

[59] *Ibid.* s.174(*a*); and see para. 3–14.

Continuation tenancies

3–08 Two types of continuation tenancy taking effect immediately after a previous long tenancy are also treated as being long tenancies. These are:

(1) *Statutory extensions*

References in the 1967 Act to a long tenancy include any period during which a long tenancy is or was continued under Part I or Part II of the Landlord and Tenant Act 1954 or the Leasehold Property (Temporary Provisions) Act 1951.[60] Under Part II of the 1954 Act (business tenancy), the tenancy of the whole of the demised property is automatically continued until determined in accordance with the 1954 Act (even if part has been sublet).[61] Such a continuation tenancy will thus comprise the whole of the relevant "house." Different considerations apply if the long tenancy is continued under Part I (residential tenancy). The long tenancy is so continued only in respect of "the premises qualifying for protection,"[62] which are defined as "the aggregate of the premises of which, if the tenancy were not one at a low rent, the tenant would be entitled to retain possession by virtue of the Rent Acts after the coming to an end of the tenancy at the term date."[63] If these premises do not comprise the whole of the "house," the tenant cannot claim the benefit of the 1967 Act.[64]

Three situations under Part I of the 1954 Act require consideration:

(i) Where the whole "house" is occupied by the tenant. In such a case, the whole house is comprised in the statutory extension and no difficulty arises.

(ii) Where part of the house has been sublet for business purposes. In such a case, only the retained part is comprised in the statutory extension.[65]

(iii) Where part of a house has been sublet for residential purposes. In such a case, the matter depends on whether the tenant has an intention to re-occupy the sublet part at some future date. If he has, "the premises qualifying for protection" will extend to the whole house.[66] But if it can be

---

[60] s. 3(5). Although the Leasehold Property (Temporary Provisions) Act 1951 is now fully spent, it is occasionally necessary to consider its effect in connection with renewal tenancies under s. 3(2), dealt with in para. 3–09, *post*.

[61] Landlord and Tenant Act 1954, s. 24(1).

[62] *Ibid.* s. 3(1).

[63] *Ibid.* s. 3(3), as amended by para. 1 of Sched. 5 to the Leasehold Reform Act 1967.

[64] s. 1(1); see *Baron* v. *Phillips* (1978) 38 P. & C.R. 91, C.A.

[65] As in *Baron* v. *Phillips*, *supra*, (in which the judgments appear to overlook s. 22(3), Landlord and Tenant Act 1954); and see *Gidden* v. *Mills* [1925] 2 K.B. 713 at p. 726 (Rent Acts).

[66] *Herbert* v. *Byrne* [1964] 1 W.L.R. 519, C.A.; *Regalian Securities Ltd.* v. *Ramsden* [1981] 1 W.L.R. 611, H.L.

shown that the tenant has abandoned any such intention, *e.g.* if the house has been permanently converted into separate self-contained flats, "the premises qualifying for protection" will only extend to the retained part.[67]

(2) *Renewal tenancies*

Certain tenancies granted by way of renewal of a previous long tenancy at a low rent are deemed to be long tenancies (but not necessarily at a low rent) for the purposes of the 1967 Act, irrespective of their terms.[68] The renewal tenancy can arise either by express grant or "by operation of law." Tenancies of this kind arising by operation of law are nowadays rare, because occupation and payment of rent by a tenant is nearly always referable to a statutory extension of the previous tenancy.[69] The renewal tenancy is deemed to be a long tenancy if all the following conditions are satisfied: **3–09**

(a) The immediately previous tenancy must have been a "long tenancy," or deemed to be such by virtue of the provision under discussion.[70] It must also have been "at a low rent"[71] at the date of its termination (but not necessarily throughout the term).

(b) The tenant under the previous tenancy must become or have become "tenant of the property or part of it under another tenancy." The tenant in question need not be the tenant claiming the benefit of the 1967 Act, but may be one of his predecessors-in-title.[72] It appears to be sufficient if the later tenancy is granted to the previous tenant jointly with one or more tenants, and it may also be sufficient if the later tenancy is granted to one of two or more tenants (although this is perhaps more doubtful). But it is not sufficient if the later tenancy is granted to some different person—albeit that such person is the wife of the previous tenant,[73] a company controlled by the previous tenant, or a purchaser from the previous tenant. In such a case, the matter is likely to depend on the precise form of the transaction under which the later tenancy is granted, and in particular on whether either of the two tenants concerned can be said to have been entitled in equity to the other tenancy.

(c) The tenant must have become tenant "on the coming to an end of"

---

[67] *Crowhurst* v. *Maidment* [1953] 1 Q.B. 53, C.A.; *Herbert* v. *Byrne, supra, per* Russell L.J. at p. 528; *cf. Regalian Securities Ltd.* v. *Ramsden, supra,* (which appears to have turned on rather unusual facts).

[68] s. 3(2).

[69] *Morrison* v. *Jacobs* [1945] K.B. 577, C.A.; *Sector Properties Ltd.* v. *Meah* (1973) 229 E.G. 1097, C.A. (Rent Acts); *Lewis* v. *M.T.C. Cars Ltd.* [1975] 1 W.L.R. 457, C.A.; *Baron* v. *Phillips, supra*; *Longrigg, Burrough and Trounson* v. *Smith* (1979) 251 E.G. 847, C.A.

[70] s. 3(2).

[71] See paras. 3–13 *et seq.*

[72] *Austin* v. *Dick Richards Properties Ltd.* [1975] 1 W.L.R. 1033, C.A.

[73] *Rendall* v. *Duke of Westminster* (1982) West London C.C., unreported.

the previous tenancy. There must be no interval between the two tenancies during which the property reverts to the absolute ownership of the landlord.

Renewal tenancies of this kind are frequently expressly granted in practice, often in consideration of the surrender of a short residue of the prior long tenancy. If a landlord and tenant wish to renew a long tenancy for a further term of 21 years or less without the renewal tenancy being deemed a long tenancy, this can be done by either (i) varying the rent payable under the existing tenancy so that it is not "at a low rent" at the date of its termination, or (ii) granting the renewal tenancy to a person other than the present tenant, providing there is no trust relationship between them.[73a]

Consecutive long tenancies

3-10 Where the tenant of any property under a long tenancy,[74] on the coming to an end of that tenancy, becomes or has become tenant of the property or part of it under another long tenancy,[75] there is deemed, for the purposes of the 1967 Act as amended, to be a single composite tenancy beginning at the same time as the earlier tenancy and expiring at the same time as the later tenancy.[76] Thus, a tenant may rely on improvements under the earlier tenancy in order to obtain a notional reduction in the rateable value[77] of the house and premises[78]; and for the purposes of determining whether the tenancy is "at a low rent," the first day of the term is the first day of the term granted by the earlier tenancy.[79] Furthermore, for the purpose of determining whether the house and premises are within the rateable value limits of the 1967 Act, the single composite tenancy is "created"[80] at the date of grant of the earlier tenancy.[81]

Concurrent tenancies

3-11 Provision is made[82] for cases where there are two or more concurrent long tenancies,[83] with the same landlord and the same tenant of two or

---

[73a] See paras. 17-13 and 17-14.

[74] Including any continuation or renewal tenancy which is deemed to be a long tenancy: see paras. 3-08 and 3-09.

[75] For meaning of "become tenant" see para. 3-09.

[76] s. 3(3).

[77] *i.e.* pursuant to Sched. 8 to the Housing Act 1974: see para. 2-23 *et seq.*

[78] *Rendall* v. *Duke of Westminster, supra.*

[79] s. 4(1): but the operation of s. 3(3) must be ignored in considering whether the proviso to s. 4(1) applies.

[80] For the purposes of s. 1(6), added by s. 118 of the Housing Act 1974: see para. 2-20.

[81] *Bates* v. *Pierrepoint* (1978) 37 P. & C.R. 420, C.A.

[82] s. 3(6).

[83] Including tenancies deemed to be long tenancies under subss. (2) to (5) of s. 3 discussed above: s. 3(6), proviso.

more parts of the house, or of the house or part of it and land or other premises[84] occupied therewith (*e.g.* different floors of a house, or a house and its garage, let separately). In such cases, for the purposes of the 1967 Act there is deemed to be a single long tenancy of all the property comprised in all the long tenancies. If the separate tenancies commenced[85] at different dates or have different term dates, then the commencement date and the term date[86] of the single long tenancy are deemed to be the commencement date and term date respectively of the long tenancy comprising the house (or, if there are two or more tenancies of the house, the earliest commencement date and the earliest term date of those tenancies).[87] Note that these provisions only apply to long tenancies; sometimes premises other than the house, which are part of the house and premises,[88] are not subject to a long tenancy. In such a case, only the tenancy or tenancies of the house are relevant for this purpose. (If the house or any part of it is not comprised in a long tenancy, the 1967 Act does not apply).

"The term date"

This expression is defined, and is important for several purposes; in particular, the fifty-year extension commences from the term date.[89] In the normal case of a tenancy for a fixed term, the expression means the contractual expiry date of that term.[90] This is so even if that date has passed and the tenancy is being automatically continued under Part I or II of the Landlord and Tenant Act 1954. 3–12

Where the fixed term is followed by a periodical tenancy, the meaning of the expression depends upon whether the periodical tenancy is protected by Part I of the Landlord and Tenant Act 1954. In the normal case, the periodical tenancy will be so protected, and the term date will be the first date on which at common law (and ignoring the 1954 Act) the tenancy could have been brought to an end by a landlord's notice to quit.[91] If, however, the premises are used for mixed business and residential purposes, the periodical tenancy will be protected, not by Part I of the Landlord and Tenant Act 1954, but by Part II of that Act.[92] In such a case, the term date is the date when the periodical tenancy is due to

[84] "Premises" in this context does not include another house, but means a garage, outhouse or other erection ancillary to the house in question: *Wolf* v. *Crutchley* [1971] 1 W.L.R. 99, C.A.
[85] For date of commencement of a tenancy, see para. 3–03.
[86] For meaning of term date, see para. 3–12.
[87] s. 3(6).
[88] For meaning see paras. 2–08 *et seq.*
[89] s. 14(1).
[90] s. 37(1)(*g*).
[91] s. 37(2): and see the Landlord and Tenant Act 1954, s. 19(2) and Sched. 4, para. 2.
[92] See Landlord and Tenant Act 1954, s. 43(1)(*c*), as amended.

terminate by reason of a landlord's notice to quit given before the date of the tenant's Notice of Leaseholder's Claim; and if no such notice to quit has been given, the earliest date thereafter on which at common law (and ignoring the 1954 Act) the tenancy could have been brought to an end by such a notice.[93]

The expression "extended term date" means the term date (as defined above) of a tenancy with a fifty-year extension under the Act; and "original term date" means the term date without such an extension.[94]

2. Low Rent

A. Outline

3–13 Except in relation to certain tenancies granted between August 1939 and April 1963[95] and as regards "shared ownership leases" mentioned below, a tenancy of any property is a tenancy "at a low rent" at any time only when the rent is less than two-thirds of the rateable value[96] of the property on the appropriate day,[97] or if later, the first day of the term granted by the tenancy.[98] When the first day of the term occurs has already been considered.[99] Where the tenancy is a renewal tenancy after a previous long tenancy at a low rent, the first day of the term will usually be the first day of the earlier term[1]; this point is sometimes overlooked by persons seeking to grant a renewal tenancy not within the 1967 Act. It is thought that any notional reduction in rateable value obtained by the tenant[2] should be ignored,[3] but the point is not clear.

"Rent" for this purpose includes only genuine rent payable as such (even if not recoverable by distress[4]), and not any service rent, rent in respect of maintenance, repairs or insurance payable to the landlord or to any superior landlord, or the like.[5] Any suspension or reduction of rent by reason of damage to the demised property is disregarded, as, conversely, is any penal additional rent payable by reason of a breach of covenant.[6] An entire rent payable at any time in respect of both the house and

---

[93] s. 37(3).
[94] s. 37(1)(*g*).
[95] As to which, see paras. 13–15 *et seq.*
[96] For meaning of rateable value, see para. 2–18.
[97] For meaning of the appropriate day, see para. 2–17.
[98] s. 4(1).
[99] See para. 3–03.
[1] s. 3(3); and see para. 3–10.
[2] *i.e.* under Sched. 8 to the Housing Act 1974: see paras. 2–23 *et seq.*
[3] s. 1(4A) refers to "the purposes of" s. 1, whereas the definition of low rent is in s. 4.
[4] See *Cheapside Land Development Co Ltd.* v. *Messels Service Co. Ltd.* [1978] A.C. 904.
[5] s. 4(1)(*b*).
[6] s. 4(1)(*c*).

premises (or any part thereof) and other property must be apportioned by the county court[7] (or in some cases by a leasehold valuation tribunal[8]) "as may be just according to the circumstances existing at the date of the severance giving rise to the apportionment," and the rent of the house and premises (or part thereof) is the fraction apportioned thereto.[9]

In order to be within the 1967 Act, the tenancy must have been "at a low rent" during the whole of the tenant's three-year qualifying occupation, as well as at the date of service of the Notice of Leaseholder's Claim.[10] For that purpose, the rent and rateable value of the house and premises constituted as at the date of the Notice of Leaseholder's Claim (and prior to the inclusion of other premises[11] and the exclusion of any part[12]) must be taken[13]; it is immaterial that the premises occupied with the house prior to that date may have been different. Similarly, in cases where the question arises whether a previous tenancy was at a low rent,[14] that question must be determined by reference to the rent and rateable value only of the house and premises constituted as at the date of Notice of Leaseholder's Claim, or of such part thereof as was included in the previous tenancy (but exclusive of any other land or premises so included).[15] If an apportionment of rent or rateable value is required because the previous tenancy did not include the whole of the house and premises or included other property, the apportionment is made as at the end of the previous tenancy (or, in the case of rent, the date of severance giving rise to the apportionment if that date is earlier).[16] 3–14

Shared ownership leases

A tenancy created by the grant of a "shared ownership lease" pursuant to section 143 of the Housing Act 1985 is treated as being at a low rent notwithstanding that the rent on the first day of the term is equal to or more than two-thirds of the rateable value.[17] However, so long as the rent payable under such a lease exceeds £10 per annum, neither the tenant nor any sub-tenant can exercise rights under the 1967 Act.[18]

---

[7] s. 20(3).
[8] s. 21(2)(*b*) as amended.
[9] s. 4(6); this provision may have been overlooked in *Dixon* v. *Allgood* (1986) 281 E.G. 183, C.A. (under appeal to the House of Lords at the date on which this book states the law).
[10] s. 1(1)(*b*) as amended; see para. 3–01.
[11] *i.e.* under s. 2(4): see para. 2–12.
[12] *i.e.* under s. 2(5), (6): see paras. 2–13, 2–14.
[13] s. 4(2), (4).
[14] *i.e.* for the purposes of s. 3(2): see para. 3–09.
[15] s. 4(3).
[16] s. 4(3) proviso.
[17] Housing Act 1985, s.174(*b*).
[18] *Ibid.* s.173.

B. Tenancies granted between August 1939 and April 1963

Generally

3–15 The above definition of a "low rent" is subject to a proviso if the tenancy was granted[19] after August 31, 1939, but before April 1, 1963[20] (whether or not it was granted by way of continuation of a previous long tenancy and for other purposes is treated[21] as forming a single tenancy with the previous tenancy). Except in relation to a tenancy granted by way of a building lease,[22] a tenancy is not regarded as a tenancy at a low rent "if at the commencement of the tenancy the rent payable under the tenancy exceeded two-thirds of the letting value of the property (on the same terms)."[23] Until the contrary is shown, it is to be assumed that the letting value is such that the proviso does not apply.[24] This puts the onus of proof squarely onto the landlord, but it is considered that the degree of proof required is no more than the usual "balance of probabilities" standard ordinarily adopted in civil cases.[25] In cases where the relevant tenancy derives from more than one separate tenancy of the house and premises, the proviso has effect if, but only if, it applies to one of the separate tenancies which comprise the house (or part of it).[26] If the rent at the date of service of the Notice of Leaseholder's Claim exceeds two-thirds of the rateable value on the appropriate day, the tenancy is not "at a low rent" anyway,[27] and it is unnecessary to consider the proviso.

The purpose of the proviso, which was inserted for the benefit of landlords, was to exempt tenancies which were initially granted at or near full market rents, but which as a result of inflation and subsequent rating revaluations[28] have since become tenancies at rents of less than two-thirds of the rateable value on the appropriate day.[29] Many rents which nowadays appear to have been of a modest amount were in fact substantial at the date of the grant of the tenancy, having regard to the

---

[19] For this purpose, it is the date of grant, whether at law or in equity (and not the date of commencement of the tenancy) which is the relevant date; see *Church Commissioners for England* v. *Woods* (1970) E.G.D. 509, C.A. The opposite applies in relation to the ascertainment of the letting value.

[20] This date was chosen because it was the date when the 1963 rating revaluation took effect.

[21] *i.e.* by s. 3(3): see para. 3–10.

[22] Defined by s. 4(1)(*d*): see para. 3–16.

[23] s. 4(1) proviso.

[24] s. 4(5).

[25] Notwithstanding dicta in *Church Commissioners for England* v. *Woods, supra.*

[26] s. 4(2).

[27] See para. 3–01.

[28] See *Gidlow-Jackson* v. *Middlegate Properties Ltd.* [1974] Q.B. 361, *per* Lord Denning M.R. at p. 370.

[29] In particular, the revaluation which came into effect on April 1, 1963.

value of money,[30] the levels of income[31] and the rates of taxation[32] then prevailing. It has been suggested that "the proviso envisages that the premises will have been let at a low rent in the sense that it is substantially less than a rack rent"[33] and that "the legislature must, therefore, have appreciated that when investigating the circumstances of a letting within the proviso a premium would in almost all cases have been paid for the lease unless prohibited by the Rent Act."[34] These suggestions are, with respect, somewhat illogical, and the relevant parliamentary debates[35] show clearly that in fact the legislature had in mind lettings at rack-rents or near rack-rents without a premium. Moreover, in the author's experience most cases within, or potentially within, the proviso occur in the common instance of a renewal to the sitting tenant of a previous tenancy[36] without any premium,[37] although sometimes with the surrender of the valuable residue of the previous tenancy.[38]

Unfortunately, the proviso was ill-considered and poorly drafted. It has led to substantial litigation, and has given rise to a number of unforeseen and capricious results. A major defect is the failure to define "letting value." In addition, Parliament appears to have overlooked (i) that the Rent Acts frequently applied to the tenancies in question; (ii) that such tenancies frequently reserved initial peppercorn or similar rents; and (iii) that the tenant had frequently made improvements before the commencement of the tenancy as part of the consideration for obtaining the tenancy. These problems are discussed below.

---

[30] The equivalent of £100 in December 1953 on the Retail Prices Index (All Items) was £935.6 in December 1985. Housing costs have escalated at a much higher rate; between January 1956 and December 1985, the Housing Index showed an increase from 100 to 1462, compared with an All Items Index increase from 100 to 841.

[31] In 1953, *e.g.*, the annual salary of a member of the Court of Appeal was £5,000 (exceeding that of a top civil servant) and that of a county court judge was £2,800. As late as 1956, the average weekly wage was under £10.

[32] In 1953, the standard rate of income tax was 9/- in the £1, and surtax started at £2,000 on earned as well as unearned incomes. If a member of the Court of Appeal was married but had no child allowance, his tax bill would have totalled £2,388, leaving him a net income of £2,612. The corresponding figures for a county court judge were a tax bill of £993, leaving a net income of £1,807.

[33] *Johnston* v. *Duke of Westminster* [1986] 3 W.L.R. 18, *per* Lord Griffiths at p. 23B.

[34] *Ibid.* p. 23C.

[35] See Hansard H.L., Vol. 285, col. 1361, where the Government spokesman (Lord Kennet) introducing the proviso as an amendment on Third Reading in the House of Lords said that it was intended to cover "long leases granted during the war and in the post-war years at what were then rack rents which have now become 'low rents' measured by the criterion of two-thirds of current rateable values." See also Hansard H.C., Vol. 751, col. 1575.

[36] Expressly contemplated by the bracketed words in the proviso.

[37] As in *Gidlow-Jackson* v. *Middlegate Properties Ltd., supra.*

[38] As in *Church Commissioners for England* v. *Woods* (1970) E.G.D. 509, C.A., and *Hembry* v. *Trustees of Henry Smith's Charity* (1986) West London C.C., unreported (Judge Parker Q.C.), under appeal at the date on which this book states the law.

"Building lease"

3–16 This term is defined[39] as "a lease granted in pursuance of or in consideration of an agreement for the erection or substantial rebuilding or reconstruction of the whole or part of the house in question or a building comprising it." Many leases are in practice granted partly in consideration of the tenant having already made[40] or agreeing to make improvements, often of a substantial nature. But it is relatively seldom that it can be said that such improvements involve substantial re-building or reconstruction of the whole or part of the house,[41] although the matter is one of degree depending upon the facts of the particular case.

"The commencement of the tenancy"

3–17 This expression is not defined, but presumably means the first day of the term granted by the tenancy,[42] already considered elsewhere.[43] Both the rent payable under the tenancy and also (it appears) the letting value of the property have to be ascertained as at that date.

"The letting value of the property (on the same terms)"

3–18 This important expression is not defined in the 1967 Act, and quite different considerations have been held to apply depending on whether the tenancy was at its commencement subject to the Rent Acts. In either case, however, the words "(on the same terms)" in their context do not include the payment of a premium, which is regarded rather as the consideration for which the lease was granted.[44] But they do include all the covenants and obligations under the tenancy (and, it is thought, any collateral contract), including covenants as to user, repair and so on.

Such obligations also include a tenant's covenant to make future improvements. But it seems clear that if improvements were made by the tenant before the commencement of the tenancy,[45] either pursuant to a prior agreement or by way of early compliance with the tenant's covenant under the tenancy (as commonly happened in practice), they cannot be ignored in ascertaining "the letting value" at that date. It is thus frequently necessary to ascertain exactly when the improvements were

---

[39] s. 4(1)(*d*).

[40] For the position where the tenant has made improvements before the commencement of the tenancy, see para. 3–18.

[41] See, *e.g. Gidlow-Jackson* v. *Middlegate Properties Ltd., supra.*

[42] The expression "the first day of the term" is used in the main part of s. 4(1) and the expression "the commencement of the tenancy" in the proviso. It is considered that the expressions are nevertheless synonymous, and the difference arises merely from the poor drafting of the section and has no significance.

[43] See para. 3–03.

[44] *Manson* v. *Duke of Westminster* [1981] Q.B. 323, C.A., following *Hill* v. *Booth* [1930] 1 K.B. 381.

[45] See para. 3–03.

done. Moreover, although it made no difference at the time when the tenancy was granted, the difference may well be crucial in ascertaining whether or not the Proviso applies. Thus if the tenant agreed to do modernisation works to a house as a condition precedent to the grant of a tenancy of the house, the tenancy will have commenced when the house had been modernised and the "letting value" will reflect the modernisation, albeit that it was done by the tenant. But if there was an immediate grant of the tenancy containing a tenant's covenant to do the modernisation works, the "letting value" will reflect only the unmodernised condition of the house and the tenant's covenant. The Proviso may well apply in the latter case but not the former. An even more capricious result sometimes occurs if in the latter case the tenant has in fact completed the modernisation works before the tenancy is granted; unless he was then entitled to the tenancy in equity, it appears inescapable that the letting value must nevertheless reflect the modernisation.

"*Letting value*" 3–19

The "letting value" was intended by Parliament to mean,[46] and was originally assumed by the courts to mean, "the rent which a landlord could have obtained in the market if he had offered the property for letting on the terms of the lease,"[47] but without a premium, *i.e.* the market rack rent. However, the expression has been construed by the House of Lords in *Johnston* v. *Duke of Westminster*[48] to mean "the best annual return obtainable in the open market for the grant of a long lease on the same terms whether this is achieved by letting at a rack rent or letting it at a lower rent plus the payment of a premium." For this purpose any premium (insofar as it is attributable to the granting of the tenancy and not to collateral matters such as furniture, fittings, etc.) has to be "decapitalised", *i.e.* expressed in annual terms, and added to the rent.[49] The appropriate method and rate of interest to be adopted on the decapitalisation matters are for expert evidence.[50] It seems probable that it should be done on a purely actuarial basis without any allowance for a

---

[46] See Hansard H.L., Vol. 285, col. 1361, where the Government spokesman (Lord Kennet) said the expression meant "the full market rent which the property could command."

[47] *Gidlow-Jackson* v. *Middlegate Properties Ltd.* [1974] Q.B. 361, *per* Stamp L.J. at p. 375C; see also *Duke of Westminster* v. *Johnston* (1985) 51 P. & C.R. 162, *per* Browne-Wilkinson L.J. at p. 172 and *per* Sir George Waller at p. 175.

[48] [1986] 3 W.L.R. 18 at p. 23D, affirming *Duke of Westminster* v. *Johnston, supra.*

[49] This frequently results in a higher figure than the market rent, as found on the evidence by the trial judge in *Johnston* v. *Duke of Westminster, supra.* The Court of Appeal ((1986) 51 P. & C.R. 162) expressed surprise at the finding, but it accords with the common market experience. In practice tenants have been, and indeed still are, willing to pay premiums but not substantial rents, partly (but not entirely) because of the different tax treatment of interest and rent.

[50] *Ibid.* at p. 25E.

sinking fund.[51] The result of the decapitalisation should be the same whether the recipient is a mesne landlord or a freeholder.[52]

In the *Johnston* case, it was said that "unless there is any reason to suppose that the bargain between landlord and tenant was not made at arms length, the combination of rent and premium will be very strong prima facie evidence of the open market letting value of that particular house let on those terms at that date, in which case the only calculation that has to be made to see if the tenant is entitled to the freehold is to apply a mathematical formula based on actuarial principles to convert the premium into an annual sum."[53] However, this statement was based on the assumption that "a premium will have been paid for almost all the houses covered by the proviso."[54] Whether it will be applied to cases of lettings without a premium,[55] and/or to lettings to sitting tenants, is not clear. As a matter of logic, the statement certainly ought to be applied equally, but it may be doubtful whether the courts will accept that consequence. In such cases, the tenant usually alleges (somewhat ungraciously) that at the time of the letting the landlord acted with generosity to sitting tenants, or failed to negotiate a proper market rent as a result of being unaware of rents and premiums then obtainable or for some other reason. The tenant endeavours to support that allegation by evidence of lettings of comparable properties shortly before or after the commencement of the tenancy, often supported by evidence of so-called "premiums" (*i.e.* purchase prices) paid on assignments of the property itself or comparable properties shortly after the lettings.[56] Despite dicta to the contrary,[57] it seems inevitable that in considering such evidence, the court will have to consider both rack rents and combinations of rent and premiums.[58]

Other evidence of letting value usually comprises market lettings of

---

[51] *Ibid.* at p. 25B.

[52] *Ibid.* at p. 25A. However, the House of Lords, like the Court of Appeal, felt unable to depart from the agreed expert evidence in this respect.

[53] *Ibid.* at p. 23F. On this footing, *Church Commissioners for England* v. *Woods* [1970] E.G.D. 509 appears to have been wrongly decided.

[54] An erroneous assumption: see para. 3–15.

[55] Which in fact were frequently made, particularly on renewal tenancies: see para. 3–15. The market situation is rather more complicated than the House of Lords appears to have envisaged.

[56] Such "premium" evidence may, however, be unreliable as a guide to letting value: *Hembry* v. *Trustees of Henry Smith's Charity* (1986) West London C.C., unreported (Judge Parker Q.C.), under appeal at the date on which this book states the law.

[57] *Johnson, supra,* at p. 23E. The argument of counsel for the landlord on this point appears sound, and the answer given to it by the House of Lords is unsatisfactory and based on an erroneous factual assumption: see para. 3–15.

[58] The difficulty can be illustrated by considering what would have happened if in *Johnston,* the lease had been granted without a premium at the maximum rent of £250, but evidence had been given that a letting could have been effected at a rent of £200 with a premium of £1,250 (as in fact occurred), or other rent and premium combinations.

comparable properties shortly before or after[59] commencement of the tenancy. Often, however, the only evidence available consists of renewals of leases to existing tenants, usually involving the surrender of the residue of an existing term, and the evidence is less satisfactory even if contemporaneous detailed valuation calculations are available.[60] It is normally unnecessary for the court to determine the exact letting value in order to decide whether or not the proviso applies, and the usual practice is for the letting value to be expressed as a figure appearing in brackets. It has been said that it would be preferable for a single figure to be determined,[61] but this usually involves the court going into unnecessary detail, and it is respectfully suggested that the usual practice is to be preferred.

"The rent payable under the tenancy"

As mentioned above, this must be ascertained as at the commencement of the tenancy.[62] The meaning of rent has already been considered.[63] Where the rent remains constant throughout the first year of the term (calculated from the commencement date), it is clear that such rent is the relevant rent, even though it may be only a peppercorn or other low rent.[64] However, it frequently happens that the rent is subject to an increase during the first year of the term, *e.g.* after an initial peppercorn or similar low rent period allowed for the time when the tenant is doing works to the property. Although the contrary may be arguable,[65] it is considered that the rent payable under the tenancy at the commencement of the tenancy means the peppercorn or other low rent payable during such initial period, and not the total amount of rent payable in respect of the whole of the first year. 3–20

The failure of Parliament to deal with initial peppercorn or other low rent periods in the proviso is unfortunate. Many tenancies which fall within the spirit of the proviso do not fall within its wording, and the landlord is unfairly precluded from relying on the proviso in such cases.

---

[59] Post-valuation date evidence is clearly admissible: *Melwood Units Pty. Ltd.* v. *Commissioner of Main Roads* [1979] A.C. 426, *per* Lord Russell of Killowen at p. 436E; *Segama N.V.* v. *Penny Le Roy Ltd.* (1983) 269 E.G. 322.

[60] See *Church Commissioners for England* v. *Woods* [1970] E.G.D. 509.

[61] *Gidlow-Jackson* v. *Middlegate Properties Ltd., supra, per* Lord Denning M.R. at p. 371C.

[62] See para. 3–15.

[63] See para. 3–13.

[64] And despite the fact that a peppercorn rent, being only nominal, is not strictly "payable" at all: *Moody* v. *Yates* (1885) 28 Ch. D. 661; 30 Ch. D. 344.

[65] The argument relies on the words "rent . . . at a yearly rate" in s. 4(1), and may derive some support from dicta of Stephenson L.J. in *Manson* v. *Duke of Westminster* [1981] Q.B. 323 at p. 329H.

Tenancies subject to Rent Acts

3–21 It has been held in the Court of Appeal[66] that the Rent Acts[67] must be taken into account in ascertaining "the letting value" under the proviso.[68] Except in cases where a premium could lawfully have been demanded by the landlord,[69] the letting value thus cannot exceed the maximum recoverable rent under the Acts. It is not practicable in this book to incorporate a full discussion of the relevant law as to tenancies affected by the Rent Acts and the maximum rent recoverable thereunder.[70] The following is a summary which, it is thought, will cover most of the problems which arise in practice in applying the proviso.

Qualifying Tenancies

3–22 In order to ascertain whether a tenancy granted in the period September 1, 1939 to March 31, 1963 was within the Rent Acts at the date of its grant, three questions have to be considered:

(a) *Whether the premises were let as a separate dwelling*

The Rent Acts applied only to premises "let as a separate dwelling."[71] A letting wholly for business purposes was outside the Acts, even if the premises had formerly been used as a dwelling-house. Until October 1, 1954, a letting partly for business purposes and partly as a residence was within the Acts,[72] even though the dominant user was for business purposes[73]; but a similar letting on or after that date[74] (unless made to an existing controlled tenant) was within Part II of the Landlord and Tenant Act 1954, and outside the Rent Acts.

(b) *Whether the premises were within the rateable value limits*

Two periods require consideration:

---

[66] *Gidlow-Jackson* v. *Middlegate Properties Ltd.* [1974] Q.B. 361.

[67] The principal relevant Acts were the Increase of Rent and Mortgage Interest (Restriction) Act 1920 (the "Act of 1920"); the Rent and Mortgage Restrictions (Amendment) Act 1933 ("the Act of 1933"); the Rent and Mortgage Restrictions Act 1939 ("the Act of 1939"); the Landlord and Tenant (Rent Control) Act 1949 (the "Act of 1949"); and the Rent Act 1957.

[68] This conclusion was criticised by Brandon L.J. in *Manson* v. *Duke of Westminster* [1981] Q.B. 323 at p. 334. But his reasoning in that passage appears to be based on a misunderstanding of the purposes of the proviso (as to which see para. 3–15), and the author does not find it convincing. Dicta in the House of Lords in the *Johnston* case *supra*, at p.24, on the other hand, suggest that the conclusion in the *Gidlow-Jackson* case was correct.

[69] As to which see para. 3–26.

[70] For full discussions, see Megarry; *The Rent Acts* (8th ed., 1955, 9th ed., 1961).

[71] s. 12(2) of the Act of 1920.

[72] s. 12(2)(ii) of the Act of 1920; s. 3(3) of the Act of 1939.

[73] *Vickery* v. *Martin* [1944] K.B. 679, C.A.

[74] When the 1954 Act came into force: s. 70(2).

(i) *September 1, 1939 to July 5, 1957.* The Rent Acts applied to a letting during this period, only if the April 1939[75] rateable value did not exceed £100 in London[76] or £75 elsewhere.[77]

(ii) *6 July, 1957 to 31 March, 1963.* The Rent Act applied to a letting during this period only (a) if the April 1939 rateable value[78] did not exceed £40 in London[79] or £30 elsewhere or[80] (b) if the letting was to an existing Rent Act tenant of the same (or partly the same) premises.[81]

(c) *Whether the tenancy was excepted from the Rent Acts*

There were several classes of tenancies which were exempted from the Rent Acts. Much the most important class for present purposes were lettings where the rent payable was less than two-thirds of the April 1939 rateable value.[82] "Rent" for this purpose meant the total sum payable by the tenant, even if inclusive of rates and other outgoings paid by the landlord.[83] After July 6, 1957, another class was a "long tenancy"[84] (*i.e.* "a tenancy granted for a term exceeding 21 years, whether or not subsequently extended by act of the parties or by any enactment").[85] The remaining classes[86] are unlikely to be relevant. A letting to a company was within the Acts so as to control the recoverable rent (and is thus relevant for the purposes of the proviso), even though a company cannot be a statutory tenant.[87]

Recoverable rent under the Rent Acts prior to July 6, 1957

From September 1, 1939, to July 6, 1957, the rent payable under any 3–23
tenancy within the Rent Acts granted between those dates was limited to

[75] April 6, 1939, for the administrative county of London, and April 1, 1939, elsewhere: s. 7(1) of the Act of 1939.
[76] The then Metropolitan Police District and the City of London.
[77] s. 3(1) of Act of 1939.
[78] See n. 76, *supra.*
[79] See n. 77, *supra.*
[80] s. 11(2) of the Rent Act 1957.
[81] s. 11(2) proviso of the Rent Act 1977.
[82] s. 12(1)(*e*) of the Act of 1920; Sched. 1 to the Act of 1939.
[83] *Mackworth* v. *Helland* [1921] 2 K.B. 755, C.A.
[84] s. 21(1) of the Rent Act 1957.
[85] s. 2(4) of the Landlord and Tenant Act 1954, incorporated by s. 25 of the Rent Act 1957.
[86] These include Crown property, local authority property, houses let with a substantial quantity of land or other premises, public houses, parsonage houses, agricultural holdings, certain new or reconstructed houses (after August 20, 1954) and furnished lettings: see Megarry, *supra* (8th ed., pp. 84 *et seq.*; 9th ed., pp. 83 *et seq.*).
[87] *Carter* v. *S.V. Carburettor Co. Ltd.* [1942] 2 K.B. 288, C.A.

the recoverable rent consisting of the "standard rent" plus "the permitted increases."[88]

The standard rent

As a general rule, the standard rent was the rent at which the premises were genuinely[89] and lawfully[90] let (or sub-let)[91] for purposes within the Rent Acts at a particular date. Such date was usually September 1, 1939.[92] If the premises were not so let on that date, the standard rent is the rent at which it was last previously so let. If the premises were so let for the first time after that date (or if there was no evidence of the amount of rent under a previous letting), the standard rent was the rent at which it was first so let.

The rule (which was established by judicial construction) that the letting must have been for the purposes of the Rent Acts excluded many tenancies, such as furnished lettings,[93] lettings for business purposes[94] and lettings at less than two-thirds of the rateable value.[95] But the rule did not require that the letting should have been within the Acts, so that lettings of premises over the rateable value limits,[96] or to a company,[97] established a standard rent. If the rent was a "progressive rent," *i.e.* a rent which rose automatically during the continuance of the tenancy,[98] the maximum rent payable constituted the standard rent.[99] Any necessary apportionments of rent were made, even if the premises previously formed part of a larger unit outside the Rent Acts by reasons of its rateable value.[1]

One exception to the above general rule should be noted. If at the date the standard rent was ascertained the rent was less than the rateable value,[2] the standard rent was the rateable value.[3]

---

[88] s. 1 of the Act of 1920; s. 16(1) of the Act of 1933; Sched. 1. to the Act of 1939.

[89] *Conqueror Property Trust Ltd.* v. *Barnes Corporation* [1944] K.B. 96, D.C. (sham letting).

[90] *Edgeware Estates Ltd.* v. *Coblenz* [1949] 2 K.B. 717, C.A. (sub-letting in breach of covenant).

[91] *Prout* v. *Hunter* [1924] 2 K.B. 736, C.A.

[92] s. 12(1)(*a*) of the Act of 1920; Sched. 1 to the Act of 1939. Except in the relatively rare cases of "old control," where the date is August 3, 1914. For "old control" see n. 4, *infra*.

[93] *Signey* v. *Abbey National B.S.* [1944] K.B. 449, C.A.

[94] *Mitchell* v. *Barnes* [1950] 1 K.B. 448, C.A.; *Court* v. *Robinson* [1951] 2 K.B. 60, C.A.

[95] *Joy* v. *Eppner* [1925] 1 K.B. 362.

[96] *Minns* v. *Moore* [1950] 1 K.B. 241, C.A.

[97] *Anspach* v. *Charlton Steam Shipping Co. Ltd.* [1955] 2 Q.B. 21, C.A.

[98] *Wheeler* v. *Wirral Estates Ltd.* [1935] 1 K.B. 294, C.A.; *Bryston Property Ltd.* v. *Edwards* [1944] K.B. 327, C.A. (overruled on a different point by *Regional Properties Ltd.* v. *Oxley* [1945] A.C. 347).

[99] s. 12(1)(*a*) of the Act of 1920.

[1] *Capital and Provincial Property Trust Ltd.* v. *Rice* [1952] A.C. 142.

[2] But not less than two-thirds of the rateable value, because the rent would not then constitute a standard rent anyway: *Joy* v. *Eppner, supra*.

[3] s. 12(1)(*a*) of the Act of 1920.

The permitted increases

There were six classes of permitted increases, but four of these applied only to properties subject to "old control"[4] and so will rarely be relevant in the present context. 3–24

(i) **Improvements or structural alterations.**[5] If after September 2, 1939,[6] the landlord incurred expenditure on improvements or structural alteration of the premises, including additional or improved fixtures and fittings[7] but not decoration or repairs,[8] he was entitled to recover as rent an increase equal to 8 per cent. per annum of the cost.[9]

It has been suggested by Lord Denning M.R. in a dissenting judgment that the "letting value" under the proviso should reflect not only the cost of improvements made by the landlord, but also the cost of improvements made by the tenant (who could recover 8 per cent. per annum of the cost from any sub-tenant).[10] It is considered that this suggestion is wrong and ought not to be followed. The wording of the proviso shows in referring to the "letting value (on the same terms)" that Parliament had in mind the landlord letting in the same way as he had let to the tenant, and not the tenant sub-letting.[11] If Lord Denning M.R. is right, the purpose of the proviso would be frustrated, and the injustice to a landlord who had let at the maximum rent recoverable by him would be manifest.

(ii) **Rate increases.** A landlord who paid the rates could recover an increase of rates as compared with the rating period which included September 1, 1939.[12]

(iii) **Other increases.** In the case of "old control" only,[13] the landlord could recover an increase of 15 per cent. of the standard rent (less any

[4] The rules for ascertaining whether a property was subject to "old control" or "new control" were very complicated, and for details reference should be made to Megarry, *The Rent Acts* (8th ed.), pp. 142 *et seq.* If in April 1931 the rateable value of the property exceeded £35 in London or £20 elsewhere, with one minor exception (substantial part sub-let), the premises could not be subject to "old control."

[5] The rules stated below relate to property subject to "new control." As to properties subject to "old control" (see n. 4, *supra*), the rules are slightly different: see Megarry, *supra*, pp. 333 *et seq.*

[6] This limitation was anomalous: see Megarry, *supra*, p. 335.

[7] s. 7(1) of the Act of 1933.

[8] See *Wates* v. *Rowland* [1952] 2 Q.B. 12, C.A. and *Morcom v. Campbell-Johnson* [1956] 1 Q.B. 106, C.A.

[9] s. 2(1)(*a*) of the Act of 1920; Sched. 1 to the Act of 1939.

[10] *Gidlow-Jackson* v. *Middlegate Properties Ltd.* [1974] Q.B. 361 at pp. 372. The majority of the Court of Appeal (Stamp and Roskill L.JJ.) did not consider the point, which had not been argued.

[11] This appears to have been overlooked by Lord Denning M.R.

[12] s. 2(1)(*b*) of the Act of 1920: Sched. 1 to the Act of 1939.

[13] See n. 4, *supra*.

rates paid by the landlord), and certain further increases relating to repairs, lettings to railway employees, and sub-letting.[14]

Recoverable rent under the Rent Acts from July 6, 1957

3–25 As mentioned above,[15] most tenancies granted between July 6, 1957, and March 31, 1963, were not subject to Rent Act control. The maximum rent recoverable under the remaining such "controlled tenancies" was twice the 1956 gross value if the landlord was responsible for repairs,[16] or four-thirds of the 1956 gross value if the tenant was responsible for repairs (with adjustment if the responsibility for repairs was shared),[17] plus (a) rates if borne by the landlord and (b) a reasonable charge for services or furniture provided by the landlord or any superior landlord.[18]

Premiums

3–26 Although the Rent Acts restricted the recoverable rent in the manner summarised above, a landlord could sometimes nevertheless lawfully take a premium as consideration for the grant of the tenancy. Three periods are relevant and require consideration:

(i) Up to June 1, 1949. A premium could be lawfully demanded for the grant of a term of 14 or more years, but not otherwise.[19]
(ii) From June 2, 1949, to July 5, 1957. No premium could be lawfully demanded for the grant of a term of any length.[20]
(iii) From July 6, 1957, onwards. A premium could be lawfully demanded for the grant of a term of 21 or more years, but not otherwise.[21]

Any premium which could be lawfully demanded must be taken into account in ascertaining the letting value.[22] It is considered that any illegal premium which was in fact paid (and so could have been recovered by the tenant) must be ignored.

---

[14] See further Megarry, *op. cit.* pp. 339 *et seq.*
[15] See para. 3–22, *supra.*
[16] s. 1(1) of the Rent Act 1957.
[17] Para. 1 of the Sched. 1 to the Rent Act 1957.
[18] s. 1(1) of the Rent Act 1977.
[19] s. 8 of the Act of 1920.
[20] s. 2 of the Act of 1949.
[21] s. 21 of the Rent Act 1957, repealed by s. 39 of the Leasehold Reform Act 1967 (itself repealed by s. 81 of the Housing Act 1969).
[22] See para. 3–19.

CHAPTER 4

PERSONS QUALIFYING

1. TENANT

Only a tenant (including a sub-tenant[1]) of the whole[2] of the house can exercise the rights conferred by the 1967 Act.[3] He ceases to be entitled to any such rights after he has assigned his tenancy in respect of the whole or any part of the house[4]; but not if he has sub-let part, even though retaining only a nominal reversion to that part. The tenant must be an individual, not a company nor a corporation sole.[5] On the other hand, trustees (including a corporate trustee) holding a leasehold house in their fiduciary capacity can exercise the rights conferred by the Act.[6] **4–01**

2. QUALIFYING OCCUPATION

Generally

The tenant must be in occupation of the house "as his residence"[7] at the date of service of his Notice of Leaseholder's Claim,[8] and also have been in such occupation for the previous three years,[9] or for periods amounting to three years in the previous ten years.[10] But his occupation need only be of part of the house, and the fact that he has sub-let part is immaterial.[11] Furthermore, the occupation of the tenant must both at the date of service of his Notice and throughout the qualifying period have been "in right of the tenancy," *i.e.* a long tenancy at a low rent[12] (although the house need only be a "house" as defined by the Act at the date of the **4–02**

---

[1] s. 5(4) and Sched. 1.
[2] s. 1(1).
[3] However, it is apparently sufficient if the tenant of part is also already the freehold of the remainder: *Harper* v. *Harris* (1968) 112 S.J. 954, Wandsworth C.C.; and see *Peck* v. *Anicar Properties Ltd.* [1971] 1 All E.R. 517, *per* Lord Denning M.R. at p. 519c.
[4] The tenant can probably exercise rights under the Act after contract but before completion. Notwithstanding the purchaser's equitable interest during that period, the vendor remains tenant and entitled to possession, so he can remain in occupation "in right of" the tenancy.
[5] s. 37(5)
[6] s. 6; and see para. 15–03.
[7] For meaning see para. 4–03.
[8] s. 1(1). The date of service is "the relevant time"; s. 37(1)(*d*).
[9] Formerly five years, reduced to three by para. 1(1) of Sched. 21 to the Housing Act 1980.
[10] s. 1(1)(*b*) as amended.
[11] s. 1(2)(*a*); *Harris* v. *Swick Securities Ltd.* [1969] 1 W.L.R. 1604, C.A.
[12] s. 1(2)(*b*); *Harris* v. *Plentex Ltd.* (1980) 40 P. & C.R. 483.

Notice.)[13] This means that the tenancy must confer on the tenant a direct and subsisting right of possession. Thus a tenant who has underlet and taken a rack-rent lease back from his under-tenant cannot claim the benefits of the Act, although he is otherwise qualified to do so; and a claim by a tenant in reliance on a lease which was subject to an underlease in favour of himself and his wife has been held invalid.[14] Similarly, a tenant who holds the tenancy as nominee for a company occupies only as a licensee of the company and so not "in right of" the tenancy.[15] Further, a purchaser who is allowed into occupation before completion of his contract to purchase likewise occupies until completion only as a licensee of the vendor[15a] and not in right of the tenancy.[15b] But for this purpose any mortgage term (that is to say, the term of a still subsisting mortgage[16]) and any attornment clause in a mortgage must be disregarded[17]; however, if the mortgagee has entered into possession and permits temporary occupation by the tenant, such occupation is not "in right of the tenancy."[18] Occupation by a beneficiary under a trust, including one of two or more beneficial joint tenants holding on the statutory trusts for sale, is counted as occupation by the trustees "in right of the tenancy."[19] A tenant who has ceased to be in occupation has no rights even though he has the three-year qualification. But once he has served his Notice of Leaseholder's Claim, his rights crystallise and are not lost if he subsequently moves out.

"As his residence"

4–03 The tenant's occupation must be "as his only or main residence,"[20] a phrase also found in tax legislation.[21] Which of two or more residences is a person's "main" residence is a question which must be considered objectively. All residences must be taken into account, including residences abroad and residences in which the tenant has no legal or beneficial interest (such as his or her parents' home). It is often difficult to say which of two or more residences is a person's "main" residence, for example if a man has a town house where he and his family live during the

---

[13] *Gaidowski* v. *Gonville and Caius College Cambridge* [1975] 1 W.L.R. 1066. per Ormrod L.J. at p. 1070B.
[14] *Hurst* v. *Earl Grosvenor* (1979) Westminster C.C., unreported (Judge Ruttle).
[15] *Duke of Westminster* v. *Oddy* (1984) 270 E.G. 945, C.A.
[15a] See Megarry and Wade, *The Law of Real Property* (5th ed.), p. 602.
[15b] *Manley* v. *Duke of Westminster* (1984) West London C.C., unreported (Judge Harris Q.C.); and see para. 15–06.
[16] *Re Fairview, Bromyard* [1974] 1 W.L.R. 579.
[17] s. 1(2)(*b*).
[18] *Poland* v. *Earl Cadogan* [1980] 3 All E.R. 544, C.A.
[19] s. 6(1), (3); see para. 15–05.
[20] s. 1(2).
[21] See s. 101, Capital Gains Tax Act 1979 (which, however, gives the taxpayer a right of election); para. 4(1)(*a*) of Sched. 1 to the Finance Act 1974 (mortgage interest relief).

working week and a country house where they go for weekends. "In such a case the judge has to come down on one side of the line or the other."[22] The question is "one of fact and degree which has to be looked at in a commonsense way,"[23] and "there is an infinity of circumstances to be taken into account in deciding which is a man's main home."[24] Such circumstances include the relative sizes, values, furnishings, periods of occupation and the lengths and types of ownership of the residences. Other important factors are where the tenant's immediate family usually live and which residence is regarded as the family's "home"; but a happily married couple may nevertheless in some circumstances have separate main residences.[25]

Degree of occupation required

It is provided that references to the tenant occupying the house "are to be construed as applying where, but only where, the tenant is . . . occupying it as his only or main residence."[26] "Occupying" is therefore construed more strictly than in other contexts[27] such as under the Rent Acts[28] or for rating purposes (where merely furnishing the house and keeping it available for living in may suffice).[29] In most cases occupation by virtue of the actual physical presence of the tenant himself is required and "once it becomes clear that the tenant is not physically in occupation the onus is firmly on him to show that the steps which he has taken to maintain occupation are clear."[30] Nevertheless, any period when the tenant is temporarily absent on holiday[31] or on business or by reason of illness (provided there is a real possibility of his returning within a reasonable time[32]) will usually still count if he can still be said to reside there.[32a] Furthermore, a tenant may occupy through his wife and family,[33] even though he himself is absent for long periods, *e.g.* on military service; 4–04

---

[22] *Fowell* v. *Radford* (1969) 21 P. & C.R. 99, *per* Lord Denning M.R. at p. 101.

[23] *Byrne* v. *Rowbotham* (1969) 210 E.G. 823, *per* Salmon L.J. See also *Frost* v. *Feltham* [1981] 1 W.L.R. 452 (on the Finance Act 1974, Sched. 4, para. 4(1)(*a*)), which, however, appears to be unduly favourable to the taxpayer.

[24] *Ibid.*

[25] *Fowell* v. *Radford, supra.*

[26] s. 1(2).

[27] *Poland* v. *Earl Cadogan* [1980] 3 All E.R. 544, C.A.

[28] See s. 2(1)(*a*), Rent Act 1977 and *Brown* v. *Brash* [1948] 2 K.B. 247, C.A.

[29] See *R.* v. *St. Pancras Assessment Committee* (1877) 2 Q.B.D. 581, *per* Lush J. at p. 588 (cited in *Poland* v. *Earl Cadogan, supra*).

[30] *Poland* v. *Earl Cadogan, supra, per* Waller L.J. at p. 549d.

[31] *Ibid*; and *Manley* v. *Duke of Westminster, supra.*

[32] *Cf. Tickner* v. *Hearn* [1960] 1 W.L.R. 1406 (Rent Acts), particularly *per* Ormrod L.J. at p. 1410.

[32a] Similarly, if the demised premises have been rendered uninhabitable by fire: *Bolhah* v. *Jigwood Securities Continuation* [1987] 2 C.L. 173, Lambeth C.C. (Judge Pearce, Q.C.).

[33] *Poland* v. *Earl Cadogan, supra, per* Waller L.J. at p. 549d.

but probably not if he has deserted them.[34] To infer continued occupation merely by leaving furniture in the house, or because a caretaker is there, may be easy in the case of a short period, "but where many months are concerned very much more doubtful."[35]

4–05 If the tenant sub-lets (or attempts to sub-let) the house otherwise than for minimal periods, he will not be in occupation; for during such periods he has (or has in his mind) put it out of his power to reside in the house and so has no "*animus possidendi.*"[36] And if he sets up a permanent residence elsewhere, his occupation may cease to be "as his only or main residence."

It is usually immaterial that the tenant also uses the house for other purposes.[37] Thus the use of part of the house as, for example, a shop or a doctor's surgery does not debar him from obtaining the necessary residential qualification.

Exceptions

4–06 There are, however, two exceptions to the above:

(i) **House which is ancillary.** The tenant is treated as not occupying as his residence a house which is let to and occupied by him, together with other land or premises to which it is ancillary.[38] Thus, occupation of a cottage let with a factory occupied by him will not suffice; but the position appears to be otherwise if the tenant sub-lets the factory, albeit to his family company.

(ii) **Agricultural holding.** The tenant is also treated as not occupying as his residence a house which is for the time being comprised in an agricultural holding within the meaning of the Agricultural Holdings Act 1986.[39] "Agricultural holding" is defined by that Act as "the aggregate of the land (whether agricultural or not) comprised in a contract of tenancy which is a contract for an agricultural tenancy."[40] Such a contract is one where, having regard to the terms of the tenancy, the actual or contemplated use of the land and any other relevant circumstances, the whole of the land, subject to such exceptions as do not substantially affect the character of the tenancy, is let for use as agricultural land;[41] and such use must be for

---

[34] It is considered that the rating cases, such as *Cardiff Corporation* v. *Robinson* [1957] 1 Q.B. 39 and *De Salles d'Epinoix* v. *Royal Borough of Kensington and Chelsea* [1970] 1 W.L.R. 179 are distinguishable.

[35] *Poland* v. *Earl Cadogan*, *supra*, *per* Waller L.J. at p. 549e.

[36] *Ibid. per* Megaw L.J. at p. 551d.

[37] s. 1(2).

[38] s. 1(3)(*a*).

[39] s. 3(1)(*b*).

[40] Agricultural Holdings Act 1986, s.1(1).

[41] *Ibid.*, s. 1(2).

the purposes of a trade or business.[42] As regards a "mixed" holding, these definitions appear to codify the effect of cases, decided under the Agricultural Holdings Act 1948, in which it was held that there could be no severance of the demised premises for the purposes of the 1948 Act,[43] and the relevant test was whether the tenancy, regarded in a common-sense way, was in substance a tenancy of agricultural land.[44] But if the tenant ceases to use the land for trade or business, the tenancy is no longer an agricultural tenancy.[45]

Evidence of occupation

The facts relating to a tenant's occupation of a house are usually outside the landlord's direct knowledge, and it is often difficult for him to disprove a tenant's claim to have been in occupation of the house as his only or main residence. The evidence provided by electoral rolls, telephone directories and the like is unsatisfactory and cannot be relied upon[46]; but it can provide a starting-point for investigations and material for cross-examination, particularly if it tends to show that the tenant was in fact residing elsewhere. In appropriate cases, discovery of documents relating to residence may be obtained.[47] An election for capital gains tax purposes[48] is considered to be of no evidential value. 4–07

At any time after receipt of the tenant's Notice of Leaseholder's Claim, the landlord may, by notice in writing, require the tenant "to furnish a statutory declaration as to the particulars of occupation of the property on which the tenant relies in the tenant's notice."[49] Frequently, such a statutory declaration simply says that the property "has been my only or main residence," but that is clearly insufficient. The statutory declaration should either state expressly that the tenant has had no other residence (if that be the case), or should give full factual details as to his occupation of every residence of his.[50]

---

42 *Ibid.* s. 1(4).
43 *Howkins* v. *Jardine* [1951] 1 K.B. 614, C.A.
44 *Howkins* v. *Jardine, supra*; *Dunn* v. *Fidoe* [1950] 2 All E.R. 685, C.A.; *cf. Lord Monson* v. *Bound* [1954] 1 W.L.R. 1321.
45 See *Wetherall* v. *Smith* [1980] 1 W.L.R. 1290, C.A.
46 See *Metropolitan Property Co. Ltd.* v. *Griffiths* (1982) 43 P. & C.R. 38, C.A.
47 As in *Nwokeji* v. *Northumberland Court (Streatham) Ltd.* (1978) 247 E.G. 733, C.A. (tenant's application struck out for failure to comply with order for discovery).
48 Pursuant to s. 101 of Capital Gains Taxes Act 1979 (formerly Finance Act 1965, s. 29).
49 Para. 2, Pt. I and para. 1, Pt. II, Sched., Leasehold Reform (Enfranchisement and Extension) Regs. 1967.
50 See further para. 6–04.

3. Succession to Tenancy on Death

4–08 The personal representatives of a deceased tenant have no rights under the 1967 Act. Except as mentioned below, any accrued rights die with the tenant, unless he has served a Notice of Leaseholder's Claim in his lifetime.[51]

However, where a tenant dies while occupying the house as his only or main residence, a member of his family who succeeds to the tenancy can count any period of the deceased tenant's occupation as his own for the purpose of the three-year qualifying occupation, provided (i) during that period he also resided in the house as his only or main residence, and (ii) he was still so resident at the date of the tenant's death.[52] A member of the tenant's family for this purpose includes the tenant's spouse and any child (including a stepchild, illegitimate child or adopted child), son-in-law, daughter-in-law, or parent of either the tenant or his or her spouse.[53] Such a member of the tenant's family is treated as succeeding to the tenancy not only if he becomes entitled under the deceased's intestacy or will or codicil[54] or under the terms of any settlement[55] (including the termination of the settlement),[56] but also as a result of an appropriation by the deceased's personal representatives towards a legacy, share of residue or other interest,[57] or an appropriation by the trustee of such a settlement,[58] or even as a result of a purchase from such personal representatives[59] or trustees.[60] For the purpose of calculating the three-year period, the successor's interest is treated as having commenced at the date of the deceased tenant's death.[61] Any interest solely as a personal representative must be disregarded.[62]

---

[51] In which case the benefit of the notice forms part of his estate.
[52] s. 7(1).
[53] s. 7(7).
[54] s. 7(2)(*a*).
[55] s. 7(3), (4).
[56] s. 7(5).
[57] s. 7(2)(*b*).
[58] s. 7(3), (4)(*b*).
[59] s. 7(2)(*b*).
[60] s. 7(3), (4)(*b*).
[61] s. 7(2)(*a*), (*b*).
[62] s. 7(2)(*c*).

CHAPTER 5

STATUTORY NOTICES AND THEIR EFFECT

A qualified tenant who wishes to acquire the freehold or have an extended lease under the 1967 Act must serve a notice, known as a Notice of Leaseholder's Claim, exercising his right to do so.[1] This Chapter deals with the form and service of such a notice, the legal consequences and effect of the notice, and the rights and duties of the recipient. **5–01**

1. NOTICE OF LEASEHOLDER'S CLAIM

Requirements of Notice

Prescribed form

A tenant's notice must[2] be in the prescribed form[3] of Notice of Leaseholder's Claim,[4] or in a form "substantially to the like effect."[5] Whether a notice is substantially to the like effect depends on a comparison of the words used with the corresponding words in the prescribed form to see whether in their ordinary significance the words compared bear the same meaning.[6] Sometimes the notes which form part of the prescribed form are by mistake omitted altogether. It is considered that this omission makes it difficult to say that the notice is in a form substantially to the like effect, and so renders the notice invalid[7]; but as the notes are either directed to the tenant or (usually) irrelevant to the transaction, and a reasonable landlord is unlikely to be misled, the contrary may be arguable.[7a] The notice must indicate whether the tenant **5–02**

---

[1] ss.8(1), 14(1).

[2] A notice given before January 1, 1968 in respect of a tenancy then expired or shortly due to expire did not have to comply with these requirements: s.34(4)(*a*).

[3] Form 1 in the Appendix to the Leasehold Reform (Notices) Regs. 1967 (S.I. 1967 No. 1768), reg. 4(i) (as amended by S.I. 1969 No. 1481), made under Landlord and Tenant Act 1954, s.66(1), as applied by Leasehold Reform Act 1967, s.22(5).

[4] Form 1 is set out in Appendix C.

[5] Leasehold Reform (Notices) Regulations, 1967 *supra*, para. 4.

[6] *Sun Alliance & London Assurance Co. Ltd.* v. *Hayman* [1975] 1 W.L.R. 177, C.A. *per* Stephenson L.J. at p. 182F (use of replaced prescribed form of notice under s.25 of the Landlord and Tenant Act 1954). See also *Rainsbury* v. *Bass* (1961) 105 S.J. 1009; *Falcon Pipes Ltd.* v. *Stanhope Gate Property Co. Ltd.* (1967) 204 E.G. 1234 and *Tegardine* v. *Brooks* (1977) 36 P. & C.R. 261, C.A.

[7] *Cf. Tegardine* v. *Brooks* supra; and see *Lewis* v. *Harries* (1971) 22 P. & C.R. 905, C.A.

[7a] Note 4 of the prescribed form informs the landlord of the need to serve a Notice in Reply, but the landlord is not prejudiced if he fails to do so (see para. 5–18) and the other matters in note 4 are seldom material.

is claiming the freehold or an extended lease, and a tenant cannot claim in the alternative.[8] This involves the deletion of one of the alternatives set out in paragraph 1 of the prescribed form.[9] Failure to make such a deletion renders the notice invalid even though the landlord knows from other sources (*e.g* previous correspondence or conversations with the tenant) which alternative the tenant is intending to claim,[10] unless the tenant has made his intentions clear elsewhere in the notice[11] or in an accompanying letter (which, it appears, can be read as part of the notice).[12] However, failure to delete the inapplicable alternative in paragraph 2 of the prescribed form does not affect the validity of the notice if the tenant's intention is otherwise apparent from the notice.[13]

Particulars

5–03 The Notice of Leaseholder's Claim must contain the following particulars: (a) the address of the house, and sufficient particulars of the house and premises to identify the property to which the claim extends[14]; (b) such particulars of the tenancy and of the rateable value of the house and premises as serve to identify the instrument creating the tenancy and show that (i) (ignoring the operation of the proviso to s.4(1)) the tenancy is and has at the material times been a long tenancy[15] at a low rent,[16] and (when para. 7 of Sched. 21 to the Housing Act 1980 has been brought into effect) (ii) that at the material time the rateable value was within the limits specified in section 1[17]; (c) the date on which the tenant acquired the tenancy[18]; and (d) the periods for which since the beginning of the previous 10 years and since acquiring the tenancy the tenant has and has not occupied the house as his residence, together with additional particulars concerning his periods of occupation as to (i) what parts, if

---

[8] *Byrnlea Property Investments Ltd.* v. *Ramsey* [1969] 2 Q.B. 253, C.A.

[9] The wording of para. 1 of the prescribed form was amended by S.I. 1969 No. 1481 after criticism of the original form by the Court of Appeal in the *Byrnlea* case, *supra*.

[10] As in *Byrnlea, supra,* itself.

[11] *e.g.* if the tenant has deleted the inapplicable alternative in para. 2 of the prescribed form (the converse of *Lewis* v. *Harries, supra*).

[12] *Per* Edmund Davies L.J. in *Byrnlea, supra,* at p. 267A; and see *Stidolph* v. *American School in London Educational Trust Ltd.* (1969) 20 P. & C.R. 802, C.A.

[13] *Lewis* v. *Harries, supra.*

[14] Sched. 3, para. 6(1)(*a*).

[15] In order to show that a renewal tenancy granting a term of under 21 years is a long tenancy (see para. 3–09), it is necessary to give particulars of the prior tenancy.

[16] Para. 6(1)(*b*); Sched. 3. In order to show that the tenancy is at a low rent, it is necessary to state the rateable value on "the appropriate day," which is usually March 23, 1965: see para. 3–13.

[17] Sub-para. (ii) is added by the Housing Act 1980, Sched. 21, para. 7, but at the date when this book states the law that para. had not been brought into effect. It was specifically excluded from the Housing Act 1980 (Commencement No. 1) Order 1980 (S.I. 1980 No. 1406).

[18] Sched. 3, para. 6(1)(*c*).

any, of the house have not been in his own occupation and for what periods, and (ii) what other residence, if any, he has had and for what periods, and which was his main residence.[19] Furthermore, where the tenant is qualified by reason of his trusteeship or other interest under a trust,[20] or as a result of succeeding to the tenancy on the death of an occupying tenant,[21] the notice must contain sufficient particulars to show this.[22] The schedule to the prescribed form requires all the above particulars to be completed, and if this is done the notice will clearly be valid.[23] The notice must also state whether copies of it are being served on anyone other than the recipient.[24] This involves the proper completion of paragraph 4 of the prescribed form.

It is expressly provided that a Notice of Leaseholder's Claim is not invalidated by any "inaccuracy" in the particulars required or by any misdescription of the property to which the claim extends; and an error as to the correct "house and premises" may be amended with leave of the court.[25] Provided that particulars are given, an omission to give full particulars is such an "inaccuracy,"[26] unless (it seems) the omission was a deliberate fraud or misrepresentation.[27] Thus the completion of paragraph 6(i) of the schedule to the prescribed form ("periods for which in the last ten years and since acquiring the tenancy the claimant has not occupied the house as his residence") by the word "None," in a case where the tenant had in fact lived abroad and sub-let the house for a period, has been held to be an inaccuracy.[28] **5–04**

Sometimes, one or more of the paragraphs of the schedule to the prescribed form are not completed at all, so that one or more of the required particulars are omitted altogether. It has been suggested that although a failure to give any particulars at all would not be an "inaccuracy," an omission of one of the required particulars might be.[29] But this appears to be unsound, and it is considered that a failure to

---

19 *Ibid.* para. 6(1)(*d*).
20 See paras. 15–03 *et seq.*
21 See para. 4–08.
22 Sched. 3, para. 6(2).
23 After the enactment of the Housing Act 1974, s. 118, the schedule to the prescribed form became defective in failing to require the tenant to state the rateable value of the house and premises on April 1, 1973, in a case where the tenant relies on s.1(5) or (6) of the 1967 Act as amended; see para. 5–04.
24 Sched. 3, para. 8(1)(*c*).
25 *Ibid.* para. 6(2). No guidance is given as to the matters the court should have taken into account in considering whether to grant leave. It is considered that in practice the court would only refuse leave in exceptional cases.
26 *Cresswell* v. *Duke of Westminster* (1986) 275 E.G. 461, C.A.
27 *Ibid. per* Donaldson M.R. at p. 462.
28 *Ibid.* The tenant in fact had the necessary residential qualification; *quaere* whether the decision would have been the same if he had not.
29 *Ibid. per* Donaldson M.R. at p. 462; but the reference to "particulars as a whole" may be to the batch of particulars in each of sub-paras. (*a*)-(*d*) of Sched. 3, para. 6(1).

include one or more of the required particulars (as opposed to a mistake in doing so) is an omission and not an "inaccuracy," and so renders the notice invalid.[30]

One common error deserves special mention. As stated above, it is not at present[31] necessary for the Notice of Leaseholder's Claim to contain particulars of the rateable value of the house and premises so as to show that it is within the rateable value limits, although it is necessary for the notice to contain such particulars so as to show that the tenancy is at a low rent.[32] Paragraph 3 of the schedule to the prescribed form is thus correct in requiring (and requiring only) particulars of "the rateable value of the house and premises on March 23, 1965 (or on the date such a value was first shown in the valuation list, if this date is after March 23, 1965)." Since the amendments to the rateable value limits in 1974, some claimants have, understandably but wrongly, omitted to furnish those particulars and instead have inserted the rateable value on April 1, 1973. It is arguable that this constitutes an omission, and not a mere "inaccuracy," and renders the notice invalid. But it is considered that the court will be reluctant to hold a notice invalid on this somewhat technical ground[33] and is likely to decide that although the particulars given were not given for the stipulated purpose of showing that the tenancy is at a low rent, the insertion of the rateable value on the wrong date can be nevertheless treated as an "inaccuracy."

In practice, it is not often that the formal validity of the notice is an important point. The tenant will usually be in a position to serve a second notice, without prejudice to the validity of the first notice, and the tenant can then rely upon both of them in the alternative.[34] In many cases, the landlord either expressly or impliedly by his conduct agrees to accept a notice as valid nothwithstanding its defects, and the landlord is then estopped from subsequently denying its validity.[35] The question of the validity of a notice thus usually only arises if the tenant is unable to serve a second notice (*e.g.* because he has assigned the tenancy or is for other reasons no longer in occupation) or if the period of time between the first and second notices has a significant effect on the purchase price.

Signature of notice

5–05 The Notice of Leaseholder's Claim must be given by the tenant and signed either by him personally (as envisaged in the prescribed form) or

[30] *Cf.* Housing Act 1985, s.177(1) ("error in or omission from").
[31] *i.e.* until the Housing Act 1980, Sched. 21, para. 7, is brought into force.
[32] See para. 5–03.
[33] But see *Tegardine* v. *Brooks* (1977) 36 P. & C.R. 261, C.A. *per* Roskill L.J. at p. 266.
[34] *Scott-Brown* v. *Pitt* (1971) West London C.C., unreported, (Judge Baxter).
[35] See *Farrow* v. *Orttewell* [1933] Ch. 480, *per* Lord Hanworth M.R. at pp. 498–9; and *Re Swanson's Agreement* [1946] 2 All E.R. 628.

by a duly authorised agent.[36] However, an unsigned notice may be valid if accompanied by a signed covering letter.[37] Difficult questions arise when the tenancy is held by joint tenants, but the notice is signed by only one or some of them. It is reasonably clear that one or some only of the joint tenants cannot claim rights under the 1967 Act,[38] and if the notice contains no indication that it is given on behalf of all of them, it is probably invalid.[39] If the notice (or, probably, a covering letter[40]) does contain such an indication, but is signed only by one of them, the question is whether he then had authority to sign on behalf of both[41]; however, in most cases (and in particular in the common case where the tenancy is held jointly by husband and wife) the tenants will usually have little difficulty in proving sufficient authority.

Service of notice

The Notice of Leaseholder's Claim can be served on the freeholder or on any intermediate landlord[42] (including a person holding a tenancy reversionary on the claimant's tenancy[43]). Service on any one of such persons is sufficient to initiate the tenant's claim, and the time-limits laid down by the 1967 Act start from the date of such service.[44] However, if the tenant knows of any such persons other than the recipient of the notice, or believes any other persons to have an interest in the property superior to his own, he must also serve copies on them[45]; and the notice must state whether any such copies are being served and, if so, on whom.[46] If the tenant fails to serve a copy of the notice on any such other person of whom he has knowledge or belief, or is guilty of unreasonable delay in doing so, he will be liable to that person for any consequent loss.[47] As a 5–06

---

[36] It has been held in other legislation that signature by an agent suffices, notwithstanding what is envisaged by the prescribed form: *Tennant* v. *London County Council* (1957) 121 J.P. 428, C.A. Landlord and Tenant Act 1954, s.25.

[37] See *Stidolph* v. *American School in London Educational Trust Ltd.* (1969) 20 P. & C.R. 802, C.A.

[38] See *Leek & Morelands B.S.* v. *Clark* [1952] 2 Q.B. 788, *per* Somervell L.J. at p. 793 (option of renewal): *Jacobs* v. *Chaudhuri* [1968] 2 Q.B. 470, C.A. (Landlord and Tenant Act 1954, Pt. II); and *Newman* v. *Keedwell* (1977) 244 E.G. 469 (counter-notice under Agricultural Holdings Act 1948, s.24(1)).

[39] *Cf. Lemon* v. *Landeur* [1946] K.B. 613, C.A. (notice to quit).

[40] *Byrnlea Property Investments Ltd.* v. *Ramsey* [1969] 2 Q.B. 253, *per* Edmund Davies L.J. at p. 267A.

[41] It is doubtful if the notice can be ratified subsequently: see *Doe. d. Mann* v. *Walters* (1830)10 B. & C. 626; *Doe d. Lyster* v. *Goldwin* (1841) 2 Q.B. 143; and *Jones* v. *Phipps* (1868) L.R. 3 Q.B. 567.

[42] Sched. 3, para. 8(1)(*a*).

[43] *Ibid.* para. 8(4).

[44] *Ibid.* para. 8(1)(*a*).

[45] *Ibid.* para. 8(1)(*b*).

[46] *Ibid.* para. 8(1)(*c*).

[47] *Ibid.* para. 8(3).

general rule service on the mortgagee of the landlord will not suffice; but the contrary applies where the landlord's mortgagee is in possession, or a receiver of the landlord's interest has been appointed either by the mortgagee or by the court.[48] In these cases the notice can be served either on the landlord or on the mortgagee in possession or the receiver (as the case may be).

The mode of service of a Notice of Leaseholder's Claim is that laid down in the Landlord and Tenant Act 1927, s.23(1).[49] The notice can be served on the landlord either personally, or by leaving it for him at his last known abode in England or Wales (which in appropriate cases will include his last known business address[50]) or by sending it by registered or recorded delivery post[51] addressed to him there.[52] There is also sufficient service if it is proved that the notice in fact reached the landlord, although wrongly addressed.[53] If the landlord is a company or a local or public authority, the notice can be sent to its secretary or other proper authority at its principal office. Service on an agent of the landlord duly authorised to receive it will also suffice,[54] and in practice most notices are served on such persons, *e.g.* the solicitors or surveyors of the landlord. An agent with authority to demand and accept rent will usually have sufficient authority for this purpose.[55]

Time for service of notice

5–07 Subject to three exceptions, a qualified tenant can be served a Notice of Leaseholder's Claim at any time during the continuance of his long tenancy,[56] even if the contractual term has expired and the tenancy is being automatically continued under Part I or II of the Landlord and Tenant Act 1954.[57] The exceptions are:

(i) Where the tenant has previously given a notice terminating his tenancy[58] (unless it has been superseded by a subsequent express or implied new tenancy).[59] Such a notice given by the tenant after service of

---

[48] *Ibid.* para. 9(1).
[49] s.22(5), incorporating Landlord and Tenant Act 1954, s.66(4).
[50] *Stylo Shoes Ltd.* v. *Prices Tailors Ltd.* [1960] Ch. 397; *Price* v. *West London Investment Ltd. B.S. Ltd.* [1964] 1 W.L.R. 616, C.A.
[51] Recorded Delivery Act 1972.
[52] Landlord and Tenant Act 1927, s.23(1).
[53] *Stylo Shoes Ltd.* v. *Prices Tailors Ltd., supra.*.
[54] *Townsends Carriers Ltd.* v. *Pfizer Ltd.* (1977) 22 P. & C.R. 361.
[55] *Ibid.*
[56] For meaning of long tenancy, see para. 3–02 *et seq.*
[57] See s. 3(2) and para. 3–08.
[58] Including a request for a new tenancy under s.26 of the Landlord and Tenant Act 1954 or a notice under s.27 of that Act: Sched. 3, para. 1(3).
[59] Sched. 3, para. 1(1).

his Notice of Leaseholder's Claim and during the currency of his claim[60] is invalid.[61]

(ii) During the subsistence of an agreement for a future tenancy of business premises to which section 28 of the Landlord and Tenant Act 1954 applies.[62]

(iii) If over two months have elapsed since the date of service of a landlord's notice under the Landlord and Tenant Act 1954, section 4 or 25 terminating the tenancy,[63] unless either (a) the landlord has given written consent to the later service of a Notice of Leaseholder's Claim[64] (a very unlikely event) or (b) the tenant gives notice of his desire to have an extended lease at the same time as withdrawing[65] a claim to acquire the freehold.[66] However, a landlord's notice under section 4 or 25 of the 1954 Act in respect of a house[67] held on a long tenancy or a low rent given to one or more individuals[68] will itself be ineffective unless, in addition to complying with the requirements of the 1954 Act, it also informs the tenant of his rights under the 1967 Act and contains certain other prescribed particulars.[69] If the tenant in fact serves a Notice of Leaseholder's Claim after service on him of a landlord's purported notice under section 4 or 25 of the 1954 Act not complying with these requirements, the landlord is barred from exercising his overriding rights to possession[70] (except after the grant of an extended lease).[71] As to the consequences of a Notice of Leaseholder's Claim served after a landlord's notice under section 4 or 25 of the 1954 Act, see below.[72]

2. Effect of Service of Tenant's Notice

Formation of contract

Once the tenant has served a Notice of Leaseholder's Claim, the landlord and the tenant become contractually bound respectively to grant **5–08**

---

[60] For meaning of currency of claim, see *ibid.* para. 5(1)(*c*). See also para. 5–12.
[61] *Ibid.* para. 1(2).
[62] Sched. 3, para. 1(1).
[63] Sched. 3, para. 2(1).
[64] Sched. 3, para. 2(1)(*a*).
[65] *i.e.* under s.9(3): see para. 6–32.
[66] Sched. 3, para. 2(1)(*b*).
[67] *i.e.* as defined for the purposes of the 1967 Act: see paras. 2–02 *et seq.*
[68] If the notice is given under s.25 of the 1954 Act: para. 10(1)(*b*) of Sched. 3 to the 1967 Act. However, a notice under s.4 of the 1954 Act will only be appropriate in similar cases.
[69] Set out in Sched. 3, para. 10(2)(3). The prescribed form of additional notes is contained in Landlord and Tenant (Notices) Regulations 1967 (S.I. No. 1831), reg. 6.
[70] *i.e.* under ss. 17 and 18: see para. 8–09.
[71] Sched. 3, para. 10(4).
[72] Para. 5–13.

and accept the freehold or extended lease (as the case may be).[73] In this respect, a Notice of Leaseholder's Claim is comparable to a notice to treat under compulsory purchase legislation.[74] The contract so formed carries with it the normal rights and remedies of an ordinary *inter partes* contract.[75] Thus, the usual remedies of specific performance,[76] rescission and damages are available, when appropriate. In the case of the acquisition of the freehold, either party can have questions of title and other conveyancing matters determined on a vendor and a purchaser summons,[77] although nowadays this is rarely done. Unless the claim is for damages or other pecuniary compensation, any such proceedings should be brought in the county court.[78] In practice, however, the remedy usually claimed is an appropriate declaration; as once the applicant has established his rights, the court does not in any real sense have any discretion but should make the appropriate declaration.[79]

The contract created by a Notice of Leaseholder's Claim incorporates the Conditions of Sale[80] prescribed by the Lord Chancellor,[81] except insofar as the parties otherwise agree.[82] Different sets of Conditions are prescribed for claims to the freehold and to an extended lease, and are considered in detail elsewhere.[83] The Conditions appear to be comprehensive, but the contract is otherwise on the terms and conditions of an "open contract" for the sale or lease of land[84] (not made by correspondence).[85] The contract thus created, but not the tenancy itself,[86] is registrable[87] under the Land Charges Act 1972[88] or may be the subject of a notice or caution under the Land Registration Act 1925[89] (but it is not an

---

[73] s.5(1).
[74] Compulsory Purchase Act 1965, s.5.
[75] s.5(3).
[76] This remedy cannot be obtained until the contents of the conveyance or the extended lease (as the case may be) and, in the case of a claim to acquire the freehold, the purchase price have been agreed or determined.
[77] s.22(4). A vendor and purchaser summons is brought under Law of Property Act 1925, s.49, which can alternatively be brought in the High Court: s.20(5).
[78] s.20(2)(*c*).
[79] *Collin* v. *Duke of Westminster* [1985] Q.B. 581 at p. 604.
[80] Set out in the Schedule to the Leasehold Reform (Enfranchisement and Extension) Regulations 1967 (S.I. 1967 No. 1879) set out in Appendix C.
[81] Under s.22(2).
[82] Paras. 2 and 3 of the Leasehold Reform (Enfranchisement and Extension) Regulations 1967 (S.I. 1967 No. 1879.)
[83] See paras. 6–02 *et seq.* (freehold) and 7–05 *et seq.* (extended lease).
[84] s.22(2).
[85] s.22(4); Law of Property Act 1925, s.46, and the Lord Chancellor's conditions made thereunder, thus do not apply.
[86] It might otherwise be suggested that the tenancy included an option to purchase the freehold or acquire a new lease, registrable as a Class C(iv) land charge.
[87] s.5(5).
[88] As a class C(iv) land charge ("estate contract"): Land Charges Act 1972, s.2(4).
[89] See the Land Registration Act 1925, ss. 49, 53, 54.

overriding interest under that Act, notwithstanding that the tenant is in actual occupation)[90]; however, if the tenant subsequently gives notice withdrawing his claim[91] or the landlord is otherwise discharged the obligations arising out of the Notice of Leaseholder's Claim, the tenant must on request and at his own cost procure the cancellation of the registration.[92] The tenant's rights created by the service of a Notice of Leaseholder's Claim are rights *in rem*.[93] They form part of the estate of a deceased tenant who has served a notice, and are enforceable against the estate of a deceased landlord.[94] If the tenant is made bankrupt, the benefit of the notice, together with the tenancy, vests in his trustee-in-bankruptcy.[95] The successor in title of a landlord is bound by a notice, unless it has not been registered as above and he is a purchaser for value.[96]

Assignment of benefit

However, special rules govern the assignment of the benefit of a tenant's notice, which is "assignable with, but not capable of subsisting apart from, the tenancy of the entire house and premises."[97] If the tenancy is assigned or vests otherwise than as affecting the whole of the house and premises, the notice ceases to have effect; and in that event the tenant may become liable to pay "such compensation as may be just to the landlord in respect of the interference (if any) by the notice with the exercise by the landlord of his power to dispose of or deal with the house and premises or any neighbouring property."[98] **5–09**

The clear purpose of requiring the benefit of the notice only to be assignable with the tenancy is to ensure that only the tenant for the time being can benefit from the notice, but the requirement is sometimes overlooked in the common case where the tenant has agreed to sell to a purchaser with the benefit of a notice.[99] The best and safest course in such circumstances is to incorporate an express assignment of the benefit of the notice in the assignment or transfer of the tenancy,[1] but an assignment by

---

[90] s.5(5).
[91] *i.e.* under ss.9(3) or 19(14): see paras. 6–32 and 10–26.
[92] Condition 11, part 1 and condition 6, part 2 of Schedule to Leasehold Reform (Enfranchisement and Extension) Regulations 1967 (S.I. 1967 No. 1879), set out in Appendix C.
[93] s.5(1).
[94] *Ibid.*
[95] See Bankruptcy Act 1914, ss.53 and 167.
[96] *Buckley* v. *S.R.L. Investments Ltd.* (1970) 22 P. & C.R. 756, L.T.
[97] s.5(2).
[98] *Ibid.* It is difficult to envisage circumstances in which such compensation might be claimed, and the author has no experience of any claim under this head.
[99] This will nearly always enhance the price the tenant can obtain in the market.
[1] For a precedent see Appendix A, Precedent No. 23.

a contemporaneous document would certainly suffice.[2] If there is a condition under a prior contract under which the tenant is obliged to assign the benefit, but no formal assignment is made on completion, it is considered that the purchaser will nevertheless be entitled to the benefit of the notice, which will thus not cease to have effect, on three alternative grounds, *viz.*: (1) upon payment of the purchase price, the condition operates as an equitable assignment of the benefit of the notice[3]; (2) the purchaser is entitled to a retrospective[4] rectification of the assignment or transfer of the tenancy to include an express assignment of the benefit of the notice, in accordance with the condition; (3) a later assignment of the benefit of the notice, in accordance with the condition and as part of the same transaction, is sufficient. Furthermore, it is considered that, provided there has been a clear antecedent agreement (which need not amount to an enforceable contract[5]) to assign the benefit of the notice, it is immaterial that such agreement is a collateral term rather than an express condition of the prior contract.

Abandonment of claim

5–10 The statutory contract created by a Notice of Leaseholder's Claim may be terminated by mutual consent,[6] which can be either express or inferred from the conduct of the parties.[7] In addition, a representation or promise made by one party (either expressly or by conduct), which has been relied on by the other party, can give rise to an estoppel preventing the former enforcing the contract.[8] But there can be no unilateral abandonment, and mere inactivity (*e.g.* as a result of a grudging acceptance of what was erroneously thought by both parties to be the legal position[9]) will not suffice.[10]

---

[2] It has been said that if such document is contemporaneous with a registered land transfer, it should be worded so as to take effect only when the transfer is completed by registration: Ruoff & Roper, *Registered Conveyancing* (5th. ed.), p. 546. But as the tenancy is transferred in equity on completion between vendor and purchaser, this seems unnecessary.

[3] Under the principle of *Walsh* v. *Lonsdale* (1882) 21 Ch. D. 9.

[4] Rectification operates retrospectively: Snell, *Principles of Equity* (28th ed.), p. 619.

[5] *Joscelyn* v. *Nissen* [1970] 2 Q.B. 86, C.A.

[6] The anti-avoidance provisions of s.23(1) do not apply: see subs. (2).

[7] *Collin* v. *Duke of Westminster* [1985] Q.B. 581, C.A., at pp. 595 *et seq.*

[8] *Collin*, *supra*, p. 595F.

[9] *Ibid.* p. 599, applying dicta of Buckley L.J. in *James* v. *Heim Gallery (London) Ltd.* (1980) 41 P. & C.R. 269 at p. 277.

[10] *Collin*, *supra*, at pp. 598–9. *Sed quaere*; there seems no reason why inactivity (particularly mutual inactivity) should not amount to conduct from which abandonment could be inferred.

Limitation Act 1980

It is not clear whether the enforcement of the statutory contract can be barred by limitation.[11] It is considered that enforcement is not barred by any statutory period under the Limitation Act 1980, but that a statutory period would nevertheless be applied in equity ("following the law") by analogy.[12] The relevant period has been held by the Court of Appeal[13] (rather surprisingly and perhaps wrongly[14]) to be the 12-year period applicable to claims on a "speciality."[15] It is considered that the period starts to run when the expiry of two months from the date of service of the tenant's Notice of Leaseholder's Claim or (if earlier) the date of service of any landlord's Notice in Reply.[16] **5–11**

Continuation of tenancy

A tenant's Notice of Leaseholder's Claim has the effect of automatically continuing the current tenancy of the house until three months after the end of the "currency of the claim."[17] During that period, the tenancy does not terminate by effluxion of time or in pursuance of a notice to quit served by the landlord or by the termination of a superior tenancy.[18] If a superior tenancy is forfeited, relief can be obtained in the usual way.[19] It is immaterial that the tenant's claim is invalid because he is not entitled to acquire the freehold or an extended lease; and, rather surprisingly, it is also immaterial that the person who serves the notice is not the tenant.[20] It is considered that the tenancy is continued as above even if the notice is defective in form or omits the required particulars.[21] However, the landlord has remedies if the tenant's claim is made otherwise than in good faith.[22] The "currency of the claim" is defined as the period until the notice is effective (*i.e.* upon the freehold or extended lease being acquired[23]), or ceases to have effect or is set aside by the court or is withdrawn.[24] The date when a notice is set aside by the court is the date **5–12**

---

[11] This point was left open by the Court of Appeal in *Collin, supra.*

[12] See Snell, *Principles of Equity* (28th ed.), p. 35, and Limitation Act 1980, s.36.

[13] *Collin, supra.*

[14] It is considered that the correct principles are to be found in *Re Compania de Electricidad de la Provincia de Buenos Aires Ltd.* [1980] Ch. 146, cited in argument but ignored in the judgments in *Collin.*

[15] Limitation Act 1980, s.8.

[16] The tenant cannot bring proceedings until then: Sched. 3, para. 7(5); see para. 5–18.

[17] Sched. 3, para. 3(1). As to forfeiture of the tenancy, see para. 5–14.

[18] *Ibid.*

[19] *i.e.* under Law of Property Act 1925, s.146, or Landlord and Tenant Act 1954, s.16(2) or 1967 Act, Sched. 5, para. 9.

[20] Sched. 3, para. 5(1).

[21] See paras. 5–02 *et seq.*

[22] s.20(5): see para. 17–07.

[23] *Ibid.* para. 5(1)(*b*).

[24] *Ibid.* para. 5(1)(*c*).

when the court's order becomes final,[25] *viz.* if the order is not appealed against when the time for appeal has expired, and otherwise when the appeal (and any further appeal) is finally disposed of or abandoned.[26] It has been said, however, that the period of any such continuation after the "term date"[27] is not part of a "long tenancy."[28]

During the "currency of the claim," any landlord's notice under section 4 or 25 of the Landlord and Tenant Act 1954 is of no effect.[29] The relation between the above statutory continuation and the automatic continuation of a tenancy under Part I or II of the Landlord and Tenant Act 1954 is far from clear. In most cases, however, it makes no difference which statutory continuation is relevant, for in each case the rent will be the same as the rent payable under the tenancy before the contractual expiry date ("the term date"), and the rights and liabilities of the tenant correspond to those under the tenancy. It may, however, be arguable that the effect of a Notice of Leaseholder's Claim is to displace the Landlord and Tenant Act 1954, Part I or II, so that the statutory continuation is under the provisions of the 1967 Act alone.

A device is sometimes suggested whereby a tenant who has insufficient time before the contractual term of his tenancy expires (or before the landlord can serve a notice under section 4 or 25 of the Landlord and Tenant Act 1954[30]) within which to acquire the necessary three-year residential qualification can effectively extend that time. It is said that if he immediately serves a Notice of Leaseholder's Claim (despite not being qualified to do so), as a result of the above continuation provisions of the 1967 Act he can effectively obtain a statutory extension under either the 1967 Act or Part I or II of the Landlord and Tenant Act 1954, and can subsequently serve a second Notice of Leaseholder's Claim after acquiring the residential qualification; and if necessary to obtain sufficient time, he can serve more than one invalid Notice of Leaseholder's Claim. If it is correct that such a notice displaces the 1954 Act (and that the continuation beyond the term date is not part of a long tenancy[31]), the device will be unsuccessful. However, in most such cases the landlord is likely to have little difficulty in showing that the tenant's claim has not been made "in good faith," in which case the court has power to order that any further Notice of Leaseholder's Claim shall be

---

[25] *Ibid.* para. 5(2).
[26] s.37(5), the wording of which follows the Landlord and Tenant Act 1954, s.64(2).
[27] Defined in s.37(1)(*g*): see para. 3–12.
[28] *Duke of Westminster* v. *Oddy* (1984) 270 E.G. 945, C.A. at p. 948.
[29] Sched. 3, para. 2(2); and see para. 5–13.
[30] Thereby making a two-month time-limit for the service of a Notice Leaseholder's Claim: see Sched. 3, para. 2(1) and see para. 5–07.
[31] See *Duke of Westminster* v. *Oddy*, *supra*.

void if given within five years after the date of the order.[32] The best and safest course for a landlord is to apply for such an order.

Effect on Landlord and Tenant Act 1954 notices

If the tenant serves a Notice of Leaseholder's Claim within due time[33] after service on him of a landlord's notice under section 4 or 25 of the Landlord and Tenant Act 1954, the latter ceases to have effect[34] (at any rate for the purposes of the 1954 Act[35]). But if the tenant's claim subsequently becomes ineffective, *i.e.* because it is withdrawn or the court decides that it is invalid, then within one month after the period of the currency of the claim[36] (or any subsequent permitted claim made out of time[37]), the landlord is entitled to serve a fresh 1954 Act notice specifying as the earliest date of termination of the tenancy whichever is the later of (i) the date of termination specified in the previous notice and (ii) three months from the giving of the new notice[38]; and consequential adjustments are made to the other time-limits laid down by the 1954 Act.[39] 5–13

As mentioned above, a landlord's notice under section 4 or 25 of the Landlord and Tenant Act 1954 served during the currency of a claim is of no effect.[40] Similarly a tenant's notice terminating the tenancy (including a tenant's request for a new tenancy under section 26 of the 1954 Act and a tenant's notice under section 27[41]) is of no effect if given during the currency of the claim.[42] Further, if the property is potentially enfranchiseable and the tenant is an individual, but no claim has been made, a notice under section 4 or 25 of the 1954 Act must contain prescribed additional notes[43] drawing attention to the tenant's possible rights under the 1967 Act.[44]

Forfeiture proceedings

The service of a Notice of Leaseholder's Claim prevents the landlord 5–14

[32] s.20(5), (6): see para. 17–06.
[33] Usually two months, under Sched. 3, para. 2(1): see para. 5–07.
[34] Sched. 3, para. 2(2).
[35] It has been held that the 1954 Act notice remains effective to preserve the time-limits of Sched. 3, para. 2(1) of the 1967 Act: *St. John's College, Cambridge* v. *Bailey* (1968) Cambridge C.C., unreported: *sed quaere.*
[36] For meaning of currency of claim see para. 5–12.
[37] *i.e.* pursuant to Sched. 3, para. 2(1), proviso.
[38] Sched. 3, para. 2(3).
[39] Sched. 3, para. 2(4).
[40] Sched. 3, para. 2(2).
[41] *Ibid.* para. 1(3).
[42] *Ibid.* para. 1(2).
[43] The prescribed form of additional notes is contained in the Landlord and Tenant (Notices) Regulations 1967 (S.I. 1967 No. 1831), reg. 6.
[44] *Ibid.* para. 10; see para. 5–07.

from taking forfeiture proceedings except with the leave of the court.[45] Moreover, the court[46] cannot grant leave unless it is satisfied that "the claim was not made in good faith."[47] It might be thought that the court can thus grant leave only if the tenant does not have a *bona fide* belief that he is entitled to the benefit of the 1967 Act. But it has been held that the court can also give leave where the claim is made recklessly or "with an ulterior motive," such as avoiding a forfeiture against which the court would not grant relief, *e.g.* where the tenant has been convicted of keeping a brothel.[48] If the house is in a very bad state of repair which the tenant will be unable to remedy, leave will be granted if the tenant's claim is for an extended lease,[49] but probably not if the claim is to acquire the freehold[50] (unless the property will be subject to a management scheme under section 19 imposing a comparable obligation to repair). If leave is given, the tenant's claim ceases to have effect,[51] and the court can order the tenant to pay compensation to the landlord.[52]

Any forfeiture proceedings which have previously been commenced when the tenant's Notice of Leaseholder's Claim is served do not terminate[53]; but the tenancy (which technically is determined by the mere issue and service of the forfeiture proceedings[54]) is deemed to continue, and any order for forfeiture may be set aside or varied as appropriate.[55] However, if it appears to the court that the tenant's claim was not made in good faith, or there was unreasonable delay in making it, the court may enforce the forfeiture[56]; and if the claim was not made in good faith the court can order the tenant to compensate the landlord for any loss he has suffered as a result.[57]

A tenant serving a notice under section 16 of the Landlord and Tenant Act 1954 (under which he is relieved from an order for possession but his tenancy is cut short) also loses the benefit of the 1967 Act.[58]

---

[45] Sched. 3, para. 4(1).
[46] *i.e.* the county court: s.20(1).
[47] Sched. 3, para. 4(1).
[48] *Central Estates (Belgravia) Ltd.* v. *Woolgar* [1972] 1 Q.B. 48, C.A., but the assumption that relief would never be granted in such a case seems unjustified: see *Glass* v. *Kencakes Ltd.* [1966] 1 Q.B. 611.
[49] *Liverpool Corporation* v. *Husan* [1972] 1 Q.B. 48, C.A. (an extreme case).
[50] *London and Winchester Properties Ltd.* v. *Felton* (1979) Liverpool C.C., unreported, not following dicta of Lord Denning M.R. in *Liverpool Corporation* v. *Husan, supra,* at p. 59D.
[51] Sched. 3, para. 4(1).
[52] Sched. 3, para. 4(3)(*a*).
[53] Sched. 3, para. 4(2).
[54] *Canas Property Co. Ltd.* v. *K.L. Television Services Ltd.* [1970] 2 Q.B. 433, C.A.
[55] Sched. 3, para. 4(2).
[56] Sched. 3, para. 4(2), proviso.
[57] Sched. 3, para. 4(3)(*b*).
[58] Sched. 3, para. 4(4).

Third parties

The service of a Notice of Leaseholder's Claim may sometimes have the effect of automatically discharging a landlord's contract made previously with a third party, insofar as that contract relates to the sale, lease or other disposal of the landlord's interest in the whole or any part of the house and premises. Such a contract is discharged if (a) the notice is effective, *i.e.* the tenant's claim is a valid one; (b) the contract does not provide for the eventuality of a tenant's Notice of Leaseholder's Claim being served; and (c) in the case only of a notice claiming an extended lease, the contract was entered into on the basis, common to both parties, that vacant possession of the house and premises or part thereof would or might be obtainable on the termination of the existing tenancy.[59] **5–15**

Compulsory purchase

A duly authorised local authority or other body with powers of compulsory acquisition may serve a notice to treat on the tenant or the landlord, or enter into a contract with either of them, for the purchase of their respective interests in the whole or any part of the house and premises. If the notice to treat or contract remains in force, it is provided that a subsequent Notice of Leaseholder's Claim is "of no effect."[60] It appears that some acquiring authorities argue that this results in the tenant's rights under the 1967 Act having to be ignored in assessing the compensation[61]; but this is clearly incorrect, because the effect of the compulsory purchase must be disregarded.[62] The compensation payable to the tenant is thus the open market value of the tenant's interest, including the right to the benefits of the 1967 Act as and when the tenant becomes duly qualified.[63] **5–16**

If the tenant has already served a Notice of Leaseholder's Claim, it will cease to have effect on the service of a notice to treat.[64] It is expressly provided that the compensation payable to either party is nevertheless to be determined on the assumption that the notice remains valid and binding.[65] If the tenant has claimed the freehold, his interest will thus be valued at the freehold vacant possession value, less the estimated enfranchisement price and costs of enfranchisement.[66]

---

[59] s.5(7).
[60] s.5(6)(*a*).
[61] See 248 E.G. 756.
[62] Land Compensation Act 1961, s.5(2); see 248 E.G. 217 (W. A. Leach).
[63] *Boaks* v. *Greater London Council* (1978) R.V.R. 17, L.T.; *Johnson* v. *Sheffield City Council* (1981) 43 P. & C.R. 272, L.T.; and see 249 E.G. 720 (T. Cockerton).
[64] s.5(6)(*b*).
[65] *Ibid.*
[66] *Sharif* v. *Birmingham City Council* (1979) 249 E.G. 147, L.T.

3. Obligations of Recipient of Tenant's Notice

Generally

5–17 The recipient of a Notice of Leaseholder's Claim or of a copy (unless he has no interest at all in the property) must forthwith serve copies on any further persons not mentioned in the tenant's notice known or believed by him to be the freeholder or an intermediate landlord,[67] adding the names of such further persons in the copies so served[68]; and he must also inform the claimant of such further persons.[69] Further, in cases where there is an intermediate landlord, if the recipient knows who is or believes himself to be "the reversioner" under paragraph 2 of Schedule 1,[70] the recipient must give written notice to that effect to the claimant, and serve copies on all the other persons interested in the property.[71] If he fails to comply with these requirements, or is guilty of any unreasonable delay in doing so, he will be liable for any consequent loss to the claimant or to any other person with an interest superior to the claimant's tenancy.[72]

The recipient of a tenant's notice whose interest is in mortgage (other than under a floating charge only[73]) must inform his mortgagee of the tenant's claim, and give him such further information as he reasonably requires from time to time.[74] If the recipient's mortgagee is in possession, or a receiver has been appointed by him or by the court, the recipient must also send the notice or copy of it to the mortgagee or receiver, as the case may be.[75]

Landlord's Notice in Reply

5–18 Provision is made for the landlord to serve a Notice in Reply to a tenant's Notice of Leaseholder's Claim.[76] Such a notice must be in the prescribed form[77] of Notice in Reply to Leaseholder's Claim[78] or in a form "substantially to the like effect,"[79] and should be served within two

---

[67] Sched. 3, para. 8(1)(*d*).
[68] Sched. 3, para. 8(1)(*e*).
[69] Sched. 3, para. 8(2)(*a*).
[70] See para. 11–05.
[71] Sched. 3, para. 8(2)(*b*).
[72] Sched. 3, para. 8(3).
[73] Sched. 3, para. 9(3). Debenture holders with fixed charges need not be informed if their securities are liable to be overreached without any part of the purchase price for the freehold being paid to them: see s.12(5) and para. 13–07.
[74] Sched. 3, para. 9(2).
[75] Sched. 3, para. 9(1).
[76] Sched. 3, para. 7.
[77] Form 2 in the Appendix to the Leasehold Reform (Notices) Regulations 1967 (S.I. 1967 No. 1768), made under the Landlord and Tenant Act 1954, s.66(1), as applied by the Leasehold Reform Act 1967, s.22(5).
[78] Form 2 is set out in Appendix C.
[79] Leasehold Reform Act (Notices) Regulations, reg. 4, *supra*.

months after the date of service of the tenant's notice.[80] The prescribed form includes a paragraph[81] indicating that the landlord reserves the right to give notice under section 2 of the 1967 Act objecting to the inclusion or exclusion of any premises in the "house and premises"[82]; and unless the landlord either reserves this right (and subsequently duly gives notice within two months after the date of service of the tenant's notice) or gives such notice within the two-month period with his Notice in Reply, he will lose his right to object under section 2.[83]

Otherwise, however, failure to serve a Notice in Reply, either within the two-month time-limit or at all, does not prevent the landlord from later challenging the validity of the tenant's claim.[84] The tenant cannot institute any court proceedings to enforce his rights until the landlord has given a Notice in Reply or the two-month period has elasped without his doing so.[85] In the latter case, the landlord is usually ordered to pay any costs unnecessarily incurred as a result of the landlord's failure to serve a Notice in Reply. Similarly, the landlord should indicate in his Notice in Reply[86] that he intends to apply for possession under section 17 or 18[87]; but even if he fails to do so, he does not lose his rights in that respect, although he will usually be ordered to pay any costs incurred as a result of such failure.

The prescribed form of Notice in Reply also requires the landlord to state whether he admits the tenant's claim.[88] If he does admit the claim, that admission is usually binding on him "so far as relates to section 1(1)(*a*) and (*b*)" of the 1967 Act, *i.e.* that the tenancy is a long tenancy at a low rent, that the house and premises are within the rateable value limits, and that the tenant has the three-year residential qualification. But the admission is not binding as regards other matters, such as whether the property comprises a "house" within the 1967 Act or the tenant was occupying the house as his only or main residence at the date of his Notice of Leaseholder's Claim; and in particular the admission does "not conclude any question whether the particulars of the house and premises in the tenant's notice are correct." Furthermore, the admission is not

---

[80] Sched. 3, para. 7.

[81] Para. 4.

[82] *i.e.* under subss. (4) and (5) of s.2, as to which see paras. 2–12 *et seq.*

[83] Sched. 3, para. 7(3), and s.2(4)(*a*) and (5)(*a*).

[84] *Church Commissioners for England* v. *Woods* (1969) Bloomsbury and Marylebone C.C., unreported (not challenged on appeal at (1970) 215 E.G. 301); *Manley* v. *Duke of Westminster* (1984) West London C.C., unreported (Judge Harris Q.C.); *Duke of Westminster* v. *Rendall* (1986) West London C.C., unreported (Judge Oddie). Clear words, such as in *e.g.* Landlord and Tenant Act 1954, s.30(1), would be required for that purpose, and there are none in the 1967 Act.

[85] Sched. 3, para. 7(5).

[86] Sched. 3, para. 7(3); see para. 3 of Form 2.

[87] See Chap. 8.

[88] Sched. 3, para. 7(1); see para. 2 of Form 2.

binding on the landlord even on the matters mentioned in section 1(1)(*a*) and (*b*), if the landlord (on whom the onus lies) "shows that he was induced to make the admission by misrepresentation or the concealment of material facts."[89] Information given in the tenant's Notice of Leaseholder's Claim which is incorrect in a material respect (such as *e.g.* putting in an erroneous figure for the rateable value or referring to the wrong tenancy[90]) will thus usually negative any admission by the landlord, irrespective of whether or not the tenant has any intention to mislead. The fact that the information is incorrect sometimes can only be ascertained by the landlord at a later stage, *e.g.* on receipt of the tenant's Statutory Declaration as to residence or when the tenant deduces his title, in which case the landlord will have little difficulty in discharging the onus of proof upon him. But even if the information could have been checked by the landlord, *e.g.* if the stated rateable value is incorrect, the landlord will often nevertheless be able to prove that he was thereby induced to admit the tenant's claim.

If the landlord does not admit the tenant's claim, his Notice in Reply must state the grounds on which it is not admitted.[91] It is sufficient for the grounds to be set out briefly (*e.g.* "your tenancy is not a 'long tenancy' as defined by the Act"), but it is often helpful to set out some short details and reasoning, particularly in cases where the landlord is relying on the proviso to section 4(1). However, it is clear that the landlord is not confined to the grounds set out in his Notice in Reply,[92] and can rely on further grounds at the hearing.[93] A convenient course often adopted in practice is for the landlord to serve a further Notice in Reply setting out any additional grounds on which he intends to dispute the tenant's claim. But it is not essential for the landlord to take this course, although a failure to state all grounds beforehand is usually taken into account by the court in exercising its discretion as to the costs of any proceedings to determine the validity of the tenant's claim.

89 Sched. 3, para. 7(4).

90 *Hurst* v. *Earl Grosvenor* (1979) Westminster C.C., unreported (Judge Ruttle).

91 Sched. 3, para. 7(1); and see para. 2 of Form 2.

92 There are no words in Sched. 3, para. 7 comparable with those in Landlord and Tenant Act 1954, s.30(1).

93 *Roberts* v. *Church Commissioners for England* (1971) Bloomsbury & Marylebone C.C., unreported, (not challenged on appeal at [1972] 1 Q.B. 278).

CHAPTER 6

ACQUISITION OF FREEHOLD

Upon serving a Notice of Leaseholder's Claim to acquire the freehold,[1] a qualified tenant becomes entitled to acquire the freehold of the "house and premises."[2] Such compulsory acquisition of the freehold is commonly referred to as "enfranchisement" by the tenant.[3] The 1967 Act and the Regulations made under it make detailed provisions as to the terms and conditions of the acquisition, the estate which the landlord is bound to convey, the contents of the appropriate conveyance or registered land transfer,[4] the costs of enfranchisement and other consequences of a Notice. This Chapter deals with these matters (but not the purchase price[5]). **6–01**

1. CONDITIONS OF STATUTORY CONTRACT

The statutory contract for sale which is created by the service of a Notice of Leaseholder's Claim[6] to acquire the freehold incorporates the Conditions[7] prescribed by the Lord Chancellor,[8] except in so far as the parties otherwise agree.[9] As regards any matters not covered by the Conditions, the contract is on the terms and conditions of an "open contract" for the sale of land (not made by correspondence[10]). Detailed reference should be made to the Conditions themselves, which appear to be comprehensive. What appears below is a brief summary of the Conditions, with comment on some of the more important provisions. **6–02**

Deposit

The landlord may by notice require a sum equal to three times the **6–03**

---

[1] As to the contents, service and effect of such a Notice, see Chap. 5.
[2] ss. 1(1), 8(1).
[3] But see Woodfall, *The Law of Landlord and Tenant* (28th ed.), para. 3–0951 for a narrower view of the meaning of enfranchisement.
[4] In the rest of this Chapter, "conveyance" is used to include a registered land transfer where appropriate.
[5] As to which see Chap. 9.
[6] See para. 5–07.
[7] Contained in Pt. I, Sched. to the Leasehold Reform (Enfranchisement and Extension) Regulations 1967 (S.I. No. 1879), set out in Appendix C.
[8] Under s. 22(2).
[9] Paras. 2 and 3 of the 1967 Regulations.
[10] s. 22(2), (4).

annual rent for the property[11] or £25 (whichever is the greater), to be paid to him or some person nominated by him, either as agent or stakeholder.[12] Most landlords require such a deposit to be paid to their solicitor or surveyor as agent, and (particularly as no interest is payable on the purchase price until after the completion date[13]) it is always in the landlord's interest to do so. The deposit fulfils the same function as a deposit under an ordinary contract for sale of land, and can be forfeited if, in breach of the statutory contract, the tenant fails to complete.[14] But it is considered that the deposit is repayable if the tenant withdraws after ascertaining the purchase price or the likely purchase price,[15] because the tenant is then exercising a right under the statutory contract, and is not in breach of it.

Evidence of tenant's right to enfranchise

6–04 The landlord may by notice require the tenant (i) to deduce his title to the tenancy and (ii) to furnish a Statutory Declaration as to the particulars of occupation of the property on which the tenant relies in his Notice of Leaseholder's Claim.[16] As to (i), the tenant should always be asked to deduce his title, except in plain cases. It may sometimes appear from his abstracted title that the tenant is not entitled to enfranchise for some reason, *e.g.* because he is not in fact the tenant, or holds as a trustee for a company[17] or is only one of two or more joint-tenants.[18] As to (ii), the Statutory Declaration (which must be made on oath[19]) should give full factual particulars of the tenant's occupation, and not (as is often the case) merely be a statement by the tenant that "I have occupied the property as my only or main residence for at least three out of the previous ten years," or the like. The purpose of the Statutory Declaration is to enable the landlord to check the accuracy of the claim made by the tenant in his Notice of Leaseholder's Claim as to his qualifying occupation.

Delivery of proof of landlord's title

6–05 The tenant may by notice require the landlord to deduce his title if he has not received a Notice in Reply within two months of giving his Notice

[11] *i.e.* the "house and premises" of which the tenant is entitled to acquire the freehold: see para. 1(2) of the 1967 Regulations.
[12] Condition 1 in Pt. I of Sched. to the 1967 Regulations. For a precedent see Precedent No. 25 in Appendix A.
[13] See para. 6–08.
[14] Condition 10(2).
[15] *i.e.* under s. 9(3): see para. 6–32.
[16] Condition 2. For a precedent see Precedent No. 25 in Appendix A.
[17] See para. 4–02.
[18] See para. 15–05.
[19] See Statutory Declarations Act 1835. For a precedent see Precedent No. 26 in Appendix A.

of Leaseholder's Claim.[20] If he has received a Notice in Reply, he can require the landlord to deduce title only if the Notice in Reply admits his claim or (if his claim is denied) he has established his right to the freehold either by agreement or by an order of the court and, in either case, if the extent of the property to be conveyed to him has been likewise established.[21] When validly required to do so, the landlord must deduce title in the usual way, *i.e.* in the case of registered land by delivery of office copies and an authority to inspect the register,[22] or in the case of unregistered land by delivery of a proper abstract of title.[23] Provision is made for the delivery and answering of objections and requisitions.[24]

The service by the tenant of a notice requiring the landlord to deduce his title may have serious consequences as to the rights of way and provisions concerning restrictive covenants to be included in the conveyance.[25] These consequences, which are frequently overlooked, are discussed below,[26] and must be carefully considered by the tenant before he serves such a notice and by the landlord when he has received one.

Particulars of rights of way and restrictive covenants

When or at any time after giving his Notice in Reply to Leaseholder's Claim, the landlord may by notice require the tenant within four weeks to state what rights of way and provisions concerning restrictive covenants he requires to be included in the conveyance.[27] Such notice must contain a statement as to the rights of way and restrictive covenants the landlord himself requires to be included[28]; and it is considered that the absence of such a statement renders the landlord's notice invalid, even if the landlord in fact requires none. If the tenant fails to comply with the notice, he is deemed to require no rights of way or provisions concerning restrictive covenants to be included in the conveyance.[29] Furthermore, even if the landlord has served no such notice, the same result follows if the tenant fails to comunicate a statement of the rights and provisions he requires when or before serving on the landlord a notice to deduce title.[30] **6–06**

At any time after he has become entitled to require the landlord to deduce title, the tenant may by notice require the landlord within four weeks to state what rights of way over the property and provisions

[20] Condition 3(1)(*i*). For a precedent see Precedent No. 27 in Appendix A.
[21] Condition 3(1)(*ii*).
[22] Condition 3(1)(*a*); and see s. 110 of the Land Registration Act 1925.
[23] Condition 3(1)(*b*).
[24] Condition 4.
[25] See Condition 5(4), (5).
[26] See para. 6–06.
[27] Condition 5(1).
[28] Condition 5(3).
[29] Condition 5(4).
[30] *Ibid.*

concerning restrictive covenants he requires to be included in the conveyance.[31] Such notice must contain a statement as to the rights of way and provisions concerning restrictive covenants the tenant himself requires to be included[32]; and it is considered that the absence of such a statement renders the tenant's notice invalid, even if the tenant in fact requires none. If the landlord fails to comply with the notice he is deemed to require no rights of way over the property or provisions concerning restrictive covenants (including, it appears, a covenant under section 29 of the 1967 Act[33]) to be included in the conveyance.[34] Furthermore, even if the tenant has served no such notice, but has served a notice on the landlord requiring him to deduce title[35] within a stipulated time, the same result follows if the landlord fails to communicate to the tenant a statement of the rights and provisions he requires within that stipulated time.[36]

Preparation of conveyance

6–07 It is provided that the conveyance shall be prepared by the tenant.[37] This accords with normal conveyancing practice, but in practice the initial drafts of most conveyances under the 1967 Act are provided by landlords who prefer the conveyances on their estate to be in a standard form. Provision is made for delivery of the draft conveyance and its engrossment,[38] and for duplicates in cases where the conveyance contains any covenant by the tenant or the grant or reservation of rights affecting other property of the landlord.[39] Further, if the conveyance is to contain any restrictive covenant and the tenant intends contemporaneously with the conveyance to execute a mortgage or convey any interest to a third party, he must inform the landlord of that intention and, if necessary, allow the landlord time to give a priority notice[40] for the registration of the covenants at least 14 days before completion.[41]

Completion and apportionment

6–08 The date for completion is fixed by either party, not earlier than one

---

[31] Condition 5(2). For a precedent see Precedent No. 27 in Appendix A.
[32] Condition 5(3).
[33] See paras. 14–09 *et seq.*
[34] Condition 5(5).
[35] *i.e.* under Condition 3.
[36] It appears that, for this purpose, the tenant's notice to deduce title must specifically stipulate a time for compliance, even though Condition 3 does not require it to do so.
[37] Condition 9(1).
[38] Condition 9(2).
[39] Condition 9(4).
[40] *i.e.* under Land Charges Act 1972, s. 11 (unregistered land).
[41] Condition 9(3).

month after the purchase price has been determined by agreement or otherwise, giving written notice to the other requiring completion. The completion date is the first working day after the expiration of four weeks from the giving of the notice.[42] Completion is at the office of the landlord's solicitor or (if the landlord so requires) at the office of his mortgagee's solicitor.[43]

Prima facie, rent is payable by the tenant up to the date of actual completion (whether or not the date fixed for completion as above), and any necessary apportionments of rent, rates and other outgoings are made as on that date.[44] But if completion is delayed beyond the date fixed (unless the delay is attributable to the default of the landlord or his mortgagee or Settled Land Act trustees[45]), the landlord can by notice elect that in lieu of rent the tenant should pay interest on the purchase price (or the balance outstanding if a deposit has been paid) from the giving of such notice until actual completion "at a rate per annum of two per cent. above the bank rate from time to time in force."[46] There is no longer any "bank rate" as such, but it is thought that this would be interpreted as equal to the Bank of England Minimum Lending Rate. The tenant has the usual option to deposit the purchase price (or the balance thereof) at a bank.[47]

The fact that the landlord is restricted only to rent, and cannot obtain interest in lieu until the date fixed for completion at the earliest, works unfairly against a landlord and has been the subject of considerable criticism. The purchase price is fixed as at the date of service of the Notice of Leaseholder's Claim,[48] but (particularly if there are any court or leasehold valuation tribunal proceedings[49]) it may be many months or even years before the purchase price is received; and the rent almost always falls a long way short of the interest which would be payable.

Extension of time-limits

The time-limits mentioned above are extended in three cases: 6–09

(a) *Where the claimant is a sub-tenant.* "The reversioner"[50] can by notice require that any period affecting the landlord (other than

---

[42] Condition 6(1).
[43] Condition 6(2).
[44] Condition 7.
[45] Condition 8(2).
[46] Condition 8(1).
[47] Condition 8(1), proviso.
[48] See s. 9(1)(1A) and para. 9–13.
[49] In which case the time-limits are extended: see para. 6–09.
[50] For definition, see para. 2, Sched. 1 to the 1967 Act and para. 11–05.

complying with a default notice under Condition 10[51]) should be doubled.[52]

(b) *Court or tribunal proceedings.* Any period when court or tribunal proceedings are pending is disregarded.[53]

(c) *Death or mental incapacity.* Any period laid down by the Conditions is extended for such further period as may be reasonable in all the circumstances in the event of the death or mental incapacity of either party.[54]

Failure to comply with obligations

6–10 If either party fails to comply with his obligations under the Conditions in due time, the other party may serve at least two months notice on the party in default. Such a notice must refer to Condition 10, specify the default and require him to make it good before the expiration of the notice.[55] If the tenant fails to comply with such a notice, then (without prejudice to the landlord's other remedies) the contract is discharged[56] and the landlord can forfeit the deposit.[57] This is a valuable remedy to the landlord. If the landlord fails to comply with such a notice, then (without prejudice to the tenant's other remedies[58]) the contract is discharged, the tenant is released from his obligation to pay the landlord's costs, and the deposit is returnable[59]; this is seldom a remedy of any value to the tenant, who will usually prefer to bring specific performance or other appropriate proceedings.

2. Estate to be Conveyed

The freehold

6–11 The landlord is "bound to make to the tenant, and the tenant to accept . . . a grant of the house and premises for an estate in fee simple absolute."[60] Thus, the landlord must execute a conveyance of the freehold to the tenant. As to the position where there are intermediate tenancies, *i.e.* other tenancies superior to that of the enfranchising tenant (and consequently more than one "landlord"), see Chapter 11.

---

[51] See para. 6–10.
[52] Condition 13(1).
[53] Condition 13(2).
[54] Condition 13(3).
[55] Condition 10(1). For a precedent, see Precedent No. 28 in Appendix A.
[56] Except for the tenant's obligation to pay the landlord's costs under s. 9(4), as to which see para. 6–33.
[57] Condition 10(2).
[58] *i.e.* under s. 9(4).
[59] Condition 10(3).
[60] s. 8(1).

"Incumbrances" and "Tenant's Incumbrances"

6–12 With certain exceptions,[61] the grant of the fee simple absolute must be made "subject to the tenancy and the tenant's incumbrances, but otherwise free from incumbrances."[62]

The expression "incumbrances" usually has a wide meaning, covering subsisting third party rights such as leases, mortgages, easements and restrictive covenants,[63] and these are clearly included. In addition, the expression is defined to include rentcharges[64] and (with certain exceptions[65]) "personal liabilities attaching in respect of the ownership of land or an interest in land though not charged on that land or interest."[66] It is considered that such liabilities include indemnity covenants for the performance of both positive and restrictive covenants, and also equitable interests which arise under constructive trusts.[67]

The expression "tenant's incumbrances" is defined as including[68] "any interest directly or indirectly derived out of the tenancy, and any incumbrance on the tenancy or any such interest (whether or not the same matter is an incumbrance also on any interest reversionary on the tenant)."[69] Under the earlier part of this definition, the expression thus plainly covers sub-tenancies, mortgages of the leasehold interest, and other incumbrances created by the tenant or any predecessor of his. Such interests would naturally be considered as "tenant's incumbrances," but the later part of the definition gives to that expression a much wider and somewhat artificial meaning. It includes any incumbrance affecting the freehold (or any superior tenancy or other superior interest) which also affects the tenancy, and any interest derived out of the tenancy. The great majority of incumbrances affecting the freehold (or other superior interest) are binding on the tenant,[70] and so are "tenant's incumbrances." The conveyance can thus be made subject to them. In practice, the landlord is seldom in a position to procure their removal or to convey free

---

[61] The exceptions are certain rentcharges (see Chap. 12) and interests capable of being overreached (see para. 6–15).

[62] s. 8(4)(*b*).

[63] See Megarry and Wade, *The Law of Real Property* (5th ed.), p. 611.

[64] See para. 6–13.

[65] Set out in s. 8(3).

[66] s. 8(2); the same definition appears in para. 7, Sched. 7, Housing Act 1985.

[67] As in, *e.g. Binion* v. *Evans* [1972] Ch. 359, C.A. and *Peffer* v. *Rigg* [1977] 1 W.L.R. 285.

[68] The definition nevertheless appears to be exhaustive. Compare the wording ("means") in the comparable provision in para. 7(*b*) of Sched. 7 to the Housing Act 1985.

[69] s. 8(2).

[70] Any incumbrances existing at the date of grant of the lease are normally binding, because the landlord is usually unable to make a grant free from them. But incumbrances affecting the freehold created after the grant of the tenancy will normally not be "tenant's incumbrances."

of them; and he is not bound to acquire any better title than he already has or could reasonably require to be vested in him.[71]

6–13 Certain interests affecting the landlord's estate merit particular consideration:

Tenancies

The freehold can be conveyed subject to the enfranchising tenant's lease, and any sub-tenancies created under it.[72] As to the position where there are intermediate tenancies, see Chapter 11.

Mortgages

Mortgages are probably "tenant's incumbrances," but a conveyance of the freehold under the 1967 Act automatically discharges mortgages affecting the freehold or any intermediate tenancy,[73] provided that the requirements of the 1967 Act as to payment of the purchase price are observed: see Chapter 13.

Rentcharges

Rentcharges affecting the freehold or any intermediate tenancy are expressly included in the definition of incumbrances,[74] but the freehold can usually be conveyed subject to them[75] (unless they are capable of being overreached[76]): see further Chapter 12.

Easements

Easements which affect the freehold or any intermediate lease as well as the tenancy are "tenant's incumbrances" and the freehold may be conveyed subject to them.[77] As to easements generally, see paras. 6–17 *et seq.*

Restrictive covenants

A conveyance may be made subject to any existing restrictive covenant affecting the landlord's interest, and the landlord is entitled to the usual covenant for indemnity against a breach of the covenant.[78] It is thus

---

[71] s. 10(1).
[72] s. 8(1).
[73] s. 12(1).
[74] s. 8(2).
[75] But not if the amount of the rentcharges exceeds the rent; s. 11(2).
[76] s. 8(4)(*b*).
[77] s. 8(2); and see para. 6–12.
[78] s. 10(4)(*a*).

immaterial whether or not a restrictive covenant is a tenant's incumbrance. See further paras. 6–25 *et seq.*

Other burdens

Certain burdens affecting the landlord's estate are not treated as incumbrances, and the conveyance can be made subject to them.[79] Such burdens are: 6–14

(i) **"Burdens originating in tenure."** These are any manorial incidents affecting former copyhold land. The only such manorial incidents now capable of existing are (i) rights of the lord of the manor to mines and minerals, (ii) rights of the lord of the manor in respect of fairs, markets and sporting, and (iii) liabilities for the upkeep of dykes, ditches, sea-walls, bridges and the like.[80]

(ii) **"Burdens in respect of the upkeep and regulation for the benefit of any locality of any land, building, structure, works, ways or watercourses."**[81] These appear to include positive obligations which are reciprocal to the benefits enjoyed,[82] such as a requirement to contribute towards the costs of maintaining estate roads used in common.[83] (Note, however, that burdens of this kind which arise under the tenancy are not within this provision[84]).

Equitable interests

The landlord must convey free from all equitable interests which are capable of being overreached.[85] For this purpose, the normal statutory requirements for a conveyance by a tenant for life or statutory owners of a settlement subject to the Settled Land Act 1925,[86] or by the trustees of a settlement on trust for sale,[87] must be observed. This normally necessitates the tenant paying the purchase monies to two or more trustees (or a trust corporation), and obtaining a receipt from them. However, it is provided that a conveyance in due form will be effective to overreach such equitable interests as are capable of being overreached, even though the purchase monies are paid to a mortgagee in accordance with the Act, 6–15

---

[79] s. 8(3).
[80] Law of Property Act 1922, ss. 128(2), 138 and paras. (5), (6), Sched. 12.
[81] Such burdens are probably not "incumbrances": see *Re Hodgson's S.E.* [1912] 1 Ch. 784.
[82] Enforceable under the principle of *Halsall* v. *Brizell* [1957] Ch. 109. See *Tito* v. *Waddell (No. 2)* [1977] Ch. 106 at pp. 289 *et seq.* and Megarry and Wade, *The Law of Real Property* (5th ed.), pp. 768–70.
[83] As in *Halsall* v. *Brizell, supra.*
[84] See para. 6–20, n. 20.
[85] s. 8(4).
[86] s. 18(1).
[87] Law of Property Act 1925, ss. 2(1), 27(2).

or into court in order to discharge a rentcharge[88] or a mortgage[89] in accordance with the Act, instead of to the trustees.[90]

A tenant acquiring the freehold under the Act takes free from any equitable interests which are void against him for want of registration or of which he has no actual or constructive notice. For this purpose, the tenant is to be treated as a purchaser "for money or money's worth" even if the purchase price payable by him is nil or only nominal.[91]

3. CONTENTS OF CONVEYANCE

Parcels clause

6–16 The property conveyed is the "house and premises" let to the tenant, subject to any permitted exclusion of part or the inclusion of other premises.[92] Where a part of the "house and premises" let to the tenant is excluded, it appears that the conveyance of the freehold will also operate as an automatic surrender to the landlord of the tenancy of that part[93]; but it is considered advisable for the tenant to make an express surrender in respect of that part, either in the conveyance of the freehold itself or by a separate contemporaneous document, so that the landlord will be able to show a clear title to it.[94]

Easements to be granted

6–17 Detailed provision is made as to what easements are to be granted with the house and premises.

Section 62 of the Law of Property Act 1925

This section is implied in all conveyances, in the absence of any contrary intention which is expressed,[95] and sometimes has a very wide operation which is frequently overlooked. Under the section, any conveyance of land passes with it "... all ... liberties, privileges, easements, rights and advantages whatsoever appertaining or reputed to appertain to the land, or any part thereof, or, at the time of the conveyance, ... enjoyed with ... the land or any part thereof."[96] Thus a

---

[88] s. 11(4).
[89] s. 13.
[90] s. 8(4)(*a*).
[91] s. 8(5). Such a case might arise where the tenancy is for a very long term at a peppercorn rent.
[92] See s. 2 and Chap. 2.
[93] s. 2(7).
[94] See Precedent Nos. 8 and 14, Appendix A.
[95] L.P.A. 1925, s. 62(4).
[96] L.P.A. 1925, s. 62(1); see also s. 62(2).

conveyance will not only pass all the existing easements which benefit the land, but also may have the effect of converting into full legal easements any quasi-easements and rights in fact then enjoyed with the land over any other land of the grantor, even where these have been used only by the licence of the grantor.[97] Thus, in one case, a tenant was allowed to use a roadway leading into a yard belonging to his landlord, and on the purchase of the freehold reversion by the tenant, it was held that he acquired a full legal easement to use the roadway, notwithstanding that his previous user was purely precarious.[98]

Section 62 will be implied in a conveyance of the freehold under the 1967 Act in the usual way. However, it is thought that an easement which is expressly or impliedly[99] conditional (*e.g.* upon payment of part of the costs of maintaining the subject-matter of the easement), will pass only subject to the same condition. Normally, section 62 can be excluded or its operation restricted,[1] and its sometimes unfair consequences[2] thereby mitigated. But this is not permitted in the case of conveyance under the 1967 Act, except with the consent of the tenant.[3] Consequently, a landlord who has granted to an enfranchising tenant a licence or permission which may be converted by section 62 into a full legal easement should expressly terminate that licence or permission before executing the conveyance, unless the tenant agrees to a clause in the conveyance expressly excluding any such easement.

Specific rights

Certain easements and rights are granted automatically (and independently of section 62 of the Law of Property Act 1925) by a conveyance under the 1967 Act. There is thus no need for them to be mentioned specifically in the conveyance, but the conveyance should expressly state that it is made under section 8 of the 1967 Act,[4] or otherwise indicate that it is made in order to give effect to the tenant's claim under the Act. In the case of a transfer of registered land to a tenant, or the first registration of a title founded on a conveyance under the 1967 Act, the Land Registry as a matter of course makes entries on the register in general terms, indicating 6–18

[97] *Wright* v. *Macadam* [1949] 2 K.B. 744, C.A.; *Goldberg* v. *Edwards* [1950] Ch. 247, C.A.; but see *Green* v. *Ashco Horticulturist Ltd.* [1966] 1 W.L.R. 889.

[98] *International Tea Stores Ltd.* v. *Hobbs* [1903] 2 Ch. 165.

[99] As in *Halsall* v. *Brizell* [1957] Ch. 169: see para. 6–20.

[1] L.P.A. 1925, s. 62(4).

[2] "I may perhaps regret that the decision in this case may tend to discourage landlords from acts of kindness to their tenants" *per* Tucker L.J. in *Wright* v. *Macadam*, *supra*, at p. 755. Reform is suggested in Law Comm. No. 36, para. 92.

[3] s. 10(1).

[4] See Precedents Nos. 1 *et seq.* and 9 *et seq.*, Appendix A.

that the property has the benefit of the easements and rights.[5] Such easements and rights relate to (a) rights of support for any building or part of a building; (b) rights to the access of light and air to any building or part of a building; (c) rights to the passage of water or of gas or other piped fuel, or to the drainage or disposal of water, sewage, smoke or fumes, or to the use or maintenance of pipes or other installations for such passage, drainage or disposal; and (d) rights to the use or maintenance of cables or other installations for the supply of electricity, for the telephone or for the receipt directly or by landline of visual or other wireless transmissions.[6] These rights appear to cover all usual domestic supplies and services.

The easements and rights of this kind automatically granted are all those (so far as the landlord is capable of granting them) as are necessary to secure to the tenant as nearly as may be the same rights as, at the date of service of his Notice of Leaseholder's Claim, were available to him under or by virtue of (a) the tenancy or any agreement collateral thereto, or (b) any grant, reservation or agreement made on the severance of the house and premises or any part thereof from other property then comprised in the same tenancy.

Rights of way

6–19 The conveyance must include a grant of such rights of way (so far as the landlord is capable of granting them) as are "necessary for the reasonable enjoyment of the house and premises as they have been enjoyed during the tenancy and in accordance with its provisions."[7] There must thus have been actual use of the way; but it is thought that such use need not have continued right up to the date of the tenant's Notice of Leaseholder's Claim, and that any use during any substantial period of the tenancy will suffice so long as that use has not been altogether abandoned. In addition, the use must have been in accordance with the provisions of the existing tenancy, *e.g.* under an implied grant in the tenancy itself, or an express grant in the tenancy or any collateral agreement.[8] However, even if these conditions are satisfied, no such right of way need be granted if it would be unreasonable to do so having regard to changes in the circumstances since the tenancy was granted,[9] or the interests of neighbouring properties also subject to similar tenancies.[10]

---

[5] See Ruoff and Roper, *Registered Conveyancing* (5th ed.), p. 549. Unless the relevant transfer or conveyance expressly states that it is made under the 1967 Act, the Land Registry should be given notice of that fact by a suitable document lodged with the application for registration.

[6] s. 10(2)(*i*).

[7] s. 10(3)(*a*).

[8] See *Grime* v. *Robinson* (1972) 24 P. & C.R. 427, L.T.

[9] s. 10(5)(*a*).

[10] s. 10(5)(*b*).

A tenant who requires the conveyance to include a right of way must duly comply with a landlord's notice under Condition 4 of the statutory Conditions of Sale, or communicate his requirement to the landlord when serving a notice under Condition 3 of those Conditions.[11] Otherwise, he will be deemed to require no right of way to be included. See further para. 6–06.

Common facilities

On some estates, the landlord owns and is responsible for the 6–20
maintenance of other property (such as a private road, private sewers, a common garden or other amenity)[12–13] which is used in common by the tenant and other persons. Except where there is a management scheme under section 19,[14] the 1967 Act fails to provide satisfactory machinery for dealing with such cases. The tenant cannot be required to enter into a direct covenant to pay a proportionate part of the maintenance and other costs of such facilities[15]; and even if he in fact agrees to give such a covenant (usually continuing such a covenant contained in his lease), being a positive covenant it is not directly enforceable against his successors in title.[16]

However, it is considered that in such cases any easement relating to such facilities can be made conditional upon the tenant contributing a fair proportion of the maintenance and other costs of the facilities.[17] Such a condition is enforceable against successors in title of the tenant, at any rate if and so long as they wish to take the benefit of the easement[18] (though not, it appears, if they do not wish to do so[19]). By this means, the burden of an obligation to pay can indirectly be made to run with the land.[20] Moreover, if there is a right of re-entry (which should be limited to a suitable perpetuity period) in the event of default of the tenant in contributing his fair proportion, such right is enforceable even though the

[11] Condition 5(4) of Sched. 1 to the Leasehold Reform (Enfranchisement and Extension) Regulations 1967 (S.I. 1879).

[12–13] Other examples which the author has encountered include communal swimming-baths, sauna baths, tennis-courts and children's play areas.

[14] See s. 19(8)(*c*), (*d*) and para. 10–19.

[15] But if the tenant refuses to continue such a covenant, the landlord can, it is thought, require an increased purchase price for the freehold.

[16] *Austerberry* v. *Oldham Corporation* (1885) 29 Ch. D. 750 at pp. 781–5; Megarry and Wade, *The Law of Real Property* (5th ed.), p. 761.

[17] Under s. 10(2), (3), where applicable, and otherwise under s. 62, L.P.A. 1925.

[18] *Halsall* v. *Brizell* [1957] Ch. 169; *Tito* v. *Waddell* (No. 2) [1977] Ch. 106 at pp. 289 *et seq.*; Megarry and Wade, *The Law of Real Property*, *supra*, pp. 768 *et seq.*

[19] *Parkinson* v. *Reid* (1966) 56 D.L.R. (2nd.) 315 (Canada). There is no clear English authority, but see *Tito* v. *Waddell* (No. 2), *supra*, at p. 295H.

[20] It is sometimes suggested that the burden can be made to run under s. 8(3). This is incorrect, because s. 8(3) is dealing only with existing obligations already affecting the freehold, and not with obligations arising solely under the tenancy.

burden of the covenant does not run with the land[21]; but it is considered that the tenant cannot be required to accept such a right of re-entry in his conveyance.

The landlord cannot be required to enter into a covenant to continue to maintain the facilities, even if (as is often the case) the lease contains a covenant to that effect. But this is usually of little comfort to the landlord, who nearly always remains liable to other tenants on the estate who have not enfranchised on similar covenants in their leases. Moreover, there is seldom any way in which the landlord can divest himself of his obligations under such covenants except under some arrangement with the tenants.

Easements and rights to be reserved

6–21 The following provisions are made as to what easements and rights are to be excepted and reserved out of the conveyance.

Specific rights

Certain easements and rights are automatically reserved by a conveyance under the 1967 Act. This is contrary to the normal rule, under which no easements are impliedly reserved to the grantor except easements of necessity and certain other intended easements.[22] It is therefore important (though not strictly essential) that the conveyance should expressly indicate that it is made in order to give effect to the tenant's claim under the Act.[23] In the case of a transfer of registered land to a tenant, or the first registration of a title founded on a conveyance under the 1967 Act, the Land Registry, as a matter of course, makes entries on the register in general terms that the property is subject to the easements and rights.[24] Such easements and rights relate to the same category of rights as those mentioned in para. 6–18.

The easements and rights of this kind automatically reserved are all those for the benefit of other property as are capable of existing in law and are necessary to secure to the person interested in the other property (usually, but not necessarily, the landlord) as are nearly as may be the same rights as at the date of the tenant's Notice of Leaseholder's Claim were available against the tenant under, or by virtue of, (a) the tenancy or

---

[21] *Shiloh Spinners Ltd.* v. *Harding* [1973] A.C. 691.

[22] *Wheeldon* v. *Burrows*, *supra*, and see Megarry and Wade, *The Law of Real Property* (5th ed.), p. 859.

[23] See Precedents Nos. 1 *et seq.* and 9 *et seq.*, Appendix A.

[24] See Ruoff and Roper, *Registered Conveyancing* (5th ed.), p. 549. Unless the relevant transfer or conveyance expressly states that it was made under the 1967 Act, the Land Registry should be given notice of that fact by a suitable document lodged with the application for registration.

any agreement collateral thereto, or (b) any grant, reservation or agreement made on the severance of the house and premises from other property then comprised in the tenancy.[25] It is thought that this will preserve any right to build notwithstanding obstruction of light to the house and premises if such a right was reserved to the landlord in the tenant's lease (as is commonly the case), and that it will amount to a written consent under section 3 of the Prescription Act 1832, thus preventing the acquisition of a prescriptive right to light after 20 years.[26] However, in cases where this is of importance, it is suggested that any express reservation of such a right should be incorporated in the conveyance in order to remove doubts on the matter.

Rights of way

The landlord is entitled to reserve expressly any right of way necessary **6–22**
for the reasonable enjoyment of other property in which he has an interest at the date of service of the tenant's Notice of Leaseholder's Claim.[27] Such enjoyment must relate to the occupational enjoyment of the retained property, and the landlord is not entitled to reserve a right of way for the purposes of a possible future development of the retained land.[28] A landlord who requires the conveyance to include such a right of way must duly comply with a tenant's notice under Condition 5 of the Statutory Conditions of Sale, or communicate his requirement to the tenant within the time fixed for compliance with a tenant's notice under Condition 3.[29] Otherwise, the landlord will be deemed to require no right of way to be included.[30]

Minerals

The landlord is entitled to except the underlying minerals, even if they **6–23**
were not excepted from the tenancy, provided that proper provision is made for the support of the house and premises as they have been enjoyed during the tenancy and in accordance with its terms.[31]

---

[25] s. 10(2)(*ii*).
[26] See *Haynes* v. *King* [1893] 3 Ch. 439; *Foster* v. *J. Lyons & Co. Ltd.* [1927] 1 Ch. 219; and *Willoughby* v. *Eckstein* [1937] Ch. 167.
[27] s. 10(2)(*b*). This right is subject to the limitations of s. 10(5), but it is unlikely that these would be relevant.
[28] *Grime* v. *Robinson* (1972) 24 P. & C.R. 427, L.T.
[29] See para. 6–06.
[30] Reg. 5(5) of Sched. 1 to the Leasehold Reform (Enfranchisement and Extension) Regulations. 1967 (S.I. 1879).
[31] s. 2(6): see para. 2–14.

Existing easements affecting landlord's estate

6–24 The conveyance must be made subject to rights of way granted or agreed to be granted before the date of service of the tenant's Notice of Leaseholder's Claim by the landlord or by the person then entitled to the reversion on the tenancy.[32] Moreover, the landlord is not obliged to convey to the tenant any better title than he already has.[33] It is considered that he can thus convey subject to any other existing easements affecting the freehold, which will probably be "tenant's incumbrances." Such easements should not be reserved (*i.e.* they should not be mentioned in the parcels clause before the habendum), but the conveyance should be made subject to them.

Restrictive covenants

Generally

6–25 Restrictive covenants are referred to in the 1967 Act as "any covenant or agreement restrictive of the user of any land or premises."[34] Notwithstanding this reference, it is considered that this expression covers all negative covenants and not merely "user covenants" in the strict sense.[35] Thus, it has been held that negative covenants as to alterations and as to outside painting are "restrictive covenants" for the purposes of the Act.[36]

The Act permits certain provisions as to restrictive covenants to be included in a conveyance, discussed below; but neither the landlord nor the tenant can require the inclusion of any provision which is unreasonable in all the circumstances, in view of (a) the date at which the tenancy commenced and changes since that date which affect the suitability at the date of service of the tenant's Notice of Leaseholder's Claim, and (b) where the tenancy is or was one of a number of tenancies of neighbouring houses, of the interests of those affected in respect of other houses.[37]

Any landlord or tenant who requires provisions as to restrictive covenants to be included in the conveyance must be careful to comply with the requirements of Condition 5 of the statutory Conditions of Sale. If he fails to do so, he will be deemed to have required no such provisions.[38]

---

[32] s. 10(3)(*b*).
[33] s. 10(1).
[34] s. 10(4).
[35] Compare the wording of s. 84(1) of the Law of Property Act 1925, as amended, which has always been assumed to cover all kinds of negative covenants.
[36] *Le Mesurier* v. *Pitt* (1972) 23 P. & C.R. 389, L.T. at p. 398.
[37] s. 10(4).
[38] Condition 5(4), (5) of Sched. 1 to the Leasehold Reform (Enfranchisement and Extension) Regulations 1967 (S.I. 1879): see para. 6–06.

Affecting landlord's estate

The conveyance must be made subject to any existing restrictive covenants affecting the landlord's estate, which are enforceable for the benefit of other property; and the landlord can require the inclusion of the usual covenant for indemnity in respect of such covenants.[39] In practice many old restrictive covenants are to be found on titles, and it is frequently uncertain whether or not they are enforceable. It is considered that the landlord is entitled to an indemnity in such cases without having to prove that the covenants remain enforceable. **6–26**

Restrictive covenants in tenant's lease

The basic rule is that the landlord cannot require the continuance of any of the covenants imposed by the tenant's lease. But an exception is made in the case of any restrictive covenant which is capable of benefiting other property,[40] and which also fulfils one of two further alternative conditions. These are as follows: **6–27**

(i) The covenant is enforceable by one or more persons other than the landlord.[41] An example is a tenant's covenant in a post-1925 lease which is expressed to be made with other persons. Even though they are not parties to the lease, such persons have the benefit of the covenant and can enforce it directly against the tenant, by virtue of section 56 of the Law of Property Act 1925.[42]

(ii) The covenant, although enforceable only by the landlord, is "such as materially to enhance the value of the other property."[43] A covenant falls within this category if it is likely to maintain the value of other property which might otherwise deteriorate.[44] Thus a covenant which controls the use of a house (*e.g.* by restricting its use to residential purposes,[45] or that of a single family residence), or its appearance (*e.g.* by preventing painting except in a manner uniform with other properties), and which is found in other leases of neighbouring properties can generally be repeated in the conveyance.

The landlord can require[46] any such restrictive covenant to be continued "with suitable adaptations," *i.e.* adapted as a freehold

---

[39] s. 10(4)(*a*).

[40] See *Marten* v. *Flight Refuelling Ltd.* [1962] Ch. 115.

[41] s. 10(4)(*b*)(*i*).

[42] *Re Ecclesiastical Commissioners for England's Conveyance* [1936] Ch. 430; and see generally Megarry and Wade, *The Law of Real Property* (5th ed.), p. 763.

[43] s. 10(4)(*b*)(*ii*).

[44] *Peck* v. *Trustees of Hornsey Parochial Charities* (1970) 22 P. & C.R. 789, L.T. at p. 799; *Le Mesurier* v. *Pitt* (1972) 23 P. & C.R. 389, L.T. at p. 398.

[45] As in *Barrable* v. *Westminster City Council* (1984) 271 E.G. 1273, L.T.

[46] Subject to the limitations in s. 10(5): see para. 6–25.

covenant; but not subject to any modification,[47] which can only be made under other legislation.[48] However, any statutory modifications made to a leasehold covenant, *e.g.* by section 19 of the Landlord and Tenant Act 1927, must be reproduced in the conveyance.[49] It is advisable[50] to follow the usual conveyancing practice of including in the conveyance an express annexation of the benefit of the covenant to the landlord's other property (and any other property benefited) and each and every part thereof[51]; and if there is such other property benefited, the covenant should be expressed to be made with the owner of such property.[52]

Covenants affecting other property

6–28 In addition, the tenant can[53] require the continuance of any restrictive covenant contained in the lease which affects other property and enhances the value of that property.[54] One method of doing this is to include in the conveyance an express declaration against merger[55]; indeed, this is probably the only method in cases where the landlord is no longer (or never was) the owner of the other property. In such a case, the landlord can limit his liability to breaches of covenant for which he is responsible.[56]

New restrictive covenants

The landlord may[57] also require the inclusion in the conveyance of any further restrictive covenants which will not interfere with the existing use of the house and premises, but which will materially enhance the value of other property of his.[58] Thus, the landlord may restrict the use of a dwelling-house to residential purposes (unless it has also been used for other purposes during the tenancy), if he has neighbouring property which will be materially benefited by such a covenant.

---

[47] *Le Mesurier* v. *Pitt*, *supra*, at p. 398.
[48] *e.g.* s. 84(1) of the Law of Property Act 1925, as amended.
[49] *Peck* v. *Trustees of Hornsey Parochial Charities*, *supra*, at p. 801.
[50] But probably not necessary: see s. 78, L.P.A. 1925 and *Federated Homes Ltd.* v. *Mill Lodge Properties* [1980] 1 W.L.R. 594, C.A.
[51] See clause 5 in the form of conveyance printed as an Annex to the report of *Le Mesurier* v. *Pitt*, *supra*.
[52] Who will then take the benefit even though not party to the conveyance: s. 56, L.P.A. 1925; Megarry and Wade, *supra*, at p. 763.
[53] Subject to the limitations in s. 10(5): see para. 6–25.
[54] s. 10(4)(*b*)(*ii*).
[55] See para. 6–31.
[56] s. 10(6).
[57] Subject to the limitations in s. 10(5): see para. 6–25.
[58] s. 10(4)(*c*).

Miscellaneous contents of conveyance

All-estate clause

The conveyance must not be framed to exclude or restrict section 63 of the Law of Property Act 1925 (which is implied in all conveyances), unless the tenant consents.[59] 6–29

Covenants for title

The landlord, whatever his capacity, need give only the covenant for title implied in a conveyance "as trustee" or "as mortgagee,"[60] *i.e.* that the grantor has not himself encumbered or charged the freehold.[61] Where the landlord is in fact the beneficial owner, even this limited covenant may not be implied if he conveys "as trustee" (for it has been said that the grantor must actually have the capacity in which he purports to convey if the statutory covenants are to be implied[62]), and there should also be included in the conveyance a clause such as follows: "It is hereby declared that the same covenants for title (but no further covenant for title) shall be implied herein as if the Vendor was conveying and was expressed to convey the said property as Trustee."

Where the freehold is registered land, it is doubtful if the above covenant for title is of any practical value. There do not appear to be any incumbrances affecting the freehold which is not itself already registered or of which the purchasing leaseholder will inevitably obtain notice when the normal conveyancing procedure is carried out.

Declaration of merger

See para. 6–30.

Acknowledgment for production

In the case of unregistered land, the landlord must give the usual acknowledgment for production of any deeds affecting the property retained by him. But he need not give an undertaking for safe custody, even if he is in fact the beneficial owner.[63]

---

[59] s. 10(1).
[60] *Ibid.*
[61] L.P.A. 1925, s. 76(1)(*f*), Sched. 3, Pt. VI.
[62] *Fay* v. *Miller, Wilkins & Co.* [1941] Ch. 360, C.A. at p. 363; *Re Robertson's Application* [1969] 1 W.L.R. 109 at p. 113; but see Megarry and Wade, *supra*, at p. 160.
[63] s. 10(6).

Other clauses

The landlord is not entitled to require any further clauses to be included in the conveyance. In particular, no option of re-purchase or right of pre-emption can be included.

4. MERGER

6–30 The acquisition of the freehold by the tenant will sometimes, but by no means always, result in there being a merger of the lease in the freehold. "Merger" is the opposite of surrender (where the landlord acquires the lease), but the effect is the same. In each case the lease is absorbed by the freehold and is altogether extinguished. However, in order for a merger to take place, the lease and the freehold must be vested in the same person in the same right and there must be no intervening interest.[64] There will be no merger if the lease is the subject-matter of an outstanding legal or equitable mortgage[65] (except perhaps, in the case of mortgage by sub-demise, as to the tenant's nominal reversion).

Merger is not automatic, even where there is no impediment to it. Both at common law[66] and in equity, whether or not there is a merger is a question of the intention of the person becoming entitled to both estates.[67] Such intention is a question of fact, and may be implied from subsequent acts.[68] In the absence of any direct evidence of intention, the court will look to the interests of the party becoming entitled to both estates, and if it is against his interest will presume that merger was not intended.[69] If it is in his interest, or if no interest or intention can be shown either way, a merger will be presumed.[70]

Often, the intention is made clear by an express declaration of merger (or, more rarely, against merger) contained in the conveyance. But a declaration of merger is sometimes included in cases where no merger is possible or where it is contrary to the interests of the tenant[71]; and it should not be included in the conveyance of the freehold as a matter of course. Two cases deserve particular mention:

---

[64] See Megarry and Wade, *supra*, at p. 686.

[65] It is submitted that the law is as stated, but there is no direct modern authority. See, however, *Doe* d. *Beadon* v. *Pyke* (1816) 5 M. & S. 146, *per* Lord Ellenborough C.J. at p. 154 (a case on surrender).

[66] Which in this instance has been made to follow equity: L.P.A. 1925, s. 185.

[67] *Re Fletcher* [1917] 1 Ch. 339, C.A.

[68] *Ibid.*

[69] *Ingle* v. *Vaughan Jenkins* [1900] 2 Ch. 368; *Capital and Counties Bank Ltd.* v. *Rhodes* [1903] 1 Ch. 631, C.A.

[70] *Re Fletcher*, *supra*, at p. 342, *per* Cozens-Hardy M.R.

[71] See, *e.g.* *Golden Lion Hotel (Hunstanton) Ltd.* v. *Carter* [1965] 1 W.L.R. 1189 ("faulty conveyancing": *per* Cross J. at p. 1192).

(1) *Lease in mortgage*

As mentioned above, there can be no merger where the lease is mortgaged. A declaration of merger in such circumstances will be of no effect (at any rate while the mortgage is still subsisting), unless the mortgage security is extended to the freehold, and may be positively misleading. 6–31

(2) *Easements or restrictive covenants annexed to lease*

An easement may be granted otherwise than by the landlord (although not acquired by prescription, except for an easement of light)[72] so as to be coterminous with the lease. Such an easement may be extinguished together with the lease if there is a merger.[73] Similarly, the benefit of a restrictive covenant may run only with the leasehold term, and will be no longer enforceable if that term is extinguished by a merger. To avoid these consequences it is suggested that in such circumstances an express declaration *against* merger should be included in the conveyance.

5. Costs of Enfranchisement

Purchase price

This is discussed in Chapter 9. 6–32

Tenant's right to withdraw

The price will be ascertained by agreement between the parties, and in default will be fixed by a leasehold valuation tribunal, subject to appeal to the Lands Tribunal.[74] Prima facie, the tenant will be bound to complete the purchase at that price.[75] But he is entitled at any time until[76] one month after the purchase price has been so ascertained to give written notice to the landlord that he is unable or unwilling to purchase at that price,[77] with the following consequences:

(a) his Notice of Leaseholder's Claim ceases to have effect[78];
(b) he is liable to compensate the landlord for any loss suffered by reason of the interference caused by the Notice with the landlord's

[72] An easement acquired by a tenant by prescription will enure for the benefit of his landlord: see Megarry and Wade, *supra*, at p. 873.
[73] *Golden Lion Hotel* (*Hunstanton*) *Ltd.* v. *Carter*, *supra*.
[74] s. 21(1) as amended.
[75] s. 5(1).
[76] Strictly only "on ascertaining the amount payable or likely to be payable", but the practical effect is as stated.
[77] s. 9(3).
[78] s. 9(3)(*a*).

right to dispose of or deal with the house and premises or any neighbouring property[79]; and

(c) he is barred for three years from serving another Notice of Leaseholder's Claim to acquire the freehold (but not from serving a Notice of Leaseholder's Claim to acquire an extended lease[80]). Furthermore, he will have to pay the landlord's costs mentioned below; but not, apparently, any costs incurred by the landlord before a leasehold valuation tribunal or the Lands Tribunal (except by reason of an order for costs). He can, however, recover any deposit he has paid.[81]

Other costs

6–33 Apart from the purchase price, the tenant must pay certain other costs, in addition to his own valuation costs and conveyancing and other legal costs.[82] He is, moreover, obliged to pay these costs even if the purchase is never in fact completed, unless the landlord successfully resists his Notice of Leaseholder's Claim on the ground of his own occupation,[83] or the tenant withdraws his notice after the grant of a minister's certificate under section 19 (or while an application for one is pending[84]). The costs for which the tenant is liable are:

(a) The landlord's valuation costs. Often, the landlord's valuer, as well as providing the landlord with a valuation, conducts the negotiations on the purchase price. The negotiating costs of the landlord are not payable by the tenant, and the valuer should accordingly charge separate valuation and negotiating fees.
(b) The landlord's ordinary conveyancing costs.
(c) The reasonable costs of or incidental to "any investigation by the landlord of that person's right to acquire the freehold."[85] This item includes the landlord's costs of investigating the claimant's title to the leasehold, and whether the tenant has been in occupation of his residence for the relevant three-year period; but not the landlord's costs of preparing and serving a Notice in Reply, serving copies on other persons interested, and taking general advice as to his rights under the Act.

---

79 *Ibid.*
80 s. 9(3)(*b*) as amended.
81 See para. 6–03.
82 s. 9(4).
83 s. 18(6)(*b*).
84 s. 19(14)(*b*).
85 s. 9(4)(*a*).

The landlord has the usual vendor's lien for the unpaid purchase price. This lien is extended to cover also all costs payable by the tenant as above, and all rent and other sums due under the tenancy, up to the date of conveyance.[86]

[86] s. 9(5).

CHAPTER 7

EXTENDED LEASE

7–01 As an alternative to acquiring the freehold, a qualified tenant may take an extended lease. On the tenant serving a Notice of Leaseholder's Claim to an extended lease,[1] the landlord is bound to grant to the tenant, in substitution for his existing tenancy, a new tenancy of "the house and premises" for a term expiring 50 years after the "term date" (*i.e.* in the usual case the contractual expiry date)[2] of his existing term.[3] The 1967 Act and the regulations made under it make detailed provisions as to the terms and conditions of the grant and the term, the rent and the covenants and conditions of the extended lease, the costs of the grant and other consequences of a notice. This Chapter deals with these matters (except for the rent[4]).

1. FREEHOLD OR EXTENDED LEASE?

Generally

7–02 It is suggested that, except as mentioned below, any tenant who can possibly do so should be advised to acquire the freehold rather than to take an extended lease[5]. This will, of course, involve a greater capital outlay. But it is thought that in most cases there is little difficulty in obtaining mortgage facilities for this purpose, commonly by way of a further loan from the existing mortgagee of the lease. The expenditure of the capital outlay will almost always be well worthwhile.

The 50–year extension is a hybrid and unsatisfactory estate. It has no statutory protection, and does not carry the right to acquire the freehold.[6] Moreover, it carries little security of tenure, for it is liable to be determined by the landlord at any time if he wishes to redevelop (although the landlord must thereupon compensate the tenant for the residue of the term he has lost).[7] A 50–year extension is thus a somewhat unsatisfactory security for would-be mortgagees. The difficulties in obtaining a mortgage encountered by long leaseholders with 30 or less

[1] As to the contents, service and effect of such a notice, see Chap. 5.
[2] s.37(1), (2), (3); and see para. 3–12.
[3] s.14(1).
[4] As to which see Chap. 9.
[5] See Precedents Nos. 21 and 22, Appendix A.
[6] s.16(1); and see para. 7–15.
[7] s.17: see Chap. 8.

years of their term to run, which in turn result in difficulties in finding a purchaser, will recur (and be more serious) in a few years' time. It is these difficulties which mainly led to the demand for enfranchisement, and (in the view of the author) there is certain to be a similar demand from the holders of 50–year extensions in the foreseeable future.

Properties in higher rateable value brackets

Different considerations apply in cases where the rateable value of the house and premises is over £1,000 in Greater London or £500 elsewhere.[8] In such cases (and also, if the tenancy was created by the grant of a lease under "the right to buy" provisions, a sub-tenancy directly or indirectly derived out of such a tenancy or an extended lease under the 1967 Act granted in substitution for such a tenancy or sub-tenancy[9]), the purchase price payable for the freehold is determined on the basis of valuation in section 9(1A) rather than section 9(1) of the 1967 Act.[10] But there is no corresponding difference in the terms of an extended lease. As the section 15 rent payable as from the original term date[11] under an extended lease is based on the letting value of the site only, ignoring the value of any buildings on the site,[12] the main financial advantage to the tenant of the 1967 Act in its original form can be obtained under an extended lease. It was formerly possible for the tenant to reap the benefit of that advantage on acquiring the freehold, by first obtaining an extended lease and then claiming the freehold.[13] But this is no longer possible,[14] unless a Notice of Leaseholder's Claim for an extended lease was served before March 4, 1986.[14a] See further paras. 9–41 *et seq.* 7–03

2. Form of Extended Lease

The 1967 Act plainly requires the grant of a new single tenancy, commencing on the date of grant and being for a term including both the unexpired term of the existing tenancy and the 50–year extension. The new tenancy is in substitution for the unexpired part of the existing 7–04

[8] After any notional reduction under the Housing Act 1974, Sched. 8, discussed in paras. 2–23 *et seq.*

[9] Housing Act 1985, s.175.

[10] See para. 9–14.

[11] For meaning, see para. 3–12.

[12] See paras. 9–03 *et seq.*

[13] *Mosley* v. *Hickman* (1986) 278 E.G. 728, C.A. affirming L.J. *sub. nom. Hickman* v. *Phillimore Kensington Estate Trustees* (1985) 274 E.G. 1261.

[14] The effect of *Mosley* v. *Hickman, supra,* was reversed by the Housing and Planning Act 1986, s. 23.

[14a] See the Housing and Planning Act 1986 s.23(2)(*c*). March 4, 1986 was the date of the decision of the Court of Appeal in *Mosley* v. *Hickman.*

tenancy,[15] which is thus surrendered to the landlord by operation of law.[16] Tenants sometimes suggest that the 50–year extension should be granted by way of a deed of variation of the existing tenancy, or by the grant of a future 50–year term[17]; often this would result in a saving of stamp duty and conveyancing costs (payable by them). Landlords should refuse any such suggestion (unless the proposed deed of variation or future lease is approved by the court[18]), and insist on the grant of the single new tenancy contemplated by the 1967 Act, for the following reasons. It is clear that the single new tenancy is in full satisfaction of the tenant's rights under the Act (except that he may acquire the freehold prior to the original term date[19]). The tenant has no further rights under the Act, and no further statutory protection under other Acts,[20] and the landlord is entitled to recover possession if he proposes to redevelop.[21] But it is far from clear that a deed of variation of the existing lease, or the grant of a future 50–year term, will similarly be considered to be in full satisfaction of the tenant's rights, even if there is an express declaration in the deed or grant to that effect. There is therefore a considerable danger that the 50–year extension made will be treated as a normal "long tenancy at a low rent," with the result that during the extension the tenant will still be able to exercise the rights given by the Act, and the landlord will be unable to obtain possession for the purposes of redevelopment.

3. Conditions of Statutory Contract

Preliminary

7–05 The statutory contract for the grant of a tenancy which is created by the service a Notice of Leaseholder's Claim[22] to acquire an extended lease incorporates the Conditions[23] prescribed by the Lord Chancellor,[24] except insofar as the parties otherwise agree.[25] As regards any matters not covered by the Conditions, the contract is on the terms and conditions of

---

[15] s.14(1); *Mosley* v. *Hickman, supra.*

[16] *Lewis (Jenkin R.) & Son* v. *Kerman* [1971] Ch. 477, C.A.; Megarry and Wade, *The Law of Real Property* (5th ed), p. 685.

[17] Such a future term would be void if commencing over 21 years from the grant: Law of Property Act 1925, s.149(3).

[18] Under s.23(4): see para. 7–19.

[19] s.16(1)(*a*).

[20] s.16(1)(*b*),(*c*) and (1A): see para. 7–15.

[21] s.17: see Chap. 8.

[22] See paras. 5–02 *et seq.*

[23] Contained in Part II of the Schedule to the Leasehold Reform (Enfranchisement and Extension) Regulations 1967 (S.I. No. 1879), set out in Appendix C.

[24] Under s.22(2).

[25] Paras. 2 and 3 of the 1967 Regulations.

an open contract for such a grant.[26] Detailed reference should be made to the Conditions, which appear to be comprehensive. What appears below is a brief summary of some of the more important provisions.

Evidence of tenant's right to extended lease

The landlord may by notice require the tenant to (i) deduce his title to the tenancy, and (ii) furnish a statutory declaration as to the particulars of occupation of the property on which the tenant relies in his Notice of Leaseholder's Claim.[27] This corresponds with an identical condition of the statutory contract to acquire the freehold.[28] **7–06**

Terms of the tenancy

The tenant may by notice require the landlord within four weeks to state what modifications in the terms of the existing tenancy, and what further provisions (other than as to payment of rent) are to be made by the terms of the new tenancy, in either of the following situations: (a) he has not received a Notice in Reply within two months of giving his Notice of Leaseholder's Claim; or (b) he has received a Notice in Reply admitting his claim or (if his claim has been denied by such a notice) he has established his right to an extended lease either by agreement or by an order of the court and, in either case, the extent of the property to be leased has been likewise established.[29] If condition (b) is satisfied, the landlord can serve a similar notice on the tenant.[30] Any such notice must contain a statement by the person giving it of which modifications and further provisions are required by him.[31] If the recipient of the notice does not comply with it in due time, or the donor does not give such a statement either when or before serving his notice, he is deemed to require no modifications or further provisions (other than as to payment of rent).[32]

Preparation of lease

In accordance with normal conveyancing practice, it is provided that the lease shall be prepared by the landlord and submitted to the tenant.[33] The tenant must approve the draft, with or without amendments, within 21 days thereafter, and if he fails to do so within that time, he is deemed **7–07**

---

[26] s.22(2).
[27] Condition 1.
[28] *i.e.* the 1967 Regulations, Sched., Pt. I, Condition 2, as to which see para. 6–04.
[29] 1967 Regs, Sched., Pt. II, Condition 2(1).
[30] *Ibid.* Condition 2(2).
[31] *Ibid.* Condition 2(3).
[32] *Ibid.* Condition 2(4).
[33] *Ibid.* Condition 3(1).

to have approved the landlord's draft.[34] Provision is made for preparation, execution and delivery on completion of the lease and any counterparts reasonably required by the landlord.[35]

Completion

The date for completion is fixed by either party, after the expiration of the time for approval of the draft lease, giving written notice to the other requiring completion; and the completion date is the first working day after the expiration of four weeks from the giving of the notice.[36] Completion is at the office of the landlord's solicitor.[37]

Extension of time-limits, failure to comply with obligations, etc.

There are further provisions extending the prescribed time-limits,[38] and dealing with the failure of either party to comply with the Conditions[39] and other matters,[40] corresponding to parallel Conditions of a statutory contract to acquire the freehold.[41]

4. Subject-Matter, Term and Rent Provisions of New Tenancy

Premises to be demised

7–08 The premises demised will be "the house and premises" let to the tenant, subject to any permitted exclusion of part or the inclusion of other premises.[42] Where a part of the "house and premises" let to the tenant is excluded, it appears that the grant of the extended lease will also operate as an automatic surrender of that part;[43] but it is considered advisable for the tenant to make an express surrender in respect of that part, preferably by a separate document, so that the landlord will be able to show a clear title to it. The 1967 Act makes no provision as to what easements are to be excepted and reserved, but it is generally assumed that those relating to "the house and premises" should be continued.

Length of new term

7–09 As mentioned above, the term to be granted must be a term expiring 50

---

[34] *Ibid.* Condition 3(2).
[35] *Ibid.* Condition 3(3).
[36] *Ibid.* Condition 4(1).
[37] *Ibid.* Condition 4(2).
[38] *Ibid.* Condition 8.
[39] *Ibid.* Condition 5.
[40] *i.e.* cancellation of land charges, etc. (Condition 6) and service of notices (Condition 7).
[41] See paras. 6–09 and 6–10.
[42] s.2: see Chap. 2.
[43] s.2(7).

years after the "term date" of the existing tenancy.[44] The grant of any other term without the prior approval of the court will not be in satisfaction of the tenant's rights under the 1967 Act, and the tenant will be able to exercise his rights during its continuance.[45]

Provisions as to rent

These are considered in detail in Chapter 9.

5. Other Terms of New Tenancy

Generally

In default of agreement, the terms of the new tenancy will, subject to the matters mentioned below, be the same as those of the existing tenancy, so far as those terms apply at the date of the tenant's Notice of Leaseholder's Claim.[46] In addition, the terms of a collateral agreement must be incorporated, or at any rate continued by a suitable instrument collateral to the new tenancy.[47] Only the usual landlord's implied covenants for the title need be included; and the landlord can limit his liability for any breaches of the landlord's covenants to those occurring while he remains the landlord, *i.e.* he can require the covenants to be enforceable only under privity of estate.[48] However, the parties are at liberty to agree other terms, and this will not prevent the new tenancy being in satisfaction of the tenant's rights under the 1967 Act.[49] **7–10**

Existing terms which are excluded

The new tenancy will not include any term of the existing tenancy or any collateral agreement which (i) provides for the renewal of the tenancy, (ii) grants an option of purchase or right of pre-emption in respect of the house and premises, or (iii) provides for the early determination of the tenancy otherwise than by way of forfeiture for breach of covenant.[50] Nor need any other term be included which would be unreasonable having regard to changes since the existing tenancy was granted.[51] It is arguable that the rent payable until the original term date should be adjusted to reflect these omissions. **7–11**

---

[44] s.14(1).
[45] See para. 7–04.
[46] s.15(1).
[47] s.15(4).
[48] s.15(9).
[49] s.15(7).
[50] s.15(5).
[51] s.15(7).

Existing terms which may be modified

It may be necessary to modify certain terms of the existing tenancy to take account of (i) differences between the property thereby demised and the "house and premises,"[52] (ii) the different terms of two or more separate tenancies of the "house and premises,"[53] and (iii) any changes since the existing tenancy which render it unreasonable for those terms to remain unchanged.[54]

Landlord's services

7–12 If the landlord will under the new tenancy be under any obligation to provide services, or to repair, maintain or insure, the new tenancy must make provision for payment by the tenant to the landlord for those matters.[55] Such payments will be in addition to the rent otherwise payable, and, if desired, can be reserved as additional rent. If the existing tenancy does not provide for any such payment, or only for payment of a fixed amount, no further amounts can be made payable until the original term date.[56] Thereafter the tenant can be obliged to make suitable payments related to the costs from time to time of the landlord's obligations. Thus the payments can be made subject to a periodic review, or can be automatically adjusted by an appropriate formula varying with the costs to the landlord. Moreover, it appears that the landlord can retain a modest profit in consideration of his obligations, expressed either as a percentage of the costs or in some other way, as is frequently done in modern flat schemes. But any provision for payment is subject to the overriding requirement that it must be "just."

Additional terms

7–13 The 1967 Act expressly requires two additional terms to be included in the new lease. First, the lease (and also any further lease granted in continuation of it) must state that no long tenancy created immediately or derivatively by way of sub-demise under the tenancy shall confer on the sub-tenant any right to the freehold or an extended lease as against the tenant's landlord.[57] Secondly, the landlord's right to resume possession under section 17 must be reserved.[58] However, it does not appear that the absence of such a reservation will prevent the landlord from exercising that right, at any rate if the lease includes a statement to the effect that the

---

[52] s.15(1)(*a*), (*b*).
[53] s.15(1)(*c*).
[54] s.15(7).
[55] s.15(3).
[56] *i.e.* in the usual case, the date of expiry of the existing tenancy: see para. 3–12.
[57] ss.15(8), 16(4).
[58] s.15(8).

new tenancy is being extended under the Act. It is always advisable (but not, it appears, obligatory) to include such a statement, which is conclusive in favour (but not against) any person who is not a party to the new lease, unless it is untrue on the face of it.[59] There are criminal safeguards against the inclusion of such a statement which is untrue.[60]

6. Registration of Title

Existing tenancy unregistered

7–14 Even if the existing tenancy is unregistered, it is necessary to apply for registration of the extended lease if either (a) the landlord's title to the house and premises is registered,[61] or (b) the landlord's title is unregistered but the house and premises (or any part of them) are in an area of compulsory registration.[62] In cases under (a) if the existing tenancy is noted against the landlord's title, an application for cancellation of that notice (in form 92) should be made. In either case, the Land Registry also requires evidence of the tenant's interest under the existing tenancy, in order to be satisfied that there is no subsisting mortgage which might affect the extended lease[63] and so make it necessary for an appropriate entry to be made protecting the mortgagee's rights.

If there is no subsisting mortgage, the original lease and the other tenant's title documents should therefore accompany the application for registration.

Existing tenancy registered

If the existing tenancy is already registered, an application for registration of the extended lease must be made. The application should include an application to give effect to the surrender of the existing lease by closing the title relating to it. For that purpose, the land certificate together with the original lease must be produced.

7. Rights Under Extended Lease

7–15 The tenant's rights under an extended lease are limited. He cannot require the grant of any further extension under the 1967 Act, and can

---

[59] s.16(7).
[60] s.16(8).
[61] Land Registration Act 1925, s.19(2); the grant of an extended lease constitutes a disposition which must be completed by registration.
[62] *Ibid.* s.123(1). For the procedure on an application for registration see Ruoff & Roper, *The Law and Practice of Registered Conveyancing* (5th ed.), Chap. 12.
[63] Leasehold Reform Act 1967, s.14(6): see para. 7–18.

acquire the freehold only if he serves his Notice of Leaseholder's Claim to the freehold before the original term date.[64] (There is one limited exception to this rule, relating to any part of the property except the house which has subsequently become held as part of another "house and premises" qualified for the benefits of the Act[65]). Moreover, neither his extended lease, nor any tenancy granted by way of continuation of it,[66] will be entitled to the protection of Part I or Part II of the Landlord and Tenant Act 1954.[67] The Rent Act 1977 does not apply to an extended lease.[68]

The rights of a sub-tenant are also limited if his sub-tenancy is derived (directly or indirectly) out of an extended lease. After the expiry of the extended lease, he will not be entitled to the protection of Part I or II of the 1954 Act or the Rent Act 1977;[69] nor can he claim the benefits of the 1967 Act as against the landlord.[70] A person granting or negotiating the grant of such a subtenancy must inform the other party that there has been an extension of the lease under the Act.[71] However, there is no penalty if he fails to do so, although the sub-tenant may have a civil right of action against him for breach of statutory duty or perhaps for misrepresentation.

8. Miscellaneous

Payments to be made by the tenant

7–16 No premium is payable upon the grant of the extended lease. But, whether or not he is in fact eventually granted an extended lease (unless the landlord successfully resists the Notice of Leaseholder's Claim on the ground of redevelopment[72] or own occupation[73]), the tenant must pay the following[74]:

(i) The landlord's costs of investigating his right to the extended lease.
(ii) The costs of the new lease. These will include the landlord's solicitor's costs and disbursements, and any stamp duty payable.

---

[64] s.16(1)(*a*), (*b*).
[65] s.16(2), (3).
[66] s.16(4).
[67] s.16(1)(*c*).
[68] s.16(1A), inserted by the Housing Act 1980, Sched. 21, para. 4, which included transitional provisions relating to existing extended leases of dwelling-houses with a registered rent under the Rent Act 1977.
[69] s.16(1)(*d*).
[70] s.16(4).
[71] s.16(7).
[72] s.17(4)(*b*): see para. 8–02.
[73] s.18(6)(*b*): see para. 8–05.
[74] s.14(2).

(iii) Any valuation of the house and premises obtained by the landlord before the grant of the extended lease for the purpose of fixing the rent payable thereunder as from the original term date; however, there can only be such a valuation if that date has already passed or if there is only a year or less of the original term unexpired at the date of the grant of the extended lease.[75] But the tenant is not liable to pay the landlord's costs of negotiation of the rent or other terms of the extended lease.

The landlord can refuse to grant the extended lease until the tenant has paid all the foregoing costs, together with all rent and other sums due under the existing tenancy or any agreement collateral thereto.[76] In cases where the extended lease is granted after the original term date, the tenant must as a condition of the grant also pay the amount of the section 15 rent during the period from the original term date until the grant.[77] If, however, the exact amount of any such costs, rent or other sums has not been ascertained, it is sufficient for the tenant to offer reasonable security for their payment.[78]

Landlord's estate subject to a mortgage

Most modern mortgages exclude the mortgagor's statutory power of granting leases,[79] and prevent the mortgagor granting a lease without the mortgagee's consent. If the mortgagor does in fact grant a lease without consent, it is not binding on the mortgagee,[80] unless the mortgagee is estopped from asserting this.[81] But, with one exception, an extended lease granted under the 1967 Act is valid and binding against the mortgagee, notwithstanding it is not authorised by him and even though the existing tenancy was not authorised by him and is invalid as against him.[82] Save where the exception applies, the Land Registry accordingly does not require evidence of the mortgagee's consent or an application to register an extended lease. 7–17

The only exception to the foregoing arises where the existing tenancy has been granted after October 27, 1967.[83] If such existing tenancy is not binding on the mortgagee, the extended lease will not be either. But the

---

75 s.15(2)(*c*).
76 s.14(3).
77 s.15(6).
78 *Ibid.*
79 *i.e.* under L.P.A. 1925, s.99.
80 *Corbett* v. *Plowden* (1884) 25 Ch.D. 678, C.A.; *Dudley and District Benefit Building Society* v. *Emerson* [1949] Ch. 707, C.A.
81 *Lever Finance Ltd.* v. *Needleman's Trustee* [1956] Ch. 375; *Stroud Building Society* v. *Delamont* [1960] 1 W.L.R. 431.
82 s.14(4).
83 s.14(4), proviso.

Act obliges the landlord in such a case to take all necessary steps to ensure that the extended lease will be valid.[84]

Where the mortgagee is entitled to possession of the title-deeds (as will almost invariably be the position in the case of a first mortgagee), the landlord must, within one month after granting an extended lease, deliver the counterpart, duly executed by the tenant, to the mortgagee.[85] The mortgage is deemed to include an obligation on the landlord to that effect, and the mortgagee can exercise all his rights under the mortgage if the landlord fails duly to deliver the counterpart.

Tenant's estate subject to a mortgage

Generally

7–18 Normally, a tenancy which is subject to a mortgage cannot be surrendered, either expressly or by operation of law, except with the consent of the mortgagee.[86] But the provisions of the 1967 Act appear to override this general rule, for it is expressly provided that an extended lease is "in substitution" for the existing tenancy,[87] and there is no saving to protect a mortgagee. However, it is provided that the extended lease "takes effect subject to a subsisting charge on the existing tenancy,"[88] which seems clearly to imply that the burden of any mortgage affecting it is transferred to the extended lease, which therefore constitutes a substituted security for the mortgage.[89] It is also provided that the mortgagee is entitled to possession of the tenant's title deeds (as is almost always the position in the case of a first mortgage), the tenant must hand over the new extended lease to the mortgage within one month of its grant; and if he fails to do so "the instrument creating or evidencing the charge shall apply . . . as if the obligation to do so were included in the terms as set out in that instrument."

Registered land

Where the existing lease is registered subject to a registered charge, the Land Registry serves notice on the proprietor of the registered charge of the application to register the extended lease and to give effect to the surrender of the existing lease. A similar notice is served on any mortgagee whose interest is protected by other means, *e.g.* the entry of a

---

[84] s.14(7).
[85] s.14(5).
[86] *Doe d. Beadon* v. *Pyke* (1816) M. & S. 146, *per* Lord Ellenborough C.J. at p. 154.
[87] s.14(1): see para. 7–04.
[88] s.14(6).
[89] But see Ruoff & Roper, *The Law and Practice of Registered Conveyancing* (5th ed.) pp. 550 *et seq.*

notice of deposit of the land certificate. Unless the mortgagee objects, the registered title to the existing lease is closed, and a protective entry made on the new title to the extended lease to the effect that the land is subject to such rights as may be subsisting in favour of the mortgagee under the charge affecting the existing lease. If the charge is a registered charge, the mortgagee is also invited to produce the charge certificate. If he does so, the certificate is endorsed to a similar effect and reissued.[90]

Extended lease with approval of the court

The county court is given power to approve the grant of a new lease on terms other than those provided by the 1967 Act, in satisfaction of the tenant's rights under the Act.[91] Such a lease can exclude the tenant's right to acquire the freehold altogether (*i.e.* even before the original term date)[92]; but unless express provision is made to the contrary, the new lease will have only the limited rights of a normal extended lease under the Act, and the landlord will be entitled to recover possession for redevelopment purposes.[93] Provision is made for the inclusion in the lease of a statement to the effect that the lease is being extended under the Act,[94] and for criminal sanctions if that statement is untrue.[95] 7–19

In some areas, considerable use has been made of this power. In particular certain estate landlords who were refused certificates under section 19[96] have been anxious not to lose control of houses on their estates and have offered tenants who have claimed the benefit of the 1967 Act attractive terms for a new lease in satisfaction of their claims. Provided that the tenant in any particular case has received independent professional advice, there is usually little difficulty in obtaining the approval of the court to such a lease. Application for approval is made by originating application under the County Court Rules, Order 3, rule 4.

---

[90] See generally, Ruoff & Roper, *supra*.
[91] s.23(4).
[92] s.23(5)(*a*).
[93] s.23(5)(*b*).
[94] s.23(6).
[95] s.23(7).
[96] See Chap. 10.

CHAPTER 8

LANDLORD'S OVERRIDING RIGHTS

8–01 A landlord is sometimes able to recover possession of the house and premises in order to redevelop[1] or for his own (or his family's) occupation.[2] Much the more important of these is the former; but, as will be seen, even this right can usually be defeated by the service of a tenant's Notice of Leaseholder's Claim to acquire the freehold. In practice, the main importance of the provisions discussed arises from their incorporation into the powers of certain public bodies under sections 28 and 29.[3]

1. REDEVELOPMENT

Generally

8–02 In certain cases, the landlord can apply to the court for an order for possession on the ground that "for the purposes of redevelopment he proposes to demolish or reconstruct the whole or a substantial part of the house and premises."[4] These words follow closely those of section 12(1) of the Landlord and Tenant Act 1954.[5] They differ, however, from the much-litigated words of section 30(1)(*f*) of that Act; but probably the only difference of importance concerns the word "proposes" as compared with "intends."[6] There is a lighter burden on a landlord to show a sufficient "proposal," and his redevelopment plans need not be so advanced or certain as is necessary to establish an "intention" within section 30(1)(*f*), *supra*.[7] Thus, it is envisaged that the landlord may have made a successful application although he has not obtained the planning and other consents necessary[8]; but a landlord would be unlikely to establish a sufficient intention under section 30(1)(*f*), *supra*, without having done so. The fact

---

[1] s. 17.
[2] s. 18.
[3] See Chap. 15.
[4] s. 17(1).
[5] Which was repealed (except as regards public bodies within s. 28 of the 1967 Act) by s. 38(1), in Part II of the 1967 Act.
[6] The leading case on "intends" is *Betty's Cafés Ltd.* v. *Phillips Furnishing Stores Ltd.* [1959] A.C. 20, in which the House of Lords approved the definition of that word by Asquith L.J. in *Cunliffe* v. *Goodman* [1950] 2 K.B. 237 at p. 253.
[7] *Magdalen and Lasher Charity Trustees* v. *Shelower* (1968) 19 P. & C.R. 389, C.A.
[8] Para. 2(3), Sched. 2.

that a sub-tenant may have some statutory protection as against the landlord must be disregarded in this connection.[9]

Time for landlord's application

8–03 Where the tenant has already been granted an extended lease, the landlord may make his application for possession not earlier than 12 months before the original term date,[10] or at any time thereafter.[11] If the tenant has not yet been granted an extended lease, the landlord can make his application only (a) after the tenant has given a Notice of Leaseholder's Claim to an extended lease,[12] and (b) within the 12 months before the original term date[13] or the date specified in any landlord's notice to quit which has previously been given, whichever is the earlier.[14] In the latter case, in order to be able to apply to the court for possession on this ground, the landlord must, within two months after service of the tenant's notice, serve a notice in reply stating that he intends to do so.[15] On the landlord making his application, the tenant's Notice of Leaseholder's Claim is suspended until the outcome of the application,[16] and ceases to have effect if the landlord is successful (but without the tenant being liable for any costs incurred thereunder).[17]

Tenant's notice to acquire the freehold

8–04 By contrast, the service by the tenant of a Notice of Leaseholder's Claim to acquire the freehold does not give the landlord any right to apply for possession. Indeed such a notice (which, however, must be served on or before the original term date if the lease has already been extended under the 1967 Act[18]) effectively prevents the landlord from making any application. Moreover, even the service of such a notice after the landlord has already made his application will usually automatically defeat that application, and no order or further order can be made on it except as to costs (although the landlord can subsequently make a further application if for some reason the tenant does not in fact acquire the freehold).[19] But a Notice of Leaseholder's Claim will not defeat a landlord's application already made, but will itself be invalid, if either (a) it is not given before

---

[9] Para. 3(3), Sched. 2.
[10] *i.e.* the contractual date of expiry of the existing tenancy: see para. 3–12.
[11] s. 17(1).
[12] s. 17(4).
[13] s. 17(1), (4).
[14] s. 17(5).
[15] Para. 7(2), Sched. 3.
[16] s. 17(4)(*a*).
[17] s. 17(4)(*b*).
[18] s. 16(1)(*a*).
[19] s. 17(6)(*b*).

the date of the court order fixing the termination of the tenancy or (b) the tenant has previously given a Notice of Leaseholder's Claim to an extended lease (whether or not it has been acted upon) and the landlord's application has been made within 12 months thereafter.[20] However, the value (if any) of the landlord's right to possession for redevelopment must be reflected in the purchase price payable by the tenant for the freehold.[21]

Orders on landlord's application and compensation

These are dealt with below.[22]

2. Residential Rights

Generally

8–05 A landlord may oppose any tenant's Notice of Leaseholder's Claim, whether to acquire the freehold or an extended lease, and apply to the court for possession, on the ground that he reasonably requires the property for his own occupation or that of an adult member of his family.[23] However, the circumstances in which the landlord can successfully obtain possession are narrow, and even then the landlord must pay compensation to the tenant. It is thought that this right has been exercised only in very rare cases, if at all.

Landlord's interest

8–06 The landlord's interest in the property must have been purchased by him or created on or before February 18, 1966. A leasehold reversion purchased or created before that date of a term of at least five years longer than the tenancy will also suffice, even if it has subsequently merged in the freehold or a superior lease purchased or created before that date. For this purpose, the duration of any tenancy is taken to be the period until it is due to expire (or, if capable of earlier determination by a landlord's notice, the date or earliest date which has been or could be specified in such a notice).[24]

Time for landlord's application

8–07 The landlord can make his application only after the tenant has given a Notice of Leaseholder's Claim to acquire the freehold or an extended

[20] s. 17(6)(*a*).
[21] See para. 9–25.
[22] See paras. 8–09 *et seq.*
[23] s. 18(1).
[24] s. 18(2).

lease, but before effect has been given to such notice.[25] Further, in order to be able to apply to the court for possession on this ground the landlord must, within two months after service of the tenant's notice, serve a Notice in Reply stating that he intends to do so.[26] On the landlord making his application, the tenant's notice is suspended until the outcome of the application, and ceases to have effect if it is successful[27] (but without the tenant being liable for any costs incurred thereunder).[28]

Grounds of application

The landlord must show that the property or part of it is reasonably required at the termination of the tenancy[29] by him for occupation as his own only or main residence, or as such residence of a person who, at the date of his application, is an adult member of his family.[30] An adult member of the landlord's family includes for this purpose the landlord's spouse, and any child,[31] son-in-law or daughter-in-law (over the age of 18), or parent of either the landlord of his or her spouse.[32] However, even if the landlord establishes this, the court is prevented from making an order for possession against the tenant if it is satisfied that, having regard to all the circumstances of the case, including the question of whether other accommodation is available for the landlord or the tenant, "greater hardship" would be caused by making the order than by refusing to make it.[33] But the fact that a sub-tenant may have some statutory protection as against the landlord must be ignored.[34] 8–08

3. Orders on Landlord's Application and Compensation

Common provisions are made[35] with regard to the procedure to be followed on a landlord's application for possession and as to the compensation payable to the tenant. 8–09

---

[25] s. 18(1).
[26] Para. 7(3), Sched. 3; and see para. 5–18.
[27] s. 18(6)(*a*).
[28] s. 18(6)(*b*).
[29] *Gurvidi* v. *Mangat* (1972) 116 S.J. 255, C.A., a decision which severely limits the possibilities of a landlord opposing on this ground.
[30] s. 18(1).
[31] Including a stepchild, adopted child or illegitimate child.
[32] s. 18(4); *cf.* s. 7(7).
[33] s. 18(4), proviso. The wording follows that of para. 1, Part III of the Rent Act 1977 (relating to Case 9 under Part I): see generally Megarry, *The Rent Acts* (10th ed.), pp. 293 *et seq.*
[34] Sched. 2, para. 3(4).
[35] By Sched. 2: see ss. 17(3), 18(5).

Possession

Proceedings for possession involve two stages. First, the landlord must make his application under the relevant section for an order for possession. The application is to the County Court[36] and should be made by an originating application.[37] If satisfied that the landlord has established his right to possession, the court will thereupon merely make a declaration to that effect.[38] Contrary to the normal practice in possession proceedings, the court cannot then fix a date for possession. This must be done on a separate later application, made by either the landlord or the tenant, when the amount of the compensation payable has been ascertained.[39] On the second application, the court will fix a date when both possession is to be given and the compensation is to be payable.[40] There appears to be no reason why the parties should not agree to dispense with either or both of these applications. Any occupying sub-tenant can, with the leave of the court, be heard on either of the applications leading to possession.[41]

The date fixed by the court for possession and payment of compensation must be not earlier than the original term date (or the expiry of a landlord's notice to quit, if earlier)[42]; and, unless the court sees special reason to the contrary, the date must be at least four months, but not more than twelve months, from the order fixing it.[43] In deciding upon the date, the court must have regard to the conduct of the parties, and, in a case where the landlord is proposing to redevelop, to what extent he has made reasonable preparations for that purpose, such as by obtaining planning and other necessary consents[44]; but the fact that a sub-tenant may have some statutory protection against the landlord must be ignored.[45] The tenancy is automatically continued until the date fixed for possession.[46]

Sub-tenancies

Termination

8–10 Any sub-tenancy (whether or not immediate) will terminate automati-

---

[36] s. 20(1).
[37] C.C.R., Ord. 3, r. 4.
[38] ss. 17(2), 18(4).
[39] Sched. 2, paras. 1(1)(*a*), 2(1).
[40] *Ibid.* para. 2(1).
[41] *Ibid.* para. 3(4).
[42] *Ibid.* para. 1(2); for meaning of "original term date," see para. 3–12.
[43] *Ibid.* para. 2(2).
[44] *Ibid.* para. 2(3).
[45] *Ibid.* para. 3(3).
[46] *Ibid.* para. 2(1).

cally with the tenancy on the date fixed for possession, and the tenant must thereupon deliver up possession to the landlord "except in so far as he is precluded from doing so by the rights of other persons to retain possession under and by virtue of any enactment."[47] An occupying residential sub-tenant within the Rent Act 1977 will thus be entitled to retain possession against the landlord, although, as his contractual tenancy will have been terminated, he will do so as a statutory tenant and not a contractual tenant.[48] But such a sub-tenant whose interest was created after the date of the landlord's application for possession (or, in the case of public bodies, the date when the Minister's certificate was served on the tenant) cannot retain possession after the date fixed for possession.[49]

By contrast, it appears that an occupying business sub-tenant within Part II of the Landlord and Tenant Act 1954 will not be entitled to retain possession against the landlord, for with the termination of his contractual tenancy his right to possession disappears.[50] This view is supported by the special provision that such a business sub-tenant can claim a share of the tenant's compensation.[51] Moreover, any request for a new tenancy under section 26 of the 1954 Act will be of no effect if made by him after the landlord has made an application for possession, and if made before will cease to have effect on the making of the application.[52]

Share of compensation

A business sub-tenant whose sub-tenancy is terminated as above[53] may claim that the compensation payable to the tenant should be shared between the tenant and himself in such proportions as may be just, regard being had to their respective interests and to any loss arising from the termination of those interests.[54] Moreover, if the tenant has agreed with the landlord to accept less than the proper amount of compensation, such a sub-tenant can recover any increased share he has thereby lost from the tenant.[55] But he cannot obtain any compensation for improvements under Part I of the Landlord and Tenant Act 1927.[56] 8–11

---

47 *Ibid.* para. 3(1).
48 Rent Act 1977, s. 2(1)(*a*).
49 Sched. 2, para. 3(2).
50 See the Landlord and Tenant Act 1954, s. 24.
51 Sched. 2, para. 6(2); and see para. 8–13.
52 *Ibid.* para. 6(1).
53 Thereby depriving him of any compensation under Landlord and Tenant Act 1954, s. 37 as amended. Presumably, the provision under discussion is intended to replace such compensation.
54 Sched. 2, para. 6(2).
55 *Ibid.* para. 6(3).
56 *Ibid.* para. 6(1).

Compensation

Amount

8–12 As mentioned above, the tenant must be compensated for loss of his tenancy.[57] If there has not already been a 50-year extension of the tenancy under the 1967 Act, in assessing the amount of compensation it must be assumed that it was to be so extended[58]; but nothing is to be payable for the loss of the right to acquire the freehold.[59] The compensation is assessed as at the date when the order for possession (which means the declaration on the landlord's original application, not the order fixing the date for possession[60]) becomes final,[61] *i.e.* when any appeal is concluded or the time for appealing (or further appealing) has expired.[62] It is to be assumed that the tenant is a willing seller in the open market,[63] but that he is selling his tenancy

(i) subject to the rights of any sub-tenant who is protected as against the landlord, but otherwise with vacant possession[64];
(ii) subject to any incumbrances which do not terminate with the tenancy and for which the tenant is liable (unless he has a right to be indemnified by the landlord), but otherwise free from incumbrances[65]; and
(iii) subject to any restrictions (in addition to those in the lease) limiting the use of the property to uses to which it has been put during the tenancy, and preventing the erection of any new house or other buildings except ordinary domestic outbuildings.[66]

Any dispute as to the amount of compensation payable is determined by a leasehold valuation tribunal.[67] For an example of the calculation of compensation, see para. 9–38.

Payment

8–13 As mentioned above, the compensation is payable on the date fixed by the court for possession.[68] The landlord is entitled to deduct from the

[57] ss. 17(2), 18(4). See also s. 28(1)(*b*), and for an example *Cottingham-Munday* v. *Dover B.C.* (1971) 220 E.G. 817, L.T.
[58] Sched. 2, para. 5(2).
[59] *Ibid.* para. 5(1).
[60] *Ibid.* para. 1(1)(*b*).
[61] *Ibid.* para. 5(1).
[62] s. 37(7).
[63] Sched. 2, para. 5(1).
[64] *Ibid.* para. 5(1)(*a*).
[65] *Ibid.* para. 5(1)(*b*).
[66] *Ibid.* para. 5(1)(*c*).
[67] s. 21(1)(*c*), as amended by the Housing Act 1980, Sched. 22, para. 8(1).
[68] Sched. 2, para. 2(1).

compensation any arrears of rent up to that date or other sums due under the tenancy or any agreement collateral thereto.[69] The court can order all or part of the compensation moneys to be paid into court in order to protect a tenant's mortgagee, or to facilitate a division with a business sub-tenant, or for any other purpose.[70] And if the tenant's estate is settled land or held on trust for sale, the compensation must be paid to two or more trustees as if it were purchase moneys on a sale.[71] But in any other case the landlord will obtain a good receipt from the tenant and is not further concerned with the application of the compensation.[72] The county court has jurisdiction to enforce payment of the compensation, whatever the amount.[73]

Delay or default

The court is given various powers where there is delay or default by either party in connection with the application for possession and any matters arising out of it, including the giving up of possession and the payment of compensation.[74] Also, if the original application itself is dismissed or withdrawn, the court has power to order that no similar application shall be made for a further five years if either the application was not made in good faith, or the landlord otherwise attempted to obtain possession by any misrepresentation or concealment.[75] **8–14**

---

[69] *Ibid.* para. 7(2).
[70] *Ibid.* para. 2(4).
[71] *Ibid.* para. 7(1), (3).
[72] *Ibid.* para. 7(1).
[73] *Ibid.* para. 4.
[74] *Ibid.* para. 8(1).
[75] *Ibid.* para. 8(3).

CHAPTER 9

VALUATION

Outline

9–01 This Chapter deals with the ascertainment of the purchase price which the tenant must pay to the landlord in order to acquire the freehold of his house and premises. It also deals with the ascertainment of "the section 15 rent" or the "modern ground rent"[1] which is payable under an extended lease after the original term date.[2] Such rent cannot be determined until one year before the original term date[3] at the earliest,[4] and so cases in which it has to be agreed or determined directly are comparatively infrequent.[5] But where the current rateable value of the house and premises is under £1,000, the freehold is valued on the assumption that an extended lease has previously been granted (if it has not actually been granted).[6] This assumption results in the modern ground rent prospectively payable after the original term date having to be estimated in all cases (except where that date is very distant[7]), as an essential step in the valuation of the landlord's interest.

Prior to 1980 all valuation disputes were determined by the Lands Tribunal,[8] but they are now referred to special leasehold valuation tribunals, subject to appeal to the Lands Tribunal.[9] See further paras. 16–06 *et seq*, where the relevant procedure and practice are also discussed.

---

[1] The former expression is preferable: see para. 9–05.

[2] For meaning see para. 3–12.

[3] *Ibid.*

[4] s.15(2)(*c*).

[5] The only reported cases are *Hancock* v. *Margrove Properties Ltd.* (1974) 229 E.G. 1231, L.T.; *Carthew* v. *Estates Governors of Alleyns College* (1974) 28 P. & C.R. 489, L.T.; *Duke of Norfolk and Barbinder Trust* v. *Bell* (1982) 263 E.G. 445, L.V.T.; *Riversea Lodge Ltd.* v. *Howe* (1983) 267 E.G. 363, L.V.T.; and *Burford Estate & Property Co. Ltd.* v. *Creasey* (1986) 277 E.G. 73, L.V.T.

[6] s.9(1).

[7] See paras. 9–31 *et seq.*

[8] s.21(1), as originally enacted.

[9] Housing Act 1980, s.142 and Sched. 22.

1. Rent Under Extended Lease

A. Up to the original term date

Until the original term date,[10] which is usually the date of expiry of the tenant's original term, the rent is normally the same as that payable under the existing tenancy.[11] However, it seems clear that such rent (like other terms of the existing tenancy) must be altered as "appropriate to take account of" the omission from the extended lease of property comprised in the existing tenancy.[12] If the tenant holds two or more tenancies of parts of the house and premises, the rent is the aggregate of the rents payable under those tenancies.[13] In addition, it is thought that any rent, or other consideration equivalent to rent, payable under an agreement collateral to the existing tenancy, must also be included in the rent payable under the extended lease .[14] 9–02

Some leases contain a tenant's option to purchase a right of pre-emption or right of renewal, or a landlord's break clause (*i.e.* a right of termination otherwise than by forfeiture for non-payment of rent or breach of covenant). Such rights, which may be of value to the tenant or the landlord as the case may be, must be excluded from the extended lease.[15] It is considered that the rent under the existing lease must be suitably adjusted to take account of the exclusion,[16] but there is at present no reported decision on the point.

B. After the original term date

General principles

The profit[17] rent payable after the original term date, commonly called "the section 15 rent" or "the modern ground rent"[18] is defined[19] as follows: 9–03

> "the rent shall be a ground rent in the sense that it shall represent the letting value of the site (without including anything for the value of the buildings on the site) for the uses to which the house and premises have been put since the commencement of the tenancy,

[10] For meaning see para. 3–12.
[11] s.15(1).
[12] s.15(1) (*a*). No alteration of rent under s.15(1)(*b*) seems appropriate to take account of alterations to the property itself.
[13] s.15(1)(*c*).
[14] s.15(4).
[15] s.15(5).
[16] Compare the final words of s.15(5) with s.15(1).
[17] A service or insurance rent may sometimes also be reserved: see para. 7–12.
[18] The former expression is preferable: see para. 9–05.
[19] By s.15(2)(*a*).

other than uses which by the terms of the new tenancy are not permitted or are permitted only with the landlord's consent."

The letting value for this purpose is, in the first instance, ascertained as at the original term date.[20] Prima facie, it remains payable throughout the 50 year extension of the extended lease, but the landlord has a right to have the rent revised after 25 years, exercisable by written notice claiming a revision served on the tenant during the 25th year.[21] If such notice is served, the revised rent is bound to be substituted, even if it is lower than the previous rent; however, the landlord can avoid that consequence by refraining from serving a notice, and there is no right for the tenant to claim a revision. The determination of the rent at either date, *i.e.* on the original term date or the date of expiry of 25 years thereafter, cannot be made earlier than 12 months before that date.[22]

Assumption as to uses

9–04 The "uses" referred to in the definition set out above mean the actual uses to which the house and premises have been put. They do not include general residential use in a broad town-planning sense, involving either development of the site to a higher density or multi-occupation of the house itself.[23] Thus, in the ordinary case of a house in single residential occupation, only that use can be considered, *i.e.* the site must be valued only as a site for a single residential house and any potential use as or conversion into flats must be ignored. But if the house is already used as flats, whether or not properly converted for that use, the site can be valued as a site for a building containing the same number of flats.[24] However, the assumed "uses" do not refer to the actual physical layout of the existing building, so that (for example) although the existing house has no bathroom, the site can be valued as a site for a house with a bathroom.[25] Further, it is to be noted that the assumed "uses" are not confined to those uses existing at the date of the tenant's Notice of Leaseholder's Claim. All other uses to which the property has been put since the commencement of "the existing tenancy" (which in the case of a

[20] s.15(2)(*b*).

[21] s.15(2)(*c*). The extended lease should provide that time is to be "of the essence" of the time-limits for service of the notice. Otherwise the ordinary rule that time is not "of the essence" (see *Burnley B.C.* v. *United Scientific Holdings Ltd.* [1978] A.C. 904) will probably apply, even though the rent revision provision is included as a statutory requirement.

[22] s.(15)(2)(*c*).

[23] *Buckley* v. *S.R.L. Investments Ltd.* (1970) 22 P. & C.R. 756, L.T., at p. 762; *County & Metropolitan Developments Ltd.* v. *Brewer Trust* (1971) 22 P. & C.R. 1135, L.T., at p. 1140; *Ruhan* v. *Attenborough* (1983) 269 E.G. 1175, L.V.T.

[24] *Lake* v. *Bennett* (1971) 219 E.G. 945, L.T.

[25] *Williams* v. *Davies* (1973) 225 E.G. 1679, L.T.

continuation tenancy will nevertheless also include the prior tenancy[26]) can be also taken into account even though they have been discontinued, unless prohibited or permitted only with the landlord's consent by the terms of the new tenancy.[27]

Assumptions as to other matters

The letting value of the site must be ascertained on the basis that it is an isolated site, and not part of a larger site.[28] However, what has to be valued is the site as it is (*i.e.* with the existing buildings on it), but disregarding the value of the buildings, as opposed to a new development site.[29] So the letting value should reflect the cost of all site works and be on the basis that all the available services have been brought to the site and, generally, that no road charges are payable;[30] but it should not reflect the cost of any drains, foundations, driveways, etc., on the site itself, which are part of the "buildings" and so must be disregarded.[31] The letting value is thus ascertained on a basis different from that of the ground rent payable under the usual form of building lease. The expression "modern ground rent" may therefore be a little misleading, and it is preferable to use the expression "section 15 rent." Despite one decision to that effect,[32] it seems to be unsound and unduly artificial in determining the letting value of a developed site to take into account "a proportion of the amount formerly representing the builders' profit and risk."[33] The fact that the property is in a general improvement area and that grants for the improvement and repair of buildings are available can be taken into account (but the effect on site values is likely to be marginal).[34] 9–05

The letting value must also reflect the terms of the new tenancy. These include the landlord's rights to possession under sections 17 and 18 upon payment of compensation,[35] but only in special circumstances are such rights likely to have any appreciable effect on the letting value.[36] They also

[26] s.3(3): see para. 3–10.

[27] s.15(2)(*a*); for an example see *Barrable* v. *Westminster City Council* (1984) 271 E.G. 1273, L.T. (house previously used as three flats).

[28] *Taylor* v. *Cornwall Properties Ltd.* (1970) 213 E.G. 381 at p. 383; *King* v. *Peureula Investments Ltd.* (1982) 265 E.G. 139, L.V.T.

[29] *Wilson* v. *Reardon* (1970) 214 E.G. 1294; *Farr* v. *Millersons Investments Ltd.* (1971) 22 P. & C.R. 1055 at p. 1060; and *Wood* v. *Cardiff Corporation* (1973) 229 E.G. 1476 at p. 1479.

[30] *B.P. Pension Trust Ltd.* v. *Blake* (1982) 264 E.G. 721, L.T., at p. 722. See also *Kemp* v. *Josephine Trust Ltd.* (1970) 22 P. & C.R. 804 at p. 811; and *Siggs* v. *Royal Arsenal Co-operative Society* (1971) 23 P. & C.R. 79, L.T.

[31] *Williams* v. *Davies, supra.*

[32] *Kemp* v. *Josephine Trust Ltd, supra,* at p. 811.

[33] *B.P. Pension Trust Ltd.* v. *Blake, supra,* at p. 722.

[34] *Duke of Norfolk and Barbinder Trust* v. *Bell* (1982) 262 E.G. 445, L.T.

[35] See paras. 8–12 *et seq.*

[36] *Carthew* v. *Estates Governors of Alleyns College* (1974) 28 P. & C.R. 489 at pp. 504–7.

include the effect of any restrictive covenant imposed, or easement reserved, by the landlord.

If the extended lease is granted after the original term date, the section 15 rent is prima facie payable only from the date of grant.[37] This accords with the well-settled common law rule that a tenancy cannot commence before the date of its grant.[38] But on the grant, the tenant must pay the excess of the section 15 rent over the rent payable under the existing tenant (after making any necessary apportionments) as from the original term date, or (if later) the date of his Notice of Leaseholder's Claim, up to the date of grant.[39] The letting value for this purpose is, in the first instance, "the letting value at the date from which the rent based on it is to commence."[40] In a case where the Notice of Leaseholder's Claim was served after the original term date, this has been interpreted by a leasehold valuation tribunal as meaning the date of service of the Notice of Leaseholder's Claim.[41] But the tribunal's reasoning is clearly erroneous in treating the provision for payment of the excess up to the date of grant as if it were rent, and it is considered that the correct date in that case was the date of the tribunal hearing.[42]

Method of ascertaining section 15 rent

9–06 The statutory formula for ascertaining the section 15 rent is an artificial one. In practice, no landlord ever lets a site (or indeed any property at all) on the terms stipulated by the 1967 Act, *i.e.* for a 50–year term with just one rent review after 25 years, except when obliged to do so by the 1967 Act itself. So there are no comparable open market lettings which a valuer can utilise to determine the section 15 rent. In almost every case, the valuer has found himself with no real alternative except first to ascertain the capital value of the site, and then to consider what rate of income return the freeholder might expect if he were to grant a 50–year lease of the site on the terms set out in the 1967 Act. The valuer thus "decapitalises" the site value to arrive at the section 15 rent.[43] Most

[37] s.15(2) as varied by s.15(6).

[38] *Roberts* v. *Church Commissioners for England* [1972] 1 Q.B. 278, C.A.; *cf. Bradshaw* v. *Pawley* [1980] 1 W.L.R. 10.

[39] s.15(6). The position is thus akin to the normal contractual position where a lease is granted after the date of commencement of the term therein specified, as explained in *Bradshaw* v. *Pawley, supra.*

[40] s.15(2)(*b*).

[41] *Riversea Lodge Ltd.* v. *Howe* (1983) 267 E.G. 363.

[42] As suggested by counsel for the landlord, whose argument appears to be correct in this respect. The difficulty "that no firm date for valuation is ascertainable," which led the tribunal to reject the arguments, is one that frequently arises, *e.g.* on the grant of a new tenancy, under Part II of the Landlord and Tenant Act 1954, and in practice is readily overcome by a valuation at the date of the hearing.

[43] See *Official Custodian of Charities* v. *Goldridge* (1973) 26 P. & C.R. 191, *per* Lord Denning M.R. at p. 205.

valuation cases which have come before the Lands Tribunal and leasehold valuation tribunals, including those concerned with the determination of the freehold price (in which the ascertainment of the section 15 rent is usually an essential step), have therefore been largely concerned with the questions of site value and percentage rate of return. Attempts to ascertain the section 15 rent by other means, *e.g.* as a fraction of the "fair rent" under the Rent Acts, have proved unreliable and have always been rejected.[44]

Site value

(1) The "cleared site" approach

The most obvious method of valuing the site is "by reference to the prices of sites for development, or redevelopment, for comparable uses."[45] It has been said that this method is particularly suitable for cases where the house in question is nearing the end of its economic life,[46] and even "that it is only when the subject house is nearing the end of its economic life that the required site value is helpfully to be ascertained by reference to the prices of sites sold for development or redevelopment."[47] But it is considered that there is no reason for such limitation, and that the "cleared-site approach" can be used even if the subject house has an indefinite future.[48] 9–07

In some cases, it may be appropriate in using this method to arrive at the site value by reference to area, *i.e.* ascertaining the value of development land per square yard and multiplying the area of the site in question by that value. But the calculations of this kind are open to criticism[49] and should be used with caution. The values of single-house plots in a district in practice seldom vary in direct proportion to the area of the plots; and several extra square yards of garden land may only add marginally to the purchase price of a development plot. Another, and sometimes more reliable, way of using this method, particularly in valuing the site of lower-priced terrace or semidetached houses, is by reference to the frontage, making a small allowance for the relative depth of the plot. These are several instances where the Lands Tribunal has

---

[44] *Gajewski* v. *Anderton* (1971) 217 E.G. 885; *Kemp* v. *Josephine Trust Ltd.* (1970) 22 P. & C.R. 804; *Carthew* v. *Estates Governors of Alleyns College* (1974) 28 P. & C.R. 489.

[45] *Farr* v. *Millersons Investments Ltd.* (1971) 22 P. & C.R. 1055 at p. 1061.

[46] *Ibid.*

[47] *Nash* v. *Castell-y-Mynach Estate* (1975) 234 E.G. 293, cogently criticised at (1976) 237 E.G. 569 (W. A. Leach).

[48] See further para. 9–10.

[49] See *e.g. Briddon* v. *Field* (1975) 234 E.G. 840.

accepted evidence of site value on this basis.[50] In the case of a large site, it may be appropriate to apply the area value of development land to part only of the site, and to value the remainder as garden land at a much lower figure.[51]

The main difficulty in using the cleared site approach is usually the practical one of finding evidence of sales or other transactions relating to comparable development sites. Often, *e.g.* in fully developed residential areas, there is simply no such evidence available at all. In other cases, the available evidence may relate only to multiple sites, which tend to attract proportionately higher prices because of the flexibility and economies of scale available to a developer; or to sites which permit development for non-comparable uses, *e.g.* for flat development, when the site value must be ascertained on basis of use for a single dwelling only. In such cases, appropriate adjustments will have to be made, thereby greatly reducing the reliability of the comparable evidence. Sometimes the only evidence available consists of a sale of a large development site. In such cases, adjustments have to be made to take account of the cost of site works and the exclusion of areas to be occupied by estate roads and other common parts, as well as the economies of scale; and in practice evidence of this kind is usually of minimal value.

(2) The "standing house" approach

9–08 Most houses within the 1967 Act are situated in areas which have long since been fully developed, and in which it is difficult to find evidence of sales or lettings of comparable vacant sites. As a result, a frequently used method of arriving at the site value of a property is by first ascertaining the freehold value with vacant possession of the whole property including the buildings, usually referred to as "the entirety value." The site value is then taken as a proportion of the entirety value, the appropriate proportion being a matter of evidence. After some early reluctance to accept this method of valuation,[52] commonly called "the standing house approach," the Lands Tribunal came to recognise and frequently to adopt it, at any rate in cases where the house in question was likely to remain in standing for the foreseeable future.

Entirety value

The "entirety value" in this context must represent the value of the property assumed to be modernised, "otherwise the letting value of the

---

[50] *e.g. O'Leary* v. *Radford* (1969) 211 E.G. 1191; *Siggs* v. *Royal Arsenal Co-operative Society* (1971) 23 P.& C.R. 79.

[51] As in *Ruhan* v. *Attenborough* (1983) 269 E.G. 1175, L.V.T.

[52] See *e.g. Hall* v. *Davies* (1970) 22 P. & C.R. 780.

site (without including anything for the value of the buildings on the site) would differ for identical sites in the same street that happened to be modernised houses on some sites but unmodernised houses on other."[53] For similar reasons, the property must be assumed to be in good condition[54] and any tenant's improvements must be included in its value.[55] Indeed, it has been said that the entirety value must represent the value of the property "fully developing the value of the site."[56] This needs qualification, because the statutory formula restricts the uses of the property to that which "it has been put since the commencement of the tenancy,"[57] and so excludes any development inconsistent with such uses. But it does require the assumption that, if the house is already in multiple-occupation, it has been properly converted for that use.[58] No deduction falls to be made for the costs of conversion.[59] It may be appropriate in certain cases, *e.g.* where the house is small in relation to the site or to the neighbouring properties, to assume that the house has been extended or even wholly or partially replaced by a larger house.[60]

In practice the valuers on each side are frequently able to agree the entirety value, or at any rate the differences between them fall within a relatively narrow range. There is usually ample good comparable evidence available to enable a determination of the entirety value to be made with little difficulty. The standing house approach, obviating the necessity to find comparable cleared-site evidence, has therefore proved popular, particularly with estate landlords, who are able to quote purchase prices based on a site value percentage common to the estate.

Site value proportion

The problem (and the inherent weakness) of the standing house approach is the selection of the appropriate percentage of the entirety value attributable to the site. In 1971 it was said that "the proportion normally adopted outside central London varies, on the evidence, 9–09

---

[53] *Kemp* v. *Josephine Trust Ltd.* (1970) 22 P. & C.R. 804 at p. 810.

[54] *Machin* v. *Redspring Ltd.* (1973) 225 E.G. 2037; *Lake* v. *Bennett* (1971) 219 E.G. 945; *Official Custodian of Charities* v. *Goldridge* (1973) 26 P. & C.R. 191 at p. 201; *Nash* v. *Castell-y-Mynach Estate* (1975) 234 E.G. 293.

[55] *Horsham* v. *Cefn Estates Ltd.* (1983) 267 E.G. 527, L.V.T.

[56] *Lake* v. *Bennett*, *supra*, at p. 948; see also *Official Trustee of Charity Lands* v. *Goldridge*, *supra*, at p. 201; *Patten* v. *Wenrose Investments Ltd.* (1976) 241 E.G. 396.

[57] See para. 9–04.

[58] *Lake* v. *Bennett*, *supra*; *Barrable* v. *Westminster City Council* (1984) 271 E.G. 1273, L.T.

[59] *Official Custodian of Charities* v. *Goldridge*, *supra*; *Barrable* v. *Westminster City Council*, *supra*.

[60] *County and Metropolitan Developments Ltd.* v. *Brewer Trust*, *supra*.

between one-quarter and one-third," but that "in central or near-central London or in other areas of highly-priced residential land, the proportion adopted is commonly higher, of the order of (plus or minus) 40 per cent."[61] The proportions of the entirety value in cases decided by the Lands Tribunal and leasehold valuation tribunals have usually been in line with that statement. Thus 40 per cent. has been found to be the appropriate figure for houses in higher-priced London areas such as Barnes,[62] Chelsea,[63] Dulwich,[64] Edgware,[65] Hampstead,[66] South Kensington,[67] Muswell Hill,[68] St. Johns Wood[69] and Wandsworth.[70] In other areas of London, the adopted percentage has been lower, as in Battersea (30 per cent.),[71] Bowes Park, N. 22 (30 per cent.),[72] Chiswick (27½ per cent.),[73] Clapton (30 per cent.),[74] Ealing (30 per cent.),[75] Hammersmith (35 per cent.),[76] Highgate (30 per cent.),[77] Kilburn (30 per cent.)[78] and Pimlico (35 per cent.).[78a] Similar percentages have been adopted outside London, as in Barnstaple, Devon (27½ per cent.),[79] Erdington, Birmingham (30 per cent.),[80] South Glamorgan (33 per cent.),[81] Halesowen (25 per cent.),[82] Hamble, South Hants (33 per cent.),[83] Liverpool 15 (25 per cent. for a

---

[61] *Farr Millersons Investments Ltd.* (1971) 22 P. & C.R. 1055, at p. 1061 (R. C. Walmsley F.R.I.C.S.).

[62] *Dangey* v. *General Management Ltd.* (1973) 227 E.G. 993, L.T.

[63] *Kemp* v. *Josephine Trust Ltd., supra.*

[64] *Carthew* v. *Estates Governors of Alleyn's College* (1974) 28 P. & C.R. 489, L.T.

[65] *Lead* v. *J. & L. Estates Ltd.* (1975) 31 P. & C.R. 495, L.T.

[66] *Lake* v. *Bennett, supra*; *Official Custodian of Charities* v. *Goldridge, supra*; but see *Embling* v. *Wells and Campden Charity Trustees* (1978) 247 E.G. 909, L.T.

[67] *Le Mesurier* v. *Pitt* (1972) 23 P. & C.R. 389, L.T. at p. 405 (2½ per cent. reduction for small size of site); *Machin* v. *Redspring Ltd.* (1973) 225 E.G. 2037, L.T.; *Grainger* v. *Gunter Estate Trustees* (1977) 246 E.G. 55, L.T.

[68] *Pearson* v. *Piercy* (1973) 226 E.G. 1417, L.T.

[69] *Middleton-Smith* v. *Harrow School Road Trust* (1981) 262 E.G. 73, L.V.T. (favourable position in mews).

[70] *Farr* v. *Millersons Investments Ltd. supra.*

[71] *Westmore Holdings Ltd.* v. *Simpson* (1981) 261 E.G. 261, L.V.T.

[72] *Burford Estate and Property Co. Ltd.* v. *Creasy* (1986) 277 E.G. 73, L.V.T. (reduction to 27½ per cent. by reason of disadvantages of size).

[73] *Gajewski* v. *Anderton* (1971) 217 E.G. 885, L.T.

[74] *Patten* v. *Wenrose Investments Ltd.* (1976) 241 E.G. 396, L.T.

[75] *Ward* v. *Radford* (1974) 28 P. & C.R. 346, L.T.

[76] *Lang* v. *Cornock* (1977) 241 E.G. 605, L.T.

[77] *Riversea Lodge Ltd.* v. *Howe* (1983) 267 E.G. 363, L.V.T. ("modest dimension in its frontage and tightly located in a terrace of similar properties").

[78] *Barrable* v. *Westminster City Council* (1984) 271 E.G. 1273, L.T.

[78a] *Pilgrim* v. *Central Estates (Belgravia) Ltd.* (1986) 278 E.G. 1373, L.V.T. (awkward shape and proximity to high buildings).

[79] *Chilcott* v. *Clinton Devon Estates* (1973) 27 P. & C.R. 282, L.T.

[80] *King* v. *Peureula Investments Ltd.* (1982) 265 E.G. 139, L.V.T.

[81] *Nash* v. *Castell-y-Mynach* (1975) 243 E.G. 293 (on estimated figure for property fully developed).

[82] *Collins* v. *Jones* (1981) 261 E.G. 1001, L.T.

[83] *Mimmack* v. *Solent Land Investments Ltd.* (1973) 26 P. & C.R. 139, L.T.

cramped site),[84] Oxford (approx. 30 per cent.),[85] Saltley, Birmingham (27 per cent.),[86] and Swansea (25 per cent.).[87]

However, as mentioned above, the percentage adopted depends on the evidence and the individual circumstances of each case.[88] Such evidence may well show that the appropriate proportion to be markedly different from the above. Thus, in certain particularly fashionable parts of London, such as Mayfair, Belgravia, Knightsbridge and Westminster, purchase prices have been negotiated on the basis of percentages substantially higher than 40 per cent. At the other end of the scale, the appropriate percentage for a small site in a poor inner city area in places such as Cardiff (19 per cent.)[89] and Sheffield (11½ per cent.)[90], or other areas such as Tyne and Wear (20 per cent. for poor site),[90a] may be much lower than 25 per cent. Despite a decision to the contrary in one case,[91] it seems clear that the percentage should be adjusted upwards if the site contributes a materially above-average proportion of the site value (*e.g.* if the property has a large garden),[92] and downwards if the reverse applies (*e.g.* if the house occupies most of the site).[93] Further,

> "if a particular house should have a value above or below the value of an average house of its type in the same locality . . . some adjustments may have to be made to the percentage of such standing-house value to arrive at the site value; otherwise anomalies might arise."[94]

Thus a corner site may be marginally more valuable than other sites,[95] and conversely a site which is unattractive, awkwardly shaped and overlooked may be less valuable.[96]

---

[84] *Ewing* v. *London & Winchester Properties Ltd.* (1981) 261 E.G. 61, L.V.T.; but see the case on appeal, *sub nom. London and Winchester Properties Ltd.'s Appeal* (1983) 45 P. & C.R. 429 (value increased to equivalent of 27 per cent. on different grounds).

[85] *Haresign* v. *St. John the Baptist's College, Oxford* (1980) 255 E.G. 711, L.T.; and see *Miller* v. *St. John the Baptist's College, Oxford* (1977) 243 E.G. 535, L.T. (reduction to 25 per cent by reason of cramped site).

[86] *Wilkes* v. *Larkcroft Properties Ltd.* (1981) 257 E.G. 1160, L.T., affirmed (1983) 268 E.G. 903, C.A.

[87] *Lewis* v. *James* (1981) 258 E.G. 651, L.T.

[88] *Nash* v. *Castell-y-Mynach Estate, supra.*

[89] *British Petroleum Pension Trust Ltd.* v. *Blake* (1982) 264 E.G. 721, L.T.; *cf. Horsham* v. *Cefn Estates Ltd.* (1983) 267 E.G. 527 (22½ per cent.).

[90] *Duke of Norfolk and the Barbinder Trust* v. *Bell* (1982) 263 E.G. 445, L.V.T.

[90a] *Cunningham* v. *Morrison-Bell* (1986) 278 E.G. 741, L.T.

[91] *Lake* v. *Bennett* (1971) 219 E.G. 945, L.T., at p. 949.

[92] *Nash* v. *Castell-y-Mynach Estate, supra.*

[93] *Le Mesurier* v. *Pitt* (1972) 23 P. & C.R. 389 L.T. at p. 405; *Chilton* v. *Clinton Devon Estate, supra*; *Burton* v. *Kolup Investments Ltd.* (1979) 251 E.G. 1290, L.T. (other disadvantages); *Miller* v. *St. John the Baptist's College, Oxford* (1977) 243 E.G. 535, L.T.; *Ewing* v. *London & Winchester Properties Ltd., supra*; *Riversea Lodge Ltd.* v. *Howe, supra*; *Middleton-Smith* v. *Harrow School Road Trust, supra.*

[94] *Horsham* v. *Cefn Estates Ltd., supra,* at p. 578.

[95] *Hall* v. *L.F. Rosen Settlement Trustees* (1984) 269 E.G. 329, L.V.T.

[96] *Burford Estate and Property Co. Ltd.* v. *Creasy* (1986) 277 E.G. 73, L.V.T.

Criticism of standing house approach

9–10 For several years, the Lands Tribunal appeared to prefer the standing house approach to other methods of valuing the site in cases where the house was likely to remain for the forseeable future. Indeed, in one case, a valuer was even told that in such circumstances any other approach was incorrect and that "it is only when the subject house is nearing the end of its economic life that the required 'site value' is helpfully to be ascertained by reference to the price of sites sold for development or redevelopment."[97] In recent years, however, the standing house approach has been the subject of trenchant criticism from one member of the Lands Tribunal,[98] being described by him as "an artificial and arbitrary basis of valuation (if 'valuation' is apt to describe it)" which should not be applied "except as a last resort,"[99] *e.g.* if no other evidence of site value is available.[1] It usually "requires the use of a fiction that the house has been repaired, improved and modernised notwithstanding that the cost of putting it into that condition is quite unknown and may be of major proportions"; and "the selection of a percentage attributable to site value is a matter of guess-work, albeit intelligent guess-work."[2] While there is obvious force in this criticism, it is respectfully suggested that the foregoing remarks go too far. The "fiction" referred to is in fact only assuming a state of affairs frequently assumed by valuers; and the cost of repair, improvement and modernisation of a house is irrelevant for the purposes of the standing-house approach.[3] It is, of course, true that the selection of the percentage attributable to the site depends on "the *ipse dixit* of the valuer,"[4] and the real weakness of the standing house approach is that (particularly in cases where there is a substantial entirety value and the tenancy has only a short time to run) a small difference in the site value percentage selected can lead to quite a large difference in the purchase price. But nevertheless the selection of a percentage by an experienced professional valuer cannot fairly be stigmatised as guess-work. For various reasons, sales of development plots often do not

---

[97] *Nash* v. *Castell-y-Mynach Estate* (1975) 234 E.G. 293 (R.C. Walmsley F.R.I.C.S); and see para. 9–07.

[98] V. G. Wellings Q.C., who is also the editor of the current (28th) edition of *Woodfall on Landlord and Tenant*, in which it is stated (Vol. 3, para. 3–1054, note 85) that the standing house approach "is an artificial basis which is not recommended."

[99] *Embling* v. *Wells and Campden Charity's Trustees* (1978) 247 E.G. 909.

[1] As was in fact the case in each of the *Embling* and the *Miller* and *Haresign* cases mentioned below.

[2] *Miller* v. *St. John Baptist's College, Oxford* (1977) 243 E.G. 535. See also *Haresign* v. *St. John Baptist's College Oxford* (1980) 255 E.G. 711 and *British Petroleum Pension Trust Ltd.* v. *Blake* (1982) E.G. 721.

[3] *Official Trustees of Charity Lands* v. *Goldridge* (1983) 26 P. & C.R. 191; *Barrable* v. *Westminster City Council* (1984) 271 E.G. 1273.

[4] *Mann* v. *Appleby Magna Parish* (1977) 244 E.G. 309 (W. H. Rees F.R.I.C.S).

provide satisfactory evidence, and in many cases the standing house approach may still provide the most reliable guide to the site value.

The practical effect of the above criticisms has been to make leasehold valuation tribunals (and the Lands Tribunal) reluctant to use the standing house approach.[5] Much greater reliance than formerly is placed on sales of comparable development plots, and (if used at all) the standing house approach has been used only where there is no evidence of such sales, or by way of a check valuation.[6] Furthermore, evidence of settlements achieved by the landlord or others showing a roughly uniform standing house percentage is treated with considerable caution.[7]

(3) The "new-for-old" approach

A further possible method of valuing the site suggested in one case 9–11

> "is by reference to what the property as whole would be worth if a new building were to be substituted for the existing building, and then taking a proportion of the value or alternatively substituting the present-day cost of putting up such a building."[8]

Although referred to in the guidance offered by one member of the Lands Tribunal in a general statement,[9] in practice this approach seems to have been little used by valuers. It is suggested that this approach is inherently unsatisfactory, containing too many imponderables to be dependable. In particular, subtracting the present day cost of putting up a new building involves a "residual valuation."

> "Only in exceptional cases does the tribunal attach weight to residual calculations prepared solely for the purpose of the arbitration proceedings; it is a phenomenon well demonstrated over the years that when valuers let themselves loose on such exercises they can prove almost anything."[10]

---

[5] *e.g. Francis* v. *Reginald Clifford & Co Ltd.* (1981) 261 E.G. 61, L.V.T.; *Ruhan* v. *Attenborough* (1983) 269 E.G. 1175, L.V.T.

[6] *e.g. Lewis* v. *James* (1981) 258 E.G. 61, L.T.: *Larkcroft Properties Ltd.* v. *Adkins* (1981) 259 E.G. 257, L.T.; *Middleton-Smith* v. *Harrow School Road Trust* (1981) 262 E.G. 73, L.V.T.; *King* v. *Peuruela Investments Ltd.* (1982) 265 E.G. 139, L.V.T.; *Riversea Lodge Ltd.* v. *Howe* (1983) 267 E.G. 363, L.V.T.

[7] *British Petroleum Pension Trust Ltd.* v. *Blake* (1982) 264 E.G. 721, L.T.; *Horsham* v. *Cefn Estates Ltd.* (1983) 267 E.G. 527, L.V.T.

[8] *Farr* v. *Millersons Investments Ltd.* (1971) 22 P. & C.R. 1055, L.T. at p. 1061.

[9] *Ibid.* (R. C. Walmsley F.R.I.C.S); see also *Mimmack* v. *Solent Land Investments Ltd.* (1973) 26 P. & C.R. 139, L.T.

[10] *Machin* v. *Redspring Ltd.* (1973) 225 E.G. 2037, L.T. (R. C. Walmsley); see also *Dangey* v. *General Management Ltd.* (1973) 227 E.G. 933, L.T. and *Burton* v. *Kolup Investments Ltd.* (1979) 251 E.G. 1290, L.T.

Decapitalisation of site value

9–12 The site value when agreed or determined must be "decapitalised" (or "rentalised") to arrive at the section 15 rent. The percentage rate of decapitalisation reflects the rate of return a landlord would expect to achieve on a letting of the site on the terms laid down by the 1967 Act, *i.e.* for a 50-year term with a rent review after 25 years, but with a full reversion of the site and its buildings at the end of the term. In cases of freehold valuations under section 9(1), the rate for decapitalisation is inevitably linked with the rate for recapitalisation and deferment.[11]

The percentage rate is a matter for evidence, but with very few exceptions[12] the rate determined by both the Lands Tribunal and leasehold valuation tribunals has varied between 6 per cent. and 8 per cent. Attempts to obtain substantially higher rates[13] have failed.[14] In 1971, it was said that the adoption of a 6 per cent. rate had become "stabilised,"[15] and in 1973 that there was a "convention of decapitalising the site value at 6 per cent. in order to arrive at the section 15 rent."[16] But more recently although 6 per cent. has sometimes been adopted,[17] slightly higher rates have been used, including $6\frac{1}{2}$ per cent.[18] and 8 per cent.[19] Much the most common rate is 7 per cent., which has frequently been either agreed between valuers[20] or adopted in several cases by both the Lands Tribunal[21] and leasehold valuation tribunals.[22]

---

[11] See para. 9–23.

[12] See, *e.g.* *Hancock* v. *Margrove Properties Ltd.* (1974) 229 E.G. 1231 (4 per cent. agreed between valuers).

[13] Paradoxically made by the tenants acquiring the freehold in order to obtain a high rate to be used for recapitalisation and deferment in the calculation of the purchase price under section 9(1): see paras. 9–27 *et seq.*

[14] *Nash* v. *Castell-y-Mynach Estate* (1975) 234 E.G. 293; *Briddon* v. *Field* (1975) 234 E.G. 840; *Grainger* v. *Gunter Estate Trustees* (1977) 246 E.G. 55.

[15] *Farr* v. *Millersons Investments Ltd.* (1971) 22 P. & C.R. 1055.

[16] *Mimmack* v. *Solent Land Investments Ltd.* (1973) 26 P. & C.R. 139; see also *Carthew* v. *Estates Governors of Alleyns College* (1974) 27 P. & C.R. 282.

[17] *Miller* v. *St. Johns College, Oxford* (1977) 243 E.G. 535; *Emden* v. *Wells and Campden Charity's Trustees* (1978) 247 E.G. 909; *Haresign* v. *St. John's College* (1980) 255 E.G. 711.

[18] *Mann* v. *Appleby Magna Parish, etc.* (1977) 244 E.G. 309.

[19] *Patten* v. *Wenrose Investments Ltd.* (1976) 241 E.G. 396; *Lead* v. *J. & L. Investments Ltd.* (1975) 31 P. & C.R. 495.

[20] As in *Chilcott* v. *Clinton Devon Estates* (1973) 27 P. & C.R. 282; *Burton* v. *Kulop Investments Ltd.* (1978) 251 E.G. 1290; *O'Connor* v. *Treffrey Estate Trustees* (1981) 259 E.G. 165; *Westmore Holdings Ltd.* v. *Simpson* (1981) 261 E.G. 61.

[21] *Lang* v. *Cornock* (1976) 241 E.G. 605; *Grainger* v. *Gunter Estate Trustees* (1977) 246 E.G. 55; *Larkcroft Properties Ltd.* v. *Adkins* (1981) 259 E.G. 257.

[22] *Francis* v. *Reginald Clifford & Co. Ltd.* (1981) 261 E.G. 61; *Middleton-Smith* v. *Harrow School Road Trust* (1981) 262 E.G. 73; *Duke of Norfolk and the Barbinder Trust* v. *Bell* (1982) 263 E.G. 445.

Example valuations—section 15 rent

Example 1—standing house valuation[23]

A mews house in St. John's Wood, London, has a 1973 rateable value of £438. The vacant possession value of the house, deemed modernised and in good condition, is £44,000: 9–13

Entirety value	£44,000	
Site value @ 40%	17,600	
Section 15 rent @ 7%	×0.07	
	£1,232	per annum

Example 2—cleared site valuation[24]

A semi-detached house in Birmingham has a 1973 rateable value of £250. The area of its site is 325 sq.yds. and its frontage is 16 ft. 6ins.

Site value 325 sq. yrds. @ £20 per sq. yrd.	£6,500	
Section 15 rent @ 7%	×0.07	
	£455	per annum

(Check valuation)		
Site value $16\frac{1}{2}$ ft. frontage @ £400 per f.f.	£6,600	
Section 15 rent @ 7%	×0.07	
	£462	per annum
	(say, £460 per annum)	

2. Basis of Valuation of Freehold

The purchase price which the tenant must pay to the landlord in order to acquire the freehold of his house and premises is calculated on one of two bases of valuation, depending on the rateable value of the house and 9–14

[23] Based on *Middleton-Smith* v. *Harrow School Road Trust* (1981) 262 E.G. 73.
[24] Based (loosely) on *Francis* v. *Reginald Clifford & Co. Ltd.* (1981) 261 E.G. 61.

premises.[25] If that rateable value "is above £1,000 in Greater London and £500 elsewhere," the valuation is made under section 9(1A).[26] In any other case (with one exception)[27] the valuation is under section 9(1), which is nearly always much more beneficial to the tenant. It is considered that the word "is" in the foregoing relates to the date by reference to which the freehold is valued, *i.e.* "the relevant time" (the date of service of the Notice of Leaseholder's Claim),[28] and not April 1, 1973, or the date on which the value happens to be agreed or determined.

The basis of valuation in section 9(1A) was introduced by the Housing Act 1974 which also increased the rateable values limits of the 1967 Act.[29] It was clearly intended to apply primarily to properties first brought within the 1967 Act as a result of such increases. But several such properties have, either in the rating list or as a result of a notional reduction under Schedule 8 to the 1974 Act,[30] a rateable value of £1,000 or under in Greater London or £500 or under elsewhere, and the freehold of any such property also clearly falls to be valued under s.9(1). Conversely, there are a few properties which were within the original rateable value limits of the 1967 Act (£400 in Greater London and £200 elsewhere)[31] but which as a result of the 1973 revaluation or any later revaluation now have a rateable value of over £1,000 in Greater London or £500 elsewhere. If a duly qualified tenant of such a property had served a Notice of Leaseholder's Claim prior to 1974, the freehold would have been valued under section 9(1), but if he serves such a notice subsequently, the purchase price must be determined under section 9(1A).[32] It may be doubted whether this consequence was really intended by Parliament, but it is considered that the wording of section 9(1A) leaves no room for doubt on the point.

Any notional reduction in rateable value to take account of tenant's improvements must be taken into account in determining the correct basis of valuation.[33] But for this purpose, the tenant must have followed the procedure of Schedule 8 to the Housing Act, 1974, and obtained a certificate of the Valuation Officer thereunder.[34] Otherwise any tenant's

---

[25] As to ascertainment of the rateable value, see paras. 2–18 *et seq.*
[26] s.9(1A), inserted by Housing Act 1974, s.118(4).
[27] See para. 9–15.
[28] See ss.9(1), 9(1A) and 37; and see cases cited in n. 32 *infra.*
[29] Housing Act 1974, s.118.
[30] See paras. 2–23 *et seq.*
[31] s.1(1)(*b*).
[32] *Chada* v. *Norton Estate Trustees* (1985) 276 E.G. 312, L.V.T.; *Oliver* v. *Central Estates (Belgravia) Ltd.* (1985) 276 E.G. 1358, L.V.T.
[33] s.9(1B) inserted by s.118(4) Housing Act 1974.
[34] See paras 2–33 *et seq.*

improvements have to be ignored for this purpose, however favourable the tenant's prospects of obtaining a sufficient notional reduction might be.[35] It has been said that a notional reduction must be taken into account even if the agreement on the Valuation Officer's certificate as to the reduction is obtained pursuant to a tenant's Schedule 8 notice served after the date of valuation; *sed quaere.*[36]

Exception

If the tenancy has (i) been created by the grant of a lease under "the right to buy" provisions now contained in Housing Act 1985, Part V (formerly in Part I of the Housing Act 1980 and Part I of the Housing and Building Control Act 1984), or (ii) is a sub-tenancy directly or indirectly derived out of such a tenancy or (iii) is an extended lease under the 1967 Act graded in substitution for such a tenancy or sub-tenancy, the purchase price is determined under section 9(1A), whatever the rateable value of the house and premises.[37] 9–15

3. Valuation of Freehold under Section 9(1)

Basis of valuation

As originally enacted,[38] the purchase price payable by the tenant was the amount which at the relevant time,[39] "the house and premises, if sold in the open market by a willing seller, might be expected to realise" on the assumptions mentioned below. This wording bears a close resemblance to that of Rule 2 in section 5 of the Land Compensation Act 1961,[40] and the price is thus "the amount which a purchaser in a friendly negotiation would be willing to pay in acquiring a freehold interest and as though no compulsory powers of acquisition had been obtained."[41] The tenant is a willing, but not an anxious, purchaser.[42] However, the purchase price must take into account any defect in the landlord's title.[43] 9–16

[35] *Effra Investments Ltd.* v. *Stergios* (1982) 264 E.G. 449, L.V.T.
[36] For a discussion of this point see paras. 2–36 *et seq.*
[37] Housing Act 1985, s.175.
[38] s.9(1), omitting words added by the Housing Act 1969, s.82.
[39] *i.e.* the date of service of the tenant's Notice of Leaseholder's Claim: s.37(1)(*d*).
[40] Replacing r. (2) in s.2 of the Acquisition of Land (Assessment of Compensation) Act 1919.
[41] *Lambe* v. *Secretary of State for War* [1955] 2 Q.B. 612, *per* Parker L.J. at p. 621, applying *Raja Vyricherla Narayana Gajapatiraju* v. *Revenue Divisional Officer, Vizagapatam* [1939] A.C. 302.
[42] *Lloyd-Jones* v. *Church Commissioners for England* (1981) 261 E.G. 471, L.T., following the cases in the last note.
[43] s.9(2).

Marriage value and section 82 of the Housing Act 1969

9–17 An occupying tenant is usually anxious to obtain the fullest possible security of tenure for himself and his family. He is also usually anxious to maintain the value of his leasehold interest, which will inevitably depreciate with the passage of time, particularly in the last 40 or so years of its term. The occupying tenant thus has a special incentive to purchase the freehold reversion and is usually willing to offer a higher price for it than other persons. Moreover, if the tenant does purchase the freehold reversion to his leasehold, he will be able to merge, or "marry," the two interests together and so obtain an unencumbered freehold interest. The tenant thus has a further special incentive to purchase the freehold, for in most cases the market value of such an unencumbered freehold interest exceeds the aggregate of the value of his leasehold interest and the purely investment value of the freehold reversion. The excess is commonly known as "the marriage value," and the higher offer expected to result from the tenant's special incentives to purchase is commonly referred to as "the tenant's bid" or "the tenant's overbid."

In two early cases before the Lands Tribunal,[44] it was ruled that the tenant himself must be considered a competitor for the freehold in the open market stipulated by section 9(1) in its original form, so that his overbid had to be taken into account in ascertaining the purchase price. However, Parliament at once took steps to reverse that ruling, and by section 82 of the Housing Act 1969 (which came into effect on July 25, 1969), section 9(1) of the 1967 Act was amended by restricting the hypothetical open market by the words "(with the tenant and members of his family residing in the house not buying or seeking to buy)."[45] This amendment, commonly referred to as "the section 82 amendment," excluded any element of the marriage value being included in the purchase price, which thus was restricted to the purely investment value of the landlord's interest. The section 82 amendment was expressly made retrospective, except as regards any purchase price agreed or determined before it came into effect.[46]

Valuation assumptions

(a) *Estate sold*

9–18 It is to be assumed that "the vendor was selling for an estate in fee-

---

[44] *Custins* v. *Hearts of Oak B.S.* (1969) 209 E.G. and *Haw* v. *Peek* (1969) 210 E.G. 347. These decisions are consistent with the cases mentioned in note 41, *supra*, and also with *I.R.C.* v. *Clay* [1914] 3 K.B. 466, C.A., although none of them were apparently cited in argument before the Lands Tribunal.

[45] See *per* Lord Denning M.R. in *Official Custodian of Charity Lands* v. *Goldridge* (1973) 26 P. & C.R. 191 at p. 207.

[46] s.82(2) of the Housing Act 1969.

simple, subject to the tenancy, but . . . that this Part of this Act conferred no right to acquire the freehold, and if the tenancy has not been extended under this Part of this Act . . . that (subject to the landlord's rights under section 17) it was to be so extended."[47] This assumption has three parts. The first part, that the vendor is selling for an estate in fee simple, means that it is the landlord's reversionary interest which must be valued. The second part, that the 1967 Act conferred no right to acquire the freehold, requires that the purchase price must be ascertained as if the sale were voluntary and not a compulsory sale. It protects the freeholder against any depreciation in the value of his interest which the right to enfranchise might be said to cause, and also protects the tenant against any addition to the purchase price because the sale is compulsory.[48]

It is the third part of this assumption, that if the tenancy has not already been extended, then (subject to the landlord's rights under section 17) it was to be extended, which is the most important. It requires that the freehold reversion which must be valued is the reversion to an extended lease under the 1967 Act. As has been seen,[49] the rent under the 50-year extension is the letting value of the site of the house and premises, without including anything for the value of the buildings on the site.[50] It is by means of this assumption[51] that the 1967 Act gave effect to the so-called principle "that the land belongs in equity to the landowner and the house belongs in equity to the occupying leaseholder" stated in the 1966 White Paper which led to the Act.[52] Moreover, the assumption means that every consequence of an extended lease being granted has to be taken into account, exactly as if there had been an actual grant of an extended lease,[53] whether such consequence favours the landlord or the tenant.[54] It

---

[47] s.9(1)(*a*).

[48] *Cf.* r. 1 in s.5(1) of the Land Compensation Act 1961, replacing s.2 of the Acquisition of Land (Assessment of Compensation) Act 1919 which excluded the ten per cent. addition which previously had customarily been added on a compulsory purchase; see *Harvey* v. *Crawley Development Corporation* [1957] 1 Q.B. 485, *per* Denning L.J. at p. 493 and Cripps, *Compulsory Acquisition of Land* (11th ed.), para. 4–046.

[49] See para. 9–03.

[50] s.15(2)(*a*).

[51] Although the value of the buildings is not excluded from the ultimate reversion expectant on the expiry of the 50-year extension, this is rarely of any value: see para. 9–22.

[52] Para. 4, Cmnd. 2916 published on February 18, 1966, and (contrary to the rules of statutory interpretation) directly quoted by Lord Denning M.R. in *Official Trustee of Charity Lands* v. *Goldridge* (1973) 26 P. & C.R. 191, at p. 204.

[53] Except as provided by the Leasehold Reform Act 1979, reversing the effect of *Jones* v. *Wrotham Park Settled Estates* [1980] A.C. 74, discussed at para. 11–22.

[54] *Jones* v. *Wrotham Park Settled Estates*, *supra*, *per* Lord Russell of Killowen at p. 111, disapproving dicta of Goff L.J. in the Court of Appeal ([1980] A.C. at p. 87). The author had the doubtful distinction of arguing the point in opposite ways (in the Court of Appeal in defence of a concession he made in the Lands Tribunal and in the House of Lords in support of Goff L.J.'s view that the concession had been wrongly made), and losing on both occasions.

is thus necessary to ignore any tenant's option of renewal, option of purchase or right of pre-emption in the existing lease, as well as any landlord's break clause.[55] Note, however, that the landlord's right under section 17 to determine the extended lease for redevelopment purposes[56] must be taken into account.[57]

(b) *Rentcharges and other charges*

9–19 It is to be assumed that the vendor was selling subject to the same rentcharges as those affecting the freehold which the conveyance is being made subject to.[58] It is also to be assumed that "the purchaser would otherwise be effectively exonerated until the termination of the tenancy from any liability or charge in respect of tenant's incumbrances."[59] The meaning and purpose of this latter provision is obscure.

(c) *Rights and burdens*

It is to be assumed that the vendor was selling "with and subject to the rights and burdens with and subject to which the conveyance to the tenant is to be made."[60] These include the various easements and rights impliedly granted by or reserved out of the conveyance, existing easements and rights benefiting other property which are automatically continued,[61] and all provisions concerning rights of way and restrictive covenants included in the conveyance under the Act.[62] This assumption clearly may benefit either the landlord or the tenant.

Purchase price

9–20 The purchase price payable by the tenant for the landlord's freehold interest under section 9(1) as amended thus comprises, and (subject as mentioned below) in valuations made for the purposes of the Act can be broken down into the following elements:

(1) the capitalised value of the rent payable under the tenancy from the date of service of the Notice of Leaseholder's Claim until the original term date;

---

[55] s.15(7); but see para. 9–02.
[56] See paras. 8–02 *et seq.*
[57] As to the valuation of this right, see para. 9–25.
[58] See as to such rentcharges, para. 12–02.
[59] s.9(1)(*b*). For meaning of "tenant's incumbrances," see para. 6–12.
[60] s.9(1)(*c*).
[61] *i.e.* under s.10(1),(2): see paras. 6–17 *et seq.*
[62] *i.e.* under s.10(3),(4),(5): see paras. 6–21 *et seq.*

(2) the capitalised value of the section 15 rent payable from the original term date until the expiry of the 50-year extension (due regard being had to the provision for review after the first 25 years of the extension);
(3) the value of the landlord's reversion to the house and premises after the expiry of the 50-year extension, all statutory rights of the tenant and any sub-tenant under Part I or II Landlord and Tenant Act 1954 or the Rent Act 1977 being excluded[63];
(4) the value (if any) of the landlord's right under section 17 to determine the 50-year extension for redevelopment purposes;
(5) the effect of new easements and restrictive covenants in the conveyance[64];
(6) the value (if any) of any other rights under the extended lease extinguished on the acquisition of the freehold.

It is necessary to consider these six elements in turn; however, in practice it is only rarely that the purchase price is affected by (4), (5) or (6).

(1) Capitalised value of the rent payable for the period of the unexpired term of the existing tenancy

The first stage in the ascertainment of the purchase price[65] is to determine the value of the rent payable for the period of the unexpired term of the existing tenancy, *i.e.* from the date of service of the Notice of Leaseholder's Claim until the original term date.[66] This is done by multiplying that rent by the figure for the "years' purchase" shown in Parry's Valuation Tables, and the only difficulty is the selection of the appropriate rate of return to assume for that purpose. This is a matter for evidence. The generally adopted percentage is 7 per cent.,[67] although lower percentages of 6 per cent.[68] and 5½ per cent.[69] have been used, as have higher percentages. Some of these percentages might seem relatively low by comparison with interest rates prevailing at the relevant time, but 9–21

[63] s.16.
[64] The effect of existing easements and restrictive covenants in the lease will be taken into account in the ascertainment of the section 15 rent.
[65] Under s.9(1A), as well as under s.9(1): see para. 9–50.
[66] For definition see para. 3–12.
[67] *Hall* v. *Davies* (1970) 22 P. & C.R. 780, L.T.; *Farr* v. *Millersons Investments Ltd.* (1976) 22 P. & C.R. 780, L.T.; *Siggs* v. *Royal Arsenal Co-operative Society Ltd.* (1971) 23 P. & C.R. 79, L.T.; *Grainger* v. *Gunter Estate Trustees* (1977) 246 E.G. 55, L.T. (15 per cent. contended for); *Middleton-Smith* v. *Harrow School Road Trust* (1982) 262 E.G. 73, L.V.T.
[68] *e.g., Le Mesurier* v. *Pitt* (1972) 23 P. & C.R. 389, L.T.; *Briddon* v. *Field* (1975) 234 E.G. 840, L.T.; *Lang* v. *Cornock* (1977) 241 E.G. 605, L.T.
[69] *Lloyd-Jones* v. *Church Commissioners for England* (1982) 261 E.G. 471, L.T. (s.9(1A)).

this is justifiable because the existing rent is followed on its termination by a greatly increased rent of substantial value, and has thus to be valued as part of a package deal involving a larger interest.[70] On this basis it has been said that the rate should be adjusted depending on the length of the unexpired term,[71] and this is considered to be the logical and correct approach.[72] In practice the amounts involved in this stage of the calculation are relatively small. The adoption of different rates of return usually results in only insignificant variations in the overall purchase price, and the appropriate capitalised amount is almost always agreed between the parties.

(2) Capitalised value of the section 15 rent

(3) Value of the landlord's ultimate reversion

9–22 It is convenient (and usual) to consider these two items together. The section 15 rent is payable as from the original term date up to the extended term date, subject to review after the first 25 years.[73] The ascertainment of the section 15 rent has already been dealt with in detail above. It is not possible to make a separate valuation of the rent payable after such review, and in any event the fact of the review is already reflected in the percentage figure adopted as the appropriate yield from the site value in order to ascertain the section 15 rent. Furthermore, it is usually considered inappropriate to make a separate valuation of the landlord's ultimate reversion at the end of the 50-year extension, because the additional value of the bricks and mortar over the value of the site alone is problematical and rarely increases the market value (but see the discussion of "the *Haresign* addition" below). Accordingly, the generally recognised method of approach at this stage is "to capitalise the section 15 rent as if in perpetuity, deferred for the period of the unexpired term of the existing tenancy, not seeking to quantify any different rent that might become substituted at the expiration of 25 years from the original term date, and not quantifying separately the value in reversion at the expiration of 50 years from the original term date."[74]

---

[70] *Siggs* v. *Royal Arsenal Co-operative Society Ltd.* (1971) 23 P. & C.R. 79, at p. 85.

[71] See the evidence of M. St. J. Hooper FRICS in *Kemp* v. *Josephine Trust* (1970) 22 P. & C.R. 804, at p. 813.

[72] Thus higher rates have been used in cases where there is a long term unexpired: see, *e.g.* *Mimmack* v. *Solent Land Investments Ltd.* (1973) 26 P. & C.R. 139, L.T.; *Lead* v. *J. & L. Estates Ltd.* (1975) 31 P. & C.R. 495, L.T.

[73] s.15(2).

[74] *Farr* v. *Millersons Investments Ltd.* (1971) 22 P. & C.R. 1055 L.T., at p. 1060.

Capitalisation

The capitalisation is made by multiplying the section 15 rent by the appropriate figure for the "Years' Purchase of a Reversion to a Perpetuity"[75] shown in Parry's Valuation Tables after the unexpired residue of the original term. It is now settled[76] that, in the absence of any special factors established by evidence, the percentage rate to be adopted for capitalisation and deferment must be the same rate as that adopted for decapitalising the site value to ascertain the section 15 rent.[77] Neither section 82 of the Housing Act 1969,[78] nor any other factors common to every case, justify the adoption of a higher (or, indeed, lower) rate of interest for capitalisation and deferment than that adopted for decapitalisation, resulting in an "adverse differential" (see paras. 9–27 *et seq.*). **9–23**

The Haresign addition

As mentioned above, it is usually considered inappropriate to attribute a separate value to the landlord's ultimate reversion. At that stage, *i.e.* at the end of the 50-year extended term, the buildings are likely to be old, and at the valuation date the market is unlikely to give anything for them over and above the site value. Thus the general practice has been to ignore the ultimate reversion, and to capitalise the section 15 rent in perpetuity. **9–24**

However, in *Haresign* v. *St. John the Baptist's College, Oxford*[79] the Lands Tribunal accepted the uncontradicted evidence of the landlord's valuer[80] that an additional value ("the *Haresign* addition") should be attributed to the reversion to a 3-storey Victorian house in Oxford falling in 53 years ahead. Although a similar addition has been made in other cases,[81] it is considered that it should not be made unless there is clear evidence that the house will remain standing and be of value at the end of

[75] Without any allowance for income tax: see *Custins* v. *Hearts of Oak Building Society* (1969) 209 E.G. 239, L.T., at p. 243; *Haw* v. *Peek* (1969) 210 E.G. 347, L.T., at p. 348; *The Goldsmith's Company* v. *Guardian Assurance Co. Ltd.* (1970) 216 E.G. 595, L.T., at p. 599; *Perrin* v. *Ashdale Land & Property Co. Ltd.* (1971) 218 E.G. 573, L.T., at p. 577.

[76] *Official Trustee of Charities* v. *Goldridge* (1973) 26 P. & C.R. 191, C.A.; *Wilkes* v. *Larcroft Properties* (1983) 268 E.G. 903, C.A.

[77] See para. 9–27.

[78] See para. 9–17.

[79] (1980) 255 E.G. 711.

[80] The tenant appeared in person and did not call any expert valuation witness.

[81] *British Petroleum Trust Ltd.* v. *Blake* (1981) 259 E.G. 777, L.V.T. (but see next footnote); *Horsham* v. *Cefn Estates Ltd.* (1983) 267 E.G. 527, L.V.T.

the 50-year extension.[82] One serious weakness of the *Haresign* addition is that, owing to the long deferment period, a small variation in the percentage rate adopted results in a substantial variation in the value of the addition.[83]

(4) Section 17—Development value

9–25 It was the intention of Parliament in passing the 1967 Act that the landlord should be entitled to the benefit of any development value of the site of the house and premises.[84] As a result of the restriction on use which is assumed in assessing the section 15 rent,[85] it is seldom that such rent reflects any development value.[86] However, one of the landlord's rights as owner of the reversion to an extended lease is the right under section 17 to determine the lease during the 50-year extension for redevelopment purposes (on paying compensation).[87] The purchase price must reflect the value (if any) to the landlord of this right.

If the landlord exercises his section 17 right so that the tenancy terminates on "the original term date," he must pay to the tenant the compensation payable under Schedule 2, which is approximately the value of the buildings for the 50-year extension.[88] In addition, the landlord of course loses the section 15 rent which otherwise would have been payable (subject to review after 25 years) throughout the extension. If, but only if, the value of the land as a development site exceeds the aggregate of the compensation and the capitalised value of the section 15 rent, the section 17 right will be of value. The value to be added to the other elements of the purchase price will thus be such excess deferred for

---

[82] It should certainly not be used if neither valuer has used it: see *British Petroleum Trust Ltd.* v. *Blake* (1982) 264 E.G. 721 L.T., disagreeing with the leasehold valuation tribunal determination, *supra*, on this point. In that case, the house was a 100-year-old inner-city terrace house fronting directly onto a road, and it is considered that the *Haresign* addition was clearly inappropriate on the facts. See further *Pilgrim* v. *Central Estates (Belgravia) Ltd.* (1986) 278 E.G. 1373, L.V.T.

[83] For instance, on the figures in the *Haresign* case itself, the adoption of nine per cent., instead of the seven per cent used, would have reduced the value of the addition from £349 to nil.

[84] This was specifically so stated in the 1966 White Paper which preceded the Act (see para. 13 Cmnd. 2916), and is consistent with the underlying theory of the Act that the land belongs to the landlord and the buildings to the tenant. Further, under s.24(2), now repealed, a conveyance under the Act was deemed to be a Case A disposition under the Land Commission Act 1967, so that a landlord might have to pay "betterment levy" on any realised development value.

[85] Under s.15(2)(*a*), discussed at para. 9–04.

[86] There was no provision making the grant of an extended lease a Case B disposition under the Land Commission Act 1967.

[87] For a full discussion of this right, see paras. 8–02 *et seq.*

[88] See para. 8–12.

the period from the date of service of the Notice of Leaseholder's Claim until the original term date.[89]

Rather surprisingly, at the date at which this book states the law there had not been any reported case before the Lands Tribunal or a leasehold valuation tribunal in which a claim for the value of the landlord's section 17 right has been made. The explanation for this is that the right is only of value in exceptional cases, *e.g.*, where there is extensive developable land comprised in the house and premises, or where the site can be intensively redeveloped (such as by replacing a single house with a block of flats). On the other hand, there appears to be no reason why the value of the site to the landlord as part of a larger site should not be taken into account. But clearly no value can be attributed to the landlord's section 17 right if the conveyance imposes restrictive covenants preventing redevelopment.[90]

(5) Effect of new easements and restrictive covenants in the conveyance

The purchase price must also take account of the grant or reservation of **9–26**
any new easements[91] and the imposition of any new restrictive covenants[92] (affecting either the reversion being purchased or neighbouring property retained by the landlord), effected by the conveyance. The price must also reflect any variation of the existing easements and covenants affecting the tenant's leasehold.[93] Thus the imposition of strict user covenants may result in a reduction of the purchase price,[94] but will probably not do so if the covenants are common to the area and necessary to maintain the standards of the area.[95]

(6) The value (if any) of any other rights extinguished on the acquisition of the freehold

Either the landlord or the tenant may have other rights under the tenancy which will be extinguished by its merger in the freehold. The purchase price may have to be adjusted to compensate the party affected for the loss of such rights.[96] For example, the price must reflect any loss to the landlord of a right to agency commission on a fire insurance policy.[97]

---

[89] See (1972) 223 E.G. 1753 (C. C. Hubbard), and Example 7, para. 9–38. For possible contrary arguments, see (1972) 223 E.G. 2041.
[90] See (1973) E.G. 137, 333, and 432.
[91] *i.e.*, under s.10(2): see para. 6–22.
[92] *i.e.*, under s.10(4),(5): see para. 6–28.
[93] The effect of the existing easements and restrictive covenants will be taken into account in the ascertainment of the section 15 rent.
[94] As in *Peck* v. *Trustees of Hornsey Parochial Charities* (1970) 22 P. & C.R. 789, L.T.
[95] *Cf.* schemes under s.19, which have not affected the purchase price: see para. 10–25.
[96] The rights will normally have been taken into account in the ascertainment of the section 15 rent.
[97] *Re Castleberg Investments (Jersey) Ltd.'s Appeal* (1985) 275 E.G. 46, L.T.

Sometimes a tenant refuses to accept the continuation of an obligation to contribute to the landlord's costs of the upkeep of common parts, and it seems clear that in such cases the purchase price must be increased appropriately.[98] Conversely, the price may be reduced if a valuable landlord's covenant is not continued.

The "Adverse Differential"

Outline

9–27 In the first cases to reach the Lands Tribunal after the passing of section 82 Housing Act 1969 ("the section 82 amendment"), the valuers on both sides continued the previous practice of using the same percentage rate for recapitalisation (*i.e.* capitalisation and deferment of the section 15 rent) as for decapitalisation, and the Tribunal's determination was made on that basis.[99] However, in one case the Tribunal commented that it was "far from convinced that the same percentage rate is necessarily appropriate, certainly since the passing of the 1969 Act, for arriving at the ground rent from capital value, as for capitalising the deemed ground rent when ascertained"[1]; and in several subsequent cases the Tribunal accepted the evidence of the tenant's surveyor that the recapitalisation rate should be higher than the decapitalisation rate.[2] This difference became known as the "adverse differential," being adverse to the interests of the landlord. In the case of a tenancy with a negligible residue of the term outstanding at the valuation date, and adopting the usual rates of six per cent. for decapitalisation and eight per cent. for recapitalisation, this led to the landlord suffering a 25 per cent. "instant loss."[3]

The adverse differential was not, however, applied in all cases,[4] and it was seldom used by the landlord's valuer. Nevertheless in *Farr* v.

---

[98] See para. 6–20.

[99] *Taylor* v. *Cornwall Property (Holdings) Ltd.* (1970) 213 E.G. 38; *Orford* v. *Davies* (1970) 214 E.G. 912; *Buckley* v. *S.R.L. Investments Ltd.* (1970) 22 P. & C.R. 756; *Wilson* v. *Reardon* (1970) 214 E.G. 1294; *Delaforce* v. *Evans* (1970) 22 P. & C.R. 770.

[1] *Orford* v. *Davies* (1970) 214 E.G. 912, at p. 914; and see also *Wilson* v. *Reardon*, (1970) 214 E.G. 1294.

[2] *Hall* v. *Davies* (1970) 22 P. & C.R. 780; *Harrison* v. *Representative Body of the Church in Wales* (1970) 215 E.G. 713; *Peck* v. *Trustees of Hornsey Parochial Charities* (1970) 22 P. & C.R. 789; *Petroff* v. *Trustees of Gunter Estate* (1970) 22 P. & C.R. 818; *Gajewski* v. *Anderton* (1971) 217 E.G. 885 (containing an elaborate and artificial justification for the adverse differential, subsequently disapproved in *Official Custodian for Charities* v. *Goldridge* (1973) 26 P. & C.R. 191, discussed in para. 9–29); *Perrin* v. *Ashdale Land & Property Co. Ltd.* (1971) 218 E.G. 573; *Finney* v. *St. Pier* (1971) 218 E.G. 867.

[3] For a lucid explanation, see *Official Custodian for Charities* v. *Goldridge* (1973) 26 P. & C.R. 191, *per* Lord Denning M.R., at pp. 205 *et seq.*

[4] See *The Goldsmiths Company* v. *Guardian Assurance Co. Ltd.* (1970) 216 E.G. 595; *Wolff* v. *Clifton Properties Ltd.* (1970) 22 P. & C.R. 553; *Kemp* v. *Josephine Trust Ltd.* (1970) 22 P. & C.R. 804.

Millersons Investments Ltd.[5] the Tribunal (R. C. Walmsley FRICS) felt able to say that not only was there a "generally recognised method of approach to the ascertainment of the price payable on enfranchisement of the freehold, but also that "several of the valuation factors involved have become stabilised," including the use of the six per cent. rate for decapitalisation and eight per cent. for recapitalisation. Mr. Walmsley, sitting as the Tribunal, applied the same rates in the next two cases.[6]

The Siggs case and "marriage-by-sale"

Siggs v. *Royal Arsenal Co-operative Society*[7] concerned three typical properties on an extensive estate owned by the landlord. The tenant's valuer originally lodged valuations showing no adverse differential, but amended his valuations in accordance with the Tribunal's guidance in *Farr* v. *Millersons Investments Ltd.*; he was however unable to put forward any valuation principle why an adverse differential should be used. The landlord's valuer, on the other hand, "was firmly of the opinion that there were no grounds either in valuation principles or in valuation practice to justify using an adverse differential," and counsel for the landlord submitted that there was nothing in the 1967 Act or the section 82 amendment which required the landlord to lose a proportion of his site value in addition to losing the value of the buildings on the site.[8] The Tribunal (again R. C. Walmsley FRICS) applying *Farr* v. *Millersons Investments Ltd.* and other earlier decisions,[9] decided that the effect of section 82 amendment was to impose on the landlord the "instant loss" inherent in the use of the adverse differential.[10] The Tribunal attempted to justify this decision by calculations in respect of one of the properties showing a separate quantification of the marriage value, and the subtraction of the tenant's bid (taken as one-half of the marriage value) from a valuation using the same rate (six per cent.) for decapitalisation and recapitalisation. In truth, however, those calculations in fact illustrated that the Tribunal had excluded the tenant's bid twice, by deducting it from a figure in which it was already excluded.[11] 9–28

However, the Tribunal went on to hold that the bid of a purchaser-investor would be influenced by the fact that he would in the future

[5] (1971) 22 P. & C.R. 1055; cogently criticised Ch.Surv. July 1971 p. 49 (M. Beaman).

[6] *Country & Metropolitan Developments Ltd.* v. *Brewer Trust* (1971) 22 P. & C.R. 1135; *Lake* v. *Bennett* (1971) 219 E.G. 945.

[7] (1971) 23 P. & C.R. 79.

[8] *Siggs* v. *Royal Arsenal Co-operative Society* (1971) 23 P. & C.R. 79, at pp. 90–91.

[9] However, the Tribunal's summary of the previous decisions omitted several cases in which neither valuer allowed an adverse differential; see the cases cited in notes 99 and 4, *supra*.

[10] *Siggs*, *supra*, at p. 94.

[11] If the Tribunal's second calculation is re-worked with a seven per cent. or eight per cent. rate for decapitalisation and recapitalisation, very different figures result; indeed, in the case of the eight per cent. rate, a purchase price of a minus figure results!

probably be able to buy in the leasehold and thus reap the benefit of the inherent marriage value, which it termed a "marriage-by-sale" incentive; and that on the facts of the case (and having regard particularly to the fact that the properties were comprised in a large estate in the common freehold ownership of the landlord), this factor counterbalanced the adverse differential.[12] In the result, the Tribunal accordingly determined prices based on calculations containing the same rate of return for decapitalisation and recapitalisation.

Despite the Tribunal's dicta in *Farr* v. *Millerson Investments Ltd.* and the *Siggs* case, valuers on behalf of landlords continued not to use an adverse differential. However, tenants' valuers usually did so, and the Tribunal's determination usually allowed a differential[13] (reduced in two cases by a *Siggs* "marriage-by-sale" factor[14]). But in one case, neither valuer used an adverse differential, and the Tribunal felt bound to accept their evidence.[15]

The Goldridge case

9–29 However, in *Official Custodian for Charities* v. *Goldridge*,[16] the Court of Appeal firmly rejected the notion that the section 82 amendment required or justified the use of an adverse differential. It also considered that the "marriage-by-sale" incentive was too speculative to be taken into account. The majority[17] however considered that there might be evidence of other special factors operating in the market which would show "that an investor-purchaser would expect a greater return on his money than an owner of land is content to take on granting a 50-year lease at a ground rent,"[18] and thereby justify the use of an adverse differential.[19] The *Goldridge* case was therefore remitted to the Lands Tribunal for

---

[12] *Siggs, supra*, at p. 97.

[13] *Sandford* v. *Mooring Aldridge* (1972) 222 E.G. 1119; *Lane* v. *Steeds* (1972) 225 E.G. 276; *Machin* v. *Redspring Ltd.* (1973) 225 E.G. 2037; and see *Cohen* v. *Bridgepoint Properties Ltd.* (1972) 224 E.G. 509 (landlord's valuer revised valuation to exclude adverse differential by reason of *Siggs* "marriage-by-sale" factor); *Pierson* v. *Piercy* (1973) 226 E.G. 1417 (only tenant appeared); *Mimmack* v. *Solent Land Investments Ltd.* (1973) 26 P. & C.R. 139 (landlord's valuer used favourable reverse differential).

[14] *Le Mesurier* v. *Pitt* (1972) 23 P. & C.R. 389; *Official Custodian for Charities* v. *Goldridge* (1973) 26 P. & C.R. 191.

[15] *Ball* v. *Johnson* (1973) 25 P. & C.R. 536, following the dicta of Lord Evershed M.R. in *Sheffield City Council* v. *Meadow Dairy Ltd.* (1958) 2 R.R.C. 395 that the Lands Tribunal, expert though it is, should be careful to act only on evidence.

[16] (1973) 26 P. & C.R. 191.

[17] Megaw and Scarman L.JJ.

[18] *Ibid. per* Scarman L.J. at p. 213.

[19] Scarman L.J. considered that such evidence might have been given in *Lake* v. *Bennett* (1971) 219 E.G. 945 at p. 949; but in fact the tenant's valuer only used an adverse differential because he had been advised by the author that the Lands Tribunal considered it correct to do so.

reconsideration and further evidence, but was shortly afterwards settled by agreement.

In practice little attempt has been made to adduce market evidence supporting an adverse differential. In the great majority of cases since the *Goldridge* decision, the valuers have not used differential rates, but used the same rate of return (usually seven per cent.) for both decapitalisation and recapitalisation.[20]

Subsequent attempts to justify an adverse differential

9–30 In *Chilcott* v. *Clinton Devon Estates*,[21] which was the first case to come before the Lands Tribunal after the decision of the Court of Appeal in the *Goldridge* case, both valuers adopted the same rate of return for both decapitalisation and recapitalisation, and no question of adverse differential therefore arose on the evidence. The Tribunal nevertheless expressed the view that its decision in the *Goldridge* case and the reasons for applying an adverse differential might have been misunderstood in the arguments addressed to the Court of Appeal,[22] and took the opportunity to put forward a previously prepared explanation of how the adverse differential had come to be applied.[23] This explanation concluded that the adverse differential "does not rest on any theory or principle of valuation; nor does it involve any question of law; it is indeed no more than a by-product of the cumulative factual and opinion evidence which the tribunal has received under this branch of its jurisdiction."[24] In the view of the author, an analysis of the previous decisions of the Lands Tribunal does not justify this statement. Moreover, as mentioned above, only in very few instances have valuers subsequently attempted to use an adverse differential.[25]

The ground usually relied on by those who support its use is that decapitalisation has to be considered in an open market in which the

---

[20] See, *e.g. Nash* v. *Castell-y-Mynach* (1975) 234 E.G. 293 at p. 295, discussed at (1976) 237 E.G. 569 (W. A. Leach).

[21] (1974) 27 P. & C.R. 282 (J. Stuart Daniel Q.C. and R. C. Walmsley FRICS) cogently criticised at (1974) 229 E.G. 1053 (W. A. Leach).

[22] In fact, every previous Lands Tribunal decision dealing with the adverse differential was read to the Court of Appeal. If there was any misunderstanding, the fault lay with the Tribunal itself and not with those addressing the Court of Appeal.

[23] In *Wilkes* v. *Larkcroft Properties Ltd.* (1983) 268 E.G. 903, C.A., the *Chilcott* decision was attributed to Mr. Stuart Daniel. However, both the characteristic reasoning and the individual prose style of the comments on the adverse differential proclaim them as vintage Walmsley.

[24] *Chilcott* v. *Clinton Devon Estates* (1974) 27 P. & C.R. 282 at pp. 284 *et seq.* The author considers that this explanation bore little resemblance to the reasons previously put forward by the Tribunal.

[25] See however *Lead* v. *J. & L. Estates Ltd.* (1975) 31 P. & C.R. 495, L.T., cogently criticised at (1976) 237 E.G. 569 (W. A. Leach); and also *Wilkes* v. *Larkcroft Properties Ltd.* (1981) 257 E.G. 1160, L.T.

tenant himself is a bidder, whereas he is excluded as a bidder on recapitalisation by reason of the section 82 amendment.[26] The Court of Appeal has been "tempted by this reasoning," but considered it inconsistent with the *Goldridge* decision.[27] However, the reasoning leads, with respect, to exactly the opposite conclusion, since the tenant-bidder might be expected to offer a higher rent to outbid the rest of the market (*i.e.* he would give the landlord a higher return).[28] It is to be hoped the artificial and illogical adverse differential, together with the equally artificial and illogical "marriage-by-sale," have now been firmly put to sleep by the *Goldridge* decision and that no further attempts at resuscitation will be made.

Long term unexpired

9-31 It is usually accepted by valuers that the reversion to a term of about 60 years or longer is so far distant[29] as to be of a negligible present value, apart from the ground rent it carries in the meantime. Although it is possible to calculate a value for such a distant reversion by reference to the estimated section 15 rent and Parry's Valuation Tables, and this has occasionally been done,[30] such a calculation is somewhat unreal and inherently unreliable. For one thing, a minor variation in the percentage rate of return adopted leads to a substantial alteration in the figure resulting from the calculation.[31] It is considered that a purchaser in the actual market would not in practice make or take any account of the calculation, and would not pay anything for the ultimate reversion.

Accordingly, in the common case where the ground rent is a fixed sum payable for the remainder of an outstanding term of 60 or more years, the value of the freehold is taken as the capitalised value of the ground rent as if it were payable in perpetuity. Prior to the decision of Court of Appeal in

---

[26] As in *Lead* v. *J. & L. Estates Ltd.* (1975) 31 P. & C.R. 495.

[27] *Wilkes* v. *Larkcroft Properties Ltd.* (1983) 268 E.G. 903.

[28] See *Official Custodian for Charities* v. *Goldridge* (1973) 26 P. & C.R. 191, *per* Lord Denning M.R. at p. 208.

[29] Small amounts have been attributed to distant reversions in *Gordon* v. *Lady Londesborough's M.S. Trustees* (1974) 230 E.G. 509, L.T. (56 years); *Uziell-Hamilton* v. *Hibbert-Foy* (1974) 230 E.G. 509, L.T. (57½ years); *Adams* v. *Lloyd* (1975) 232 E.G. 1370, L.T. (55¾ years); and *Collins* v. *Jones* (1981) 261 E.G. 1001, L.V.T. (50 years); *cf. Shutt* v. *Phillips* (1974) 227 E.G. 1186, L.T. (58 years).

[30] See, *e.g. Mimmack* v. *Solent Land Investments Ltd.* (1973) 26 P. & C.R. 139, L.T. (67 years); *Lead* v. *J & L Estates* (1975) 236 E.G. 819 (61 years); *Lowther and others* v. *Strandberg* (1985) 273 E.G. 53 L.T. (on appeal from L.V.T. *sub. nom. Silver* v. *Holland House Estates Trustees* (1983) 266 E.G. 913) (81 years); and see para. 9-24 ("the *Haresign* addition").

[31] Thus, if in the *Lowther* case the adopted percentage had been ten per cent. instead of nine per cent., the ultimate reversion in relation to 65 Abbotsbury Road would have been valued at £62 and not £130. Conversely if eight per cent. had been used the valuation would have been £273.

Gallaher Estates Ltd. v. *Walker*,[32] it had become settled in the Lands Tribunal that, particularly having regard to general interest rates then current and the lack of attraction of such a long fixed-interest investment, the purchase price should be the ground rent multiplied by a figure, called the "years' purchase" (Y.P) usually between 10 and 13.[33] The actual figure depended on factors such as the locality of the property and the amount of the ground rent.

The Court of Appeal in delivering judgments dismissing the landlord's appeal in the *Gallaher Estates* case expressed the view that the money market was not "a safe guide in making valuations of land"[34] and that "the important market is the land market in the vicinity."[35] Lord Denning M.R. suggested that other persons in the neighbourhood apart from the sitting tenant might bid for the freehold in order to enforce the covenants of the lease and maintain the amenities of the environment.[36] He might have added the landlord himself, who is not excluded from the hypothetical market.[37] Lord Denning M.R. and Sachs L.J. also considered that there might be purchasing institutions[38] not concerned with a low current yield but looking to the long-distant future.[39] However these remarks were merely obiter dicta and were not based on any evidence before the court. For a time, these remarks caused a change in the Lands Tribunal practice, despite the fact that (predictably, in the author's view) no evidence was ever adduced in support of them. In reliance mainly on comparable sales to tenants,[40] the Tribunal determined values reflecting higher figures of years' purchase.[41] 9–32

However, the continuing absence of any such evidence appears to have caused both the Lands Tribunal[42] and leasehold valuation tribunals[42a] to 9–33

---

[32] (1973) 28 P. & C.R. 113.

[33] *Jenkins* v. *Bevan Thomas* (1972) 23 P. & C.R. 258; *Barber* v. *Trustees of Eltham United Charities* (1972) 221 E.G. 1343; *Gallaher Estates Ltd.* v. *Walker* (1972) 221 E.G. 1379; *Shutt* v. *Phillips* (1974) 227 E.G. 1186.

[34] (1973) 28 P. & C.R. 113 at pp. 117, 121.

[35] *Ibid.* p. 117, *per* Lord Denning M.R.

[36] *Ibid.* p. 117.

[37] See *e.g. Siggs* v. *Royal Arsenal Co-operative Society* (1972) 23 P. & C.R. 79 at p. 97.

[38] "Corporations and insurance companies" (*per* Lord Denning): "institutions ... of a charitable nature and large estates" (*per* Sachs L.J.).

[39] (1973) P. & C.R. 113 at pp. 117, 121.

[40] Such reliance is usually considered unsafe by reason of the "*Delaforce* effect" see para. 9–61.

[41] *Finkel* v. *Simon* (1974) 28 P. & C.R. 509 (26 YP); *Valentine* v. *Somerset* (1974) 231 E.G. 632 (32 YP).

[42] *Cohen* v. *Metropolitan Property Realisations Ltd.* (1976) 239 E.G. 666; *Janering* v. *English Property Corporation Ltd. and Nessdale Ltd.* (1977) 22 P. & C.R. 523 (9.1 YP); *Ugrinic* v. *Shipway (Estates) Ltd.* (1977) 244 E.G. 893.

[42a] *Betts* v. *G. and D. Developments Ltd.* (1981) 261 E.G. 787; *cf. Jevons* v. *Carbury Investments Ltd.* (1984) 271 E.G. 637 (figure based on evidence and tribunal's own knowledge).

revert to much lower figures of years' purchase, more related to rates of interest current at the date of the tenant's Notice of Leaseholder's Claim. The precise years' purchase depends on all the circumstances of the case.[43] In particular, the trouble and costs of collection of a small ground rent tends to reduce the value of the reversion, and in some cases the reversion has been valued at a nominal amount only.[44] But the purchase price may be determined on the basis of a sale as part of a parcel of ground rents, as opposed to a sale of the reversion on its own,[45] and may reflect the value to a purchaser of an agency commission on any fire insurance premium which the tenant is under covenant to pay.[46]

An attempt to determine the value of a reversion by reference to the difference between original sale offers for freehold and leasehold sites on the same estate was unsuccessful.[47] The statutory algebraic formula for the redemption of rentcharges[48] is not applicable.[49]

Example valuations—freehold price under section 9(1)

9–34 *Example 3—Short term unexpired, standing house valuation*[50]

A detached house in Ealing, London, has a 1973 rateable value of £650. It is held on a lease at a ground rent of £20 per annum, and there are 18 years of the term unexpired at the date of service of the Notice of Leaseholder's Claim. The vacant possession value of the house, deemed modernised and in good condition, is £90,000:

[43] For a case in which there were phased increases in the ground rent, see *Divis* v. *Middleton* (1983) 268 E.G. 157, L.T.

[44] *Yates* v. *Bridgewater Estates Ltd.* (1982) 261 E.G. 1001, L.V.T.; *Williams* v. *Walsh* (1983) 268 E.G. 915, L.V.T.

[45] *Re Castleberg Investments (Jersey) Ltd.'s Appeal* (1985) 275 E.G. 46, L.T.; but see *Williams* v. *Walsh* (1983) 268 E.G. 915, L.V.T.

[46] *Re Castleberg Investments (Jersey) Ltd.'s Appeal, supra.*

[47] *Divis* v. *Middleton* (1983) 268 E.G. 157, L.T.

[48] In s.10 of the Rentcharges Act, 1977 (and see para. 7A, Sched. 1 to the 1967 Act, discussed at para. 11–07).

[49] *Williams* v. *Walsh* (1983) 268 E.G. 915, L.V.T.

[50] See paras. 9–08 *et seq.*

Ground rent	£20	
Years' purchase for 18 years @ 7%	10.06	
		£201.20
Entirety value	£90,000	
Site value @ 30%	£27,000	
Section 15 rent @ 7%	£ 1,890	
Years' purchase in perpetuity deferred 18 years @ 7%	×4.227	
		£7,989.03
		£8,190.23
	say	£8,190

Example 4—Short term unexpired, cleared site valuation[51] 9–35

A semi-detached house in Birmingham has a 1973 rateable value of £450. It is held on a lease at a ground rent of £15 per annum, and there are 33 years of the term unexpired at the date of service of the Notice of Leaseholder's Claim. The area of its site is 400 sq.yds. and it has a frontage of 18 ft. (*See overleaf*).

[51] See para. 9–07.

Ground rent	£15		
Years' purchase for 33 years @ 7%	×12.75		
			£191.25
Site value 40 sq. yds. @ £30 per sq. yd.		£12,600	
(Check valuation)			
Site value 18ft. frontage @ £600 per f.f.	£10,800		
Adjust (i) extra depth compared to average +10%	£1,080		
(ii) better location compared to average +5%	£540		
		£12,420	
	say	£12,500	
Section 15 rent @ 7%		£875	
Years' purchase in perpetuity deferred 33 years at 7%		×1.531	
			£1,339.62
			£1,520.87
		say	£1,520

9–36 *Example 5—Term expired, standing house valuation*[52]

A terrace house in Cardiff has a 1973 rateable value of £300. It is held on a lease at a ground rent of £5 per annum, and there are only 12 days of the term unexpired at the date of service of Notice of Leaseholder's Claim. The vacant possession value of the house, deemed modernised and in good condition, is £32,000:

Ground rent for original term		Nil
Entirety value	£32,000	
Site value @ 25%	£8,000	
Section 15 rent @ 7%[53]	£560	
Years' purchase in perpetuity @ 7%	×14.2857	
		£8,000

[52] See paras. 9–08 *et seq.*

[53] It is not really necessary to ascertain the section 15 rent. As there is no deferment, and the same interest rate is used for decapitalisation and recapitalisation, the calculation could stop at the site value. But in accordance with the provisions of the Act, it is customary to include a calculation of the section 15 rent.

Example 6—Long term unexpired[54] **9–37**

A semi-detached house in a new town has a 1973 rateable value of £400. It is held on a lease at a ground rent of £30 per annum, and there are 87 years of the term unexpired at the date of service of the Notice of Leaseholder's Claim:

Ground rent	£30	
Years' purchase in perpetuity @ 10%	× 10	
		£300

Example 7—Short term unexpired, with addition for development potential[55] **9–38**

An old house, standing on a 1.5 acre site in a suburb of Greater London, has a 1973 rateable value of £950. It is held on a lease at a ground rent of £20, and there are 15 years of the term unexpired at the date of service of the Notice of Leaseholder's Claim. The vacant possession value of the property, deemed modernised and in good condition, but with its use restricted to that of a single private dwelling-house and grounds, is £60,000. However, the value of the site for redevelopment purposes is £100,000. (*See overleaf*).

[54] See paras. 9–31 and 9–32.
[55] See para. 9–25.

Ground rent		£20	
Years' purchase for 15 years @ 7%			×9.17
			£183
Entirety value[56]		£60,000	
Site value @ 35%		£21,000	
Section 15 rent @ 7%		£1,470	
Years purchase for 50 years @ 7%[57]		×13.80	
		£20,286	
Defer 15 years @ 7%		×0.3264	
			£6,621
Full site value		£100,000	
Defer 65 (15+50) years		×0.0123	
			£1,230
			£8,034
Addition for s.17 right			
Full site value		£100,000	
Less (1) Schedule 2 compensation[58]			
Annual value (say)	£4,500		
Less section 15 rent	£1,470		
Net benefit per annum	£3,030		
Y.P. for 50 years @ 7%	×13.80		
		£41,814	
Less (2) Y.P. for 50 years @ 7% of s.15 rent (as above)		£20,286	
		£37,900	
Defer 15 years @ 7%		×0.3264	
		£12,371	
			£20,405
		say	£20,400

[56] The "standing house" valuation approach is used in this example, as to which see paras. 9–08 *et seq*. Note that the section 15 rent must be ascertained on the assumption that the house site can be used only as the site of a single private residence: see para. 9–04.

[57] In this example, a "*Haresign*" addition has been used: see para. 9–24. As the value of the ultimate reversion after the expiry of the 50-year extension is attributable wholly to the site itself (and not to the buildings), it is considered that this is an exceptional case where the use of a *Haresign* addition can be justified.

[58] See para. 8–12.

4. Valuation of Freehold under Section 9(1A)

Basis of valuation

The purchase price payable by the tenant in cases where the freehold falls to be valued under section 9(1A) of the 1967 Act[59] is the amount which at the relevant time,[60] "the house and premises, if sold in the open market by a willing seller, might be expected to realise" on the assumptions mentioned below. This wording bears a close resemblance to that of Rule 2 in section 5 of the Land Compensation Act 1961,[61] and the price is thus "the amount which a purchaser in a friendly negotiation would be willing to pay in acquiring a freehold interest and as though no compulsory powers of acquisition had been obtained."[62] The tenant is a willing, but not an anxious, purchaser.[63] However, the purchase price must take into account any defect in the landlord's title.[64] **9–39**

Marriage value

The wording of section 9(1A) mentioned above is identical to that in section 9(1) as originally enacted, *i.e.* before the words "(with the tenant and members of his family residing in the house not buying or seeking to buy)" were introduced by section 82 of the Housing Act 1969. But that amendment plainly cannot be read as amending section 9(1A), and it is clear that the purchasing tenant and his family are therefore not excluded from the market.[65] It follows that the purchase price is not limited to the purely investment value of the freeholder's interest and must reflect the existence of any "marriage value" and any special "tenant's bid" likely to be made as a result.[66] This has been accepted in both the Lands Tribunal[67] and leasehold valuation tribunals.[68] It is sometimes suggested that only a **9–40**

---

[59] Introduced by the Housing Act 1974, s.118. As to whether the valuation should be under s.9(1) or s.9(1A), see para. 9–14.

[60] *i.e.* the date of service of the tenant's Notice of Leaseholder's Claim: s.37(1)(*d*).

[61] Replacing Rule (2) in s.2 of the Acquisition of Land (Assessment of Compensation) Act 1919.

[62] *Lambe* v. *Secretary of State for War* [1955] 2 Q.B. 612, *per* Parker L.J. at p. 621, applying *Raja Vyricherla Narayana Gajapatiraju* v. *Revenue Divisional Officer, Vizagapatam* [1939] A.C. 302, P.C.

[63] *Lloyd-Jones* v. *Church Commissioners for England* (1981) 261 E.G. 471, L.T., following the cases in the last note.

[64] s.9(2).

[65] *Norfolk* v. *Trinity College, Cambridge* (1976) 32 P. & C.R. 147, L.T.

[66] See generally as to marriage value and tenant's bid para. 9–17.

[67] *Norfolk* v. *Trinity College, Cambridge, supra*; *Lloyd-Jones* v. *Church Commissioners for England* (1981) 261 E.G. 471, L.T.; *Lowther* v. *Strandberg* (1985) 273 E.G. 53.

[68] *Silverman* v. *Catherine Investments Ltd.* (1984) 271 E.G. 381; *Henry Smith's Charity Kensington Estates Trustees* v. *Frampton* (1985) 273 E.G. 990.

small nominal value should be attributed to "the tenant's bid," because the tenant need only make one further bid to be able to outbid the other potential purchasers in the hypothetical market. This "one more bid" argument is fallacious[69] and has been decisively rejected in other valuation contexts concerning a special purchaser[70] and by the Lands Tribunal in cases under section 9(1A).[71]

As to the valuation of the tenant's bid, which involves the quantification of the marriage value and its division between the freeholder and the enfranchising tenant, see paras. 9–54 and 9–55.

Valuation assumptions

(a) *Estate sold*

9–41 It is to be assumed that "the vendor was selling for an estate in fee-simple, subject to the tenancy, but on the assumption that this Part of this Act conferred no right to acquire the freehold."[72] The first limb of this assumption means that it is the landlord's freehold reversion which must be valued. The second limb requires that the purchase price must be ascertained as if the sale were a voluntary and not a compulsory sale. It protects the freeholder against any depreciation in the value of his interest which the right to enfranchise might be said to cause, and also the tenant against any addition to the purchase price because the sale is compulsory.[73] These assumptions are similar to the first two assumptions which have to be made on a valuation under section 9(1).[74]

These assumptions do not, however, repeat the final part of section 9(1)(*a*), *viz.* that, if the tenancy has not been extended under Part I of this

---

[69] It ignores both (1) the fact that the vendor must be assumed to be "willing" and so able to use his bargaining power to obtain a fair share of any additional value to a special purchaser, and (2) the existence of speculators in the hypothetical market confident of obtaining a higher offer from the special purchaser: see the cases mentioned in the next footnote.

[70] See *I.R.C.* v. *Clay and Buchanan* [1914] 3 K.B. 466, C.A.; and *Raja Vyricherla Narayana Gajapatiraju* v. *Revenue Divisional Officer, Vizagatapam* [1939] A.C. 302, P.C.

[71] *Norfolk* v. *Trinity College, Cambridge* (1976) 32 P. & C.R. 147, L.T.; *Lloyd-Jones* v. *Church Commissioners for England* (1981) 261 E.G. 471, L.T.

[72] s.9(1A)(*a*).

[73] *Cf.* r. (1) in s.5(i) of the Land Compensation Act 1961, replacing s.2 of the Acquisition of Land (Assessment of Compensation) Act 1919, which excluded the ten per cent. addition which previously had customarily been added on a compulsory purchase: see *Harvey* v. *Crawley Development Corporation* [1957] 1 Q.B. 485, *per* Denning L.J. at p. 493; and Cripps, *Compulsory Acquisition of Land* (11th ed.) para. 4–046.

[74] See para. 9–18.

1967 Act, it is to be assumed that (subject to the landlord's rights under section 17) it was to be so extended.[75] This contrast with section 9(1)(*a*), coupled with the assumption that at the end of the tenancy the tenant has the right to remain in possession of the house and premises under Part I Landlord and Tenant Act 1954,[76] made it reasonably clear that the tenant's right to an extended lease had to be ignored,[77] even prior to the amendment enacted by section 23 of the Housing and Planning Act 1986. That amendment (which is considered in more detail below)[78] expressly provides that it is to be assumed now that Part I of the 1967 Act conferred no right to an extended lease.

Mosley v. Hickman. However, in *Mosley* v. *Hickman*,[79] the Court of Appeal held that different considerations applied in cases where the tenant had previously claimed and had been duly granted an extended lease.[80] Prior to "the original term date,"[81] the extended lease is of necessity a "long tenancy at a low rent," and the tenant is not precluded from exercising his right to acquire the freehold.[82] Moreover, although the extended lease will have been granted after February 18, 1966, it is treated for the purposes of the 1967 Act as a single composite long tenancy beginning at the same time as the term of the earlier tenancy[83] and thus "created" at that time (at the latest) for the purposes of section 1(6)(*c*), so that the upper £750/£1500 rateable value limit will apply.[84] An extended lease must be granted for the residue of the term of the existing tenancy plus 50 years and is "in substitution" for the original tenancy[85] which is thereby surrendered.[86] It was held by the Court of Appeal in *Mosley* v. *Hickman* that "the tenancy" in the above assumption concerning the estate sold meant the extended lease and could not be construed as referring to the original tenancy. 9–42

---

[75] s.9(1)(*a*); see para. 9–18.

[76] s.9(1A)(*b*); see para. 9–45.

[77] *Lowther* v. *Strandberg* (1985) 273 E.G. 53 at p. 55, affirming the decision of the leasehold valuation tribunal on this point *sub. nom. Silver* v. *Holland House Estates Trustees* (1983) 266 E.G. 913.

[78] See para. 9–44.

[79] (1986) 278 E.G. 728, C.A., affirming the decision of the Lands Tribunal acting as an arbitrator reported *sub. nom. Hickman* v. *Phillimore Kensington Estate Trustees* (1985) 50 P. & C.R. 476. For a helpful discussion see (1985) 276 E.G. 614 (C. C. Hubbard).

[80] Under s.14.

[81] Defined by s.37: see para. 3–12.

[82] s.16(1)(*a*).

[83] By s.3(3), which clearly applies to an extended lease: see s.16(5).

[84] *Bates* v. *Pierrepoint* (1978) 37 P. & C.R. 420, C.A.

[85] s.14(1); and see para. 7–04.

[86] *Re Savile Settled Estates* [1931] 2 Ch. 210; *Jenkin R. Lewis & Son Ltd.* v. *Kerman* [1971] Ch. 477, C.A. at p. 486.

9–43 **Consequences of Mosley v. Hickman.** The result of *Mosley* v. *Hickman*[87] was that the purchase price payable for the freehold was usually lower than it would have been if the original tenancy had remained,[88] and the shorter the outstanding period until the "original term date" (*i.e.* the residue of the original tenancy if it had remained in being) the more marked this difference became.[89] So a tenant who wished to enfranchise could obtain a significant reduction in the purchase price by first obtaining an extended lease and then immediately claiming the freehold. This was admittedly anomalous, but it was the inevitable consequence of the failure of Parliament to make the necessary connection between the freehold price and the terms of an extended lease in relation to higher rateable value properties.[90] Note, however, that *Mosley* v. *Hickman* did not effectively equate the section 9(1A) basis of valuation with the section 9(1) basis, as has sometimes been mistakenly suggested. Under the former, "the marriage value" element is not excluded.[91]

9–44 **Reversal of Mosley v. Hickman.** The effect of *Mosley* v. *Hickman* was reversed, save as mentioned below, by section 23(1) of the Housing and Planning Act 1986. This provided that in addition to the assumption in section 9(1A) of the 1967 Act that Part I of that Act conferred no right to acquire the freehold, it was also to be assumed that it conferred no right to acquire an extended lease "and, where the tenancy has been extended under this Part of this Act, that the tenancy will terminate on the original term date."[92] So any extended lease is effectively ignored. The result is illogical and unsatisfactory, because the purchase price no longer has any relationship to the true value of the landlord's interest, but is artificially raised to a figure that is usually considerably higher. Parliament has retained the valuable right to an extended lease, but chosen to disregard it when the freehold price comes to be ascertained. The result is anomalous.[93]

The amendment made by section 23(1) of the 1986 Act does not however apply in any of the following three cases: (a) where the enfranchisement price has been determined, by agreement or otherwise,

---

[87] See note 79, *supra.*

[88] Because the section 15 rent payable during the 50-year extension is lower than the "fair rent" payable under Part I of the 1954 Act would be.

[89] In *Mosley* v. *Hickman*, which concerned 3 houses in Argyll Road, Kensington, London, at the valuation date (*i.e.* the date of service of the Notice of Leaseholder's Claim to the freehold) the relevant period was approximately 15 years. The purchase prices had been agreed between the parties on the alternative bases of ignoring and taking into account the extension, as follows: 13 Argyll Road, £49,500/£110,000; 27 Argyll Road, £45,000/£98,000; and 46 Argyll Road, £56,000/£137,500.

[90] See the comments at para. 1–17.

[91] See para. 9–40.

[92] For meaning of original term date, see s.37(1)(*g*) and para. 3–12.

[93] See further para. 1–21.

before January 7, 1987[94]; (b) where a Notice of Leaseholder's Claim to the freehold was served before November 7, 1986[95]; or (c) where a Notice of Leaseholder's Claim to an extended lease was served before March 5, 1986[96] (the date of the decision of the Court of Appeal in *Mosley* v. *Hickman*).[97] It is likely that para. (c) will prove to be much the most important of these dates, for there have been few, if any, cases covered by paras. (a) or (b) which are not also covered by para. (c).

(b) *Part I of the Landlord and Tenant Act 1954*

It is to be assumed that "at the end of the tenancy the tenant has the right to remain in possession under the provisions of Part I of the Landlord and Tenant Act 1954."[98] Under these provisions, the tenancy is automatically continued[99] until certain steps are taken,[1] and upon its termination the tenant becomes entitled to a statutory tenancy under the Rent Act 1977[2] at a "fair rent."[3] **9–45**

It is to be observed that the assumption is only that the tenant has the right to remain under Part I of the 1954 Act, and not that he will in fact do so. A statutory tenancy is regarded by most tenants of houses in the higher rateable value brackets as an unsatisfactory holding. It is non-assignable, the fair rent is subject to review every two years, and the tenant cannot deduct the rent against income tax. A long tenancy acquired for a premium, on the other hand, is a marketable and assignable interest giving better security, and interest payable under a mortgage raised to acquire it (up to the current maximum principal sum of £30,000)[4] will be deductible against income tax. In practice, few tenants of properties in the higher rateable value brackets allow their tenancies to expire and then rely on their rights under Part I of the 1954 Act. Nearly all tenants seek a grant of a longer term before then, and this is a market factor which has

---

[94] *i.e.* the date when s.23 came into force.

[95] The date of the passing of the 1986 Act.

[96] s.23(3).

[97] It is difficult to see why this date was chosen in preference to the date of the Lands Tribunal's decision (May 15, 1985). The effect of that decision was well publicised before the date of the decision of the Court of Appeal: see, *e.g.*, (1985) 276 E.G. 614 (C. C. Hubbard).

[98] s.9(1A)(*b*).

[99] s.3(1) of the 1954 Act.

[1] Normally the service of a "landlord's notice proposing a statutory tenancy" under s.4(3) of the 1954 Act.

[2] ss.6 and 7 of the 1954 Act.

[3] s.70 of the Rent Act 1977. For discussion, see Woodfall, *Landlord and Tenant* (28th ed.) Vol. 3, para. 3–0094.

[4] *i.e.* as regards loans made after March 26, 1974: see para. 24(3), Sched. 1 to the Finance Act 1974 and s.20 of the Finance Act 1986.

been recognised by the Lands Tribunal as affecting the purchase price.[5] See further para. 9–51.

(c) *Repairs*

9–46 It is to be assumed that "the tenant has no liability to carry out any repairs maintenance or redecoration under the terms of the tenancy or Part I of the Landlord and Tenant Act 1954."[6] Any logical purpose or plausible justification for this assumption remains undetected by the author. The second limb of the assumption does not cause much difficulty. If it is to be assumed that the tenant has no repairing liabilities under his statutory tenancy arising under Part I of the 1954 Act, then clearly the "fair rent" will have to be correspondingly higher to compensate the landlord. It is considered that the landlord's net profit rental should remain the same, so that this part of the assumption has little practical effect.

The first limb of the assumption, relating to the existing tenancy, is a different matter. It appears to lead inevitably to the conclusion that a tenant who at the date of his Notice of Leaseholder's Claim has let his house fall into disrepair will pay a lower purchase price than if he had complied with his repairing obligations; and the worse the tenant's breach of his repairing covenant, the cheaper his freehold will be. In the normal way, a landlord would be compensated by a dilapidations claim (*i.e.*, for damages for breach of the repairing covenant),[7] but this part of the assumption appears clearly to negate any such claim. It is considered that this anomalous and inequitable result cannot be avoided, however anxious the court would be to avoid it, for the words used are too clear and unambiguous to admit of any other construction.[8]

However, this assumption will probably only affect the purchase price in rare cases. Most tenants of properties in the higher rateable value brackets do in fact keep their properties in reasonable repair. It is considered that this fact would be taken into account by the market, and thus that the possibility of any serious disrepair should be largely ignored in the valuation.[9]

---

[5] *Lloyd-Jones* v. *Church Commissioners for England* (1981) 261 E.G. 471.

[6] s.9(1A)(*c*).

[7] Under Pt. I of the 1954 Act, the landlord would be liable to do "initial repairs," *i.e.* repairs necessary to bring the house into good repair having regard to its age, character and location (s.9); but he would be entitled to a "payment for accrued tenant's repairs," a payment from the tenant of the cost of such of the initial repairs as required in consequence of the tenant's failure to fulfil his repairing obligations under his former tenancy (s.8(1)).

[8] *Cf. Vacher & Sons Ltd.* v. *London Society of Compositors* [1903] A.C. 107, and *Stock* v. *Frank Jones (Tipton) Ltd.* [1978] 1 W.L.R. 231, H.L.

[9] The assumption has not affected any of the valuations made in the cases on s.9(1A) so far reported, but in each of them the house was in good repair.

(d) *Improvements*

9–47 It is to be assumed "that the price be diminished by the extent to which the value of the house and premises has been increased by any improvement carried out by the tenant or his predecessors in title at their own expenses."[10] "Improvements" in this context has its usual meaning, and excludes maintenance and renewal. However, the improvement does not have to be structural, so that non-structural improvements such as the installation of sinks and cookers, cupboards, bookshelves and the like are within the assumption.[11] It is considered that the improvement must have been carried out by the tenant or his predecessor during the current tenancy (or a prior tenancy which under section 3(3) of the 1967 Act is treated as a single composite tenancy with the current tenancy)[12]; improvements made during any other tenancy are not included.[13] In this connection, it is to be noted that if the grant of a tenancy is made conditional upon the making of the improvement (as is frequently the case in practice), there is no tenancy, either at law or in equity until the improvements have been completed.[14] But otherwise it appears to be immaterial that the improvement was made pursuant to an obligation of the tenant under his lease, so that the landlord has in effect given consideration for the improvement. (On the other hand it is considered that the building of the house itself is not an "improvement" in this context).[15] It is also immaterial that the improvement was made in breach of covenant and without the consent of the landlord.

The wording of the assumption is curious, and on one reading could lead to the conclusion that the value of the improvements related to the freehold in possession (*i.e.* without any deferment in respect of the outstanding term) should be deducted from the price. However, this construction, which could in some circumstances not difficult to imagine result in a nil or negative price, can hardly accord with the intention of Parliament and has been rejected by the Lands Tribunal.[16] The manner in which the assumption is given effect is for the property to be valued (at all stages in the valuation[17]) as if the improvements had not been made, *i.e.*

---

[10] s.9(1A)(*d*).
[11] *Cf.* para. 1(2), Sched. 8 to the Housing Act 1974, discussed at para. 2–25.
[12] See *Hemmings* v. *Trustees of Henry Smith's Charity* (1982) 45 P. & C.R. 377, C.A. (similar words in s.70(3)(*b*) of the Rent Act 1977).
[13] *Cf.* para. 2–27.
[14] *Cornish* v. *Brook Green Laundry Ltd.* [1959] 1 Q.B. 394, C.A.
[15] Although there is no reference to para. 1(2), Sched. 8 to the Housing Act 1974, it is thought that the words will be given a similar meaning.
[16] *Norfolk* v. *Trinity College, Cambridge* (1976) 32 P. & C.R. 147, L.T.
[17] Including the calculation of the marriage value: see para. 9–54.

as if the property had been in the same condition as when originally let[18]; and it is their value, and not their cost, which falls to be disregarded.[19]

(e) *Rentcharges and other charges*

(f) *Rights and burdens*

9–48 These assumptions are identical to assumptions (b) and (c) in valuations under section 9(1) and are dealt with at para. 9–19.

Purchase price—generally

9–49 Except in cases where the tenant has previously claimed an extended lease and section 23 of the Housing and Planning Act 1986 does not apply,[20] the purchase price payable by the tenant for the landlord's interest under section 9(1A) as amended thus comprises, and (subject as mentioned below) in valuations for the purposes of the Act can be broken down into the following elements:

(1) the capitalised value of the rent payable under the tenancy from the date of service of the Notice of Leaseholder's Claim until the original term date;
(2) the present value of the landlord's reversion after the original term date, on the assumptions as to Part I of the Landlord and Tenant Act 1954, repairs and improvements mentioned above;
(3) a share of the "marriage value" of the freehold and leasehold interests;
(4) the effect of new easements and restrictive covenants in the conveyance;
(5) the value (if any) of any other rights under the existing tenancy extinguished on the acquisition of the freehold.

It is necessary to consider these five elements in turn; however, in practice it is only rarely that the purchase price is affected by either (4) or (5).

(1) Capitalised value of the rent payable for the period of the unexpired term of the existing tenancy

9–50 The first stage in the ascertainment of the purchase price is to determine the value of the rent payable for the period of the unexpired

---

[18] *Cf. GREA Property Investments Ltd.* v. *Williams* (1979) 250 E.G. 65 and *Estates Projects Ltd.* v. *Greenwich L.B.C.* (1979) 251 E.G. 851, (both cases concerning rent reviews).
[19] *Henry Smith's Charity Kensington Estate Trustees* v. *Frampton* (1985) 273 E.G. 990, L.V.T.
[20] See para. 9–44.

term of the existing tenancy, *i.e.* from the date of service of the Notice of Leaseholder's Claim until the original term date. This is done in the same manner as in valuations under s.9(1), as to which see para. 9–21. As to the position where there is a long term outstanding, see para. 9–53.

(2) Value of landlord's reversion after the original term date, on the assumptions as to Part I of the Landlord and Tenant Act, 1954, repairs and improvements mentioned above

Generally

For the reasons given in para. 9–45, experience has shown that it is comparatively rare for a tenant of a property in the higher rateable value brackets to allow his tenancy to expire and then rely on his rights under Part I of the 1954 Act. Nearly all such tenants seek to obtain the grant of a longer tenancy well before the term date, though doubtless the possibility of the exercise of the tenant's rights under Part I of the 1954 Act is a factor which the parties take into account in negotiating the terms of a new longer tenancy. This is a market factor which has been recognised by the Lands Tribunal as affecting the purchase price.[21] In one leading case,[22] the Tribunal accepted evidence that a purchaser of such a property would be mainly concerned with its vacant possession value and would pay only small regard to the amount of any "fair rent" currently payable or likely to become payable, and that "the primary approach to a valuation of a freehold interest in a house which is let at a fair rent was to take a percentage of the vacant possession value, not to capitalise the net income."[23] On the evidence in that case, the Tribunal held that the landlord's reversion after the original term date should be valued at the vacant possession value (less the value of tenant's improvements[24]), less a ten per cent. deduction for the risk of the tenant claiming a tenancy under Part I of the Landlord and Tenant Act 1954, the resulting figure then being deferred at an appropriate percentage[25] for the period of the unexpired term of the tenancy. **9–51**

This approach and method of valuation has been followed and adopted in the subsequent reported cases before the Lands Tribunal[26] and leasehold valuation tribunals,[27] and it is considered to be correct, at any

---

[21] See *Lloyd-Jones* v. *Church Commissioners for England* (1981) 261 E.G. 471; *Lowther* v. *Strandberg* (1985) 273 E.G. 53.

[22] *Lloyd-Jones* v. *Church Commissioners for England* (1981) 261 E.G. 471.

[23] See at p. 473.

[24] See paras. 9–47 and 9–52.

[25] In that case, 6 per cent., which is a low figure.

[26] *Lowther* v. *Strandberg, supra.*

[27] *Silverman* v. *Catherine Investments Ltd.* (1984) 271 E.G. 381; *Henry Smith's Charity Kensington Estate Trustees* v. *Frampton* (1985) 273 E.G. 990.

rate if there is an appreciable residue of the term of the tenancy outstanding.[28] The percentage deduction of ten per cent. has also been adopted in the reported cases, but the appropriate deduction to take account of the tenant's rights under Part I of the Landlord and Tenant Act 1954 must inevitably be a matter of valuation and evidence in each case. The percentage rate to be used for deferment is also a matter of valuation and evidence in each case, but as in the case of valuations under section 9(1),[29] the rate usually adopted is seven per cent.[30]

Repairs and Improvements

9–52 This part of the valuation must also take into account the statutory assumptions as to repairs and improvements which have to be made, as to which see paras. 9–46 and 9–47 above. In the case of improvements, it is their value, and not their cost, which must be disregarded.[31]

Long term unexpired

9–53 As in the case of valuations under section 9(1),[32] it is unusual for any separate value to be attributed to a reversion to a term of about 60 years or longer, although this has occasionally been done.[33] It is considered that the value of the freehold (apart from a share of the marriage value) should be taken as the capitalised value of the ground rent as if it were payable in perpetuity, or ascertained by reference to comparable freehold sales.[34]

(3) Share of marriage value of freehold and leasehold interests

Calculation of marriage value

9–54 As mentioned above, the purchase price under section 9(1A)[35] must reflect the existence of any "marriage value" and any special "tenant's bid" likely to be made as a result.[36] The method of calculation of the marriage value which has now become established by decisions of the

---

[28] If the term has expired or is due shortly to expire, the evidence may be that the amount of the "fair rent" should assume a greater importance.

[29] See para. 9–23.

[30] *Silverman* v. *Catherine Investments Ltd.* (1984) 271 E.G. 381; *Henry Smith's Charity Kensington Estate Trustees* v. *Frampton* (1985) 273 E.G. 990.

[31] *Henry Smith's Charity Kensington Estate Trustees* v. *Frampton*, *supra.*

[32] See paras. 9–31 *et seq.*

[33] See *Lowther* v. *Strandberg* (1985) 273 E.G. 53, L.T., and the comments in note 30 to para. 9–31.

[34] As in *Norfolk* v. *Trinity College, Cambridge* (1976) 32 P. & C.R. 147, L.T.

[35] Whether or not affected by the Housing and Planning Act 1986, s.23.

[36] See generally para. 9–40.

Lands Tribunal[37] and leasehold valuation tribunals[38] is as follows. There are ascertained: (1) the value of the tenant's interest ignoring tenant's improvements (and ignoring also the right to enfranchise); (2) the enfranchisement price (ignoring any marriage value); and (3) the value of the freehold in possession ignoring tenant's improvements. The aggregate of (1) and (2) is then substracted from (3). This method is considered to be entirely logical, for it directly assesses the increase in value released by the marriage of the interests of the landlord and the tenant.[39]

Division of marriage value

It has also become established by decisions of the Lands Tribunal and leasehold valuation tribunals that the marriage value calculated as above should be divided equally between the freeholder and the tenant.[40] This is considered to be correct as a matter of logic, because the bargaining powers of the freeholder and the tenant (both of whom are assumed to be "willing"[41]) are equal, and the agreement of both of them is required in the hypothetical sale postulated by section 9(1A). Tenants who have long terms outstanding sometimes argue that the division of the marriage value ought to be proportionate to the value of the respective interests of the freeholder and the tenant; but that argument is fallacious, because those values do not reflect the relative bargaining powers of the two parties.[42] However, the question is properly one of valuation, *i.e.* what the market would in fact do, and not one of logic. It would be open to either party to bring evidence that in sales to tenants outside the 1967 Act, the division of the marriage value is generally in some proportion other than 50:50, but no attempt has yet been made to adduce such evidence. **9–55**

If there is an intermediate lessee whose interest is also being acquired by the enfranchising tenant, it is considered that the one-half of the marriage value to which the freeholder is normally entitled should be divided equally between him and the intermediate lessee. However, in the only reported case[43] in which such a situation has been considered, a leasehold valuation tribunal held that such one-half of the marriage value

---

[37] *Norfolk* v. *Trinity College, Cambridge* (1976) 32 P. & C.R. 147; *Lloyd-Jones* v. *Church Commissioners for England* (1981) 261 E.G. 471; *Lowther* v. *Strandberg* (1985) 273 E.G. 53.

[38] *Silverman* v. *Catherine Investments Ltd.* (1984) 271 E.G. 381; *Henry Smith's Charity Kensington Estate Trustees* v. *Frampton* (1984) 273 E.G. 990.

[39] But see criticisms at 238 E.G. 544 and 239 E.G. 181 and 623.

[40] See the cases cited in the last two footnotes.

[41] See *Lloyd-Jones* v. *Church Commissioners for England, supra.*

[42] If the argument were correct, the freeholder would receive the lion's share of the marriage value in cases where the tenant has only a short term outstanding.

[43] *Silverman* v. *Catherine Investments Ltd.* (1984) 271 E.G. 381.

should be apportioned[44] between the freeholder and the intermediate lessee in shares proportionate to the values of their respective interests.[45]

(4) The effect of new easements and restrictive covenants in the conveyance

(5) The value (if any) of any other rights under the existing tenancy extinguished on the acquisition of the freehold

9–56 The same considerations apply as in the case of a valuation under section 9(1), as to which see paras. 9–26 and 9–27.

Example valuations—freehold price under section 9(1A), if there has been no extended lease or section 23(1) of the Housing and Planning Act 1986 is applicable

9–57 *Example 8—Long term unexpired*[46]

A detached house in Kensington has a 1973 rateable value of £1,400. It is held on a lease at a ground rent of £150 per annum and there are 75 years of the term unexpired at the date of service of the Notice of Leaseholder's Claim. The freehold vacant possession value of the house is £250,000, of which £20,000 is attributable to improvements carried out by a previous tenant:

---

[44] The report (1984) 271 E.G. 381 at p. 383 misprints "apportionment" as "appointment."

[45] The evidence given before the tribunal was unsatisfactory, because neither valuer indicated separate prices for the freehold and the intermediate leasehold interest, as required by the 1967 Act: see para. 11–14.

[46] Based on *Norfolk* v. *Trinity College, Cambridge* (1976) 32 P. & C.R. 147, L.T. and *Lowther* v. *Strandberg* (1985) 273 E.G. 53, L.T.

Ground rent		£150	
Years' purchase in perpetuity @ 7%[47]		×14.28	
			£2,142
Marriage value[48]			
Freehold	£250,000		
Less tenant's improvements	£20,000		
		£230,000	
Less (1) Value of freeholder's interest (apart from marriage value)	£2,142		
Less (2) Value of tenant's interest, ignoring tenant's improvements, (apart from marriage value)[49]	£215,000		
		£217,142	
Gain on marriage of interest		£12,858	
Freeholder's share at 50%[50]			£6,429
			£8,671
		say	£8,670

Example 9—Short term unexpired[51] 9–58

A house in Knightsbridge, London, has a 1973 rateable value of £1,545, but the tenant has obtained a certificate from the Valuation Officer under Schedule 8 to the Housing Act 1974 certifying a notional reduction of £75 in respect of tenant's improvements.[52] It is held on a lease at a ground rent of £35 per annum and there are 18 years of the term unexpired at the date of service of the Notice of Leaseholder's Claim. The freehold vacant

---

[47] See para. 9–53.

[48] See para. 9–54.

[49] This figure must be established by valuation evidence, usually supported by sales of comparable leasehold properties (not reflecting the value of any rights under the 1967 Act).

[50] See para. 9–55.

[51] Based on *Lloyd-Jones* v. *Church Commissioners for England* (1981) 261 E.G. 471, L.T. and *Henry Smith's Charity Kensington Estate Trustees* v. *Frampton* (1985) 273 E.G. 990, L.V.T.

[52] See paras. 2–23 *et seq.*

possession value of the house is £250,000, of which £40,000 is attributable to improvements carried out by a previous tenant:

Ground rent		£35	
Years' purchase for 18 years @ 7%[53]		×10.06	
			£35.2
Freehold vacant possession value	£250,000		
Less tenant's improvements	£40,000		
	£210,000		
Less 10% for risk of tenant claiming Part I of the 1954 Act rights[54]	£21,000		
		£189,000	
Defer 18 years @ 7%		×0.2959	
			£55,925
			£56,277
Marriage value[55]			
Freehold (less tenant's improvements)		£210,000	
Less (1) Value of freeholder's interest (apart from marriage value)	£56,277		
Less (2) Value of tenant's interest (apart from marriage value)[56]	£90,000		
		£146,277	
Gain on marriage of interests		£63,723	
Freeholder's share at 50%[57]			£31,861
			£88,138
		say	£88,140

[53] See para. 9–50.
[54] See para. 9–51.
[55] See para. 9–54.
[56] This figure must be established by valuation evidence, usually supported by sales of comparable leasehold properties (not reflecting the value of any rights under the 1967 Act). The appropriate deduction for tenant's improvements is frequently arrived by deducting the same proportion from the leasehold value as is deducted from the freehold value, as in *Henry Smith's Charity Kensington Estate Trustees* v. *Frampton, supra.*
[57] See para. 9–55.

Purchase price where the tenant has previously been granted an extended lease and section 23 of the Housing and Planning Act 1986 does not apply

In a few cases, and in particular where the tenant has been granted an extended lease pursuant to a Notice of Leaseholder's Claim served before March 5, 1986,[58] section 23 of the Housing and Planning Act 1986 has no application[59] and "the tenancy" in the valuation assumption in section 9(1A)(*a*) of the 1967 Act as amended means the extended lease.[60] In such cases, the purchase price can be broken down into the five elements set out in para. 9–49, except that element (2) is the present value of the landlord's reversion after the extended term date,[61] on the assumptions as to Part I of the 1954 Act, repairs and improvements mentioned above.[62] However, in the valuation of this element, those assumptions have little or no practical consequence, because the 50-year extension is at the section 15 rent, which ignores the value of the buildings on the site.[63] **9–59**

The valuation thus effectively differs from a valuation under section 9(1) only in that "the tenant's bid" or share of the "marriage value" is not excluded.[64] This latter element remains important, and in cases where there is a long term outstanding may represent the greater part of the purchase price.[65] The above assumptions, particularly the assumption as to improvements, may be relevant in calculating the value of "marriage value" element.

Example valuation—freehold price under section 9(1A) if an extended lease has previously been granted and section 23(1) of the Housing and Planning Act 1986 is not applicable[66]

Example 10—Short term unexpired, standing house valuation[67] **9–60**

The facts are the same as in Example 9 above, except that an extended lease has been granted pursuant to a Notice of Leaseholder's Claim served prior to March 5, 1986:[68]

---

58 The date of the decision of the Court of Appeal in *Mosley* v. *Hickman* (1986) 278 E.G. 728.
59 See subs. (4) and para. 9–44.
60 *Mosley* v. *Hickman, supra*: see paras. 9–42 and 9–43.
61 *i.e.*, the date of expiry of the 50-year extension.
62 See paras. 9–45 to 9–47.
63 See paras. 9–03 *et seq.*
64 See paras. 9–40, 9–54 and 9–55.
65 As in *Norfolk* v. *Trinity College, Cambridge* (1976) 32 P. & C.R. 147, L.T. and *Lowther* v. *Strandberg* (1985) 273 E.G. 53.
66 The relevant "tenancy" is thus the extended lease, in accordance with *Mosley* v. *Hickman* (1986) 278 E.G. 728, C.A.
67 Apart from the marriage value element, the valuation is the same as a valuation under s.9(1): see para. 9–59. As to the standing house approach, see paras. 9–08 *et seq.*
68 See s.23(3) of the Housing and Planning Act 1986 and para. 9–44.

Ground rent		£35	
Years' purchase for 18 years @ 7%		×10.06	
			£35.2
Entirety value[69]		£250,000	
Site value @ 40%		£100,000	
Section 15 rent @ 7%		£7,000	
Years purchase in perpetuity deferred 18 years @ 7%		×4.227	
			£29,589
			£29,941
Marriage value[70]			
Freehold (less tenant's improvements)		£210,000	
Less (1) Value of freeholder's interest (apart from marriage value)	£29,941		
Less (2) Value of tenant's interest less tenant's improvements (apart from marriage value)[71]	£150,000		
		£179,941	
Gain on marriage of interests		£30,059	
Freeholder's share at 50%[72]			£15,029
			£44,970

[69] *i.e.* the freehold vacant possession value. No deduction should be made in respect of tenant's improvements at this stage of the valuation, because in arriving at the site value by the "standing house" approach, the property must be assumed to be modernised and in good condition: see para. 9–08.

[70] See para. 9–54.

[71] This figure must be established by suitable valuation evidence. The appropriate deduction for tenant's improvements is frequently arrived at by deducting the same proportion from the leaseholds value as is deducted from the freehold value, as in *Henry Smith's Charity Kensington Estates Trustees* v. *Frampton* (1985) 273 E.G. 990, L.V.T. As a result of the 50-year extension, this figure is (in the case of short terms unexpired) substantially higher than the value of an unextended term, with the consequence that the marriage value is significantly smaller.

[72] See para. 9–55.

5. Evidence of Comparable Settlements

In many cases before the Lands Tribunal and leasehold valuation tribunals, the landlord's valuer has given evidence of previous agreed transactions under the 1967 Act in support of his valuation. Such "settlement comparables" evidence is regarded with considerable caution. It was early recognised by the Lands Tribunal in *Delaforce* v. *Evans*[73] that the great majority of tenants are usually anxious to settle and thus often willing to pay something in excess of the proper price in order to achieve a settlement. Tenants also are unwilling to risk the potentially considerable expense of a hearing before a tribunal, particularly if (as is frequently the case) such expense would be out of proportion to the amount at stake. They are also unwilling to undergo the delay involved in a tribunal hearing. Moreover, in the case of freehold valuations under section 9(1), the purchase price arrived at on a settlement in practice often includes an element of the tenant's bid, excluded by the amendment introduced by section 82 of the Housing Act 1969,[74] and is higher than the proper price for that reason.[75] 9–61

These factors commonly referred to as "the *Delaforce* effect,"[76] have resulted in settlement evidence being given little weight except where it provides solid support for the landlord's case.

> "Unless the settlement evidence is shown to provide solid support, the tribunal attaches little weight to it: for instance, if the tenants who settled had done so without professional advice, or despite such advice; or if there is no clear evidence as to the basis on which the settlements were negotiated; or if the valuer producing the settlement evidence was not personally engaged in the negotiations[77]; or if there is market evidence which puts in doubt the site value contended for; then in any or all of these circumstances the evidence afforded by settlements is readily displaced by other evidence."[78]

And even where the settlement evidence does provide solid support, it is

---

[73] (1970) 22 P. & C.R. 770. See also *Kemp* v. *Josephine Trust Ltd.* (1970) 22 P. & C.R. 804 at pp. 814–815 (where the rival contentions on this matter were clearly put by counsel for each party); *Gajewski* v. *Anderton* (1971) 217 E.G. 885; and other cases cited below.

[74] See para. 9–17.

[75] *Delaforce* v. *Evans* (1970) 22 P. & C.R. 770; *Janering* v. *English Property Corporation Ltd. and Nessdale Ltd.* (1977) 33 P. & C.R. 523; *Miller* v. *St. John's College, Oxford* (1977) 243 E.G. 535 (but the statement that the schedule of comparables was inadmissible for this reason is clearly too wide); *Pilgrim* v. *Central Estates (Belgravia) Ltd.* (1986) 278 E.G. 1373, L.V.T.

[76] An expression first used in *The Goldsmiths Co.* v. *Guardian Assurance Co. Ltd.* (1970) 216 E.G. 395 at p. 599.

[77] This example is open to question.

[78] *Farr* v. *Millersons Investments Ltd.* (1971) 22 P. & C.R. 1055 at p. 1061.

often considered appropriate to make a suitable deduction to take account of the *Delaforce* effect.

CHAPTER 10

MANAGEMENT SCHEMES

1. INTRODUCTION

Background

Nearly every long lease at a low rent under which a tenant may be qualified for the benefits conferred by the 1967 Act was originally granted as one of a number in an area and as part of an estate. The common landlord, in his capacity as the freeholder (or sometimes a long leaseholder) of the area, usually granted building leases of the whole or part of the area, or developed the whole or part of the area himself and disposed of it on long leases at premiums. In such cases, it is likely that the leases impose similar covenants on all or most of the tenants. Such covenants, if they have been duly enforced by the common landlord, ensure the maintenance of the character and standards of the estate as a whole, and consequently are of considerable benefit to the tenants themselves as well as to the landlord. In many cases, of course, the former common landlord's ownership of the estate has become fragmented, or the covenants have not in practice been enforced. But it was recognised[1] that in other cases it would be unfortunate, and unfair to the other tenants of the estate, if the exercise of the right to acquire the freehold by any one or more tenants prevented the former unified management and control from being any longer effective. **10–01**

Outline

Accordingly, special provision was made by section 19 of the 1967 Act for the retention of the management powers of a common landlord of an estate area for the general benefit of the owners and occupiers of properties within that area. The procedure for permitting this to be done involved two stages. First, a certificate had to be obtained from the Minister[2] in respect of the area. As originally enacted, the application for such a certificate had to be made within two years after the date when Part I of the 1967 Act came into force, *i.e.* before January 1, 1970.[3] However in **10–02**

---

[1] See the White Paper (Cmnd. 2916), para. 22.

[2] In Wales and Monmouthshire, the Secretary of State for Wales; elsewhere formerly the Minister of Housing and Local Government, now the Secretary of State for the Environment: s. 19(1).

[3] s. 19(1).

relation to any area which comprised property within the increased rateable value limits introduced by the Housing Act, 1974, the time-limit for such an application was extended to July 31, 1976.[4] Secondly, if (but only if) the Minister gave a certificate, within one year thereafter application had to be made to the High Court for the approval of a scheme setting out the management powers to be retained.[5] Once a scheme is approved, its terms are binding on any tenant who acquires the freehold[6]; and provision is made for the tenant's right to do so to be suspended in the meanwhile.[7]

The permissible contents of any scheme are, however, rather limited. In particular, it must be appreciated that the landlord can neither (a) prevent a duly qualified tenant from acquiring the freehold, nor (b) recover possession from a tenant who has acquired the freehold, in order to redevelop.[8] These are serious limitations, and have been the subject of a good deal of criticism. Most applications under the section have been made (i) by landlords whose other properties in the area are not liable to enfranchisement (*e.g.* because they consist of flats and maisonettes, or are over the rateable value limits) and who wish to keep up the standards of the area; (ii) by landlords who are under obligations to repair or redecorate the relevant house and/or other premises used in common and who wish to avoid difficulty in recovering the appropriate fraction of the costs of complying with such obligations after enfranchisement; or (iii) by tenants' associations.

2. Area and Applicants

Area

10-03 An application to the Minister[9] for a section 19 certificate could[10] only be made in the case of an "area which is occupied directly or indirectly by him or his licensees or for the time being unoccupied."[11] The common landlord is usually the freeholder, but can also be an intermediate tenant. A number of properties can form an "area" for this purpose, even though they are not adjoining. A joint application could be made by the landlords of two or more neighbouring areas which would together form a unit.[12] It

[4] Housing Act 1974, s. 118(2).
[5] s. 19(1).
[6] s. 19(10)(*a*).
[7] s. 19(14), (15).
[8] *Re Calthorpe Estate Edgbaston, Birmingham* (1973) 26 P. & C.R. 120.
[9] See n. 2, *supra*.
[10] No further application can now be made: see para. 10-05.
[11] s. 19(1).
[12] s. 19(12).

is not clear whether the Minister could grant a certificate for an area which differs from that included in the application; it seems probable that the Minister could not include any property not comprised in the application, but that he could grant a certificate for part only of the area in respect of which the application was made.

A certificate which includes property which at its date is no longer in the ownership of the common landlord (*e.g.* property sold off between the date of application and the date of the certificate) is invalid,[13] unless perhaps such land is *de minimis* in relation to the area as a whole.[14] However, the certificate may on its proper construction exclude such property even though the property is shown as part of the area on a plan referred to in the certificate, and so be valid.[15] Furthermore, an invalid certificate could be amended by the Minister, the amended certificate being treated as made pursuant to the original application.[16] Otherwise, the certificate is final and cannot be varied, although the High Court may exclude any part of the area comprised in it from a scheme.[17]

Who could apply

Except in two cases, only a person who is the common landlord could apply under section 19 to the Minister for a certificate and to the High Court for a scheme in respect of an area,[18] although different common landlords of the same area (*e.g.* the freehold and a long leaseholder) could make separate applications.[19] The two exceptions were: **10–04**

(a) *Two or more landlords*

Two or more common landlords of neighbouring areas could make joint application.[20] Where it appeared to the Minister that a certificate would, if the interests of the joint applicants were held by a single person, otherwise be given for those areas as a unit, he could grant a single certificate for those areas as a whole, and the applicants then jointly constituted "the landlord." In addition, however, it had also to appear to the Minister that the applicants were willing to be bound by any scheme approved by the High Court to co-operate in the management of their respective properties as a whole; and such scheme must be made subject to conditions (enforceable as provided by the scheme) for securing that

---

[13] *Cadbury* v. *Woodward* (1972) 23 P. & C.R. 281.
[14] *Re Dulwich College's Application* (1972) 224 E.G. 1039.
[15] *Ibid.* (area correctly described in the Schedule supplied to the Minister).
[16] *Cadbury* v. *Woodward (No. 2)* (1972) 24 P. & C.R. 335.
[17] s. 19(4); see further para. 10–11.
[18] s. 19(11).
[19] *New Hampstead Garden Suburb Ltd.* v. *Barrabell* (1974) C.A., unreported, C.A.T. Ub. 332.
[20] s. 19(12).

the applicants and their successors in title do co-operate. The most common example of a joint application is where parts of an estate are held by different members of the same family or the trustees of different family settlements.

(b) *Tenants' representative body*

Provision was made[21] for cases where it appeared to the Minister (i) that a certificate would be granted on the application of one or more landlords,[22] and (ii) that a "body of persons" (which it could be either incorporate or unincorporated) was so constituted as to be capable of representing the tenants in the area, or such of them as should become entitled to acquire their landlord's interest under the 1967 Act, and that such body was a suitable one.[23] The usual kind of tenants' or residents' association frequently constituted such a body, but it was sometimes found convenient to incorporate a company (or a society under the Industrial and Provident Societies Acts 1965–1968) for the purpose. Such a representative body could make an application to the Minister either alone or jointly with the landlord, and the Minister could grant a certificate accordingly. See further para. 10–24.

3. Minister's Certificate

Time for application

10–05 As originally enacted, the application to the Minister[24] for a certificate had to be made before January 1, 1970.[25] However, in relation to any area which comprised property within the increased rateable value limits introduced by the Housing Act 1974, the time-limit for such an application was extended to July 31, 1976.[26] Since that date, no further application can be entertained. It follows that, with very few exceptions, the benefits of section 19 can be obtained only with regard to estates existing prior to those dates. No comparable provision is made with regard to future long leasehold estates, notwithstanding that the rights conferred by the 1967 Act apply equally to qualified leaseholders of houses on such estates.

Preliminary notices

10–06 The applicant for a certificate, after making his application, had to give

[21] s. 19(13).
[22] s. 19(13)(*a*).
[23] s. 19(13)(*b*).
[24] For the meaning of "Minister" see note 2 *supra*.
[25] i.e. within 2 years after Part I of the 1967 Act came into force: s. 19(1).
[26] Housing Act 1974, s. 118(3).

adequate notice of it to all persons interested, either by advertisement or otherwise, as required by the Minister.[27] The Minister usually required notice to be given by post to all the occupying tenants. The notice had to inform the persons interested of the application and its purpose, and invite them to make representations for or against the application within a time which appeared to the Minister to be reasonable. Before giving a certificate, the Minister had to consider all the representations so made within that time.[28]

Holding of inquiry

If it appeared to the Minister from the representations made to him that there was among the persons making them substantial opposition to the application for a certificate, he was required to afford to those opposing the application an opportunity to appear at an inquiry and be heard by a person appointed for that purpose.[29] A few inquiries of this kind were held.[30] **10–07**

Matters to be considered by the Minister

The Minister could grant a certificate only if **10–08**

> "in order to maintain adequate standards of appearance and amenity and regulate redevelopment in the area in the event of tenants acquiring the landlord's interest in their house and premises . . . it is in the minister's opinion likely to be in the general interest that the landlord should retain powers of management in respect of the house and premises or have rights against the house and premises arising from the exercise elsewhere of his powers of management."[31]

The kind of powers of management and other rights envisaged are discussed below.

The Minister, in considering whether or not to grant a certificate (and also the High Court in considering whether to approve a scheme), had to

> "have regard primarily to the benefit likely to result from the scheme to the area as a whole (including houses likely to be acquired from

---

[27] s. 19(2).
[28] *Ibid.*
[29] *Ibid.*
[30] Examples were the Calthorpe Estate, Edgbaston (see *Re Calthorpe Estate, Edgbaston, Birmingham* (1973) 26 P. & C.R. 120), the Dulwich College Estate (see *Re Dulwich College Estate's Application* (1973) 231 E.G. 845; Hampstead Garden Suburb (see *New Hampstead Garden Suburb Ltd* v. *Barrabell* (1974) C.A., unreported, C.A.T. U.b. 332), in respect of which certificates were granted; and the Blundellsands Estate, Lancashire, in respect of which a certificate was refused.
[31] s. 19(1).

the landlord under this Part of this Act), and the extent to which it is reasonable to impose, for the benefit of the area, obligations on tenants so acquiring their freeholds; but regard may also be had to the past development and present character of the area and to architectural or historical considerations, to the neighbouring area and to the circumstances generally."[32]

4. Approval and Contents of Scheme

Application to High Court for a scheme

(a) *Who may apply*

10–09 This has already been discussed: see para. 10–04.

(b) *Time*

The application must be made within one year after the granting of the Minister's certificate.[33] This time-limit is absolute and there is no provision for any extension.

(c) *Practice and procedure*

The proceedings are assigned to the Chancery Division,[34] and are begun by originating summons. Unless any one or more tenants have previously indicated that they desire to be joined as defendants, the originating summons can be made *ex parte*.[35] All tenants should then be sent a circular letter informing them of the proceedings, stating that they are entitled, if they so wish, to be joined as defendants, and either enclosing a copy of the proposed scheme or indicating a convenient place where it can be inspected. When the summons comes before the Master, he must satisfy himself that all the tenants have been duly circularised; and if any of them have indicated a wish to be joined as defendants, the Master will order them to be so joined, and provide them with an opportunity to file affidavit evidence.

The originating summons is supported by an affidavit sworn on behalf of the applicant. This sets out the history of the matters and the reasons for the application, and should exhibit examples of common-form leases used in the area. It should also show that the Minister's certificate has

---

[32] s. 19(3).
[33] s. 19(1).
[34] R.S.C., Ord. 93, r. 15.
[35] *St. Mary Abbott's Place Properties Ltd's Application* (1970) 214 E.G. 413 (Pennycuick J.). The practice is similar to that under s. 84(2) of the Law of Property Act 1925, as to which see *Re Sunnyfield* [1932] 1 Ch. 79 at p. 83.

been obtained, and exhibit the proposed scheme (which is often annexed to draft minutes of order). The affidavit should also show that all the tenants have been circulated, and exhibit any consents and correspondence with them. In one early case,[36] it was suggested that the summons should also be supported by an affidavit sworn by a surveyor dealing with the benefits that would accrue to the area from the scheme. However, evidence of this kind usually only stated the obvious and proved to be of little or no value, and in practice evidence of this kind has not been required.

(d) *Preliminary application*

The applicant is entitled, if he thinks fit, to make a preliminary application to the court, before submitting his scheme for approval.[37] On such a preliminary application the court can (i) give general directions as to the matters properly to be included in the scheme, and (ii) order that any part of the scheme comprised in the Minister's certificate should be excluded from the scheme, or that no scheme at all can be approved for the area.[38] A preliminary application of this kind is made by way of a summons in the originating summons, and not by separate proceedings. This power was exercised in one important case,[39] but otherwise does not appear to have been used. **10–10**

(e) *Hearing*

If there is little or no opposition to the proposed scheme, the Master will usually direct the originating summons to be heard by the judge in chambers.[40] In other cases, the Master may adjourn it into the non-witness list or the witness list as appropriate. In either case, a tenant is usually permitted to appear and present arguments, even if he has not previously been joined as a defendant.

(f) *Matters to be considered*

The matters to be considered by the High Court in deciding whether or not to grant a scheme are the same as those to be considered by the minister in deciding whether or not to grant a certificate[41]: see para. 10–08.

---

[36] *Re Sherwood Close (Barnes) Management Co's Application* [1972] Ch. 208.
[37] s. 19(4).
[38] *Ibid.*
[39] *Re Calthorpe Estate, Edgbaston, Birmingham, supra.*
[40] *Re St. Mary Abbott's Place Properties Ltd.'s Application, supra.*
[41] s. 19(3).

(g) *Costs*

The court has its usual full discretion as to the costs of the proceedings.[42] There is no reported case in which the objectors have been ordered to pay any part of the applicant's costs, and it is thought that such an order would only be made in a case where the objections were wholly frivolous or vexatious. In one contested case in which the objectors were largely unsuccessful, there was no order as to costs and it was suggested that this would be "the ordinary rule in a case where everybody was seeking to produce the best scheme."[43] But this suggestion has found little favour, and in the author's experience the general practice has been to allow at any rate one set of costs to objectors who have acted responsibly and assisted the court.

Powers of the High Court

(a) *Area*

10–11 Prima facie, any scheme approved by the court must cover the whole of the area comprised in the Minister's certificate,[44] although it may make different provision for different parts of the area.[45] But any part of that area which has been conveyed away by the common landlord between the date of the certificate and the date of approval of the scheme can,[46] and probably must,[47] be excluded from the scheme. Further, if having regard to (i) the matters which have to be taken into account by the Minister when considering whether to grant a certificate, (ii) the provisions which it is practical to make by a scheme and (iii) any change in the circumstances since the giving of the certificate, the court thinks if proper so to do, it may either exclude from the scheme any area comprised in the certificate, or declare that no scheme at all can be approved for the area.[48] In addition, any scheme must include provision for excluding (either automatically or by or with the approval of the court) any part of the area from its operation if a change of circumstances makes it appropriate.[49] On the other hand, the court has no power to include in the scheme property not included in the certificate, such as land acquired by the landlord after the date of the certificate.[50]

---

[42] Supreme Court of Judicature (Consolidation) Act 1925, s. 50.
[43] *Re Dulwich College Estate's Application* (1973) 231 E.G. 845.
[44] s. 19(5).
[45] s. 19(6).
[46] See s. 19(1).
[47] *Cadbury* v. *Woodward* (1972) 23 P. & C.R. 281.
[48] s. 19(4).
[49] s. 19(6).
[50] *Cadbury* v. *Woodward*, supra.

(b) *Properties affected*

The scheme can, and generally should, extend to all properties of which the common landlord subsequently disposes of his freehold or other interest. The property need not be a house or other residential property, and the disposition need not be in favour of a tenant qualified under the 1967 Act.[51] In practice, tenants are usually anxious that no property within the area should be disposed of free from the obligations of the scheme. However, it must be appreciated that the scheme does not "bite" on any property unless and until the common landlord disposes of his interest. In particular, the scheme does not operate over any property of which the tenant has acquired only an extended lease under the 1967 Act. The tenant remains subject only to the covenants and conditions of his lease, unless and until the landlord's interest is acquired; but thereupon these are replaced by the provisions of the scheme. **10–12**

(c) *Approval of scheme*

Section 19 is concerned with the retention of the landlord's powers of management,[52] and a scheme can only be approved by the court if it appears "not to give the landlord a degree of control out of proportion to that previously exercised by him or to that required for the purposes of the Scheme."[53] (If the applicant is not a landlord, this provision is taken to mean "not to give to the applicant a degree of control out of proportion to that previously exercised by the landlord,"etc.)[54] It is plain from these requirements that the scheme must broadly be based on the existing leases of properties in the area. But it does not follow that nothing can be included in the scheme by way of such powers except any such powers which the landlord actually had and exercised at the date of the scheme, or that only provisions common to all leases of properties in the area can be included. Suitable new powers of management can be included, provided that these are not "out of proportion" to those previously exercised.[55] The scheme must also appear to the court to be "fair and practical," but this does not mean that a scheme must be perfect or impossible to improve.[56] **10–13**

The court can approve a scheme as originally submitted, or with any subsequent modifications proposed or agreed to by the applicant.[57] There

---

[51] s. 19(9).
[52] See sidenote and subs. (1).
[53] s. 19(5).
[54] *New Hampstead Garden Suburb Ltd.* v. *Barrabell* (1974), unreported, C.A.T. U.b. 332.
[55] *Re Dulwich College Estate's Application, supra.*
[56] *Ibid.*
[57] s. 19(5).

is no power to approve a scheme without the consent of the landlord[58] (except, apparently, as to the grant of powers enabling a tenant's representative body which has obtained a certificate to participate).[59] However, the court can, if it is of the opinion that the applicant is unwilling to agree to a suitable scheme or is not proceeding in the matter with due dispatch, dismiss the application altogether.[60] So if a landlord is unwilling to accept an amendment to a proposed scheme, the court's only sanction is the somewhat unsatisfactory one of dismissing the application altogether, which may be against the best interests of the tenants.[61] Otherwise the court can only dismiss the application "if no scheme can be approved for the area,"[62] a circumstance which has not occurred in practice and which the author finds hard to envisage.

Obligatory contents of scheme

10–14 There are three matters which must be included in any scheme, and it appears that the court cannot approve the scheme if any of them are omitted. The three matters are:

(a) *Change of circumstances*

The scheme must provide for terminating or varying all or any of the provisions of the scheme, or for excluding part of the area covered by the scheme, if a change of circumstances makes it appropriate.[63] This can be done by including a term in the scheme "for enabling it to be done by or with the approval of the High Court." The usual way of dealing with this matter is to grant any person concerned liberty to apply to the court for an appropriate modification of the scheme if a change of circumstances occurs. In some schemes, however, provision is made for discouraging frivolous applications of this nature, *e.g.* by requiring the application to be made by a specific number of tenants. It is considered that the usual power of the court to award costs is sufficient for this purpose, and that a specific provision of this kind is unnecessary and in some cases could prove unfair.

(b) *Change of landlord*

The scheme must also include suitable provision for identifying the

[58] *New Hampstead Garden Suburb Ltd.* v. *Barrabell, supra.*
[59] s. 19(13)(*ii*).
[60] s. 19(5)(*b*).
[61] This happened in *Pollock* v. *Westmacott* (1981) Foster J. (unreported), but the landlords appealed to the Court of Appeal which approved a compromise scheme agreed in the meantime between the landlords and the tenants.
[62] s. 19(4)(*b*).
[63] s. 19(6).

person who is, for the purposes of the scheme, to be treated as the landlord for the time being.[64] Save as regards straightforward matters (such as *e.g.* a change in the trusteeship of a landlord's estate or the transfer of the entirety of the landlord's estate in the area as a whole), this is not easy to do, at any rate in the comprehensive manner which appears to be contemplated. Particular difficulty arises in cases where the landlord's interest becomes fragmented. In practice, schemes seldom deal properly with this and other situations, and if necessary an application to the court for an appropriate "change of circumstances" variation must be made.[65]

(c) *Two or more landlords*

Where the Minister grants a certificate to two or more landlords on a joint application by them, the scheme must "be made subject to conditions (enforceable in such manner as may be provided by the scheme) for securing that the landlords co-operate" in the management of their properties and the administration of the scheme.[66]

Other contents of scheme

The matters which may be governed by a scheme are fairly wide. For the most part, they are the kind of matters which are commonly dealt with in well-drafted leases of an estate area, and include the following: **10–15**

(a) *Redevelopment*

The scheme can impose regulations regulating the redevelopment of property.[67] However, the landlord can only control the redevelopment by negative obligations: he cannot recover the property from the owner and redevelop it himself.[68] Most schemes include a prohibition on development or redevelopment without the consent of the landlord. Arguments that planning control makes this kind of prohibition unnecessary or undesirable have always been rejected. However, in order that the landlord should not have "a degree of control out of proportion to that previously exercised by him"[69] such prohibition is usually made subject to a proviso that the landlord's consent is not to be unreasonably withheld, thus reproducing the effect of the Landlord and Tenant Act 1927, s.19(2)

---

[64] s. 19(7)(*a*).
[65] Under s. 19(6) discussed above.
[66] s. 19(12).
[67] s. 19(8)(*a*).
[68] *Re Calthorpe Estate, Edgbaston, Birmingham* (1973) 26 P. & C.R. 120 (landlord's proposed right of repurchase for development purposes not within s. 19).
[69] s. 19(5).

(which applies only to covenants in leases).[70] It is thought that consent can be reasonably withheld if the tenant's proposals conflict with the landlord's plans for the area; and in one case the scheme as approved contained a further clause expressly prohibiting development in a manner inconsistent with the landlord's plans and proposals for the area.[71] Most schemes require the enfranchised owner to submit plans of any proposed development and to pay the landlord's reasonable surveyor's and other costs of considering such plans.

(b) *Use*

10–16 The scheme can impose provisions regulating the use of the property.[72] Most schemes include restrictions on the user, generally to that of a single private dwelling-house or other permitted use at the date of enfranchisement,[73] except with the consent of the landlord. Unless the covenant is in the common form of lease so provided, it is not necessary for the qualifying words "such consent not to be unreasonably withheld" to be included.[74] Other restrictions on use commonly found in schemes include not to hang washing except at prescribed times,[75] not to park caravans, etc., at the front of the house,[76] not to hold auctions, not to keep animals which may be or become a nuisance, not to commit a nuisance or use the property for illegal or immoral purposes,[77] and not to vitiate insurance. Restrictions of this kind are apparently subject to the power of modification or discharge conferred on the Lands Tribunal by section 84 of the Law of Property Act 1925 as amended.[78] As to the user of common parts, see para. 10–19.

Most restrictions on the user of property can often also be included in the conveyance or transfer on enfranchisement by the landlord (other

---

[70] *e.g. Re Copse Hill Estate, Wimbledon* (1971) 219 E.G. 1604; *Re Dulwich College Estate's Application* (1973) 231 E.G. 845 (not fully reported on this point); *Re Grosvenor Belgravia Estate* (1973) (unreported, Pennycuick V.C.); Re *Calthorpe Estate, Edgbaston, Birmingham, supra*; *Re Prudential Kensington Estate* (1978) (unreported); *Re Phillimore Kensington Estate* (1980) (unreported, Oliver J.).

[71] *Re Calthorpe Estate Edgbaston, Birmingham, supra.*

[72] s. 19(8)(*a*).

[73] Usually mentioned in the initial transfer or conveyance of the freehold, *e.g. Re Grosvenor Belgravia Estate* (1973) (unreported, Pennycuick V-C); *Re Calthorpe Estate, Edgbaston, Birmingham, supra* (not reported on this point).

[74] *Re Calthorpe Estate, Edgbaston, Birmingham, supra* at p. 127.

[75] A restriction that can "raise considerable heat": *Re Dulwich College Estates' Application* (1973) 231 E.G. 845, at p. 849.

[76] *Re Dulwich College Estate's Application, supra* at p. 849; *Re Calthorpe Estate, Edgbaston, Birmingham* (not reported on this point).

[77] It does not matter that these are also matters for the police or for individual action: *Commission for the New Towns* v. *Berman* (1973) 226 E.G. 617.

[78] *Re Calthorpe Estate, Edgbaston, Birmingham, supra* at p. 127.

than a tenants' association) independently of any scheme.[79] But it is nevertheless helpful to include them in a scheme for three reasons: (1) it avoids possible disputes with individual tenants as to whether such restrictions should be so included; (2) it avoids any difficulty of enforcement by the landlord due to his no longer owning neighbouring property capable of being benefited[80]; and (3) it enables the restrictions to be enforced by a body, such as a residents' association, to which the rights of the landlord have been transferred[81] but which does not own any neighbouring property.

(c) *Appearance*

The scheme can impose provisions regulating the appearance of property.[82] Most schemes include prohibitions on external alterations or additions without the consent of the landlord, usually subject to a proviso that such consent shall not be unreasonably withheld.[83] Other restrictions under this head commonly found in schemes include not to decorate except in approved colours and materials,[84] not to cut down trees except with consent,[85] not to erect television or other aerials[86] and not to erect signs or placards except for specified limited purposes.[87] Restrictions of this kind are apparently subject to the power of modification conferred on the Lands Tribunal by section 84 of the Law of Property Act 1925 as amended.[88] **10–17**

(d) *Maintenance and repair of property*

The scheme can impose on persons from time to time occupying or interested in enfranchised property obligations in respect of the maintenance or repair (including redecoration) of the property.[89] Most schemes include repairing and redecoration obligations of this kind. However, **10–18**

---

[79] *i.e.* under s. 10(4), (5): see paras. 6–25 *et seq.*

[80] A covenantee who has parted with all property capable of being benefited cannot enforce a restrictive covenant against a successor of the original covenantor: *London County Council* v. *Allen* [1914] 3 K.B. 642, C.A.

[81] Under s. 19(7)(*b*): see para. 10–24.

[82] s. 19(8)(*a*).

[83] Thus reproducing the effect of s. 19(2), Landlord and Tenant Act 1927: see para. 10–15.

[84] *e.g. Re Grosvenor Belgravia Estate, supra.* This provision is important in cases where it is desirable to maintain uniformity of appearance.

[85] *e.g. Re Calthorpe Estate, Edgbaston, Birmingham* (1973) 26 P. & C.R. 120 (not reported on this point).

[86] *e.g. Re Grosvenor Belgravia Estate, supra.*

[87] *e.g. Re Dulwich College Estate's Application* (1973) E.G. 845 at p. 849. *Re Calthorpe Estate, Edgbaston, Birmingham, supra* (not reported on this point); *Re Grosvenor Belgravia Estate, supra*; *Re Prudential Kensington Estate* (1978) (unreported); *Re Phillimore Kensington Estate* (1980) (unreported, Oliver J.).

[88] See *Re Calthorpe Estate, Edgbaston, Birmingham,* supra at p. 127.

[89] s. 19(8)(*c*).

such obligations must be limited to the external or internal structural parts of the property, and internal non-structural repairs and internal decorations are outside the purposes of the section.[90] Other obligations under this head commonly found in schemes include the maintenance and repair of boundary walls and fences, and the maintenance and cultivation of the garden. It is considered that all such positive obligations can be enforced directly against successors-in-title of the enfranchising tenant,[91] the provisions of the scheme constituting statutory exceptions to the general rule that the burden of positive covenants do not run with the land.[92] However, the landlord can be given power to inspect,[93] and to carry out repairs himself[94] and recover the costs of so doing from the owner.[95] Most schemes include these powers, and this indirect method of enforcement is the most practical and effective.

Some schemes permit the landlord to redecorate the property as part of periodic communal redecoration, and to recover the appropriate share of the cost from the owner.[96] Provisions of this kind often require the enfranchised owner to contribute the whole or part of his share before the redecoration takes place, and this is essential in cases where "the landlord" is a residents' association without independent funds.[97]

(e) *Common parts*

10–19 The scheme can impose obligations on owners of property to repair and maintain parts of the area used in common,[98] or to contribute to the costs incurred by the landlord in doing so.[99] Many schemes include provisions of the latter kind, obliging the enfranchised owners to contribute to the costs of maintaining private roads and paths serving the area, communal gardens and other amenities.[1] Sometimes the scheme has set out these obligations in detail; but in other cases (particularly where the area concerned is a large one with several forms of common lease relating to

---

[90] *Re Sherwood Close (Barnes) Management Co's Application* [1972] Ch. 208.
[91] For a contrary view see (1975) 39 Conv. 398 (M. Vitoria) at p. 402.
[92] See Megarry and Wade *The Law of Real Property* (5th ed.), p. 741.
[93] s. 19(8)(*d*).
[94] s. 19(8)(*b*).
[95] s. 19(8)(*c*).
[96] *Pollock* v. *Westmacott* (1981) (*unreported*).
[97] *Re Uplands Estate Highfield, Southampton* (1975) (unreported, Templeman J.). *Re Nos. 1–22 Regents Park Terrace* (1976) (unreported).
[98] s. 19(8)(*c*).
[99] s. 19(8)(*d*).
[1] *Re Copse Hill Estate, Wimbledon* (1971) 219 E.G. 1604: *Re Grosvenor Belgravia Estate* (1973) (unreported, Pennycuick V.-C.); *Re Nos. 1–22 Regents Park Terrace, supra*; *Re Uplands Estate, Highfield, Southampton, supra*; *Re Prudential Kensington Estate* (1978) (unreported).

different parts of the area), the scheme has provided that the provisions of the existing lease concerning the common parts should be deemed to remain in force notwithstanding enfranchisement.[2] Several schemes, particularly those where the "landlord" is a tenants' association or management company,[3] or where it is intended that the freeholder's power should in due course be transferred to such an association or management company,[4] have been applied for, primarily in order to enable the provisions in the leases concerning maintenance of common parts to be effectively perpetuated.

The scheme can also impose regulations concerning the user of common parts.[5] In some schemes, a provision has been included enabling the landlord to make rules or by-laws for that purpose, and to revoke or vary those rules.[6]

(f) *Insurance and reinstatement*

Most schemes include an obligation on the enfranchised owner to insure to the full replacement value of the buildings comprised in the property, and to rebuild after destruction.[7] Some landlords have attempted to go further and reproduce powers in the leases to effect insurance themselves and recover the cost from the owner, or to oblige the tenant to insure with an insurance company nominated by the landlord (arguing that otherwise it would be difficult to enforce compliance with the obligation to insure satisfactorily). Such attempts have generally been rejected by the court as outside the purposes of the section and incompatible with freehold ownership.[8] **10–20**

(g) *Financial obligations*

The scheme may provide for any sums due to the landlord to be charged on the owner's property and for the landlord to enforce such a charge by means of the powers and remedies open to him under the Law of Property Act 1925, as if he were a mortgagee by deed and having powers of sale and leasing and of appointing a receiver.[9] Most schemes **10–21**

---

[2] *Re Calthorpe Estate, Edgbaston, Birmingham, supra* (not reported on this point); *Re Garden City Estate of Letchworth* (1972) (unreported).

[3] *Re Uplands Estate, Highfield, Southampton, supra.*

[4] *Re Nos. 1–22 Regents Park Terrace, supra.*

[5] s. 19(8)(*a*).

[6] *Re Copse Hill Estate, Wimbledon, supra.*

[7] *Re Sherwood Close (Barnes) Management Co's Application* [1972] Ch. 208; and see *Commission for New Towns* v. *Berman* (1973) 226 E.G. 617, and *Re Dulwich College Estate's Application* (1973) 231 E.G. 845 (confining obligation to rebuild to owners of freehold or leases of seven years).

[8] *Re Phillimore Kensington Estate* (1980) (unreported, Oliver J.); *Pollock* v. *Westmacott* (1981) (unreported, Foster J.).

[9] s. 19(8). The powers and remedies referred to are contained in L.P.A. 1925, ss. 99 and 101.

include such a provision. In 1972 the Building Societies Association pointed out that a building society is absolutely prohibited from advancing money on a property subject to a prior charge.[10] To avoid this difficulty, the Association suggested a proviso to be included in schemes postponing any charge arising under the scheme to any existing or future charge which is either a first charge or one under which the chargee is entitled to possession of the title-deeds.[11] That proviso has been incorporated in several schemes without opposition from the landlord,[12] but it is unsatisfactory, being both wider than necessary to meet the difficulty and insufficient to protect a second mortgagee. A preferable form of proviso, approved in other cases,[13] postpones any charge under the scheme to any other charge created before the charge under the scheme has both arisen and been registered (or made the subject of a notice or caution) under the Land Registration Act 1925 or the Land Charges Act 1972, as the case may be.

(h) *Other obligations*

10–22 Schemes approved by the court have included the following further obligations on enfranchised owners:

(i) To become a member of a residents' association or a management company.[14]
(ii) To give notice of devolution of interest to the landlord and pay a registration fee.[15]
(iii) To allow the landlord to enter in order to repair adjoining properties or common parts.
(iv) To pay a general management charge for the administration of the scheme.[16] It is usually impractical, or unduly cumbersome and expensive, for the costs of administration of the scheme to be satisfactorily apportioned from the landlord's administration costs relating to unenfranchised properties,[17] and many schemes there-

[10] By the Building Societies Act 1962, s. 32.
[11] The proviso is set out in *Re Abbots Park Estate (No. 2)* [1972] 1 W.L.R. 1597.
[12] *e.g. Re Abbots Park Estate (No. 2), supra.*
[13] *e.g. Re Calthorpe Estate Birmingham* (1973) 26 P. & C.R. 120 (not reported on this point); *Re Grosvenor Belgravia Estate* (1973) (unreported, Pennycuick V.-C.); *Re Prudential Kensington Estate* (1978) (unreported).
[14] *Re Abbots Park Estate* [1972] 1 W.L.R. 598 (residents' association), not following *Re Sherwood Close (Barnes) Management Co's Application* [1972] Ch. 208 (management company), which is considered wrongly decided on this point.
[15] *Re Dulwich College Estate's Application* (1973) 231 E.G. 847 at p. 851 (confining obligation to owners of freehold or leases of seven years or more); *Re Calthorpe Estate, Edgbaston, Birmingham* (1973) 26 P. & C.R. 120 (not reported on this point); *Re Grosvenor Belgravia Estate, supra.*
[16] But see *Re Dulwich College Estate's Application, supra* at p. 851.
[17] *Ibid.*

fore provide for a small annual fixed amount suitably index-linked against inflation.[18]

(v) To pay the landlord's costs specifically incurred in relation to the enfranchised owner's property (*e.g.* costs of considering applications for consent to alterations or change of user, preparation and service of notices requiring compliance with the scheme, making inspections to see if such notice complied with, and so on). It is considered that costs of this kind should not be included in the management charge payable by all enfranchised owners.[19]

(i) *Transfer of powers of landlord*

The scheme may provide for the transfer of the powers and rights thereunder of the landlord to a local authority or other body, including a management company or other body constituted for the purpose.[20] A transfer to a local authority would seldom be appropriate, and is not usually acceptable to the tenants; and in most schemes, in order to safeguard the interests of the tenants, the power to transfer is made exercisable only with the consent of the court. **10–23**

(j) *Representative bodies*

As mentioned above, a Minister's certificate may be granted to a tenant's representative body, either alone or jointly with the landlord or landlords.[21] In that event, the application to the High Court for a scheme may be made by the representative body alone, or by the landlord or landlords alone, or by both jointly.[22] Further, by leave of the High Court, an application may be proceeded with by the representative body alone or by the landlord or landlords alone, though not the applicant or applicants.[23] **10–24**

In the event of a certificate being granted to a representative body, where alone or jointly with the landlord or landlords, the scheme may, with the consent of the latter "or on such terms as to compensation or otherwise as appear to the High Court to be just" confer on the representative body the right to participate in the administration of the scheme or in the management of the landlord's property in the area. The author is not aware of any case in which compensation has been paid. The

[18] *Re Calthorpe Estate, Edgbaston, Birmingham, supra* (not reported on this point); *Re Grosvenor Belgravia Estate, supra*; *Re Prudential Kensington Estate, supra.*
[19] *Ibid.*
[20] s. 19(7)(*b*).
[21] s. 19(13).
[22] s. 19(13)(i).
[23] s. 19(13)(ii).

appropriate "participation" depends on the facts, but in cases where the landlord applies for a scheme it is usually limited to a right to be consulted,[24] as opposed to a sharing of executive rights of management.

Practical difficulties arise where the scheme is granted to a representative body alone, because the management powers over the relevant area are necessarily divided. The scheme will affect only enfranchised properties,[25] and unless and until a tenant acquires the freehold, he will remain liable only to the landlord under the covenants in the lease. Section 19 fails to deal with this problem. The possible solutions appear to be:

(i) The landlord can agree with the representative body to enforce the covenants in the leases on its behalf on being given a suitable indemnity as to costs. However, such an agreement would not bind the landlord's successors-in-title.

(ii) The landlord can grant an intermediate lease of the whole estate, subject to but with the benefit of the leases, thus reproducing the position in many flat schemes. But this involves the representative body in the collection and payment of rent; and it is for that, and other reasons, not usually suitable.

(iii) The landlord can grant a long lease of the common parts to the representative body at a peppercorn rent and enter into a covenant as under (i) above in that lease. It is considered that such a covenant "touches and concerns" the common parts and will be enforceable against a successor-in-title of the landlord. This is the best solution, which has been adopted in practice.[26]

In some cases, the certificate has been granted to the landlord alone, *e.g.* because at the date of application to the Minister there was no suitable representative body in existence, but the landlord is not concerned to manage the scheme himself. Examples occur where all the leases in the area are likely to be enfranchised, and there is a private road or other common parts which require maintenance, or it is agreed that a common painting scheme should be continued. In such cases, the convenient course has been for the landlord to apply for the scheme, but on the footing (sometimes incorporated in an undertaking contained in the order of the court) to transfer his powers immediately[27] to a suitable tenants' body.[28]

---

[24] As in *Re Calthorpe Estate, Edgbaston, Birmingham, supra* (where however the representative body had not been granted a certificate).

[25] See para. 10–12.

[26] *Re Uplands Estate, Highfield, Southampton, supra.*

[27] *i.e.* under s. 19(7)(*b*): see para. 10–23.

[28] This course was adopted in *Re Nos. 1–22 Regents Park Terrace, supra.*

5. Registration and Interim Provisions

Registration

Both the Minister's certificate and an approved scheme are registrable as local land charges under the Land Charges Act 1972.[29] Where an approved scheme has been duly registered, its obligations, both positive and negative, are enforceable against the enfranchising tenant and his successors in title.[30] The conveyance or registered land transfer must be drafted accordingly, and the enfranchisement price must be adjusted to take account of the scheme[31]; but it is generally considered that the benefits to the tenant of a scheme fully compensate for its burdens, and that the existence of a scheme does not materially affect the price.[32] **10–25**

Interim provisions

Suspension of tenant's claim to acquire freehold

It would obviously have been inconvenient if a tenant could acquire the freehold of his house and premises before the landlord had a proper opportunity to obtain the approval of a scheme. The 1967 Act therefore provides for the suspension of the tenant's claim to acquire the freehold if the Minister has given a certificate, or an application for one is pending.[33] The landlord need take no further proceedings in relation to a tenant's Notice of Leaseholder's Claim to acquire the freehold, beyond those which appear to him reasonable in the circumstances.[34] However, the tenant can withdraw such a Notice at any time during its suspension, without being liable for the landlord's conveyancing and valuation costs[35] (which a tenant usually has to pay if he withdraws his Notice),[36] and without being precluded from serving another such Notice within the following three years.[37] **10–26**

Cesser of suspension

The suspension of the tenant's claim ceases, and the tenant's Notice to acquire the freehold becomes fully effective, on the approval of a scheme

[29] s. 19(10).
[30] s. 19(10)(*a*).
[31] s. 19(10)(*b*).
[32] *Silver* v. *Holland House Estates Trustees* (1983) 266 E.G. 913 at p. 1009. L.V.T., affirmed on this point (*sub. nom. Lowther* v. *Strandberg*) (1985) 273 E.G. 53 at p. 55, L.T.
[33] s. 19(14).
[34] s. 19(14)(*a*).
[35] s. 19(14)(*b*).
[36] s. 9(4).
[37] *Cf.* s. 9(3)(*b*), which appears to be inapplicable.

by the court or the happening of any event as a result of which it is no longer possible to obtain a scheme.[38]

Extended lease

A tenant's claim for an extended lease is not suspended under the provisions discussed above.[39] The claim must be duly proceeded with, and an extended lease granted, notwithstanding that application has been made for a certificate or a scheme. It is presumably envisaged that all the landlord's powers of management which are likely to be included in an approved scheme will be incorporated into the extended lease.

[38] The events are listed in s. 19(15).
[39] s. 19(14) does not apply.

CHAPTER 11

SUB-TENANTS

IT frequently happens that a tenant who is duly qualified to claim the benefits of the 1967 Act does not hold directly from the freeholder, but as a sub-tenant through one or more intermediate tenancies. With one exception mentioned below, a qualified sub-tenant is entitled to all the benefits of the Act[1] and it is immaterial that his sub-tenancy may not extend to the whole of the premises demised by one or more of the intermediate tenancies. Conversely, all the intermediate tenants (as well as the freeholder) have all the rights and obligations of "the landlord" under the Act, in so far as their interests are affected.[2] The relevant machinery of the Act is adapted to cases where there is a qualified sub-tenant by the detailed provisions of Schedule 1 to the 1967 Act, which are considered in this Chapter. **11–01**

Exception

There is one exception to the foregoing. The rights conferred by the Act cannot be exercised in any case (which, it is thought, is encountered only very rarely) where all three of the following conditions apply: **11–02**

(a) The otherwise duly qualified sub-tenant's interest was granted by sub-demise out of a superior tenancy other than a long tenancy at a low rent (ascertained presumably at the date of the sub-demise which, it appears, need not be immediate from the superior tenancy).
(b) The grant was made in breach of the terms of the superior tenancy.
(c) There has been no waiver of the breach by the superior landlord (*e.g.* by acceptance of rent with knowledge of the breach).[3]

1. GENERAL PROVISIONS

"The claimant"

In Schedule 1 to the 1967 Act, a sub-tenant who serves a Notice of Leaseholder's Claim to acquire the freehold or an extended lease is **11–03**

---

[1] s. 5(4).
[2] Sched. 1, para. 1(1)(*a*).
[3] s. 5(4).

referred to as "the claimant."[4] For convenience such a sub-tenant will be similarly referred to in this Chapter.

Reversionary tenancy

11–04 A tenancy which is reversionary on the claimant's tenancy (that is to say, a future tenancy limited to take effect only on or after the expiry of the claimant's tenancy), is treated as if it were a concurrent intermediate tenancy.[5] Such a reversionary tenancy will, however, be void if limited to take effect more than 21 years from the date of its grant[6]; but a contract for such a tenancy is valid, so long as, when granted, the tenancy will take effect within 21 years of the date of the grant.[7]

"The reversioner"

11–05 There would often be considerable practical difficulties if the owners of the freehold and all the intermediate tenancies each had to deal separately with the claimant. The 1967 Act therefore provides that one of those persons, generally the one with the greatest monetary interest in the reversion (ignoring the rent payable during the claimant's sub-tenancy), is to be selected in order to conduct the proceedings arising out of the claimant's Notice of Leaseholder's Claim on behalf of all of them.[8] This person is defined as "the reversioner," and the persons for whom he is authorised to act are defined as "the other landlords."[9]

The reversioner is, prima facie, the intermediate tenant who has an expectation[10] of at least 30 years' possession of the house after the termination of the sub-tenancy,[11] on the assumption that the claimant's tenancy would terminate on the later of (a) its term date[12] (or, in the case of a tenancy which has already been extended, its original term date), and (b) the date of service of the Notice of Leaseholder's Claim.[13] If there are two or more such intermediate tenancies, the reversioner will be the holder of that one which is most immediate to the claimant's sub-tenancy.[14] And where, as is commonly the case, there is no such

---

[4] Sched. 1, para. 1(1).
[5] *Ibid.* para. 1(2).
[6] L.P.A. 1925, s. 149(3).
[7] *Re Strand and Savoy Properties* [1960] Ch. 582; *Weg Motors Ltd.* v. *Hales* [1962] Ch. 49, C.A.
[8] Sched. 1, para. 1(1)(*b*).
[9] *Ibid.* para. 1(3).
[10] On the assumption that his tenancy will terminate on its term date: *ibid.* para. 13(1)(*b*).
[11] *Ibid.* para. 2(*a*).
[12] On the earlier expiry of a notice to quit served before the date or the Notice of Leaseholder's Claim: *ibid.* para. 13(2).
[13] Sched. 1, para. 13(1)(*a*). For the meanings of "term date" and "original term date," see para. 3–12.
[14] *Ibid.* para. 2(*a*).

intermediate tenancy with an expectation of 30 years' possession, the freeholder is the reversioner.[15] Where there is a Crown interest in the property, the appropriate Crown authority[16] has power to act as "the reversioner."[17]

However, any of the other landlords may apply to the county court for the appointment of himself or any other person as the reversioner in place of the person so designated.[18] The court can make such appointment, on such terms and conditions as it thinks fit, if it considers: 11-06

(a) That having regard to the respective interests of the other landlords, or the absence or incapacity of the reversioner, or other special circumstances, one of the other landlords ought to act as the reversioner; or
(b) That the reversioner is unwilling to act, and that one of the other landlords could appropriately replace him and is willing to do so; or
(c) That by reason of complications in the title, the statutory provisions designating "the reversioner" are inapplicable.

The court may also remove the reversioner and appoint another person in his place if it appears to the court proper to do so having regard to any delay or default, actual or apprehended, on the part of the reversioner; and an application for this purpose can be made by the claimant as well as by any of the other landlords.[19]

Service of Notice of Leaseholder's Claim

Detailed provisions are made for the service of the claimant's Notice of Leaseholder's Claim and copies on all the persons interested in the property, either by the claimant himself or by the recipient of any such Notice or copy.[20] These provisions, which are intended to ensure that every person concerned will be aware both of the Notice and also of the interests of the other persons concerned, have already been discussed.[21] 11-07

Powers and duties of the reversioner

Except with regard to applications for possession,[22] and as mentioned 11-08

---

[15] *Ibid.* para. 2(*b*).
[16] As to which see s. 33(2).
[17] Sched. 1, para. 14(1).
[18] *Ibid.* para. 3(1).
[19] *Ibid.* para. 3(2).
[20] Sched. 3, para. 8.
[21] See para. 5-06.
[22] As to which see Chap. 8.

below,[23] the reversioner has power, and also (it appears) a duty,[24] to act on behalf of all the other landlords in all matters arising from the service of the claimant's Notice of Leaseholder's Claim.[25] These include the question of whether or not the claimant is duly qualified to acquire the freehold or an extended lease, and the contents of any transfer or conveyance or any extended lease. They also include all matters concerning title, and the ascertainment and payment of the purchase price, but subject to the modifications discussed below.[26] The authority of the reversioner extends to the taking and defending of legal proceedings on behalf of the other landlords as well as himself.[27] It is not necessary to join any of the other landlords as parties to any such proceedings, but it is usually advisable to send them copies of the proceedings. The acts of the reversioner in any such matter are fully binding on the other landlords.[28] However, if there is a dispute as to how the reversioner should act, either he or any of the other landlords can apply to the court for directions.[29] Provided that the reversioner acts in good faith and with reasonable care and diligence, he is not liable for any loss or damage to any of the other landlords.[30]

In particular, it is provided that (except as regards the Crown[31]) the reversioner "may on behalf and in the name of the other landlords execute" any conveyance (or registered land transfer) or extended lease.[32] The other landlords must be named as parties to such conveyance or extended lease, which must be appropriately worded so as to operate over their respective separate interests. But the reversioner can himself execute the conveyance or extended lease, at any rate by signing his name and adding "on behalf and in the name of the Duke of Barsetshire" (if the latter is one of the other landlords), or apparently even simply by signing "Barsetshire" in his own handwriting. However, this procedure is unsatisfactory from the point of view not only of the claimant, who will be unable to know if the reversioner has carried out the statutory duties laid down,[33] but also of the other landlords. It is accordingly suggested that, except in cases of difficulty, the relevant deeds should be properly executed by all the parties named in them in the usual way.

---

[23] See paras. 11–09 and 11–14.
[24] The wording of Sched. 1, para. 1(1)(*b*) seems to be mandatory.
[25] Sched. 1 para. 1(1)(*b*).
[26] See respectively paras. 11–09 and 11–14.
[27] Sched. 1, para. 4(1)(*b*).
[28] *Ibid.* para. 4(2).
[29] *Ibid.* para. 4(2).
[30] *Ibid.* para. 4(4).
[31] *Ibid.* para. 14(1) proviso.
[32] *Ibid.* para. 4(1)(*a*).
[33] *Quaere* whether the claimant will receive a good title if the reversioner has not done so; probably he will, but the position is not clear, particularly where the reversioner does not act in good faith.

Title

Prima facie, the title of the other landlords will be deduced by the reversioner,[34] and the other landlords must supply him with all the necessary information and assistance for that purpose.[35] However, a landlord may deal with the deducing, evidencing and verifying of his title directly with the claimant, if he gives written notice to the reversioner and the claimant to that effect; and moreover, he must do so if the claimant so requires by a written notice given to him and to the reversioner.[36] In practice, it is nearly always more convenient if the other landlords deal directly with the claimant on all matters of the landlord's title. In any event, each of the other landlords is entitled to have his reasonable conveyancing costs paid by the claimant.[37] In addition, each of the other landlords is entitled to be separately represented in any legal proceedings in which his title comes into question, *e.g.* if there is a dispute as to what easements and restrictive covenants affecting or benefiting other land of his ought to be included in the transfer or conveyance of the freehold.[38] 11–09

Covenant against assignment or sub-letting

An intermediate tenancy may be subject to a covenant on the part of the tenant not to assign or sub-let, either absolute or without the consent of the landlord. Such a covenant can be ignored. On the claimant acquiring the freehold, he will simultaneously acquire the relevant landlord's interest, so that the question of whether there will be a breach of covenant becomes academic. Moreover, it is settled that the compulsory sale of a lease under statutory provisions does not constitute a breach of the covenant anyway.[39] It would appear that a compulsory sub-letting would similarly not constitute a breach, but the matter is put beyond doubt by a specific provision to that effect.[40] 11–10

Duties of other landlords

Each of other landlords must give the reversioner such information and assistance as he requires, except in so far as the claimant deals directly with him in relation to matters of title and the ascertainment of the purchase price on the acquisition of the freehold.[41] Where the claimant is acquiring the freehold, each landlord must also make available on 11–11

[34] Sched. 1, para. 1(1)(*a*).
[35] *Ibid.* para. 5(3)(*a*).
[36] *Ibid.* para. 5(2).
[37] ss. 9(4), 14(2); and see paras. 6–32 and 7–16.
[38] Sched. 1, para. 5(1).
[39] *Slipper* v. *Tottenham and Hampstead Junction Ry.* (1867) L.R. 4 Eq. 112.
[40] Sched. 1, para. 12(1).
[41] *Ibid.* para. 5(5)(*a*).

completion all deeds and other documents which must then be handed over to the claimant, including the land certificate in the case of registered land.[42] He must also make "such contribution as may be just" towards the reversioner's costs and expenses which are not recoverable, or which cannot in fact be recovered, from the claimant.[43]

Missing landlord

11–12 If any of the other landlords cannot be found, or the landlord's identity cannot be ascertained, the reversioner must apply to the court for directions.[44] But subject to any such directions, the reversioner must proceed as in other cases.[45] The reversioner can execute the conveyance or extended lease on behalf of the missing landlord by such description as will enable him and his interest to be identified.[46] In such a case, it is suggested that the missing landlord should not be made a party, but the reversioner should be expressed to convey his interest, or concur in the grant of the extended lease (as the case may be), in pursuance of the power conferred on him by the Act. If the freehold is conveyed, the purchase price of the missing landlord's interest must be paid into court[47] (*i.e.* the county court).[48] Any such conveyance or extended lease is effective even if the missing landlord turns out to be the Crown.[49]

Landlord's proceedings for possession

11–13 The reversioner has no authority to bring proceedings on behalf of another landlord for possession under section 17 (redevelopment) or section 18 (own or family's occupation). But any landlord, including a reversionary tenant whose interest will commence only after the expiration of the claimant's interest, is entitled to make his own application for that purpose.[50]

2. Acquisition of Freehold

Purchase price

11–14 A separate price must be ascertained for each of the separate interests

---

[42] *Ibid.* para. 5(5)(*b*).
[43] *Ibid.* para. 5(6).
[44] *Ibid.* para. 4(3).
[45] *Ibid.* para. 4(3)(*a*).
[46] *Ibid.* para. 4(3)(*b*).
[47] *Ibid.* para. 4(3)(*c*).
[48] Compare the position where no landlord at all can be found, when the purchase price must be paid into the High Court: s. 27(3), and see para. 17–24.
[49] Sched. 1, para. 14(2).
[50] Sched. 1, para. 6(1).

of all the landlords.[51] Except in the case of a "minor superior tenancy" (discussed below[52]), each separate price will be ascertained on the usual basis set out in section 9 of the 1967 Act as amended, modified as appropriate to relate it to the sale of the interest in question. It is not correct to ascertain a single price for whole reversion to the claimant's tenancy on that basis and then to apportion it between the separate reversionary interests.[53] Prima facie, the reversioner has full power to agree each separate price on behalf of the other landlords,[54] and such agreement is binding on them.[55] But any of the other landlords may deal directly with the claimant for the purpose of agreeing the price payable for his interest, on giving written notice to that effect to the reversioner and the claimant.[56] Moreover, whether he does so or not, he can require the reversioner to apply to a leasehold valuation tribunal for that price to be fixed by that tribunal. He is entitled to be separately represented in such proceedings, and in any other proceedings relating to the price payable for his interest.[57] The claimant is obliged to pay his reasonable valuation costs.[58]

The reversioner can also accept payment of the purchase price on behalf of any other landlord.[59] But the latter may require the claimant to pay the purchase price in respect of his interest direct to him or his agent.[60] However, if thereafter he or his agent fails to attend the completion, after being given details of the time and place fixed for completion, then (unless he has made other arrangements to receive the purchase price and has notified the reversioner of them) his purchase price can be validly accepted by the reversioner who can give a good receipt for it.[61] The other landlord can also be separately represented in any legal proceedings concerning the payment of the purchase price.[62]

Contents of conveyance

All the landlords must be made parties to the transfer or conveyance, and must convey their respective interests to the claimant.[63] All the **11–15**

---

[51] Sched. 1, para. 7(1)(*b*); *Silverman* v. *Catherine Investments Ltd.* (1984) 271 E.G. 381, L.V.T.; *Pilgrim* v. *Central Estates (Belgravia) Ltd.* (1986) 278 E.G. 1373, L.V.T.
[52] See para. 11–17.
[53] *Jones* v. *Wrotham Park Settled Estates* [1980] A.C. 74, at pp. 108H, 111D.
[54] Sched. 1, para. 1(1)(*b*).
[55] *Ibid.* para. 4(2).
[56] *Ibid.* para. 5(3) as amended by Housing Act 1980, Sched. 22, para. 10.
[57] *Ibid.* para. 5(1).
[58] s. 9(4)(*e*); and see para. 6–33.
[59] Sched. 1, para. 1(1)(*b*).
[60] *Ibid.* para. 5(4).
[61] *Ibid.* para. 5(4).
[62] *Ibid.* para. 5(1).
[63] *Ibid.* para. 1(1)(*a*). See Precedent No. 20, Appendix A.

provisions regarding the contents of the transfer or conveyance,[64] rentcharges[65] and mortgages[66] are applicable, in so far as they are relevant to the particular landlord's interests. But an intermediate tenant need not make any payment towards the redemption of a rentcharge[67] where that is necessary.[68] Nor need any landlord make any payment towards the discharge of a mortgage affecting the interest of another landlord[69] where that is necessary.[70]

Nominal reversions

Generally

11–16 In many cases, an intermediate tenancy has only a nominal reversion. Thus, a common type of development involves the grant of a 99 year lease to a builder, who erects a house (or more frequently, a number of houses) on it and then grants an underlease (or a number of underleases) for the residue of the 99 year term, less a few days. Prima facie, the purchase price for any such intermediate tenancy of a house, unless it is a "minor superior tenancy" (considered below), must be ascertained and paid by the claimant in the usual way.[71] However, as there is generally no value in his reversion apart from the rent it carries, the purchase price is in practice limited to the capitalised value of his profit rent, *i.e.* the difference between the rent he receives from the sub-tenant and the rent (after any necessary apportionment[72]) which he has to pay to the freeholder.[73] It is considered that this is the position even if the valuation falls to be made under section 9(1A), for a nominal reversion would probably not affect any share of the "marriage value" of the various interests in the house.[74] If there is no profit rent, the purchase price is nominal only.[75]

It was formerly possible for the claimant to require that the profit rent should instead be reserved as an irredeemable terminable rentcharge,[76] but that right was repealed by the Rentcharges Act 1977.

---

64 *Ibid.* para. 7(1)(*a*).
65 *Ibid.* para. 7(1)(*b*).
66 *Ibid.* para. 7(1)(*c*).
67 *Ibid.* para. 7(2).
68 *i.e.* under s. 11(2): see para. 12–03.
69 Sched. 1, para. 7(2).
70 *i.e.* under s. 12(8), proviso: see para. 13–02.
71 See para. 11–14.
72 By the county court or a leasehold valuation tribunal: s. 20(3) or s. 21(2)(*b*).
73 *Cf.* para. 9–31.
74 See further para. 9–55.
75 See, *e.g.* *Hameed* v. *Hussain* (1977) 242 E.G. 1063, L.T. (decided before the enactment of Sched. 1, para. 7A).
76 Sched. 1, para. 8, repealed by the Rentcharges Act 1977, s. 17(2) and Sched. 2.

"Minor superior tenancy"

In the case of a "minor superior tenancy," which is defined[77] as a tenancy superior to the claimant's tenancy having an expectation of possession of not more than one month and in respect of which the profit rent (after any necessary apportionment[78]) is not more than £5 per year, the purchase price is calculated by applying a formula instead of on the basis set out in section 9 of the 1967 Act.[79] The formula, which is the same as that used for calculating the redemption price of a rentcharge under the Rentcharges Act 1977, is: 11–17

$$P = £\frac{R}{Y} - \frac{R}{Y(1+Y)^n}$$

where P = the price payable, R = the profit rent, Y = the yield expressed as a decimal fraction from $2\frac{1}{2}$ per cent. Consols (the price of which is taken to be the middle market price at the close of business on the last trading day in the week before service of the Notice of Leaseholder's Claim to the freehold[80]), and n = the period expressed in years (counting any part of a year as a whole year) which the minor superior tenancy would have to run if it were not being extinguished by enfranchisement.[81]

The first part of this formula ($£\frac{R}{Y}$) capitalises the profit rent as if in perpetuity, and the second part then makes an appropriate deduction to compensate for its earlier termination. The formula applies whether the valuation is being made under section 9(1) or section 9(1A), and in the latter case thus automatically deprives the holder of the minor superior tenancy of any share in the "marriage value" of the various interests in the house.[82]

Right to withdraw Notice

A sub-tenant may withdraw his Notice of Leaseholder's Claim to acquire the freehold, within one month after all the purchase prices payable to the landlords have been ascertained.[83] But he can do so only in respect of the interests of all the landlords, and not those of some only.[84] 11–18

---

[77] In Sched. 1, para. 7A(2).
[78] *Ibid.* para. 7A(3), (4). If the profit rent is subject to variation, the tenancy will not be within the definition of minor superior tenancy.
[79] Sched. 1, para. 7A, inserted into the 1967 Act by the Housing Act 1980, Sched. 21, para. 6.
[80] *Ibid.* para. 7A(6).
[81] *Ibid.* para. 7A(5).
[82] See para. 9–55.
[83] s. 9(3); see para. 6–32.
[84] Sched. 1, para. 9.

3. Extended Lease

Person to grant extended lease

11–19 The extended lease must be granted by the landlord "having an interest sufficient in point of duration, which is not superior to another such interest"[85]; that is to say, the most immediate tenant with more than 50 years' reversion to the claimant's tenancy, or if there is no such tenant, the freeholder. Such grantor will usually, but not necessarily, be "the reversioner."[86] If there is no one landlord having such an interest in the whole of the house and premises, then those having appropriate interests in separate parts must grant the extended lease jointly, and for that purpose are treated as jointly entitled to the whole until immediately after the grant.[87]

Contents of extended lease

11–20 Although it is not specifically so provided, it seems clear that all the landlords who hold subsisting tenancies intermediate between those of the grantor and the claimant should also be joined as parties. The extended lease will have effect as if there had been a surrender and re-grant of any such subsisting intermediate tenancies, and all the covenants and other provisions of the lease must be framed accordingly.[88] But if the claimant himself has an intermediate tenancy, even though it may be superior to that of the grantor, the lease must include a surrender of that tenancy by him, without any re-grant.[89]

The extended lease must contain the provisions for rent review permitted by the 1967 Act,[90] modified as necessary to ensure that the grantor and the intermediate landlords (or, it appears, any of them) will be able to call for a review of the rent.[91] Similarly, provision must be made in respect of the cost of any landlord's obligations as to services, maintenance or insurance.[92] And the lease must contain a declaration that no long tenancy created immediately or derivatively by way of sub-demise shall confer on the sub-tenant the right to acquire the freehold or an extended lease as against any of the claimant's landlords (including any who are not parties to the extended lease).[93]

---

[85] *Ibid.* para. 10(1).
[86] See para. 11–05.
[87] Sched. 1, para. 10(3).
[88] *Ibid.* para. 10(2). The intermediate tenancies thus become "leases of the reversion."
[89] *Ibid.* para. 11(1).
[90] See s. 15(2) and para. 9–03.
[91] Sched. 1, para. 10(4).
[92] s. 15(3) and Sched. 1, para. 10(4).
[93] s. 16(4) and Sched. 1, para. 10(4).

Onerous or valueless intermediate tenancy

A person holding an intermediate tenancy which is onerous, or of little or no value, is enabled to surrender his tenancy when the extended lease is granted to the claimant. An intermediate tenancy comes within this category if the rent payable by the intermediate tenant in respect of the house and premises (after any necessary apportionment[94]) is either greater,[95] or less by no more than £4 a year,[96] than the like rent he will receive after the extended lease has been granted (which may or may not be material for this purpose). In that event, the intermediate tenant may give written notice to his immediate landlord of his desire to surrender; if he does so, and neither of them is the reversioner, he must also give a similar notice to the reversioner. The extended lease must thereupon contain an actual surrender of the intermediate tenancy without any regrant.[97] Moreover, if the result of such a surrender would be that the difference in the rents payable by and to another intermediate tenant becomes as above, he too can exercise this power of surrender. If the person to grant the extended lease surrenders his interest under this power, he will be replaced for that purpose by the next superior landlord.[98] **11–21**

In addition, any intermediate tenant may, by a like notice, require that the extended lease confers on him the right to surrender his interest, if, by reason of a revision of the rent payable under the extended lease, his rent will thereafter be either greater, or less by no more than £4 a year, than the rent in respect of the house and premises, or if his rent will be such after another intermediate tenant has similarly surrendered his interest.[99] Until there is a prospect of the revised rent being less than the rent currently payable under the claimant's sub-tenancy for the house and premises, it is difficult to envisage how this right can be of any practical value.

There is nothing in the 1967 Act to prevent an intermediate tenant contracting out of his right of surrender. A covenant to that effect in the intermediate lease was an essential part of the device for increasing the purchase price payable by the enfranchising tenant successfully employed by the landlords in *Jones* v. *Wrotham Park Settled Estates*[1] considered below.

---

[94] Sched. 1, para. 11(5).
[95] *Ibid.* para. 11(2)(*a*).
[96] *Ibid.* para. 11(2)(*b*).
[97] *Ibid.* para. 11(2).
[98] *Ibid.* para. 11(4).
[99] *Ibid.* para. 11(3).
[1] [1980] A.C. 74.

4. Leasehold Reform Act 1979

Background

11–22 This Act was passed to reverse the effect of the decision of the House of Lords in *Jones v. Wrotham Park Settled Estates*,[2] and can only be properly understood by reference to the facts of that case. These were complicated, but the essential features can be shortly summarised as follows:

(1) The tenant held a lease directly from the freeholders of a house for a term expiring in the year 2048 at the yearly rent of £15, and was entitled to acquire the freehold under the 1967 Act.
(2) Shortly before service of the tenant's Notice of Leaseholder's Claim, the freeholder granted an intermediate lease to an associated company for a term of 300 years, at a peppercorn rent during the tenant's lease and a rack rent thereafter.
(3) The intermediate lease contained a provision that if the company granted a sub-lease, the rent would be increased to a rack rent for the duration of the sub-lease.
(4) The intermediate lease also contained a covenant by the company not to exercise the power of surrender discussed above.[3]
(5) It was agreed between the parties that if the intermediate lease was ignored, the purchase price under section 9 of the Act would be £300, but if it was not ignored and it was assumed that pursuant to (3) above the rent payable by the company was increased to a rack rent, the purchase prices under the section would be £4,000 for the freehold and nil for the intermediate term (which on that assumption clearly had a substantial negative value).

The House of Lords, reversing the Court of Appeal, held, first, that the assumption required by section 9(1) that the tenant's lease had been extended under the 1967 Act necessarily involved the further assumption that the company had granted a sub-lease and that consequently the rent payable under the intermediate lease had been increased to a rack rent[4]; and secondly, that the anti-avoidance provisions of the 1967 Act[5] did not affect the matter. The purchase price for the freehold was accordingly determined at £4,000.

---

[2] [1980] A.C. 74. For a full discussion see (1982) 45 M.L.R. 121 (G. Woodman).
[3] See para. 11–21.
[4] This point had in fact been conceded by counsel for the tenant before the Lands Tribunal and the Court of Appeal, but the correctness of the concession had been doubted in the Court of Appeal, particularly by Goff L.J.: see at p. 87. However, the point was fully argued before the House of Lords, which decided that counsel's concession had been rightly made: see p. 111C. See further para. 9–18.
[5] Under s. 23, considered in Chap. 17.

The 1979 Act

The 1979 Act was passed "to provide further protection, for a tenant in possession claiming to acquire the freehold under the Leasehold Reform Act 1967, against artificial inflation of the price he has to pay."[6] It provides that as against a tenant in possession who serves a Notice of Leaseholder's Claim to the freehold, the price payable 11–23

> "cannot be made less favourable by reference to a transaction since February 15, 1979[7] involving the creation or transfer of an interest superior to (whether or not preceding) his own, or an alteration since that date of the terms on which such an interest is held."[8]

It applies to all Notices of Leaseholder's Claim served on or after April 4, 1979,[9] and any prior Notices served before that date unless the price had been agreed or determined before that date.[10]

The wording of the 1979 Act is hardly satisfactory, perhaps as a result of the haste with which it was enacted.[11] It is difficult to discern any purpose in the words "in possession," for a non-occupying tenant cannot validly serve a Notice of Leaseholder's Claim anyway. Possibly, the words confine the benefit of the 1979 Act to tenants remaining in possession at the date when the purchase price is agreed or determined, but such a limitation is illogical and serves no useful purpose. "Less favourable" presumably means "higher," and "by reference to" seems to mean "as a result of." "An interest superior to (whether or not preceding) his own" means an intermediate tenancy, whether granted before or after the claimant's tenancy. Such an intermediate tenancy is not invalidated, and remains fully effective as between all persons interested in the property. All the 1979 Act does is to provide that it cannot have the effect of increasing the purchase price above what it would have been if it had not been granted.[12]

---

[6] See the preamble to the Act; and see also para. 1–19.

[7] The date the Bill was first introduced in Parliament. This limitation prevented the 1979 Act applying to the tenant in the *Jones* case: see para. 1–19.

[8] Leasehold Reform Act 1979, s. 1(1).

[9] The date the 1979 Act was passed.

[10] *Ibid.* s. 1(3).

[11] See para. 1–19.

[12] See further (1979) 123 S.J. 311 (T. Aldridge); (1979) 19 R.V.R. 308 (C. Lewsley).

CHAPTER 12

RENTCHARGES

12–01 THE 1967 Act makes special provision for cases where the freehold interest is subject to a rentcharge (otherwise called a "chief rent"[1] or a "fee farm rent"). In general, if the tenant exercises his right to acquire the freehold, the landlord can, at his option, convey either subject to the rentcharge or free from it.

Conveyance subject to rentcharge

12–02 Although a rentcharge is an "incumbrance"[2] the conveyance[3] can, except in two special cases (dealt with below), nevertheless be made subject to it.[4] Moreover, if the rentcharge affects other property as well as the house and premises, the landlord can apportion the rentcharge in accordance with section 190(1) of the Law of Property Act 1925.[5] Such an apportionment requires the consent of the tenant, but the tenant may not withhold his consent unreasonably.[6] On the other hand, the consent of the rentcharge owner to an apportionment is not required, although unless it is obtained, the apportionment is not binding on the rentcharge owner and he retains his full rights over all the properties charged.[7] However, the freeholders for the time being of each of the properties amongst which the rentcharge is apportioned without consent have statutory rights against each other in the event of non-payment.[8] In practice, reliance is usually placed on those statutory rights, and the consent of the rentcharge owner is not obtained. If the conveyance is made subject to the rentcharge, this will, of course, be reflected in the purchase price.[9]

Conveyance free from rentcharge

12–03 As an alternative, the landlord can arrange for the redemption of the rentcharge.[10] There is usually no difficulty in doing this with the agreement of the rentcharge owner. But in default of such agreement, the

---

[1] Particularly in Lancashire.
[2] s. 8(2).
[3] Or registered land transfer, as the case may be.
[4] s. 8(4)(*b*).
[5] s. 11(1).
[6] s. 11(1).
[7] L.P.A. 1925, s. 190(1).
[8] *Ibid.* s. 190(2).
[9] s. 9(1)(*b*), (1A)(*e*).
[10] s. 11(1).

landlord can obtain the compulsory redemption of the rentcharge under sections 8 to 10 of the Rentcharges Act 1977 on paying to the person named[11] in the Secretary of State's "instructions for redemption" under that Act[12] (or in certain cases into court[13]), the "redemption price"[14] specified therein[15] after any necessary apportionment has been made,[16] thus obtaining a redemption certificate[17] under that Act.

Exceptions

There are two exceptions to the above: 12–04

(a) *Rentcharge under settlement*

Some rentcharges arise under settlements and take effect in equity only, *e.g.* a wife's "pin-money" rentcharge under a marriage settlement. Such rentcharges are capable of being overreached, and the conveyance of the freehold must normally be made free from them.[18] It is, however, submitted that a landlord who is absolutely entitled subject only to a family rentcharge may convey subject to it (upon giving a full indemnity) under section 1(1) of the Law of Property (Amendment) Act 1926,[19] and certainly it would be most unreasonable of a tenant not to accept such a conveyance.

(b) *Rentcharge exceeding current rent*

The conveyance may not be made subject to a rentcharge exceeding the rent[20] currently payable in respect of the house and premises[21] under the tenant's lease at the date of service of his Notice of Leaseholder's Claim.[22] However, only the amount of the rentcharge for which the tenant will become primarily liable is taken into account for this purpose, and there must be ignored any amounts charged on or apportioned to other

---

[11] Who will be the rentcharge owner's mortgagee, or (if none) the trustees of any settlement affecting the rentcharge or (if none) the rentcharge owner: Rentcharges Act 1977, s. 10(2).
[12] *Ibid.* s. 9(4)(*b*).
[13] *Ibid.* s. 10(4).
[14] Calculated under the formula set out in *ibid.* s. 10(1). The same formula is used to ascertain the price payable for "a minor superior tenancy" under L.R.A. 1967, Sched. 1, para. 7A (inserted by Housing Act 1980, Sched. 21, para. 6), as to which see para. 11–07.
[15] Rentcharges Act 1977, s. 9(4)(*a*).
[16] L.P.A. 1925, s. 191(7).
[17] *Ibid.* ss. 8(1), 9(5).
[18] s. 8(4)(*b*).
[19] As to which, see Megarry and Wade *The Law of Real Property* (5th ed.), p. 347–8.
[20] *i.e.* rent reserved as such, excluding any service, maintenance or insurance rent: ss. 4(1)(*b*), (*c*) and 11(2).
[21] After any necessary apportionment: ss. 4(5) and 11(2).
[22] s. 11(2).

property,[23] or against which the landlord has the benefit of an indemnity to which the tenant will become entitled[24]; and there must also be ignored any rentcharge for which the tenant is already primarily liable by reason of a provision for indemnity in his lease.[25] Unless the landlord is able to arrange that there will be no excess in some other way (*e.g.* by apportioning part of the rentcharge to other property[26]), he must procure the redemption at least of the excess.[27] There is no provision for compulsory redemption of part only of a rentcharge affecting a single property, so the landlord will be able to redeem the excess alone only by agreement with the owner of the rentcharge. Otherwise, he will have to redeem compulsorily the whole of the rentcharge as it affects the house and premises. In most cases of difficulty[28] the landlord can require the tenant to pay into the County Court[29] for the district in which the property is situated[30] up to the whole of his purchase price towards the redemption (but must pay any balance necessary himself).[31] The conveyance will thereupon discharge the house and premises from the rentcharge, and the sole remedies of the rentcharge owner will be against the fund in court.[32]

Reservation of rentcharge

12–05 There can no longer be any reservation of a new rentcharge.[33] The former right of an enfranchising sub-tenant to require the reservation of a rentcharge in lieu of paying a purchase price for the intermediate tenant's interest in certain cases where there was an intermediate tenancy with only a nominal reversion,[34] has been abolished.[35]

---

[23] s. 11(3)(*a*).
[24] s. 11(3)(*b*).
[25] s. 11(8).
[26] Under L.P.A. 1925, s. 190(1).
[27] s. 11(2).
[28] *i.e.* those arising for any of the reasons mentioned in s. 13(2) (as to which see para. 13–10): s. 11(4). It is thought that these reasons in practice cover all cases of difficulty.
[29] For the procedure, see C.C.R. 1981, Ord. 46, r. 20(2).
[30] C.C.R. Ord. 46, r. 20(2)(*d*).
[31] s. 11(4), (6), (7).
[32] s. 11(5).
[33] Rentcharges Act 1977, s. 1.
[34] Granted by L.R.A. 1967, Sched. 1, para. 8, now repealed.
[35] By the Rentcharges Act 1977, Sched. 2.

CHAPTER 13

MORTGAGES

1. ACQUISITION OF FREEHOLD—MORTGAGE OF LANDLORD'S ESTATE

Outline

The conveyance[1] to the tenant of the freehold must be made "free from incumbrances,"[2] and so the estates of the freeholder and of any intermediate landlords must be discharged from all legal or equitable mortgages or charges affecting them. Certain equitable charges, *e.g.* family charges arising under a settlement,[3] would be overreached on a conveyance anyway. But apart from these, in the absence of any special provision in the 1967 Act, it would be necessary either for the mortgage to be redeemed before conveyance, *i.e.* by the mortgagor paying off all principal moneys, interest and other moneys secured, or for the mortgagee to release the property conveyed from the mortgage. Each of these alternatives could have caused considerable difficulty, particularly in the very common case where the mortgage affects a number of properties; the mortgagor might well not be in a financial position to redeem, and the mortgagee could justifiably refuse to release the property from his security. The Act therefore provides for the automatic discharge of the mortgage so far as it affects the property being enfranchised upon the tenant paying his purchase price either to the mortgagee[4] or into court,[5] in the manner described below. **13–01**

Types of mortgage affected

The special provisions of the 1967 Act discussed below apply to all mortgages and charges, whether legal or equitable, affecting the whole or any part of the house and premises being conveyed, except for: **13–02**

(a) rentcharges[6];
(b) charges capable of being overreached, *e.g.* family charges[7];

---

[1] This expression includes a registered land transfer.
[2] s. 8(1).
[3] See s. 8(4).
[4] s. 12.
[5] s. 13.
[6] s. 12(9); see Chap. 12.
[7] s. 12(1); see Chap. 15.

(c) specific and floating debenture-holders' charges, as to which see paragraph 13–07; and

(d) "tenant's incumbrances."[8] This expression is defined[9] as including "any incumbrance on the tenancy or on any interest directly or indirectly derived out of the tenancy (whether or not it is an incumbrance also on any interest reversionary on the tenancy)." The expression would thus normally include a mortgage created prior to the tenancy, if the tenancy was not authorised as against the mortgagee. But a mortgage affecting such an unauthorised tenancy[10] is treated for this purpose as not being a "tenant's incumbrance" (and so must be discharged before conveyance),[11] unless (a) it was granted after January 1, 1968,[12] and (b) the tenancy has not become binding on the mortgagee[13] by the date of the conveyance.[14]

Payment to mortgagee

13–03 The mortgagee of the freehold or any intermediate tenancy can, if he so wishes, join in the conveyance for the purpose of releasing the property conveyed from the security of the mortgage, either without any payment at all or on payment of a smaller sum than that to which he would otherwise be entitled.[15] A mortgagee who has ample other security may be prepared to take this course. But otherwise, the enfranchising tenant must pay his purchase price ascertained in accordance with section 9 of the Act as amended[16] (reduced by any amount required to redeem a rentcharge[17]), or so much of it as is necessary to redeem the mortgage, direct to the mortgagee, and not to the landlord.[18] If there are two or more mortgagees, the tenant must pay the purchase price to the mortgagees according to their priority[19]; and if the tenant himself has the benefit of a mortgage affecting the freehold, he can retain the appropriate amount in respect of it.[20] Any right of the mortgagee to consolidate the mortgage with a

---

[8] s. 8(1).
[9] By s. 8(2).
[10] Which will be binding against the mortgagor: see para. 3–01.
[11] s. 12(8).
[12] The "appointed day" when the 1967 Act came into force.
[13] As to which see para. 7–17 and cases there cited.
[14] s. 12(8), proviso.
[15] s. 12(7).
[16] See Chap. 9.
[17] ss. 11(4), 12(9).
[18] s. 12(2).
[19] s. 12(2).
[20] s. 12(3).

mortgage of other property (preventing the redemption of one mortgage without the other) is excluded for this purpose.[21]

Consequences of payment to mortgagee

Generally

Provided the purchase price is paid either directly to the mortgagee in the manner discussed above, or else into court,[22] the conveyance will have the effect of automatically discharging the property conveyed from the mortgage and from any court order made for the purpose of enforcing it.[23] Any term of years created for the purposes of the mortgage is also discharged as regards the property conveyed.[24] These consequences follow even if the mortgagee neither is a party to the conveyance nor executes it.[25] However, except so far as the payment to the mortgagee satisfies the obligations of the mortgagor, his personal liability remains unaffected, as also are the mortgagee's rights in respect of other properties subject to the mortgage or (as a result of a consolidation) any other mortgage.[26] Moreover, the mortgage will not be discharged as regards the property conveyed in so far as the purchase price is neither paid to the mortgagee nor into court.[27] **13–04**

Registered land

Where the landlord's estate is comprised in a registered land title, the tenant must also apply for the cancellation of any mortgage which is entered in the charges register but which is being discharged. In cases where there is no express discharge by the mortgagee, and the tenant relies only on the automatic discharge under the 1967 Act outlined above, the Chief Land Registrar requires sufficient evidence of this to be lodged before cancelling the entry of the mortgage on the register of the land transferred.[28] The evidence must prove that sufficient money has been paid to the mortgagee (or into court[29]) for the statutory provisions to operate. Similar evidence must also be supplied on any application by the tenant for first registration. In cases where the mortgagee has expressly discharged the mortgage as regards the land transferred, the Chief Land **13–05**

---

[21] s. 12(3).
[22] Under s. 13: see para. 13–09.
[23] s. 12(1).
[24] s. 12(1).
[25] s. 12(1) ("by virtue of this section"); and see s. 12(7).
[26] s. 12(6).
[27] s. 12(2).
[28] Land Registration Rules 1925, r. 46.
[29] See paras. 13–09 to 13–11.

Registrar requires a copy of a written receipt signed by the mortgagee acknowledging the discharge.[30]

In either of these cases, the tenant's application to cancel the charge should if possible be accompanied by the charge certificate,[31] and the Chief Land Registrar will then accept such evidence in place of an express discharge. If the mortgagee does not co-operate and the charge certificate cannot therefore be lodged, it is the practice of the Chief Land Registrar to serve a special notice on mortgagee explaining to him the nature of the tenant's application and asking him to consent to the registration of his charge. The Chief Land Registrar will usually thereafter cancel the registration, unless the mortgagee in reply shows prima facie grounds for maintaining it.[32] In the latter event, the registration remains until the matter is resolved by agreement or by a decision of the Chief Land Registrar in his judicial capacity, or of the High Court, either on a reference by him[33] or in ordinary *inter partes* proceedings.

Obligations of mortgagee

Discharge of property

13–06 Although the 1967 Act provides for the mortgage to be discharged on the payment of the purchase price direct to the mortgagee,[34] there is no express duty cast upon the mortgagee to give the mortgagor an effective discharge. The mortgagor should nevertheless always demand a formal discharge, either incorporated in the conveyance itself[35] or by a separate document. Otherwise, although the mortgage will in fact be discharged, it will be impossible to satisfy a subsequent purchaser of this; for it will be extremely difficult to give satisfactory conveyancing proof that the correct amount (or indeed anything at all) was paid to the mortgagee. If the mortgagee refuses to give a discharge, the mortgagor should threaten to pay the purchase price into court, on the ground that difficulty arises because the mortgagee "refuses or fails to make out a title, or to accept payment and give a proper discharge."[36] It is thought that all the costs of payment into court, as well as the costs of obtaining payment out, would be payable out of the moneys paid in (and so be borne by the mortgagee) in such circumstances.

---

[30] See Ruoff and Roper, *Registered Conveyancing* (5th ed.), p. 551; and see para. 13–06.
[31] Land Registration Act 1925, s. 64(1).
[32] Ruoff and Roper, *supra*, at p. 552.
[33] Land Registration Rules 1925, r. 298.
[34] s. 12(1), (2).
[35] See Precedents Nos. 6, 7, 16 and 17, Appendix A.
[36] s. 13(2)(*b*); see para. 13–10.

Notice of payment off

Most mortgages require notice of a specific period before they can be redeemed; and in some cases the right to redeem is postponed for some time.[37] Where the tenant is acquiring the freehold under the 1967 Act, the mortgagee is obliged to accept not less than three months' notice of the intention to pay the whole or any part of the principal sum secured, together with interest up to the date of payment, notwithstanding anything to the contrary in the mortgage.[38]

Debenture-holders' charges

As a general rule, any debenture-holders' charge is automatically discharged by a conveyance of the freehold to the tenant under the 1967 Act.[39] The tenant need not pay any part of the purchase price to the debenture-holders; and their charge must be ignored in determining any question of priorities.[40] As regards a floating charge, this rule would accord with the ordinary law. But, with two exceptions, this rule also applies even if the charge was a specific charge on the house and premises under the debenture itself or if (as a result of the crystallisation of a floating charge) it has subsequently become one. This departure from the ordinary law is, however, minimised by the two exceptions which, it is thought, will cover nearly all debenture-holders' charges and under which a specific charge is treated as an ordinary mortgage for the purposes of the Act. The two exceptions arise where at the date of the conveyance the charge is a specific charge as regards the house and premises and either: **13–07**

(a) the charge is in favour of trustees for the debenture-holders[41]; or
(b) there is only one debenture-holder. It may be that he must hold only a single debenture[42] (this is not clear); but it is considered that a single debenture-holder holding all of a series of debentures is also excluded.

Rights of mortgagee

Where the mortgage is compulsorily discharged under the Act, the mortgagee is entitled, if he so requires, "to receive such additional payment as is reasonable in the circumstances in respect of the costs of re- **13–08**

[37] The postponement is not necessarily a "clog on the equity": *Knightsbridge Estates Trust Ltd.* v. *Byrne* [1939] Ch. 441, C.A.
[38] s. 12(4).
[39] s. 12(5).
[40] For the purpose of s. 12(2).
[41] s. 12(5) proviso.
[42] An ordinary mortgage made by a company is probably a debenture for this purpose: see the *Knightsbridge Estates Trust* case in the House of Lords [1940] A.C. 631.

investment or other incidental costs and expenses and in respect of any reduction in the rate of interest obtainable on re-investment."[43] The circumstances in which the mortgagee will be able to exercise this right will occur where he is adversely affected by the Act, *e.g.* by an enforced early redemption of a mortgage under which the mortgagor's right to redeem is postponed. It is not clear who is to make the additional payment; presumably, it must be made by the enfranchising tenant, for it would be very harsh to throw this further liability onto the landlord.

Payment into court

Outline

13–09 A mortgage is also automatically discharged, so far as it affects the house and premises, where the tenant makes a payment into court[44] on account of his purchase price[45] (reduced by any amount required to redeem a rentcharge).[46] In certain cases of difficulty, the tenant is given power to pay into court; and in certain other cases, the tenant is obliged to do so. If less than the correct amount is paid in, it is doubtful whether the mortgage is effectively discharged.

Cases of difficulty

13–10 The cases of difficulty when the tenant has the option to pay into court are:

(a) where difficulty arises in ascertaining how much is payable in respect of the mortgage[47];
(b) because the mortgagee is missing or cannot be ascertained[48];
(c) because the mortgagee "refuses or fails to make out a title, or to accept payment and give a proper discharge, or to take any steps reasonably required of him to enable the sum payable to be ascertained and paid"[49]; and
(d) "because a tender of the sum payable cannot, by reason of complications in the title to it or the want of two or more trustees

---

[43] s. 12(4).
[44] Normally, the county court of the district in which the property is situated: County Court Rules 1981, Ord. 49, r. 8(2)(*d*). (There is an exception where the obligation to make the payment in arises out of proceedings in another court: s. 13(3). See para. 13–11.) For the procedure, see C.C.R. 1981, Ord. 49, r. 8, set out at para. 20–163.
[45] s. 13(1).
[46] s. 13(4).
[47] s. 13(1)(*a*).
[48] s. 13(2)(*a*).
[49] s. 13(2)(*b*); see paras. 12–05 and 13–06.

or for other reasons, be effected, or not without incurring or involving unreasonable cost and delay."[50]

In any of those cases, the tenant may pay into court his purchase price or such part of it as is required to cover the amount due under the mortgage.[51] If that amount is unknown, the tenant can pay in the whole of his purchase price or such lesser sum as he thinks right to cover the amount due.[52]

Mandatory payment in

The tenant *must* pay his purchase price into court if prior to the conveyance he is given written notice that the landlord or a mortgagee requires him to do so, for the purpose of protecting the rights of any mortgagee, or because the landlord has made or is going to make application to the court for relief against the mortgage,[53] or because the landlord is bankrupt or in liquidation.[54] The tenant must likewise pay his purchase price into court if prior to the conveyance he is given written notice that steps have been taken to enforce the mortgage by the bringing of any court proceedings, or by the appointment of a receiver, or otherwise.[55] It is difficult to see the purpose of this latter mandatory direction to the tenant. Furthermore, questions may arise as to what constitutes "written notice" for this purpose; on a strict reading, it would appear that a merely informative letter to the tenant, without any request to pay into court, makes it obligatory to the tenant to pay into court. However, there is no reason why the landlord's estate should not be discharged from the mortgage by agreement between all parties concerned, without the necessity for invoking the Act at all, thus saving unnecessary costs. Where the obligation for payment in arises from proceedings in a court specified in the notice other than the county court, payment must be made into the court so specified.[56] 13–11

Registered land

As in the case where payment is made to the mortgagee,[57] where the landlord's estate is comprised in a registered land title, the tenant must also apply for the cancellation of any mortgage which is entered in the charges register but which is being discharged. The application should be 13–12

[50] s. 13(2)(*c*).
[51] s. 13(1).
[52] s. 13(1). The tenant apparently has a complete discretion.
[53] Under s. 36: see para. 13–16.
[54] s. 13(3)(*a*).
[55] s. 13(3)(*b*).
[56] s. 13(3).
[57] See para. 13–05.

accompanied by a copy of the affidavit sworn for that purpose[58] and a copy of the official receipt of the court for the payment in.

2. Extended Lease—Mortgage of Landlord's Estate

13–13 The position where the tenant claims an extended lease, and the landlord's estate is subject to a mortgage, has already been dealt with: see paragraph 7–17.

3. Mortgagee of Landlord's Estate in Possession or Receiver Appointed

Mortgagee in possession

13–14 Where the landlord's mortgagee has gone into possession, the tenant's Notice of Leaseholder's Claim to acquire the freehold or an extended lease can be served either on the mortgagor or the mortgagee.[59] However, all the proceedings arising from the Notice are conducted by the mortgagee; and any conveyance or lease can be executed either by the landlord at the direction of the mortgagee or by the mortgagee in the name and on behalf of the landlord.[60] The mortgagee can oppose a tenant's claim to acquire an extended lease and obtain possession under section 17 (redevelopment)[61] as if he were the landlord.[62] Any compensation paid by him on obtaining possession (whether an application is made for possession or the tenant gives up possession by agreement) is added to the mortgage security, and the tenant must pay interest on it at the same rate as is payable under the mortgage on the principal sum secured; but the compensation sum is not recoverable from the mortgagor on his personal covenant alone.[63] If the mortgagee acting as landlord receives any compensation under the Act, such compensation is dealt with as if it were proceeds of sale of the mortgaged property.[64]

Receiver appointed

13–15 Where a receiver has been appointed, whether by the mortgagee or by the court, the tenant's Notice of Leaseholder's Claim can be served on any one of the mortgagor, the mortgagee or the receiver.[65] Prima facie, the

---

[58] *i.e.* under County Court Rules 1981, Ord. 49 r. 8(2)(*a*): see para. 20–163.
[59] Sched. 3, para. 9(1): and see para. 5–06.
[60] s. 25(1).
[61] See paras. 8–02 *et seq.*
[62] s. 25(2).
[63] s. 25(3).
[64] s. 25(4).
[65] Sched. 3, para. 9(1).

proceedings under the tenant's Notice will be conducted by the landlord himself in the usual way; although he may not oppose the tenant's claim and apply for possession under section 17 (redevelopment)[66] or section 18 (occupation as own or family's residence)[67] without the mortgagee's consent.[68] But the mortgagee can give the landlord written notice that the proceedings under the tenant's Notice shall be conducted, either generally or in relation to section 17 only, by the mortgagee himself as if he were a mortgagee in possession.[69] In certain cases, the tenant may have to pay the purchase price into court.[70]

4. Transitional Relief against Mortgages of Landlord's Estate

One of the results of the 1967 Act was to depreciate the value of the freehold or intermediate tenancy of a house subject to a long tenancy at a low rent, particularly one due to expire in a relatively short time. This is because the compensation provisions proceeded on the basis that only the site belonged to the landlord, who was thus deprived of the reversionary value of the bricks and mortar.[71] This could cause hardship to the landlord if his interest was subject to a mortgage. The Act made special provision in the case of certain mortgages in existence when it was passed[72] for relief to be given to the landlord against such hardship, at the expense of the mortgagee[73] (but not at the expense of the tenant who might be considered to be the person substantially benefiting in such circumstances). Similar relief could also be obtained by a second or later mortgagee.[74] **13–16**

The mortgages qualifying for this relief, however, were confined to those which both (i) were made before October 27, 1967[75] and (ii) affected the estate of the freeholder or an intermediate tenant of a house held on a long tenancy with 20 years or less unexpired on that date (or then capable of being determined within 20 years from that date by a landlord's notice).[76] The relief was thus of a transitional nature only, and, in the author's experience, has seldom been claimed. As the relevant provisions

---

66 See paras. 8–02 *et seq.*
67 See paras. 8–05 *et seq.*
68 s. 25(5)(*a*).
69 s. 25(5)(*b*).
70 s. 13(3)(*b*); see para. 13–11.
71 ss. 9(1), 15(2).
72 *i.e.* on October 27, 1967. No consequential amendment was made when the Housing Act 1974, s. 118 (which brought further houses within the ambit of the 1967 Act) came into force.
73 s. 36.
74 s. 36(3).
75 s. 36(1)(*b*).
76 s. 36(1)(*a*).

are almost spent as this book goes to press, they are not discussed further.[77]

5. Mortgage Affecting Tenant's Estate

Acquisition of freehold

13–17 The acquisition of the freehold by the tenant does not affect any mortgage of the tenant's leasehold. As a general rule, the tenant's lease will thus remain as a separate estate, and any declaration of merger will be of no effect as against the mortgagee.[78] However, in many cases, and particularly where the purchase price is being raised by the tenant by way of further loan from his mortgagee, it is desirable and convenient for the mortgage security to be extended to cover the freehold,[79] and a declaration of merger then will be valid and effective. In such cases, the mortgagee should be made a party to the conveyance,[80] although this is not essential unless a part of the house and premises is excluded from enfranchisement and so surrendered to the landlord.[81]

Extended lease

13–18 Where the tenant acquires an extended lease, the rights and interests of the mortgagee are transferred to the new lease.[82] See further paragraph 7–18.

---

[77] A full discussion is to be found in the 1st edition of this book (1967) at paras. 12–14 to 12–19.

[78] See para. 6–31.

[79] See Precedent No. 19, Appendix A.

[80] See Precedent No. 20, Appendix A.

[81] See s. 2(5), (6), (7) and paras. 2–13 and 2–14.

[82] s. 14(6).

CHAPTER 14

SPECIAL CLASSES OF LANDLORD

1. PUBLIC BODIES

Right to possession

Outline

If a Minister of the Crown certifies that a property will in 10 years or less be required by a public body for development purposes, that public body has the right under section 28 of the 1967 Act to resist a tenant's claim to the freehold or an extended lease, and to claim possession for those purposes at the expiry of the contractual term of the tenancy. **14–01**

Public bodies qualifying

The public bodies entitled to the benefit of section 28 are: **14–02**

(1) Local authorities. These are county, borough and district councils, the mayor commonalty and citizens of the City of London, the Inner London Education Authority, any other London joint authority, any joint board in which all the constituent authorities are such local authorities, and any combined police authority within the meaning of the Police Act 1964.[1]
(2) New Town authorities, namely the Commission for the New Towns and any development corporation.[2]
(3) The Development Board for Rural Wales.[3]
(4) University bodies.[4]
(5) Health authorities.[5]
(6) Nationalised industries.[6]

---

[1] s. 28(5)(*a*); Local Government Act 1972, ss. 1(10), 179(3); Local Government Act 1985, Sched. 14, para. 43 and Sched. 17. The former Greater London Council was also included prior to its abolition, effective as of April 1, 1986.
[2] s. 28(5)(*b*).
[3] s. 28(5)(*bb*), inserted by Development of Rural Wales Act 1976, s. 28 and Sched. 5, para. 7.
[4] Defined by s. 28(5)(*c*). As to what constitutes a university, see *St. Davids College, Lampeter* v. *Ministry of Education* [1951] 1 All E.R. 559.
[5] Listed by s. 28(5)(*d*), as substituted by National Health Service Reorganisation Act 1973, Sched. 4, para. 111, and amended by Health Services Act 1980, Sched. 1, para. 18 and by the Family Practitioner Committees Order 1985 (S.I. 1985 No. 39) art. 5(*a*).
[6] s. 28(5)(*e*).

(7) Harbour authorities and statutory water undertakers, but only in respect of their functions as such.[7]
(8) The Royal College of Art.[8]
(9) The Wimbledon and Putney Common Conservators.[9]
(10) Other bodies of a public nature included by Order[10] of the Secretary of State for the Environment.[11]

Minister's certificate

14–03 Any Minister of the Crown may certify that the property will, in 10 years or less, be required for "relevant development."[12] "Relevant development" means development for purposes (other than investment purposes) of the public body in question,[13] but

(i) In relation to a local authority, "relevant development" includes any development to be undertaken (whether or not by that authority) in order to secure (a) the development or re-development of an area defined by a development plan under the Town and Country Planning Act 1971 as an area of comprehensive development, or (b) the treatment as a whole, by development, re-development, or improvement, or partly one and partly by another method, of any area in which the property is situated.[14]
(ii) The purposes of a county or county borough council include the purposes of a police authority which is a committee of the council.[15]
(iii) The purposes of a university body include the purposes of a related university body.[16]
(iv) In the case of a health authority, the purposes of the National Health Service Act 1977 are substituted for the purposes of that body.[17]

"Development" is not defined, but appears to have its ordinary

[7] s. 28(5)(*f*).
[8] Leasehold Reform Act 1967 (Application of section 28 to Royal College of Art) Order 1968 (S.I. 1968 No. 2022).
[9] Leasehold Reform Act 1967 (Wimbledon and Putney Commons Conservators) Order 1971 (S.I. 1971 No. 1009).
[10] s. 28(7). Any such Order may be revoked or varied by statutory instrument: s. 28(8).
[11] Secretary of State for the Environment Order 1970 (S.I. 1970 No. 1681).
[12] s. 28(1); for examples of the refusal and grant of a certificate, see [1969] J.P.L. 325, 505.
[13] s. 28(6).
[14] *Ibid.* as amended by Town and Country Planning Act 1968, Sched. 9, para. 75, and Town and Country Planning Act 1971, Sched. 23, Pt. II.
[15] s. 28(6)(*a*); Local Government Act 1972, s. 272(1), Sched. 30.
[16] s. 28(6)(*b*).
[17] s. 28(6)(*c*), as substituted by National Health Service Reorganisation Act 1973, Sched. 4, para. 111, and amended by Health Service Act 1980, Sched. 1, para. 18.

meanings of either new building or the demolition and reconstruction of existing buildings. Despite an assumption to the contrary by the Secretary of State for Education in one case,[18] it is considered that it does not include the extended artificial meaning of a material change of use, as in section 22 of the Town and Country Planning Act 1971.[19]

Before the Minister can give a certificate, the public body must give notice to the tenant (whether or not entitled to the benefit of the 1967 Act) stating that the question of giving such a certificate is under consideration by the Minister, and that any representation to the Minister which the tenant makes within 21 days will be taken into account before a certificate is given; and the Minister must duly consider any representation so made.[20] A Minister's certificate which is valid on its face cannot be challenged, except in judicial review proceedings in the High Court.[21]

Effect of Minister's certificate

If the Minister gives a certificate, any Notice of Leaseholder's Claim subsequently served is of no effect.[22] One consequence of this appears to be that the tenant is not entitled to compensation under section 17[23] unless the tenant serves a Notice within two months after the certificate,[24] which he may not be qualified to do; and for that reason a certificate is in practice never given until after the tenant has served a Notice of Leaseholder's Claim. The Notice thereupon ceases to have effect;[25] but if the tenant had a valid claim, section 17 applies as if the tenancy had been extended under the 1967 Act.[26] So the landlord can claim possession under that section on or after the original term date[27]; and the tenancy is automatically continued until the landlord does so, and is not determined by effluxion of time, by a notice to quit or by the termination of a superior tenancy.[28] The practical effect is that, although the tenant loses the security of tenure given by the 1967 Act, he retains most of the substantial financial benefit which the Act confers. 14–04

If the tenant has brought proceedings for a declaration that he is entitled to the freehold or an extended lease, and an application for a Minister's certificate is pending, the proceedings should be stood over

[18] *Gaidowski* v. *Gonville and Caius College, Cambridge* (1977) 33 P. & C.R. 528, L.T., decided on s. 29: see para. 14–11.
[19] *Cf.* ss. 17 and 38 (amending Landlord and Tenant Act 1954, s. 12(1)(*a*)).
[20] s. 28(4).
[21] *Gaidowski* v. *Gonville and Caius College, Cambridge, supra.*
[22] s. 28(1)(*a*).
[23] See para. 8–12.
[24] s. 28(1)(*b*)(ii).
[25] s. 28(1)(*a*).
[26] s. 28(1)(*b*).
[27] See para. 8–03.
[28] s. 28(2).

until the result of the application is known.[29] In the case of a business tenancy, a certificate under section 57 of the Landlord and Tenant Act 1954 has the same effect as a Minister's certificate (but no compensation under section 59 of that Act is payable).[30]

Once the tenant has acquired the freehold or an extended lease, a Minister's certificate is of no effect. It follows that, if he is qualified to do so, a tenant of a qualified public body should acquire the freehold under the 1967 Act at a time when there are over 10 years to go before the original term date.

Application

14–05 When a qualified public body makes the necessary application to the county court for possession under section 17, the Minister's certificate is conclusive that the public body proposes to demolish or reconstruct the whole or a part of the house and premises.[31] Otherwise, the application is treated exactly as an application by a private landlord for possession under section 17, and the same provisions as to procedure and compensation for the tenant are applicable.[32]

Shared ownership leases—generally

14–06 Many public bodies operate "equity-sharing" schemes, whereby a person can purchase a percentage interest in a property, paying a rack-rent for the remainder, coupled with a "staircasing" arrangement under which the purchaser can acquire further percentage interests in the property. Schemes of this kind usually involve the grant of long "shared ownership leases." Provision has been made[33] for tenancies granted by such leases to be excluded from the operation of the 1967 Act, which might otherwise become applicable when the tenant has a substantial percentage in the property and so enable him to enfranchise at a lower price than that provided for under the terms of his lease.

The original exclusion provisions were contained in section 140 of the Housing Act 1980, and these provisions remain in force as regards tenancies granted before the coming into operation of section 18 of and Schedule 4 to the Housing and Planning Act 1986[34]. The latter introduced a new section 33A and Schedule 4A into the 1967 Act, and replace section 140 of the Housing Act 1980 as regards tenancies granted after the date

---

[29] *Hadfield* v. *Greater London Council* (1968) 207 E.G. 627, C.A.
[30] s. 28(3).
[31] s. 28(1)(*c*).
[32] s. 28(1)(*b*): see Chap. 8.
[33] Housing Act 1980, s. 140. This section also exempts certain similar tenancies granted by registered housing associations, considered in paras. 14–22 *et seq.*
[34] Housing and Planning Act 1986, Sched. 4, para. 11.

when they come into operation[35]. It is thus necessary to consider both the original and the replacement exclusion provisions.

Shared ownership leases granted before the coming into force of section 33A and Schedule 4A

Bodies qualifying 14–07

The bodies entitled to the benefit of the exclusion from the 1967 Act under this head are narrower than those with a right of possession under section 28 of the 1967 Act discussed above. They are confined to the Inner London Education Authority, other London joint authorities,[36] certain local authorities (but not county councils),[37] New Town authorities[38] and the Development Board for Rural Wales.[39]

Tenancies excluded

In order for a tenancy to be excluded under this head, it must satisfy all of the following requirements:

(a) It must have been granted after August 8, 1980.[40]
(b) It must have been created by the grant by a qualifying public body of a lease at a premium.[41]
(c) The lease must provide (i) for the tenant to be able to acquire the freehold for a consideration which is to be calculated in accordance with the terms of the lease and which is reasonable having regard to the premium or premiums paid by the tenant under the lease[42] (the onus of showing reasonableness being on the landlord[43]); and (ii) state the landlord's opinion that by virtue of the Housing Act 1980, s. 140 the tenancy will not be a long tenancy at a low rent for the purposes of the 1967 Act when the interest of the landlord belongs to a qualifying public body.[44]

Extent of exclusion

If the above requirements are complied with, the tenancy is treated as not being a long tenancy at a low rent for the purposes of the 1967 Act, if

---

[35] No such date had been prescribed at the date at which this book states the law.
[36] Housing Act 1980, s. 140(2)(*aa*), (*ab*), inserted by the Local Government Act 1985, Sched. 14, Part II, para. 58(*e*).
[37] *Ibid.* s. 140(2)(*a*).
[38] *Ibid.* s. 140(2)(*b*)(*c*).
[39] *Ibid.* s. 140(2)(*d*).
[40] *i.e.* when s. 140 came into operation on the passing of the 1980 Act: s. 153(3).
[41] *Ibid.* s. 140(1).
[42] *Ibid.* s. 140(3)(*a*).
[43] *Ibid.* s. 140(5).
[44] *Ibid.* s. 140(3)(*b*).

and so long as the interest of the landlord belongs to a qualifying public body (not necessarily the grantor).[45]

Shared ownership leases granted after the coming into force of section 33A and Schedule 4A

14–08 *Bodies qualifying*

The bodies entitled to the benefit of the exclusion from the 1967 Act under this head are narrower than those with the right of possession under section 28 of the 1967 Act discussed above (but wider than those under section 140 of the Housing Act 1980). They are certain local authorities (including county councils), the Inner London Education Authority, other London joint authorities,[46] New Town authorities, urban development corporations[47] and the Development Board for Rural Wales.[48]

Tenancies excluded

In order for a tenancy to be excluded under this head, it must satisfy all of the following requirements:

(a) It must have been granted after section 33A of and Schedule 4A to the 1967 Act came into operation.[49]
(b) It must have been created by the grant by a qualifying public body of a lease at a premium.[50]
(c) The lease must (i) provide for the tenant to acquire the freehold for a consideration which is to be calculated in accordance with the terms of the lease and which is reasonable, having regard to the premium or premiums paid by the tenant under the lease[51] (the onus of showing reasonableness being on the landlord[52]); and (ii) state the landlord's opinion that by notice of para. 2 of Schedule 4A the tenancy will be excluded from the operation of Part I of the 1967 Act or any time when the interest of the landlord belongs to a qualifying public body.[53]

Extent of exclusion

If the above requirements are complied with, the tenancy is excluded

---

[45] *Ibid.* s. 140(1).
[46] *i.e.*, established by Part IV of the Local Government Act 1985.
[47] As defined by Part XVI of the Local Government, Planning and Land Act 1980.
[48] Sched. 3A, para. 2(2).
[49] Housing and Planning Act 1986, Sched. 4, para. 11.
[50] Sched. 4A, para. 2(1)(*a*).
[51] *Ibid.* para. 2(3)(*a*).
[52] *Ibid.* para. 2(4).
[53] *Ibid.* para. 2(3)(*b*).

from the operation of Part I of the 1967 Act at any time when the interest of the landlord belongs to a qualifying public body.[54]

Shared ownership leases granted pursuant to the "right to buy" provisions

If a secure tenant[55] (i) has validly exercised the "right to buy" conferred by the Housing Act 1980, Pt. I, now in the Housing Act 1985, Pt. V, (ii) has also claimed the right to a mortgage[56] but (iii) (by reason of the restrictions on the amount he can leave outstanding on mortgage[57]) his right to a mortgage does not cover the full amount of the purchase price and costs for which he is liable, he has the right to a "shared ownership lease" of the kind mentioned above.[58] If the landlord owns the freehold, once the tenant has acquired a total share[59] in the house of 100 per cent. he is entitled to a conveyance of the freehold.[60] But if the landlord does not own the freehold, the tenant has no such right. The tenant will then have tenancy of the unexpired term of the landlord's lease less five days[61] (or 125 years, if less[62]), at a rent of £10 per annum.[63] 14–09

Such a shared ownership lease is treated as a "long tenancy" even if it was granted for a term of 21 years or less.[64] It is also treated as a tenancy "at a low rent" before the tenant has acquired a total share in the house of 100 per cent. notwithstanding that the rent is more than two-thirds of the rateable value on the first day of the term.[65] So if the house is within the rateable value limits of the 1967 Act[66] and the tenant has the necessary residential qualification,[67] he will become entitled to the freehold or an extended lease under the 1967 Act. But the tenant (and also any tenant under a sub-tenancy directly or indirectly derived out of the shared ownership tenancy) is precluded from exercising that right so long as the rent payable under the lease exceeds £10 per annum.[68] If the tenant (or any such sub-tenant) exercises the right to acquire the freehold, the purchase price is assessed under the valuation basis of section 9(1A) of the 1967 Act, whatever the rateable value of the house and premises[69];

---

[54] *Ibid.* para. 2(1).
[55] Defined by Housing Act 1985, ss. 79, 185.
[56] *i.e.* under *ibid.* s. 132.
[57] *Ibid.* s. 133.
[58] *Ibid.* ss. 143–151, replacing the Housing and Building Control Act 1984, ss. 12–17.
[59] Defined by *ibid.* s. 187.
[60] *Ibid.* Sched. 9, para. 8.
[61] *Ibid.* Sched. 7, para. 12(2).
[62] *Ibid.* Sched. 7, para. 12(1).
[63] *Ibid.* Sched. 9, para. 5.
[64] *Ibid.* s. 174(*a*).
[65] *Ibid.* s. 174(*b*).
[66] See paras. 2–21 *et seq.*
[67] See Chap. 4.
[68] *Ibid.* s. 173.
[69] *Ibid.* s. 175(1), (2): see further para. 9–15.

and that valuation basis applies in relation to any continuation or substituted tenancy, and any sub-tenancy directly or indirectly derived out of it.[70]

2. Local Authorities

Rights to possession

14–10 A local authority is a public body within section 28 of the 1967 Act, and is accordingly entitled to the rights under that section discussed in paras. 14–01 *et seq.*.

Shared ownership leases

Shared ownership leases held from certain local authorities are excluded from the 1967 Act, as discussed in para. 14–06. Special provisions apply in relation to such leases granted pursuant to the "right to buy" provisions, as discussed in para. 14–09.

Overspill areas

A local authority which has responsibility for an overspill area (*i.e.* the council of a "receiving district" under the Town Development Act 1952 as extended[71]), has the same powers as a New Town authority to reserve in any conveyance or extended lease granted by it covenants against leasing without consent and selling without giving the right of first refusal. See paras. 14–15 and 14–16, "New Town authorities".

Reservation of development rights

14–11 In addition, a local authority[72] can, under section 29, impose in any conveyance or extended lease granted by it under the 1967 Act (or in any lease granted in satisfaction of a tenant's rights under the Act[73]) such covenants "restricting the carrying out of development or clearing of land as are necessary to reserve the land for possible development by the authority,"[74] The expression "development" is not defined, but it appears from its context to include only its ordinary meaning of new building, or the substantial demolition or reconstruction of existing buildings,[75] and

[70] *Ibid.* s. 175(3), (4), (5).
[71] Local Government Act 1972, s. 185(3), 272(1), Sched. 30.
[72] As defined in s. 28(5)(*a*): see s. 29(5).
[73] s. 29(8); as to such leases see s. 23(4) and para. 7–19.
[74] s. 29(1), (2).
[75] s. 29(1) uses the word "land," by way of distinction from "house and premises" which seems to indicate that the section is concerned mainly with the site.

not, for instance, conversion into flats[76] or a change of use. However, in one case[77] the Secretary of State for Education (whose consent was necessary because the landlord was a "university body"[78]) appears to have assumed that a change of use would involve "development," and that the word should thus be given the wider meaning contained in section 22 of the Town and Country Planning Act 1971. It is considered that the Secretary of State's consent in that case could have been successfully challenged on a judicial review.[79] But development is not confined to "relevant development" as under section 28,[80] and can thus include development for investment purposes.

Form of covenant

A local authority can, of course, use its ordinary powers of compulsory purchase in order to obtain land for development,[81], and it might have been thought that the purpose of section 29 was to preserve all development value in the land to the local authority. But this view has been rejected by the Lands Tribunal,[82] which considered that it was sufficient if the covenants merely "facilitate the reservation of the property for possible development" by the local authority; and the Tribunal decided[83] that the covenants should not be absolute but should be qualified by the words "not without the consent in writing of the vendors first obtained (such consent not to be unreasonably withheld)." However, it is thought that a local authority would not be unreasonably withholding consent to any proposed development which would (to any substantial extent) increase the compensation payable on a compulsory purchase, particularly if such purchase is likely to take place in the near future. **14–12**

Requirements as to covenant

It is considered that a section 29 covenant is a restrictive covenant (in the case of enfranchisement) or a modification of the terms of the existing tenancy (in the case of an extended lease), and cannot be required by the **14–13**

[76] Note that Housing Act 1985, s. 610 (which permits the court to authorise the conversion of a house into flats notwithstanding a restrictive covenant to the contrary) has not been excluded. *Cf.* Law of Property Act 1925, s. 84, which is excluded by Sched. 4, para. 1(5).

[77] *Gaidowski* v. *Gonville & Caius College, Cambridge* (1977) 33 P. & C.R. 528 (a case concerning a university body, which has the same powers).

[78] See s. 29(6) and para. 14–18.

[79] But not in any other manner: see the *Gaidowski* case, *supra.*

[80] See para. 14–03.

[81] *e.g.* under the Housing Act 1985 Pt. XVII or the Town and Country Planning Act 1971, s. 112.

[82] The *Gaidowski* case, *supra.*

[83] The Tribunal also decided in the *Gaidowski* case that there should be no restriction at all on development within the 10 per cent. tolerance for which there is deemed planning consent under para. 1 of Class 1 of the General Development Order then current.

local authority unless the terms of the statutory conditions are duly complied with.[84] Such a covenant must be specifically expressed to be entered into under section 29.[85] It is registrable as a Class D (ii) land charge under section 2 (5) of the Land Charges Act 1972, or section 59 (2) of the Land Registration Act 1925, as appropriate.[86] It is binding on successors of the covenantor,[87] including a body with compulsory purchase powers (unless that body also acquires the benefit of the covenant)[88]; but if not duly registered it will be void against a purchaser for money or money's worth.[89] However, the covenant is clearly personal to the local authority and its benefit cannot be assigned. Further, the covenant is not subject to the rule against perpetuities,[90] and it cannot be discharged or modified by the Lands Tribunal under section 84 of the Law of Property Act 1925, as amended.[91] Any development in breach of the covenant must be ignored on assessing the compensation payable on a compulsory purchase or on the exercise of the landlord's right to possession for development purposes under section 17.[92]

Enforcement of covenant

14–14 The covenant cannot be enforced by injunction nor, in the case of a lease, by forfeiture proceedings.[93] Enforcement must be by the procedure prescribed by Part I of Schedule 4 (which procedure, however, closely resembles that which a landlord must follow if he wishes to enforce a right of re-entry for a breach of covenant other than non-payment of rent).[94] The local authority may serve written notice on the covenantor (or successor of his)[95] specifying the covenant and the alleged breach.[96] The notice must state that, within a stipulated time (not less than six weeks) thereafter, the local authority proposes to execute a vesting declaration unless in the meantime the recipient of the notice serves a counter-notice.[97] Such a counter-notice may object that there has been no breach of the covenant, or no breach in respect of land in which the recipient of

[84] Leasehold Reform (Enfranchisement and Extension) Regulations 1967 (S.I. 1967 No. 1879) Sched., Pt. I, para. 5 and Pt. II, para. 2.
[85] s. 29(3).
[86] Sched. 4, para. 1(2)(*a*), (3)(*a*).
[87] Defined by Sched. 4, para. 1(4).
[88] Sched. 4, para. 1(7).
[89] Sched. 4, para. 1(2)(*b*), (3)(*b*).
[90] Sched. 4, para. 1(6).
[91] Sched. 4, para. 1(5).
[92] s. 29(4).
[93] Sched. 4, para. 1(1).
[94] The enforcement procedure was based on the procedure for enforcing "crownhold covenants" under the Land Commission Act 1967, ss. 19–21 (now repealed).
[95] Sched. 4, para. 2(1).
[96] Sched. 4, para. 2(2)(*a*).
[97] Sched. 4, para. 2(2)(*b*).

the notice has any interest; and, in addition, or as an alternative, the counter-notice may claim relief.[98] If a counter-notice is duly served, the local authority can only proceed with the proposed vesting declaration on obtaining the leave of the court.[99] If there is an objection in the counter-notice, the court can grant leave only if the local authority (on whom the onus lies) satisfies the court that such objection is not well-founded.[1] If there is a claim for relief in the counter-notice, the court has full power to grant such relief on terms that it considers just.[2]

Where the covenantor (or his successor, as the case may be) fails to serve a counter-notice within the time stipulated in the local authority's notice, or the court grants leave, the local authority may at any time within the next six months execute a vesting declaration in a prescribed form,[3] vesting the interest to which the declaration relates in itself.[4] However, it must then pay compensation as if it had compulsorily acquired the interest under a notice to treat served on the date of the vesting declaration,[5] but without any compensation for severance or disturbance,[6] nor for any development which has been carried out in breach of the covenant.[7]

3. New Town Authorities

Right to possession

14–15 A New Town Authority (*i.e.* the Commission for the New Towns and any development corporation within the New Towns Act 1965[8]) is a public body within section 28, and is accordingly entitled to the rights under that section discussed above.[9]

Shared ownership leases

Shared ownership leases held from New Town authorities are excluded from the 1967 Act, as discussed in para. 14–06 *et seq.* above. Special provisions apply in relation to such leases granted pursuant to the right to buy, as discussed in para. 14–12 above.

98 Sched. 4, para. 2(3).
99 Sched. 4, para. 2(4).
1 Sched. 4, para. 2(4)(*a*).
2 Sched. 4, para. 2(4)(*b*).
3 Sched. 4, para. 3(2).
4 Sched. 4, para. 3(1), (3).
5 Sched. 4, para. 3(4).
6 Sched. 4, para. 3(5).
7 s. 29(4).
8 The New Towns Act 1965 was repealed by the New Towns Act 1981, but the Commission for the New Towns and development corporations continue in being.
9 See paras. 14–01 *et seq.*

Reservation of development rights

A New Town authority also has the same power as a local authority under section 29 to impose in any conveyance or extended lease granted by it a covenant restricting the development of clearing of land.[10] For such covenants and their enforcement, see under "Local Authorities" above.[11] Such a covenant would, however, be of no value to a New Town authority if it could not subsequently acquire the property. Accordingly, powers of compulsory purchase akin to the ordinary powers of a local authority are given to the Commission for the New Towns if it desires to redevelop for its own purposes (other than those of investment).[12]

Reservation of other rights

14–16 A New Town authority (and also the council of an overspill area[13]) may also require the inclusion in any conveyance[14] or extended lease (and any further lease)[15] granted by it the following:

(i) A covenant against leasing without the written consent of the authority. If such a covenant is included in a lease, the usual proviso that such consent is not to be unreasonably withheld[16] is excluded.
(ii) A covenant granting right of pre-emption (*i.e.* of first refusal) at a price equal to the price payable by way of compensation under a vesting declaration under Schedule 4.[17]

Any such covenant must be expressed to be entered into to give effect to section 30, and can only be enforced in the same manner as a covenant under section 29.[18] See under "Local Authorities" above.

4. Development Board for Rural Wales

14–17 This board[19] is a public body akin to a New Town authority, and has all the powers of such an authority under sections 28, 29 and 30 discussed

[10] s. 29(1), (6)(*a*).
[11] Paras. 14–11 to 14–14.
[12] s. 29(7) and Sched. 4, para. 4.
[13] s. 30(7)(*b*).
[14] s. 30(1).
[15] s. 30(2).
[16] *i.e.* under the Landlord and Tenant Act 1927, s. 19(1).
[17] s. 30(4); and see para. 14–12.
[18] s. 30(3).
[19] Constituted by the Development of Rural Wales Act 1976.

above.[20] The provisions concerning shared ownership leases in relation to public bodies also apply to the Board.[21]

5. University Bodies

Right to possession

A university body (which includes any university, university college or college of a university) is a public body within section 28, and is accordingly entitled to the rights under that section discussed above.[22] 14–18

Reservation of development rights

A university body also has the same powers as a local authority to impose in any conveyance or extended lease granted by it a covenant restricting the development or clearing of land[23] (see under "Local Authorities" above[24]); but in order to exercise this power the university body must first obtain the consent of the Secretary of State for Education and Science.[25] Further, the Secretary of State is given powers of compulsory acquisition of property subject to such a covenant, for development for the purposes (other than investment purposes) of the university body[26] or any related university body.[27]

A university body which is subject to the Universities and College Estates Act 1925, and which receives purchase moneys on the sale of a freehold in accordance with the 1967 Act or other payments by way of compensation under the Act, must deal with them as if they were amounts payable as consideration on a sale effected under the 1925 Act[28]; and it can apply capital moneys in the payment of compensation to a tenant for the loss of his tenancy on obtaining an order for possession under section 17.[29]

---

[20] s. 28(5)(*bb*), 29(6A), 30(7), all inserted by *ibid.* Sched. 7, para. 5.
[21] See paras. 14–06 *et seq.*
[22] See paras. 14–01 *et seq.*
[23] By s. 29.
[24] Paras. 14–12 *et seq.*
[25] s. 29(6).
[26] Sched. 4, para. 5.
[27] s. 29(6B), inserted by the Housing Act 1980, Sched. 21, para. 5, which were based on "concessionary crownhold covenants" under the Land Commission Act 1967, s. 13 (now repealed).
[28] s. 24(1)(*b*).
[29] Sched. 2, para. 9(2).

6. Ecclesiastical Landlords

14–19 The sanction of the Church Commissioners is required as to the contents of any conveyance or extended lease to be granted by any ecclesiastical landlord,[30] and as to valuation and certain other matters under the 1967 Act.[31] The Church Commissioners are also entitled to appear and be heard in any proceedings under the Act in which an ecclesiastical landlord is concerned. Further detailed provision is made[32] for other matters concerning ecclesiastical property.

7. National Trust

14–20 Only an extended lease, and not the freehold, can be acquired by a tenant of the National Trust.[33]

8. Housing Associations

Shared ownership leases—generally

14–21 Some housing associations operate "equity-sharing" schemes whereby a person can purchase a percentage interest in a property, paying a rack-rent for the remainder, coupled with a "staircasing" arrangement under which the purchaser can acquire further percentage interests in the property. Schemes of this kind usually involve the grant of long "shared ownership leases." Provision has been made[34] for tenancies granted by such leases to be excluded from the operation of the 1967 Act, which might otherwise become applicable when the tenant has a substantial percentage in the property and so enable him to enfranchise at a lower price than that provided for under the terms of his lease.

The original exclusion provisions were contained in section 140 of the Housing Act 1980, and these provisions remain in force as regards tenancies granted before the coming into operation of section 18 of and Schedule 4 to the Housing and Planning Act 1986.[35] The latter introduced a new section 33A and Schedule 4A into the 1967 Act, and replaced section 140 of the Housing Act 1980 as regards tenancies granted after the

---

[30] Defined by s. 31(1).
[31] s. 31(2).
[32] By s. 31.
[33] s. 32.
[34] Housing Act 1980, s. 140. This section also exempts certain similar tenancies granted by public bodies; considered in para. 14–06 *et seq.*
[35] Housing and Planning Act 1986, Sched. 4, para. 11.

date when they come into operation[36]. It is thus necessary to consider both the original an the replacement exclusion provisions.

Shared ownership leases granted before the coming into force of section 33A and Schedule 4A

Extent of exclusion

Such a tenancy is only excluded if (i) it was granted by a housing association registered under the Housing Associations Act 1985,[37] (ii) it fulfills the conditions set out below, and (iii) the landlord's interest belongs, for the time being, to a registered housing association (not necessarily the grantor[38]). 14–22

Conditions of tenancy

In order for a tenancy to be excluded, it must satisfy all the following conditions:

(i) It must have been granted after August 8, 1980.[39]
(ii) It must have been granted at a premium calculated by reference to a percentage of the value of the house or the cost of providing it.[40]
(iii) When granted it must have complied with the requirements made by the Secretary of State for this purpose.[41] The present requirements[42] are that either (a) the tenancy provides for the tenant to acquire the landlord's interests in the property, whether under an option or otherwise, for a consideration which is to be calculated in accordance with the terms of the lease and which is reasonable, having regard to the premium or premiums paid by the tenant under the lease, or (b) it is a "lease for the elderly," *i.e.* it relates to one of a group of dwelling-houses providing accommodation for elderly persons with social service or special facilities nearby and contains certain specified conditions.[43]
(iv) It must state the landlord's opinion that by virtue of the Housing Act 1980, s. 140 the tenancy will not be a long tenancy at a low rent

---

[36] No such date had been prescribed at the date at which this book states the law.
[37] *Ibid.* s. 140(6) as amended. If granted prior to the enactment of the 1985 Act, the housing association must have been registered under Housing Act 1974, s. 13.
[38] *Ibid.* s. 140(1).
[39] *i.e.* when s. 140 came into effect on the passing of the 1980 Act: s. 153(3).
[40] *Ibid.* s. 140(4)(*a*).
[41] *Ibid.* s. 140(4)(*b*).
[42] Housing (Exclusion of Shared Ownership Tenancies from the Leasehold Reform Act 1967) Regs. 1982 (S.I. 1982 No. 62), set out in Appendix C.
[43] *Ibid.* regulations 2 and 3, where the qualifications are set out in detail.

for the purposes of the 1967 Act when the interest of the landlord belongs to a registered housing association.[44]

Shared ownership leases granted after the coming into force of section 33A and Schedule 4A

14–23 *Extent of exclusion*

Such a tenancy is excluded if (i) it was granted by a housing association registered under the Housing Associations Act 1985 and (ii) it fulfills the conditions set out below.[45] It is immaterial whether or not the interest of the landlord still belongs to such an association.[46]

Condition of tenancy

In order for a tenancy to be excluded under this head, it must satisfy all the following conditions:

(i) It must have been granted after section 33A and Schedule 4A of the 1967 Act came into force.[47]
(ii) It must have been granted (a) for a term of 99 years or more and must not be (and cannot become) terminable except in pursuance of a provision for re-entry or forfeiture[48] and (b) at a premium calculated by reference to the value of the house or the cost of providing it, of not less than 25 per cent (or such other percentage as may be prescribed) of the figure by reference to which it was calculated.[49]
(iii) It must (a) provide for the tenant to acquire additional shares, and also the balance of the landlord's interest in the house on terms specified in the lease and complying with prescribed requirements[50]; (b) does not restrict the tenant's powers to assign mortgage or charge his interest in the house[51]; and (c) if it enables the landlord to require payment for outstanding shares in the house, do so only in such circumstances as may be prescribed.[52]
(iv) It must state the landlords opinion that by virtue of paragraph 3 of Schedule 4A the lease is excluded from the operation of Part I of

---

44 *Ibid.* s. 140(4)(*c*).
45 Sched. 3A, para. 3(1).
46 *Cf.* Housing Act 1980, s.140(1).
47 Housing and Planning Act 1986, Sched. 4, para. 11.
48 Sched. 3A, para. 3(2)(*a*).
49 *Ibid.*, para. 3(2)(*b*).
50 *Ibid.*, para. 3(2)(*c*), (*f*).
51 *Ibid.*, para. 3(2)(*d*).
52 *Ibid.*, para. 3(2)(*e*).

the 1967 Act.[53] However, in any proceedings the court can waive this requirement if of opinion that it is just and equitable to do so.[54]

Leases for the elderly

Extent of exclusion 14–24

A lease within the prescribed description of a "lease for the elderly"[55] is excluded if (i) it was granted by a housing association registered under the Housing Associations Act 1985, (ii) it fulfills the conditions set out below, and (iii) the interest of the landlord belongs to such a housing association (not necessarily the grantor).[56]

Condition of tenancy

In order for a tenancy to be excluded under this head it must satisfy all the following conditions:

(i) It must have been granted after the coming into operation of section 33A and Schedule 4A.[57]
(ii) It must have been granted at a premium which is calculated by reference to a percentage of the value of the house or of the cost of providing it.[58]
(iii) It must have complied, or the time when it was granted, with prescribed requirements.[59]
(iv) It must state the landlo^rd's opinion that by virtue of paragraph 4 of Schedule 4A the lease is excluded from the operation of Part I of the 1967 Act at any time when the interest of the landlord belongs to a registered housing association.[60]

Shared ownership leases granted pursuant to the right to buy

Tenants of many housing associations are "secure tenants" entitled to exercise the right to buy.[61] If such a tenant exercises a right to a shared ownership lease, the provisions discussed in para. 14–10 apply. 14–25

---

[53] *Ibid.*, para. 3(2)(*g*).
[54] *Ibid.*, para. 3(3).
[55] *Ibid.*, para. 4(3). No description had been prescribed at the date at which this book states the law.
[56] *Ibid.*, para. 4(1).
[57] Housing and Planning Act 1986, Sched. 4, para. 11.
[58] *Ibid.*, Sched. 4A, para 4(2)(*a*).
[59] *Ibid.*, para. 4(2)(*b*).
[60] *Ibid.*, para. 4(2)(*c*).
[61] Housing Act 1985, ss. 79, 80, 118. Note, however, that the right to buy does not arise if the housing association is a charity: *ibid.* Sched. 6, para. 1.

Other leases granted pursuant to the right to buy

The 1967 Act does not apply in the case of a tenancy granted pursuant to the right to buy where the landlord is a housing association and the freehold is owned by a charity.[62] Nor does it apply to a further tenancy granted by way of continuation of such a tenancy,[63] or a sub-tenancy directly or indirectly granted out of such a tenancy or any such further tenancy.[64]

9. Charities

14–26 Apart from the charitable bodies mentioned in this Chapter (and subject to the exception below) the 1967 Act makes no special provisions for charities; and they are accordingly bound by the provisions of the Act. As any property subject to the Act will necessarily not be "functional land" of a charity, the consent of the Charity Commissioners will not be required to the grant, conveyance or extended lease, unless the property forms part of the permanent endowment of the charity.[65] If the legal estate is vested in the Official Custodian of Charities, he must execute any conveyance or transfer.[66]

Exception

The 1967 Act does not apply in the case of a tenancy granted pursuant to the right to buy where the landlord is a housing association and the freehold is owned by a charity, and in the case of certain other associated tenancies,[67] see further para. 14–25.

10. The Crown

14–27 The Crown is not bound by the Act. But, during the passage of the 1967 Act through Parliament, the Minister of Land and Natural Resources (Mr. F. Willey, M.P.) stated in a Written Reply[68]

"The various Crown authorities will agree to enfranchisement and

---

[62] *Ibid.* s. 172(1), (2).
[63] *Ibid.* s. 142(3), referring (indirectly) to s. 3(3) of the 1967 Act: see para. 3–10.
[64] *Ibid.* s. 142(4).
[65] Charities Act 1960, ss. 29, 45(3); the word "expressly" in s. 29(3) appears to preclude reliance on that subsection in the case of a permanent endowment.
[66] Charities Act 1960, s. 17(2) authorises charity trustees to execute on behalf of the Official Custodian only if the transaction is authorised by an order of the court or of the Charity Commissioners.
[67] Housing Act 1985, s. 172.
[68] H.C. Deb., Vol. 747, Col. 42 (March 31, 1967).

extension of leases for qualified leaseholders holding from the Crown on the terms provided for in the Leasehold Reform Bill, except that enfranchisement will be refused where the house is of special architectural or historic interest or adjoins such houses and is important in safeguarding them and their surroundings . . . "

The Act contains certain enabling provisions for this purpose.[69] It is also made clear that the fact that the Crown has, or formerly had, an interest in the property will not prevent the Act from operating as between other persons.[70]

Where a sub-tenant[71] exercises his rights under the Act in respect of property in which the Crown has a freehold or intermediate leasehold interest, and the Crown has indicated that it will concur in the conveyance of the freehold or grant of an extended lease, "the reversioner"[72] can act on behalf of the Crown (as one of the "other landlords") for all purposes[73] except the execution of the conveyance or extended lease.[74] The appropriate Crown authority[75] can also itself act as "the reversioner."[76] A conveyance or extended lease executed on behalf of a missing or unascertainable landlord[77] is effective even if the Crown transpires to be that landlord.[78]

11. Bodies Owning Estates Regulated by Statute or Trust Deed

The 1967 Act does not contain any exemption from the Act[79] in favour of landlords owning estates regulated by private Act of Parliament[80] or by a trust deed.[81] The tenants of such bodies are thus entitled to exercise in full the rights conferred by the Act. However, such bodies often qualified 14–28

[69] s. 33(3), (4), (5).
[70] s. 33(1).
[71] See generally Chap. 11.
[72] As to who is "the reversioner," see para. 11–05.
[73] Sched. 1, para. 14(1).
[74] *Ibid.* para. 14(1) proviso.
[75] See s. 33(2).
[76] Sched. 1, para. 14(1).
[77] *i.e.* under s. 27(3) (see para. 17–22) or Sched. 1, para. 4(1)(*a*) (see para. 11–08).
[78] s. 27(8) and Sched. 1, para. 14(2).
[79] Strenuous efforts in Parliament to obtain exemption failed.
[80] Such as the Letchworth Garden City Corporation Act 1962. Under the proviso to s. 11(2) of that Act, the rent payable on a renewal by the Corporation of a long lease must be at site value only, *i.e.* the rent is assessed on the same basis as the revised rent payable from the original term date under an extended lease granted under the 1967 Act: see s. 15(2) and para. 7–12.
[81] Such as the Bournville Village Trust, Birmingham, and the Jordans Village Trust, Bucks.

and were granted a Minister's certificate under section 19, and so were able to apply to the High Court for a Scheme under that section.[82]

A body of this kind (not being a local authority, New Town authority or university body[83]) is unable to reserve the development rights in the property enfranchised. During the passage of the 1967 Act through Parliament, the Minister of State, Ministry of Housing and Local Government (Mr. Niall MacDermot, Q.C., M.P.) indicated that in suitable cases[84] the Government would consider sympathetically any Private Bill to enable such a body to do so,[85] but no such Private Bill has been enacted.

12. Bodies Holding Land which is Inalienable by Statute

14-29 It is understood that there are a few bodies owning freehold property which is made inalienable by a local or private Act of Parliament. The 1967 Act fails to make any provision with regard to such inalienable property,[86] and it is uncertain whether a qualified tenant of such property will be able to enfranchise or whether he will be able only to have an extended lease, as in the case of the National Trust,[87] (or such other lesser interest as permitted by the private Act). It is thought that the private Act will prevail, and that the tenant will not be entitled to enfranchise, for "where there are general words in a later Act capable of reasonable and sensible application without extending them to subjects specially dealt with by earlier legislation, you are not to hold that earlier legislation indirectly repealed, altered, or derogated from merely by force of such general words, without any indication of a particular intention to do so."[88]

[82] See Chap. 10. The bodies mentioned in the last two footnotes each obtained a scheme under s. 19.

[83] And so unable to take advantage of s. 29: see para. 14-16.

[84] The Minister was dealing primarily with Letchworth Garden City Corporation.

[85] H.C. Deb., Vol. 751, col. 1541 (October 24, 1967).

[86] Compare the Housing Act 1985, s. 182 (power in connection with the right to buy to repeal or amend local Acts).

[87] s. 32; and see para. 14-20.

[88] *Per* Lord Selborne L.C. in *Seward* v. *The Vera Cruz* (1884) 10 App.Cas. 59 at p. 68. See also *Blackpool Corporation* v. *Starr Estate Co.* [1922] 1 A.C. 27 *per* Lord Haldane at p. 34; *R.* v. *Minister of Health, ex p. Villiers* [1936] 2 K.B. 29 at p. 44; *Craies on Statute Law* (7th ed.), p. 377 *et seq.*; and *Maxwell on Interpretation of Statutes* (12th ed.), pp. 196 *et seq.*

CHAPTER 15

SETTLEMENTS AND TRUSTS

1. AFFECTING LANDLORD'S INTEREST

Obligations under the 1967 Act

Generally

Landlords who hold their interests upon trust have the same obligations under the 1967 Act as landlords who hold beneficially. So if the tenant serves an effective Notice of Leaseholder's Claim to acquire the freehold, the trustees must convey their interest free from all equitable interests capable of being overreached,[1] observing the usual statutory requirements for a conveyance by a tenant for life or statutory owners of a settlement subject to the Settled Land Act 1925,[2] or by the trustees of a settlement on trust for sale.[3] This usually means that the purchase price must be paid to two or more trustees or a trust corporation.[4] However, the equitable interests will also be overreached[5] if the purchase price is paid to a mortgagee or into court in or towards the discharge of a mortgage or a rentcharge pursuant to the provisions of the 1967 Act.[6] If the tenant serves an effective Notice of Leaseholder's Claim to an extended lease,[7] the trustees must likewise grant the extended lease, even if it is outside their powers, as is usually the case if the settlement contains no express power of leasing.[8] Where the landlord's interest is vested in a custodian trustee, the managing trustees or committee of management are deemed to be the trustees for the purposes of the 1967 Act, and the landlord's interest is deemed to be vested in them, except as regards the execution of any conveyance or extended lease.[9] **15–01**

---

[1] s. 8(1).
[2] S.L.A. 1925, s. 18(1).
[3] L.P.A. 1925, ss. 2(1), 27(2).
[4] The tenant is considered a purchaser for money or money's worth even if the purchase price is nil or nominal: s. 8(5).
[5] s. 8(4)(*a*).
[6] ss. 11–13: see paras. 12–04, (rentcharges) and 13–03 *et seq.* (mortgages).
[7] s. 14(1).
[8] The statutory powers in S.L.A. 1925, ss. 41, 42 are seldom wide enough.
[9] s. 26(1).

15–02 A purchase price paid to Settled Land Act trustees will be held by them as capital moneys. They, or the High Court on the application of any beneficiary, can require the tenant for life to reinvest the purchase price in a manner which gives the beneficiaries similar benefits to those they would have received if no sale had been made.[10] If there are no Settled Land Act trustees, or only one (not being a trust corporation), the purchase price can be paid into the High Court.[11]

Trust for sale

15–03 A purchase price paid to trustees for sale must be dealt with by them as ordinary proceeds of sale.[12] Difficulties may arise if there are no trustees, or only one (not being a trust corporation), for, unlike in the case of a Settled Land Act settlement, there is no power to pay the purchase price into court in order to overreach the beneficial interests. The author has seen it suggested that, by refusing to appoint another trustee, a single trustee for sale can effectively prevent a conveyance under the 1967 Act overreaching the beneficial interests, particularly as he is not bound to convey to the tenant any better title than he has.[13] But it is considered that in such circumstances the tenant could successfully apply to the High Court for the appointment of a new trustee or trustees (and also probably the removal of the existing trustee).[14] It is also considered that the tenant would be a "person interested" entitled to apply to the High Court to dispense with the consent of any person whose consent is required for a sale but who refuses to give his consent.[15]

Rights under the 1967 Act

15–04 Conversely, landlords who hold their interests on trust have the same rights under the 1967 Act as landlords who hold beneficially. In particular, trustees can oppose a tenant's claim under section 18 (occupation for own or family's residence) if the property is reasonably required for the occupation of a beneficiary, whether or not he is also a trustee, or an adult member of the beneficiary's family.[16] Furthermore, capital moneys under the settlement can be applied in paying compensa-

---

[10] S.L.A. 1925, s. 79.
[11] *Ibid.* ss. 18(1), 113.
[12] s. 24(1).
[13] s. 10(1).
[14] *i.e.* under the Trustee Act 1925, s. 41. Alternatively, an order might be sought under L.P.A. 1925, s. 30, but the opening words of that provision do not appear to cover the circumstances under consideration.
[15] *i.e.* under L.P.A. 1925, s. 30.
[16] s. 18(3); see para. 8–08.

tion to the tenant for the loss of his tenancy under that section or section 17 (redevelopment), whether possession is obtained with or without any application to the court, and the trustees can raise money by way of mortgage for that purpose.[17]

2. Affecting Tenant's Interest

Occupation by beneficiary

The occupation of a house by a person beneficially interested under a settlement (including one of two or more co-owners) for the qualifying three-year period will suffice for the purposes of the 1967 Act.[18] A "person beneficially interested" in this context means a personal beneficiary under a private settlement, whether his interest is under fixed or discretionary trusts; and it is sufficient if he is only "derivatively" interested, *e.g.* as a purchaser of a beneficial interest or as a beneficiary under a sub-settlement. If that beneficiary is the sole tenant for life under the Settled Land Act 1925, he can acquire the freehold or extended lease as if he were the absolute owner, for the benefit of the settlement.[19] In any other case, the trustees of the settlement can exercise the like rights which the beneficiary would have if he had been the absolute owner.[20] Trustees for this purpose include joint tenants for life and statutory owners under the Settled Land Act 1925, co-owners holding upon the statutory trusts for sale[21] (as well as any other trustees for sale), and nominees for an absolute owner. The beneficiary must have occupied the house "as his only or main residence" for the qualifying three-year period[22]; but he need not necessarily have been entitled under the trusts to occupy the house, and it is sufficient if he was merely permitted to do so by reason of his beneficial interest, *e.g.* as one of several discretionary beneficiaries.[23] However, if he is not entitled directly under the trusts to occupy, his occupation must be referable to his beneficial interest, so that (for example) occupation by a remainderman during a subsisting prior life-tenancy will not suffice. 15–05

It is expressly provided that an absolute owner may also count any previous periods of occupation as a beneficiary under a settlement towards his qualifying three-year period.[24] The converse case where a 15–06

---

[17] Sched. 2, para. 9(1); see para. 8–13.
[18] s. 6(3); see *Marsh* v. *Gilbert* (1980) 256 E.G. 715.
[19] s. 6(2).
[20] s. 6(3). The trustees thus have any rights which the beneficiary, if an absolute owner, would have acquired under s. 7 (succession on death), as to which see para. 4–08.
[21] s. 6(1).
[22] s. 1(2); and see paras. 4–02 *et seq.*
[23] s. 6(3).
[24] s. 6(1).

beneficiary was previously the absolute owner (*e.g.* where the absolute owner has transferred the tenancy into the joint names of himself and his wife, or settled it on himself for life with the remainder to his children) is not expressly covered; but it seems clear that the trustees can similarly count his period of occupation as absolute owner towards the three-year period.[25] The position is different if a husband who was an absolute owner has transferred the tenancy to his wife or settled it on his wife for life. The husband's continued occupation is not referable to any beneficial interest, and there is nothing in the 1967 Act to equate the occupation of one spouse to that of the other, or to enable one spouse to count the other's occupation towards the three-year occupation period (except on the death of the other spouse[26]).

The trustees of a public or charitable trust cannot take the benefit of these provisions, because there are only charitable objects and no persons beneficially interested under the trust. It is immaterial that a person is allowed to occupy the house by virtue of the trust, *e.g.* as in the case of a trust to use a house as a residence of a minister of a church,[27] or as a convent.

The fiduciary relationship between vendor and purchaser which arises on a contract for sale of land[27a] does not constitute a settlement or trust within these provisions, and so a purchaser cannot count any occupation prior to completion towards his qualifying three-year period.[27b]

Succession on death

15–07 The period of occupation of a deceased beneficiary can in certain cases be added to that of a member of his family who succeeds to the tenancy, whether under the trusts of the settlement or otherwise.[28] This has already been dealt with.[29]

Acquisition of freehold or extended lease

15–08 Where the trustees of a settlement, or a tenant for life under the Settled Land Act 1925, are entitled to the benefits of the 1967 Act as discussed above, they are given a statutory power to acquire the freehold or an

---

[25] Because, if during his occupation as beneficiary he had been the absolute owner, he would have the qualification: see s. 6(3).

[26] Under s. 7: see para. 4–08.

[27] But the trustees may have rights under the Places of Worship (Enfranchisement) Act 1920 as amended: see Chap. 19.

[27a] See Megarry and Wade, *The Law of Real Property* (5th Ed.) p. 602.

[27b] *Manley* v. *Duke of Westminster* (1984) West London C.C., unreported (Judge Harris Q.C.), and see para. 4–02.

[28] s. 7(3)–(6).

[29] See para. 4–08.

extended lease.[30] The powers of a tenant for life under the Settled Land Act 1925, which are also exercisable by trustees for sale,[31] have always included the power to acquire the freehold reversion to a settled tenancy.[32] These powers now also include the acceptance of an extended lease under the 1967 Act[33]; and the power to expend capital moneys, or raise moneys by way of mortgage, in order to acquire the freehold reversion, now also covers the payment of all expenses incurred in doing this or in acquiring an extended lease.[34] A conveyance of the freehold[35] or the grant of an extended lease[36] in favour of the tenant for life or statutory owners under the Settled Land Act 1925 will be a subsidiary vesting deed, and must accordingly contain (a) particulars of the last or only principal vesting instrument, (b) a statement that the property is to be held on the same trusts as the land comprised therein, (c) the names of the trustees of the settlement, and (d) the name of the person (if any) with the power to appoint new trustees.[37]

Any interest acquired by trustees, including a tenant for life under the Settled Land Act 1925, will be held on the trusts of the settlement, whether or not the machinery of the 1967 Act is used. Moreover an interest acquired by a trustee in his own name will usually be treated as having been acquired by him in his fiduciary capacity, whether or not it is acquired pursuant to a claim under the 1967 Act.[38] Any compensation payable by the landlord if he obtains possession pursuant to section 17 (redevelopment) or section 18 (occupation as own or family's residence), whether or not the landlord makes an application to the court for that purpose, is payable to the trustees of a settlement under the Settled Land Act 1925[39] and will be held by them as capital money.[40] Such compensation paid to trustees for sale will be held by them as proceeds of sale.[41]

---

[30] s. 6(4); but not if there is an explicit direction to the contrary in a trust instrument made after October 27, 1967.
[31] L.P.A. 1925, s. 28.
[32] S.L.A. 1925, s. 73(1)(x).
[33] s. 6(5).
[34] s. 6(5); it appears that the purchase price itself can be raised by mortgage.
[35] S.L.A. 1925, s. 10(1).
[36] s. 6(2)(*b*); S.L.A. 1925, s. 53(2).
[37] S.L.A. 1925, s. 10(2).
[38] *Griffith* v. *Owen* [1907] 1 Ch. 195, *per* Parker J. at p. 204; *Protheroe* v. *Protheroe* [1968] 1 W.L.R. 519, C.A.
[39] Sched. 2, para. 7(1).
[40] There is no express provision, but see S.L.A. 1925, s. 81.
[41] Sched. 2, para. 7(3).

Chapter 16

COURT AND TRIBUNAL PROCEEDINGS

1. High Court

16–01 The jurisdiction of the High Court under the 1967 Act is as follows:

(a) *Management schemes.* All proceedings for the approval[1] or for the variation[2] of a management scheme under section 19 must be brought in the High Court, and are assigned to the Chancery Division.[3] The procedure is discussed in Chapter 10. However, a restrictive covenant in a scheme can also be discharged or modified by the Lands Tribunal under section 84(1), Law of Property Act 1925 as amended.[4]

(b) *Missing landlord.* A tenant who wishes to acquire the freehold, but who is prevented from doing so because the landlord cannot be found, may apply for an order vesting the freehold in him.[5] Such an application must be made to the High Court and is assigned to the Chancery Division.[6] As to the procedure, see Chapter 17.

(c) *Forfeiture.* Forfeiture proceedings may be commenced in the usual way in the Queen's Bench or the Chancery Division of the High Court, as well as in the county court, notwithstanding that the tenant has served a Notice of Leaseholder's Claim.[7] However, in such a case, the leave of the court is required, and can only be granted if the court is satisfied that the tenant's claim was not made "in good faith."[8] The High Court may also make certain other orders in connection with forfeiture proceedings.[9]

(d) *Damages.* A claim arising out of the 1967 Act for damages or pecuniary compensation only may be brought in the High Court, as well as in the county court.[10]

16–02 In addition, the High Court has a general power[11] to order the removal into the High Court of any proceedings in a county court, if the High

---

[1] s. 19(1).
[2] s. 19(4).
[3] R.S.C. Ord. 93, r. 15.
[4] *Re Calthorpe Estate, Edgbaston, Birmingham* (1973) 26 P. & C.R. 120.
[5] s. 27.
[6] R.S.C. Ord. 93, r. 15.
[7] Sched. 3, para. 3.
[8] *Ibid.* para. 4(1). For a full discussion, see para. 5–14.
[9] *Ibid.* para. 4(3).
[10] s. 20(7).
[11] Under s. 41, County Courts Act 1984, replacing s. 115, County Courts Act 1959, specifically referred to in s. 20(1), (2) of the 1967 Act.

Court or a judge thereof thinks it desirable that the proceedings should be heard and determined in the High Court.[12] The High Court has an absolute discretion in this respect,[13] and one ground on which an application for that purpose has sometimes succeeded is that a difficult point of law is involved.[14] However, as the 1967 Act expressly confers a general jurisdiction on the county court and there is a direct appeal on a point of law to the Court of Appeal, it is considered that an application will succeed only in very exceptional circumstances.

Although "the Court" in the 1967 Act usually means the county court, the High Court has in fact accepted jurisdiction in at least two cases[15] concerning the construction of a particular section of the Act. In one case this was done notwithstanding that there were contemporaneous proceedings pending in the county court, it being said that the originating summons was not one involving "any jurisdiction expressed to be conferred on the county court" by the 1967 Act[16]; but this statement appears to have been made *per incuriam.*[17] Nevertheless, the jurisdiction is useful in cases where the tenant is unable to make a claim, *e.g.* because he does not yet satisfy the three-year residential requirement but it is desired to establish whether he will have a valid claim when he does so; it is doubtful if the county court has jurisdiction to make an appropriate declaration in such circumstances.[18]

2. County Court

Outline

16–03 Generally speaking, the county court has jurisdiction in all matters arising under the 1967 Act,[19] and is the proper forum for all proceedings under that Act, except in relation to the following:

(a) *Management schemes and missing landlords.* As seen above,[20] the High Court has sole jurisdiction as to these matters.

---

[12] Application may be made to a Master or (outside London) to a District Registrar who may order any county court proceedings to be stayed pending the final hearing of the application: R.S.C. Ord. 107, r. 2.

[13] *Challis* v. *Watson* [1913] 1 K.B. 547.

[14] *Rees* v. *Williams* (1851) 7 Exch. 51.

[15] *Harris* v. *Plentex Ltd.* (1980) 40 P. & C.R. 483; *Eton College* v. *Bard* [1983] Ch. 321 (unreported before Whitford J. at first instance).

[16] *Harris* v. *Plentex Ltd. supra,* per Vinelott J. at p. 484.

[17] The case seems to fall within s. 20(2)(*a*).

[18] The wording of s. 22 appears not to be wide enough to confer jurisdiction.

[19] See s. 20.

[20] See para. 16–01.

(b) *Valuation matters.* Leasehold valuation tribunals (and formerly the Lands Tribunal[21]) have sole jurisdiction on questions of valuation.[22]

16–04 In particular, the 1967 Act expressly provides[23] that the county court is the proper forum for the following:

1. Proceedings to determine whether a person is entitled to acquire the freehold or an extended lease of a house and premises, or to what property his right extends. (However, as mentioned above, there appears to be no jurisdiction to determine a question of construction of the 1967 Act if there is no current claim[24]).
2. Proceedings to determine the contents of any conveyance of the freehold or extended lease.[25]
3. Proceedings relating to the performance or discharge of obligations arising from the service of a Notice of Leaseholder's Claim,[26] including proceedings for specific performance[27] or for payment of damages[28] or compensation.[29]
4. Proceedings to determine the amount of a sub-tenant's share of compensation in the event of the landlord exercising his right to possession, or for establishing or giving effect to his right to it.[30]
5. Proceedings to determine any question of apportionment of rent.[31]
6. Proceedings to determine any question of appointment or aggregation of rateable value.[32]

However, leasehold valuation tribunals (and formerly the Lands Tribunal[33]) have concurrent jurisdiction in respect of matters within categories 2, 4 and 5 above, either by agreement or where an application is made with reference to the same transaction.[34] In appropriate cases the county court has power to transfer those matters to a leasehold valuation tribunal.[35]

---

[21] See para. 16–07.
[22] See paras. 16–06 *et seq.*
[23] s. 20(2), (3).
[24] See para. 16–02.
[25] *i.e.* under s. 9 or s. 15 as the case may be.
[26] See generally Chap. 5.
[27] It seems clear that specific performance proceedings arising out of the 1967 Act can be brought in the county court even if the purchase price, or the value of the property in the case of an extended lease, exceeds the usual county court limit of £30,000.
[28] *i.e.* under the general law: see s. 5(3).
[29] *i.e.* under the special provisions in, *e.g.* ss. 9(3) and 20(5).
[30] *i.e.* under ss. 17 and 18 and Sched. 2: see Chap. 8.
[31] s. 20(3).
[32] *i.e.* under s. 37(6), incorporating s. 25(2) Rent Act 1977: see para. 2–18.
[33] See para. 16–07.
[34] s. 21(2).
[35] s. 21(3): see para. 16–06.

Procedure

Most applications under the 1967 Act should be brought by Originating Application under Order 3, rule 4 of the County Court Rules 1981, and the appropriate relief is usually one or more declarations.[36] The venue for the proceedings is usually the court for the district in which the house in question is situated.[37] Such proceedings can be (and often are) brought by landlords, *e.g.* for a declaration that the tenant is not entitled to acquire the freehold under the 1967 Act, particularly in cases where the contractual tenancy has expired, or is due to expire shortly.[38] **16–05**

Special rules are made[39] for (a) payments into court[40] in respect of rentcharges and mortgagees, (b) the transfer of proceedings to a leasehold valuation tribunal and (c) applications by the landlord for possession.[41]

Appeal

Appeal from the county court lies to the Court of Appeal in the usual way.[42] An appellant cannot raise a point on appeal unless it was taken in the county court[43]; but a respondent can support the decision of the county court on any ground, whether or not taken previously.[44]

3. Leasehold Valuation Tribunals

Jurisdiction

Leasehold valuation tribunals have exclusive jurisdiction on matters of **16–06**

---

[36] The remedy of specific performance is sometimes claimed but is seldom appropriate. A specific performance order cannot properly be made until (in the case of the acquisition of the freehold) the purchase price and the terms of the conveyance or transfer have been agreed or determined, or (in the case of the grant of an extended lease) the terms of the extended lease have been agreed or determined.

[37] Order 4, rule 8 of the C.C.R. 1981. The district in which the respondent or one of the respondents resides or carries on business is a possible alternative.

[38] *i.e.* in order to enable the landlord to serve a notice under s. 4 or s. 25, Landlord and Tenant Act 1954 and to prevent the automatic continuation of the tenancy: see paras. 2 and 3, Sched. 3 and para. 5–12.

[39] By Order 49, rule 8 of the C.C.R. 1981, set out in Appendix C.

[40] *i.e.* under ss. 11(4) or 13(1) or (3).

[41] *i.e.* under ss. 17 or 18: see Chap. 8. No form of notice to the occupants is prescribed, but Form No. 426 can be used.

[42] County Courts Act 1984, s. 77.

[43] *Smith* v. *Baker and Sons Ltd.* [1891] A.C. 325; *Boyer* v. *Warbey* [1953] 1 Q.B. 234. For examples under the 1967 Act, see *Peck* v. *Anicar Properties Ltd.* [1971] 1 All E.R. 517 and *Gaidowski* v. *Gonville and Caius College, Cambridge* [1975] 1 W.L.R. 1066 at p. 1070E.

[44] *Weller and Son Ltd.* v. *Thomas* [1921] 1 K.B. 541, D.C., approved in *Thomas* v. *Marconi's Wireless Telegraph Co. Ltd.* [1965] 1 W.L.R. 850, C.A.

valuation arising under the 1967 Act, subject to appeal to the Lands Tribunal. These may concern the following[45]:

(a) the price payable on the acquisition of the freehold[46];
(b) the revised ground rent payable under an extended lease, both from the original term date or from the 25th anniversary thereof[47];
(c) the compensation payable to the tenant[48] if the landlord obtains an order for possession for the purpose of redevelopment (section 17) or for his own or his family's occupation[49] (section 18).

The author has seen a suggestion that this jurisdiction is linked to the determination of figures, and that the tribunal has no jurisdiction to determine whether the freehold purchase price ought to be on the valuation basis of section 9(1) or section 9(1A) of the 1967 Act, as amended. So, it is said, the tribunal cannot determine whether a Valuation Officer's Certificate under Schedule 8 of the Housing Act 1974, given after the date of service of the tenant's Notice of Leaseholder's Claim has a retroactive effect for that purpose, even though the right to enfranchise is admitted and only the purchase price remains in dispute.[50] This suggestion appears clearly erroneous. There are numerous examples in other fields of a tribunal deciding a point of law which is necessary for the determination of a matter within the tribunal's jurisdiction[51]; and the question of the correct basis of valuation is no different in this respect from any other point of law. Leasehold valuation tribunals have (correctly, it is submitted) in fact determined the valuation basis in several cases.[52]

16–07 If an application is made to a leasehold valuation tribunal to determine one of the above matters of valuation, the tribunal may also determine questions as to the contents of any conveyance or extended lease or as to the apportionment of rent or compensation[53]; and the parties can by agreement confer jurisdiction on a leasehold valuation tribunal to determine such questions.[54] Further, if an application has been made to

---

[45] s. 21(1), as amended by para. 8(1), Sched. 22 of the Housing Act 1980.
[46] *i.e.* under s. 9(1) or 9(1A).
[47] *i.e.* under s. 15(2).
[48] Para. 5, Sched. 2.
[49] See Chap. 8.
[50] For a discussion of this difficult point, see paras. 2–36 *et seq.*
[51] *e.g.* by the Lands Tribunal under s. 1 of the Land Compensation Act 1961.
[52] *Effra Investments Ltd.* v. *Stergios* (1982) 264 E.G. 449; *Chada* v. *Norton Estate Trustees* (1985) 276 E.G. 312; *Oliver* v. *Central Estates (Belgravia) Ltd.* (1985) 276 E.G. 1358. See also *Burford Estate & Property Co. Ltd.* v. *Creasy* (1986) 277 E.G. 73 (other preliminary issues determined); and *Hickman* v. *Phillimore Kensington Estate Trustees* (1985) 274 E.G. 1261 (basis of valuation determined by Lands Tribunal appointed as arbitrator).
[53] s. 21(2), as amended by para. 8(3), Sched. 22 of the Housing Act 1980.
[54] *Ibid.*

the court to determine any of such questions and an application is subsequently made to a leasehold valuation tribunal to determine a valuation matter, the court can by order transfer those questions to the leasehold valuation tribunal if it appears convenient that the matters arising on the two applications should be considered together.[55] However, a leasehold valuation tribunal has no power to deal with the costs incurred in the court proceedings or subsequently to the transfer[56]; and it is suggested that this is a factor which the court ought to take into consideration in deciding whether or not to order a transfer.

The above jurisdiction was originally exercised by the Lands Tribunal, but as from March 31, 1981, was transferred to leasehold valuation tribunals.[57] However, provision is made for appeal to the Lands Tribunal.[58]

Constitution

A leasehold valuation tribunal is a rent assessment committee under Schedule 10 to the Rent Act 1977, when constituted to make any determination under the 1967 Act.[59] At least one of its members must be a person who has experience in the valuation of land.[60] Like rent assessment committees generally,[61] they regard themselves as entitled to rely on their own general knowledge and experience, whatever the evidence or representations (or absence of such) submitted by the parties; and there is nothing in the legislation which restricts their determination to the limits indicated by the amounts considered appropriate by the parties.[62] However, it is considered that if evidence is given by experienced valuers on each side, a tribunal should be slow to depart from those limits or to arrive at its decision by a method not adopted by either valuer; and it should certainly not do so without giving the parties an opportunity to comment before giving its decision.[63] **16–08**

Procedure

The procedure before a leasehold valuation tribunal is governed by the **16–09**

[55] s. 21(3), as amended by para. 8(4), Sched. 22 of the Housing Act 1980.
[56] Unlike the Lands Tribunal under s. 21(4) as originally enacted (replaced by para. 8(5), Sched. 22 of the Housing Act 1980).
[57] Housing Act 1980, s. 142(1).
[58] *Ibid.* para. 2, Sched. 22; see paras. 16–11 *et seq.*
[59] *Ibid.* s. 142(1), (2).
[60] *Ibid.* para. 1, Sched. 22.
[61] See *Crofton Investment Trust Ltd.* v. *Greater London Rent Assessment Committee* [1967] 2 Q.B. 955, D.C.; and *Metropolitan Properties Co. (F.G.C.) Ltd.* v. *Lannon* [1968] 1 W.L.R. 815, D.C.
[62] See the comments of the tribunals in *Yates* v. *Bridgewater Estates Ltd.* (1982) 261 E.G. 1001 and *Blake* v. *British Petroleum Pension Trust Ltd.* (1981) 259 E.G. 777.
[63] *British Petroleum Pension Trust Ltd.* v. *Blake* (1982) 264 E.G. 721, L.T., at p. 724.

Rent Assessment Committee (England and Wales) (Leasehold Valuation Tribunal) Regulations 1981, to which detailed reference should be made.[64] Any application must be in the prescribed Form 1, 2 or 3 set out in the Schedule to the Regulations, or in a form substantially to the like effect.[65] Where the application relates to price for the freehold, it can only be made if the landlord has informed the tenant of the price his is asking or if two months from service of the Notice of Leaseholder's Claim have elapsed without his doing so.[66]

Where a matter is referred to it, a tribunal may by notice in writing served on the tenant or landlord or on any superior landlord require him to give to the tribunal, within such period (being not less than 14 days from service of the notice) as may be specified in the notice, such information as the tribunal may reasonably require.[67] The tribunal must take all reasonable steps to ensure such information, and the results of any other enquiries it has made, are supplied to each of the parties before the hearing.[68] The tribunal must also take all reasonable steps to ensure that a copy of, or sufficient extracts from or particulars of, any relevant document received by it from one party are supplied to the other parties before the hearing.[69] The tribunal endeavours to ensure that the parties exchange particulars of their valuations and of all comparable transactions on which they intend to rely, but there is no power to require an exchange.[70] If any new valuation or comparable is introduced at the hearing, the tribunal must adjourn to afford the other party sufficient opportunity to deal with it, unless the other party consents or the tribunal considers that he will have a sufficient opportunity without an adjournment.[71]

The Regulations make provisions as to the hearing before the tribunal,[72] which must be in public unless for special reasons the tribunal otherwise decides.[73] A party may appear either in person or by any person authorised by him, whether or not such person is a counsel or a solicitor.[74] At least 14 days' notice of the leasing, stating its date, time and place,

---

[64] S.I. 1981 No. 271, made under s. 21(4A) (inserted by para. 8(6), Sched. 22, Housing Act 1980), set out in Appendix C.
[65] s. 21(4A) and reg. 3.
[66] s. 21(1B) inserted by para. 8(2), Sched. 22, Housing Act 1980.
[67] Para. 7(1), Sched. 22, Housing Act 1980. If any person fails without reasonable cause to comply with such a notice, he is liable on summary conviction to a fine not exceeding £200; para. 7(2).
[68] reg. 9(1)(*b*).
[69] reg. 9(1)(*a*).
[70] *Hall* v. *L. F. Rosen Settlement's Trustees* (1983) 269 E.G. 329, L.V.T.
[71] reg. 9(2).
[72] regs. 5 to 8.
[73] reg. 5(5).
[74] reg. 6(c).

must be given to the parties, and a copy of such notice sent to any other person who has given notice of his intention to appear.[75] The tribunal may proceed to deal with an application in the absence of a party, if satisfied that such party has been duly notified of the hearing.[76] The tribunal's decision must be recorded in a signed document containing the reasons for the decision, but containing no reference to the decision being by a majority (if that be the case) or to any opinion of a minority[77]; and a copy must be sent by the tribunal to each party.[78]

Costs

The tribunal has no power to make any order as to costs; and the landlord's valuation costs which a tenant must pay[79] do not include the landlord's costs before the tribunal.[80] 16–10

Appeal

Appeal from the leasehold valuation tribunal lies only to the Lands Tribunal, as to which see para. 16–11. Unlike the case of a rent assessment committee, no appeal lies to the High Court,[81] and it is not possible to apply for a Case Stated.[82]

4. Lands Tribunal

Appeal from leasehold valuation tribunal

Any person who is dissatisfied with the decision of a leasehold valuation tribunal in proceedings to which he was a party may appeal to the Lands Tribunal if (but only if) he appeared before the tribunal.[83] The appeal can be brought on matters of fact and valuation, as well as on points of law, and (unless the parties otherwise agree) involves a complete re-hearing.[84] 16–11

---

[75] regs. 5(2) and 13.
[76] reg. 7.
[77] reg. 11(1).
[78] reg. 11(3).
[79] *i.e.* under s. 9(4) or s. 1(2).
[80] Housing Act 1980, para. 5, Sched. 22.
[81] *i.e.* by virtue of s. 13(1), Tribunals and Inquiries Act 1971.
[82] Housing Act 1980, para. 2, Sched. 22.
[83] *Ibid.*
[84] *Re London and Winchester Properties Ltd.'s Appeal* (1983) 45 P. & C.R. 429 (which, despite the appellant's name, concerned a house in Liverpool); and see *British Petroleum Pension Trust Ltd.* v. *Blake* (1982) 264 E.G. 721, L.T. and *Lowther* v. *Strandberg* (1985) 274 E.G. 53.

Procedure

16–12 Notice of appeal must be given, by written notice in Form 3A[85] and sent to the registrar of the Lands Tribunal, within 28 days after delivery of the tribunal's decision,[86] *i.e.* the date endorsed on the document issued by the tribunal recording its decision.[87]

There is no power to extend the time for appealing.[88] The notice of appeal must state the grounds on which the appellant intends to rely, and he is not entitled to rely on any other grounds unless the Lands Tribunal thinks it just in all the circumstances, and on such terms as to costs or adjournment or otherwise as it may think fit, to allow such additional grounds to be put forward.[89] However, it has been said that as the appeal involves a complete re-hearing the grounds of appeal can be stated quite generally (as in the case of rating appeals)[90] *e.g.* "the purchase price determined by the leasehold valuation tribunal is excessive." The appellant must also inform the registrar of the names and addresses of the other parties to the dispute.[91] If any such other party wishes to appear, he must give notice to the registrar within 21 days, stating (*inter alia*) the grounds on which he relies[92]; but a respondent is not limited to the grounds stated in his notice.[93] The Rules provide that the registrar can direct the parties to exchange statements of their cases.[94] It has been suggested,[95] on the authority of a rating case,[96] that if another party also wishes to challenge the tribunal's decision, he should also serve a notice of appeal, because the Lands Tribunal only has power to depart from the decision of the tribunal in favour of a party appealing. But this seems doubtful,[97] particularly as the hearing before the Lands Tribunal is a re-hearing[98] and the Rules make no provision for a cross-appeal.

16–13 The Lands Tribunal sits in public,[99] unless it is determining the appeal without a hearing[1] (or is sitting as an arbitrator).[2] Leave must be obtained

---

[85] Set out at para. 20–144.
[86] r. 12, Lands Tribunal Rules 1975 as amended.
[87] r. 2(2), as amended.
[88] *Cf. James* v. *Gerrard (V.O.)* [1972] R.A. 45, L.T.
[89] r. 43.
[90] *Re London and Winchester Properties Ltd.'s Appeal, supra*, at p. 431.
[91] r. 12.
[92] r. 13.
[93] *Croydon Corporation* v. *Hardiman (V.O.)* (1962) 9 R.R.C. 382, L.T.
[94] rr. 11(1) and 14.
[95] In *British Petroleum Pension Trust Ltd.* v. *Blake, supra.*
[96] *Ellerby* v. *March* [1954] 2 Q.B. 357, C.A.
[97] The decision in *Ellerby* v. *March, supra*, turned on the wording of ss. 48 and 49 of the Local Government Act 1948, (now ss. 76 and 77 of the General Rate Act 1967), and the wording of para. 2, Sched. 22 to the Housing Act 1980 is different.
[98] *Cf. Croydon Corporation* v. *Hardiman (V.O.)* and *Wates Ltd., supra.*
[99] r. 33.
[1] *i.e.* under r. 33A. It is thought that an appeal from a leasehold valuation tribunal will not be heard without a hearing, unless all parties consent.
[2] See para. 16–15.

to call more than one expert witness.[3] If more than one party intends to call an expert witness, copies of their valuations (including particulars and computations in support of their valuations) and particulars of the comparables on which they intend to rely must be sent to the registrar[4]; and when he has received all such documents, the registrar must send copies to each party within seven days.[5] The Lands Tribunal can admit new evidence which was not before the leasehold valuation tribunal,[6] and has a discretion to admit further evidence between the hearing and its decision.[7]

It has been said that as the appeal is a complete re-hearing, the appeal must be determined solely on the evidence presented before the Lands Tribunal, without regard to the evidence given to the leasehold valuation tribunal.[8] This seems questionable and unfortunate, particularly as the respondent to the appeal is put to the expense of repeating his valuation evidence and the main purpose of the introduction of leasehold valuation tribunals was to avoid expense. Previous decisions of the Lands Tribunal are of high persuasive authority, but the Lands Tribunal is not bound by them.[9]

Although the statutory provisions do not expressly so provide[10], it has been held that the Lands Tribunal has all the powers conferred on leasehold valuation tribunals, and can make an appropriate order determining the purchase price.[11]

Costs

The Lands Tribunal has a full discretionary power to award costs, either on the High Court or any county court scale.[12] And where the county court gives a certificate of unreasonable delay or default,[13] the 16–14

---

[3] r. 42(2). Leave should normally be sought under r. 45 before the hearing. If leave is sought at the hearing, the tribunal may adjourn the hearing "on such terms as to costs and otherwise as it thinks fit" (r. 42(6)), which usually involves the applicant in paying the costs of the adjournment.

[4] r. 42(3).

[5] r. 42(4).

[6] *Croydon Corporation* v. *Hardiman* (V.O.), *supra.*

[7] *Wexler* v. *Playle* (V.O.) [1960] 1 Q.B. 217, C.A.

[8] *Re London and Winchester Properties Ltd.'s Appeal* (1983) 45 P. & C.R. 429. The tenant did not appear before the Lands Tribunal, doubtless because the expense of so doing would have been wholly disproportionate to the amount in dispute.

[9] *West Midland Baptist (Trust) Association* v. *Birmingham Corporation* [1968] 2 Q.B. 188, *per* Salmon L.J. at p. 210.

[10] *Cf.* s. 77 of the General Rate Act 1967 (appeal from local valuation court).

[11] *Re London and Winchester Properties Ltd.'s Appeal, supra.* ("these inept provisions").

[12] Lands Tribunal Rules 1975, r. 56(1), (2).

[13] *i.e.* under s. 20(4) or para. 8(1), Sched. 2 of the 1967 Act.

Lands Tribunal may make a similar order for costs in relation to the matter in question as the county court is authorised to make.[14]

When it acted as a tribunal of first instance in valuation matters, the Lands Tribunal at first accepted that the tenant's position was analagous to that of an acquiring authority in compulsory purchase cases, and awarded costs to the landlord if he obtained a price higher than that offered by the tenant.[15] But this approach seems to have been tacitly abandoned, and the Lands Tribunal frequently made no order as to costs in cases where the figure determined fell between those contended for by the parties.[16] However, the "sealed offer" procedure was made expressly applicable,[17] and was commonly invoked by tenants[18] so if the landlord only obtained a figure below the tenant's sealed offer, he was ordered to pay the tenant's costs as from the date of the offer[19]; but if he obtained a higher figure, the tenant was usually ordered to pay his costs.[20] A sealed offer from the landlord was of less importance, and he sometimes was awarded costs even if the figure obtained was below his sealed offer.[21]

However, it is considered that the foregoing has little applicability to the question of costs before the Lands Tribunal in its appellate capacity, and that rather different factors should govern the exercise of the discretion. As the main reason for the introduction of leasehold valuation tribunals was to avoid the expense of a hearing before the Lands Tribunal, it would be incongruous if an unsuccessful respondent were ordered to pay the appellant's costs of an appeal and thus be considerably worse off than if there had been only a Lands Tribunal hearing. It is therefore suggested that in the normal case (and in particular if the appeal is brought by the landlord on a test case), there should be no order as to the costs of a successful appeal. In one case,[22] in which the tenant did not appear before the Lands Tribunal and the landlord obtained an increase of £80 in the purchase price, the Tribunal refused the landlord's application for costs, partly because by failing to appear the tenant "may

---

[14] Housing Act 1980, para. 6, Sched. 22.

[15] See, *e.g. Haw* v. *Peek* (1969) 210 E.G. 347; *Rees* v. *Scott* (1969) 211 E.G. 415.

[16] *The Goldsmith's Company* v. *Guardian Assurance Co. Ltd.* (1970) 216 E.G. 597; *County & Metropolitan Developments Ltd.* v. *Brewer Trust* (1971) 219 E.G. 775; *Baker* v. *Cox* (1979) 250 E.G. 1094; *Stopa* v. *Trotter* (1981) 257 E.G. 75, L.T.

[17] Lands Tribunal Rules 1975, r. 50(2).

[18] The offer had to be unconditional for this purpose: *Williams* v. *Davies* (1973) 225 E.G. 1679.

[19] See *e.g. Harrison* v. *Representative Body of the Church in Wales* (1970) 215 E.G. 713; *Wolff* v. *Clifton Properties Ltd.* (1970) 22 P. & C.R. 553; *Farr* v. *Millersons Investments Ltd.* (1971) 22 P. & C.R. 1055; *Norfolk* v. *Trinity College Cambridge* (1976) 32 P. & C.R. 147.

[20] See *e.g. Petroff* v. *Trustees of the Guenter (Cedars) Estate* (1970) 22 P. & C.R. 818; *Kemp* v. *Josephine Trust Ltd.* (1970) 22 P. & C.R. 804; *Finney* v. *St. Pier* (1971) 218 E.G. 867; *Adams* v. *Lloyd* (1974) 232 E.G. 1370.

[21] See *e.g. Gajewski* v. *Anderton* (1971) 217 E.G. 885.

[22] *Re London and Winchester Properties Ltd.'s Appeal, supra.*

have assisted the appellants in their success" and partly because the landlord would probably benefit from the decision in relation to other properties. It is considered that this was an entirely correct exercise of the Tribunal's discretion, although it might have been further justified by the wider considerations outlined above. In the other cases which have so far reached the Lands Tribunal on appeal, the successful party did not ask for costs and no order to costs was made.

Legal Aid is available in the Lands Tribunal,[23] and this can afford the tenant an effective safeguard against any award of costs against him.[24] In such cases, there must be an order for taxation in accordance with Schedule 2 of the Legal Aid Act 1974.

Appeal to Court of Appeal

An appeal from the Lands Tribunal lies directly to the Court of Appeal, **16–15**
but only on a point of law.[25] Any person aggrieved (but not the leasehold valuation tribunal itself)[26] may require the Lands Tribunal to state a case for the decision of the Court of Appeal.[27] As to the procedure, see R.S.C. Order 61, rule 1. At the time of going to press there have been only four such appeals.[28] There is a further appeal to the House of Lords, with leave of the Court of Appeal or the House of Lords.[29]

Arbitration

The Lands Tribunal can sit as an arbitrator in valuation matters,[30] with **16–16**
a right of appeal on a point of law direct to the Court of Appeal.[31] Several procedural and other provisions of the Arbitration Act 1950[32] are applicable to an arbitration by the Lands Tribunal. But the Arbitration Act 1979 does not apply, so the appeal to the Court of Appeal is as of right and does not require the prior leave of a High Court judge under that Act. When leasehold valuation tribunals were introduced, there was no

---

[23] Legal Aid Act 1974, para. 5, Pt. I, Sched. 1.
[24] *Ibid.* s. 8(1)(*e*).
[25] Lands Tribunal Act 1949, s. 3(4).
[26] Housing Act 1980, para. 3, Sched. 22.
[27] *Ibid.*
[28] *Official Custodian of Charities* v. *Goldridge* (1973) 26 P. & C.R. 191; *Gallaher Estates Ltd.* v. *Walker* (1973) 28 P. & C.R. 113; *Jones* v. *Wrotham Park Settled Estates* (1977) 37 P. & C.R. 289 (reversed by the House of Lords [1980] A.C. 74); and *Wilkes* v. *Larkcroft Properties Ltd.* (1983) 268 E.G. 903. See also *Mosley* v. *Hickman* (1986) 52 P. & C.R., 248, an appeal from the Lands Tribunal sitting as an arbitrator, *sub. nom Hickman* v. *Phillimore Kensington Estates Trustees* (1985) 274 E.G. 1261.
[29] Administration of Justice (Appeals) Act 1934, s. 1.
[30] Lands Tribunal Act 1949, s. 1(5).
[31] *Ibid.* s. 3(4). See *Mosley* v. *Hickman, supra.*
[32] Listed in Lands Tribunal Rules 1975, r. 38 (S.I. 1975 No. 299), set out in Appendix C.

machinery for transfer of proceedings then already pending in the Lands Tribunal, and the Lands Tribunal accepted its appointment by consent of all parties in such cases.[33] Parties in other cases, particularly where the amounts involved are substantial, sometimes wish to appoint the Lands Tribunal as arbitrator so as to effectively by-pass the leasehold valuation tribunal with a view to a saving of expense and time. It is understood that the Lands Tribunal is willing to accept appointment as an arbitrator in suitable cases, *e.g.* if the amounts involved are substantial and the matters in issue are largely questions of law.[34]

[33] *Lloyd-Jones* v. *Church Commissioners for England* (1982) 261 E.G. 471 is an example of such a case.
[34] As in *Hickman* v. *Phillimore Kensington Estate Trustees* (1985) 274 E.G. 1261.

CHAPTER 17

MISCELLANEOUS

1. CONTRACTING OUT

Generally

Not surprisingly, the 1967 Act contains provisions which prevent the landlord and the tenant contracting out of the Act or otherwise avoiding its effect. With certain exceptions dealt with below, "any agreement relating to a tenancy (whether contained in the instrument creating the tenancy or not and whether made before the creation of the tenancy or not) shall be void insofar as it purports to exclude or modify" any of the tenant's rights under the Act, "or provides for the termination or surrender of the tenancy in the event of a tenancy acquiring or claiming any such right or for the imposition of any penalty or disability on the tenant in that event."[1] Several points arise out of this. **17–01**

"Agreement relating to the tenancy"

An agreement may "relate to" a tenancy even though one or both of the landlord or the tenant is not a party to it. Thus a contract made by the tenant with a company in which the landlord is interested is such an agreement, as is a contract by the landlord with a relative of the tenant.[2] Similarly, a concurrent lease granted to a third party subject to and with the benefit of a tenancy has been held by the Court of Appeal to relate to the tenancy.[3]

"Purports to"

In the context, "purports to" is not limited to its primary meaning of "is expressed to but not effectively," but has the wider meaning of "has the effect of."[4]

---

[1] s.23(1), the wording of which is similar to that of Landlord and Tenant Act 1954, s.38(1); and see also 1954 Act, s.17.

[2] *Jones* v. *Wrotham Park Settled Estates* [1980] A.C. 74, *per* Orr L.J. at pp. 85–6; and see *per* Goff L.J. at p. 88F, and *per* Stephenson L.J. at p. 91F.

[3] *Ibid.* reversing the Lands Tribunal at (1977) 33 P. & C.R. 304. The point was left open in the House of Lords: [1980] A.C. 74 at p. 114D.

[4] *Ibid.* at pp. 85G, 89D, applying dicta of Lord Denning M.R. and Diplock L.J. in *Joseph* v. *Joseph* [1967] Ch. 78 (decided on Landlord and Tenant Act 1954, s.38(1)), followed in *Allnatt London Properties Ltd.* v. *Newton* [1984] 1 All E.R. 423, C.A. This point was also left open in the *Jones* case in the House of Lords: [1980] A.C. 74 at p. 114D.

"Modify"

An example of a modification of the tenant's rights is a provision postponing the right of enfranchisement until the end of the term of the tenancy.[5] It seems probable that an artificial alteration of the rent payable under the tenancy (or of the length of the term or some other provision of the tenancy), in a way that would affect the purchase price on enfranchisement, would also involve such a modification.[6] But a "modification of the situation to which the statutory system of calculation of the price applies" is not a modification of the tenant's rights of enfranchisement "which remain untouched save as to the cost of enforcing the right."[7] On this basis, a complicated device involving a concurrent lease granted by the landlord to an associated company under which the rent became a full rack rent if the tenant under the original tenancy enfranchised (thus increasing the market value of the landlord's interest[8]) was held not to "modify" the tenant's rights under the Act, notwithstanding that the obvious purpose of the device was to increase substantially the aggregate purchase price payable by the tenant.[9]

"Provides for"

It is considered that in the context this expression is not limited to "provides expressly for" but has the wider meaning of "has the effect of providing for,"[10] but the point remains undecided.[11]

"Termination or surrender"

Any term providing, directly or indirectly, for the automatic cesser of the term of a tenancy, or for the landlord to have a right of determination or forfeiture of the term, in the event of the service of a Notice of Leaseholder's Claim, is clearly rendered invalid.

"Penalty or disability"

The precise meaning and ambit of these expressions is uncertain. The context plainly precludes "penalty" having either of its usual legal meanings of a fine or other imposition in criminal proceedings and of a fixed sum payable upon the breach of a contract. The word appears to

---

[5] *Ibid.* [1980] A.C. 74 at p. 114B.
[6] As suggested by counsel for the tenant at *ibid.* p. 103F.
[7] *Ibid.* at p. 114A.
[8] Determined separately under Sched. 1 of the 1967 Act: see para. 11–14.
[9] *Jones* v. *Wrotham Park Settled Estates, supra*, discussed at para. 11–23. The effect of the decision has been reversed by the Leasehold Reform Act 1979: see para. 11–24.
[10] *Cf. I.R.C.* v. *Jamieson* [1964] A.C. 1445.
[11] The dicta of Orr and Goff L.JJ. in *Jones* v. *Wrotham Park Settled Estates, supra*, at pp. 87B and 90B, suggest the contrary view, but this appears to be unduly narrow.

mean (and to be restricted to) a sum of money or its equivalent which becomes due; as an obvious example, a covenant on the part of the tenant to pay a sum of money on the service of a Notice of Leaseholder's Claim would involve a "penalty." A "disability" probably covers other adverse consequences of a Notice, such as the tenant being precluded from occupying the property or his use of it being otherwise restricted. But the device involving a concurrent lease mentioned above was held not to involve any "penalty or disability."[12]

Exceptions

The provisions discussed above do not, however, prevent the tenant surrendering his tenancy.[13] Nor do they invalidate any agreement of the following kinds: 17–02

(a) Agreements under which the tenant is entitled to acquire the freehold or any intermediate tenancy, or an extended lease, on terms different from those provided for by the 1967 Act.[14]
(b) Agreements whereby any Notice of Leaseholder's Claim (whether to acquire the freehold or an extended lease) served by the tenant ceases to have effect, and the tenant is prevented from serving a further notice for three years thereafter.[15]
(c) Agreements fixing the amount of any compensation to which the tenant has become entitled where the landlord has successfully obtained an order for possession under section 17 or 18.[16]

But in each of these cases, the court has power to set aside or vary the agreement,[17] discussed below.

2. Powers of Court

The court is given special powers in the following cases. 17–03

Insufficient recompense for tenant

The court,[18] if it is of the opinion that the tenant is not adequately recompensed for his rights under the Act, has wide powers to set aside or

[12] *Ibid.* at p. 114C, affirming the decision of the Court of Appeal on this point.
[13] s.23(2).
[14] s.23(2)(*a*).
[15] s.23(2)(*b*), as amended by Housing Act 1980, Sched. 21, para. 1(2); *cf.* the power of the court under s.20(6) as amended, discussed at para. 17–07.
[16] s.23(2)(*c*). For such orders for possession, see para. 8–09.
[17] s.23(3).
[18] *i.e.* the county court, or any other court in which proceedings are brought against the tenant on the agreement: s.23(3).

vary two types of agreement and give such relief as it thinks just "having regard to the situation and conduct of the parties." The first type of agreement is one for the surrender of the tenancy or for the acquisition by the tenant of the freehold or any intermediate tenancy or of any extended lease; but in such a case the power is exercisable only if two conditions are satisfied, *viz.* (i) the tenant is duly qualified under the 1967 Act to acquire the freehold or an extended lease,[19] and (ii) the court has not previously given its approval to the transaction.[20] Condition (i) is a serious limitation. If, for instance, the landlord persuades the tenant to enter into a bad bargain before the tenant has acquired the three-year residential qualification,[21] the court is powerless under this provision, and the tenant can rely only on any common law or other remedy (*e.g.* under the Misrepresentation Act 1967) which he may have. The second type of agreement[22] is one made (without the prior approval of the court) for the surrender of an extended lease on the landlord claiming possession for purposes of development.[23]

There is no reported decision giving guidance as to how the court should exercise this jurisdiction. It is considered that the onus of proof is on the tenant to show (i) that he was not adequately recompensed and (ii) that it is a proper case in which the jurisdiction should be exercised. The court will thus have to investigate the transaction impugned to see if the tenant made a satisfactory bargain, and this will involve consideration of such matters as the personal situation of each of the parties, and their relative wealth and experience in property dealings. It is thought that a tenant who has been separately represented by competent professional advisers is unlikely to be able to invoke this jurisdiction.[24] It is not clear whether the court can exercise the above power where the agreement impugned has been completed, *e.g.* after an actual surrender by the tenant or the transfer of the freehold. On the face of it, the wording of the Act appears not to permit such a completed transaction to be set aside or varied; but the court, which will probably be reluctant to decide that it can then no longer exercise the power, may find itself able to achieve the same result by making an order setting aside or varying the prior agreement, and then ordering the consequential rectification of the completed transaction.[25]

---

[19] Although the contrary is arguable, it is thought that the tenant need not have served a Notice of Leaseholder's Claim.

[20] s.23(3)(*a*).

[21] See para. 4-02.

[22] s.23(3)(*b*).

[23] *i.e.* under s.17. It is unclear why there is no parallel provision covering the case of the landlord claiming possession for his own occupation under s.18; but such cases are rarely found in practice.

[24] But in such a case the prior approval of the court will nearly always have been obtained.

[25] See *Clark* v. *Barnes* [1929] 2 Ch. 368.

Prior approval of transactions

17–04 Although it is not expressly so provided, it is clear[26] from the provisions discussed above that the prior approval of the court may be obtained to any of the transactions otherwise liable to be set aside or varied, and that if such approval is obtained it will be conclusive that the tenant has been adequately recompensed.

Furthermore, the court is given express power to approve the grant to a tenant who is duly qualified to acquire the freehold or an extended lease under the Act,[27] or entitled to the benefit of a previous tenant's Notice of Leaseholder's Claim,[28] of a new tenancy on such terms as the court may approve.[29] Those terms may exclude the right to acquire the freehold[30]; and, except insofar as it otherwise provides, the new tenancy is treated as if it were an extended lease under the Act for the purposes of (i) excluding further rights under the Act for the new tenancy (and any sub-tenancy created out of it) as well as the normal statutory rights,[31] but (ii) including the landlord's right to possession for redevelopment purposes.[32] Moreover, such a tenancy approved by the court is binding on all persons entitled to any interest or charge on the landlord's estate,[33] notwithstanding that the tenancy would not otherwise be authorised or would be outside the landlord's statutory or other power of leasing.[34] But if the landlord's estate is charitable or ecclesiastical property, the prior consent of the Charity Commissioners[35] or the Church Commissioners[36] may be necessary. If a lease at a low rent contains a statement that it is being made pursuant to this power, that statement is conclusive in favour of other persons, unless it appears from the lease that the statement is untrue[37]; and there are criminal sanctions if the statement is untrue.[38]

This latter power is extensively used by landlords who wish to retain control over properties in an estate area but who have failed to obtain a

---

[26] From the words "without the prior approval of the court" in s.23(3)(*a*) and (*b*).

[27] The wording is "where a tenant . . . is under this Part of this Act entitled to acquire . . . ", but it is not considered necessary for the tenant to have served a Notice of Leaseholder's Claim.

[28] *e.g.* by assignment, gift, succession under a Will or intestacy: see paras. 5–08 *et seq.*

[29] s.23(4).

[30] s.23(5)(*a*).

[31] *i.e.* under Landlord and Tenant Act 1954, Parts I and II, and the Rent Act 1977.

[32] s.23(5)(*b*), incorporating s.16(1)–(6).

[33] Unless the existing tenancy (i) was granted on or after January 1, 1968, (ii) was granted subsequently to a charge on the landlord's estate, and (iii) is not binding on the persons interested in the charge: s.23(4), proviso.

[34] s.23(4).

[35] *i.e.* under Charities Act 1960, s.29: see para. 14–21.

[36] *i.e.* under 1967 Act, s.31.

[37] s.23(6).

[38] s.23(7).

management scheme under section 19.[39] A tenant who serves a Notice of Leaseholder's Claim is offered a new lease on sufficiently attractive terms in satisfaction of all his rights under the 1967 Act, but containing appropriate covenants dealing with repair, decoration, user, insurance, etc. A difficulty arises if the tenant's claim is of doubtful validity, but it is considered that once the court has made an order approving the new lease, that order cannot be challenged for want of jurisdiction.[40]

Delay or default

17–05 If either the landlord or the tenant is guilty of unreasonable delay or default in carrying out their respective obligations arising from the service of a Notice of Leaseholder's Claim, the other party has the various remedies conferred by the statutory Conditions,[41] as well as the usual remedies of specific performance, rescission or damages.[42] In addition, and without prejudice to those remedies, the court can also revoke vary and make other orders as to any costs already awarded in any proceedings, or award costs if none have been awarded.[43] Also, the court can certify any delay or default to enable the Lands Tribunal to deal similarly with the costs of any proceedings before it,[44] but the transfer of jurisdiction to leasehold valuation tribunals[45] appears to have rendered this power of minimal practical use.

Bad faith, etc., of tenant

17–06 In two types of case where a Notice of Leaseholder's Claim is given and the notice is set aside by the court or withdrawn[46] or otherwise ceases to have effect (or would, if valid, cease to have effect)[47] the court has powers intended to safeguard the landlord's position.[48] The two types of case are where it appears to the court[49] that *either*:

(a) The Notice of Leaseholder's Claim was not given "in good faith."[50] A notice given by a tenant who knows he is not entitled (*e.g.* because he

---

[39] See Chap. 10.

[40] *Cohen* v. *Jonesco* [1926] 2 K.B. 1, C.A.; *Re Gale* [1966] Ch. 236, *per* Russell L.J. at p.247G.

[41] Contained in the Schedule to the Leasehold Reform (Enfranchisement and Extension) Regs. 1967 (S.I. No. 1879): see paras. 6–02 *et seq.*

[42] s.5(1): see para. 5–08.

[43] s.20(4)(*a*).

[44] s.20(4)(*b*) and Housing Act 1980, Sched. 21, para. 6.

[45] Which have no power to award costs: see para. 16–10.

[46] A voluntary withdrawal by the tenant of his Notice thus does not avoid the exercise of these powers.

[47] An example is where the court makes a declaration that the tenant is not entitled to acquire the freehold or an extended lease.

[48] s.20(5), (6).

[49] The onus of proof is on the landlord.

[50] s.20(5)(*a*).

does not have the necessary three-year residential period) will not be "in good faith." But it seems also that a notice given recklessly or "with an ulterior motive," such as avoiding a forfeiture against which the court would not give relief, will also not be "in good faith."[51] *Or*

(b) The person giving the notice attempted in any material respect to support it by misrepresentation or the concealment of material facts.[52] In most cases of this kind, the notice itself will not have been given in good faith, but this alternative also covers cases where a notice originally given in good faith is subsequently supported by a misrepresentation or concealment of material facts. It appears that even an entirely innocent misrepresentation or concealment suffices, although doubtless the court would be less inclined to exercise its discretionary power in such a case.

The powers of the court exercisable in the above cases on the application of the landlord are (i) to order the person giving the notice to pay to the landlord such sum as appears sufficient as compensation for damage or loss sustained by the landlord as the result of the giving of the notice[53]; and (ii) (whether or not such a compensation order is made) to order that any further Notice of Leaseholder's Claim giving by that person in respect of the same house or any part of it, with or without other property, shall be void if given within the five years beginning with the date of the order.[54] The second of these powers is useful in cases where a tenant who has not yet acquired the three-year residential qualification (or is for some other reason not entitled to the benefits of the 1967 Act) serves a Notice of Leaseholder's Claim in order to prolong his tenancy[55] or prevent the service of a landlord's notice under Part I or II of the Landlord and Tenant 1954.[56] But it is to be noticed that the court can only declare void a further notice served *after* the date of the order. There is no power to declare void a further notice served before then, even one served after commencement of the proceedings. In extreme cases, however, it may be possible to obtain an injunction against service of a further notice. **17–07**

[51] *Central Estates (Belgravia) Ltd.* v. *Woolgar* [1972] 1 Q.B. 48, C.A., decided on similar words in Sched. 3, para. 4(1). See also *Liverpool Corporation* v. *Husan* [1972] 1 Q.B. 72, C.A., and para. 5–14.

[52] s.20(5)(*b*).

[53] s.20(5). It is thought that the landlord has to prove such damage or loss, which usually is limited to legal and similar costs but may extend to other matters.

[54] s.2(6). Unlike the five-year residential qualification period, this five-year period was not reduced to 3 years by the Housing Act 1980.

[55] *i.e.* under Sched. 3, para. 3(1): see para. 5–12.

[56] Sched. 3, para. 2(2): see para. 5–12.

3. Avoiding the 1967 Act

Generally

17–08 Cases sometimes arise where the landlord is willing only to grant a lease outside the 1967 Act, and the tenant wishes to take such a lease. The question then arises as to how this result can be achieved. No difficulty arises if the tenant already has a tenancy in respect of which he has previously served, or is able to serve, a Notice of Leaseholder's Claim. In such cases the parties can, with the approval of the county court, agree a new tenancy providing expressly for the Act to be excluded.[57] But otherwise such an exclusion provision is rendered void by the anti-avoidance provisions discussed above, and it is not possible directly to contract out of the Act.[58]

There are, however, several methods at present open whereby it is considered that the effect of the Act can nevertheless be avoided. These methods involve transactions that may be somewhat artificial, but that is immaterial provided that the transaction is not a sham. The mere fact that it is artificial and plainly intended to avoid the effect of the Act does not make it a sham or otherwise enable the court to disregard it or say that it is for that reason within the anti-avoidance provisions of the Act.[59] But the transactions are, of course, vulnerable to future legislation. Moreover, they may well affect the marketability of the tenancies granted and thus prove of limited attraction to prospective tenants and their mortgages.

The methods of avoiding the Act all depend on the transaction being arranged so that one of the qualifications under the Act cannot be satisfied. They are conveniently discussed under four heads.

(1) *"House"*

17–09 In a few exceptional cases, it is possible by ensuring in the design of new or converted houses that there is a sufficient overlap to remove the property in question from the definition of "house." For this purpose, a material part of the property "must lie above or below a part of the structure not comprised in the house."[60] One possibility which involves only a modest overlap is for adjoining houses to have intertwining staircases.

The 1967 Act can otherwise only be avoided under this head by excluding (say) the roof and/or the outside walls, and/or a basement and foundations, from the demise, so that the tenant does not have a tenancy

[57] s.23(2): see para. 17–04.
[58] s.23(1): see para. 17–01.
[59] See *Jones* v. *Wrotham Park Settled Estates* [1980] A.C. 74.
[60] s.2(2); see paras. 2–05 *et seq.*

of the whole house. Although the landlord would thereby retain full ownership of the excluded parts, a tenant's covenant to repair those parts can be included in the lease. As such a covenant is of direct benefit to the premises demised, it "touches and concerns" the demised premises and it will be binding on successors-in-title of the tenant.[61]

(2) *"Long tenancy"*

Except in cases of a renewal of a long tenancy at a low rent in favour of an existing tenant,[62] the 1967 Act can be avoided by the grant of a term of under 21 years. An alternative which may be more acceptable to tenants is to grant an initial term of under 21 years, together with one or more options for renewal for further terms of under 21 years on payment of a premium on their exercise.[63] The premium should be something more than a merely nominal sum. Such options of renewal do not offend the rule against perpetuities.[64] However, care must be exercised in the drafting of the options to ensure (i) that the tenancy is not perpetually renewable,[65] and (ii) that any option is not exercisable until not more than 21 years before the grant of the new term and so not invalidated by section 149(3) of the Law of Property Act 1925.[66] The frequently used (but questionable[67]) device of making the tenancy terminable by the tenant by notice after a death or marriage is no longer available.[68] 17–10

(3) *"Low rent"*

A tenancy is not at a low rent, and therefore outside the 1967 Act, if the rent is over two-thirds of the rateable value on "the appropriate day"[69] or, if later, the first day of the term thereby granted.[70] (Note, however, that if the tenancy is granted by way of a renewal of a previous long tenancy, there is deemed to be a single composite tenancy commencing on the first day of the earlier term.[71]) But such a tenancy has three disadvantages; 17–11

(i) the rent may be unacceptably high;
(ii) the tenancy will usually be a "protected tenancy" under the Rent

[61] *Easterby* v. *Sampson* (1830) 6 Bing. 644.
[62] s.3(2) renders the renewal tenancy a "long tenancy": see paras. 3–09 and para. 17–13.
[63] A premium is essential to avoid s.3(4): see para. 3–07.
[64] Perpetuities and Accumulation Act 1964, s.9(1).
[65] Converted to a 2,000 year term by Law of Property Act 1922, Sched. 15.
[66] *Re Strand and Savoy Properties Ltd.* [1960] Ch. 582; *Weg Motors Ltd.* v. *Hales* [1962] Ch. 49, C.A.
[67] See para. 3–05.
[68] By reason of the amendment to the proviso to s.3(1) made by Housing Act 1980, Sched. 21, para. 3.
[69] For definition, see para. 2–17.
[70] s.4(1); see para. 3–13.
[71] s.3(3); *Bates* v. *Pierrepoint* (1978) 37 P. & C.R. 420, C.A.; and see para. 3–10.

Act 1977, which can create problems in relation to the taking of a premium on assignment[72] (although if the tenancy is a long tenancy and certain conditions are satisfied the exemption afforded by the Rent Act 1977, s.127, may apply);

(iii) there may be future alterations in the formula for determining whether the tenancy is "at a low rent," *e.g.* on a rating revaluation. Theoretically it would be possible to combat this eventuality by including a provision that the rent should automatically be increased to (say) £5 above the maximum rent payable with the tenancy remaining at a low rent. But the rent would then be subject to possibly substantial increases, and this solution appears to be unsatisfactory.

(4) *Company tenant*

17–12 A company cannot claim under the 1967 Act, except in a fiduciary capacity.[73] So if a tenancy is taken in the name of a company beneficially, the 1967 Act does not apply.

Renewal of tenancies

17–13 Further cases arise in practice where it is desired to renew a long tenancy at a low rent by the grant of a further term of under 21 years at a premium. In such cases, section 3(2) of the 1967 Act will operate to render the renewal tenancy a "long tenancy," notwithstanding that it is granted for a term of under 21 years. There are two methods[74] by which it is considered that the effect of section 3(2) can be successfully avoided.

(1) *Renewal to different tenant*

In order for section 3(2) to bite, the tenant under the first lease must "become tenant of the property or part of it under another tenancy." So the section will not apply if the new tenant is a different person from the first tenant, even if the former is the first tenant's spouse,[75] or another member of his family, or a company controlled by him; there is nothing in the 1967 Act to equate the ownership of one with the ownership of the other. However, it is not sufficient if a previous joint tenant becomes the sole new tenant, or (the reverse situation) a sole tenant becomes one of two or more joint tenants.[76] Furthermore, care must be taken to ensure

---

[72] See Rent Act 1977, s.126.

[73] s.37(5); *Duke of Westminster* v. *Oddy* (1984) 270 E.G. 945, C.A.

[74] The remarks in para. 17–08, *supra*, apply equally to these.

[75] s.3(2) has been held by the Court of Appeal not to apply in such a case: *Rendall* v. *Duke of Westminster* (1982), C.A. (unreported) C.A.T. No. 203.

[76] It is considered that the wording of s.3(2) is wide enough to cover both these cases.

that the new tenant is the new tenant beneficially as well as legally. If the first tenant held the previous tenancy in trust for the new tenant, or (the reverse situation) the new tenant takes the renewal tenancy in trust for the previous tenant, it is considered that section 3(2) will apply; and a similar situation will arise if there is any enforceable contract for sale between them.[77] It is advisable for the landlord to obtain written admissions from both that there is no trust or contractual relationship between them as regards the house.

(2) *Alteration of rent at end of tenancy*

Section 3(2) operates only where a long tenancy *at a low rent* comes to an end. If, therefore, the rent is increased to over two-thirds of the rateable value[78] for (say) the last quarter of the earlier tenancy, it will cease to be at a low rent and section 3(2) will not apply. If the contractual term of the previous tenancy is still subsisting, such an increase of rent does not involve any implied surrender of the previous tenancy.[79] If the contractual term has come to an end, but the tenancy is being automatically continued under the Landlord and Tenant Act 1954, Pts. I or II, the increase in rent may involve the determination of the continuation tenancy and the grant of a short new one. But this is immaterial, for although section 3(2) will render such new tenancy a long tenancy, it will not be at a low rent, and the section will have no further operation on the tenancy thereafter granted. 17–14

4. Missing Landlord

Acquisition of freehold only

A special procedure is laid down to deal with cases where the landlord cannot be found or his identity cannot be ascertained.[80] Cases of this kind are quite common, especially where the rent reserved by the lease is a nominal or very small amount. The procedure is, however, limited to cases where the tenant wishes to acquire the freehold. A tenant who wishes to acquire an extended lease from a missing landlord cannot do so. Further, a tenant who wishes to obtain a notional reduction in the rateable value of the house and premises[81] appears to be unable to do so, 17–15

[77] Thus creating a trust in favour of the purchaser: see *Lysaght* v. *Edwards* (1876) 2 Ch.D. 499 at pp. 506–10, and Megarry and Wade, *The Law of Real Property* (5th ed.), p. 601.
[78] On "'the appropriate day" or the first day of the term, if later: see s.4(1) and para. 2–17.
[79] *Lewis (Jenkin R.) & Son* v. *Kerman* [1971] Ch. 477, C.A.; Megarry and Wade, *The Law of Real Property, supra*, p. 685.
[80] s.27.
[81] *i.e.* under Housing Act 1974, Sched. 8: see paras. 2–23 *et seq.*

at any rate directly.[82] It is difficult to see any cogent reason for these apparent omissions.

Sub-tenant

17–16 It is, however, unnecessary to use this procedure if (as is often the case) there is some other interest superior to the tenancy. For the owner of that interest may be "the reversioner," or can be appointed as such by the county court if he is not[83]; and in that capacity he can, subject to the directions of the county court, agree all matters affecting the missing landlord, including the purchase price for the latter's interest.[84] Moreover, he can execute a conveyance of the freehold or an extended lease on behalf of the missing landlord, provided he pays the purchase price for the missing landlord's interest into the county court.[85] This procedure is a good deal simpler than that outlined below.

Procedure

17–17 It has been said that the course of events likely to be followed involves five stages.[86]

(1) **Preliminary**

The tenant must satisfy two initial conditions:

(i) he must be entitled to acquire the freehold under the 1967 Act, *i.e.* the property must comprise a house let on a long tenancy at a low rent and be within the rateable value limits, and he must have the necessary residential qualifications; and
(ii) he must be unable to serve a Notice of Leaseholder's Claim because the person to be served "cannot be found, or his identity cannot be ascertained."[87]

Much the most frequent case which arises in practice is where the identity of the landlord is unknown. One step which the applicant should always take in such a case is to ascertain if the freehold title is registered under the Land Registration Acts 1925 to 1971. A search of the index

---

[82] But it may be that a possible reduction, so that the freehold is valued under the Land Registration Act 1925, s.9(1) as opposed to s.9(1A), can be taken into account by the surveyor appointed by the President of the Lands Tribunal: see para. 17–20.
[83] Sched. 1, paras. 2, 3; and see para. 11–05.
[84] Sched. 1, para. 4(3); and see para. 11–08.
[85] Sched. 1, para. 4(3)(*c*).
[86] *Re Robertson's Application* [1969] 1 W.L.R. 109, in which Megarry J. made general observations as to the procedure to be followed and the form of conveyance to be used under s.27.
[87] s. 27(1).

map will reveal this information,[88] but not the name and address of the registered proprietor. There appears to be jurisdiction[89] for the Chief Land Registrar to permit the tenant (who appears clearly to be a "person interested"[90] in the freehold title) to inspect the proprietorship register of the freehold title, but the Chief Land Registrar takes the view that he is unable to permit such inspection or otherwise reveal the identity of the registered proprietor if the latter refuses consent,[91] without an order of the court. However, the court now has an express power to permit inspection and the making of copies of entries on the register,[92] and it is thought will normally make such an order so as to enable the tenant to trace his landlord in this kind of case.

(2) **Application to court**

The tenant must apply to the High Court, which has power to "make such order as the court thinks fit with a view to the house and premises being vested in him . . . as if he had at the date of his application to the High Court given notice of his desire to have the freehold."[93] The application has the effect of a Notice of Leaseholder's Claim to acquire the freehold, even if the landlord is subsequently traced.[94] Such applications are assigned to the Chancery Division,[95] and should be made by an originating summons[96–98] in the *ex parte* form. The originating summons should be supported by an affidavit sworn by the applicant proving that the preliminary requirements set out above are satisfied. The affidavit should thus exhibit the lease (or a copy if the original is not available), fully setting out the history of the matter, proving the right of the applicant to acquire the freehold, and stating what enquiries have been made by the applicant to trace the landlord. The affidavit should also state the date up to which the ground rent has been paid. It is sometimes convenient for the applicant's affidavit to be supplemented by an affidavit sworn by his solicitor. **17–18**

[88] Land Registration Rules 1925, r. 286.
[89] Under Land Registration Act 1925, s.112 and Land Registration Rules 1925, r. 288(2).
[90] *i.e.* under r. 288(2) *supra*: see Ruoff & Roper, *Registered Conveyancing* (5th ed.), p. 548.
[91] See Ruoff & Roper, *ibid.* The authority there cited is r. 288(2), *supra*, but it is difficult to see that it supports the Chief Land Registrar's view.
[92] Land Registration Act 1925, s.112, as substituted by Administration of Justice Act 1982, s.67 and Sched. 5.
[93] Leasehold Reform Act 1967, s.27(1).
[94] s.27(2)(*a*): see para. 17–26.
[95] R.S.C., Ord. 93, r. 15.
[96–98] R.S.C., Ord. 5, r. 3: *Re Robertson's Application, supra*, at p. 111B. If appropriate, the originating summons should also ask for an order under Land Registration Act 1925, s.112: see n. 89.

(3) **Advertisement, valuation and conveyance**

17–19 The third stage consists of complying with the procedure laid down by the 1967 Act relating to advertisement, the ascertainment of the sum to be paid into court and the preparation of the conveyance or transfer.[99] These are all matters as to which the Master will usually give directions when the originating summons comes before him on the first appointment.

(a) *Advertisement*

The court "may require the applicant to take such further steps by way of advertisement or otherwise as the court thinks proper for the purpose of tracing the landlord."[1] Provided that the applicant has already made all reasonable enquiries, the only requirement is usually that advertisements are inserted in specified newspapers circulating in the locality where the property in question is situated and also in any other locality where there is some possibility of the landlord being traced. As to what happens if as a result the landlord is traced, see para. 17–26.

(b) *Ascertainment of sum to be paid into court*

17–20 This sum (defined as "the appropriate sum") comprises the purchase price for the freehold together with unpaid rent due up to the date of the conveyance.[2]

(i) **Purchase price.** The purchase price is "such amount as a surveyor selected by the President of the Lands Tribunal may certify to be at a fair valuation the price payable" under s.9 of the 1967 Act.[3] The application to the President of the Lands Tribunal is made by letter, and the Registrar of the Lands Tribunal will notify the applicant's solicitors of the surveyor selected. It is considered that it should be made clear to the surveyor whether the valuation is to be made under subsection (1) or subsection (1A) of section 9,[4] and in the latter case what "improvements have been carried out by the tenant or his predecessors in title at their own expense" for the purposes of subsection (1A) para. (d).[5] It is not clear whether the surveyor can also take into account the prospect of a notional reduction of the rateable value at the date of the application by reason of structural improvements under the Housing Act 1974, Sched. 8, bringing the

[99] *Re Robertson's Application, supra*, at p. 111C.
[1] s.27(2).
[2] s.27(5).
[3] s.27(5). As to such price, see Chap. 9.
[4] See para. 9–14.
[5] See para. 9–47.

rateable value to under £500 or (in Greater London) £1,000 so that subsection (1) of section 9 is applicable[6]; it is suggested that the wording of section 27(5) of the 1967 Act (particularly the reference to a "fair valuation") is wide enough to permit the surveyor to do this.[7] The surveyor should also be informed as to the contents of the proposed conveyance to the applicant.[8] It seems that he should assume that the landlord can show a good title, and not make any deduction for possible defects of title.[9] The surveyor's certificate is usually given by letter, and it should specifically refer to the provisions of the 1967 Act which he bore in mind in making his valuation.[10] When received, the surveyor's certificate should be put in evidence.

(ii) **Unpaid rent.** The appropriate sum must include "the amount of estimated rent remaining unpaid (as determined by the High Court) of any pecuniary rent payable for the house and premises up to the date of the conveyance."[11] If the rent has any pecuniary value, however small, (*i.e.* is not merely a peppercorn[12] or the like), the court must determine the arrears up to a specified date when it is anticipated that the conveyance will be ready for execution.[13] However, the arrears are limited to six years,[14] which are not statute-barred.[15] **17–21**

(c) *Conveyance*

The conveyance (or registered land transfer[16]) will be in a form determined by the court and for this purpose it is assumed, unless the contrary is shown, that the landlord has no interest in any neighbouring property.[17] The conveyance will usually be made between "the person or persons in whom the property hereby conveyed is on the date hereof vested for an estate in fee simple" (or some other suitable innominate grantor)[18] as owner (or vendor) and the applicant as purchaser. It should briefly recite the lease and the devolution of title to the applicant, the satisfaction of the requirements of section 27 of the 1967 Act, the order of **17–22**

---

[6] See para. 2–23.
[7] Notwithstanding that he cannot take into account the prospect of a notional reduction to bring the house and premises within the rateable value limits in s.1.
[8] Which may, at least in theory, affect the purchase price: see para. 9–16.
[9] Under s.9(2).
[10] *Re Robertson's Application, supra,* at p. 111F.
[11] s.27(5).
[12] As in *Re Robertson's Application, supra.*
[13] *Re Frost's Application* [1970] 1 W.L.R. 1145 (one penny arrears).
[14] *Re Howell's Application* [1972] Ch. 509.
[15] *i.e.* under Limitation Act 1980, s.19.
[16] If the freehold title is registered it will usually be possible to trace the landlord: see para. 17–17.
[17] s.27(4).
[18] *Re Robertson's Application, supra,* at p. 114H.

the court and the payment into court. The operative part should be a straightforward conveyance of the freehold, omitting any references to easements,[19] restrictive covenants and minerals.[20] The owner should not convey as beneficial owner, but the following clause, or a clause to the like effect, should be included: "It is hereby declared that the same covenants for title but no further covenant for title shall be implied herein as if the owner was conveying and was expressed to convey the property hereby conveyed as trustee."[21] If appropriate, the conveyance can include a declaration of merger.[22] A certificate of value for stamp duty purposes will almost always be appropriate.[23-24] The testimonium and attestation clauses will be in an unusual form, because they will refer to the order of the court. It has been suggested that the Master should refer the matter to conveyancing counsel to the court, to investigate the tenant's title and draft the conveyance,[25] but the procedure is now sufficiently standardised to make the costs[26] and delay in taking this step unnecessary except in difficult cases.

(4) **Approval by the court**

17–23 The fourth stage is the approval by the court. A Chancery Master (or a District Registrar) is empowered to exercise the powers of the court under section 27.[27] The Master nearly always requires draft minutes of the order he will be asked to make to be lodged in chambers prior to the hearing. The applicant must be prepared to prove his right to enfranchisement sufficiently and "to satisfy all inquiries which might be made by a conveyancer who is prudent and suspicious but not, I hope, obstinate."[28] The order[29] should first recite the jurisdiction, and then

(i) either approve a previously lodged conveyance, or order that a proper conveyance be settled by the Master (or by conveyancing counsel to the court),[30]

(ii) nominate a named Master to execute the conveyance[31];

---

[19] *Ibid.* at p. 113E.

[20] *Ibid.* at p. 113H: see ss.2(6) and 27(4).

[21] ss.10(1) and 27(3); *Re Robertson's Application, supra,* at p. 112H; and generally para. 6–29.

[22] See para. 6–30. A declaration of merger will not be appropriate (and would probably be ineffective) if the lease is subject to any mortgage or charge.

[23-24] Under Finance Act 1963, s.55, as amended.

[25] *Re Robertson's Application, supra,* at p. 114D.

[26] Payable by the applicant: *ibid.* at p. 115E. See para. 17–25.

[27] R.S.C., Ord. 32, r. 14; Practice Direction (Chancery: Masters' Powers) [1976] 1 W.L.R. 637, para. 3(*w*).

[28] *Re Robertson's Application, supra,* at p. 113H.

[29] See Precedent No. XXIV, Appendix A.

[30] See para. 17–22.

[31] *Re Robertson's Conveyance, supra,* at p. 114F.

(iii) declare the amount of unpaid rent remaining recoverable[32];
(iv) give liberty to pay into court the total of the sum certified by the surveyor[33] and such unpaid rent, and contain an appropriate lodgment schedule[34]; and
(v) direct that upon payment into court, the nominated Master should execute the approved conveyance and deliver it to the applicant.[35–37]

(5) **Completion**

17–24 The fifth and final stage is completion by the execution of the conveyance upon payment into court, in accordance with the order. When the order has been passed and entered, the applicant should lodge a draft conveyance in chambers, and issue a summons to proceed. Once the conveyance has been settled, it will be engrossed and examined by the applicant and the engrossment lodged in chambers. When the payment into court has been made, the Master will execute the engrossment and hand it over to the applicant. It is prudent for the applicant to preserve with the title deeds the document selecting the surveyor and his valuation. The order may not necessarily constitute adequate conveyancing proof of these matters.

Costs

17–25 The court cannot order the applicant's costs to be paid out of the amount to be paid into court, and consequently the applicant must bear his own costs.

Landlord subsequently traced

17–26 If, after the tenant has made his application, the landlord is found or ascertained, the application is treated as a Notice of Leaseholder's Claim to acquire the freehold duly served on him.[38] No further proceedings can be taken under the application,[39] except that the court can give directions as to the steps to be taken for giving effect to the landlord's rights and obligations, including directions modifying or dispensing with any of the requirements of the 1967 Act or regulations made under it.[40] The tenant can in such a case only withdraw his application before any further steps are taken either by the landlord or himself.[41] Thereafter, he must obtain

[32] See para. 17–21.
[33] See para. 17–20.
[34] *Re Robertson's Application, supra*, at p. 114G.
[35-37] *Ibid.* at p. 114H.
[38] s.27(2)(*a*).
[39] s.27(2).
[40] s.27(2)(*a*).
[41] s.27(7).

either the consent of the landlord or the leave of the court, and the court cannot give leave unless it appears just to do so by reason of matters coming to the tenant's knowledge in consequence of the landlord being traced.[42] It appears that the tenant cannot even exercise the usual right to withdraw within one month after the purchase price has been determined,[43] although it is difficult to see why this should be so.

5. Landlord under Disability

17–27 Where a landlord is a "patient" within section 94(2) of the Mental Health Act 1983,[43a] his receiver or (if none) any person so authorised can, under an order of the Court of Protection, act for all purposes of Part I of the 1967 Act.[44]

6. Covenants against Assignment or Sub-Letting

Generally

17–28 Many tenancies contain the usual tenant's qualified covenant against assignment or sub-letting, *i.e.* a covenant not to assign or sub-let without the prior consent of the landlord subject to an express or statutory[45] proviso that such consent may not be unreasonably withheld. The question frequently arises whether a landlord can reasonably withhold consent on the ground that the proposed assignee (or sublessee) would be able to acquire the freehold under the 1967 Act when he has acquired the three-year residential qualification. It is settled that if the existing tenant would never have been able to claim the benefit of the 1967 Act, *e.g.* because the tenant is a company[46] or has sub-let for substantially the whole of the residue of the demised term,[47] the landlord can justifiably withhold consent.[48]

It is immaterial in such cases that the tenancy in question has many years of its term outstanding, or that it was originally granted to an individual.[49] It is also immaterial that all or some of the landlord's other

[42] s.27(7).
[43] Under s.9(3).
[43a] Formerly the Mental Health Act 1959, s.101.
[44] s.26(2).
[45] Under Landlord and Tenant Act 1927, s.19(1).
[46] *Norfolk Capital Group Ltd.* v. *Kitway Ltd.* [1977] 1 Q.B. 507, C.A.
[47] *Bickel* v. *Duke of Westminster* [1977] 1 Q.B. 517, C.A.; and see *Welch* v. *Birrane* (1974) 29 P. & C.R. 102 (Lawson J.).
[48] See the cases cited in notes 46 and 47 above. The two Court of Appeal cases were decided by different divisions of that court independently of each other (the *Kitway* case was heard and decided after the hearing but before judgement in the *Bickel* case).
[49] See the *Kitway* case (35 years outstanding of term originally granted to an individual), *supra.*

properties have already been enfranchised so that he has lost control of the area and the possibility of a comprehensive redevelopment; the financial detriment to the landlord if the proposed assignee would in time be able to enfranchise is enough to make it reasonable for the landlord to refuse consent.[50] On the other hand, it is reasonably clear that it is not possible for the landlord to refuse consent in cases where the assignor or sublessor is an individual, and thus either actually[51] or potentially (*i.e.* on acquiring the residential qualification) entitled to the benefit of the 1967 Act.[52]

Consent is sometimes requested to an assignment or sub-letting of part of the premises comprised in a tenancy, so that as a result of the exclusion of part of the former "premises," the rateable value of the house and premises[53] is reduced below the rateable value limits.[54] It is considered that the landlord can justifiably withhold his consent in such cases, on principles similar to those discussed above.

A property transfer order under the Matrimonial Causes Act 1973 is an assignment falling within a covenant against an assignment.[55] But such a covenant usually covers only voluntary assignments of the legal estate,[56] and does not extend to a succession on the death of a tenant,[57] a vesting order under the Trustee Act 1925[58] or a declaration of trust by the tenant.[59] Such matters are effectively covered by a covenant against parting with possession, but such a covenant is usually to be found only in relatively modern long tenancies.

Avoidance

In cases where the covenant is in a narrow form, *i.e.* prohibiting assignment or sub-letting without prior consent but not prohibiting parting with possession, it is often possible for parties to an intended sale 17–29

---

[50] *Ibid.* It is also immaterial that the lease was granted after the 1967 Act came into force: *Sungate (U.K.) Ltd.* v. *Howard de Walden Estates Ltd.* (1983) unreported (Falconer J.).

[51] If the tenant has already acquired the residential qualification, it will nearly always be to his financial advantage to serve a Notice of Leaseholder's Claim and sell together with the benefit of the Notice: see para. 5–09.

[52] The point was raised but not decided in *Marsh* v. *Gilbert* (1980) 256 E.G. 715.

[53] See para. 2–20.

[54] Either enabling the tenant to claim the benefit of the 1967 Act, or to make the purchase price determined under s.9(1) rather than s.9(1A): see para. 9–14.

[55] If a landlord refuses consent, the Family Division will refuse a property transfer order, leaving the question of the reasonableness of the landlord's refusal to be considered elsewhere: *Regan* v. *Regan* [1977] 1 W.L.R. 84.

[56] The covenant may contain words (*e.g.* prohibiting parting with possession) which give it a wider effect.

[57] *Seers* v. *Hind* (1791) 1 Ves. 294; *Doe d. Goodbehere* v. *Bevan* (1815) 3 M. & S. 353; and Woodfall's *Law of Landlord and Tenant* (28th ed.), Vol. 1, para. 1–1207.

[58] *Marsh* v. *Gilbert* (1980) 256 E.G. 715.

[59] *Gentle* v. *Faulkner* [1900] 2 Q.B. 267, C.A.

of a leasehold interest to arrange matters so that the landlord's consent is not required. In practice, many potentially enfranchiseable leases contain a covenant only in a narrow form of this kind. It is settled that such a covenant only prevents an assignment by deed of the legal estate without consent, and not a declaration of trust, even though the tenant parts with the whole of his beneficial interest.[60] By means of a declaration of trust, the purchaser can effectively claim the benefit of the 1967 Act when he has acquired the three-year residential qualification. Two possible schemes are as follows:

(1) The purchaser (P) forms a company, and application is made to the landlord for consent to an assignment. If unconditional consent is given, the tenancy can be assigned to P's company which can execute a contemporaneous declaration of trust in favour of P, in consideration of P having provided the purchase price.[61] If P occupies the house as his only or main residence for three years, the company can then claim the benefit of the 1967 Act relying on P's residential qualification.[62] However, the landlord can defeat this scheme being put into effect by imposing a condition preventing the creation of a trust as a term of his consent to the assignment. It is considered that the imposition of such a condition is not unreasonable.[63]

(2) If the landlord does impose such a condition, the vendor (V) can simply declare itself trustee for P, in consideration of the purchase price. If desired, V can thereafter resign as trustee, and P (in exercise of an appropriate power contained in the declaration of trust) can appoint (say) his company and himself as new trustees in place of V.[64] The legal estate would not vest in the new trustees by virtue of the deed of appointment, and the landlord's consent to its transfer to them would be required.[65] However, it is considered that as the assignment does not alter the position under the 1967 Act, such consent cannot be reasonably withheld. But even if it can, the position would be that V would remain as bare trustee for P and could (at P's request and expense) in due course claim the benefits of the 1967 Act on behalf of P.

---

[60] *Ibid.* See particularly *per* Romer L.J. at pp. 276–7.

[61] As an alternative, P.'s company can purchase beneficially, with P. loaning the purchase price, and subsequently declare itself a trustee in consideration of the extinguishment of the loan. But this course would involve two payments of *ad valorem* stamp duty.

[62] Under s.6(3), which is not limited to trusts entered into voluntarily; see para. 15–05.

[63] This follows from the *Norfolk* and *Bickel* cases, *supra.*

[64] Two new trustees are required: Trustee Act 1925, s.36.

[65] There is no implied vesting in the case of tenancies assignable only with the landlord's consent: Trustee Act 1925, s.40(4)(*b*).

Chapter 18

ENLARGEMENT OF LONG TERMS

Outline

In a few cases, a long term can be unilaterally enlarged by the tenant into a freehold, without involving the landlord or paying him any compensation, under Section 153 of the Law of Property Act 1925.[1] This right of enlargement extends to a term under a sub-lease, provided that the superior term out of which it has been created is itself capable of enlargement.[2] However, the conditions necessary for this right to arise are strict, and are seldom encountered in practice. **18–01**

Conditions

The conditions which must be fulfilled are as follows: **18–02**

(1) The term as originally created was for at least 300 years, of which at least 200 years remain unexpired.[3] For this purpose this term is created at the earliest on the date of grant of the lease, and not on any previous date from which the term is expressed to run.[4]

(2) There is no trust or right of redemption in favour of the freeholder or any reversion.[5] This condition excludes mortgage terms, unless the right to redeem has become statute-barred under the Limitation Act 1939.[6]

(3) There is no rent or "merely a peppercorn or other rent having no money value" reserved, or having been reserved has ceased to be payable.[7] A rent of "one silver penny if lawfully demanded" is a rent having no money value for this purpose.[8] But a rent of three shillings was held to have a money value even though not regularly paid.[9] However, a rent of £1 or less which has not been paid for a continuous period of 25

---

[1] Replacing s. 65 of the Conveyancing Act 1881 and s. 11 of the Conveyancing Act 1911.

[2] s. 153(2).

[3] s. 153(1).

[4] See *Roberts* v. *Church Commissioners for England* [1972] Q.B. 278 and para. 3–03.

[5] s. 153(1)(*a*).

[6] s. 153(3); and see L.P.A. 1925, s. 88(3).

[7] s. 153(1)(*b*).

[8] *Re Chapman and Hobbs* (1885) 29 Ch.D. 1007.

[9] *Re Smith and Stott* (1883) 29 Ch.D. 1007n. In *Blaiberg* v. *Keeves* [1906] 2 Ch. 175, a rent of one shilling was assumed to have a money value. Today the reversions to such leases would probably be unmarketable, and it might be argued that as a result the rents have no money value.

years (five having elapsed since 1925), is deemed to have ceased to be payable and can no longer be recovered.[10]

(4) The term is not "liable to be determined by re-entry for condition broken."[11-12] Leases without a forfeiture clause are very rare, and it is seldom that this condition is fulfilled.

Mode of enlargement

18–03 The right of enlargement can be exercised by the legal owner of the term, whether entitled beneficially or as trustee or personal representative. Such person has power by deed (a "Deed of Enlargement"[13]) to declare that as from the date of the deed the term is enlarged into a fee simple.[14] He thereupon acquires a fee simple instead of the term, in respect of all the land subject to the term,[15] including all mines and minerals unless they have been previously severed[16]; but such fee simple is held on the same trusts (if any) as affected the term, and must be dealt with accordingly.[17]

Effect of enlargement

18–04 The fee simple acquired by enlargement is subject

> "to all the same covenants and provisions relating to user and enjoyment, and to all the same obligations of every kind, as the term would have been subject to if it had not been enlarged."[18]

It has occasionally been suggested that the right of enlargement may provide a means for making positive covenants run with the land.[19] But many practical difficulties arise, in particular as to the persons entitled to enforce such covenants.[20] Schemes based on the right are "untried and artificial"[21] and are not recommended.

---

[10] s. 153(4).
[11-12] s. 153(5).
[13] For precedents see Key & Elphinstone, *Precedents in Conveyancing* (15th ed, 1953) Vol. 1, pp. 949 *et seq.*
[14] s. 153(6).
[15] s. 153(7). It is considered that the freeholder's estate is destroyed; but see *Challis on Real Property* (3rd ed., 1911), pp. 333–4, and (1958) 22 Conv. (N.S.) 101 at pp. 106–112 for different views.
[16] s. 153(10).
[17] s. 153(7),(9); subs. (9) contains some elaborate conveyancing provisions.
[18] s. 153(7).
[19] See (1958) 22 Conv. (N.S.) 101 (T.P.D. Taylor).
[20] *Cf.* para. 19–13, dealing with a comparable provision in the Places of Worship (Enfranchisement) Act 1920.
[21] Wilberforce Report on Positive Covenants 1965 (Cmnd. 2719), para. 8(vi). See also the Law Commission Report on the Law of Positive and Negative Covenants, 1984 (Law Comm. No. 127), para. 3.41.

Chapter 19

PLACES OF WORSHIP

By the Places of Worship (Enfranchisement) Act 1920, the trustees of certain leasehold premises held on trust to be used for the purposes of a place of worship, or attached to and used in connection with a place of worship and held on the same trusts, were given a right to enlarge their interest into a fee simple. By section 40 of the Leasehold Reform Act 1967, the 1920 Act was extended to minister's houses held by trustees on different trusts and to Church of England parsonage houses held by the incumbent, and other amendments were also made.[1] **19–01**

Premises within the 1920 Act

Whether or not premises are within the 1920 Act depends entirely on whether they are held upon certain religious trusts, and not on their physical description.[2] The premises may comprise parts of buildings which are divided horizontally, notwithstanding that enfranchisement may create a flying freehold.[3] **19–02**

The premises which qualify are:

(a) Premises "held on trust to be used for the purposes of a place of worship," whether in conjunction with other purposes or not.[4] A place of worship (i) means any church, chapel or other building used for "public religious worship,"[5] which expression can include worship to which, on some or even all occasions, only certain sections of the public are admitted[6]; and (ii) includes any burial ground, Sunday or Sabbath school or caretaker's house attached to or used with and held on the same trusts as a place of worship.[7] Such use need not be exclusive, so that (for instance) the intermittent use of a church hall as a Sunday school is sufficient.[8]

(b) Premises held on trust to be used, in connection with a place of

---

[1] The text of the 1920 Act as amended is set out in Sched. 6 of the Leasehold Reform Act 1967.

[2] s. 1(1), (1A) of the 1920 Act as amended.

[3] The legal difficulties and disadvantages of this are mitigated by the statutory continuation of the tenant's covenants under s. 3: see para. 19–13.

[4] *Ibid.* s. 1(1).

[5] *Ibid.* s. 5.

[6] *Stradling* v. *Higgins* [1932] 1 Ch. 143.

[7] The 1920 Act, s. 5.

[8] *Stradling* v. *Higgins*, supra.

worship,[9] for the purpose of a minister's house, whether in conjunction with other purposes or not.[10] Prior to the amendments made by the Leasehold Reform Act 1967, the minister's house had to be held on the same trusts as the place of worship itself, but this is no longer necessary.

(c) A parsonage house, *i.e.* the residence house of a benefice, held by the incumbent.[11] Such a house will be held by the incumbent as a "corporation sole," and is outside the provisions of the Leasehold Reform Act 1967.[12] In such a case, the provisions of the 1920 Act have effect (with any necessary modifications) as if the residence house were vested in trustees.[13] The provisions of the Parsonages Measure 1938, as amended, apply in relation to the acquisition of the freehold reversion.[14]

Use of premises

19–03 The 1920 Act only applies if the premises are being used for the purposes of the appropriate trust.[15] Further, the Act only contemplates the whole of the premises held under a lease being enfranchised, and (except as mentioned below[16]) provides no machinery for severance of different parts. It seems, therefore, that the whole, or at any rate substantially the whole,[17] of the premises comprised in the lease must be being used for the purposes of the appropriate trust; and it would be odd if, for instance, the use of one room in a building as a Sunday school were to enable the whole building to be enfranchised.

Exclusion of part of premises

19–04 In two cases, however, the 1920 Act makes provision for severance of part of the premises comprised in the lease. These are as follows:

(i) *Land over two acres.* If the premises exceed two acres, the right of enfranchisement is limited to two acres only.[18] It is not clear how the two acres is to be determined, but it is thought that the trustees entitled to enfranchise can elect which two acres they will acquire.

(ii) *Minerals.* Where the person entitled to the freehold or to an intermediate reversion requires that the underlying minerals be excepted, the trustees are not entitled to acquire his interest in the minerals if

---

[9] Defined as above: *ibid.* s. 5.
[10] *Ibid.* s. 1(1).
[11] The 1920 Act, s. 1(1A).
[12] Leasehold Reform Act 1967, s. 37(5).
[13] s. 1(1A) of the 1920 Act as amended.
[14] *Ibid.* In particular the incumbent must obtain certain consents before acquiring the freehold reversion: Parsonages Measure, s. 2.
[15] s. 1(1) of the 1920 Act as amended.
[16] *Ibid.* s. 1(1), proviso (*a*), (*aa*), discussed in para. 19–04.
[17] See *Stradling* v. *Higgins*, supra at p. 152.
[18] The 1920 Act, s. 1(1), proviso (*a*).

proper provision is made for the support of the premises as they have been enjoyed during the lease and in accordance with the terms of the lease and the trust.[19]

Exceptions

There are two cases in which premises which would otherwise qualify are excepted from the operation of the 1920 Act, and the right to enfranchise cannot be exercised. These are as follows: 19–05

(i) *Breach of covenant.* The Act does not apply where the premises are used or are proposed to be used for the purposes of a place of worship[20] in contravention of any covenant contained in the lease under which the premises are held or in any lease superior thereto.[21] Covenants of this kind are frequently found in leases entered into after 1920.

(ii) *Public bodies.* The Act does not apply where the premises form part of land which has been acquired or is vested in any municipal, local or rating authority, or in the owners thereof for the purposes of a railway, dock, canal or navigation under any Act of Parliament, Provisional Order or Order having the force of an Act of Parliament and the freehold reversion in the premises is held or retained by such owners for those purposes.[22] It is to be noted that ownership of an intermediate lease is not within this exception.

Tenancies within the 1920 Act

The Act applies to all leases (including underleases and agreements for leases and underleases) whenever made (a) for lives or a life or (b) for "a term of years where the term as originally created was a term of not less than 21 years, whether determinable on a life or lives or not."[23] A term cannot be created before the date of its grant,[24] so that there must be at least 21 years from the date of grant of the lease until the last day of the term grant, whatever the length of the term specified in the habendum to the lease. However, it will be sufficient if there was a prior specifically enforceable agreement for a lease made at least 21 years before the last day of the term.[25] It is considered that the purpose of the words "as originally created" is merely to make it clear that it is the original length of the term (and not the outstanding residue at the date of the trustees' 19–06

[19] *Ibid.* s. 1(1), proviso (*aa*), inserted by L.R.A. 1967, s. 40(2).
[20] As defined in *ibid.* s. 5: see para. 19–02.
[21] *Ibid.* s. 1(1), proviso (*c*).
[22] *Ibid.* s. 1(1), proviso (*d*).
[23] *Ibid.* s. 1(2).
[24] *Roberts* v. *Church Commissioners for England* [1972] 1 Q.B. 278, C.A., following *Shaw* v. *Kay* (1847) 1 Exch. 412 and *Earl Cadogan* v. *Guiness* [1936] Ch. 515.
[25] See further para. 3–03.

claim) which is relevant, and that the words are not sufficient to bring within the Act a renewal term of under 21 years coming into effect on the termination of a term of over 21 years.[26]

There is no restriction on the rent payable under the tenancy, so that the Act applies whether the rent is a nominal rent, a ground rent, a rack rent or any other rent. The Act also applies notwithstanding any agreement to the contrary, either in the lease or elsewhere (not being an agreement against the enlargement of the leasehold interest into a freehold contained in a lease granted or made before the passing of the Act).[27]

Rights under the Act

19–07 Trustees who hold a qualified leasehold interest under the provisions discussed above are (subject to the exception mentioned above) entitled to enlarge their interest into a fee simple; and for that purpose, they may acquire both the freehold and all intermediate reversions.[28]

The procedure for acquiring the reversionary interests is that laid down by Part I of the Compulsory Purchase Act 1965, as if the trustees were an authority authorised to acquire the premises under a compulsory purchase order made under the Acquisition of Land (Authorisation Procedure) Act 1946.[29] In order to exercise their rights under the 1920 Act, the trustees must therefore serve a notice to treat on each owner of a reversionary interest,[30] and there is no time-limit for so doing.[31] (A full discussion of this procedure is beyond the scope of this book.[32]) The notice to treat must (a) give particulars of the land to which it relates, (b) demand particulars of the recipient's estate and interest in the land, and of the claim made by him in respect of that land, and (c) state that the trustees are willing to treat for the purchase of the land.[33] Any disputes as to whether the trustees are entitled to rights under the 1920 Act and as to the effect of the exercise of such rights must be decided by the High

[26] The 1920 Act contains no provision equivalent to s. 3(3) of the Leasehold Reform Act 1967, as to which see para. 3–09.

[27] s. 1(1) of the 1920 Act.

[28] *Ibid.* s. 1(1). "Intermediate reversion" is defined as "any leasehold interest in the land (whether under a lease or underlease or under an agreement for a lease or underlease) superior to the lease held by the trustees": s. 5.

[29] *Ibid.* s. 2. For the purpose of the Compulsory Purchase Act 1965, Part I, "land" includes easements in or relating to land: the 1920 Act, s. 2(*a*).

[30] See s. 5(1) of the Compulsory Purchase Act 1965. It is thought that all the reversionary interests must be acquired at the same time.

[31] Compulsory Purchase Act 1965, s. 4, is excluded by the 1920 Act, s. 2(*a*).

[32] Reference should be made to the *Encyclopaedia of Compulsory Purchase and Compensation* (Sweet and Maxwell).

[33] Compulsory Purchase Act 1965, s. 5(2).

Court,[34] but disputes as to the amount of compensation payable are determined by the Lands Tribunal.[35]

Compensation

Subject to the qualification as to buildings and improvements dealt with below,[36] the compensation payable for the freehold and any intermediate reversions is that which would be payable if the trustees were an acquiring authority with powers of compulsory acquisition.[37] The compensation is thus calculated in accordance with the Rules set out in section 5 of the Land Compensation Act 1961, and in particular Rule 2 which provides that, subject to certain qualifications, the value of the land is to be taken as "the amount which the land, if sold in the open market by a willing seller, might be expected to realise." The date of valuation is the date of agreement or determination by the Lands Tribunal.[38] In addition, the owner of a reversionary interest may be able to claim compensation for severance or injurious affection,[39] *e.g.* if the property acquired is included in a proposed development. 19–08

It is expressly provided that "no allowance shall be made on account of the acquisition being compulsory."[40] This provision, which is in the same terms as s. 2(1) of the Acquisition of Land (Assessment of Compensation) Act 1919,[41] merely excludes the 10 per cent. addition to the compensation which, prior to that Act, it had become customary to add simply because the acquisition was compulsory.[42] Also, it is provided that

> "in determining the amount of compensation in any case where the rent reserved under the lease is less than the full annual value of the land, the compensation, so far as it is payable in respect of the interest of the lessor expectant or the termination of the term of the lease, shall not be ascertained on the basis of the rent so reserved, but . . . on the estimated full value of the land at the expiration of the terms of the lease."[43]

This is a puzzling provision which appears merely to state the obvious,

---

[34] There is no provision conferring jurisdiction on the County Court.
[35] Land Compensation Act 1961, s. 1, and Compulsory Purchase Act 1965, s. 6.
[36] See para. 19–09.
[37] s. 2 of the 1920 Act.
[38] *W. & S. (Long Eaton) Ltd.* v. *Derbyshire County Council* (1975) 31 P. & C.R. 99, C.A.; *Washington Development Corporation* v. *Bamblings (Washington) Ltd.* (1985) 273 E.G. 980, following *Birmingham Corporation* v. *West Midland Baptist (Trust) Association Inc.* [1970] A.C. 874 (rule 5).
[39] Under s. 7 of the Compulsory Purchase Act 1965.
[40] s. 2(*d*) of the 1920 Act.
[41] Now r. 1 in s. 5(1) of the Land Compensation Act 1961.
[42] See *Encyclopaedia of Compulsory Purchase*, para. 2–1060.
[43] s. 2(*e*) of the 1920 Act.

i.e. that the ultimate reversion must be valued at its actual value, without reference to the rent payable during the term. However, it precludes any argument that the compensation must be limited to the rent capitalised in perpetuity. But it does not carry any implication that the "marriage value" or "tenant's bid" must be ignored.[44]

As to the effects on the compensation of the automatic continuation of certain tenant's covenants and other obligations after the freehold has been acquired, see below.[45]

Buildings and improvements

19–09 It is provided that "in determining the amount of any compensation the value of any building erected, or improvements made by the trustees, shall be excluded."[46] Despite an inappropriately placed comma, it seems clear that in order for its value to be excluded, a building must have been erected by the trustees (*i.e.* it is not the value of every building which is excluded). For if all buildings were excluded, the word "erected" would be otiose, and there would be no need to mention improvements at all.

"Trustees" are defined to mean the trustees in whom the leasehold premises are vested for the time being "and includes their predecessors in title."[47] "Predecessors in title" has a wider meaning than predecessors in office, and includes all non-trustee previous owners of the leasehold interest. However, it is considered that in order for the value of any buildings or improvements to be excluded, they must have been erected or made during the currency of the existing tenancy[48]; and that buildings erected or improvements made, whether by the trustees or any predecessor in title, during a previous tenancy or as a condition of being granted the existing tenancy (*i.e.* under a building agreement), must be taken into account in assessing the compensation. A particular difficulty arises in connection with a building lease, *i.e.* when the lease is granted before the building is erected, but with a covenant to build. Although the consequence seems illogical and unfair to the landlord, on the language of the 1920 Act it seems inescapable that the value of the building erected in accordance with a covenant must be excluded.

Marriage value or tenant's bid

19–10 It is settled that the "special suitability or adaptability of the land,"

---

[44] See para. 19–10.
[45] See para. 19–13.
[46] s. 2(*c*) of the 1920 Act.
[47] *Ibid.* s. 5.
[48] *Cf. Trustees of Henry Smith's Charity* v. *Hemmings* (1983) 265 E.G. 383, C.A..

which under rule (3) in section 5 of the Land Compensation Act 1961 must be ignored in assessing the compensation, does not cover what is commonly referred to as a share of "the marriage value" or "the tenant's bid," *i.e.* the additional value which market experience shows that a tenant will pay in, to be able to "marry" his interest with the freehold.[49] The amount of the marriage value is usually ascertained by deducting the aggregate of the value of the tenant's leasehold interest and the purchase price (ignoring any marriage value element) from the unencumbered freehold value; and the share of the marriage value or "the tenant's bid," which is included in the purchase price, is usually one half of the marriage value so calculated.[50]

Intermediate reversion

It is provided that "the consideration payable in respect of any intermediate reversion may, at the option of the person entitled to that reversion, be an annual rentcharge for a term corresponding to the unexpired residue of the term of the reversion."[51] This provision is in conflict with section 2 of the Rentcharges Act 1977, which prohibits the creation of new rentcharges (except in certain circumstances, none of which are relevant), and it is thought that the failure to repeal it expressly is an oversight.[52] It may be arguable that the above provision has been impliedly repealed, and for that reason it is unsafe to rely upon it. Moreover, in any event, any annual rentcharge created in this way is liable to be compulsorily redeemed,[53] so there appears little purpose in the owner of the intermediate reversion opting for it. 19–11

Trusts affecting freehold

It is expressly provided that the estate in fee simple acquired by the trustees, must be held by them upon the same trusts as those upon which the leasehold interest would have been held by them if it had not been enlarged into a fee simple.[54] This spells out what would be the consequence under the general law.[55] 19–12

---

[49] *Lambe* v. *Secretary of State for War* [1955] 2 Q.B. 612, C.A., following *Raja Vyricherla Narayana Gajapatiraju* v. *Revenue Divisional Officer, Vizagapatam* [1939] A.C. 302, P.C.

[50] See *Norfolk* v. *Trinity College, Cambridge* (1976) P. & C.R. 32; P. & C.R. 147, C.A. and *Lloyd-Jones* v. *Church Commissioners for England* (1981) 261 E.G. 471, L.T.; and see paras. 54 *et seq.*

[51] s. 2(*b*) of the 1920 Act.

[52] Compare the provisions of para. 8, Sched. 1 of the Leasehold Reform Act 1967 (as originally enacted), repealed by the Rentcharges Act 1977.

[53] Under The Rentcharges Act 1977, s. 8.

[54] s. 3 of the 1920 Act.

[55] See *e.g. Protheroe* v. *Protheroe* [1968] 1 W.L.R. 519, C.A.

Continuation of covenants

19–13 The 1920 Act contains unusual[56] provisions for the automatic continuation of both positive and negative covenants and other obligations of the tenant. It is provided that the estate in fee simple acquired by the trustees

> "shall be subject to all the same covenants and provisions relating to user and enjoyment and to all the same obligations of every kind other than the payment of rent as those to which the leasehold interest would have been subject if it had not been so enlarged."[57]

However, covenants to insure and reinstate after fire "and any other covenant to do any act which may or will be beneficial to the demised premises alone" are excepted from such continuation (unless the consideration was payable in the form of a rentcharge and that rentcharge is still payable).[58] Thus positive covenants, such as covenants to repair, or to contribute to common expenses, will only be continued if they are capable of benefiting other property, *i.e.* where the freeholder retains neighbouring property which may be adversely affected by a breach of the covenant. It appears that such continuation is automatic, and it is unnecessary for the covenants and obligations to be mentioned in the conveyance or transfer to the trustees. Nevertheless, it is considered advisable for them to be expressly referred to in such documents. It is to be noted that any restrictive covenants affecting unregistered land must be registered as Class D (ii) land charges, and must be registered at the Land Charges Registry.[59] Such restrictive covenants are, however, subject to discharge or modification by the Lands Tribunal exercising its jurisdiction under s. 84(1) of the Law of Property Act 1925 as amended.[60] All the landlord's obligations under the lease will be extinguished on the merger of the leasehold with the freehold, and are not thus continued.

Some difficulty may arise as to the persons entitled to enforce the covenants. It is provided that

> "all such covenants provisions and obligations shall be enforceable against the trustees and their successors in title by the persons who, but for the enlargement of the leasehold interest under this Act, would for the time being have been entitled to enforce such covenants, provisions or obligations."[61]

---

[56] The only comparable provisions are in the Law of Property Act 1925, s. 153(8), as to which see para. 18–04.
[57] s. 3 of the 1920 Act.
[58] *Ibid.* s. 3 proviso.
[59] *i.e.* under the Land Charges Act 1972.
[60] *Cf. Re Calthorpe Estate, Edgbaston, Birmingham* (1973) 26 P. & C.R. 120 (covenant under s. 19, L.R.A. 1967).
[61] s. 3 of the 1920 Act.

The effect of this provision remains to be judicially decided. The former freeholder (or owner of relevant intermediate interest) will usually be the person entitled to enforce the covenants, etc. It is thought that the benefit will devolve as part of his estate on his death. If his interest was settled, it is thought that the benefit devolves under the settlement. But if any neighbouring land capable of benefiting from the covenants is sold, it is thought that the benefit will pass to the purchaser only if it is expressly assigned to him.

Abandonment of claim

Strictly speaking, the trustees cannot withdraw or abandon a notice to treat served by them, without the consent of the owners of the freehold and any intermediate reversions,[62] except during two periods. These are (i) within six weeks after any of such owners has served on the trustees a notice stating the compensation claimed by him,[63] and (ii) within six weeks after the Lands Tribunal has determined the compensation payable by the trustees.[64] In practice, however, there is nothing to be gained by the owners forcing the trustees to wait for one of those periods; and even if the trustees fail to withdraw their notice to treat, it may be difficult to enforce an order for specific performance against them. The trustees will have the protection of Part II of the Landlord and Tenant Act 1954 at the expiry of their contractual terms.[65] 19–14

[62] *Cf. Tawney* v. *Lynn and Ely Rly* (1847) 16 L.J.Ch. 202.
[63] Land Compensation Act 1961, s. 31(1).
[64] *Ibid.* s. 31(2).
[65] *Parkes* v. *Westminster Roman Catholic Diocese Trustee* (1978) 36 P. & C.R. 22, C.A.

APPENDIX A

Precedents

1

20–01 **TRANSFER of whole of land in registered title by freeholder absolutely entitled in favour of leaseholder absolutely entitled. Short form, without reserving easements or imposing fresh restrictive covenants**[1]

H.M. LAND REGISTRY

Land Registration Acts 1925–1971

TRANSFER OF WHOLE
(NOT imposing fresh restrictive covenants) for giving effect to section 8 of the Leasehold Reform Act 1967[2]

County and district *or* London borough:
Title no.:
Property:
Date:

1. In consideration of ____ pounds (£____) the receipt whereof is hereby acknowledged I AB of ____ [formerly of ____ *registered address if different*] HEREBY TRANSFER to CD of ____ the land comprised in the title above referred to[3]

2. There shall be implied in this Transfer such covenant for title on the part of the transferor as under section 76(1)(F) of the Law of Property Act 1925 and rule 76 of the Land Registration Rules 1925 is implied in the case of a person transferring and expressed to be transferring as trustee[4]

3. And I the said CD HEREBY DECLARE that the term created by the registered lease of which I am the registered proprietor under Title No. ____ [*leasehold title no.*] shall forthwith merge and be extinguished in the fee simple thereof hereby transferred[5] And I HEREBY APPLY for the said Title No. ____ [*leasehold title no.*] to be closed[6]

[*Or if the lease is unregistered*

And I the said CD HEREBY DECLARE that the term created by a Lease dated ____ made between ____ and ____ and noted against the above-mentioned title shall forthwith merge and be extinguished in the fee simple of the land hereby transferred and I hereby apply for the cancellation of the said note][7]

4. It is hereby certified that the transaction hereby effected does not form part of a larger transaction or of a series of transactions in respect of which the amount or value or aggregate amount or value of the consideration exceeds £____[8]

SIGNED SEALED AND DELIVERED, *etc.*[9]

Notes

[1] This precedent follows Form 19 (Transfer of Whole) set out in the Schedule to the Land Registration Rules 1925.

[2] It is necessary to give notice to the Land Registry that the transfer is being made under the 1967 Act, in order to ensure that an entry is made on the register to that effect, showing in particular that the property has the benefit of and is subject to the easements and rights mentioned in s.10(2): see para. 6–21, note 24. Such notice is conveniently incorporated in the transfer itself, either in the heading (as in this Precedent) or in the operative part after the acknowledgment of receipt of the purchase price.

[3] It is not necessary to mention any subsisting easements affecting the land transferred, nor to state that the transfer is made subject to the lease.

[4] It is not necessary for an absolute owner to give the full "beneficial owner" covenants for title: see s.10(1) and para. 6–29. It may be sufficient for the transferor merely to transfer "as trustee," but in view of the doubts raised in *Fay* v. *Miller Wilkins & Co.* [1941] Ch. 360, it is preferable to include clause 2 of this Precedent.

[5] As to merger, see para. 6–30. It is not always to the tenant's advantage to include a declaration of merger, and in exceptional cases it may even be desirable to include a declaration against merger: see para. 6–31.

[6] If preferred, the application to close can be made by letter. Both the freehold and leasehold land certificates must be lodged for this purpose.

[7] See n. 5, above.

[8] A certificate of value for stamp duty purposes will almost always be appropriate.

[9] The transfer should be executed by both parties.

2

TRANSFER of part of land in registered title by freeholder absolutely entitled. Short form, without reserving easements or imposing fresh restrictive covenants[1] 20–02

H.M. LAND REGISTRY

Land Registration Acts 1925–1971

TRANSFER OF PART
(NOT imposing fresh restrictive covenants) for giving effect to section 8 of the Leasehold Reform Act 1967[2]

County and district *or* London borough:
Title no.:
Property:
Date:

1. In consideration of ____ pounds (£____) the receipt whereof is hereby acknowledged I AB of ____ [formerly of ____ *registered address if different*] HEREBY TRANSFER to CD of ____ the land shown and edged red on the accompanying plan[3] and known as ____ being part of the land comprised in the title above referred to
[*Continue as in Precedent No. 1*]

Notes

[1] This Precedent follows Form 20 (Transfer of Part) set out in the Schedule to the Land Registration Rules 1925.
[2] See note 2 to Precedent No. 1.
[3] The plan must be signed by the transferor, and by or on behalf of the transferee, unless the part transferred is clearly defined on (and transferred by reference to) the filed plan or general map: see the Land Registration Rules 1925, r. 79.

3

20–03 **TRANSFER by landlord, under rule 72, of unregistered land in a compulsory area**[1]

H.M. LAND REGISTRY

Land Registration Acts 1925–1971

TRANSFER UNDER RULE 72
(NOT imposing fresh restrictive covenants) for giving effect to section 8 of the Leasehold Reform Act 1967

County and district *or* London borough:
Title no.:
Property:
Date:

1. In consideration of ____ pounds (£____) the receipt whereof is acknowledged I AB of ____ HEREBY TRANSFER to CD of ____ the land shown and edged red on the accompanying plan and known as ____[2]

2. [*As clause 2 of Precedent No. 1*]

3. And I the said CD HEREBY DECLARE that the term created by the registered lease of which I am the registered proprietor under Title No. ____. [*leasehold title no.*] shall forthwith merge and be extinguished in the fee simple thereof hereby transferred And I HEREBY APPLY for the said Title No. ____ [*leasehold title no.*] to be closed

[*Or if the lease is unregistered* And I the said CD HEREBY DECLARE that the term created by a Lease dated ____ made between ____ and ____ shall forthwith merge and be extinguished in the fee simple of the land hereby transferred]

[*Continue as in Precedent No. 1*]

Notes

[1] Rule 72 of the Land Registration Rules 1925 provides that a person entitled to apply for first registration may deal with the land as if he were the registered proprietor.

[2] Alternatively, the land can be described by reference to a previous document of title, provided the description is adequate to identify the land.

4

TRANSFER by freeholder absolutely entitled in favour of leaseholder absolutely entitled. Full form, including provision for the grant and reservation of easements, for the imposition of fresh restrictive covenants, and where there are subsisting restrictive covenants[1] 20–04

H.M. LAND REGISTRY

Land Registration Acts 1925–1971

TRANSFER OF PART

[NOT imposing fresh restrictive covenants] for giving effect to section 8 of the Leasehold Reform Act 1967[2]

County and district *or* London borough:
Title no.:
Property:
Date:

1. In consideration of ____ (£____) the receipt whereof is hereby acknowledged I AB of ____ [formerly of ____ *registered address if different*] (hereinafter called "the Vendor") HEREBY TRANSFER to CD of ____ (hereinafter called "the Purchaser") the land shown and edged red on the accompanying plan[3] and known as ____ being part of the land comprised in the title above referred to [*if appropriate* Together With the rights specified in the First Schedule[4]] [and] except and reserving and subject as hereinafter provided

2. The rights specified in the Second Schedule are excepted and reserved unto the Vendor in fee simple for the benefit of the remainder of the land comprised in the above title number[5]

[3. *If there are subsisting restrictive covenants*[6] With the object of affording to the Vendor a full and sufficient indemnity in respect thereof (but not further or otherwise) the Purchaser HEREBY COVENANTS with the Vendor to observe and perform the covenants and provisions referred to in entry no. ____ of the charges register of the title above referred to (so far as they relate to the land hereby transferred and still subsisting and capable of being enforced) And to indemnify and keep indemnified the Vendor and his estate from and against all actions proceedings costs claims and demands in respect thereof]

[4. *If restrictive covenants are being imposed*[7] The Purchaser HEREBY

COVENANTS with the Vendor to the intent that the burden of this covenant may run with and bind the land hereby transferred and to the intent that the benefit of the same may be annexed to and run with the remainder of the land comprised in the above title number and each and every part thereof to observe and perform the covenants and stipulations set out in the Third Schedule hereto]

[*Here insert Clauses 2, 3 and 4 of Precedent No. 1*]

THE FIRST SCHEDULE

1. The right at all times and for all purposes connected with the existing use of the land hereby transferred with or without motor and other vehicles and animals to go pass and repass over and along the roadway tinted brown[8] on the accompanying plan[9]

2. [*etc. as appropriate*]

THE SECOND SCHEDULE

1. The right at all times and for all purposes connected with the existing use of the remainder of the land comprised in the above title number with or without motor or other vehicles and animals to go pass and repass over and along the roadway tinted blue[10] on the accompanying plan and included in the land hereby transferred[11]

2. [*etc. as appropriate*]

THE THIRD SCHEDULE

[*Here set out any restrictive covenants in the Lease which materially enhance the value of other property of the Vendor, and also any other restrictive covenants required by the Vendor which will not interfere with the existing use of the land transferred but which will materially enhance the value of other property of his*[12]]

SIGNED SEALED AND DELIVERED, *etc.*[13]

Notes

[1] This Precedent sets out in full the appropriate contents of a transfer where (i) the freehold is subject to subsisting covenants; (ii) easements are to be granted and reserved; and (iii) restrictive covenants are to be imposed. It is seldom necessary to use this form in full and it should be adapted as appropriate. Compare Precedent No. 10.

[2] See note 2 to Precedent No. 14.

[3] The plan must be signed by the transferor, and by or on behalf of the transferee, unless the part transferred is clearly defined on (and transferred by reference to) the filed plan or general map: see the Land Registration Rules 1925, r. 79.

[4] Law of Property Act 1925, s.62 will apply, and so it may not be imperative to include an

express grant of easements. Nevertheless it is thought desirable to make express mention of easements of the kind set out in the First Schedule to this Precedent. See s.10(3)(*a*) and paras. 6–17 and 6–19.

[5] Any easements (apart from those mentioned in s.10(2)) which the vendor wishes to reserve must be expressly mentioned. The vendor can require the reservation of easements of the kind set out in the Second Schedule to this Precedent. See s.10(3)(*b*) and paras. 6–22 *et seq.*

[6] The vendor is entitled to an indemnity in respect of subsisting restrictive covenants: see s.10(4)(*a*) and para. 6–26.

[7] See s.10(4)(*b*), (*c*) and paras. 6–27 and 6–28. If there are any restrictive covenants in the lease which are expressed to be made with any persons other than the landlord (and which may thus be enforceable by those persons under Law of Property Act 1925, s.56), the purchaser should also covenant with those persons. In addition, the landlord can be required to enter into any restrictive covenants in the lease (or any agreement collateral thereto) affecting other property of his which materially enhance the value of the house and premises: see s.10(4)(*b*) and para. 6–28. In such cases the landlord will similarly covenant with the tenant, but there should be added the following proviso: "Provided that the Vendor shall not be liable for any breach of the said covenants and stipulations for which he is not responsible": see s.10(6).

[8] Rights appurtenant to the land are usually tinted brown on the Registry plan.

[9] As to rights of way, see s.10(3)(*a*) and para. 6–19.

[10] Land subject to a right of way is usually tinted blue on the Registry plan.

[11] As to rights of way, see s.10(3)(*b*) and para. 6–22.

[12] See note 7, *ante.*

[13] The transfer must be executed by both parties.

5

TRANSFER by trustees for sale to tenant[1] **20–05**

[*Heading as Precedents No. 1, 2 or 4*]

1. In consideration of ____ pounds (£____) the receipt whereof is acknowledged We AB of ____ and CD of ____ [*if appropriate* (hereinafter called "the Vendors")] as trustees HEREBY TRANSFER to EF of ____ [*if appropriate* (hereinafter called "the Purchaser")] the land [*continue as in Precedent No. 1, 2 and 4*]

[*Remainder as Precedents No. 1, 2 or 4, but omitting clause 2 of Precedent No. 1*]

Notes

[1] This form adapts Precedent Nos. 1, 2 or 4 to cases where the freehold is held on a trust for sale. See s.8(4) of the 1967 Act, Law of Property Act 1925, s.2(1)(ii) and para. 15–01.

[2] As the transferors are in fact trustees, the "trustee" covenant for title mentioned in s.10(1) will be incorporated, and clause 2 of Precedent No. 1 should be omitted: see para. 6–29.

6

TRANSFER of part by freeholder absolutely entitled subject to a mortgage in favour of leaseholder absolutely entitled, where freeholder's mortgagee is joined.[1] **VARIATIONS where whole, part or none of the purchase price is** **20–06**

paid to the mortgagee[2]

H.M. LAND REGISTRY

Land Registration Acts 1925–1971

TRANSFER AND DISCHARGE OF PART (FREEHOLD)
to give effect to section 8 of the Leasehold Reform Act 1967[3]

County and district *or* London borough:
Title no.:
Property:
Date:

1. In consideration of ___ pounds (£___) paid [*if the whole purchase price is being paid to the Mortgagee* at the request of AB of ___ (hereinafter called "the Vendor") to CD of ___ (hereinafter called "the Mortgagee") in reduction of the moneys owing to him under the charge hereinafter mentioned the payment and receipt of which is acknowledged] [*if part of the purchase price is being paid to the Mortgagee* to AB of ___ (hereinafter called "the Vendor") the receipt whereof the Vendor hereby acknowledges and of ___ pounds (£___) paid at the request of the Vendor to CD of ___ (hereinafter called "the Mortgagee") in reduction of the moneys owing to him under the charge hereinafter mentioned the payment and receipt of which is acknowledged] [*if no part of the purchase price is being paid to the Mortgagee* to AB of ___ (hereinafter called "the Vendor") with the consent of CD of ___ (hereinafter called "the Mortgagee") the receipt whereof the Vendor hereby acknowledges] the Vendor HEREBY TRANSFERS to EF of ___ the land shown and edged red on the accompanying plan[4] and known as ___ being part of the land comprised in the title above referred to And the Mortgagee As Mortgagee HEREBY DISCHARGES the land hereby transferred from the Legal Charge dated ___ and registered on the ___ of which he is the proprietor and from all liability in respect thereof
[*Continue as rest of Precedent No. 2 or 4 as appropriate*]

Notes

[1] It is recommended that any transfer of a landlord's interest which is subject to a subsisting mortgage should be in one of the alternative forms of this Precedent. If the mortgagee refuses to join in the transfer, or otherwise to give a proper discharge on being tendered the purchase price payable under the Act, the tenant should threaten to pay the purchase price into court under s.13. See para. 12–05.

[2] This Precedent, including each variation, follows Form 55 (Transfer and Discharge) set out in the Schedule to the Land Registration Rules 1925. Compare Precedent No. 16.

[3] See note 2 to Precedent No. 1.

[4] See note 3 to Precedent No. 2.

7

TRANSFER of part by freeholder absolutely entitled subject to a mortgage in favour of a leaseholder absolutely entitled, where freeholder's mortgagee is not joined.[1] VARIATION where purchase price is paid into court[2] 20–07

[*Heading as in Precedent No. 6*]

1. In consideration of ____ pounds (£____) paid to EF of ____ as mortgagee under the charge hereinafter mentioned [*or* into the ____ County Court to the credit of an action the short title and reference to which is ____] the payment of which is acknowledged I AB of ____ HEREBY TRANSFER to CD of ____ [*continue as Precedent No. 2 or No. 4*]

2. It is HEREBY DECLARED that the land hereby transferred is now freed and discharged from the Legal Charge dated ____ [*date*] and registered on ____ [*date*] of which the said EF is the proprietor and from all liability in respect thereof under and by virtue of the provisions of section 12 [*or if there is a payment into court*) section 13] of the said Act[3]
[*Continue as Precedent No. 2 or No. 4*]

Notes

[1] This Precedent should only be used in exceptional cases where the mortgagee refuses to join in the transfer or to give a proper discharge. See generally paras. 13–06 and 13–09.
[2] *i.e.* under s.13: see paras. 13–09 *et seq.*
[3] It is advisable to refer specifically to s.12 or s.13.

8

TRANSFER by freeholder absolutely in favour of leaseholder absolutely entitled, where part of "the house and premises" is excluded and surrendered to freeholder[1] 20–08

[*Heading as in Precedent No. 4*]

[*Clauses 1, 2, 3 and 4 of Precedent No. 4, as appropriate*]

5. (1) The Purchaser as Beneficial Owner[2] HEREBY SURRENDERS AND ASSIGNS to the Vendor [if the lease is registered] the registered Lease of which the Purchaser is the proprietor under Title No. ____ [*leasehold title no*] [*or if the lease is unregistered* the Lease dated the ____ and made between ____ and ____ and noted against the above-mentioned title] so far as regards the land specified in the ____ Schedule hereto but not further or otherwise

(2) In consideration of the surrender the Vendor HEREBY RELEASES AND

DISCHARGES the Purchaser from all (if any) claims and liability for past breaches of covenant under the said Lease[3]

6. The Purchaser HEREBY DECLARES that the term created by the said registered Lease [*or if the lease is unregistered* by the said Lease] shall (so far as the same relates to the land hereby transferred) forthwith merge and be extinguished in the fee simple thereof[4] AND HEREBY APPLIES for the cancellation of the said note

[*Clauses 2 and 4 of Precedent No. 1*]

THE ____ SCHEDULE

Particulars of premises surrendered to Vendor
[*As appropriate*]

Notes

[1] As to when the landlord can require part of the "house and premises" to be excluded from the transfer, see s.2(5) and para. 6–13. It may be that, by virtue of s.2(7), the transfer would impliedly operate as a surrender of the excluded part, even if there is no express surrender. But the subsection is by no means clear, and it is considered preferable for the transfer to incorporate an express surrender, as in this Precedent. If preferred, the surrender can be made by a separate document. Compare Precedent No. 14.
[2] It may be that the Purchaser need only give the "trustee" covenants for title: *cf.* s.10(6).
[3] The surrender alone will not relieve the tenant from past breaches of covenant: *Richmond* v. *Savill* [1926] 2 K.B. 530, C.A.
[4] See as to merger para. 6–30.

9

20–09 **CONVEYANCE by freeholder absolutely entitled in favour of leaseholder absolutely entitled. Short form, where there are no subsisting easements and covenants, and without reserving easements or imposing fresh restrictive covenants.**[1]

THIS CONVEYANCE is made the ____ day of ____ BETWEEN AB of ____ (hereinafter called "the Vendor") of the one part AND CD of ____ (hereinafter called "the Purchaser") of the other part

WHEREAS:—

(1) The Vendor is the estate owner in fee simple of the property hereby conveyed subject to but with the benefit of the Lease[2] short particulars whereof are set out in the First Schedule hereto (hereinafter called "the Scheduled Lease") but otherwise free from encumbrances

(2) The Vendor has agreed[3] with the Purchaser for the sale to him for the sum of £____ of the fee simple of the property hereby conveyed subject as aforesaid but otherwise free from encumbrances

(3) The term of years granted by the Scheduled Lease is now vested in the Purchaser[4]

NOW THIS DEED WITNESSETH as follows:—

1. In pursuance of the said agreement and in consideration of the sum of £____ now paid by the Purchaser to the Vendor and to give effect to section 8 of the Leasehold Reform Act 1967[5] the Vendor as Trustee[6] HEREBY CONVEYS unto the Purchaser ALL THAT [*parcels*[7]] TO HOLD the same UNTO the Purchaser Subject to but with the benefit of the Scheduled Lease

2. It is HEREBY DECLARED that the same covenants for title (but no further covenants for title) shall be implied herein as if the Vendor was conveying and expressed to convey the property hereby conveyed as trustee[8]

3. The Purchaser HEREBY DECLARES that the said term of years granted by the Scheduled Lease shall forthwith merge and be extinguished in the fee simple of the property hereby conveyed[9]

[4. *If documents of title are being retained by the Vendor* The Vendor HEREBY ACKNOWLEDGES the right of the Purchaser to the production of the documents specified in the Second Schedule hereto (possession of which is retained by the Vendor) and to delivery of copies thereof][10]

5. It is hereby certified that the transaction hereby effected does not form part of a larger transaction or of a series of transactions in respect of which the amount or value or the aggregate amount or value of the consideration exceeds £____ [*as appropriate*][11]

IN WITNESS whereof the parties hereto have hereunto set their respective hands and seals the day and year first before written

THE FIRST SCHEDULE

The Scheduled Lease
[*Here set out short particulars of Lease*]

THE SECOND SCHEDULE

Particulars of documents retained by the Vendor
[*Here set out short particulars of any documents retained by the Vendor*]

SIGNED SEALED AND DELIVERED, *etc.*[12]

Notes

[1] This Precedent is for use only in straightforward cases. If the property in question is unregistered but in a compulsory registration area, it is suggested that the transaction

should be effected by a transfer under rule 72 of the Land Registration Rules 1925: see Precedent No. 3, *supra*.

[2] *i.e.* the "long tenancy at a low rent" giving the tenant his right to enfranchise.

[3] It is not necessary to mention the 1967 Act in the recitals; but see note 5, *post*.

[4] There is no need to recite the Purchaser's title in any further detail.

[5] All conveyances under s.8 of the 1967 Act should contain an express statement to that effect, to draw attention to the automatic grant and reservation of certain easements under s.10(2). See para. 6–18.

[6] It is not necessary for an absolute owner to give the full "beneficial owner" covenants for title: see s.10(1) and para. 6–29. However, to ensure that the "trustee" covenants for title are implied, in view of the doubts raised by *Fay* v. *Miller Wilkins & Co* [1941] Ch. 360, C.A., Clause 2 of this Precedent should be included unless the Vendor is in fact a trustee.

[7] See para. 6–16. Preferably a full modern description of the property (if possible with a plan) should be inserted, particularly in cases where the parcels clause is out of date. If there is a suitable modern description in the Lease, the parcels can read: "the property comprised in and demised by the Scheduled Lease."

[8] See note 6, *ante*.

[9] As to merger, see para. 6–30. It is not always to the tenant's advantage to include a declaration of merger, and in exceptional circumstances it may even be desirable to include an express declaration *against* merger: see para. 6–31.

[10] In most cases, the Vendor will retain title deeds relating to other property, so that this clause will be appropriate. However, no undertaking as to safe custody need be given: see s.10(6).

[11] A certificate of value will usually be required for stamp duty purposes.

[12] If it contains a declaration of merger, the conveyance should be executed by the Purchaser, as well as by the Vendor.

10

20–10 **CONVEYANCE by freeholder absolutely entitled in favour of leaseholder absolutely entitled. Full form, including provisions where freehold is subject to subsisting easements and covenants, for the grant and reservation of easements, and for the imposition of restrictive covenants.**[1]

THIS CONVEYANCE is made the ____ day of ____ BETWEEN AB of ____ (hereinafter called "the Vendor") of the one part and CD of ____ (hereinafter called "the Purchaser") of the other part

WHEREAS:—

(1) The Vendor is the estate owner in fee simple of the property hereby conveyed subject to [*if appropriate*[2] the subsisting rights easements and covenants hereinafter mentioned and subject also to] but with the benefit of the Lease[3] short particulars whereof are set out in the First Schedule hereto (hereinafter called "the Scheduled Lease") [*if appropriate*[4] so far as the same affects the property hereby conveyed] but otherwise free from encumbrances

(2) The Vendor has agreed[5] with the Purchaser for the sale to him for the sum of £____ of the fee simple of the property hereby conveyed subject as aforesaid [*if easements are being reserved*[6] and except and reserving as hereinafter provided] [*if restrictive covenants are being*

imposed[7] and subject as hereinafter provided] [*if both easements are being reserved and restrictive covenants are being imposed* and except and reserving and subject as hereinafter provided] but otherwise free from encumbrances

(3) The term of years granted by the Scheduled Lease [*if appropriate* so far as the same affects the property hereby conveyed] is now vested in the Purchaser[8] [*if appropriate* at the apportioned yearly rent of £____]

NOW THIS DEED WITNESSETH as follows:—

1. In pursuance of the said agreement and in consideration of the sum of £____ now paid by the Purchaser to the Vendor (the receipt whereof the Vendor hereby acknowledges) and to give effect to section 8 of the Leasehold Reform Act 1967 the Vendor as Trustee[9] HEREBY CONVEYS unto the Purchaser ALL THAT[10] [*parcels*[11]] [*if appropriate* TOGETHER WITH the rights and easements specified in the Second Schedule hereto (so far as the Vendor is capable of granting the same)[12]] [*if appropriate* EXCEPT AND RESERVING unto the Vendor in fee simple the rights and easements specified in the Third Schedule hereto[13]] TO HOLD the same UNTO the Purchaser in fee simple Subject to [*if appropriate* the subsisting rights and easements specified in the Fourth Schedule hereto and subject also to] [*if appropriate* the subsisting covenants specified in the Fifth Schedule hereto (so far as the same affect the property hereby conveyed and are still subsisting and capable of being enforced) and subject also to] but with the benefit of the Scheduled Lease [*if appropriate* so far as the same affects the property hereby conveyed]

[2. *If there are subsisting covenants*[14] With the object of affording to the Vendor a full and sufficient indemnity in respect thereof (but not further or otherwise) the Purchaser HEREBY COVENANTS with the Vendor to observe and perform the said covenants specified in the Fifth Schedule hereto (so far as the same affect the property hereby conveyed and are still subsisting and capable of being enforced) And to indemnify and keep indemnified the Vendor and his estate from and against all actions proceedings costs claims and demands in respect thereof]

[3. *If restrictive covenants are being imposed*[15] The Purchaser HEREBY COVENANTS with the Vendor to the intent that the burden of this covenant may run with and bind the property hereby conveyed and to the intent that the benefit of the same may be annexed to and run with the adjoining or neighbouring property of the Vendor [*short description of Vendor's property e.g.* known as ____ *or* shown coloured brown on the plan annexed hereto] and each and every part thereof[16] to observe and perform the covenants and stipulations set out in the Sixth Schedule hereto]

4. It is HEREBY DECLARED that the same covenants for title (but no further covenants for title) shall be implied herein as if the Vendor was

conveying and was expressed to convey the property hereby conveyed as Trustee[17]

5. The Purchaser HEREBY DECLARES that the said term of years granted by the Scheduled Lease [*if appropriate* (so far as the same affects the property hereby conveyed)] shall forthwith merge and be extinguished in the fee simple of the property hereby conveyed[18]

[6. *If documents of title are being retained by the Vendor* The Vendor HEREBY ACKNOWLEDGES the right of the Purchaser to the production of the documents specified in the Seventh Schedule hereto (possession of which is retained by the Vendor) and to delivery of copies thereof)][19]

7. It is hereby certified that the transaction hereby effected does not form part of a larger transaction or of a series of transactions in respect of which the amount or value or the aggregate amount or value of the consideration exceeds [*as appropriate*][20]

IN WITNESS whereof the parties hereto have hereunto set their respective hands and seals the day and year first before written.

THE FIRST SCHEDULE

Particulars of the Scheduled Lease

A Lease dated the ____ and made between (1) ____ and (2) ____ for the term ____ years from the ____ at the yearly rent of £____ [*or as appropriate*]

THE SECOND SCHEDULE

Particulars of rights and easements granted

(so far as the Vendor is capable of granting the same)[21]

1. The right in common with the Vendor and all other persons having the like right at all times and for all purposes connected with the existing use of the property hereby conveyed with or without motor and other vehicles and animals to go pass and repass over and along the roadway shown coloured green on the plan annexed hereto [*or as appropriate*][22]

2. [*etc., as appropriate*]

THE THIRD SCHEDULE

Particulars of rights and easements excepted and reserved to the Vendor[23]

1. The right in common with the Purchaser and all other persons having the like right at all times and for all purposes connected with the existing use of the adjoining or neighbouring property of the Vendor with or without motor and other vehicles and animals to go pass and repass over and along the roadway forming part of the property hereby conveyed shown coloured blue on the plan annexed hereto [*or as appropriate*][24]

2. [*etc., as appropriate*]

THE FOURTH SCHEDULE

Particulars of subsisting rights and easements[25]

[*Here set out particulars of subsisting rights and easements affecting the property conveyed, e.g. by reference to the documents by which they were granted or reserved*]

THE FIFTH SCHEDULE

Particulars of subsisting covenants

[*Here set out particulars of subsisting covenants affecting the property conveyed, e.g. by reference to the documents by which they were imposed*]

THE SIXTH SCHEDULE

Particulars of restrictive covenants imposed[26]

[*Here set out any restrictive covenants in the Scheduled Lease which materially enhance the value of other property of the Vendor, and also any other restrictive covenants required by the Vendor which will not interfere with the existing use of the property conveyed but which will materially enhance the value of other property of his*]

THE SEVENTH SCHEDULE

Particulars of documents retained by the Vendor

[*Here set out short particulars of any documents retained by the Vendor*]

SIGNED SEALED AND DELIVERED, *etc.*[27]

Notes

[1] This Precedent sets out in full the appropriate contents of a conveyance where (i) the freehold is subject to subsisting easements and covenants, (ii) easements are to be granted and reserved and (iii) restrictive covenants are to be imposed. It is seldom necessary to use this form in full, and it should be adapted as appropriate. Compare Precedent No. 4.

[2] *i.e.* where there are existing easements and/or covenants affecting the freehold. If there are only easements (and no covenants), or vice versa, the words in square brackets must be amended appropriately.

[3] *i.e.* the "long tenancy or a low rent" giving the tenant his right to enfranchise.

[4] *i.e.* where the tenant holds only part of the property originally comprised in the lease.

[5] It is not necessary to mention the 1967 Act in the recitals; but see note 9, *post.*

[6] See note 13, *post.*

[7] See note 15, *post.*

[8] There is no necessity to recite the Purchaser's title in any further detail.

[9] All conveyances under s.8 of the 1967 Act should contain an express statement to that effect, to draw attention to the automatic grant and reservation of certain easements under s.10(2). See para. 6–18.

[10] It is not necessary for an absolute owner to give the full "beneficial owner" covenants for title: see s.10(1) and para. 6–29, *ante.* However, to ensure that the "trustee" covenants for title are implied, in view of the doubts raised by *Fay* v. *Miller Wilkins & Co* [1941] Ch. 360, C.A., clause 4 of this Precedent should be included unless the Vendor is in fact a trustee.

[11] See para. 6–16. Preferably, a full modern description of the property (if possible with a plan) should be inserted, particularly in cases where the parcels clause in the lease is out of date. If there is a suitable modern description in the lease, the parcels can read: "the property comprised in and demised by the Scheduled Lease."

[12] S.62 of the Law of Property Act 1925 will apply, and so it may not be imperative to include an express grant of easements. Nevertheless it is thought desirable to make express mention of easements of the kind set out in the Second Schedule to this Precedent. See s.10(3)(*a*) and paras. 6–17 and 6–19.

[13] Any easements (apart from those mentioned in s.10(2)) which the vendor wishes to reserve must be expressly mentioned. The vendor can require the reservation of easements of the kind set out in the Third Schedule to this Precedent. See s.10(3)(*b*) and paras. 6–22 *et seq.*

[14] The vendor is entitled to this indemnity as regards restrictive covenants: see s.10(4)(*a*) and para. 6–26.

[15] See s.10(4)(*b*), (*c*) and paras. 6–27 and 6–28. If there are any restrictive covenants in the lease which are expressed to be made with any persons other than the landlord (and which may thus be enforceable by those persons under s.56 of the Law of Property Act 1925), the purchaser should also covenant with those persons. In addition, the landlord can be required to enter into any restrictive covenants in the lease (or any agreement collateral thereto) affecting other property of his which materially enhance the value of the house and premises: see s.10(4)(*b*) and para. 6–28. In such cases, the landlord will covenant similarly with the tenant, but there should be added the following proviso: "Provided that the Vendor shall not be liable for any breach of the said covenants and stipulations for which he is not responsible": see s.10(6).

[16] These words ensure that the benefit of the covenants are fully annexed; but see para. 6–27.

[17] See note 10, *ante.*

[18] As to merger, see para. 6–30. It is not always to the tenant's advantage to include a declaration of merger, and in exceptional cases it may even be desirable to include a declaration *against* merger: see para. 6–31.

[19] No undertaking for safe custody need be given: see s.10(6).

[20] A certificate of value will nearly always be appropriate.

[21] See note 12, *ante.*

[22] As to rights of way, see s.10(3)(*a*) and para. 6–19.

[23] See note 13, *ante.*

[24] As to rights of way, see s.10(3)(*b*) and para. 6–22.

[25] The vendor will only be able to convey subject to existing rights and easements (except any capable of being overreached) and the conveyance should be made subject to them: see s.8(1) and para. 6–24.
[26] See note 15, *ante*.
[27] If the conveyance contains any reservation or covenant in favour of the vendor, it must be executed by both parties, and a duplicate should be retained by the vendor; see Condition 9(4) in Part I of the Sched. to the Leasehold Reform (Enfranchisement and Extension) Regs 1967 (S.I. 1967 No. 1879), set out in Appendix C, and para. 6–07.

11

CONVEYANCE by trustees for sale of the freehold in favour of leaseholder who is absolutely entitled[1] 20–11

THIS CONVEYANCE is made the ____ day of ____ BETWEEN AB of ____ and CD of ____ (hereinafter called "the Vendors") of the one part and EF of ____ (hereinafter called "the Purchaser") of the other part

WHEREAS:—

(1) [*As recital* (1) *of Precedent No. 9 or 10 as appropriate, substituting* "Vendors" *for* "Vendor" *and making consequential amendments*]

(2) The property hereby conveyed is vested in the Vendors as trustees upon the trust for sale declared by a Conveyance [*or* Assent] dated the ____ and made between ____ [*set out parties*] and in exercise of the trust for sale aforesaid[2] the Vendors have agreed [*continue as in recital* (2) *of Precedent No. 9 or 10*]

(3) [*As recital* (3) *of Precedent No. 9 or 10*]

NOW THIS DEED WITNESSETH as follows:—

[*Continue to end of Precedent No. 1 or 2 as appropriate, but (i) substituting* "Vendors" *for* "Vendor" *and making consequential amendments and (ii) omitting Clause 2 of Precedent No. 9/Clause 4 of Precedent No. 10*]

Notes

[1] This form adapts Precedents Nos. 9 or 10 to cases where the freehold is held on a trust for sale. See s.8(4) of the 1967 Act, Law of Property Act 1925, s.2(1)(ii) and para. 15–01.
[2] Or simply "upon an immediate binding trust for sale and in exercise thereof."

12

CONVEYANCE by tenant for life under the Settled Land Act 1925 of the freehold in favour of leaseholder who is absolutely entitled[1] 20–12

THIS CONVEYANCE is made the ____ day of ____ BETWEEN AB of ____ (hereinafter called "the Vendor") of the first part CD of ____ and EF of

____ (hereinafter called "the Trustees") of the second part and GH of ____ (hereinafter called "the Purchaser") of the third part

WHEREAS:—

(1) [*As recital* (1) *of Precedent No. 9 or 10*]

(2) The property hereby conveyed is vested in the Vendor upon the trusts of a settlement subject to the Settled Land Act 1925 by a Principal Vesting Deed [*or* Subsidiary Vesting Deed *or* Vesting Assent *as the case may be*] dated the ____ and made between ____ [*set out parties*] and the Trustees were thereby [*or if there has been a subsequent appointment of new trustees* by a Deed of Declaration dated the ____ and made between ____] stated to be the trustees of the said settlement for the purposes of the said Act

(3)
[*As recitals* (2) *and* (3) *of Precedent No. 9 or 10*]
(4)

NOW THIS DEED WITNESSETH as follows:—

1. In pursuance of the said agreement and in consideration of the sum of £____ now paid by the Purchaser at the direction of the Vendor to the Trustees (the receipt and payment whereof in manner aforesaid the Trustees and the Vendor hereby respectively acknowledge) and to give effect to section 8 of the Leasehold Reform Act 1967 the Vendor as trustee in exercise of the powers conferred on him by the said Act and all other powers him enabling HEREBY CONVEYS [*continue as in Clause 1 of Precedent No. 9 or 10*]

[*Here insert the rest of Precedent No. 9 or 10 as appropriate, but omitting Clause 2 of Precedent No. 9/Clause 4 of Precedent No. 10*[2]]

Notes

[1] This form adapts Precedent Nos. 9 or 10 to cases where the freehold is settled land subject to the Settled Land Act 1925. The formalities of s.18 of that Act must be duly complied with in order that the equitable interests under the settlement are overreached: see s.8(4) of the 1967 Act, Law of Property Act 1925, s.2(1)(i) and para. 15–01, *ante*. The Precedent can be suitably adapted if the legal estate in the freehold is vested in the Settled Land Act trustees as statutory owners.

[2] As a tenant for life exercising his power of sale under the Settled Land Act 1925 is deemed to be in the position of a trustee (s.107), Clause 2 of Precedent No. 9/Clause 4 of Precedent No. 10 is unnecessary.

13

20–13 **SUBSIDIARY VESTING DEED whereby freeholder absolutely entitled conveys the freehold to leaseholder who holds his interest as tenant for life**

under a settlement subject to the Settled Land Act 1925[1]

THIS SUBSIDIARY VESTING DEED is made the ___ day of ___ BETWEEN AB of ___ (hereinafter called "the Vendor") of the first part CD of ___ (hereinafter called "the Purchaser") of the second part and EF of ___ and GH of ___ (hereinafter called "the Trustees") of the third part

WHEREAS:—

(1)

[*As recitals* (1) *and* (2) *of Precedent No. 9 or 10*]

(2)

(3) Under and by virtue of a Principal Vesting Deed [*or* Vesting Assent *as the case may be*] dated the ___ and made between ___ the term of years granted by the Scheduled Lease [*if appropriate* so far as the same affects the property hereby conveyed] is now vested on the Purchaser [*if appropriate* at the apportioned yearly rent of £___] Upon the trusts of the settlement therein mentioned and the Trustees were thereby [*or if there has been a subsequent appointment of new trustees* by a Deed of Declaration dated the ___ and made between ___] stated to be the trustees of the said settlement for the purposes of the Settled Land Act 1925

NOW THIS DEED WITNESSETH as follows:—

1. In pursuance of the said agreement and in consideration of the sum of £___ paid by the Trustees at the direction of the Purchaser to the Vendor (the receipt whereof the Vendor hereby acknowledges) and to give effect to section 8 of the Leasehold Reform Act 1967 [*as in Clause 1 of Precedent No. 9 or 10 to end and continue*] Upon and subject to the same trusts and powers as are declared by the said Principal Vesting Deed [*or* Vesting Assent] with respect to the property therein comprised

[*Here insert Clauses 2–3 of Precedent No. 10 as appropriate*]

[4](1) The Trustees are the trustees of the settlement for the purposes of the Settled Land Act 1925

(2) The power of appointing new trustees of the settlement is vested in the Purchaser during his lifetime [*or as the case may be*]

[*Continue from Clause 3 of Precedent No. 9/Clause 5 of Precedent No. 10 to end as appropriate*]

Note

[1] As to the acquisition of the freehold by the tenant for life under the Settled Land Act 1925, see s.6(2) and paras. 15–05 and 15–08. The conveyance of the freehold to him must be by way of a subsidiary vesting deed containing the particulars required by s.10 of the Settled Land Act 1925.

14

20–14 **CONVEYANCE by freeholder absolutely entitled in favour of leaseholder absolutely entitled, where part of the "house and premises" is excluded and surrendered to freeholder**[1]

THIS DEED OF CONVEYANCE AND SURRENDER is made the ____ day of ____ BETWEEN AB of ____ (hereinafter called "the Vendor") of the one part and CD of ____ (hereinafter called "the Purchaser") of the other part

WHEREAS:—

(1)

[*As recitals (1) and (2) of Precedent No. 9 or 10*]

(2)

(3) The term of years granted by the Scheduled Lease so far as the same affects the property hereby conveyed is now vested in the Purchaser

(4) There is also vested in the Purchaser the term of years granted by the Scheduled Lease so far as the same affects [*where the Purchaser is entitled to the whole of the property originally comprised in the Scheduled Lease* the remainder of the property comprised in and demised by the Scheduled Lease] [*where the Purchaser is not so entitled* a further part of the property comprised in and demised by the Scheduled Lease] and upon the treaty for the said sale it was agreed that the Purchaser should surrender the same unto the Vendor in manner hereinafter appearing

NOW THIS DEED WITNESSETH as follows:—

1. [*As Clause 1 of Precedent No. 9 or 10, but ensuring that the part of the house and premises which is to be retained by the Vendor is excluded from the parcels clause*]

2. (1) In pursuance of the said agreement the Purchaser as beneficial owner[2] HEREBY SURRENDERS AND ASSIGNS unto the Vendor ALL THAT [*parcels, being description of part excluded*] TO HOLD the same UNTO the Vendor To the intent that the term of years granted by the Scheduled Lease so far as it affects the same shall forthwith merge and be extinguished in the fee simple thereof[3]

(2) In consideration of the surrender hereinbefore contained the Vendor HEREBY RELEASES AND DISCHARGES the Purchaser from all (if any) claims and liability for past breaches of covenant under the Scheduled Lease[4]

3. The Purchaser HEREBY DECLARES that the said term of years granted by the Scheduled Lease (so far as the same affects the property hereby

conveyed under Clause 1 hereof) shall forthwith merge and be extinguished in the fee simple of the same[5]

[*Here insert Clause 2 of Precedent No. 9 or Clauses 2–4 of Precedent No. 10, as appropriate*]

[5.] The Purchaser HEREBY ACKNOWLEDGES the right of the Vendor to the production of the documents specified in the [Eighth *or as appropriate*] Schedule hereto (possession of which is retained by the Purchaser) and to delivery of copies thereof And hereby undertakes for the safe custody of the same

[*Continue from Clause 4 of Precedent No. 9/Clause 6 of Precedent No. 10 to end as appropriate*]

THE EIGHTH SCHEDULE

Particulars of documents retained by the Purchaser

[*Here set out particulars of documents affecting the leasehold title retained by the Purchaser*]

SIGNED SEALED AND DELIVERED, *etc.*[6]

Notes

[1] As to when the landlord can require part of the "house and premises" to be excluded from the conveyance, see s.2(5) and para. 2–13. It may be that, by virtue of s.2(7), the conveyance would impliedly operate as a surrender of the excluded part, even though there is no express surrender. But the subsection is by no means clear, and in any case it is considered preferable, to enable the landlord to show an absolute title to the excluded part, for the conveyance to incorporate an express surrender, as in this Precedent. If preferred, the surrender can be made by separate document.

[2] It may be that the Purchaser need only give the "trustee" covenants for title: *cf.* s.10(6).

[3] See as to merger para. 6–30.

[4] The surrender alone will not relieve the tenant from past breaches of covenant: *Richmond* v. *Savill* [1926] 2 K.B. 530, C.A.

[5] See note 18 to Precedent No. 10.

[6] The deed must be executed by both parties, and a duplicate retained by the Vendor.

15

EXCEPTION of mines and minerals out of conveyance by freeholder[1]

EXCEPT AND RESERVING unto the Vendor in fee simple all mines and minerals in or under the lands hereby conveyed with full power and authority to work and get the same but by underground workings only and without entering upon or withdrawing support[2] for or in any manner affecting the surface of the property hereby conveyed and the buildings thereon erected

Notes

[1] If the lease itself excepts mines and minerals, they will not form part of the "house and premises," and the landlord need not convey them to the tenant. In such a case, the exception and reservation in the conveyance should follow the terms of that in the lease. This Precedent is designed to deal with the case where there is no such exception in the lease, but where the landlord wishes to reserve the mines and minerals: see s.10(6) and para. 2–14. The conveyance should contain an exception in the above form, and also a surrender of the mines and minerals included in the lease; Precedent No. 14 can be adapted for this purpose.

[2] No right to let down the surface can be reserved: s.10(6).

16

20–16 **CONVEYANCE by freeholder absolutely entitled subject to a mortgage or legal charge in favour of leaseholder absolutely entitled, where freeholder's mortgagee is joined.[1] VARIATIONS where whole, part or none of the purchase price is paid to the mortgagee**

THIS CONVEYANCE is made the ____ day of ____ BETWEEN AB of ____ (hereinafter called "the Vendor") of the first part CD of ____ (hereinafter called "the Mortgagee") of the second part and EF of ____ (hereinafter called "the Purchaser") of the third part

WHEREAS:—

(1) The Vendor is the estate owner in fee simple of the property hereby conveyed subject to [*if appropriate* the subsisting rights easements and covenants hereinafter mentioned and to] a Mortgage [*or* Legal Charge] dated the ____ and made between the Vendor of the one part and the Mortgagee of the other part[2] and the principal sum interest and other moneys thereby secured and subject also to but with the benefit of the Lease [*continue as recital (1) of Precedent No. 9 or 10*]

(2)

[*As recitals (2) and (3) of Precedent No. 9 or 10*]

(3)

(4) It has been agreed that [*if the whole purchase price is being paid to the Mortgagee*[3] the whole of the said sum of £____ shall be paid to the Mortgagee] [*if part of the purchase price is being paid to the Mortgagee*[4] the sum of £____ being part of the said sum of £____ shall be paid to the Mortgagee] and that the Mortgagee shall join in this deed for the purpose and in manner hereinafter appearing

[*or if no part of the purchase price is being paid to the Mortgagee*

(4) The Mortgagee being satisfied that the other property comprised in the said Mortgage [*or* Legal Charge] is a sufficient security for all moneys

thereby secured has agreed to join in this deed for the purpose and in manner hereinafter appearing]

NOW THIS DEED WITNESSETH as follows:—

1. In pursuance of the said agreement and in consideration of the sum of £____ paid by the Purchaser [*if the whole purchase price is being paid to the Mortgagee* at the request of the Vendor to the Mortgagee in reduction[5] of the moneys secured by the said Mortgage [*or* Legal Charge] (the payment and receipt whereof in manner aforesaid the Vendor and the Mortgagee hereby respectively acknowledge) [*if part of the purchase price is being paid to the Mortgagee* as to £____ part thereof at the request of the Vendor to the Mortgagee in reduction[5] of the moneys secured by the said Mortgage [*or* Legal Charge] (the receipt whereof the Mortgagee hereby acknowledges) and as to £____ the balance thereof with the consent of the Mortgagee to the Vendor (the payment and receipt of which respective sums of £____ and £____ making together the said purchase price of £____ the Vendor hereby acknowledges)] [*if no part of the purchase price is being paid to the Mortgagee* with the consent of the Mortgagee to the Vendor (the receipt whereof the Vendor hereby acknowledges)] and to give effect to section 8 of the Leasehold Reform Act 1967 the Vendor as trustee[6] HEREBY CONVEYS and the Mortgagee as mortgagee HEREBY SURRENDERS AND RELEASES unto the Purchaser ALL THAT [*parcels*[7]] TO HOLD the same UNTO the Purchaser in fee simple [*continue to end of Clause 1 of Precedent No. 9 or 10*] freed and discharged from the said Mortgage [*or* Legal Charge] and the principal sum interest and other moneys thereby secured [*if the Mortgage is by demise add* and to the intent that the term of years granted by the said Mortgage shall so far as the same affects the property hereby conveyed merge and be extinguished in the fee simple thereof]

[*Continue as Clauses 2–4 of Precedent No. 9 or Clauses 2–6 of Precedent No. 10 as appropriate*]

[7.] The Mortgagee HEREBY ACKNOWLEDGES the right of the Purchaser to the production of the documents specified in the [Eighth *or as appropriate*] Schedule hereto (possession of which is retained by the Mortgagee) and to delivery of copies thereof And the Vendor HEREBY COVENANTS with the Purchaser that as and when any of the said documents shall come into the possession of the Vendor or his successors in title he or they will at the request and cost of the Purchaser or his successors in title execute a statutory acknowledgment for the production of the same and for delivery of copies thereof[8]

[*Continue as Clause 5 of Precedent No. 9 or Clause 7 of Precedent No. 10 to end, as appropriate*]

THE [EIGHTH *or as appropriate*] SCHEDULE

Particulars of documents retained by the Mortgagee

[*Here insert particulars of documents affecting the property conveyed which are retained by the Mortgagee*]

SIGNED SEALED AND DELIVERED, *etc.*

Notes

[1] It is recommended that any conveyance of a landlord's interest which is subject to a subsisting mortgage should be in one of the alternative forms of this Precedent. If the mortgagee refuses to join in the conveyance, or otherwise to give a proper discharge on being tendered the purchase price payable under the Act, the tenant should threaten to pay the purchase price into court under s.13. See para. 13–06.

[2] If either the vendor or the mortgagee is not an original party, this part of the recital will need appropriate amendment, and it may be desirable to describe the mortgage (or legal charge) by reference to a Schedule.

[3] The property conveyed will then be automatically discharged from the mortgage: see s.12(1), (2) and para. 13–04.

[4] This alternative will usually only be appropriate where the purchase price exceeds the amount secured by the mortgage.

[5] Or "in full discharge."

[6] See note 10 to Precedent No. 10.

[7] See notes 11, 12 and 13 to Precedent No. 10.

[8] This is the usual form appropriate for cases where the deeds remain in the possession of the mortgagee. In most cases, there will be no documents retained by the vendor and if so Clause 4 and the Second Schedule to Precedent No. 9/Clause 6 and the Seventh Schedule to Precedent No. 10 will be omitted.

17

20–17 **CONVEYANCE by freeholder absolutely entitled subject to a mortgage or legal charge in favour of leaseholder absolutely entitled, where freeholder's mortgagee is not joined.[1] VARIATION where purchase price is paid into court[2]**

THIS CONVEYANCE is made the ____ day of ____ BETWEEN AB of ____ (hereinafter called "the Vendor") of the one part and CD of ____ (hereinafter called "the Purchaser") of the other part

WHEREAS:—

(1) [*As recital (1) of Precedent No. 16, but in place of* the Mortgagee *substitute* ____ [*name of mortgagee*] (hereinafter called "the Mortgagee")]

(2)

[*As recitals (2) and (3) of Precedent No. 9 or 10*]

(3)

(4) The Purchaser has paid the said sum of £____ directly to the

Mortgagee [*or if appropriate* into the ____ County Court[2] to the credit of an action the short title and reference to which is ____]

(5) This Deed is made pursuant to Part I of the Leasehold Reform Act 1967[3]

NOW THIS DEED WITNESSETH as follows:—

1. In pursuance of the said agreement and in consideration of the sum of £____ paid by the Purchaser to the Mortgagee [*or if appropriate* into court] as aforesaid (the payment whereof in manner aforesaid the Vendor hereby acknowledges[4]) and to give effect to section 8 of the said Act the Vendor [*continue as in Clause 1 of Precedent No. 9 or 10*]

2. It is HEREBY DECLARED by the Vendor and the Purchaser that the property hereby conveyed is now freed and discharged from the said Mortgage [*or* Legal Charge] and the principal sum interest and other moneys thereby secured under and by virtue of the provisions of section 12 [*or if there is a payment into court* section 13] of the said Act[5]

[*Continue as Clauses 2–3 of Precedent No. 9 or Clauses 2–5 of Precedent No. 10, as appropriate*]

[5.] The Vendor HEREBY COVENANTS with the Purchaser that as and when any of the documents specified in the [Eighth *or as appropriate*] Schedule hereto (possession of which is retained by the Mortgagee) shall come into the possession of the Vendor or his successors in title he or they will at the request and cost of the Purchaser or his successors in title execute a statutory acknowledgment for the production of the same and for delivery of copies thereof[6]

[*Continue as Clause 5 of Precedent No. 9 or Clause 7 of Precedent No. 10 to end, as appropriate*]

THE [EIGHTH *or as appropriate*] SCHEDULE

Particulars of documents retained by the Mortgagee

[*Here insert particulars of documents affecting the property conveyed which are retained by the Mortgagee*]

SIGNED SEALED AND DELIVERED, *etc.*

Notes

[1] This Precedent should only be used in exceptional cases when the mortgagee refuses to join in the conveyance, or give a proper discharge. See generally paras. 13–06 and 13–09.

[2] *i.e.* under s.13: see paras. 13–09 *et seq.*

[3] It is thought advisable to refer specifically to the Act, so that the somewhat unusual provisions of s.12(1) or s.13 are brought into operation.

[4] The vendor will require sufficient proof before giving this acknowledgment.

[5] See s.10(1) and para. 13–09.

[6] See note 8 to Precedent No. 16.

18

20–18 **CONVEYANCE by freeholder absolutely entitled in favour of leaseholder absolutely entitled subject to a legal charge.[1] Where leaseholder's mortgagee is joined and there is a merger of interests (to be used in conjunction with Precedent No. 19).[2] VARIATION where mortgagee makes further advance towards the purchase price of the freehold[3]**

THIS CONVEYANCE is made the ____ day of ____ BETWEEN AB of ____ (hereinafter called "the Vendor") of the first part CD of ____ (hereinafter called "the Purchaser") of the second part and EF of ____ (hereinafter called "the Mortgagee") of the third part

WHEREAS:—

(1)

[*As recitals (1) and (2) of Precedent No. 9 or 10*]

(2)

(3) [*As recital (3) of Precedent No. 9 or 10 and continue*] Subject to a Legal Charge dated the ____ and made between the Purchaser of the one part and the Mortgagee of the other part and the principal sum interest and other moneys thereby secured

(4) The Mortgagee has agreed to execute this deed [*if appropriate* and to lend to the Purchaser the further sum of £____ towards the purchase by the Purchaser of the property hereby conveyed] in consideration of the execution by the Purchaser of a Deed of Substituted Security[4] [*if appropriate* and Further Advance] of even date herewith and made between the Purchaser of the one part and the Mortgagee of the other part

NOW THIS DEED WITNESSETH as follows:—

[*Here set out Clauses 1–2 of Precedent No. 9 or Clauses 1–4 of Precedent No. 10, as appropriate*]

5. The Purchaser and the Mortgagee HEREBY DECLARE [*continue as Clause 3 of Precedent No. 9/Clause 5 of Precedent No. 10*]

[*Continue from Clause 4 of Precedent No. 9/Clause 6 of Precedent No. 10 to end, as appropriate*]

Notes

[1] In most cases, it is likely to be more convenient for the legal charge to be discharged immediately prior to the conveyance to the purchaser, and for a fresh legal charge to be entered into immediately thereafter. That course avoids the complications of this Precedent and Precedent No. 19.

[2] The Precedent must be used in conjunction with Precedent No. 19. The purpose of the

mortgagee being joined as a party is to enable an effective declaration of merger to be made: see para. 6–31.

[3] This occurs fairly frequently, the mortgagee advancing a further sum to cover the purchase price and other costs of acquiring the freehold. A further charge is then necessary to cover the additional advance: see the variation to Precedent No. 19.

[4] See Precedent No. 19.

19

DEED OF SUBSTITUTED SECURITY whereby the freehold is substituted for the leasehold as the security under a legal charge (to be used in conjunction with Precedent No. 18).[1] VARIATION where mortgagee makes further advance[2] **20–19**

THIS DEED OF SUBSTITUTED SECURITY [*if a further advance is made* AND FURTHER CHARGE] is made the ____ day of ____ BETWEEN CD of ____ (hereinafter called "the Borrower") of the one part and EF of ____ (hereinafter called "the Mortgagee") of the other part

WHEREAS:—

(1) This Deed is made supplemental to the following:—

(A) A Legal Charge (hereinafter called "the Original Charge") dated the ____ day of ____ and made between the same parties as are parties hereto for securing the principal sum of £____ together with interest and other moneys on the term of years therein mentioned

(B) A Conveyance (hereinafter called "the Conveyance") of even date herewith and made between AB [*name of freeholder*] of the first part the Borrower of the second part and the Mortgagee of the third part

(2) By the Conveyance the freehold reversion expectant on the said term of years was conveyed to the Borrower and it was thereby declared by the Borrower and the Mortgagee that the said term should merge and be extinguished in the fee simple of the property thereby conveyed

(3) In consideration of the execution of the Conveyance by the Mortgagee the Borrower has agreed that the property therein comprised should be substituted for the said term of years as security for the principal sum together with the interest and other moneys (if any) now due and owing under the Original Charge[3]

[(4) *If a further advance is made* The Mortgagee has also agreed to lend to the Borrower the further sum of £____ upon having the repayment thereof together with interest thereon secured in manner hereinafter appearing]

NOW THIS DEED made in pursuance of the said agreement [*if a further advance is made* and in consideration of the further sum of £____ now paid by the Mortgagee to the Borrower (the receipt whereof the Borrower hereby acknowledges)] WITNESSETH as follows:—

1. The Borrower as beneficial owner HEREBY CHARGES BY WAY OF LEGAL MORTGAGE All That the freehold property comprised in and conveyed by the conveyance with the payment to the Mortgagee of the principal sum[4] together with the interest and other moneys (if any) now due and owing under the Original Charge subject to the like right of redemption and with the like power of sale and other provisions for securing and obtaining payment of the same and with the benefit of the like covenants on the part of the Borrower and subject to the like provisions in all respects as are contained or implied in or conferred by the Original Charge to the intent that the property hereby charged may become in all respects substituted for the said term of years as the security thereby granted.

[2. *If a further advance is made* The Borrower HEREBY COVENANTS with the Mortgagee to pay to the Mortgagee on the ____ day of ____ next[5] the said sum of £____ with interest thereon at the rate of £____ per cent. per annum AND ALSO if the said sum shall not be so paid to pay to the Mortgagee interest thereon or on the principal sum for the time being hereby secured at the rate aforesaid by equal quarterly[6] payments on the usual quarter days[7] in every year

3. The Borrower as beneficial owner HEREBY FURTHER CHARGES BY WAY OF LEGAL MORTGAGE All That the freehold property comprised in and conveyed by the Conveyance with the payment to the Mortgagee of the further principal sum and interest hereinbefore covenanted to be paid and all other moneys hereby secured as well as the principal sum interest and other moneys secured by the Original Charge

4. The covenants powers and provisions contained in the Original Charge [*if appropriate* including the provisions for variation in the rate of interest] shall operate and take effect in like manner for protecting and enforcing this security as if such covenants powers and provisions were repeated in this deed]

IN WITNESS, *etc.*

SIGNED SEALED AND DELIVERED, *etc.*

Notes

[1] It is envisaged that the mortgagee has been a party to a conveyance of the freehold containing a declaration of merger, as in Precedent No. 18. The merger will extinguish the leasehold, and so the freehold must be substituted as the security.

[2] *e.g.* towards the purchase price of the freehold and expenses.

[3] If desired, the amount of principal sum and interest outstanding can be recited.

[4] If the amount of the principal sum outstanding has been recited, the figure should be inserted.

[5] *i.e.* the next date for payment of interest under the Original Charge.

[6] Or "monthly" or "half-yearly," as in the Original Charge.

[7] Or as in the Original Charge.

20

CONVEYANCE AND ASSIGNMENT by freeholder and intermediate tenant both absolutely entitled in favour of leaseholder absolutely entitled[1] 20–20

THIS CONVEYANCE AND ASSIGNMENT is made the ____ day of ____ BETWEEN AB of ____ (hereinafter called "the First Vendor") of the first part CD of ____ (hereinafter called "the Second Vendor") of the second part and EF of ____ (hereinafter called "the Purchaser") of the third part

WHEREAS:—

(1) The First Vendor is the estate owner in fee simple of the property hereby conveyed subject to [*if appropriate* the subsisting rights easements and covenants hereinafter mentioned and subject also to] but with the benefit of the Lease short particulars whereof are set out in Part I of the First Schedule hereto (hereinafter called "the Head Lease") [*if appropriate* so far as the same affects the property hereby conveyed] but otherwise free from incumbrances

(2) The First Vendor has agreed [*continue as in recital (2) of Precedent No. 9 or 10*]

(3) The term of years granted by the Head Lease [*if appropriate*[2] so far as the same affects the property hereby conveyed] is now vested in the Second Vendor [*if appropriate*[3] at the apportioned yearly rent of £____] subject to but with the benefit of the Lease short particulars whereof are set out in Part II of the First Schedule hereto (hereinafter called "the Underlease")[4] but otherwise free from incumbrances

(4) The Second Vendor has agreed with the Purchaser for the sale to the Purchaser for the sum of £____ of the property hereby conveyed for the residue of the said term of years granted by the Head Lease subject as aforesaid

(5) The term of years granted by the Underlease is now vested in the Purchaser[5]

NOW THIS DEED WITNESSETH as follows:—

1. [*As Clause 1 of Precedent No. 9 or 10 as appropriate, but in place of* the Vendor *substituting* the First Vendor *and in place of* the Scheduled Lease *substituting* the Head Lease]

2. In pursuance of the said agreement and in consideration of the sum of £____ paid by the Purchaser to the Second Vendor (the receipt whereof the Second Vendor hereby acknowledges) and to give effect to section 8 of the Leasehold Reform Act 1967 the Second Vendor as trustee[6] HEREBY ASSIGNS unto the Purchaser ALL THAT the property hereinbefore conveyed

TO HOLD the same UNTO the Purchaser for all the residue of the said term of years granted by the Head Lease and subject to the rent thereby reserved[7] [*or if there has already been an apportionment*[8] the said apportioned rent] [*or if an apportionment is necessary*[9] the yearly rent of £____ (being an apportioned part of the rent thereby reserved)] and to the covenants and conditions therein contained [*if appropriate* so far as the same relate to the property hereinbefore conveyed] subject to but with the benefit of the Underlease

[*Continue as in Clauses 2 and 3 of Precedent No. 10, adapted as appropriate*]

5. It is HEREBY DECLARED that the same covenants for title (but no further covenants for title) shall be implied herein as if the First Vendor and the Second Vendor were respectively conveying and expressed to convey as trustee

6. The Purchaser HEREBY DECLARES that the respective terms of years granted by the Head Lease and by the Underlease [*if appropriate* (so far as the same affected the property hereby conveyed)] shall forthwith merge and be extinguished in the fee simple of the property hereby conveyed

[*Continue as Clauses 4 and 5 and testimonium of Precedent No. 9/Clauses 6 and 7 and testimonium of Precedent No. 10, as appropriate*]

THE FIRST SCHEDULE

Part I
Particulars of the Head Lease

[*Complete as appropriate*]

Part II
Particulars of the Underlease

[*Complete as appropriate*]

[*Continue to end of Precedent No. 9 or 10, adapted as appropriate*]

Notes

[1] As to this Precedent, see Sched. 1, para. 7 and para. 11–15. It is provided that "the reversioner" (as to which see Sched. 1, paras. 2 and 3, and paras. 11–05 and 11–06) "may on behalf and in the name of the other landlords execute" the conveyance: see Sched. 1, para. 4(1)(*a*) and para. 11–08. But this should only be done in cases of difficulty.

[2] *i.e.* if the second vendor is no longer the leaseholder of all the property comprised in the head lease.

[3] *i.e.* if there has already been an apportionment of the rent as regards the property conveyed alone.

[4] If there are further sub-tenancies, they can be defined as "the First Underlease," "the Second Underlease" and so on.
[5] It is assumed in this Precedent that the underlease comprises only the property conveyed.
[6] See note 10 to Precedent No. 10.
[7] If the Head Lease comprises only the property conveyed.
[8] See note 2, *ante.*
[9] An informal apportionment of the rent will result in covenants between the second vendor and the purchaser being implied by s.77(1)(D) of the Law of Property Act 1925.

21

EXTENDED LEASE granted before the term date of existing lease.[1] Full form, with variation where freeholder will continue to provide services, repair, maintenance or insurance 20–21

[*Heading for registered land, if appropriate*[2]]

THIS LEASE is made the ____ day of ____ BETWEEN AB of ____ (hereinafter called "the Landlord" which expression shall where the context so admits include the person for the time being entitled to the reversion immediately expectant on the term hereby granted) of the one part and CD of ____ (hereinafter called "the Tenant" which expression shall where the context so admits include his successors in title to the said term) of the other part

WHEREAS:—

(1) The premises hereby demised are now vested in the Tenant for the residue of the term of years granted by the Lease short particulars whereof are set out in the First Schedule hereto (hereinafter called "the Scheduled Lease") at [*if appropriate* an apportioned part of] the rent thereby reserved and subject to the covenants and conditions therein contained

(2) The Tenant in exercise of the rights conferred on him by Part I of the Leasehold Reform Act 1967 as amended (hereinafter called "the Act") has required the Landlord to grant to him a lease of the premises hereby demised for an extended term under the Act in substitution[3] for the term of years aforesaid and the Landlord has agreed so to do in manner and upon the terms hereinafter appearing

NOW THIS DEED WITNESSETH as follows:—

1. In pursuance of the said agreement and in consideration of the rents hereinafter reserved and the covenants on the part of the Tenant and conditions hereinafter contained the Landlord pursuant to section 14 of the Act HEREBY DEMISES unto the Tenant ALL THAT [*parcels*[4]] (hereinafter called "the demised premises") TO HOLD the same UNTO the Tenant for the term of years ____ from the ____ day of ____ [5] (but subject to earlier

determination as hereinafter mentioned) Subject to all rights and easements or reputed and easements belonging to or enjoyed with any adjacent or neighbouring property[6] YIELDING AND PAYING therefor until the ____ day of ____ [*the original term date*] the yearly rent of ____ [*i.e. the rent or apportioned rent, as the case may be, payable in respect of the house and premises under the Scheduled Lease*] and thereafter the rent specified in the Second Schedule hereto without any deduction by equal half-yearly payments in advance on the ____ day of ____ and the ____ day of ____ in each year [*or as provided in the Scheduled Lease*][7] [AND YIELDING AND PAYING ALSO until the ____ day of ____ [8] by way of further or additional rent. *Here include any reservation of rent in respect of services repairs maintenance or insurance contained in the Scheduled Lease* and thereafter] [*or if there is no such reservation but the Landlord will remain liable for services etc.* AND YIELDING AND PAYING ALSO from the ____ day of ____ [8] by way of further or additional rent] [a sum equal to a one ____ th part of the actual cost to the Landlord from time to time of providing services repairs maintenance and insurance in accordance with the covenants on the part of the Landlord hereinafter contained such sum to be certified in writing by the accountant for the time being of the Landlord whose certificate shall be final and binding upon the Landlord and the Tenant such further or additional rent to be payable on the half-yearly date for payment of rent next occurring after the date of such certificate *or as appropriate*[9]]

2. The Tenant hereby covenants with the Landlord as follows:—

(1) To pay the rents hereby reserved at the times and in manner aforesaid

(2) To observe and perform the covenants on the part of the tenant contained in the Scheduled Lease [*if the Scheduled Lease also comprises other property* (so far as the same relate to or affect the demised premises)] as if the same had been herein set out and repeated in full[10] [*Or set out covenants in full. This will be preferable in many cases, particularly where the covenants or the Scheduled Lease include covenants no longer relevant (such as covenants to build), or are outdated or otherwise unsuitable for a modern lease.*[11]]

(3) To pay to the Landlord the reasonable costs to the Landlord of obtaining a valuation for the purposes of ascertaining the rent payable hereunder in accordance with paragraph 3 of the Second Schedule hereto[12]

3. The Landlord hereby covenants with the Tenant to observe and perform the covenants on the part of the Landlord contained in the Scheduled Lease [*if the Scheduled Lease also comprises other property* (so far as the same relate to or affect the demised premises)] as if the same had been herein set out and repeated in full.[13]

Provided That the Landlord shall not be personally liable under any of the said covenants otherwise than in respect of breaches thereof for which he is responsible[14]

[*Or set out covenants in full. Often the only covenant on the part of the landlord will be the covenant for quiet enjoyment. If there are further covenants, a proviso limiting the landlord's responsibility to breaches for which he is responsible should be added.*[15]]

4. PROVIDED ALWAYS and it is HEREBY AGREED as follows:—

(1) [*Proviso for re-entry as in the Scheduled Lease*[16]]

(2) The Landlord may at any time not earlier than twelve months before the ____ day of ____ [*the original term date*] apply to the court under section 17 of the Act for an order that he may resume possession of the demised premises on the ground that for the purposes of redevelopment he proposes to demolish or reconstruct the whole or a substantial part of the demised premises and the provisions of that section and of Schedule 2 to the Act shall apply accordingly[17]

5. It is HEREBY DECLARED by the parties hereto as follows:—

(1) This Lease is granted by way of extension of the Scheduled Lease [*if the Scheduled Lease also comprises other property* (so far as the same affects the property hereby demised)] under Part I of the Act[18]

(2) No long tenancy (as defined by section 4 of the Act) created immediately or derivatively by way of sub-demise under the term hereby granted shall confer on the sub-tenant as against the Landlord any right under Part I of the Act to acquire the freehold or an extended lease[19]

IN WITNESS, *etc.*

THE FIRST SCHEDULE

The Scheduled Lease

A Lease dated the ____ day of ____ made between (1) EF and (2) GH [*parties*] for the term of ____ years from the ____ day of ____ at the yearly rent of £____ [*if appropriate* registered under title no. ____]

THE SECOND SCHEDULE

Ascertainment of Rent

1. (1) The rent payable under this Lease as from the ____ day of ____ [*the original term date under the Scheduled Lease*] shall in accordance with section 15(2) of the Act (subject to review as hereinafter provided) be the ground rent as at that date in the sense that it shall represent the letting value of the site of the demised premises (without including

anything for the value of the buildings on the site) for the present use of the demised premises and all other (if any) the uses to which the same have been put since the commencement of the Scheduled Lease [(other than the user mentioned in clause 2(–) hereof)][20]

(2) The said rent shall be determined not earlier than twelve months prior to the date aforesaid and in default of agreement between the Landlord and the Tenant shall be determined in accordance with section 21(1) of the Act[21]

2. (1) The Landlord shall have the right to require a revision of the rent hereby reserved and payable as from the ____ day of ____ [*the twenty-fifth anniversary of the original term date under the Scheduled Lease*] on giving written notice claiming such revision to the Tenant before that date (but not earlier than twelve months prior thereto)[22]

(2) Upon such written notice being given the said rent payable as from the date aforesaid shall in accordance with section 15(2) of the Act be the ground rent as at that date in the sense aforesaid and in default of agreement between the Landlord and the Tenant shall be determined in accordance with section 21(1) of the Act[23]

3. The reasonable cost to the Landlord of obtaining a valuation for the purposes of ascertaining the rent payable hereunder in accordance with paragraph 1 or 2 of this Schedule shall on each occasion be borne and paid by the Tenant[24]

SIGNED SEALED AND DELIVERED, *etc.*

Notes

[1] This Precedent is the standard form of lease when the tenant exercises his right to a fifty-year extension. As to the form and contents, see ss.14–16 and paras. 7–08 *et seq.* If the term to be granted is for a term different to that set out in s.14(1), *i.e.* otherwise than for a term expiring fifty years after the term date of the existing tenancy, the consent of the court under s.23(4) should be obtained: see para. 7–19.

[2] See s.14(1) and para. 7–14.

[3] It is considered desirable to make express mention of the Act, to ensure that the lease will be in full satisfaction of the tenant's rights thereunder: see s.14(1) and paras. 7–04 and 7–09.

[4] Here set out modern description of the "house and premises"" see s.2 and paras. 2–02 *et seq.* If the Scheduled Lease is registered, this can usually be done by reference to the Title No. If not, but the demised premises are in a compulsory registration area, there should be a plan signed by both parties.

[5] The term of years and commencement date must be carefully chosen so that the term granted will expire fifty years after the "original term date" (*i.e.* in general the date when the existing tenancy is due to expire): see para. 3–12. It will usually be convenient for the commencement date to be last previous date of which the original term date will be an anniversary. The term of years will then be the number of years until the original term date (counting the unexpired part of a year as one) plus fifty.

[6] It is thought that the lease should be made subject to these subsisting rights. A landlord need not acquire any better title than he has or could require to be vested in him: see s.14(7).

[7] It will not usually be necessary to provide for the payment of rent in respect of part of a

half-year or other rental period. All sums due by way of rent under the existing tenancy must be paid before the lease is granted: see s.14(3)(*a*) and para. 7–16.

[8] *i.e.* the original term date.

[9] See s.15(3) and para. 7–12.

[10] See s.15(1) and paras. 7–10 *et seq.* Note that the parties are at liberty to agree other terms, and that either of them may require any term of the existing tenancy to be excluded or modified if it would be unreasonable to include it unchanged in view of the date when the existing tenancy commenced and of changes since that date: see s.15(6).

[11] See note 10, *ante.*

[12] See s.15(2)(*c*) and para. 7–16. A covenant to this effect may not be strictly necessary, but it is considered preferable to include it expressly.

[13] See note 10, *ante.* Any covenant by the landlord to grant a new tenancy or a right of pre-emption should be excluded: see s.15(5).

[14] See s.15(9).

[15] See notes 10, 13 and 14, *ante.*

[16] No further right to determine the lease (except under s.17) can be included: see s.15(5).

[17] This reservation must be included: see s.15(8) and para. 7–13.

[18] This statement is conclusive in favour (but not against) any third parties: see s.16(7) and para. 7–13.

[19] The Act requires this statement to be included: see s.15(8), referring to s.16(4), and para. 7–13.

[20] The wording of this provision follows that of s.15(2)(*a*). See para. 9–03. The final words in square brackets will be deleted unless there has been a user which by the terms of the extended lease is prohibited or permitted only with the landlord's consent.

[21] See s.15(2)(*c*) and para. 9–03.

[22] See s.15(2) and para. 9–03.

[23] See note 21, *ante.*

[24] See note 12, *ante.*

22

EXTENDED LEASE granted after (or within twelve months before) the term date of the existing lease.[1] 20–22

[*Heading for registered land, if appropriate*[2]]

THIS LEASE is made the ____ day of ____ BETWEEN [*continue as parties to Precedent No. 21*]

WHEREAS:—

(1) The premises hereby demised were formerly [*or if the term date of the existing lease has not passed* are now] vested in the Tenant for the term of years granted by the Lease short particulars whereof are set out in the First Schedule hereto (hereinafter called "the Scheduled Lease") at [*if appropriate* an apportioned part of] the rent thereby reserved and subject to the covenants and conditions therein contained

(2) [*As recital (2) of Precedent No. 21*]

NOW THIS DEED WITNESSETH as follows:—

1. [*As Clause 1 of Precedent No. 21*] YIELDING AND PAYING therefor during the term hereby granted the rent of £____ [3] (subject to revision in

accordance with the provisions contained in the Second Schedule hereto) without any deduction [*continue as in Precedent No. 21*]

[*Here insert Clauses 2 to 5 and First Schedule in Precedent No. 21, but deleting from Clause 4(2) the words* "at any time not earlier than twelve months before the ____ day of ____"]

THE SECOND SCHEDULE

Review of Rent

1. [*As paragraph 2(1) of the Second Schedule in Precedent No. 21*]
2. Upon such written notice being given the said rent payable from the date aforesaid shall in accordance with section 15(2) of the Act be the ground rent as at that date in the sense that it shall represent the letting value of the site of the demised premises (without including anything for the value of the buildings on the site) for the present use of the demised premises and all other (if any) the uses to which the same have been put since the commencement of the Scheduled Lease [(other than the user mentioned in clause 2(–) hereof)[4]] And in default of agreement shall be determined in accordance with section 21(1) of the Act
3. The reasonable cost to the Landlord of obtaining a valuation for the purpose of ascertaining the rent payable hereunder in accordance with this Schedule shall be borne and paid by the Tenant[5]

SIGNED SEALED AND DELIVERED, *etc.*

Notes

[1] In these cases, the revised ground rent under s.15(2) will be ascertained before the lease is granted. If the lease is granted after the "original term date" (as to which see para. 3–12), the revised ground rent will be payable only from the grant, but the tenant must also pay to the landlord before the grant the difference between the previous rent and the revised rent for the period from the original term date or the date of the tenant's statutory notice (whichever is the later) up to the date of the lease: see s.15(6) and para. 7–16.

[2] See note 2 to Precedent No. 21.

[3] If the original term date has passed, the lease should grant a 50-year term commencing on that date. In other cases, the wording of Precedent No. 21 should be followed: see note 5 thereto.

[4] *i.e.* the rent revised in accordance with s.15(2): see para. 9–03.

[5] *i.e.* any user not permitted or permitted only with the landlord's consent: see s.15(2)(*a*).

[6] See note 12 to Precedent No. 21.

23

ASSIGNMENT of the benefit of a Notice of Leaseholder's Claim previously given[1] 20–23

[*Insert after the parcels in the assignment or transfer*[2] *of the tenancy*]

TOGETHER WITH the full benefit of a Notice of Leaseholder's Claim dated [*date*] and given by ____ to ____ and the rights and obligations arising thereunder

Notes

[1] The benefit of a Notice of Leaseholder's Claim is assignable with, but not capable of subsisting apart from, the tenancy of the house and premises: see s.5(2) and para. 5–09. Although a contemporaneous separate assignment would almost certainly suffice, it is preferable to include an assignment in any assignment or transfer of the tenancy.

[2] As the original transfer will be retained in the Registry, it is suggested that the transfer be executed in duplicate.

24

ORDER OF COURT under s.27, where landlord cannot be found or his identity cannot be determined[1] 20–24

IN THE HIGH COURT OF JUSTICE 19__B. No__
CHANCERY DIVISION
MASTER
IN THE MATTER of [*address of property*]
and
IN THE MATTER of the LEASEHOLD REFORM ACT 1967

THE APPLICATION of A.B. by Originating Summons dated ______ 19__ coming on to be heard this day
AND UPON HEARING [Counsel] [*or* Solicitors] for the Applicant
AND UPON READING an Affidavit of A.B. filed the ______ 19__ and two Affidavits of C.D. filed the ______ 19__ and the ______ 19__ and the exhibits therein respectively referred to
AND THIS COURT being of opinion that the tenant of the property at [*address of property*] has a right under Part I of the Leasehold Reform Act 1967 to acquire the freehold thereof is prevented from giving notice of his desire to have the freehold because [the person to be served with the notice cannot be found] [*or* the identity of the person to be served with the notice cannot be ascertained]

AND with a view to the said property being vested in the Applicant for an estate in fee simple absolute in possession THIS COURT DOTH ORDER a proper [conveyance] [*or* transfer] of the said property in favour of the Applicant and giving effect so far as possible to the requirements of section 10 of the above Act be settled by the Master AND IT IS ORDERED that E.F. one of the Masters of the Supreme Court be designated pursuant to section 47 of the Supreme Court of Judicature (Consolidation) Act 1925 to execute the said [conveyance] [*or* transfer] AND THIS COURT DOTH DETERMINE AND DECLARE pursuant to the provisions of section 27(5) of the above Act that the amount of the rent payable for the said property by the Applicant as tenant which remains unpaid and will remain up to the ________ 19__ is the sum of £____[2] AND THIS COURT DOTH ORDER that the Applicant be at liberty on or before the said ________ 19__ to lodge in Court as directed in the Lodgement Schedule hereto the sum of £____ being as to £____ the amount certified as provided by section 27(5) of the above Act to be the price payable for the said property[3] and as to the balance of £____ the said amount of rent remaining unpaid as aforesaid AND IT IS ORDERED that the said sum of £____ being lodged in Court as aforesaid the said Master do execute the [conveyance] [*or* transfer] settled as aforesaid and deliver the same to the Applicant

AND the parties are to be at liberty to apply

LODGEMENT SCHEDULE

In the High Court of Justice
Chancery Division

Ledger Credit: Re [*address of property*] Re Leasehold Reform Act 1967
19__B No__

Particulars of Funds to be lodged to the account of The Accountant General	Person to make the lodgement	Amount Money	Amount Securities
CASH Invest in Capital Fund	The Applicant A.B.	£____	Nil

Notes

[1] This Precedent is adapted from the order made in *Re Frost's Application* [1970] 1 W.L.R. 1145. The Master can make the Order: para. 3(W) Practice Direction (Chancery: Masters' Powers) [1976] 1 W.L.R. 637. See para. 17–23.

[2] The amount of rent will be limited under Limitation Act 1980, s.19 to six years arrears: see *Re Howell's Application* [1972] Ch. 509 and para. 17–21.

[3] The purchase price is certified by a surveyor selected by the President of the Lands Tribunal: see s.27(5) and para. 17–20.

25

LANDLORD'S NOTICE under Conditions 1 and 2 requiring the tenant to give a deposit, to deduce title and to furnish a Statutory Declaration as to occupation[1] 20–25

Leasehold Reform Act 1967

Re [*address of house and premises*]

To AB of [*address*]
And to his Solicitors Messrs. XY & Co. of [*address*]

1. TAKE NOTICE that pursuant to Condition 1 in Part I of the Schedule to the Leasehold Reform (Enfranchisement and Extension) Regulations 1967, CD the landlord of the property described in your Notice of Leaseholder's Claim to acquire the freehold dated [____] HEREBY REQUIRES YOU to deposit with his Solicitors Messrs. PQ of [____] the sum of £[____] (being three times the annual rent payable under your tenancy) [*or* £25] to be held by them as his agent[2] on account of the purchase price payable for the property and any other sums payable by you in accordance with the provisions of the said Act.

2. AND TAKE NOTICE that pursuant to Condition 2 in Part I of the said Schedule the said CD HEREBY REQUIRES YOU to deduce your title to the tenancy and to furnish a Statutory Declaration as to the particulars of occupation of the property on which you rely in your Notice.[3]

Dated (Signed) ....

Messrs. PQ of [*address*]
Solicitors for CD

Notes

[1] See paras. 6–03 and 6–04. Separate notices can be served, but it is usual and convenient to serve a combined notice in this form.

[2] Or stakeholder, if preferred.

[3] For a precedent of an appropriate Statutory Declaration, see Precedent No. 26, *post*.

26

STATUTORY DECLARATION by tenant as to occupancy of the house and premises[1] 20–26

WE AB and CD his wife both of [____] do hereby jointly and severally solemnly and sincerely declare as follows:—

1. We are the leasehold owners of the property known as [*address of house and premises*] ("the Property"), which is held by us for the residue

of the term of [____] years from [____] granted by a Lease dated the [____] and made between (1) [*original landlord*] and (2) [*original tenant*]. Our purchase of the Property was completed on the [____] and we moved in approximately two weeks later.

[2. Since then we have resided continuously at the Property as our only residence, and were so residing at the date of service on Notice of Leaseholder's Claim dated the [____]. At no time during that period has either of us had any other residence.]

[2. Since that date we have resided continuously at the Property as our main residence, and were so residing at the date of service of our Notice of Leaseholder's Claim dated the [____].

3. From [____] until the present, I CD have also owned a small country cottage known as [*address*], the main accommodation of which is a lounge/dining-room and kitchen on the ground floor and three bedrooms and a bathroom on the first floor. We spend on average approximately one weekend into two there, and I CD and our children sometimes spend part of the school holidays there. However otherwise we reside at the Property, which at all material times has been and remains our main residence.[2]]

AND we jointly and severally make this solemn declaration believing the same to be true, and by virtue of the provisions of the Statutory Declaration Act 1835.

Notes

[1] Under Condition 2 in Part I (enfranchisement) and Condition 1 in Part II (extended lease) of the Schedule to the Leasehold Reform (Enfranchisement and Extension) Regs. 1967, the landlord may by notice require the tenant to furnish a Statutory Declaration as to the particulars of occupation of the property on which the tenant relies in his Notice of Leaseholder's Claim. See paras. 6–04 and 7–06.

[2] Full particulars of the other residence and of the applicant's occupation of it should be given, in order for the landlord to be able to check the accuracy of the claim made by the tenant as to his "main" residence. An unsupported statement that the property is the applicant's "main" residence is plainly insufficient.

27

20–27 **TENANT'S NOTICE under Conditions 3(1) and 5(2) requiring the landlord to deduce title and to state what rights and covenants he requires**

Leasehold Reform Act 1967
Re [*address of house and premises*]

To A.B of ______
And his Solicitors Messrs XY & Co of ______

1. TAKE NOTICE that pursuant to Condition 3(1) in Part I of the

Schedule to the Leasehold Reform (Enfranchisement and Extension) Regulations 1967, CD the tenant of the house and premises described in his Notice of Leaseholder's Claim to acquire the freehold dated ______ HEREBY REQUIRES YOU to deduce your title to the said house and premises in accordance with the provisions of that Condition [*if the landlord's title is registered*] by delivering an authority to inspect the register at H.M. Land Registry together with all particulars and information which may be required pursuant to section 110 of the Land Registration Act 1925 to be furnished on a sale of registered land [*or if the landlord's interest is unregistered* by delivering an Abstract of Title thereto.]

2. AND TAKE NOTICE that pursuant to Condition 5(2) in Part I of the said Schedule that the said CD HEREBY REQUIRES YOU within 4 weeks of the date of service hereof to state what rights of way over the house and premises and provisions concerning restrictive covenants you require to be included in the conveyance or transfer in accordance with the provisions of the said Act.

3. AND TAKE NOTICE that the said AB does not require any rights of way or provisions concerning restrictive covenants to be included in the said conveyance or transfer [save for a right of way in the following terms:

> "Together with the full and free right and liberty for the Purchaser and all persons authorised by him (in common with all others entitled to the like right) at all times and for all purposes with or without vehicles to pass and repass over and along the roadway shown coloured brown on the plan annexed hereto."]

28

LANDLORD'S NOTICE under Condition 10 specifying tenant's default and requiring him to make it good[1] 20–28

Leasehold Reform Act 1967
Re [*address of house and premises*]

To AB of ______
And his Solicitors, Messrs XY & Co of ______

1. TAKE NOTICE that you have neglected and failed to [pay a deposit] [deduce your title to the tenancy] [furnish a Statutory Declaration as to the particulars of occupation of the above property on which you rely in your Notice of Leaseholder's Claim to acquire the freehold dated ____][2] pursuant to a notice dated ____ served on you by or on behalf of your landlord CD.[3]

2. WE HEREBY GIVE YOU NOTICE pursuant to Condition 10(1) in

Part I of the Schedule to the Leasehold Reform (Enfranchisement and Extension) Regulations 1967 to make good such default before the expiration of two months after the date of service of this Notice upon you.[4]

3. AND TAKE NOTICE that if you fail to comply with this Notice, the said CD will either [forfeit your deposit and] treat the contract created by the service of your Notice of Leaseholder's Claim as discharged pursuant to Condition 10(2) or exercise such other or further remedies as he may be advised.

Dated Signed..

Messrs. PQ of [*address*]
Solicitors for CD

Notes

[1] See para. 6–10.
[2] Or as appropriate.
[3] *i.e.* a notice under Condition 1 and/or 2: see Precedent 25, *supra.*
[4] It is essential to refer expressly to Condition 10.

APPENDIX B

STATUTES

Leasehold Reform Act 1967

(1967 c. 88)

ARRANGEMENT OF SECTIONS

PART I

ENFRANCHISEMENT AND EXTENSION OF LONG LEASEHOLDS

An Act to enable tenants of houses held on long leases at low rents to acquire the freehold or an extended lease; to apply the Rent Acts to premises held on long leases at a rackrent, and to bring the operation of the Landlord and Tenant Act 1954 into conformity with the Rent Acts as so amended; to make other changes in the law in relation to premises held on long leases, including amendments of the Places of Worship (Enfranchisement) Act 1920; and for purposes connected therewith.

[27th October 1967]

PART I

ENFRANCHISEMENT AND EXTENSION OF LONG LEASEHOLDS

Right to enfranchisement or extension

Tenants entitled to enfranchisement or extension

1.—(1) This Part of this Act shall have effect to confer on a tenant of a leasehold house, occupying the house as his residence, a right to acquire on fair terms the freehold or an extended lease of the house and premises where— **21–01**

(*a*) his tenancy is a long tenancy at a low rent and [subject to subsections (5) and (6) below] the rateable value of the house and premises on the appropriate day is not (or was not) more than £200 or, if it is in Greater London, than £400; and

(*b*) at the relevant time (that is to say, at the time when he gives notice in accordance with this Act of his desire to have the freehold or to have an extended lease, as the case may be) he has been tenant of the house under a long tenancy at a low rent, and occupying it as his residence, for the last [three years] or for periods amounting to [three years] in that last ten years;

and to confer the like right in the other cases for which provision is made in this Part of this Act.

[1A) The references in subsection (1)(*a*) and (*b*) to a long tenancy at a low rent do not include a tenancy excluded from the operation of this Part by section 33A and Schedule 4A to this Act.]

(2) In this Part of this Act references, in relation to any tenancy, to the

tenant occupying a house as his residence shall be construed as applying where, but only where, the tenant, is, in right of the tenancy, occupying it as his only or main residence (whether or not he uses it also for other purposes); but—

(*a*) references to a person occupying a house shall apply where he occupies it in part only; and

(*b*) in determining in what right the tenant occupies, there shall be disregarded any mortgage term and any interest arising in favour of any person by his attorning tenant to a mortgagee or chargee.

(3) This Part of this Act shall not confer on the tenant of a house any right by reference to his occupation of it as his residence (but shall apply as if he were not so occupying it) at any time when—

(*a*) it is let to and occupied by him with other land or premises to which it is ancillary; or

(*b*) it is comprised in an agricultural holding within the meaning of the Agricultural Holdings Act 1948.

(4) In subsection (1)(*a*) above, "the appropriate day", in relation to any house and premises, means the 23rd March 1965 or such later day as by virtue of [section 25(3) of the Rent Act 1977] would be the appropriate day for purposes of that Act in relation to a dwelling-house consisting of that house.

[(4A) Schedule 8 to the Housing Act 1974 shall have effect to enable a tenant to have the rateable value of the house and premises reduced for purposes of this section in consequence of tenant's improvements.]

[(5) If, in relation to any house and premises, the appropriate day for the purposes of subsection 1(*a*) above fall on or after 1st April 1973 that subsection shall have effect in relation to the house and premises,—

(*a*) in a case where the tenancy was was created on or before 18th February 1966, as if for the sums of £200 and £400 specified in that subsection there were substituted respectively the sums of £750 and £1,500; and

(*b*) in a case where the tenancy was created after 18th February 1966, as if for those sums of £200 and £400 there were substituted respectively the sums of £500 and £1,000.

(6) If, in relation to any house and premises,—

(*a*) the appropriate day for the purposes of subsection (1)(*a*) above falls before 1st April 1973, and

(*b*) the rateable value of the house and premises on the appropriate day was more than £200 or, if it was then in Greater London, £400, and

(*c*) the tenancy was created on or before 18th February 1966,

subsection (1)(*a*) above shall have effect in relation to the house and premises as if for the reference to the appropriate day there were substituted a reference to 1st April 1973 and as if for the sums of £200 and £400 specified in that subsection there were substituted respectively the sums of £750 and £1,500.]

AMENDMENTS

The first set of words in square brackets in subs. (1) and those in subss. (5) and (6) were inserted by the Housing Act 1974, s.118(1) and (3). The words in square brackets in subs. (4) were substituted by the Rent Act 1977, Sched. 23, para. 42. The second set of words in square brackets in subss. (1) and (4A) were substituted by the Housing Act 1980, s.141 and Sched. 21. Subs. (1A) was inserted by the Housing and Planning Act 1986, Sched. 4, para. 3 (but had not been brought into effect at the date on which this book states the law). **21–02**

Meaning of "house" and "house and premises," and adjustment of boundary

2.—(1) For purposes of this Part this Act, "house" includes any building designed or adapted for living in and reasonably so called, notwithstanding that the building is not structurally detached, or was or is not solely designed or adapted for living in, or is divided horizontally into flats or maisonettes: and— **21–03**

(*a*) where a building is divided horizontally, the flats or other units into which it is so divided are not separate "houses," though the building as a whole may be; and

(*b*) where a building is divided vertically the building as a whole is not a "house" though any of the units into which it is divided may be.

(2) References in this Part of this Act to a house do not apply to a house which is not structurally detached and of which a material part lies above or below part of the structure not comprised in the house.

(3) Subject to the following provisions of this section, where in relation to a house let to and occupied by a tenant reference is made in this Part of this Act to the house and premises, the reference to premises is to be taken as referring to any garage, outhouse, garden, yard and appurtenances which at the relevant time are let to him with the house and are occupied with and used for the purposes of the house or any part of it by him or by another occupant.

(4) In relation to the exercise by a tenant of any right conferred by this Part of this Act there shall be treated as included in the house and premises any other premises let with the house and premises but not at the relevant time occupied and used as mentioned in subsection (3) above (whether in consequence of an assignment of the term therein or a subletting or otherwise), if—

(*a*) the landlord at the relevant time has an interest in the other premises and, not later than two months after the relevant, time, gives to the tenant written notice objecting to the further severance of them from the house and premises; and

(*b*) either the tenant agrees to their inclusion with the house and premises or the court is satisfied that it would be unreasonable to require the landlord to retain them without the house and premises.

(5) In relation to the excise by a tenant of any right conferred by this Part of this Act there shall be treated as not included in the house and premises any part of them which lies above or below other premises (not consisting only of underlying mines or minerals), if—

(*a*) the landlord at the relevant time has an interest in the other premises and, not later than two months after the relevant time, gives to the tenant written notice objecting to the further severance from them of that part of the house and premises; and

(*b*) either the tenant agrees to the exclusion of that part of the house and premises or the court is satisfied that any hardship or inconvenience likely to result to the tenant from the exclusion, when account is taken of anything that can be done to mitigate its effects and of any undertaking of the landlord to take steps to mitigate them, is outweighed by the difficulties involved in the further severance from the other premises and any hardship or inconvenience likely to result from that severance to persons interested in those premises.

(6) The rights conferred on a tenant by this Part of this Act in relation to any house and premises shall not extend to underlying minerals comprised in the tenancy if the landlord requires that the minerals be excepted, and if proper provision is made for the support of the house and premises as they have been enjoyed during the tenancy and in accordance with its terms.

(7) Where by virtue of subsection (4) above a tenant of a house acquiring the freehold or an extended lease is required to include premises of which the tenancy is not vested in him, this Part of this Act shall apply for the purpose as if in the case of those premises a tenancy on identical terms were vested in him and the holder of the actual tenancy were a sub-tenant; and where by virtue of subsection (5) or (6) above the tenant of a house acquiring the freehold or an extended lease is required to exclude property of which the tenancy is vested in him, then unless the landlord and the tenant otherwise agree or the court for the protection of either of them from hardship or inconvenience otherwise orders, the grant to the tenant shall operate as a surrender of the tenancy in that property and the provision to be made by the grant shall be determined as if the surrender had taken place before the relevant time.

Meaning of "long tenancy"

21–04 **3.**—(1) In this Part of this Act "long tenancy" means, subject to the provisions of this section, a tenancy granted for a term of certain years exceeding twenty-one years, whether or not the tenancy is (or may become) terminable before the end of that term by notice given by or to the tenant or by re-entry, forfeiture or otherwise, and includes a tenancy for a term fixed by law under a grant with a covenant or obligation for perpetual renewal unless it is a tenancy by sub-demise from one which is not a long tenancy:

Provided that a tenancy granted so as to become terminable by notice after a death or marriage is not to be treated as a long tenancy [if either—

(*a*) it was granted before 18th April 1980 or in pursuance of a contract entered into before that date: or

(*b*) the notice is capable of being given at any time after the death or marriage of the tenant, the length of the notice is not more than three months and the terms of the tenancy preclude both its assignment [otherwise than by virtue of section [92] of the Housing Act [1985] (assignments by way of exchange)] and the subletting of the whole of the premises comprised in it.]

(2) Where the tenant of any property under a long tenancy at a low rent [(other than a lease excluded from the operative of this Part by section 33A and Schedule 4A to this Act)], on the coming to an end of that tenancy, becomes or has become tenant of the property or part of it under another tenancy (whether by express grant or by implication of law), then the later tenancy shall be deemed for the purposes of this Part of this Act, including any further application of this subsection, to be a long tenancy irrespective of its terms.

(3) Where the tenant of any property under a long tenancy, on the coming to an end of that tenancy, becomes or has become tenant of the property or part of it under another long tenancy, then in relation to the property or that part of it this Part of this Act shall apply as if there had been a single tenancy granted for a term beginning at the same time as the term under the earlier tenancy and expiring at the same time as the term under the later tenancy.

(4) Where a tenancy is or has been granted for a term of years certain not exceeding twenty-one years, but with a covenant or obligation for renewal; without payment of a premium (but not for perpetual renewal), and the tenancy is or has been once or more renewed so as to bring to more than twenty-one years the total of the terms granted (including any interval between the end of a tenancy and the grant of a renewal), then this Part of the Act shall apply as it would apply if the term originally granted had been one exceeding twenty-one years.

(5) References in this Part of this Act to a long tenancy include any period during which the tenancy is or was continued under Part I or II of the Landlord and Tenant Act 1954 or under the Leasehold Property (Temporary Provisions) Act 1951.

(6) Where at any time there are separate tenancies, with the same landlord

and the same tenant, of two or more parts of a house, or of a house or part of it and land or other premises occupied therewith, then in relation to the property comprised in such of those tenancies as are long tenancies this Part of this Act shall apply as it would if at that time there were a single tenancy of that property and the tenancy were a long tenancy, and for that purpose references in this Part of this Act to the commencement of the term or to the term date shall, if the separate tenancies commenced at different dates or have different term dates, have effect as references to the commencement or term date, as the case may be, of the tenancy comprising the house (or the earliest commencement or earliest term date of the tenancies comprising it):

Provided that this subsection shall have effect subject to the operation of subsections (2) to (5) above in relation to any of the separate tenancies.

21–05 AMENDMENTS

The words within the outer square brackets in subs. (1) were added by the Housing Act 1980, Sched. 21, and the words within them in square brackets by the Housing and Building Control Act 1984, Sched. 11, para. 3. They were further amended by the Housing (Consequential Provisions) Act 1985, Sched. 2, para. 13. The words in square brackets in subs. (2) were added by the Housing and Planning Act 1986, Sched. 4, para. 4.

Meaning of "low rent"

21–06 **4.**—(1) For purposes of this Part of this Act a tenancy of any property is a tenancy at a low rent at any time when rent is not payable under the tenancy in respect of the property at a yearly rate equal to or more than two-thirds of the rateable value of the property on the appropriate day or, if later, the first day of the term:

Provided that a tenancy granted between the end of August 1939 and the beginning of April 1963 otherwise than by way of building lease (whether or not it is, by virtue of section 3(3) above, to be treated for other purposes as forming a single tenancy with a previous tenancy) shall not be regarded as a tenancy at a low rent if at the commencement of the tenancy the rent payable under the tenancy exceeded two-thirds of the letting value of the property (on the same terms).

For the purposes of this subsection—

(*a*) "appropriate day" means the 23rd March 1965 or such later day as by virtue of [section 25(3) of the Rent Act 1977] would be the appropriate day for purposes of that Act in relation to a dwelling-house consisting of the house in question; and

(*b*) "rent" means rent reserved as such, and there shall be disregarded any part of the rent expressed to be payable in consideration of services to be provided, or of repairs, maintenance or insurance to be effected by the landlord, or to be payable in respect of the cost thereof to the landlord or a superior landlord; and

(*c*) there shall be disregarded any term of the tenancy providing for suspension or reduction of rent in the event of damage to property demised, or for any penal addition to the rent in the event of a contravention of or non-compliance with the terms of the tenancy or an agreement collateral thereto; and

(*d*) "building lease" means a lease granted in pursuance or in consideration of an agreement for the erection or the substantial re-building or reconstruction of the whole or part of the house in question or a building comprising it.

(2) Where on a claim by the tenant of a house to exercise any right conferred by this Part of this Act a question arises under section 1(1) above whether his tenancy of the house is or was at any time a tenancy at a low rent, the question shall be determined by reference to the rent and rateable value of the house and premises as a whole, and in relation to a time before the relevant time shall be so determined whether or not the property then occupied with the house or any part of it was the same in all respects as that comprised in the house and premises for the purposes of the claim; but, in a case where the tenancy derives (in accordance with section 3(6) above) from more than one separate tenancy, the proviso to subsection (1) above shall have effect if, but only if, it applies to one of the separate tenancies which comprises the house or part of it.

(3) Where on a claim by the tenant of a house to exercise any right conferred by this Part of this Act a question arises under section 3(2) above whether a tenancy is or was a long tenancy by reason of a previous tenancy having been a long tenancy at a low rent, the question whether the previous tenancy was one at a low rent shall be determined in accordance with subsection (2) above as if it were a question arising under section 1(1), and shall be so determined by reference to the rent and rateable value of the house and premises or the part included in the previous tenancy, exclusive of any other land or premises so included:

Provided that where an apportionment of rent or rateable value is required because the previous tenancy did not include the whole of the house and premises or included other property, the apportionment shall be made as at the end of the previous tenancy except in so far as, in the case of rent, an apportionment falls to be made at an earlier date under subsection (6) below.

(4) For purposes of subsection (2) or (3) above a house and premises shall be taken as not including any premises which are to be or may be included under section 2(4) above in giving effect to the tenant's claim, and as including any part which is to be or may be excluded under section 2(5) or (6).

(5) Where on a claim by the tenant of a house to exercise any right

conferred by this Part of this Act a question arises whether a tenancy granted as mentioned in the proviso to subsection (1) above is or was at any time a tenancy at a low rent, it shall be presumed until the contrary is shown that the letting value referred to in that proviso was such that the proviso does not apply.

(6) Any entire rent payable at any time in respect of both a house and premises or part thereof and of property not included in the house and premises shall for purposes of this section be apportioned as may be just according to the circumstances existing at the date of the severance giving rise to the apportionment, and references in this section to the rent of a house and premises or of part thereof shall be construed accordingly.

AMENDMENT

21–07 The words in square brackets in subs. (1)(*a*) were substituted by the Rent Act 1977, Sched. 23, para. 42.

General provisions as to claims to enfranchisement or extension

21–08 **5.**—(1) Where under this Part of this Act a tenant of a house has the right to acquire the freehold or an extended lease and gives notice of his desire to have it, the rights and obligations of the landlord and the tenant arising from the notice shall insure for the benefit of and be enforceable against them, their executors, administrators and assigns to the like extent (but no further) as rights and obligations arising under a contract for a sale or lease freely entered into between the landlord and tenant; and accordingly, in relation to matters arising out of any such notice, references in this Part of this Act to the tenant and the landlord shall, in so far as the context permits, include their respective executors, administrators and assigns.

(2) Notwithstanding anything in subsection (1) above, the rights and obligations there referred to of a tenant shall be assignable with, but not capable of subsisting apart from, the tenancy of the entire house and premises; and if the tenancy is assigned without the benefit of the notice, or if the tenancy of one part of the house and premises is assigned to or vests in any person without the tenancy of another part, the notice shall accordingly cease to have effect, and the tenant shall be liable to make such compensation as may be just to the landlord in respect of the interference (if any) by the notice with the exercise by the landlord of his power to dispose of or deal with the house and premises or any neighbouring property.

(3) In the event of any default by the landlord or the tenant in carrying out the obligations arising from any such notice, the other of them shall have the like rights and remedies as in the case of a contract freely entered into.

(4) The provisions of Schedule 1 to this Act shall have effect in relation to the operation of this Part of this Act where a person gives notice of his desire to have the freehold or an extended lease of a house and premises, and either he does so in respect of a sub-tenancy or there is a tenancy reversionary on his tenancy; but any such notice given in respect of a tenancy granted by sub-demise out of a superior tenancy other than a long tenancy at a low rent shall be of no effect if the grant was made in breach of the terms of the superior tenancy and there has been no waiver of the breach by the superior landlord.

(5) No lease shall be registrable under the Land Charges Act 1925 or be deemed to be an estate contract within the meaning of that Act by reason of the rights conferred on the tenant by this Part of this Act to acquire the freehold or an extended lease of property thereby demised, nor shall any right of a tenant arising from a notice under this Act of his desire to have the freehold or to have an extended lease be an overriding interest within the meaning of the Land Registration Act 1925; but any such notice shall be registrable under the Land Charges Act 1925 or may be the subject of a notice or caution under the Land Registration Act 1925, as if it were an estate contract.

(6) A notice of a person's desire to have the freehold or an extended lease of a house and premises under this Part of this Act—

(*a*) shall be of no effect if at the relevant time any person or body of persons who has or have been, or could be, authorised to acquire the whole or part of the house and premises compulsorily for any purpose has or have, with a view to its acquisition for that purpose, served notice to treat on the landlord or on the tenant, or entered into a contract for the purchase of the interest of either of them, and the notice to treat or contract remains in force; and

(*b*) shall lease to have effect if before the completion of the conveyance in pursuance of the tenant's notice any such person or body of persons serves notice to treat as aforesaid;

but where a tenant's notice ceases to have effect by reason of a notice to treat served on him or on the landlord, then on the occasion of the compulsory acquisition in question the compensation payable in respect of any interest in the house and premises (whether or not the one to which that notice to treat relates) shall be determined on the basis of the value of the interest subject to and with the benefit of the rights and obligations arising from the tenant's notice and affecting that interest.

(7) Where any such notice given by a tenant entitled to acquire the freehold or an extended lease has effect, then (without prejudice to the general law as to the frustration of contracts) the landlord and all other persons shall be discharged from the further performance, so far as relates to the disposal in any manner of the landlord's interest in the house and premises or any part thereof, of any contract previously entered into and

not providing for the eventuality of such a notice (including any such contract made in pursuance of the order of any court):

Provided that, in the case of a notice of the tenant's desire to have an extended lease, this subsection shall not apply to discharge a person from performance of a contract unless the contract was entered into on the basis, common to both parties, that vacant possession of the house and premises or part thereof would or might be obtainable on the termination of the existing tenancy.

(8) A tenant's notice of his desire to have an extended lease under this Part of this Act shall cease to have effect if afterwards (being entitled to do so) he gives notice of his desire to have the freehold.

Rights of trustees

21–09 **6.**—(1) Where a tenant of a house is occupying it as his residence, his occupation of it at any earlier time shall for purposes of this Part of this Act be treated as having been an occupation in right of the tenancy if at that time—

(*a*) the tenancy was settled land for purposes of the Settled Land Act 1925, and he was sole tenant for life within the meaning of that Act; or

(*b*) the tenancy was vested in trustees and he, as a person beneficially interested (whether directly or derivatively) under the trusts, was entitled or permitted to occupy the house by reason of that interest.

References in this section to trustees include persons holding on the statutory trusts arising by virtue of sections 34 to 36 of the Law of Property Act 1925 in cases of joint ownership or ownership in common.

(2) Where a tenancy of a house is settled land for purposes of the Settled Land Act 1925, a sole tenant for life within the meaning of that Act shall have the same rights under this Part of this Act in respect of his occupation of the house as if the tenancy of it belonged to him absolutely, but without prejudice to his position under the settlement as a trustee for all parties entitled under the settlement; and—

(*a*) the powers under that Act of a tenant for life shall include power to accept an extended lease under this Part of this Act; and

(*b*) an extended lease granted under this Part of this Act to a tenant for life or statutory owner shall be treated as a subsidiary vesting deed in accordance with section 53(2) of that Act.

(3) Where a tenancy of a house is vested in trustees (other than a sole tenant for life within the meaning of the Settled Land Act 1925), and a person beneficially interested (whether directly or derivatively) under the trusts is entitled or permitted by reason of his interest to occupy the house, then the trustees shall have the like rights under this Part of this

Act in respect of his occupation as he would have if he were the tenant occupying in right of the tenancy.

(4) Without prejudice to any powers exercisable under the Settled Land Act 1925 by tenants for life or statutory owners within the meaning of that Act, where a tenancy of a house is vested in trustees, then unless the instrument regulating the trusts (being made after the passing of this Act) contains an explicit direction to the contrary, the powers of the trustees under that instrument shall include power, with the like consent or on the like direction (if any) as may be required for the exercise of their powers (or ordinary powers) of investment, to acquire and retain the freehold or an extended lease under this Part of this Act.

(5) The purposes authorised for the application of capital money by section 73 of the Settled Land Act 1925, or by that section as applied by section 28 of the Law of Property Act 1925 in relation to trusts for sale, and the purposes authorised by section 71 of the Settled Land Act 1925 or by that section as applied as aforesaid as purposes for which moneys may be raised by mortgage, shall include the payment of any expenses incurred by a tenant for life or statutory owners or by trustees for sale, as the case may be, in or in connection with proceedings taken by him or them by virtue of subsection (2) or (3) above.

Rights of members of family succeeding to tenancy on death

7.—(1) Where the tenant of a house dies while occupying it as his residence, and on his death a member of his family resident in the house becomes tenant of it under the same tenancy, then for the purposes of any claim by that member of the family to acquire the freehold or an extended lease under this Part of this Act he shall be treated as having been the tenant, and occupying the house as his residence, during any period when— **21–10**

(*a*) he was resident in the house, and it was his only or main place of residence; and

(*b*) the deceased person was, as the tenant under that tenancy, occupying the house as his residence (or would for the purposes of a claim made by him at the time of his death have been treated as having been so occupying it).

(2) For purposes of this section—

(*a*) a member of a tenant's family on whom the tenancy devolves on the tenant's death by virtue of a testamentary disposition or the law of intestate succession shall, on the tenancy vesting in him, be treated as having become tenant on the death; and

(*b*) a member of a tenant's family who, on the tenant's death, acquires the tenancy by the appropriation of it in or towards satisfaction of any legacy, share in residue, debt or other share in or claim against the tenant's estate, or by the purchase of it on a sale made by the tenant's personal representatives in the administration of the estate, shall be treated as a person on whom the tenancy devolved by direct bequest; and

(*c*) a person's interest in a tenancy as personal representative of a deceased tenant shall be disregarded, but references in paragraphs (*a*) and (*b*) above to a tenancy vesting in, or being acquired by, a member of a tenant's family shall apply also where, after the death of a member of the family, the tenancy vests in or is acquired by the personal representatives of that member.

(3) Where a tenancy of a house is settled land for purposes of the Settled Land Act 1925, and on the death of a tenant for life within the meaning of that Act a member of his family resident with him becomes entitled to the tenancy in accordance with the settlement or by any appropriation by or purchase from the personal representatives in respect of the settled land, this section shall apply as if the tenancy had belonged to the tenant for life absolutely and the trusts of the settlement taking effect after his death had been trusts of his will.

(4) Where in a case not falling within subsection (3) above a tenancy of a house is held on trust and—

(*a*) a person beneficially interested (whether directly or derivatively) under the trust is entitled or permitted by reason of his interest to occupy the house; and

(*b*) on his death a member of his family resident with him becomes tenant of the house in accordance with the terms of the trust or by any appropriation by or purchase from the trustees;

then this section shall apply as if the deceased person while so occupying the house had been tenant of it occupying in right of the tenancy, and as if after his death the trustees had held and dealt with the tenancy as his executors (the remaining trusts being trusts of his will).

(5) Subsections (3) and (4) above shall apply, with any necessary adaptations, where a person becomes entitled to a tenancy on the termination of a settlement or trust as they would apply if he had become entitled in accordance with the settlement or trust.

(6) The reference in section 6(3) above to the rights which a beneficiary under a trust would have if he were the tenant occupying in right of the tenancy includes any rights which he would have by virtue of this section.

(7) For purposes of this section a person is a member of another's family if that person is—

(*a*) the other's wife or husband; or

(*b*) a son or daughter or a son-in-law or daughter-in-law of the other, or of the other's wife or husband; or (*c*) the father or mother of the other, or of the other's wife or husband.

In paragraph (*b*) above any reference to a person's son or daughter includes a reference to any stepson or stepdaughter, any illegitimate son or daughter, *and any adopted son or daughter* of that person, and "son-in-law" and "daughter-in-law" shall be construed accordingly.

(8) In Schedule 2 to the Intestates' Estate Act 1952 (which gives a surviving spouse a right to require the deceased's interest in the matrimonial home to be appropriated to the survivor's interest in the deceased's estate, but by paragraph 1(2) excludes tenancies terminating, or terminable by the landlord, within two years of the death), paragraph 1(2) shall not apply to a tenancy if—

(*a*) the surviving wife or husband would in consequence of an appropriation in accordance with that paragraph become entitled by virtue of this section to acquire the freehold or an extended lease under this Part of this Act, either immediately on the appropriation or before the tenancy can determine or be determined as mentioned in paragraph 1(2); or

(*b*) the deceased's husband or wife, being entitled to acquire the freehold or an extended lease under this Part of this Act, had given notice of his or her desire to have it and the benefit of that notice is appropriated with the tenancy.

(9) This section shall have effect in relation to deaths occurring before this Act was passed as it has effect in relation to deaths occurring after.

AMENDMENT

The words in italics in subs. (7) were repealed by the Children Act 1975, Sched. 4. **21–11**

Enfranchisement

Obligation to enfranchise

8.—(1) Where a tenant of a house has under this Part of this Act a right to acquire the freehold, and gives to the landlord written notice of his desire to have the freehold, then except as provided by this Part of this Act the landlord shall be bound to make to the tenant, and the tenant to accept, (at the price and on the conditions so provided) a grant of the house and premises for an estate in fee simple absolute, subject to the tenancy and to tenant's incumbrances, but otherwise free of incumbrances. **21–12**

(2) For purposes of this Part of this Act "incumbrances" includes rentcharges and, subject to subsection (3) below, personal liabilities attaching in respect of the ownership of land or an interest in land though not charged on that land or interest; and "tenant's incumbrances" includes any interest directly or indirectly derived out of the tenancy, and

any incumbrance on the tenancy or any such interest (whether or not the same matter is an incumbrance also on any interest reversionary on the tenancy).

(3) Burdens originating in tenure, and burdens in respect of the upkeep or regulation for the benefit of any locality of any land, building, structure, works, ways or watercourse shall not be treated as incumbrances for purposes of this Part of this Act, but any conveyance executed to give effect to this section shall be made subject thereto except as otherwise provided by section 11 below.

(4) A conveyance executed to give effect to this section—

(*a*) shall have effect under section 2(1) of the Law of Property Act 1925 to overreach any incumbrance capable of being overreached under that section as if, where the interest conveyed is settled land, the conveyance were made under the powers of the Settled Land Act 1925 and as if the requirements of section 2(1) as to payment of the capital money allowed any part of the purchase price paid or applied in accordance with sections 11 to 13 below to be so paid or applied;

(*b*) shall not be made subject to any incumbrance capable of being overreached by the conveyance, but shall be made subject (where they are not capable of being overreached) to rentcharges [redeemable under sections 8 to 10 of the Rentcharges Act 1977 and those falling within paragraphs (*c*) and (*d*) of section 2(3) of that Act (estate rentcharges and rentcharges imposed upon certain enactments)] except as otherwise provided by section 11 below.

(5) Notwithstanding, that on a grant to a tenant of a house and premises under this section no payment or a nominal payment only is required from the tenant for the price of the house and premises, the tenant shall nevertheless be deemed for all purposes to be a purchaser for a valuable consideration in money or money's worth.

AMENDMENT

21–13 The words in square brackets in subs. (4) were substituted by the Rentcharges Act 1977, Sched. 2, para. 4.

Purchase price and costs of enfranchisement, and tenant's right to withdraw

21–14 **9.**—(1) Subject to subsection (2) below, the price payable for a house and premises on a conveyance under section 8 above shall be the amount which at the relevant time the house and premises, if sold in the open market by a willing seller [(with the tenant and members of the family who reside in the house not buying or seeking to buy)] might be expected to realise on the following assumptions:—

(*a*) on the assumption that the vendor was selling for an estate in fee simple, subject to the tenancy but on the assumption that this Part of this Act conferred no right to acquire the freehold, and if the tenancy has not been extended under this Part of this Act, on the assumption that (subject to the landlord's rights under section 17 below) it was to be so extended;

(*b*) on the assumption that (subject to paragraph (*a*) above) the vendor was selling subject, in respect of rentcharges *and other rents* to which section 11(2) below applies, to the same annual charge as the conveyance to the tenant is to be subject to, but the purchaser would otherwise be effectively exonerated until the termination of the tenancy from any liability or charge in respect of tenant's incumbrances; and

(*c*) on the assumption that (subject to paragraphs (*a*) and (*b*) above) the vendor was selling with and subject to the rights and burdens with and subject to which the conveyance to the tenant is to be made, and in particular with an subject to such permanent or extended rights and burdens as are to be created in order to give effect to section 10 below.

[The references in this subsection to members of the tenant's family shall be construed in accordance with section 7(7) of this Act].

[(1A) Notwithstanding, the foregoing subsection, the price payable for a house and premises, the rateable value of which is above £1,000 in Greater London and £500 elsewhere, on a conveyance under section 8 above, shall be the amount which at the relevant time the house and premises, if sold in the open market by a willing seller, might be expected to realise on the following assumptions:—

(*a*) on the assumption that the vendor was selling for an estate in fee simple, subject to the tenancy, but on the assumption that this Part of this Act conferred no right to acquire the freehold [or an extended lease and, where the tenancy has been extended under this Part of this Act, that the tenancy will terminate on the original term date];

(*b*) on the assumption that at the end of the tenancy the tenant has the right to remain in possession of the house and premises under the provisions of the Landlord and Tenant Act 1954:

(*c*) on the assumption that the tenant has no liability to carry out any repairs, maintenance or redecorations under the terms of the tenancy or Part I of the Landlord and Tenant Act 1954;

(*d*) on the assumption that the price be diminished by the extent to which the value of the house and premises has been increased by any improvement carried out by the tenant or his predecessors in title at their own expense;

(*e*) on the assumption that (subject to paragraph (*a*) above) the vendor was selling subject, in respect of rent charges *and other rents* to which section 11(2) below applies, to the same annual charge as the conveyance to the tenant is to be subject to, but the purchaser would otherwise be effectively exonerated until the termination of the tenancy from any liability or charge in respect of tenant's incumbrances; and

(*f*) on the assumption that (subject to paragraphs (*a*) and (*b*) above) the vendor was selling with and subject to the rights and burdens with and subject to which the conveyance to the tenant is to be made, and in particular with and subject to such permanent or extended rights and burdens as are to be created in order to give effect to section 10 below.

(1B) For the purpose of determining whether the rateable value of the house and premises is above £1,000 in Greater London, or £500 elsewhere, the rateable value shall be adjusted to take into account any tenants' improvements in accordance with Schedule 8 to the Housing Act 1974.]

(2) The price payable for the house and premises shall be subject to such deduction (if any) in respect of any defect in the title to be conveyed to the tenant as on a sale in the open market might be expected to be allowed between a willing seller and a willing buyer.

(3) On ascertaining the amount payable, or likely to be payable, as the price for a house and premises in accordance with this section (but not more than one month after the amount payable has been determined by agreement or otherwise), the tenant may give written notice to the landlord that he is unable or unwilling to acquire the house and premises at the price he must pay; and thereupon—

(*a*) the notice under section 8 above of his desire to have the freehold shall cease to have effect, and he shall be liable to make such compensation as may be just to the landlord in respect of the interference (if any) by the notice with the exercise by the landlord of his power to dispose of or deal with the house and premises or any neighbouring property; and

(*b*) any further notice given under that section with respect to the house or any part of it (with or without other property) shall be void if given within the following [three years].

(4) Where a person gives notice of his desire to have the freehold of a house and premises under this Part of this Act, then unless the notice lapses under any provision of this Act excluding his liability, there shall be borne by him (so far as they are incurred in pursuance of the notice) the reasonable costs of or incidental to any of the following matters:—

(*a*) any investigation by the landlord of that person's right to acquire the freehold;
(*b*) any conveyance or assurance of the house and premises or any part thereof or of any outstanding estate or interest therein;
(*c*) deducing, evidencing and verifying the title to the house and premises or any estate or interest therein;
(*d*) making out and furnishing such abstracts and copies as the person giving the notice may require;
(*e*) any valuation of the house and premises;

but so that this subsection shall not apply to any costs if on a sale made voluntarily a stipulation that they were to be borne by the purchaser would be void.

(5) The landlord's lien (as vendor) on the house and premises for the price payable shall extend—

(*a*) to any sums payable by way of rent or recoverable as rent in respect of the house and premises up to the date of the conveyance; and
(*b*) to any sums for which the tenant is liable under subsection (4) above; and
(*c*) to any other sums due and payable by him to the landlord under or in respect of the tenancy or any agreement collateral thereto.

AMENDMENTS

The words in square brackets in subs. (1) were inserted by the Housing Act 1969, s.82. The words in italics in subss. (1) and (1A) were repealed by the Rentcharge Act 1977, Sched. 2. Subss. (1A) and (1B) were added by the Housing Act 1974, s.118. The words in square brackets in subs. (3) were substituted by the Housing Act 1980, s.141 and Sched. 21. The words in square brackets in subs. (1A), para. (*a*), were added by the Housing and Planning Act 1986, s.23. **21–15**

Rights to be conveyed to tenant on enfranchisement

10.—(1) Except for the purpose of preserving or recognising any existing interest of the landlord in tenant's incumbrances or any existing right or interest of any other person, a conveyance executed to give effect to section 8 above shall not be framed so as to exclude or restrict the general words implied in conveyances under section 62 of the Law of Property Act 1925, or the all-estate clause implied under section 63, unless the tenant consents to the exclusion or restriction; but the landlord shall not be bound to convey to the tenant any better title than that which he has or could require to be vested in him, nor to enter into any covenant for title other than such covenant as under section 76(1) (F) of the Law of Property Act 1925 is implied in the case of a person conveying and expressed to convey as trustee or mortgagee. **21–16**

(2) As regards rights of any of the following descriptions, that is to say,—

(*a*) rights of support for any building or part of a building;

(*b*) rights to the access of light and air to any building or part of a building;

(*c*) rights to the passage of water or of gas or other piped fuel, or to the drainage or disposal of water, sewage, smoke or fumes or to the use or maintenance of pipes or other installations for such passage, drainage or disposal;

(*d*) rights to the use or maintenance of cables or other installations for the supply of electricity, for the telephone or for the receipt directly or by landline of visual or other wireless transmissions;

a conveyance executed to give effect to section 8 above shall by virtue of this subsection (but without prejudice to any larger operation it may have apart from this subsection) have effect—

(i) to grant with the house and premises all such easements and rights over other property, so far as the landlord is capable of granting them, as are necessary to secure to the tenant as nearly as may be the same rights as at the relevant time were available to him under or by virtue of the tenancy or any agreement collateral thereto, or under or by virtue of any grant, reservation or agreement made on the severance of the house and premises or any part thereof from other property then comprised in the same tenancy; and

(ii) to make the house and premises subject to all such easements and rights for the benefit of other property as are capable of existing in law and are necessary to secure to the person interested in the other property as nearly as may be the same rights as at the relevant time were available against the tenant under or by virtue of the tenancy or any agreement collateral thereto, or under or by virtue of any grant, reservation or agreement made as is mentioned in paragraph (i) above.

(3) As regards rights of way, a conveyance executed to give effect to section 8 above shall include—

(*a*) such provisions (if any) as the tenant may require for the purpose of securing to him rights of way over property not conveyed, so far as the landlord is capable of granting them, being rights of way which are necessary for the reasonable enjoyment of the house and premises as they have been enjoyed during the tenancy and in accordance with its provisions; and

(*b*) such provisions (if any) as the landlord may require for the purpose of making the property conveyed subject to rights of way necessary for the reasonable enjoyment of other property, being property in which at the relevant time the landlord has an interest, or to rights of way granted or agreed to be granted before the relevant time by the landlord or by the person then entitled to the reversion on the tenancy.

(4) As regards restrictive covenants (that is to say, any covenant or agreement restrictive of the user of any land or premises), a conveyance executed to give effect to section 8 above shall include—

(*a*) such provisions (if any) as the landlord may require to secure that the tenant is bound by, or to indemnify the landlord against breaches of, restrictive covenants which affect the house and premises otherwise than by virtue of the tenancy or any agreement collateral thereto and are enforceable for the benefit of other property; and

(*b*) such provisions (if any) as the landlord or the tenant may require to secure the continuance (with suitable adaptations) of restrictions arising by virtue of the tenancy or any agreement collateral thereto, being either—

(i) restrictions affecting the house and premises which are capable of benefiting other property and (if enforceable only by the landlord) are such as materially to enhance the value of the other property; or

(ii) restrictions affecting other property which are such as materially to enhance the value of the house and premises;

(*c*) such further provisions (if any) as the landlord may require to restrict the use of the house and premises in any way which will not interfere with the reasonable enjoyment of the house and premises as they have been enjoyed during the tenancy but will materially enhance the value of other property in which the landlord has an interest.

(5) Neither the landlord nor the tenant shall be entitled under subsection (3) or (4) above to require the inclusion in a conveyance of any provision which is unreasonable in all the circumstances, in view—

(*a*) of the date at which the tenancy commenced, and changes since that date which affect the suitability at the relevant time of the provisions of the tenancy; and

(*b*) where the tenancy is or was one of a number of tenancies of neighbouring houses, of the interests of those affected in respect of other houses.

(6) The landlord may be required to give to the tenant an acknowledgment within the meaning of section 64 of the Law of Property Act 1925 as regards any documents of which the landlord retains possession, but not an undertaking for the safe custody of any such documents; and where the landlord is required to enter into any covenant under subsection (4) above, the person entering into the covenant as landlord shall be entitled to limit his personal liability to breaches of the covenant for which he is responsible.

Exoneration from, or redemption of, rentcharges etc.

21–17 **11.**—(1) Where a house and premises are to be conveyed to a tenant in pursuance of section 8 above, section 8(4)(*b*) shall not preclude the landlord from releasing, or procuring the release of, the house and premises from any rentcharge *or other rent falling within section* 191 *of the Law of Property Act* 1925; and the conveyance may, with the tenant's agreement (which shall not be unreasonably withheld), provide in accordance with section 190(1) of the Law of Property Act 1925 that a rentcharge shall be charged exclusively on other land affected by it in exoneration of the house and premises, or be apportioned between other land affected by it and the house and premises.

(2) Where, but for this subsection, a conveyance of a house and premises to a tenant might in accordance with section 8 above be made subject, in respect of rents to which this subsection applies, to an annual charge exceeding the annual rent payable under the tenancy at the relevant time, then the landlord shall be bound on or before the execution of the conveyance to secure that the house and premises are discharged from the whole or part of any rents in question to the extent necessary to secure that the annual charge shall not exceed the annual rent so payable; and for this purpose the annual rent shall be calculated in accordance with section 4(1)(*b*) and (*c*) and (6) above.

(3) For purposes of subsection (2) above the house and premises shall be treated as discharged from a rent to the extent to which—

(*a*) the rent is charged on or apportioned to other land so as to confer on the tenant in respect of the house and premises the remedies against the other land provided for by section 190(2) of the Law of Property Act 1925; or

(*b*) the landlord is otherwise entitled to be exonerated from or indemnified against liability for the rent in respect of the house and premises and the tenant will (in so far as the landlord's right is not a right against the tenant himself or his land) become entitled on the conveyance to the like exoneration or indemnity.

(4) Where for the purpose of complying with subsection (2) above the house and premises are to be discharged from a rent by redemption of it (with or without prior apportionment), and for any reason mentioned in section [13(2) below] difficulty arises in paying the redemption price, the tenant may, and if so required by the landlord shall, before execution of the conveyance pay into court on account of the price for the house and premises an amount not exceeding the appropriate amount to secure redemption of the rent; and if the amount so paid by the tenant is less than that appropriate amount, the landlord shall pay into court the balance.

(5) Where payment is made into court in accordance with subsection

(4) above, the house and premises shall on execution of the conveyance be discharged from the rent, and any claim to the redemption money shall lie against the fund in court and not otherwise.

(6) For purposes of subsection (4) above "the appropriate amount to secure redemption" of a rent is (subject to subsection (7) below) the amount of redemption money agreed to be paid or in default of agreement, the amount [specified as the redemption price in instructions for redemption under section 9(4) of the Rentcharges Act 1977.]

(7) Where a rent affects other property as well as the house and premises, and the other property is not exonerated or indemnified by means of a charge on the house and premises, then—

(*a*) "the appropriate amount to secure redemption" of the rent for purposes of subsection (4) above shall, if no amount has been agreed or [specified] as mentioned in subsection (6), be such sum as, on an application under section [4 of the Rentcharges Act 1977] for the apportionment of the rent, may, pending the apportionment, be approved by the apportioning authority as suitable provision (with a reasonable margin) for the redemption money of the part likely to be apportioned to the house and premises; and

(*b*) the apportionment, when made, shall be deemed to have had effect from the date of the payment into court, and if in respect of any property affected by the rent there has been any overpayment or underpayment, the amount shall be made good by abatement of or addition to the next payment after the apportionment and (if necessary) later payments.

(8) Subsection (2) above applies to rentcharges and [redeemable under sections 8 to 10 of the Rentcharges Act 1977] which during the continuance of the tenancy are, or but for the termination of the tenancy before their commencement would have been, recoverable from the landlord without his having a right to be indemnified by the tenant.

AMENDMENTS

The words in italics in subs. (1) were repealed, and those in square brackets in subss. (4) (6) (7) and (8) substituted by Rentcharges Act 1977, Sched. 1 and 2. **21–18**

Discharge of mortgages etc. on landlord's estate

12.—(1) Subject to the provisions of this section, a conveyance executed to give effect to section 8 above shall, as regards any charge on the landlord's estate (however created or arising) to secure the payment of money or the performance of any other obligation by the landlord or any other person, not being a charge subject to which the conveyance is required to be made or which would be overreached apart from this **21–19**

section, be effective by virtue of this section to discharge the house and premises from the charge, and from the operation of any order made by a court for the enforcement of the charge, and to extinguish any term of years created for the purposes of the charge, and shall do so without the persons entitled to or interested in the charge or in any such order or term of years becoming parties to or executing the conveyance.

(2) Where in accordance with subsection (1) above the conveyance to a tenant will be effective to discharge the house and premises from a charge to secure the payment of money, then except as otherwise provided by this section it shall be the duty of the tenant to apply the price payable for the house and premises, in the first instance, in or towards the redemption of any such charge (and, if there are more than one, then according to their priorities); and if any amount payable in accordance with this subsection to the person entitled to the benefit of a charge is not so paid nor paid into court in accordance with section 13 below, then for the amount in question the house and premises shall remain subject to the charge, and to that extent subsection (1) above shall not apply.

(3) For the purpose of determining the amount payable in respect of any charge under subsection (2) above a person entitled to the benefit of a charge to which that subsection applies shall not be permitted to exercise any right to consolidate that charge with a separate charge on other property; and if the landlord or the tenant is himself entitled to the benefit of a charge to which that subsection applies, it shall rank for payment as it would if another person were entitled to it, and the tenant shall be entitled to retain the appropriate amount in respect of any such charge of his.

(4) For the purpose of discharging the house and premises from a charge to which subsection (2) above applies, a person may be required to accept three months or any longer notice of the intention to pay the whole or part of the principal secured by the charge, together with interest to the date of payment, notwithstanding that the terms of the security make other provision or no provision as to the time and manner of payment; but he shall be entitled, if he so requires, to receive such additional payment as is reasonable in the circumstances in respect of the costs of re-investment or other incidental costs and expenses and in respect of any reduction in the rate of interest obtainable on re-investment.

(5) Subsection (2) above shall not apply to any debenture-holders' charge, that is to say, any charge, whether a floating charge or not, in favour of the holders of a series of debentures issued by a company or other body of persons, or in favour of trustees for such debenture holders; and any such charge shall be disregarded in determining priorities for purposes of subsection (2):

Provided that this subsection shall not have effect in relation to a charge in favour of trustees for debenture holders which at the date of the conveyance to the tenant is (as regards the house and premises) a specified and not a floating charge.

(6) Where the house and premises are discharged by this section from a charge (without the obligations secured by the charge being satisfied by the receipt of the whole or part of the price), the discharge of the house and premises shall not prejudice any right or remedy for the enforcement of those obligations against other property comprised in the same or any other security, nor prejudice any personal liability as principal or otherwise of the landlord or any other person.

(7) Subsections (1) and (2) above shall not be taken to prevent a person from joining in the conveyance for the purpose of discharging the house and premises from any charge without payment or for a less payment that that to which he would otherwise be entitled; and, if he does so, the persons to whom the price ought to be paid shall be determined accordingly.

(8) A charge on the landlord's estate to secure the payment of money or the performance of any other obligation shall not be treated for the purposes of this Part of this Act as a tenant's incumbrance by reason only of the grant of the tenancy being subsequent to the creation of the charge and not authorised as against the persons interested in the charge; and this section shall apply as if the persons so interested at the time of the grant had duly concurred in the grant for the purpose (but only for the purpose) of validating it despite the charge on the grantor's estate:

Provided that, where the tenancy is granted after the commencement of this Part of this Act (whether or not it is, by virtue of section 3 (3) above, to be treated for other purposes as forming a single tenancy with a previous tenancy) and the tenancy has not by the time of the conveyance of the house and premises to the tenant become binding on the persons interested in the charge, the conveyance shall not by virtue of this section discharge the house and premises from the charge except so far as it is satisfied by the application or payment into court of the price payable for the house and premises.

(9) Nothing in this section shall apply in relation to any charge falling within section 11 above, and for purposes of subsection (2) above, the price payable for the house and premises shall be treated as reduced by any amount to be paid out of it before execution of the conveyance for the redemption of a rent in accordance with section 11(4).

Payment into court in respect of mortgages etc.

13.—(1) Where under section 12(1) above a house and premises are, on a conveyance to the tenant, to be discharged of any charge falling within that subsection, and in accordance with section 12(2) a person is or may 21–20 be entitled in respect of the charge to receive the whole or part of the price payable for the house and premises, then if—

(*a*) for any reason difficulty arises in ascertaining how much is payable in respect of the charge; or

(*b*) for any reason mentioned in subsection (2) below difficulty arises in making a payment in respect of the charge;

the tenant may pay into court on account of the price for the house and premises the amount, if known, of the payment to be made in respect of the charge or, if that amount is not known, the whole of the price or such less amount as the tenant thinks right in order to provide for that payment.

(2) Payment may be made into court in accordance with subsection (1)(*b*) above where the difficulty arises for any of the following reasons:

(*a*) because a person who is or may be entitled to receive payment cannot be found or ascertained;

(*b*) because any such person refuses or fails to make out a title, or to accept payment and give a proper discharge, or to take any steps reasonably required of him to enable the sum payable to be ascertained and paid; or

(*c*) because a tender of the sum payable cannot, by reason of complications in the title to it or the want of two or more trustees or for other reasons, be effected, or not without incurring or involving unreasonable cost or delay.

(3) Without prejudice to subsection (1)(*a*) above, the price payable for a house and premises on a conveyance under section 8 above shall be paid by the tenant into court if before execution of the conveyance written notice is given to him—

(*a*) that the landlord or a person entitled to the benefit of a charge on the house and premises so requires for the purpose of protecting the rights of persons so entitled, or for reasons related to any application made or to be made under section 36 below, or to the bankruptcy or winding up of the landlord; or

(*b*) that steps have been taken to enforce any charge on the landlord's interest in the house and premises by the bringing of proceedings in any court, or by the appointment of a receiver, or otherwise;

and where payment is to be made into court by reason only of a notice under this subsection, and the notice is given with reference to proceedings in a court specified in the notice other than the county court, payment shall be made into the court so specified.

(4) For the purpose of computing the amount payable into court under this section, the price payable for the house and premises shall be treated as reduced by any amount to be paid out of it before execution of the conveyance for the redemption of a rent in accordance with section 11(4) above.

Extension

Obligation to grant extended lease

14.—(1) Where a tenant of a house has under this Part of this Act a right to an extended lease, and gives to the landlord written notice of his desire to have it, then except as provided by this Part of this Act the landlord shall be bound to grant to the tenant, and the tenant to accept, in substitution for the existing tenancy a new tenancy of the house and premises for a term expiring fifty years after the term date of the existing tenancy. **21–21**

(2) Where a person gives notice of his desire to have an extended lease of a house and premises under this Part of this Act, then unless the notice lapses under any provision of this Act excluding his liability, there shall be borne by him (so far as they are incurred in pursuance of the notice) the reasonable costs of or incidental to any of the following matters:—

(*a*) any investigation by the landlord of that person's right to an extended lease;

(*b*) any lease granting the new tenancy;

(*c*) any valuation of the house and premises obtained by the landlord before the grant of the new tenancy for the purpose of fixing the rent payable under it in accordance with section 15 below.

(3) A tenant shall not be entitled to require the execution of a lease granting a new tenancy under this section otherwise than on tender of the amount, so far as ascertained,—

(*a*) of any sums payable by way of rent or recoverable as rent in respect of the house and premises up to the date of tender; and

(*b*) of any sums for which at that date the tenant is liable under subsection (2) above; and

(*c*) of any other sums due and payable by him to the landlord under or in respect of the existing tenancy or any agreement collateral thereto;

and, if the amount of any such sums is not or may not be fully ascertained, on offering reasonably security for the payment of such amount as may afterwards be found to be payable in respect of them.

(4) This section shall have effect notwithstanding that the grant of the existing tenancy was subsequent to the creation of a charge on the landlord's estate and not authorised as against the persons interested in the charge; and a lease executed to give effect to this section shall be deemed to be authorised as against the persons interested in any charge on the landlord's estate, however created or arising, and shall be binding on them:

Provided that, where the existing tenancy is granted after the commencement of this Part of this Act (whether or not it is, by virtue of section 3(3) above, to be treated for other purposes as forming a single tenancy with a previous tenancy) and, the grant being subsequent to the creation of the charge on the landlord's estate, the existing tenancy is not binding on the persons interested in the charge, a lease executed to give effect to this section shall not by virtue of this subsection be binding on those persons.

(5) Where a lease is executed to give effect to this section, and any person having a charge on the landlord's estate is by reason thereof entitled to possession of the documents of title relating to that estate, the landlord shall within one month after execution of the lease deliver to that person a counterpart of it duly executed by the tenant, and the instrument creating or evidencing the charge shall apply in the event of his failing to deliver a counterpart in accordance with this subsection as if the obligation to do so were included in the terms of the charge as set out in that instrument.

(6) Where under a lease executed to give effect to this section the new tenancy takes effect subject to a subsisting charge on the existing tenancy, and at the time of its execution the person having the charge is by reason thereof entitled to possession of the documents of title relating to the existing tenancy, then he shall be similarly entitled to possession of the documents of title relating to the new tenancy and the tenant shall within one month of the execution of the lease deliver it to him, and the instrument creating or evidencing the charge shall apply in the event of the tenant failing to deliver the lease in accordance with this subsection as if the obligation to do so were included in the terms of the charge as set out in that instrument.

(7) A landlord granting a lease under this section shall be bound to take such steps as may be necessary to secure that it is not liable in accordance with the proviso to subsection (4) above to be defeated by persons interested in a charge on his estate; but a landlord is not obliged, in order to grant a lease under this section, to acquire a better title than he has or could require to be vested in him.

Terms of tenancy to be granted on extension

21–22 **15.**—(1) Subject to the provisions of his Part of this Act, the new tenancy to be granted under section 14 above shall be a tenancy on the same terms as the existing tenancy as those terms apply at the relevant time, but with such modifications as may be required or appropriate to take account—

(*a*) of the omission from the new tenancy of property comprised in the existing tenancy; or

(*b*) of alterations made to the property demised since the grant of the existing tenancy; or (*c*) in a case where the existing tenancy derives (in accordance with section 3(6) above) from more than one separate tenancies, of their combined effect and of the difference (if any) in their terms.

(2) The new tenancy shall provide that as from the original term date the rent payable for the house and premises shall be a rent ascertained or to be ascertained as follows:—

(*a*) the rent shall be a ground rent in the sense that it shall represent the letting value of the site (without including anything for the value of buildings on the site) for the uses to which the house and premises have been put since the commencement of the existing tenancy, other than uses which by the terms of the new tenancy are not permitted or are permitted only with the landlord's consent;

(*b*) the letting value for this purpose shall be in the first instance the letting value at the date from which the rent based on it is to commence, but as from the expiration of twenty-five years from the original term date the letting value at the expiration of those twenty-five years shall be substituted, if the landlord so requires, and a revised rent become payable accordingly;

(*c*) the letting value at either of the times mentioned shall be determined not earlier than twelve months before that time (the reasonable cost of obtaining a valuation for the purpose being borne by the tenant), and there shall be no revision of the rent as provided by paragraph (*b*) above unless in the last of the twenty-five years there mentioned the landlord gives the tenant written notice claiming a revision.

(3) Where during the continuance of the new tenancy the landlord will be under any obligation for the provision of services, or for repairs, maintenance or insurance, the rent payable in accordance with subsection (2) above shall be in addition to any sums payable (whether as rent or otherwise) in consideration of those matters or in respect of the cost thereof to the landlord; and if the terms of the existing tenancy include no provision for the making of any such payments by the tenant, or provision only for the payment of a fixed amount, the terms of the new tenancy shall make, as from the time when rent becomes payable in accordance with section (2) above, such provision as may be just for the making by the tenant of payments related to the cost from time to time to the landlord, and for the tenant's liability to make those payments to be enforceable by distress, re-entry or otherwise in like manner as the liability for the rent.

(4) Subject to subsection (5) below, provision shall be made by the terms of the new tenancy or by an instrument collateral thereto for the continuance with any suitable adaptations of any agreement collateral to the existing tenancy.

(5) For purposes of subsections (1) and (4) above, there shall be

excluded any term of the existing tenancy or any agreement collateral thereto in so far as that term provides for or relates to the renewal of the tenancy, or confers any option to purchase or right of pre-emption in relation to the house and premises, or provides for the termination of the tenancy before the term date otherwise than in the event of a breach of its terms; and there shall be made in the terms of the new tenancy or any instrument collateral thereto such modifications as may be required or appropriate to take account of the exclusion of any such term as aforesaid.

(6) Where the new tenancy is granted after the original term date, the first reference in subsection (2) above to that date shall have effect as a reference to the grant of the new tenancy; but on the grant of the new tenancy there shall be payable by the tenant to the landlord as an addition to the rent payable under the existing tenancy any amount by which for the period since the relevant time or the original term date (whichever is the later) the sums payable to the landlord in respect of the house and premises (after making any necessary apportionment) for rent and matters referred to in subsection (3) above fall short in total of the sums that would have been payable for rent and matters so referred to under the new tenancy, and section 14(3)(*a*) above shall apply accordingly.

(7) Subsections (1) to (6) above shall have effect subject to any agreement between the landlord and tenant as to the terms of the new tenancy or any agreement collateral thereto; and either of them may require that for purposes of the new tenancy there shall be excluded or modified any term of the existing tenancy or an agreement collateral thereto which it would be unreasonable in the circumstances to include unchanged in the new tenancy in view of the date at which the existing tenancy commenced and of changes since that date which affect the suitability at the relevant time of the provisions of that tenancy.

(8) The new tenancy shall make provision in accordance with section 16(4) below, and shall reserve to the landlord the right to resume possession in accordance with section 17.

(9) In granting the new tenancy, the landlord shall not be bound to enter into any covenant for title beyond that implied from that grant, and a person entering into any covenant required of him as landlord shall be entitled to limit his personal liability to breaches of the covenant for which he is responsible.

(10) Nothing in this section shall affect the rights or obligations of the landlord under section 35 of and Schedule 1 to the Sexual Offences Act 1956 (which apply where the tenant or occupier of any premises is convicted of permitting the whole or part of them to be used as a brothel).

Exclusion of further rights after extension

16.—(1) Subject to subsections (2) and (3) below, where a tenancy of a house and premises has been extended under section 14 above, then as regards any property comprised in the extended tenancy— **21–23**

(*a*) the right of a tenant under this Part of this Act to acquire the freehold by virtue of the tenancy shall not be exercisable unless notice of his desire to have the freehold is given not later than the original term date of the tenancy; and

(*b*) there shall be no further right to an extension of the tenancy under this Part of this Act; and

(*c*) neither section 1 of the Landlord and Tenant Act 1954 nor Part II of that Act shall apply to the tenancy; and

(*d*) after the extended term date neither section 1 of the Landlord and Tenant Act 1954 nor Part II of that Act shall apply to any tenancy directly or indirectly derived out of the tenancy, nor shall a person be entitled by virtue of any such sub-tenancy to retain possession under [Part VII of the Rent Act 1977] or any enactment applying or extending that Part of that Act [or under the Rent (Agriculture) Act 1976].

[(1A) The Rent Act 1977 shall not apply to a tenancy extended under section 14 above; but if when this provision comes into force a rent is registered under Part IV of the 1977 Act for a dwelling-house which is the subject of an extended tenancy, the tenant shall not be obliged to pay more than the registered rent under the extended tenancy until the next rental period (within the meaning of the 1977 Act) after the landlord has served on him a notice in writing that the registered rent no longer applies.]

(2) Where—

(*a*) a tenancy of a house and premises has been extended under section 14 above; and

(*b*) any part other than the house of the property then comprised in that tenancy is afterwards (while so comprised) held or occupied with another house not so comprised;

subsection (1)(*a*) or (*b*) above shall not apply to exclude any right under this Part of this Act of a tenant of the other house to acquire the freehold or an extended lease of that part as being at the relevant time comprised in his house and premises, unless the landlord objects in accordance with subsection (3) below.

(3) If, in a case falling within subsection (2) above, a tenant of the other house gives notice of his desire to have the freehold or an extended lease under this Part of this Act, the landlord, not later than two months afterwards, may give him written notice objecting to the inclusion in his house and premises of the part in question; and, if the landlord does so,

that part shall be treated as not so included and this Part of this Act shall apply as it applies where property is excluded from a house and premises under section 2(4):

Provided that if the tenant is seeking to acquire the freehold this subsection shall apply only if his notice is given after the original term date of the tenancy under which the said part is held.

(4) Where a tenancy has been extended under section 14 above, no long tenancy created immediately or derivatively by way of sub-demises under the tenancy shall confer on the sub-tenant, as against the tenant's landlord, any right under this Part of this Act to acquire the freehold or an extended lease.

(5) Where a tenancy has been extended under section 14 above, and that tenancy and any subsequent tenancy at a low rent of property comprised in it (with or without intervening tenancies) are to be treated under section 3(3) above as a single tenancy of that property, the single tenancy shall be treated for purposes of this section as one which has been extended under section 14, and the instrument granting any such subsequent tenancy shall make provision in accordance with subsection (4) above.

(6) A person granting a sub-tenancy to which subsection (1)(*d*) above will apply, or negotiating with a view to the grant of such a sub-tenancy by him or by a person for whom he is acting as agent, shall inform the other party that the sub-tenancy is to be derived out of a tenancy extended under section 14 of this Act (or one treated for purposes of this section as so extended), unless either he knows that the other party is aware of it or he himself is unaware of it.

(7) Where an instrument extending a tenancy at a low rent, or granting a further tenancy at a low rent in substitution for or in continuance of such a tenancy, contains a statement to the effect that the tenancy is being or has been previously extended under this Part of this Act, the statement shall be conclusive for purposes of this section in favour of any person not being a party to the instrument, unless the statement appears from the instrument to be untrue.

(8) Any person who—

(*a*) includes or causes to be included in an instrument a statement to the effect mentioned in subsection (7) above, knowing the statement to be untrue; or

(*b*) executes, or with intent to deceive makes use of, any instrument, knowing that it contains such a statement and that the statement is untrue;

shall be liable on conviction on indictment to imprisonment for a term not exceeding two years, or on summary conviction to imprisonment for a term not exceeding three months or to a fine not exceeding [the prescribed sum] or to both.

AMENDMENT

The words in square brackets in subs. (1) were substituted by the Rent Act 1977, Sched. 23, para. 43, and the words at the end of para. (*d*) of that subs. by the Rent (Agriculture) Act 1976, Sched. 8, para. 17. Subs. (1A) was added by the Housing Act 1980, s.141 and Sched. 21. The words in square brackets in subs. (8) were substituted by the Magistrates' Courts Act 1980, s.32(2). **21–24**

Landlord's overriding rights

Redevelopment rights (exclusion or termination of extension)

17.—(1) Where a tenancy of a house and premises has been extended under section 14 above, the landlord may, at any time not earlier than twelve months before the original term date of the tenancy, apply to the court for an order that he may resume possession of the property on the ground that for the purposes of redevelopment he proposes to demolish or reconstruct the whole or a substantial part of the house and premises. **21–25**

(2) If on an application under subsection (1) above the court is satisfied that the landlord has established the ground mentioned in that subsection, then subject to the provisions of this section the court shall by order declare that the landlord is entitled as against the tenant to obtain possession of the house and premises and the tenant is entitled to be paid compensation by the landlord for the loss of the house and premises.

(3) Where an order is made under subsection (2) above, the tenancy shall determine and the compensation become payable in accordance with Schedule 2 to this Act; and the provisions of that Schedule shall have effect as regards the measure of compensation under any such order and the effects of the order where there are sub-tenancies, and as regards other matters relating to applications and orders under this section.

(4) Where the tenancy of a house and premises has not been extended under section 14 above, but the tenant has a right to an extended lease and gives notice of his desire to have one, then this section shall apply as if the lease had been extended under section 14; and—

(*a*) on the making by the landlord of an application under this section, the notice shall be suspended until the time when an order under subsection (2) or an order dismissing the application becomes final or the application is withdrawn; and

(*b*) on an order under subsection (2) becoming final, the notice shall cease to have effect, but section 14(2) above shall not apply to require the tenant to make any payment to the landlord in respect of costs incurred by reason of the notice.

(5) For purposes of subsection (4) above, the reference in subsection (1) to the original term date shall have effect as a reference to the term date or, in a case where before the relevant time the landlord had given notice

to quit terminating the tenancy at a date earlier than the term date, as a reference to the date specified in the notices to quit.

(6) Where a landlord makes an application under subsection (1) above, then—

(*a*) if the tenant afterwards gives notice of his desire to have the freehold of the house and premises under this Part of this Act, that notice shall be of no effect if it is not given before the date of the order fixing the date for the termination of the tenancy (in accordance with Schedule 2 to this Act), or if the tenant's notice of his desire to have an extended lease was given within twelve months before the making of the landlord's application; and

(*b*) if a notice given by the tenant (before or after the making of the landlord's application) of his desire to have the freehold has effect, no order or further order shall be made on the landlord's application except as regards costs, but without prejudice to the making of a further application by the landlord if the tenant's notice lapses without effect being given to it.

Residential rights (exclusion of enfranchisement or extension)

21–26 **18.**—(1) Subject to subsection (2) below, where the tenancy of a house and premises has not been extended under section 14 above, but the tenant has a right to acquire the freehold or an extended lease and has given notice of his desire to have it, the landlord may, at any time before effect is given to the notice, apply to the court for an order that he may resume possession of the property on the ground that it or part of it is or will be reasonably required by him for occupation as the only or main residence of the landlord or of a person who is at the time of the application an adult member of the landlord's family.

(2) A landlord shall not be entitled to apply to the court under this section if his interest in the house and premises, or an interest which has merged in that interest but would otherwise have had a duration extending at least five years longer than that of the tenancy, was purchased or created after the 18th February 1966; and for purposes of this subsection the duration of any interest in the house and premises (including the tenancy) shall be taken to be the period until it is due to expire or, if capable of earlier determination by notice given by a person as landlord, the date or earliest date which has been or could be specified in such a notice.

(3) Where the landlord's interest is held on trust, subsection (1) above shall apply as if the reference to occupation as the residence of the landlord were a reference to the like occupation of a person having an interest under the trust (whether or not also a trustee), and the reference to a member of the landlord's family were a reference to the like member

of such a person's family; and for purposes of subsection (1) a person is an adult member of another's family if that person is—

(*a*) the other's wife or husband; or

(*b*) a son or daughter or son-in-law or daughter-in-law of the other, or of the other's wife or husband, who has attained the age of eighteen; or

(*c*) the father or mother of the other, or of the other's wife or husband.

In paragraph (*b*) above any reference to a person's son or daughter includes a reference to any stepson or stepdaughter, any illegitimate son or daughter, [. . .] of that person, and "son-in-law" and "daughter-in-law" shall be construed accordingly.

(4) If on an application under subsection (1) above the court is satisfied that the landlord has established the ground mentioned in that subsection and is not disentitled by subsection (2), the court shall by order declare that the landlord is entitled as against the tenant to obtain possession of the house and premises and the tenant is entitled to be paid compensation by the landlord for the loss of the house and premises:

Provided that the court shall not make an order under this subsection if the court is satisfied that having regard to all the circumstances of the case, including the question whether other accommodation is available for the landlord or the tenant, greater hardship would be caused by making the order than by refusing to make it.

(5) Where an order is made under subsection (4) above, the tenancy shall determine and the compensation become payable in accordance with Schedule 2 to this Act; and the provisions of that Schedule shall have effect as regards the measure of compensation under any such order and the effects of the order where there are sub-tenancies, and as regards other matters relating to applications and orders under this section.

(6) Where a landlord makes an application under this section—

(*a*) any notice previously given by the tenant of his desire to have the freehold or an extended lease of the house and premises under this Part of this Act shall be suspended until the time when an order under subsection (4) or an order dismissing the application becomes final or the application is withdrawn; and

(*b*) on an order under subsection (4) becoming final, the notice shall cease to have effect, but section 9(4) or 14(2) above shall not apply to require the tenant to make any payment to the landlord in respect of costs incurred by reason of the notice;

and a notice of the tenant's desire to have the freehold shall be of no effect if given after the making of the application and before the time referred to in paragraph (*a*) above or after an order under subsection (4) above has become final.

AMENDMENT
The words omitted from subs. (3) were repealed by the Children Act 1975, Sched. 4.

Retention of management powers for general benefit of neighbourhood

21–27 **19.**—(1) Where, in the case of any area which is occupied directly or indirectly under tenancies held from one landlord (apart from property occupied by him or his licensees or for the time being unoccupied), the Minister on an application made within the two years beginning with the commencement of this Part of this Act grants a certificate that, in order to maintain adequate standards of appearance and amenity and regulate redevelopment in the area in the event of tenants acquiring the landlord's interest in their house and premises under this Part of this Act, it is in the Minister's opinion likely to be in the general interest that the landlord should retain powers of management in respect of the house and premises or have rights against the house and premises in respect of the benefits arising from the exercise elsewhere of his powers of management, then the High Court may, on an application made within one year of the giving of the certificate, approve a scheme giving the landlord such powers and rights as are contemplated by this subsection.

For purposes of this section "the Minister" means as regards areas within Wales and Monmouthshire the Secretary of State, and as regards other areas the Minister of Housing and Local Government.

(2) The Minister shall not give a certificate under this section unless his is satisfied that the applicant has, by advertisement or otherwise as may be required by the Minister, given adequate notice to persons interested, informing them of the application for a certificate and its purpose and inviting them to make representations to the Minister for or against the application within a time which appears to the Minister to be reasonable; and before giving a certificate the Minister shall consider any representations so made within that time, and if from those representations it appears to him that there is among the persons making them substantial opposition to the application, he shall afford to those opposing the application, and on the same occasion to the applicant and such (if any) as the Minister thinks fit of those in favour of the application, an opportunity to appear and be heard by a person appointed by the Minister for the purpose, and shall consider the report of that person.

(3) The Minister in considering whether to grant a certificate authorising a scheme for any area, and the High Court in considering whether to approve a scheme shall have regard primarily to the benefit likely to result from the scheme to the area as a whole (including houses likely to be acquired from the landlord under this Part of this Act), and the extent to which it is reasonable to impose, for the benefit of the area, obligations on tenants so acquiring their freeholds; but regard may also be had to the

past development and present character of the area and to architectural or historical considerations, to neighbouring areas and to the circumstances generally.

(4) If, having regard to the matters mentioned in subsection (3) above, to the provision which it is practicable to make by a scheme, and to any change of circumstances since the giving of the certificate under subsection (1), the High Court think it proper so to do, then the High Court may by order—

(*a*) exclude from the scheme any part of the area certified under that subsection; or

(*b*) declare that no scheme can be approved for the area;

and before submitting for approval a scheme for an area so certified a person may, if he sees fit, apply to the High Court for general directions as to the matters proper to be included in the scheme and for a decision whether an order should be made under paragraph (*a*) or (*b*) above.

(5) Subject to subsections (3) and (4) above, on the submission of a scheme to the High Court, the High Court shall approve the scheme either as originally submitted or with any modifications proposed or agreed to by the applicant for the scheme, if the scheme (with those modifications, if any) appears to the court to be fair and practicable and not to give the landlord a degree of control out of proportion to that previously exercised by him or to that required for the purposes of the scheme; and the High Court shall not dismiss an application for the approval of a scheme, unless either—

(*a*) the Court makes an order under subsection (4)(*b*) above; or

(*b*) in the opinion of the Court the applicant is unwilling to agree to a suitable scheme or is not proceeding in the matter with due despatch.

(6) A scheme under this section may make different provision for different parts of the area, and shall include provision for terminating or varying all or any of the provisions of the scheme, or excluding part of the area, if a change of circumstances makes it appropriate, or for enabling it to be done by or with the approval of the High Court.

(7) Except as provided by the scheme, the operation of a scheme under this section shall not be affected by any disposition or devolution of the landlord's interest in the property within the area or parts of that property; but the scheme—

(*a*) shall include provision for identifying the person who is for the purposes of the scheme to be treated as the landlord for the time being: and

(*b*) may include provision for transferring, or allowing the landlord for the time being to transfer, all or any of the powers and rights conferred by the scheme on the landlord for the time being to a local authority or other body, including a body constituted for the purpose.

In the following provisions of this section references to the landlord for the time being shall have effect, in relation to powers and rights transferred to a local authority or other body as contemplated by paragraph (*b*) above, as references to that authority or body.

(8) Without prejudice to any other provision of this section, a scheme under it may provide for all or any of the following matters:—

(*a*) for regulating the redevelopment, use or appearance of property of which tenants have acquired the landlord's interest under this Part of this Act; and

(*b*) for empowering the landlord for the time being to carry out work for the maintenance or repair of any such property or carry out work to remedy a failure in respect of any such property to comply with the scheme, or for making the operation of any provisions of the scheme conditional on his doing so or on the provision or maintenance by him of services, facilities or amenities of any description; and

(*c*) for imposing on persons from time to time occupying or interested in any such property obligations in respect of maintenance or repair of the property or of property used or enjoyed by them in common with others, or in respect of cost incurred by the landlord for the time being on any matter referred to in this paragraph or in paragraph (*b*) above;

(*d*) for the inspection from time to time of any such property on behalf of the landlord for the time being, and for the recovery by him of sums due to him under the scheme in respect of any such property by means of a charge on the property;

and the landlord for the time being shall have, for the enforcement of any charge imposed under the scheme, the same powers and remedies under the Law of Property Act 1925 and otherwise as if he were a mortgagee by deed having powers of sale and leasing and of appointing a receiver.

(9) A scheme under this section may extend to property in which the landlord's interest is disposed of otherwise than under this Part of this Act (whether residential property or not), so as to make that property, or allow it to be made, subject to any such provision as is or might be made by the scheme for property in which tenants acquire the landlord's interest under this Part of this Act.

(10) A certificate given or scheme approved under this section [shall (notwithstanding section 2(*a*) or (*b*) of the Local Land Charges Act 1975) be a local land charge and for the purposes of that Act the landlord for the area to which it relates shall be treated as the originating authority as respects such charge; and where a scheme is registered in the appropriate local land charges register.]

(*a*) the provisions of the scheme relating to property of any description shall, so far as they respectively affect the persons from time to time occupying or interested in that property, be enforceable by the landlord for the time being against them, as if each of them had covenanted with the landlord for the time being to be bound by the scheme; and

(*b*) in relation to a house and premises in the area section 10 above shall have effect subject to the provisions of the scheme, and the price payable under section 9 shall be adjusted accordingly.

[10A) Section 10 of the Local Land Charges Act 1975 shall not apply in relation to schemes which, by virtue of this section, are local land charges.]

(11) Subject to subsections (12) and (13) below, a certificate shall not be given nor a scheme approved under this section for any area except on the application of the landlord.

(12) Where, on a joint application made by two or more persons as landlords of neighbouring areas, it appears to the Minister—

(*a*) that a certificate could in accordance with subsection (1) above be given as regards those areas, treated as a unit, if the interests of those persons were held by a single person; and

(*b*) that the applicants are willing to be bound by any scheme to co-operate in the management of their property in those areas and in the administration of the scheme;

the Minister may give a certificate under this section for those areas as a whole; and where a certificate is given by virtue of this subsection, this section shall apply accordingly, but so that any scheme made by virtue of the certificate shall be made subject to conditions (enforceable in such manner as may be provided by the scheme) for securing that the landlords and their successors co-operate as aforesaid.

(13) Where it appears to the Minister—

(*a*) that a certificate could be given under this section for any area or areas on the application of the landlord or landlords; and

(*b*) that any body of persons is so constituted as to be capable of representing for purposes of this section the persons occupying or interested in property in the area or areas (other than the landlord or landlords), or such of them as are or may become entitled to acquire their landlord's interest under this Part of this Act, and is otherwise suitable;

then on an application made by that body either alone or jointly with the landlord or landlords a certificate may be granted accordingly; and where a certificate is so granted, whether to a representative body alone or to a representative body jointly with the landlord or landlords—

(i) an application for a scheme in pursuance of the certificate may be made by the representative body alone or by the landlord or landlords alone or by both jointly and, by leave of the High Court, may be proceeded with by the representative body or by the landlord or landlords though not the applicant or applicants; and

(ii) without prejudice to subsection (7)(*b*) above, the scheme may, with the consent of the landlord or landlords or on such terms as to compensation or otherwise as appear to the High Court to be just, confer on the representative body any such rights or powers under the scheme as might be conferred on the landlord or landlords for the time being, or enable the representative body to participate in the administration of the scheme or in the management by the landlord or landlords of his or their property in the area or areas.

(14) Where a certificate under this section has been given for an area, or an application for one is pending, then subject to subsection (15) below if (before or after the making of the application or the giving of the certificate) a tenant of a house in the area gives notice of his desire to have the freehold under this Part of this Act,—

(*a*) no further proceedings need be taken in relation to the notice beyond those which appear to the landlord to be reasonable in the circumstances; but

(*b*) the tenant may at any time withdraw the notice by a further notice in writing given to the landlord, and section 9(4) above shall not apply to require him to make any payment to the landlord in respect of costs incurred by reason of the notice withdrawn.

(15) Subsection (14) above shall cease to have effect by virtue of an application for a certificate if the application is withdrawn or the certificate refused, and shall cease to have effect as regards the whole or part of an area to which a certificate relates—

(*a*) on the approval of a scheme for the area or that pare of it; or

(*b*) on the expiration of one year from the giving of the certificate without an application having been made to the High Court for the approval of a scheme for the area or that part of it, or on the withdrawal of an application so made without a scheme being approved: or

(*c*) on an order made under subsection (4) above with respect to the area or that part of it, or an order dismissing an application for the approval of a scheme for the area or that part of it, becoming final.

AMENDMENTS

21-28 The words in square brackets in subs. (10) were substituted by the Local Land Charges Act 1975, s.17(2), Sched. 1, which also added subs. (10A).

Determination of questions, procedure, etc.

Jurisdiction and special powers of county court

20.—(1) Subject to section 115 of the County Courts Act 1959, any jurisdiction expressed to be conferred on the court by this Part of this Act shall, unless the contrary intention appears, be exercised by the county court. **21–29**

(2) Except as provided by this section and section 21 below, there shall also be brought in the county court any proceedings under this Part of this Act of the following descriptions:—

(*a*) proceedings for determining whether a person is entitled to acquire the freehold or an extended lease of a house and premises, or to what property his right extends;

(*b*) proceedings for determining what provisions ought to be contained in a conveyance in accordance with section 10 or 29 (1), or in a lease granting a new tenancy under section 14;

(*c*) any other proceedings relating to the performance or discharge of obligations arising out of a tenant's notice of his desire to have the freehold or an extended lease, including proceedings for the recovery of damages or compensation in the event of the obligations not being performed;

(*d*) any proceedings for determining the amount of a sub-tenants share under Schedule 2 to this Act in compensation payable to a tenant under section 17 or 18, or for establishing or giving effect to his right to it.

(3) Where in connection with any acquisition by a tenant of the freehold or an extended lease under this Part of this Act it is necessary to apportion between the house and premises (or part of them) and other property the rent payable under his tenancy or any superior or reversionary tenancy, then, subject to section 115 of the County Courts Act 1959 and to section 21 below, the apportionment shall be made by the county court.

(4) Where it is made to appear to the court that the landlord or the tenant has been guilty of any unreasonable delay or default in the performance of obligations arising from a tenant's notice of his desire to have the freehold or an extended lease under this Part of this Act, then (without prejudice to any right to damages) the court may—

(*a*) by order revoke or vary, and direct repayment of sums paid under, any provision made by a previous order as to payment of the costs of proceedings in the court in relation to the matter, or, where costs have not been awarded, award costs;

(*b*) certify particulars of the delay or default to the Land Tribunal with a view to enabling the Tribunal to exercise a like discretion in relation to costs of proceedings before the Tribunal.

(5) Where a person gives notice of his desire to have the freehold or to have an extended lease of a house and premises under this Part of this Act, and the notice either is set aside by the court or withdrawn, or ceases to have effect, or would, if valid, cease to have effect, then if it is made to appear to the court—

(*a*) that the notice was no given in good faith; or

(*b*) that the person giving the notice attempted in any material respect to support it by misrepresentation or the concealment of material facts;

the court may, on the application of the landlord, order that person to pay to the landlord such sum as appears sufficient as compensation for damage or loss sustained by the landlord as the result of the giving of the notice.

(6) In any case where under subsection (5) above the court has power, on the application of the landlord, to order a person to make a payment to the landlord, the court (whether or not it makes an order under that subsection) may, on the application of the landlord, order that any further notice given by that person under this Part of this Act of his desire to have the freehold or an extended lease of the same house or any part of it, with or without other property, shall be void if given within the five years beginning with the date of the order.

(7) Subsection (2)(*c*) above shall not prevent the bringing of proceedings in a court other than the county court where the claim is for damages or pecuniary compensation only.

Jurisdiction of Lands Tribunal

21–30 **21.**—(1) The following matters shall, in default of agreement, be determined by [a leasehold valuation tribunal] namely,—

(*a*) the price payable for a house and premises under section 9 above;

(*b*) the amount of the rent to be payable (whether originally or on a reversion) for a house and premises in accordance with section 15(2);

(*c*) the amount of any compensation payable to a tenant under section 17 or 18 for the loss of a house and premises.

[(1A) An application to a leasehold valuation tribunal under subsection (1) above must be in the prescribed form and contain the prescribed particulars.

(1B) No application may be made to a leasehold valuation tribunal under subsection (1) above to determine the price for a house and premises unless either—

(*a*) the landlord has informed the tenant of the price he is asking; or (*b*) two months has elapsed without his doing so since the tenant gave notice of his desire to have the freehold under this Part of this Act.]

(2) Notwithstanding section 20(2) or (3) above, [a leasehold valuation tribunal] shall have jurisdiction, either by agreement or in a case where an application is made to [a tribunal] under subsection (1) above with reference to the same transaction,—

(*a*) to determine what provisions ought to be contained in a conveyance in accordance with section 10 or 29(1) of this Act, or in a lease granting a new tenancy under section 14; or

(*b*) to apportion between the house and premises (or part of them) and other property the rent payable under any tenancy; or

(*c*) to determine the amount of a sub-tenant's share under Schedule 2 to this Act in compensation payable to a tenant under section 17 or 18.

(3) Where, after an application has been made to the court with respect to any matter falling within the jurisdiction of [a leasehold valuation tribunal] under subsection (2) above, an application is made to [a tribunal] under subsection (1) as it appears to the court convenient that the questions arising on the two applications should be disposed of together, the court may by order transfer to [a leasehold valuation tribunal] the proceedings on the application to the court.

[(4) Without prejudice to the generality of [section 75 of the County Courts Act 1984] or section 74 of the Rent Act 1977, the powers thereby conferred to make rules of procedure shall extend to prescribing the procedure consequent on any such transfer.]

[(4A) The Secretary of State may make regulations prescribing—

(*a*) the form of any application under subsection (1) above; and

(*b*) the particulars which it must contain;

and any such regulations shall be made by statutory instrument subject to annulment in pursuance of a resolution of either House of Parliament.]

(5) [. . .]

AMENDMENTS

The words and subss. in square brackets were added, and subs. (5) was repealed, by the Housing Act 1980, s.142 and Sched. 22, save for the words in square brackets within subs. (4), inserted by the County Courts Act 1984, Sched. 2, para. 31. 21–31

Validity of tenants' notices, effect on Landlord and Tenant Act 1954 and on notices to quit, etc., and procedure generally

22.—(1) The provisions of Schedule 3 to this Act shall have effect— 21–32

(*a*) to exclude a tenant's right to acquire the freehold or an extended lease under this Part of this Act if a notice of his desire to have it is given too late; and (*b*) to make a notice of a person's desire to have the freehold or an extended lease under this Part of this Act effectual where apart from the notice the tenancy would or might terminate by forfeiture or otherwise; and

(*c*) for adapting the procedure under Parts I and II of the Landlord and Tenant Act 1954, and for relating to one another proceedings under that Act and proceedings under this Part of this Act; and

(*d*) generally for regulating the procedure under this Part of this Act.

Where a tenant having a right under this Part of this Act to acquire the freehold or an extended lease gives the landlord notice in accordance with this Part of this Act of his desire to have it, then except as otherwise provided by this Act the procedure for giving effect to the notice, and the rights and obligations of all parties in relation to the investigation of title and other matters arising in giving effect to the notice, shall be such as may be prescribed by regulations made by [the Secretary of State] by statutory instrument (which shall be subject to annulment in pursuance of a resolution of either House of Parliament), and subject to or in the absence of provision made by any such regulations as regards any matter shall be as nearly as may be the same as in the case of a contract of sale or leasing freely negotiated between the parties.

(3) In relation to a claim to acquire the freehold, regulations under subsection (2) above may include provision—

(*a*) for a sum on account of the price payable for the house and premises and landlord's costs to be deposited with the landlord or with some person as his agent or as stakeholder, and for the return or forfeiture in any prescribed circumstances of the whole or part of the sum deposited;

(*b*) for enabling or requiring the tenant in any prescribed circumstances, instead of continuing to pay rent under the tenancy, to pay sums representing interest on the price payable or, at his option, either to pay such sums as aforesaid or to pay or deposit the price payable or the balance of it;

(*c*) for any matters incidental to or arising out of the matters mentioned above;

and in relation to any claim the regulations may provide for discharging the landlord or the tenant by reason of the other's default or delay from the obligations arising out of the claim.

(4) In the case of a claim to acquire the freehold, subsection (2) above shall not be taken in any case as applying forms prescribed under section 46 of the Law of Property Act 1925 for contracts entered into by correspondence; but, without prejudice to the generality of that subsection section 49 (which provides for the determination of questions arising between vendor and purchaser) shall apply.

(5) Section 66 of the Landlord and Tenant Act 1954 (which requires the

prescribed form for a notice to be prescribed by regulations of [the Secretary of State], and makes provisions as to the contents of prescribed forms and as to the service of notices) shall have effect as if any reference therein to that Act were a reference also to this Part of this Act.

AMENDMENT

The words in square brackets in subs. (2) and (5) were substituted by the Transfer of Functions (Lord Chancellor and Secretary of State) Order 1974 (S.I. No. 1986), Art. 3(2).

Supplementary

Agreements excluding or modifying rights of tenant

23.—(1) Except as provided by this section, any agreement relating to a tenancy (whether contained in the instrument creating the tenancy or not and whether made before the creation of the tenancy or not) shall be void in so far as it purports to exclude or modify any right to acquire the freehold or an extended lease or right to compensation under this Part of this Act, or provides for the termination or surrender of the tenancy in the event of a tenant acquiring or claiming any such right or for the imposition of any penalty or disability on the tenant in that event. **21–33**

(2) Subsection (1) above shall not be taken to preclude a tenant from surrendering his tenancy, and shall not—

(*a*) invalidate any agreement for a tenant to acquire an interest superior to his tenancy or an extended lease on terms different from those provided for by this Part of this Act; or

(*b*) where a tenant has given notice of his desire to have the freehold or an extended lease under this Part of this Act, invalidate any agreement between the landlord and the tenant that that notice shall cease to be binding or any provision of such an agreement excluding or restricting for a period not exceeding [three years] the right to give a further notice of either kind with respect to the house or any part of it; or

(*c*) where a tenant's right to compensation has accrued, invalidate any agreement as to the amount of the compensation.

(3) Where—

(*a*) a person, being entitled as tenant of a house to acquire the freehold or an extended lease under this Part of this Act, enters into an agreement without prior approval of the court for the surrender of his tenancy, or for the acquisition by him of an interest superior to his tenancy or of any extended lease; or

(*b*) a tenancy having been extended under this Part of this Act, the tenant, on the landlord claiming possession for purposes of redevelopment, enters into an agreement without the prior approval of the court for the surrender of the tenancy;

then on the application of the tenant the county court or any court in which proceedings are brought against him on the agreement may, if in the opinion of the court he is not adequately recompensed under the agreement for his rights under this Part of this Act, set aside or vary the agreement and give such other relief as appears to the court to be just, having regard to the situation and conduct of the parties.

(4) Where a tenant of a house is under this Part of this Act entitled to acquire the freehold or an extended lease, or entitled to the benefit of a previous tenant's notice of his desire to have the freehold or an extended lease, there may with the approval of the court be granted to him in satisfaction of that right a new tenancy on such terms as may be approved by the court; and, subject to section 29 of the Charities Act 1960 and to section 31 below, a tenancy may be so granted by the landlord, and shall be binding on persons entitled to any interest in or charge on the landlord's estate, notwithstanding that it would not apart from this provision be authorised as against any such persons and notwithstanding any restriction imposed by statute or otherwise on the landlord's powers of leasing:

Provided that where the existing tenancy is granted after the commencement of the Part of this Act (whether or not it is, by virtue of section 3(3) above, to be treated for other purposes as forming a single tenancy with a previous tenancy) and, the grant being subsequent to the creation of a charge on the landlord's estate, the existing tenancy is not binding on the persons interested in the charge, a tenancy so granted shall not by virtue of this subsection be binding on those persons.

(5) Where a tenancy is granted by virtue of subsection (4) above,—

(*a*) the terms of the new tenancy may exclude any right to acquire the freehold under this Part of this Act; and

(*b*) [section 9(1) and (1A) above,] section 14(5) and (6) above and, except in so far as provision is made to the contrary by the terms of the new tenancy, section 16(1) to (6) and section 17(1) to (3) (together with Schedule 2 to this Act and, so far as relevant, subsections (1) to (3) above) shall apply as if the new tenancy were granted by way of extension under this Part of this Act.

(6) Where an instrument extending a tenancy at a low rent, or granting a further tenancy at a low rent in substitution for or in continuance of such a tenancy, contains a statement to the effect that by virtue of subsection (4) above the tenancy is being or has previously been extended in satisfaction of the right to an extended lease under section 14 above, the statement shall be conclusive in favour of any person not being a party

to the instrument, unless the statement appears from the instrument to be untrue.

(7) Any person who—

(*a*) includes or causes to be included in an instrument a statement to the effect mentioned in subsection (6) above, knowing the statement to be untrue; or

(*b*) executes, or with intent to deceive makes use of, any instrument, knowing that it contains such a statement and that the statement is untrue;

shall be liable on conviction on indictment to imprisonment for a term not exceeding two years, or on summary conviction to imprisonment for a term not exceeding three months or to a fine not exceeding [the prescribed sum] or to both.

AMENDMENT

The words in square brackets in subs. (2)(*b*) were substituted by the Housing Act 1980, s.141 and Sched. 21. Those in subs. (5) were inserted by the Housing and Planning Act 1986, s.23. Those in subs. (7) were substituted by the Magistrates' Courts Act 1980, s.32(2). 21–34

Application of price or compensation received by landlord, and charge of betterment levy on enfranchisement

24.—(1) Any sum received by the landlord by way of the price payable for a house and premises under section 9 above, or by way of compensation under any provision of this Part of this Act providing for compensation to be recovered by or awarded to a landlord,— 21–35

(*a*) where the interest of the landlord is held on trust for sale shall be dealt with as if it were proceeds of sale arising under the trust; and

(*b*) where the landlord is a university or college to which the Universities and College Estates Act 1925 applies, shall be dealt with as if it were an amount payable as consideration on a sale effected under that Act.

(2) For purposes of Part III of the Land Commission Act 1967 any conveyance executed to give effect to section 8 above shall be deemed to be a conveyance on sale of any interest transferred (or, as regards a tenancy, an assignment on sale of it), and the price payable for the interest under section 9 shall be deemed to be consideration payable in respect of the disposition of that interest.

Mortgagee in possession of landlord's interest

25.—(1) Where a landlord's interest is subject to a mortgagee and the mortgagee is in possession, then subject to the provisions of this section all such proceedings arising out of a person's notice of his desire to have the freehold or an extended lease under this Part of this Act as would 21–36 apart from this provision be taken by or in relation to the landlord shall, as regards his interest, be conducted by and through the mortgagee as if he were the landlord, and any conveyance to be executed under section 8 of this Act or lease to be executed under section 14 shall, if it requires execution by the landlord, either be executed by the landlord by the direction of the mortgagee or be executed by the mortgagee in the name and on behalf of the landlord; but this subsection shall not affect the operation in relation to the mortgage of sections 12 and 13 above.

(2) Where a landlord's interest is subject to a mortgage and the mortgagee is in possession, then (without prejudice to subsection (1) above) any application under section 17 above shall be made by the mortgagee as if he were the landlord, and that section and Schedule 2 to this Act shall apply accordingly.

(3) Any compensation paid by the mortgagee in accordance with section 17 above (whether possession is obtained under that section or without an application thereunder) shall be treated as if it were secured by the mortgage, with the like priority and with interest at the same rate as the mortgage money, so however that (without prejudice to the recovery of interest) the amount shall not be recoverable from the mortgagor personally.

(4) Where a mortgagee is by virtue of this section acting as landlord and any case arises in which compensation may be recovered by or awarded to a landlord, compensation may be recovered by or awarded to the mortgagee accordingly, and shall be dealt with as if it were proceeds of sale of property subject to the mortgage.

(5) Where a landlord's interest is subject to a mortgage, and a receiver appointed by the mortgagee or by the court is in receipt of the rents and profits,—

(*a*) the landlord shall not make any application under section 17 or 18 above without the consent of the mortgagee; and

(*b*) the mortgagee may by written notice given to the landlord require that this section shall apply, either generally or so far as relates to section 17 above, as if he were a mortgagee in possession.

(6) In this section "mortgage" includes any charge or lien, and "mortgagor" and "mortgagee" shall be construed accordingly.

Person to act where landlord is custodian trustee or under disability

21–37 **26.**—(1) Where the interest of a landlord in any property is vested in a person as custodian trustee, the managing trustees or committee of management shall be deemed to be the landlord for the purposes of this Part of this Act and the interest be deemed to be vested in them, except as regards the execution of any instrument disposing of or affecting that interest.

(2) Where a landlord is incapable by reason of mental disorder within the meaning of [the Mental Health Act 1983] of managing and administering his property and affairs, his receiver [appointed under Part VII of the said Act of 1983 or Part VIII of the Mental Health Act 1959] or (if no such receiver is acting for him) any person authorised in that behalf shall, under an order of the authority [having jurisdiction under Part VII of the said Act of 1983], take his place as landlord for purposes of this Part of this Act.

AMENDMENT

The words in square brackets were substituted by the Mental Health Act 1983, Sched. 4, para. 22.

Enfranchisement where landlord cannot be found

27.—(1) Where a tenant of a house having a right under this Part of this Act to acquire the freehold is prevented from giving notice of his desire to have the freehold because the person to be served with the notice cannot be found, or his identity cannot be ascertained, then on an application made by the tenant the High Court may, subject to and in accordance with the provisions of this section, make such order as the Court thinks fit with a view to the house and premises being vested in him, his executors, administrators or assigns for the like estate and on the like terms (so far as the circumstances permit) as if he had at the date of his application to the High Court given notice of his desire to have the freehold. **21–38**

(2) Before making any such order the High Court may require the applicant to take such further steps by way of advertisement or otherwise as the Court thinks proper for the purpose of tracing the landlord; and if after an application is made to the High Court and before the house and premises are vested in pursuance of the application the landlord is traced, then no further proceedings shall be taken with a view to the house and premises being so vested, but subject to subsection (7) below—

(*a*) the rights and obligations of all parties shall be determined as if the applicant had, at the date of the application, duly given notice of his desire to have the freehold; and

(*b*) the High Court may give such directions as the Court thinks fit as to the steps to be taken for giving effect to those rights and obligations, including directions modifying or dispensing with any of the requirements of this Act or of regulations made under this Act.

(3) Where a house and premises are to be vested in a person in pursuance of an application under this section, then on his paying into the Supreme Court the appropriate sum there shall be executed by such person as the High Court may designate a conveyance in a form approved

by the High Court and containing such provisions as may be so approved for the purpose of giving effect so far as possible to the requirements of section 10 above; and that conveyance shall be effective to vest in the person to whom the conveyance is made the property expressed to be conveyed, subject as and in the manner in which it is expressed to be conveyed.

(4) For the purpose of any conveyance to be executed in accordance with subsection (3) above, any question as to the property to be conveyed and the rights with or subject to which it is to be conveyed shall be determined by the High Court, but it shall be assumed (unless the contrary is shown) that the landlord has no interest in property other than the property to be conveyed and, for the purpose of excepting them from the conveyance, any underlying minerals.

(5) The appropriate sum to be paid into the Supreme Court in accordance with subsection (3) above shall be such amount as a surveyor selected by the President of the Lands Tribunal may certify to be at a fair valuation the price payable in accordance with section 9 above, together with the amount or estimated amount remaining unpaid (as determined by the High Court) of any pecuniary rent payable for the house and premises up to the date of the conveyance.

(6) Where a house and premises are vested in a person in accordance with this section, the payment into the Supreme Court of the appropriate sum shall be taken to have satisfied any claims against the tenant, his executors, administrators or assigns in respect of the price payable under this Part of this Act for the acquisition of the freehold in the house and premises.

(7) An application under this section may be withdrawn at any time before execution of a conveyance under subsection (3) above and, after it is withdrawn, subsection (2)(*a*) shall not apply; but where any step is taken (whether by the landlord or the tenant) for the purpose of giving effect to subsection (2)(*a*) in the case of any application, the application shall not afterwards be withdrawn except with the landlord's consent or by leave of the High Court, and the High Court shall not give leave unless it appears to the Court just to do so by reason of matters coming to the knowledge of the applicant in consequence of the landlord being traced.

(8) A conveyance executed under subsection (3) above shall have effect as provided by that subsection notwithstanding any interest of the Crown in the property expressed to be conveyed.

Land held for public purposes, ecclesiastical land, etc.

Retention or resumption of land required for public purposes

21-39 **28.**—(1) Where the landlord of any property is a body to which this section applies, and a Minister of the Crown certifies that the property will in ten years or less be required for relevant development, then—

(*a*) a notice of a person's desire to have the freehold or an extended lease under this Part of this Act of a house comprised in the property shall be of no effect;

(*b*) if the tenancy of any such house has not been extended under this Part of this Act, but the tenant, being entitled to acquire the freehold or an extended lease thereunder, either—

(i) before a copy of the certificate has been served on him, has given notice of his desire to have the freehold or an extended lease; or

(ii) not later than two months after a copy of the certificate is served on him, gives the landlord written notice, in the prescribed form, claiming to be so entitled;

then section 17 above shall apply as if the tenancy had been so extended;

(*c*) for the purposes of any application by the landlord under section 17 above in relation to property comprised in the certificate (whether the application is made by virtue of paragraph (*b*) above or otherwise), the certificate shall be conclusive that the ground specified in section 17(1) is established.

(2) Where by virtue of subsection (1)(*b*) above a tenancy of any property is to be treated as having been extended, then as regards that property the tenancy shall not terminate either by effluxion of time or in pursuance of any notice given by the landlord or the tenant or by the termination of a superior tenancy.

(3) In the case of a tenancy to which Part II of the Landlord and Tenant Act 1954 applies, subsections (1) and (2) above shall have effect where a certificate is given under section 57 of that Act as they have effect where a certificate is given under this section; but where by virtue of subsection (1)(*b*) above a tenancy is to be treated as having been extended, no compensation shall be payable under section 59 of that Act in respect of the tenancy or any immediate or derivative sub-tenancy.

(4) A Minister shall not give a certificate under this section with respect to any house, unless the landlord has given to the tenant of the house written notice stating—

(*a*) that the question of giving such a certificate is under consideration by that Minister; and

(*b*) that if within twenty-one days of the giving of the notice the tenant makes to that Minister representations in writing with respect to that question, they will be considered before the question is determined;

and if the tenant makes any such representations within those twenty-one days the Minister shall consider them before determining whether to give the certificate.

(5) This section applies—

(*a*) to any local authority, that is to say, the Mayor and commonalty and citizens of the City of London, [...] [the Inner London Education Authority, any joint authority established by Part IV of the Local Government Act 1985], any county council, borough council or district council, any joint board in which all the constituent authorities are local authorities within this paragraph and any combined police authority within the meaning of the Police Act 1964; and

(*b*) to the Commission for the New Towns and to any development corporation within the meaning of the New Towns Act 1965; and

[(*bb*) to the Development Board for Rural Wales.]

(*c*) to any university body, that is to say, any university, university college or college of a university, and for this purpose "college of a university" includes, in the case of a university organised on a collegiate basis, a constituent college or other society recognised by the university and, in the case of London University, a college incorporated in the university or a school of the university; and

[(*d*) to any Regional Health Authority, any Area Health Authority [any District Health Authority] [any Family Practitioner Committee] and any special health authority; and]

(*e*) to any body corporate established by or under any enactment for the purpose of carrying on under national ownership any industry or part of an industry or undertaking; and

(*f*) to any body not included above which is a harbour authority within the meaning of the Harbours Act 1964 or a statutory water undertaker for purposes of the Water Act 1945, but in respect only of the body's functions as harbour authority or statutory water undertaker.

(6) In subsection (1) above "relevant development," in relation to any body to which this section applies, means development for purposes (other than investment purposes) of that body, but in relation to a local authority includes any development to be undertaken, whether or not by that authority, ["in order to secure—

(*a*) the development or re-development of an area defined by a development plan under the Town and Country Planning Act 1971 as an area of comprehensive development; or

(*b*) the treatment as a whole, by development, re-development, or improvement, or partly by one and partly by another method, of any area in which the property is situated.]

However—

(*a*) the purposes of a county council or *county borough* council shall be taken to include the purposes of a police authority which is a committee of the council; and

(*b*) the purposes of a university body shall be taken to include the purposes of any related university body (a university and the colleges of that university within the meaning of subsection (5) (*c*) above being related to one another within the meaning of this paragraph); and

[(*c*) in the case of a Regional Health Authority, Area Health Authority [District Health Authority] [Family Practitioner Committee] or special health authority, the purposes of the [National Health Service Act 1977] shall be substituted for the purposes of the body].

(7) If it appears to the Minister of Housing and Local Government or to the Secretary of State that this section should apply to any body or description of bodies having functions of a public nature but not included above, he may by order direct that this section shall apply to that body or description of bodies.

(8) The power to make orders under subsection (7) above shall include power to vary or revoke any order made for the purposes of that subsection, and shall be exercisable by statutory instrument of which a draft shall be laid before Parliament.

AMENDMENTS

Subs. (5) (*bb*) was added by the Development of Rural Wales Act 1976, Sched. 7, para. 5; subs. (5)(*d*) and the proviso (*c*) to subs. (6), were amended by the National Health Service Reorganisation Act 1973, s.57, Sched. 4, and the inner set of words in square brackets in the latter substituted by the National Health Service Act 1977; the words in square brackets in subs. (6) before the proviso were amended by the Town and Country Planning Acts 1968, s.106 and Sched. 9, para. 75 and 1971, s.291(1) and Sched. 23, Part II; and the words in italics in the proviso (a) to subs. (6) were repealed by the Local Government Act 1972, Sched. 30. The words in square brackets in subs. 5(*a*) were added by the Local Government Act 1985, Sched. 14, para. 43, and those omitted repealed by *ibid.* Sched. 17. The words "District Health Authority" were inserted by the Health Services Act 1980, Sched. 1, Pt. 1, para. 18, and the words "Family Practitioner Committee" by the Family Practitioner Committees (Consequential Modifications) Order 1985 S.I. 1985 No. 39, Art. 5(*a*). 21–40

Reservation of future right to develop

29.—(1) Where a tenant of a house and premises acquires the freehold under this Part of this Act, the landlord being a local authority, there shall, if so required by the local authority, be included in the conveyance under section 8 above such covenants on the part of the tenant restricting the carrying out of development or clearing of land as are necessary to reserve the land for possible development by the authority. 21–41

(2) Where a tenant of a house and premises acquires an extended lease under this Part of this Act, the landlord being a local authority, such

covenants as are mentioned in subsection (1) above shall, if so required by the local authority, be included in the instrument extending the lease under section 14 above and, if so included, then in the terms of any subsequent tenancy at a low rent which is by virtue of section 3(3) above to be treated (with or without any intervening tenancies) as a single tenancy with that under the extended lease.

(3) Where a covenant is entered into to give effect to subsection (1) or (2) above, it shall be expressed to be so entered into, and Part I of Schedule 4 to this Act shall have effect with respect to the operation and enforcement of any covenant so entered into.

(4) Where a tenant of a house and premises acquired the freehold or an extended lease under this Part of this Act, the landlord being a local authority, and afterwards the local authority or any other person acquires compulsorily any interest in the property, then for the purpose of assessing compensation in accordance with the Land Compensation Act 1961 no account shall be taken of any increase in the value of that interest which is attributable to the carrying out of development in contravention of a covenant entered into to give effect to subsection (1) or (2) above, or to any prospect of carrying out any such development; and any compensation payable to a tenant under section 17 above shall be assessed without regard to any increase in the value of his interest which under this subsection would be disregarded on a compulsory purchase of that interest.

(5) For purposes of this section "local authority" means a local authority as defined in section 28(5)(*a*) above.

(6) Subsections (1) to (4) above shall have effect in relation—

(*a*) to the Commission for the New Towns and to any development corporation within the meaning of the New Towns Act 1965; and

(*b*) to any university body as defined in section 28(5)(*c*) above;

as if any reference in those subsections or in Part I of Schedule 4 to this Act to a local authority were a reference to that Commission, corporation or university body; but a university body shall not require a covenant to be entered into under this section, unless they have first obtained the consent of the Secretary of State.

[(6A) Subsections (1) to (4) above shall have effect in relation to the Development Board for Rural Wales as if any reference in those subsections or in Part I of Schedule 4 to this Act to a local authority were a reference to the Board.]

[(6B) Where the landlord is a university body, the possible development for which land may be reserved by a covenant entered into to give effect to subsection (1) or (2) above includes development by a related university body (within the meaning of section 28 (6)(*b*) above).]

(7) Part II of Schedule 4 to this Act shall have effect to enable property

to be re-acquired compulsorily where it is subject to a covenant entered into to give effect to subsection (1) above with the Commission for the New Towns [the Development Board for Rural Wales] or a university body.

(8) This section shall apply, with the necessary adaptations where a new tenancy is granted in satisfaction of the right to an extended lease under this Part of this Act, as it applies where a lease is extended in accordance with this Part of this Act.

AMENDMENTS

Subs. (6A) and the words in square brackets in subs. (7) were added by the Development of Rural Wales Act 1976, Sched. 7, para. 5. Subs. (6B) was added by the Housing Act 1980, s.141 and Sched. 21. **21–42**

Reservation of right of pre-emption in new town or overspill area

30.—(1) Where a tenant of a house and premises acquires the freehold under this Part of this Act, the landlord being a body to which this section applies, there shall, if so required by the landlord, be included in the conveyance under section 8 above the following covenants on the part of the tenant, that is to say— **21–43**

- (*a*) a covenant that no tenancy of the property comprised in the conveyance or any part of that property shall be granted except with the consent in writing of the landlord; and
- (*b*) such covenant as appears to the landlord to be requisite for securing that, in the event of any proposal to sell that property or any part of it, the landlord will have a right of pre-emption at the price mentioned in subsection (4) below.

(2) Where a tenant of a house and premises acquires an extended lease under this Part of this Act, the landlord being a body to which this section applies, such covenants as are mentioned in subsection (1) above shall, if so required by the landlord, be included in the instrument extending the lease under section 14 above and, if so included, then in the terms of any subsequent tenancy at a low rent which is by virtue of section 3(3) above to be treated (with or without intervening tenancies) as a single tenancy with that under the extended lease.

(3) Where a covenant is entered into to give effect to subsection (1) or (2) above, it shall be expressed to be so entered into, and Part I of Schedule 4 to this Act shall have effect, with respect to the operation and enforcement of any covenant so entered into as it applies in the case of a covenant entered into with the same body to give effect to section 29(1) or (2) above.

(4) The price referred to in subsection (1)(*b*) above, in relation to an interest in any property, is a sum equal to (and in default of agreement, to be determined in the like manner as) the compensation which would be

payable for that interest if acquired by the execution, on such date as may be determined in accordance with the covenant, of a vesting declaration under Schedule 4 to this Act.

(5) Section 19 of the Landlord and Tenant Act 1927 (covenants not to assign etc. without licence or consent) shall not have effect in relation to any covenant entered into to give effect to subsection (2) above.

(6) This section shall apply, with the necessary adaptations, where a new tenancy is granted in satisfaction of the right to an extended lease under this Part of this Act, as it applies where a lease is extended in accordance with this Part of this Act.

(7) This section applies—

(*a*) to the Commission for the New Towns [to the Development Board for Rural Wales] and to a development corporation within the meaning of the New Towns Act 1965; and

(*b*) in respect of housing provided by them by virtue of section 5 of the Town Development Act 1952 (which authorises a council to exercise its powers for the purpose of relieving congestion or over-population outside their area), the council or any receiving district for purposes of that Act, [. . .].

AMENDMENT

21–44 The words in square brackets in subs. (7) were added by the Development of Rural Wales Act 1976, Sched. 7, para. 5. The words omitted from that subs. were repealed by the Housing (Consequential Provisions) Act 1985, Sched. 1.

Ecclesiastical property

21–45 **31.**—(1) The provisions of this section shall have effect as regards as operation of this Part of this Act of tenancies (including subtenancies) of ecclesiastical property, that is to say, property belonging to a capitular body within the meaning of the Cathedrals Measure 1963 or belonging to an ecclesiastical benefice; and in this section "ecclesiastical; landlord" means the capitular body or incumbent having an interest as landlord in ecclesiastical property.

(2) In relation to an interest of an ecclesiastical landlord, the consent of the Church Commissioners shall be required to sanction—

(*a*) the provisions to be contained in a conveyance in accordance with section 10 above, or in a lease granting a new tenancy under section 14, and the price or rent payable, except as regards matters determined by the court [a leasehold valuation tribunal] or the Lands Tribunal;

(*b*) any exercise of the ecclesiastical landlord's rights under section 17 above, except as aforesaid, and any agreement for the payment of compensation to a tenant in accordance with that section without an application thereunder;

(*c*) any grant of a tenancy in satisfaction of the right to an extended lease under this Part of this Act;

and the Church Commissioners shall be entitled to appear and be heard in any proceedings under this Part of this Act to which an ecclesiastical landlord is a party or in which he is entitled to appear and be heard.

(3) Where the ecclesiastical property forms part of the endowment of a cathedral church, any sum received by the capitular body by way of the price payable for the property under section 9 above, or by way of compensation under any provision of this Part of this Act providing for compensation to be recovered by or awarded to a landlord, shall be treated as part of that endowment; and the powers conferred by sections 21 and 23 of the Cathedrals Measure 1963 in relation to the investment in the acquisition of land of moneys forming part of the endowment of a cathedral church shall extend to the application of any such moneys in the payment of compensation in accordance with section 17 above (whether possession is obtained under that section or without an application thereunder).

(4) In the case of ecclesiastical property belonging to an ecclesiastical benefice—

(*a*) no consent or concurrence other than that of the Church Commissioners under subsection (2) above shall be required to a disposition under this Part of this Act of the incumbent's interest (including a grant of a tenancy in satisfaction of the right to an extended lease);

(*b*) during a vacancy in the benefice, the abeyance shall not affect the operation of this Part of this Act, but the place of the incumbent shall be taken by the person authorised to exercise in his place the powers conferred on him by the Ecclesiastical Leasing Acts, and the Ecclesiastical Commissioners (Powers) Measure 1936 (together with section 7 of the Vacancies in Sees Measure 1959) shall apply accordingly;

(*c*) any sum receivable by the incumbent by way of the price payable for the property under section 9 above, or of any such compensation as is mentioned in subsection (3) above, shall be paid to the Church Commissioners to be applied for purposes for which the proceeds of a sale by agreement of the property would be applicable under any enactment or Measure authorising such a sale or disposing of the proceeds of such a sale, and any sum required for the payment of compensation as mentioned in subsection (3) above may be paid by the Church Commissioners on behalf of the incumbent out of any moneys in their hands;

(*d*) the revenues and possessions of the benefice shall stand charged with the repayment of any sum expended by the Church Commissioners in pursuance of paragraph (*c*) above.

(5) This Part of this Act shall apply to land belonging to an ecclesiastical benefice, and this section shall have effect in relation thereto, notwithstanding that the patronage of the benefice belongs to Her Majesty in right of the Crown or the Duchy of Lancaster or to the Duchy of Cornwall.

AMENDMENT

21–46 The words in square brackets in subs. (2)(*a*) were added by the Housing Act 1980, s.142 and Sched. 22.

Saving for National Trust

21–47 **32.** This Part of this Act shall not prejudice the operation of section 21 of the National Trust Act 1907, and accordingly a person shall not be entitled under this Part of this Act to acquire the freehold of property if an interest in the property is under that section vested inalienably in the National Trust for Places of Historic Interest or Natural Beauty.

Crown land

21–48 **33.**—(1) In the case of a tenancy from the Crown this Part of this Act shall apply in favour of the tenant as in the case of any other tenancy if there has ceased to be a Crown interest in the land, and as against a landlord holding a tenancy from the Crown shall apply also if either—

(*a*) his subtenant is seeking an extended lease and the landlord, or a superior landlord holding a tenancy from the Crown, has a sufficient interest to grant it and is entitled to do so without the concurrence of the appropriate authority; or

(*b*) the appropriate authority notifies the landlord that as regards any Crown interest affected the authority will grant or concur in granting the freehold or extended lease.

(2) For purposes of this section "tenancy from the Crown" means a tenancy of land in which there is, or has during the subsistence of the tenancy been, a Crown interest superior to the tenancy, and "Crown interest" and "the appropriate authority" in relation to a Crown interest mean respectively—

(*a*) an interest comprised in the Crown Estate, and the Crown Estate Commissioners;

(*b*) an interest belonging to Her Majesty in right of the Duchy of Lancaster, and the Chancellor of the Duchy;

(*c*) an interest belonging to the Duchy of Cornwall, and such person as the Duke of Cornwall or the possessor for the time being of the Duchy appoints;

(*d*) any other interest belonging to a government department or held on behalf of Her Majesty for the purposes of a government department, and the Minister in charge of that department.

(3) The restriction imposed by section 3(2) of the Crown Estate Act 1961 on the term for which a lease may be granted by the Crown Estate Commissioners shall not apply where the lease is granted by way of extension of a long tenancy at a low rent and it appears to the Crown Estate Commissioners that, if the tenancy were not a tenancy from the Crown, there would be a right to an extended lease under this Part of this Act.

(4) Where, in the case of land belonging to Her Majesty in right of the Duchy of Lancaster or to the Duchy of Cornwall, it appears to the appropriate authority that a tenant under a long lease at a low rent would, if the tenancy were not a tenancy from the Crown, be entitled to an extended lease under this Part of this Act, then a lease corresponding to that to which the tenant would be so entitled may be granted to take effect wholly or partly out of the Crown interest by the same person and with the same formalities as in the case of any other lease of such land.

(5) In the case of land belonging to the Duchy of Cornwall, the purposes authorised by section 8 of the Duchy of Cornwall Management Act 1863 for the advancement of parts of such gross sums as are therein mentioned shall include the payment to tenants of sums corresponding to those which, if the tenancies were not tenancies from the Crown, would be payable by way of compensation under section 17 above.

[Exclusion of certain shared ownership leases

33A.—The provisions of Schedule 4A to this Act shall have effect to exclude certain shared ownership leases from the operation of this Part of this Act.] 21–49

AMENDMENT

This section was added by the Housing and Planning Act 1986, Sched. 4, para. 5. 21–50

Transitional

Tenancies terminated since 8th December 1964, or subject to early termination

34.—(1) Where, before or after the passing of this Act, but after the 8th December 1964, a long tenancy at a low rent of a house ("the former long tenancy") has terminated at or after its term date, then subject to the provisions of this section there shall be treated for purposes of this Part of this Act as a long tenancy at a low rent— 21–51

(*a*) any tenancy which was granted by way of continuation of the former long tenancy but is not or was not a tenancy at a low rent; and (*b*) any statutory tenancy arising by virtue of Part I of the Landlord and Tenant Act 1954 or of the Rent Acts on the termination of the former long tenancy or of any tenancy granted (or treated by implication of law as granted) by way of continuation of it.

For purposes of this subsection a tenancy granted to the tenant of the house under a tenancy granted by way of continuation of the former long tenancy, or to the person retaining possession of the house by virtue of any such statutory tenancy as aforesaid, shall be regarded as granted by way of continuation of the former long tenancy.

(2) A notice of a person's desire to have the freehold or an extended lease of a house and premises, if given by virtue of subsection (1) above, may be given before the appointed day, but shall be of no effect if given more than three months after the day this Act is passed.

(3) A notice of a person's desire to have the freehold or an extended lease of a house and premises may also be given before the appointed day if it is given in respect of a tenancy of which the term date falls within twelve months after the day this Act is passed, or which is to be or can be terminated within those twelve months either by notice given by the landlord or by the operation of section 26 or 28 of the Landlord and Tenant Act 1954 in relation to a request or agreement for a new tenancy made before this Act is passed.

(4) Where by virtue of subsection (2) or (3) above a notice is given before the appointed day—

(*a*) it shall contain the particulars required by Schedule 3 to this Act, but need not be in the prescribed form;

(*b*) if it is given in respect of a sub-tenancy, copies of it shall be served on the same persons other than the recipient as in the case of a notice given after the appointed day;

(*c*) the landlord shall not be required to take any further proceedings before the appointed day and no notice in reply shall be required earlier than one month after the appointed day, but subject to that and to section 35 below, as from the appointed day, the notice shall have effect as if all the provisions of this Part of this Act had come into force on the day it is passed.

(5) In relation to a notice given by virtue of subsection (2) or (3) above, Part I of Schedule 3 to this Act shall have effect from the day it is passed; but in a case where (by virtue of those subsections or otherwise) a person gives notice, within three months after that day, of his desire to have the freehold or an extended lease and does so in respect of a tenancy falling within subsection (1) above or of any such tenancy as is mentioned in subsection (3), Part I of Schedule 3 shall not have effect to invalidate the notice by reason either—

(*a*) that it is given more than two months after the landlord's notice terminating the tenancy has been given under section 4 or 25 of the Landlord and Tenant Act 1954; or

(*b*) that it is given after a tenant has made a request for a new tenancy under section 26 of that Act, or is given during the subsistence of an agreement for a future tenancy to which section 28 of that Act applies, not being an agreement entered into after the passing of this Act.

(6) Where subsection (1) above applies to a tenancy, this Part of this Act shall have effect in relation to any claim by the tenant to acquire the freehold or an extended lease, and in relation to any new tenancy granted under section 14 above, subject to the following modifications:—

(*a*) the provisions to be contained in a conveyance in accordance with section 10 above, or in a lease granting a new tenancy under section 14, shall be determined by reference to the terms of the former long tenancy as they applied immediately before its termination and to the circumstances generally of that tenancy; and

(*b*) references to the term date of the existing tenancy, or to the original term date, shall have effect as references to the term date of the former tenancy.

(7) Where a statutory tenancy of a house has arisen by virtue of Part I of the Landlord and Tenant Act 1954 and the terms of the tenancy include the carrying out of initial repairs, but (before or after it arose) a notice is by virtue of this section given by the tenant of his desire to have the freehold or an extended lease, then the rights and obligations under the statutory tenancy in relation to initial repairs (together with any order of the court made with respect thereto before the relevant time) shall be suspended during the currency of the notice, except in so far as the court on the application of the landlord or of the tenant may otherwise order; and

(*a*) if in pursuance of the notice the tenant acquires the freehold, the price payable for the house and premises shall be adjusted as may be proper (regard being had to the rent paid and to be paid under the statutory tenancy) so as to take account of any initial repairs carried out by the landlord before the relevant time, of any order or agreement for the further carrying out by him of any initial repairs thereafter and of any payments for tenant's accrued repairs received by the landlord; or

(*b*) if in pursuance of the notice the tenant acquires an extended lease, there shall be payable by the tenant to the landlord as if it were due under the statutory tenancy on its termination such sum, if any, as may be proper so as to take account of the matters aforesaid (regard being had to the rent paid under the statutory tenancy and to any terms of the new tenancy relating to repairs).

(8) Where a statutory tenancy of a house has arisen as mentioned in subsection (1)(*b*) above, and (before or after it arose) a notice is by virtue of this section given by the tenant of his desire to have the freehold or an extended lease, then so long as the notice has effect the tenancy shall continue, and on the tenant's death or bankruptcy shall devolve, as a contractual tenancy would, and the rights and obligations arising from the notice shall continue and devolve accordingly; but this shall not affect any right to retain possession by virtue of the Rent Acts which arises on a death.

Proceedings and orders under Landlord and Tenant Act 1954

21–52 **35.**—(1) Where a person's notice of his desire to have the freehold or an extended lease under this Part of this Act is given as mentioned in section 34(5)(*a*) or (*b*) above, but has effect by virtue of that subsection, then the following provisions of this section shall apply; and in those provisions "claim" and "claimant" mean that notice and the person giving it or for the time being entitled to the rights under it of the person giving it.

(2) On the making of the claim and, if any application has been made to the court under the Landlord and Tenant Act 1954 in respect of a notice given by the landlord or a request by the claimant for a new tenancy, on the claimant lodging a copy of the claim in the court, any such notice or request under that Act and anything done in pursuance thereof (including any such application and any order resulting therefrom) shall cease to have effect, except as otherwise provided by this section:

Provided that this shall not affect any order as to costs (whether of proceedings in the court or of any appeal) or preclude the making of such an order.

(3) The making of the claim shall not affect the operation—

(*a*) of any landlords' notice containing proposals for a statutory tenancy where all the terms of the statutory tenancy have been agreed or determined in accordance with section 7 of the Landlord and Tenant Act 1954; or

(*b*) of any order of the court under section 29 of that Act for the grant of a new tenancy; or

(*c*) of any agreement for a future tenancy to which section 28 of that Act applies;

but subject to the provisions of that Act and of section 34 above, the notice, order or agreement, and any statutory tenancy or tenancy arising or granted under it, shall remain unaffected by the claim unless and until effect is given to the claim.

(4) Where either—

(*a*) the landlord has made an application to the court for, or has obtained, an order for the claimant to give up possession on the ground specified in section 12(1)(*a*) (redevelopment) of the Landlord and Tenant Act 1954, and the claim is for an extended lease; or

(*b*) the landlord has made an application to the court for, or has obtained, such an order on the ground specified in paragraph 1(*e*) (residence for landlord or his family) of Schedule 3 to that Act;

then if the landlord gives notice of his willingness to pay compensation and lodges a copy of it in the court, the application may be proceeded with or, as the case may be, the order shall have effect as if the claim had not been made.

(5) Where either—

(*a*) the court has refused an order for the grant of a new tenancy under Part II of the Landlord and Tenant Act 1954 on the ground specified in section 30(1)(*f*) (redevelopment), and the claim is for an extended lease; or

(*b*) the court has refused an order as aforesaid in accordance with section 30(1)(*g*) on the ground of the landlord's intention to occupy the holding as his residence;

then if the landlord gives notice of his willingness to pay compensation, the tenancy shall terminate in accordance with Part II of that Act as if the claim had not been made.

(6) Where the claimant's tenancy is terminated by virtue of subsection (4) or (5) above, and apart from those subsections (and sections 17 and 18 above) he would have been entitled to acquire the freehold or an extended lease in pursuance of the claim, he shall be entitled to recover from the landlord, in lieu of any compensation under the Landlord and Tenant Act 1927 or under section 37 of the Landlord and Tenant Act 1954, the like compensation as is payable where a claim to acquire the freehold or an extended lease is overridden under section 17 or 18 above.

(7) If the claimant's right to compensation under subsection (6) above is disputed, he may apply to the court for an order declaring that he is entitled to the compensation; and any compensation under that subsection shall in default of agreement be assessed, and may be recovered, in like manner as compensation under section 17 or 18 above.

(8) References in this section to the landlord giving notice of his willingness to pay compensation shall be construed as references to his giving to the claimant (whether before or after the making of the claim) written notice that he is willing to pay compensation in accordance with subsection (6) above if so required by that subsection; but a notice of a landlord's willingness to pay compensation shall be of no effect if it is given after the tenancy in question would have terminated but for the claim, or if it is given more than one month after the day on which the claim is made.

(9) In this section references to the landlord shall be construed as references to the landlord proceeding under Part I or II, as the case may be of the Landlord and Tenant Act 1954.

Relief in respect of mortgages etc. on landlord's estate

21–53 **36.**—(1) Where at the passing of this Act—

(*a*) a house is held on a long tenancy not having more than twenty years unexpired, or on a long tenancy capable of being determined within twenty years by notice given by the landlord; and

(*b*) the estate of the immediate or a superior landlord is charged to secure payment of any sum (otherwise than by way of rentcharge), whether or not the landlord is personally liable as principal or otherwise for the payment of that sum;

then on an application under subsection (2) or (3) below the court may make such order authorised by the subsection as the court thinks proper for the purpose of avoiding or mitigating any financial hardship that might otherwise be caused by the rights conferred on tenants by this Part of this Act.

(2) In any of the following cases, that is to say,—

(*a*) where the landlord proposes during the tenancy (including any extension thereof under this Act) to sell or realise any property which is subject to the charge, or a tenant of the house has given notice under this Part of this Act of his desire to have the freehold;

(*b*) where during the tenancy (including any such extension) the person entitled to the benefit of the charge has taken any steps to enforce the charge or demanded payment of the sum thereby secured or, if the house or any other property subject to the charge is subject also to another charge created or arising before the commencement of this Part of this Act, a person entitled to the benefit of the other charge has taken any steps to enforce the other charge or demanded payment of the sum thereby secured;

the court may on the application of the landlord make an order providing for all or any of the following:—

(i) for discharging or modifying any liability in respect of the sum secured by the charge, whether of the landlord or of persons liable jointly with him or as surety for him;

(ii) for discharging or modifying the terms of the charge whether as respects the house or any other property subject to the charge, or the terms of any collateral charge;

(iii) for restricting the exercise of any right or remedy in respect of any such liability or charge.

(3) In any of the cases mentioned in subsection (2)(*a*) and (*b*) above the court may on the application of the person entitled to the benefit of the charge make an order providing for all or any of the following:—

(*a*) for discharging or modifying the terms of any prior charge, whether as respects the house or any other property subject to the charge;

(*b*) for restricting the exercise of any right or remedy in respect of any prior charge on the house or other property subject to the charge.

(4) Any order under this section may be made either unconditionally or subject to such terms and conditions including conditions with respect to the payment of money, as the court may think just and equitable to impose.

(5) Where steps are taken in a court other than the county court to enforce a charge or recover any sum thereby secured, that other court shall have the like powers under this section in relation to that or any other charge as the county court would have in consequence of those steps being taken or, if an application under this section is pending in the county court, may on such terms as the other court thinks just suspend the proceedings for the enforcement of the charge or recovery of the said sum or direct that they be transferred to the county court.

Construction

Interpretation of Part 1

37.—(1) For the purposes of this Part of this Act— 21–54

(*a*) "the appointed day" means the day appointed for the coming into force of the provisions of this Part of this Act other than sections 34 to 36, and references to the commencement of this Part of this Act shall be construed as referring to the commencement of those provisions;

(*b*) "incumbrance" and "tenant's incumbrance" have, subject to section 12(8) above, the meanings assigned to them by section 8;

(*c*) "notice to quit" means notice to terminate a tenancy (whether a periodical tenancy or a tenancy for a term of years certain) given in accordance with the provisions (whether express or implied) of that tenancy;

(*d*) "relevant time" means, in relation to a person's claim to acquire the freehold or an extended lease under this Part of this Act, the time when he gives notice in accordance with this Act of his desire to have it;

(*f*) "tenancy" means a tenancy at law or in equity, but does not include a tenancy at will, nor any interest created by way of security and liable to termination by the exercise of any right of redemption or otherwise, nor any interest created by way of trust under a settlement, and "demise" shall be construed accordingly;

(*g*) "term date," in relation to a tenancy granted for a term of years certain, means the date of expiry of that term, and "extended term date" and "original term date" mean respectively the term date of a tenancy with and without an extension under this Part of this Act.

(2) A tenancy to which section 19(2) of the Landlord and Tenant Act 1954 applies shall be treated for purposes of this Part of this Act as granted to expire at the date which is the term date for purposes of that Act (that is to say, the first date after the commencement of that Act on which, apart from that Act, the tenancy could have been brought to an end by notice to quit given by the landlord).

(3) Subject to subsection (2) above, where under section 3(2) of this Act a tenancy created or arising as a tenancy from year to year or other periodical tenancy is to be treated as a long tenancy, the term date of that tenancy shall be taken to be the date (if any) at which the tenancy is to terminate by virtue of a notice to quit given by the landlord before the relevant time, or else the earliest date at which it could at that time (in accordance with its terms and apart from any enactment) be brought to an end by a notice to quit given by the landlord.

(4) Subject to subsection (2) above, in the case of a tenancy granted to continue as a periodical tenancy after the expiration of a term of years certain, or to continue as a periodical tenancy if not terminated at the expiration of such a term, any question whether the tenancy is at any time to be treated for purposes of this Part of this Act as a long tenancy, and (if so) with what term date, shall be determined as it would be if there had been two tenancies, as follows—

(*a*) one granted to expire at the earliest time (at or after the expiry of the said term of years) at which the tenancy could (in accordance with its terms and apart from any enactment) be brought to an end by notice to quit given by the landlord; and

(*b*) the other granted to commence at the expiration of the first (and not being one to which subsection (2) above applies).

(5) References in this Part of this Act to a tenant occupying a house as his residence shall be construed in accordance with section 1(2) above; but no reference in this Part of this Act to a person occupying property as his residence shall be taken to extend to any occupation of a company or other artificial person nor, where the tenant is a corporation sole, shall the corporator, while in occupation, be treated as occupying as tenant.

(6) [Section 25(1), (2) and (4) of the Rent Act 1977] shall apply to the ascertainment for purposes of this Part of this Act of the rateable value of a house and premises or any other property as they apply to the ascertainment of that of a dwelling-house for purposes of that Act.

(7) For purposes of this Part of this Act an order of a court is to be treated as becoming final—

(*a*) if not appealed against, on the expiration of the time for bringing an appeal; or

(*b*) if appealed against and not set aside in consequence of the appeal, at the time when the appeal and any further appeal is disposed of by the determination of it and the expiration of the time for bringing a further appeal (if any) or by its being abandoned or otherwise ceasing to have effect.

AMENDMENTS

Subs. (1)(*e*) was repealed by the Rent Act, 1968, s.117(5) and Sched. 17. The words in square brackets in subs. (6) were substituted by the Rent Act 1977, Sched. 23, para. 44. **21–55**

PART II

AMENDMENTS OF OTHER ACTS

• • • • • •

Amendment of Places of Worship (Enfranchisement) Act 1920

40.—(1) In section 1(1) of the Places of Worship (Enfranchisement) Act **21–56**
1920 after the words "place of worship," where first occurring, there shall be inserted the words "or, in connexion with a place of worship, for the purpose of a minister's house"; and accordingly in section 5 of that Act—

(*a*) in the definition of "place of worship" for the words "caretaker's house or minister's house" there shall be substituted the words "or caretaker's house"; and

(*b*) in the definition of "trustees" after the words "place of worship" there shall be inserted the words "or minister's house."

(2) In section 1(1) of the Places of Worship (Enfranchisement) Act 1920 after paragraph (*a*) of the proviso there shall be inserted as a new paragraph (*aa*) the following paragraph:—

"(*aa*) where the person entitled to the freehold or an intermediate reversion requires that underlying minerals be excepted, the trustees shall not be entitled to acquire his interest in the minerals if proper provision is made for the support of the premises as they have been enjoyed during the lease and in accordance with the terms of the lease and of the trust; and."

(3) After section 1(1) of the Places of Worship (Enfranchisement) Act 1920 there shall be inserted as a new subsection (1A):—

"(1A) Where the residence house of a benefice is held by the incumbent under a lease to which this Act applies, this Act shall have effect (with any necessary modifications) in relation to the enlargement of the incumbent's leasehold interest into a fee simple, and in relation to the estate so acquired, as it would have effect if the residence house were vested for that interest in trustees; and the powers and provisions of the Parsonages Measure 1938 (as amended by any subsequent enactment) relating to the purchase of houses for parsonages shall apply for and in relation to the acquisition under this Act of the freehold reversion."

(4) In section 2 of the Places of Worship (Enfranchisement) Act 1920 for the words from "the Lands Clauses Acts," where first occurring, to the end of paragraph (*a*) there shall be substituted—

"Part I of the Compulsory Purchase Act 1965 shall apply as if the trustees were an authority authorised to acquire the premises by virtue of a compulsory purchase order, made under the Acquisition of Land (Authorisation Procedure) Act 1946; but in relation to any acquisition under this Act the following provisions shall have effect:—

(*a*) in Part I of the Compulsory Purchase Act 1965 section 4 (time limit for acquisition) shall not apply, and for purposes of the said Part I "land" shall include easements in or relating to land;"

and accordingly in the Places of Worship (Enfranchisement) Act 1920 there shall be omitted the definition in section 5 of "the county court" and the Schedule (which adapted for purposes of that Act the enactments originally applied by section 2, and in particular made in relation to re-sales special provision about the right to pre-emption conferred by the Lands Clauses Acts but not by the Compulsory Purchase Act 1965).

(5) Section 4 of the Places of Worship (Enfranchisement) Act 1920 (under which the trusts of a place of worship may be enforced after enfranchisement by the Charity Commissioners, and if the trusts are not observed, the Commissions may require the land to be sold) shall be omitted.

(6) In section 5 of the Places of Worship (Enfranchisement) Act 1920, in the definition of "freehold reversion," there shall be omitted the words from "and, where" onwards (being words relating to copyhold land and land of customary tenure).

(7) In accordance with the provisions of this section the Places of Worship (Enfranchisement) Act 1920 shall, subject to subsection (8) below, have effect as set out in Schedule 6 to this Act.

(8) This section and the repeals made by Part II of Schedule 7 to this

Act shall not affect the operation of the Places of Worship (Enfranchisement) Act 1920 where an interest has been acquired, or notice to treat for its acquisition has been served, under that Act before this section comes into force, except that section 4 of that Act shall cease to have effect for any purpose.

Short title, repeals, extent and commencement

41.—(1) This Act may be cited as the Leasehold Reform Act 1967. **21–57**

(2) The enactments mentioned in Schedule 7 to this Act are hereby repealed to the extent specified in the third column of that Schedule, but subject to the savings mentioned at the end of Parts I and II of the Schedule.

(3) This Act shall not extend to Scotland or Northern Ireland.

(4) Sections 34 to 36 of this Act shall come into force on the day it is passed; and, subject to section 34, the other provisions of Part I shall come into force on such day as the Minister of Housing and Local Government and the Secretary of State may appoint by order made by them jointly by statutory instrument, which shall be laid before Parliament after being made.

(5) Part II of this Act shall come into force at the end of one month following the day on which this Act is passed.

SCHEDULES

Section 5

SCHEDULE 1

ENRANCHISEMENT OR EXTENSION BY SUB-TENANTS

General

1.—(1) Where a person (in this Schedule referred to as "the claimant") gives notice of his desire to have the freehold or an extended lease of a house and premises under Part I of this Act, and does so in respect of a sub-tenancy (in this Schedule referred to as "the tenancy in possession"), then except as otherwise provided by this Schedule— **21–58**

(*a*) the rights and obligations of the landlord under Part I of this Act shall, so far as their interests are affected, be rights and obligations respectively of the estate owner in respect of the fee simple and of each of the persons in whom is vested a concurrent tenancy superior to the tenancy in possession (and references to the landlord shall apply accordingly); and

(*b*) the proceedings arising out of the notice, whether for resisting or giving effect to the claim to acquire the freehold or extended lease, shall be conducted, on behalf of all the persons referred to in (*a*) above, by and through that one of them who is identified by this Schedule as "the reversioner."

(2) Where there is a tenancy reversionary on a tenancy in respect of which a person gives notice as aforesaid, then (except in so far as special provision is made for such a reversionary tenancy) this Schedule shall apply as if the reversionary tenancy were a concurrent tenancy intermediate between the tenancy in possession and any interest superior to it.

(3) In the following provisions of this Schedule the persons for whom the reversioner is by this paragraph authorised to act are referred to as "other landlords"; and in this Schedule references to superior interests mean the estate in fee simple and any tenancy superior (or treated by sub-paragraph (2) above as superior) to the inferior interest in question.

2. Subject to paragraph 3 below, "the reversioner" shall be—

(*a*) if any person has a tenancy of the house carrying an expectation of possession of thirty years or more, that person or, if there is more than one, that one of them to whose tenancy the other tenancies are superior;

(*b*) if there is no such tenancy, the estate owner in respect of the fee simple of the house.

3.—(1) If it appears to the court, on an application made by any of the persons having an interest superior to the tenancy in possession,—

(*a*) that the respective interests of those persons, the absence or incapacity of the person designated by paragraph 2 above or other special circumstances require that one of the other landlords should act as the reversioner instead of that person; or

(*b*) that the person so designated is unwilling to act as the reversioner, and that one of the other landlords could appropriately replace him and is willing to do so; or

(*c*) that by reason of complications in the title paragraph 2 above is inapplicable;

the court may, on such terms and conditions as it thinks fit, appoint such person as it thinks fit to be the reversioner.

(2) The court may also, on the application of any of the other landlords or of the claimant, remove the reversioner and appoint another person in his place, if it appears to the court proper to do so by reason of any delay or default, actual or apprehended, on the part of the reversioner.

4.—(1) Without prejudice to the generality of paragraph 1 above, the reversioner may on behalf and in the name of the other landlords—

(*a*) execute any conveyance to give effect to section 8 of this Act, or any lease to give effect to section 14; and

(*b*) take or defend any legal proceedings under Part I of this Act in respect of matters arising out of the claimant's notice.

(2) Subject to paragraphs 5 and 6 below, in relation to all matters within the authority given to him by this Schedule the reversioner's acts shall be binding on the other landlords and on their interests in the house and premises or any other property; but in the event of dispute either the reversioner or any of the other landlords may apply to the court for directions as to the manner in which he should act on the matter in dispute.

(3) If any of the other landlords cannot be found, or his identity cannot be ascertained, the reversioner shall apply to the court for directions, and the court may make such order in the matter as it thinks proper with a view to giving effect to the rights of the claimant and protecting the interests of other persons; but subject to the directions of the court—

(*a*) the reversioner shall proceed as in other cases;

(*b*) a conveyance or lease executed by the reversioner on behalf of that landlord by such description as will identify the interest intended to be conveyed or bound shall be of the same effect as if executed in his name;

(*c*) if the freehold is to be conveyed to the claimant, any sum paid as the price for that landlord's interest shall be paid into court.

(4) The reversioner, if he acts in good faith and with reasonable care and diligence, shall not be liable to any of the other landlords for any loss or damage caused by any act or omission in the exercise or intended exercise of the authority given to him by this Schedule.

5.—(1) Notwithstanding anything in paragraph 4(2) above, any of the other landlords shall be entitled, if he so desires, to be separately represented in any legal proceedings in which his title to any property comes in question, or in any legal proceedings relating to the price payable for the house and premises under section 9 of this Act.

(2) For the purpose of deducing, evidencing or verifying his title to any property, any of the other landlords, on giving written notice to the reversioner and to the claimant, may deal directly with the claimant, if he objects to disclosing his title to the reversioner, and he shall deal directly with the claimant if the claimant by written notice given to him and to the reversioner so requires.

(3) For the purpose of agreeing the price payable for his interest under section 9 of this Act, any of the other landlords, on giving written notice to the reversioner and to the claimant,

may deal directly with the claimant; and whether he does that or not, he may require the reversioner to apply to [a leasehold valuation tribunal] for the price to be determined by [a leasehold valuation tribunal].

(4) Any of the other landlords shall be entitled to require that the price payable for his interest (or so much of it as is payable to him) shall be paid by the claimant to him or to a person authorised by him to receive it, instead of to the reversioner; but if, after being given proper notice of the time and place fixed for completion with the claimant, neither he nor a person so authorised attends to receive payment, and he has not made, and notified the reversioner of, other agreements with the claimant to receive payment, the reversioner shall be authorised to receive it for him and the reversioner's written receipt for the amount payable shall be a complete discharge to the claimant.

(5) It shall be the duty of each of the other landlords—

(*a*) subject to sub-paragraphs (2) and (3) above, to give the reversioner all such information and assistance as he may reasonably require; and

(*b*) after being given proper notice of the time and place fixed for completion with the claimant (if the claimant is acquiring the freehold), to ensure that all deeds and other documents that ought on his part to be delivered to the claimant on completion are available for the purpose, including in the case of registered land the land certificate and any other documents necessary to perfect the claimant's title;

and, if any of the other landlords fails to do so, he shall indemnify the reversioner against any liability incurred by the reversioner in consequence of the failure.

(6) Each of the other landlords shall make such contribution as may be just to the costs and expenses incurred by the reversioner and not recoverable or not recovered from the claimant.

6.—(1) The authority given by this Schedule to the reversioner shall not extend to the bringing of proceedings under section 17 or 18 of this Act on behalf of any of the other landlords, or preclude any of the other landlords from bringing proceedings under that section on his own behalf; and (without prejudice to the operation of paragraph 1(2) above) a person entitled to a tenancy reversionary on the tenancy in possession may make an application under section 17 (by virtue of subsection (4)) or section 18 as a landlord.

(2) Sections 29 and 30 of this Act shall apply, and apply only, where the authority entitled to require the covenant under the section is the estate owner in respect of the fee simple and there is no tenancy carrying an expectation of possession of thirty years or more.

(3) For purposes of section 3(6) of this Act separate tenancies shall be deemed to be tenancies with the same landlord if the immediate landlord is the same.

Enfranchisement

7.—(1) Where a conveyance is executed to give effect to section 8 of this Act— 21–59

(*a*) section 10 shall have effect in relation to rights and restrictions arising by virtue of any tenancy superior to the tenancy in possession (or by virtue of an agreement collateral to such a tenancy), so far as they are directly or indirectly to the benefit of or enforceable against the claimant during the tenancy in possession, as if they arose by virtue of that tenancy; and

(*b*) [subject to paragraph (7A] a separate price shall be payable in accordance with section 9 for each of the interests superior to the tenancy in possession, and [. . .] section 9 shall apply to the computation of that price with such modifications as are appropriate to relate it to a sale of the interest in question subject to any tenancies intermediate between that interest and the tenancy in possession, together with tenant's incumbrances relative to those tenancies; and

(*c*) so much of section 11 as relates to the application of the purchase price for redemption of rentcharges *or other rents* shall apply only to the price payable for the estate in fee simple; and

(*d*) so much of sections 12 and 13 as relates to the application of the price payable in or towards redemption of charges shall apply separately to the price payable for each interest together with the relative charges.

(2) Where by reason of section 11(2) of this Act it is necessary to make (otherwise than out

of the price payable for the house and premises) any payment for the redemption of a rentcharge *or other rent*, the reversioner, if he is not the landlord liable or primarily liable in respect of the rentcharge *or rent*, shall not be required to make that payment otherwise than out of money made available for the purpose by that landlord, and it shall be the duty of that landlord to provide for the redemption; and similarly where by reason of section 12(8) proviso of this Act it is necessary to discharge the house and premises from a charge affecting the interest of any landlord.

[7A.—(1) The price payable for a minor superior tenancy shall be calculated (except where it has been determined by agreement or otherwise before this paragraph comes into force) by applying the formula set out in sub-paragraph (5) instead of in accordance with section 9.

(2) "A minor superior tenancy" means a superior tenancy having an expectation of possession of not more than one month and in respect of which the profit rent is not more than £5 per year.

(3) "Profit rent" means an amount equal to that of the rent payable under the tenancy on which the minor superior tenancy is in immediate reversion, less that of the rent payable under the minor superior tenancy.

(4) Where the minor superior tenancy or that on which it is in immediate reversion comprises property other than the house and premises, the reference in sub-paragraph (3) to the rent payable under it means so much of that rent as is apportioned to the house and premises.

(5) The formula is—

$$P = £\frac{R}{Y} - \frac{R}{Y(1+)^n}$$

where—

P = the price payable;
R = the profit rent;
Y = the yield (expressed as a decimal fraction) from $2\frac{1}{2}$ per cent. Consolidated Stock;
n = the period, expressed in years (taking any part of a year as a whole year) which the minor superior tenancy would have to run if it were not extinguished by enfranchisement.

(6) In calculating the yield from $2\frac{1}{2}$ per cent. Consolidated Stock, the price of that stock shall be taken to be the middle market price at the close of business on the last trading day in the week before the tenant gives notice in accordance with this Act of his desire to have the freehold.]

8. [. . .]

9. Nothing in this Schedule shall be taken to entitle the claimant to give notice under section 9(3) of this Act of his inability or unwillingness to acquire particular interests superior to the tenancy in possession, but any such notice shall extend to all those interests.

Extension

10.—(1) Where a lease is executed to give effect to section 14 of this Act, then except as provided by paragraph 11 below the new tenancy shall be granted by the landlord having an interest sufficient in point of duration which is not superior to another such interest.

(2) Subject to paragraph 11 below, the lease shall have effect for the creation of the new tenancy, and for the operation of the rights and obligations conferred and imposed by it, as if there had been a surrender and re-grant of any subsisting tenancy intermediate between the interest of the landlord granting the new tenancy and the tenancy in possession, and the covenants and other provisions of the lease shall be framed and take effect accordingly.

(3) If there is no one landlord having such an interest in the whole of the house and premises as is referred to in sub-paragraph (1) above, then those having the appropriate interests in separate parts thereof shall instead grant the tenancy; and where it is necessary in accordance with this sub-paragraph for more than one landlord to join in granting the new tenancy, the lease shall have effect in accordance with sub-paragraph (2) above, but as if they had been jointly entitled to their interests and had become separately entitled by assignments taking effect immediately after the lease.

(4) The lease shall give effect to section 15(2) of this Act on the basis that the references

there to the landlord include the landlord granting the new tenancy, the immediate landlord of whom the new tenancy will be held and any intermediate landlord, and shall give effect to section 15(3) on the basis that account is to be taken of obligations imposed on any of those landlords by virtue of the new tenancy or any superior tenancy; and section 16(4) of this Act shall apply on the basis that the reference there to the tenant's landlord includes the immediate landlord of whom the new tenancy will be held and all superior landlords, including any superior to the landlord granting the new tenancy.

11.—(1) Where a tenancy in the house and premises superior to the tenancy in possession is vested in the claimant or a trustee for him, the lease under section 14 of this Act shall include an actual surrender of that superior tenancy without a regrant, and it shall accordingly be disregarded for purposes of paragraph 10 above.

(2) Where, apart from this provision, the effect of the lease under section 14 of this Act would be, as regards any tenancy superior to the new tenancy,—

(*a*) that the rent payable under that superior tenancy would be equal to or more than the rent payable under the tenancy on which it would be in immediate reversion (regard being had to the operation of this sub-paragraph in relation to any other tenancy); or

(*b*) that the difference between those rents would not be more than four pounds a year;

then the person entitled to that superior tenancy may by written notice given to his immediate landlord and, if neither of them is the reversioner, to the reversioner require that the lease shall include an actual surrender by him of his tenancy without a re-grant.

(3) Any person entitled to a tenancy superior to the new tenancy may by the like notice require that the lease shall confer on him the right to surrender his tenancy if by reason of any revision of the rent payable under the claimant's new tenancy (together with any consequent surrender under this provision of tenancies intermediate between the superior tenancy and that new tenancy) the rent payable under the superior tenancy will not thereafter be less by more than four pounds a year than the rent payable under the tenancy on which it will be in immediate reversion.

(4) Where a landlord required apart from this sub-paragraph (or by virtue of this sub-paragraph as it operates in relation to another landlord) to grant the new tenancy would do so by virtue of a tenancy in respect of which he claims, by the like notice, to have the benefit of sub-paragraph (2) or (3) above, he shall for purposes of paragraph 10 above be replaced, subject to any further operation of this sub-paragraph, by the next superior landlord.

(5) References in this paragraph to the rent payable under a tenancy mean, in relation to a tenancy comprising property other than the house and premises, so much of that rent as is apportionable to the house and premises, and any surrender or provision for the surrender of such a tenancy in accordance with this paragraph shall be limited to the house and premises.

12.—(1) No provision of any tenancy prohibiting, restricting or otherwise relating to a sub-demise by the tenant shall have effect with reference to any lease executed to give effect to section 14 of this Act.

(2) Where by reason of section 14(4) proviso of this Act it is necessary to make any payment to discharge the house and premises from a charge affecting the interest of any landlord, the reversioner, if he is not the landlord liable or primarily liable in respect of the charge, shall not be required to make that payment otherwise than out of money made available for the purpose by that landlord, and it shall be the duty of that landlord to provide for the charge being discharged.

Supplementary

13.—(1) For purposes of this Schedule the expectation of possession carried by a tenancy is the expectation which it carries at the relevant time of possession after the tenancy in possession, on the basis that—

(*a*) subject to sub-paragraph (2) below, the tenancy in possession terminates at the relevant time if its term date fell before then, or else terminates at its term date or (in the case of a tenancy which has been extended) its original term date; and

(*b*) a tenancy other than the tenancy in possession terminates at its term date.

(2) In a case where before the relevant time the claimant's immediate landlord had given notice to quit terminating the tenancy in possession at a date earlier than the term date, the

date specified in the notice to quit shall be substituted for the date in sub-paragraph (1)(*a*) above.

14.—(1) This Schedule shall apply notwithstanding that the tenancy in possession is a tenancy from the Crown within the meaning of section 33 of this Act; and, where under section 33(1)(*b*) the appropriate authority gives notice that as regards a Crown interest the authority will grant or concur in granting the freehold or an extended lease, then in relation to the Crown interest and the person to whom it belongs this Schedule shall have effect as it has effect in relation to other landlords and their interests, but with the appropriate authority having power to act as reversioner or otherwise for purposes of this Schedule on behalf of that person:

Provided that paragraph 4(1)(*a*) above shall not apply to the execution of a conveyance or lease on behalf of the person to whom a Crown interest belongs.

(2) A conveyance or lease executed in pursuance of paragraph 4(3) above shall be effective notwithstanding that the interest intended to be conveyed or bound is a Crown interest or a tenancy from the Crown.

AMENDMENTS

21-60 Para. 8 was repealed by the Rentcharges Act 1977, s.17 and Sched. 2, as were the words in italics in para. 7(1) and (2). The words in square brackets in para. 7, and para. 7A, were added, and the words omitted between square brackets in para. 7 repealed, by the Housing Act 1980, s.141 and Sched. 21, *post.* Those in square brackets in para. 5 were substituted by the Housing Act 1980, s.142 and Sched. 22.

Sections 17, 18, 20 21, 23 and 25

SCHEDULE 2

PROVISIONS SUPPLEMENTARY TO SECTIONS 17 AND 18 OF THIS ACT

21-61 1.—(1) This Schedule has effect where a tenant of a house and premises is entitled to be paid compensation under section 17 or 18 of this Act, or would be so entitled on the landlord obtaining an order for possession, or where an application for such an order is dismissed or withdrawn; and for purposes of this Schedule—

(*a*) "application for possession" means a landlord's application under section 17(1) or 18(1); and

(*b*) "order for possession" means an order under section 17(2) or 18(4).

(2) Where the tenancy has not been extended under section 14 of this Act, references in this Schedule to the original term date shall be construed as references to the term date or, in a case where before the relevant time the landlord had given notice to quit terminating the tenancy at a date earlier than the term date, as references to the date specified in the notice to quit.

2.—(1) Where an order for possession is made, the tenancy shall determine, and the compensation payable to the tenant by virtue of the order shall become payable, on such date as may, when the amount of that compensation is known, be fixed by order of the court made on the application either of the landlord or of the tenant.

(2) An order of the court under this paragraph shall not fix a date earlier than the original term date of the tenancy, nor shall it fix a date less than four months or more than twelve months after the date of the order unless the court sees special reason for doing so; and in a case under section 18 of this Act an application to [a leasehold valuation tribunal] to determine the amount of the compensation payable to the tenant shall not be made more than twelve months before the original term date.

(3) In fixing the date the court shall have regard to the conduct of the parties and, in a case under section 17 of this Act, to the extent which the landlord has made reasonable preparation for proceeding with the redevelopment (including the obtaining of or preparations relating to the obtaining of any requisite permission or consent, whether from any authority whose permission or consent is required under any enactment or from the owner of an interest in any property).

(4) The court may by order direct that the whole or part of the compensation payable to the tenant shall be paid into court, if the court thinks it expedient so to do for the purpose of ensuring that the sum paid is available for meeting charges on the tenant's interest in the house and premises, or for the purpose of division, or for any other purpose.

3.—(1) On the termination of a tenancy under an order for possession there shall terminate also any immediate or derivative sub-tenancy, and the tenant shall be bound to give up possession of the house and premises to the landlord except in so far as he is precluded from doing so by the rights of other persons to retain possession under or by virtue of any enactment.

(2) Where a sub-tenancy of property comprised in the tenancy has been created after the date of the application for possession (or any earlier date when, in the case of an application relying on section 28(1) of this Act, a copy of the Minister's certificate was served on the tenant), then no person shall in respect of that sub-tenancy be entitled under section 15(3) of the Increase of Rent and Mortgage Interest (Restrictions) Act 1920, or any enactment applying or extending it, to retain possession of that property after the termination of the tenancy under the order for possession.

(3) In exercising its jurisdiction under section 17 or 18 of this Act or this Schedule the court shall assume that the landlord, having obtained an order for possession, will not be precluded from obtaining possession by the right of any person to retain possession by virtue of the Rent Acts or otherwise.

(4) A person in occupation of the house and premises or part of them under a sub-tenancy liable to terminate under sub-paragraph (1) above may, with the leave of the court, appear and be heard on any application for possession or application under paragraph 2 above.

4. Where an order has been made under paragraph 2 above, the court making the order or another county court shall have jurisdiction to hear and determine any proceedings brought by virtue of the order to recover possession of the property or to recover the compensation, notwithstanding that by reason of the value of the property or the amount of the compensation the proceedings are not within the jurisdiction conferred on county courts apart from this provision.

5.—(1) The amount payable to a tenant, by virtue of an order for possession, by way of compensation for the loss of the house and premises shall be the amount which, if sections 17 and 18 of this Act had not been passed, the house and premises, if sold in the open market by a willing seller, might at the date when the order for possession becomes final be expected to realise, on the assumption that the vendor was selling the tenancy, and was selling—

(*a*) subject to the rights of any person who will on the termination of the tenancy be entitled to retain possession as against the landlord, but otherwise with vacant possession; and

(*b*) subject to any subsisting incumbrances which will not terminate with the tenancy and for which during the continuance of the tenancy the tenant is liable without having a right to be indemnified by the landlord, but otherwise free of incumbrances; and

(*c*) subject to any restriction which would be required (in addition to any imposed by the terms of the tenancy) to limit the uses of the house and premises to those to which they have been put since the commencement of the tenancy and to preclude the erection of any new dwelling-house or any other building not ancillary to the house as a dwelling-house;

but there shall be left out of account any value attaching to the right to acquire the freehold under Part I of this Act.

(2) The compensation payable in respect of a tenancy which has not been extended under section 14 of this Act shall be computed as if the tenancy was to be so extended.

6.—(1) Part I of the Landlord and Tenant Act 1927 (compensation for improvements on termination of business tenancies) shall not apply on the termination of the tenancy or any sub-tenancy in accordance with this Schedule; and a request for a new tenancy or any sub-tenancy shall be of no effect if made after the application for possession, or shall cease to have effect on the making of that application. **21–62**

(2) Where a sub-tenancy terminating with the tenancy in accordance with paragraph 3 above is one to which Part II of the Landlord and Tenant Act 1954 applies, the compensation payable to the tenant shall be divided between him and the sub-tenant in such proportions as

may be just, regard being had to their respective interests in the house and premises and to any loss arising from the termination of those interests and not incurred by imprudence.

(3) Where the amount of the compensation payable to the tenant is agreed between him and the landlord without the consent of a sub-tenant entitled under sub-paragraph (2) above to a share in the compensation, and is shown by the sub-tenant to be less than might reasonably have been obtained by the tenant, the sub-tenant shall be entitled under sub-paragraph (2) above to recover from the tenant such increased share as may be just.

7.—(1) The landlord shall not be concerned with the application of the amount payable to the tenant by way of compensation under an order for possession, but (subject to any statutory requirements as to payment of capital money arising under a settlement or a disposition on trust for sale and to any order under paragraph 2(4) above for payment into court) the written receipt of the tenant shall be a complete discharge for the amount payable.

(2) The landlord shall be entitled to deduct from the amount so payable to the tenant—

(*a*) the amount of any sum payable by way of rent or recoverable as rent in respect of the house and premises up to the termination of the tenancy; and

(*b*) the amount of any other sums due and payable by the tenant to the landlord under or in respect of the tenancy or any agreement collateral thereto.

(3) Where the tenancy is held on trust for sale, and compensation is paid in respect of it in accordance with section 17 or 18 of this Act (whether possession is obtained under that section or without any application for possession), the sum received shall be dealt with as if it were proceeds of sale arising under the trust.

8.—(1) Where a landlord makes an application for possession, and it is made to appear to the court that in relation to matters arising out of that application (including the giving up of possession of the house and premises or the payment of compensation) the landlord or the tenant has been guilty of any unreasonable delay or default, the court may—

(*a*) by order revoke or vary, and direct repayment of sums paid under, any provision made by a previous order as to payment of the costs of proceedings taken in the court on or with reference to the application, or, where costs have not been awarded, award costs;

(*b*) certify particulars of the delay or default to the Lands Tribunal with a view to enabling the Tribunal to exercise a like discretion in relation to costs of proceedings before the Tribunal.

(2) [. . .]

(3) Where an application for possession is dismissed or withdrawn, and it is made to appear to the court—

(*a*) that the application was not made in good faith; or

(*b*) that the landlord had attempted in any material respect to support by misrepresentation or the concealment of material facts a request to the tenant to deliver up possession without an application for possession;

the court may order that no further application for possession of the house and premises made by the landlord shall be entertained if it is made within the five years beginning with the date of the order.

9.—(1) The purposes authorised for the application of capital money by section 73 of the Settled Land Act 1925, or by that section as applied by section 28 of the Law of Property Act 1925 in relation to trusts for sale, and the purposes authorised by section 71 of the Settled Land Act 1925 or by that section as applied as aforesaid as purposes for which moneys may be raised by mortgage, shall include the payment of compensation in accordance with section 17 or 18 of this Act (whether possession is obtained under that section or without any application for possession).

(2) The purposes authorised for the application of capital money by section 26 of the Universities and College Estates Act 1925, and the purposes authorised by section 31 of that Act as purposes for which moneys may be raised by mortgage, shall include the payment of compensation in accordance with section 17 of this Act (whether possession is obtained under that section or without any application for possession).

AMENDMENTS

21–63 The words in square brackets in para. 3 were substituted by the Rent Act 1977, Sched. 23.

Those in square brackets in para. 2(2) were substituted, and para. 8(2) was repealed, by the Housing Act 1980, s.142 and Sched. 22.

Sections 22 and 34 SCHEDULE 3 21–64

Validity of Tenants' Notices, Effect on Landlord and Tenant Act 1954 etc. and Procedure Generally

Part I

Restrictions on claims by tenant, and effect of claims on other notices, forfeitures, etc.

1.—(1) A claim to acquire the freehold or an extended lease of any property shall be of no effect if made after the tenant has given notice terminating the tenancy of that property (not being a notice that has been superseded by the grant, express or implied, of a new tenancy), or if made during the subsistence of an agreement for a future tenancy to which section 28 of the Landlord and Tenant Act 1954 applies.

(2) A tenant's notice terminating the tenancy of any property, shall be of no effect if given during the currency of a claim made in respect of the tenancy to acquire the freehold or an extended lease of that property.

(3) In sub-paragraphs (1) and (2) above references to a notice terminating a tenancy include a tenant's request for a new tenancy under section 26 of the Landlord and Tenant Act 1954, and a tenant's notice under section 27(1) of that Act that he does not desire the tenancy to be continued.

2.—(1) A claim to acquire the freehold or an extended lease of any property shall be of no effect if made more than two months after the landlord's notice terminating the tenancy of that property has been given under section 4 or 25 of the Landlord and Tenant Act 1954 (whether or not that notice has effect to terminate the tenancy):

Provided that—

(*a*) this sub-paragraph shall not apply where the landlord gives his written consent to a claim being made after the end of those two months; and

(*b*) where a tenant, having given notice of his desire to have the freehold, gives after the end of those two months a further notice under section 9(3) of this Act of his inability or unwillingness to acquire the house and premises at the price he must pay, he may with the notice under section 9(3) give a notice of his desire to have an extended lease (if he then has a right thereto).

(2) A landlord's notice terminating a tenancy of any property under section 4 or 25 of the Landlord and Tenant Act 1954 shall be of no effect if given during the currency of a claim made in respect of the tenancy to acquire the freehold or an extended lease of that property, and shall cease to have effect on the making of such a claim.

(3) Where any such landlord's notice ceases (by virtue of sub-paragraph (2) above or section 35 of this Act) to have effect on the making of a claim, but the claim is not effective, then if within one month after the period of currency of that claim (or any subsequent claim made by virtue of the proviso to sub-paragraph (1) above) a landlord's notice terminating the tenancy is given under section 4 or 25 of the Landlord and Tenant Act 1954, the earliest date which may be specified therein as the date of termination shall be the date of termination specified in the previous notice or the expiration of three months from the giving of the new notice, whichever is the later.

(4) Where by virtue of sub-paragraph (3) above a landlord's notice specifies as the date of termination of a tenancy a date earlier than six months after the giving of the notice, then—

(*a*) if it is a notice proposing a statutory tenancy, section 7(2) of the Landlord and Tenant Act 1954 shall apply in relation to the notice with the substitution, for references to the period of two months ending with the date of termination specified in the notice and the beginning of that period, of references to the period of three months beginning with the giving of the notice and the end of that period; and

(*b*) if it is a notice under section 25 of that Act, an application under section 24 for a new tenancy shall not be entertained unless it is made within three months after the giving of the notice.

3.—(1) Where a tenant makes a claim to acquire the freehold or an extended lease of any property, then during the currency of the claim and for three months thereafter the tenancy in that property shall not terminate either by effluxion of time or in pursuance of a notice to quit given by the landlord or by the termination of a superior tenancy; but if the claim is not effective, and but for this sub-paragraph the tenancy would have so terminated before the end of those three months, the tenancy shall so terminate at the end of the three months.

(2) Sub-paragraph (1) above shall not be taken to prevent an earlier termination of the tenancy in any manner not there mentioned, nor affect the power under section 146(4) of the Law of Property Act 1925 to grant a tenant relief against the termination of a superior tenancy, or any right of the tenant to relief under section 16(2) of the Landlord and Tenant Act 1954 or under paragraph 9 of Schedule 5 to that Act.

4.—(1) Where a tenant makes a claim to acquire the freehold or an extended lease of any property, then during the currency of the claim no proceedings to enforce any right of re-entry or forfeiture terminating the tenancy shall be brought in any court without the leave of that court, and leave shall not be granted unless the court is satisfied that the claim was not made in good faith; but where leave is granted, the claim shall cease to have effect.

(2) Where a claim is made to acquire the freehold or an extended lease of property comprised in a tenancy, the tenancy shall be deemed for purposes of the claim to be a subsisting tenancy notwithstanding that the claim is made when proceedings are pending to enforce a right of re-entry or forfeiture terminating the tenancy and notwithstanding any order made afterwards in those proceedings, and if the claim is effective, the court in which the proceedings were brought may set aside or vary any such order to such extent and on such terms as appear to that court to be appropriate:

Provided that if it appears to that court that the claim is not made in good faith, or there has been unreasonable delay in making it, and that apart from the claim effect should be given to the right of re-entry or forfeiture, the court shall order that the tenancy shall not be treated as subsisting nor the claim as valid by virtue of this sub-paragraph.

(3) Where a court other than the county court—

(*a*) grants leave under sub-paragraph (1) above; or

(*b*) makes an order under the proviso to sub-paragraph (2) above on the ground that a claim was not made in good faith;

the court may make any such order as the county court is authorised to make by section 20(5) or (6) of this Act.

(4) A tenant who, in proceedings to enforce a right of re-entry or forfeiture or a right to damages in respect of a failure to comply with any terms of the tenancy, applies for relief under section 16 of the Landlord and Tenant Act 1954 is not thereby precluded from making a claim to acquire the freehold or an extended lease; but if he gives notice under section 16(2) (under which the tenant is relieved from any order for recovery of possession or for payment of damages, but the tenancy is cut short), any claim made by him to acquire the freehold or an extended lease of property comprised in the tenancy, with or without other property, shall be of no effect, or, if already made, shall cease to have effect.

(5) Sub-paragraph (4) above shall apply in relation to proceedings relating to a superior tenancy with the substitution for the references to section 16 and to section 16(2) of the Landlord and Tenant Act 1954 of references to paragraph 9 and to paragraph 9(2) of Schedule 5 to that Act.

5.—(1) For purposes of this Part of this Schedule—

(*a*) references to a claim to acquire the freehold or an extended lease shall be taken as references to a notice of a person's desire to acquire it under Part I of this Act and except in so far as the contrary intention appears as including a claim by a tenant not entitled to acquire it and a claim made by a person who is not a tenant; and

(*b*) references to a claim being effective shall be taken as references to the freehold or an extended lease being acquired in pursuance of the claim and

(*c*) references to the currency of a claim shall be taken as references to the period from the giving of a notice which has effect or would, if valid, have effect to the time when the notice is effective or ceases to have effect, or (not being a valid notice) is set aside by the court or withdrawn or would if valid, cease to have effect, and those references shall include any period when the notice is suspended.

(2) For purposes of sub-paragraph (1)(*c*) above the date when a notice ceases to have effect or is set aside would, if valid, cease to have effect in consequence of an order of a court shall be taken to be the date when the order becomes final.

PART II

Procedural Provisions

6.—(1) A tenant's notice under Part I of this Act of his desire to have the freehold or an extended lease of a house and premises shall be in the prescribed form, and shall contain the following particulars:— **21–65**

(*a*) the address of the house, and sufficient particulars of the house and premises to identify the property to which the claim extends;

(*b*) such particulars of the tenancy and of the rateable value of the house and premises as serve to identify the instrument creating the tenancy and show that [(i)] (apart from the operation, if any, of the proviso to section 4(1) of this Act) the tenancy is and has at the material times been a long tenancy at a low rent; [at the material time the rateable value was within the limits specified for the purposes of section 1;]

(*c*) the date on which the tenant acquired the tenancy;

(*d*) the periods for which since the beginning of the preceding ten years and since acquiring the tenancy the tenant has and has not occupied the house as his residence, together with the following additional particulars about the periods for which during that time he has so occupied the house, that is to say,—

(i) what parts, if any, of the house have not been in his own occupation and for what periods; and

(ii) what other residence, if any, he has had and for what periods, and which was his main residence.

(2) Where the tenant gives the notice by virtue of section 6 or 7 of this Act, sub-paragraph (1)(*c*) and (*d*) above shall apply with the appropriate modifications of references to the tenant, so that the notice shall show the particulars bringing the case within section 6 or 7.

(3) The notice shall not be invalidated by any inaccuracy in the particulars required by this paragraph or any misdescription of the property to which the claim extends; and where the claim extends to property not properly included in the house and premises, or does not extend to property that ought to be so included, the notice may with the leave of the court, and on such terms as the court may see fit to impose, be amended so as to exclude or include that property.

7.—(1) Where a tenant of a house gives the landlord notice in accordance with Part I of this Act of the tenant's desire to have the freehold or an extended lease, the landlord shall within two months give the tenant a notice in reply in the prescribed form stating whether or not the landlord admits the tenant's right to have the freehold or extended lease (subject to any question as to the correctness of the particulars given in the tenant's notice of the house and premises); and if the landlord does not admit the tenant's right, the notice shall state the grounds on which it is not admitted.

(2) Subject to sub-paragraph (3) below, where under Part I of this Act the landlord may object to the inclusion of any part of the house and premises as described in the tenant's notice, or may object to the exclusion of other property, the notice of his objection shall be given with or before his notice in reply, unless the right to give it later is reserved by the notice in reply.

(3) If (on the assumption, where it is not admitted, that the tenant has the right claimed) it is intended to apply to the court for possession of the house and premises under section 17 or 18 of this Act, the notice in reply shall state that it is the intention to do so, and sub-paragraph (2) above shall not apply.

(4) Where a landlord's notice in reply admits the tenant's right to have the freehold or extended lease of a house and premises, the admission shall be binding on the landlord, so far

as relates to the matters mentioned in section 1(1)(*a*) and (*b*) of this Act, unless the landlord shows that he was induced to make the admission by misrepresentation or the concealment of material facts; but the admission shall not conclude any question whether the particulars of the house and premises in the tenant's notice are correct.

(5) The tenant shall not institute proceedings in the court with a view to the enforcement of his right to have the freehold or an extended lease before the landlord has given notice in reply or two months have elapsed without his doing so since the giving of the tenant's notice.

8.—(1) Where a person ("the claimant") gives notice as tenant of a house of his desire to have the freehold or an extended lease under Part I of this Act,—

(*a*) the notice shall be regarded as served on the landlord if it is served on any of the persons having an interest in the house and premises superior to the claimant's tenancy and references to the relevant time shall be construed accordingly;

(*b*) copies of the notice shall be served by the claimant on any other persons known or believed by him to have such an interest;

(*c*) the notice shall state whether copies are being served in accordance with paragraph (*b*) above on anyone other than the recipient and, if so, on whom;

(*d*) a recipient of the notice or a copy of it (including a person receiving a copy under this paragraph), unless he is a person having no such interest, shall forthwith serve a copy on any person who is known or believed by him to have such an interest and is not stated in the recipient's copy of the notice or known by him to have received a copy;

(*e*) a recipient of the notice or a copy of it shall, in any further copies served by him in accordance with paragraph (d) above, supplement the statement under paragraph (*c*) by adding any further persons on whom he is serving copies or who are known by him to have received one,

(2) Any recipient of any such notice or a copy of it—

(*a*) if he serves further copies of it on other persons in accordance with sub-paragraph (1)(*d*) above, shall notify the claimant of the persons added by him to the statement under sub-paragraph (1)(*c*); and

(*b*) if he knows who is, or believes himself to be, the person designated as the reversioner by paragraph 2 of Schedule I to this Act, shall give written notice to the claimant stating who is thought by him to be the reversioner, and shall serve copies of it on all persons known or believed by him to have an interest superior to the claimant's tenancy.

(3) Any person who fails without reasonable cause to comply with sub-paragraph (1) or (2) above, or is guilty of any unreasonable delay in doing so, shall be liable for any loss thereby occasioned to the claimant or to any person having an interest superior to the claimant's tenancy.

(4) In this paragraph references to an interest superior to the claimant's tenancy mean the estate in fee simple and any tenancy superior to the claimant's tenancy, but shall apply also to a tenancy reversionary on the claimant's tenancy.

9.—(1) Where the interest of a landlord is subject to a charge, and the person entitled to the benefit of the charge is in possession or a receiver appointed by him or by the court is in receipt of the rents and profits, a notice by a tenant of his desire to have the freehold or an extended lease under Part I of this Act shall be duly given if served either on the landlord or on that person or any such receiver; but the landlord or that person, if not the recipient of the notice, shall forthwith be sent the notice or a copy of it by the recipient:

Provided that in the case of a debenture-holders' charge within the meaning of section 12(5) of this Act this sub-paragraph shall not authorise the service of a notice on, or require a notice or copy to be sent to, the persons entitled to the benefit of the charge, other than trustees for the debenture-holders, but where the notice is served on the landlord and there is no trustee for the debenture-holders, he shall forthwith send it or a copy of it to any receiver appointed by virtue of the charge.

(2) Where a tenant of a house gives notice of his desire to have the freehold or an extended lease under Part I of this Act, and the interest of the person to whom the notice is given, or any person receiving a copy of it under paragraph 8 above, is subject to a charge to secure the payment of money, then subject to sub-paragraph (3) below the recipient of the notice or copy shall forthwith inform the person entitled to the benefit of the charge (unless the notice was

served on him or a receiver appointed by virtue of the charge that the notice has been given and shall give him such further information as may from time to time be reasonably required from the recipient by him.

(3) References in sub-paragraph (2) above to a charge shall not include a charge falling within section 11 of this Act or a debenture-holders' charge within the meaning of section 12(5) of this Act.

10.—(1) This paragraph shall have effect in relation to a landlord's notice terminating a tenancy of a house under section 4 or 25 of the Landlord and Tenant Act 1954 if—

(*a*) no previous notice terminating the tenancy has been given under either of those sections; and

(*b*) in the case of a notice under section 25, the tenancy is a long tenancy at a low rent, and the tenant is not a company or other artificial person.

(2) The landlord's notice shall not have effect unless it states—

(*a*) that, if the tenant has a right under Part I of this Act to acquire the freehold or an extended lease of property comprised in the tenancy, notice of his desire to have the freehold or an extended lease cannot be given more than two months after the service of the landlord's notice; and

(*b*) that, in the event of a tenant having the right and giving such a notice within those two months, the landlord's notice will not operate; and

(*c*) that, in the event of the tenant giving such a notice within those two months, the landlord will be entitled to apply to the court under section 17 or 18 of this Act and proposes to do so or, as the case may be, will not be entitled or does not propose to do so.

(3) The landlord shall also in the notice give the names and addresses of any other persons known or believed by him to have an interest superior to the tenancy terminated by the notice or to be the agent concerned with the property on behalf of a person having such an interest; and for this purpose "an interest superior to the tenancy terminated by the notice" means the estate in fee simple and any tenancy superior to that tenancy, but includes also a tenancy reversionary on that tenancy.

(4) Where a tenant's notice of his desire to have the freehold or an extended lease of a house and premises under Part I of this Act is given after the service of a landlord's notice terminating the tenancy under section 4 or section 25 of the Landlord and Tenant Act 1954, and the landlord's notice does not comply with sub-paragraph (2) above, no application made under section 17 or 18 of this Act with respect to the house and premises by the landlord giving the notice shall be entertained by the court (other than an application under section 17 after the grant of an extended lease).

(5) This paragraph shall not apply, or be treated by virtue of section 34(4)(*c*) as applying, to a landlord's notice given before the appointed day.

AMENDMENT

The words in square brackets in para. 6 were inserted by the Housing Act 1980, Sched. 21, para. 7.

Sections 29 and 30 SCHEDULE 4

SPECIAL COVENANTS WITH LOCAL AUTHORITIES ETC. ON ENFRANCHISEMENT OR EXTENSION

PART I

OPERATION AND ENFORCEMENT OF COVENANTS

1.—(1) A covenant entered into in accordance with section 29 or 30 of this Act (in this Part of this Schedule referred to as "a relevant covenant") shall not be enforceable by any means other than those provided by paragraphs 2 and 3 below. **21–66**

(2) A relevant covenant affecting land other than registered land—

(*a*) may be registered under section 10 of the Land Charges Act 1925 as a restrictive covenant, if apart from this sub-paragraph it would not be registrable under that section as a restrictive covenant or as an estate contract; and

(*b*) subject to section 13 of that Act, shall be binding upon every successor of the covenantor, if apart from this sub-paragraph it would not be binding upon every such successor.

(3) Where a relevant covenant affects registered land,—

(*a*) notice of the covenant may be registered under section 59(2) of the Land Registration Act 1925 as a land charge (other than a local land charge) within the meaning of that Act, if apart from this subsection notice of the covenant would not be so registrable, and the provisions of that Act as to land charges shall apply accordingly; and

(*b*) where notice of the covenant has been so registered, the covenant shall be binding upon every successor of the covenantor, if apart from this subsection it would not be binding upon every such successor.

(4) In sub-paragraphs (2) and (3) above "successor of the covenantor," in relation to the covenants entered into on any disposition, means a person, other than the covenantor, who is for the time being entitled—

(*a*) to the interest disposed of, either in the whole or in part of the property comprised in the disposition; or

(*b*) to an interest consisting of a tenancy (whether of the whole or of part of that property) which has been created (directly or indirectly) out of the interest disposed of.

(5) Section 84 of the Law of Property Act 1925 (power to discharge or modify restrictive covenants affecting land) shall not have effect in relation to any relevant covenant.

(6) The rule against perpetuities and any enactment relating to that rule shall not apply to any right conferred by, or exercisable in relation to, a relevant covenant, if apart from this sub-paragraph it would apply to any such right.

(7) Where any such interest as is mentioned in sub-paragraph (4)(*a*) or (*b*) above is acquired (whether compulsorily or by agreement) by an authority possessing compulsory purchase powers within the meaning of the [Town and Country Planning Act 1971] (including any government department), nothing in the enactment which authorises that acquisition, or in any other enactment conferring powers on that authority, shall be construed as relieving that authority from the obligation to comply with any relevant covenant to which that interest remains subject; but the rights of the covenantee shall for purposes of any such acquisition be treated as an interest in the land affected, and as capable of being, and liable to be, extinguished by being compulsorily acquired in like manner and subject to the like conditions as other interests of the covenantee would be.

2.—(1) Where it appears to a local authority that a relevant covenant entered into on a disposition by that authority has been broken, the authority may serve written notice under this paragraph on any one or more of the following persons, that is to say—

(*a*) any person for the time being entitled to the interest disposed of either in the whole or in part of the land comprised in the disposition (in this paragraph referred to as "the land under covenant"); and

(*b*) any person entitled to an interest consisting of a tenancy (whether of the whole or of part of the land under covenant) which has been created (directly or indirectly) out of the interest disposed of.

(2) A notice served on any person under sub-paragraph (1) above shall—

(*a*) specify the covenant and the matters in respect of which it is alleged by the authority that the covenant has been broken; and

(*b*) state that, after the end of such period (not being less than six weeks from the date of service of the notice) as may be specified in the notice, the authority propose to execute a vesting declaration under paragraph 3 below in respect of that person's interest in the land under covenant unless before the end of that period he serves on the authority a counter-notice under sub-paragraph (3) below.

(3) Any person on whom a notice is served under sub-paragraph (1) above may, before the end of the period specified in the notice in accordance with sub-paragraph (2)(*b*) serve on the

authority a counter-notice in writing objecting to the notice on such one or more of the following grounds as may be specified in the counter-notice, that is to say—

(*a*) that the relevant covenant specified in the notice under sub-paragraph (1) above has not been broken as alleged in the notice;

(*b*) that if that covenant has been so broken, the breach does not relate to any part of the land under covenant in which the person serving the counter-notice has an interest;

(*c*) that in the circumstances he ought to be relieved against the execution of a vesting declaration under paragraph 3 below in respect of his interest.

(4) Where a person has served a counter-notice under sub-paragraph (3) above and that counter-notice has not been withdrawn, the authority shall not execute a vesting declaration under paragraph 3 below in respect of his interest except with the leave of the court; and on any application for such leave—

(*a*) where the grounds of objection specified in the counter-notice consist of or include that which is specified in sub-paragraph (3)(*a*) or (*b*) above, the court shall not grant leave unless satisfied that the objection on that ground is not well-founded; and

(*b*) without prejudice to paragraph (a) above, where the grounds of objection specified in the counter-notice consist of or include that which is specified in sub-paragraph (3)(*c*) above, the court, if having regard to the conduct of the parties and to all the other circumstances it appears to the court to be just and equitable to do so, may refuse to grant leave, either unconditionally or on such terms (as to costs, damages or otherwise) as the court think fit.

3.—(1) Where a local authority have served on any person a notice under paragraph 2 above in respect of such an interest as is mentioned in paragraph 2(1) (*a*) or (*b*), then subject to paragraph 2(4) above and to the provisions of any order made under it, the authority may execute a vesting declaration under this paragraph in respect of that interest—

(*a*) at any time within the six months following the end of the period specified in the notice in accordance with paragraph 2(2)(*b*) . . . if no counter-notice under paragraph 2(3) is served before the end of that period; or

(*b*) if such a counter-notice is so served but is withdrawn, at any time within the six months following the withdrawal of the counter-notice or;

(*c*) if such a counter-notice is so served and is not withdrawn, at any time within the six months following the time when the order giving leave under paragraph 2(4) becomes final.

(2) A vesting declaration under this paragraph in respect of an interest in land shall be in such form as may be prescribed by regulations made by statutory instrument by the Minister of Housing and Local Government.

(3) Where a vesting declaration is executed under this paragraph the interest to which it relates shall vest in the authority on such date as is specified in that behalf in the declaration.

(4) Any reference in the Land Compensation Act 1961 to the compulsory acquisition of land, or of an interest in land, shall be construed as including a reference to the execution of a vesting declaration under this paragraph in respect of an interest in land; and that Act shall apply in relation to the execution of such a declaration as if the authority, having been duly authorised to acquire that interest compulsorily in accordance with the [Acquisition of Land Act 1981] had served notice to treat in respect of that interest on the date of execution of the declaration.

(5) In assessing compensation in accordance with the Land Compensation Act 1961 in respect of an interest in land vested in a local authority by a vesting declaration under this paragraph—

(*a*) nothing shall be included for damage sustained by reason that the land in which the interest subsists is severed from other land held therewith, or for disturbance or any other matter not directly based on the value of land or of an interest in land; and

(*b*) in a case where immediately before the execution of the declaration the interest is subject to a right of pre-emption under a covenant entered into in accordance with section 30(1)(*b*) of this Act, no account shall be taken of any diminution of the value of the interest which is attributable to that right.

PART II

RE-ACQUISITION FOR DEVELOPMENT BY NEW TOWNS COMMISSION OR UNIVERSITY BODY

21–67 4. Where a tenant of a house and premises acquires the freehold under Part I of this Act subject to a covenant entered into under section 29(1) with the Commission for the New Towns, and the property or any part of it is afterwards required for development for purposes (other than investment purposes) of the Commission, the Commission may be authorised by the Minister of Housing and Local Government to acquire the property or that part of it compulsorily; [and the provisions of the Acquisition of Land Act 1981 shall apply to a compulsory purchase under this paragraph].

5.—(1) Where a tenant of a house and premises acquires the freehold under Part I of this Act subject to a covenant entered into under section 29(1) with a university body, and the property or any part of it is afterwards required for development for the purposes (other than investment purposes) of that or a related university body, the Secretary of State for Education and Science may at the cost and on behalf of the university body for which it is required acquire the property or that part of it by compulsory purchase.

(2) [The Acquisition of Land Act 1981 shall apply to a compulsory purchase under this paragraph.]

(3) For purposes of this paragraph a university and the colleges of that university (within the meaning of section 28(5)(*c*) of this Act) are university bodies related to one another.

[6.—(1) Where a tenant of a house and premises acquires the freehold under Part I of this Act subject to a covenant entered into under section 29(1) with the Development Board for Rural Wales, and the property or any part of it is afterwards acquired for development for purposes (other than investment purposes) of the Board the Board may be authorised by the Secretary of State to acquire the property or that part of it compulsorily.

(2) [The Acquisition of Land Act 1981 shall apply to a compulsory purchase under this paragraph.]]

AMENDMENTS

21–68 The words in square brackets in para. 1(7) were substituted by the Town and Country Planning Act 1971, s.291(1), Sched. 23, Pt. II, those in paras. 3(4), 4, 5(2) and 6(2) by the Acquisition of Land Act 1981, s.34 and Sched. 4. Para. 6 was added by Sched. 7, para. 5, to the Development of Rural Wales Act 1976.

21–69

SCHEDULE 4A

EXCLUSION OF CERTAIN SHARED OWNERSHIP LEASES

Leases granted in pursuance of right to be granted a shared ownership lease

1. A lease granted in pursuance of the right to be granted a shared ownership lease under Part V of the Housing Act 1985 is excluded from the operartion of this Part of this Act.

Certain leases granted by certain public authorities

2.—(1) A lease which—

(*a*) was granted at a premium by a body mentioned in sub-paragraph (2), and

(*b*) complies with the conditions set out in sub-paragraph (3),

is excluded from the operation of this Part at any time when the interest of the landlord belongs to such a body.

(2) The bodies are—

(*a*) a county, district or London borough council, the Common Council of the City of London or the Council of the Isles of Scilly;
(*b*) the Inner London Education Authority or a joint authority established by Part IV of the Local Government Act 1985;
(*c*) the Commission for the New Towns or a development corporation established by an order made, or having effect as made, under the New Towns Act 1981;
(*d*) an urban development corporation withing the meaning of Part XVI of the Local Government, Planning and Land Act 1980;
(*e*) the Development Board for Rural Wales;

(3) The conditions are that the lease—
(*a*) provides for the tenant to acquire the freehold for a consideration which is to be calculated in accordance with the lease and which is reasonable, having regard to the premium or premiums paid by the tenant under the lease, and
(*b*) states the landlord's opinion that by virtue of this paragraph the tenancy will be excluded from the operation of this Part of this Act at any time when the interest of the landlord belongs to a body mentioned in sub-paragraph (2) above.

(4) If, in certain proceedings in which it falls to be determined whether a lease complies with the condition in sub-paragraph (3)(*a*), the question arises whether the consideration payable by the tenant on acquiring the freehold is reasonable, it is for the landlord to show that it is.

Certain leases granted by housing associations

3.—(1) A lease granted by a housing association and which complies with the conditions set out in sub-paragraph (2) is excluded from the operation of this Part of this Act, whether or not the interest of the landlord still belongs to such an association.

(2) The conditions are that the lease—
(*a*) was granted for a term of 99 years or more and is not (and cannot become) terminable except in pursuance of a provision for re-entry or forefeiture;
(*b*) was granted at a premium, calculated by reference to the value of the house or the cost of providing it, of not less than 25 per cent., or such other percentage as may be prescribed, of the figure by reference to which it was calculated;
(*c*) provides for the tenant to acquire additional shares in the house on terms specified in the lease and complying with such requirements as may be prescribed;
(*d*) does not restrict the tenant's powers to assign, mortgage or charge his interest in the house;
(*e*) if it enables the landlord to require payment for outstanding shares in the house, does so only in such circumstances as may be prescribed;
(*f*) provides for the tenant to acquire the landlord's interest on terms specified in the lease and complying with such requirements as may be prescribed; and
(*f*) states the landlord's opinion that by virtue of this paragraph the lease is excluded from the operation of this Part of this Act.

(3) In any proceedings the court may, if of the opinion that it is just and equitable to do so, treat a lease as satisfying the conditions in sub-paragraph (2) notwithstanding that the condition specified in paragraph (*g*) of that sub-paragraph is not satisfied.

(4) In this paragraph "housing association" has the same meaning as in the Housing Associations Act 1985.

4.—(1) A lease for the elderly granted by a registered housing association and which complies with the conditions set out in sub-paragraph (2) is excluded from the operation of this Part of this Act at any time when the interest of the landlord belongs to such an association.

(2) The conditions are that the lease—
(*a*) is granted at a premium which is calculated by reference to a percentage of the value of the house or of the cost of providing it,
(*b*) complies, at the time when it is granted, with such requirements as may be prescribed, and
(*c*) states the landlord's opinion that by virtue of this paragraph the lease will be

excluded from the operation of this Part of this Act at any time when the interest of the landlord belongs to a registered housing association.

(3) In this paragraph—

"lease for the elderly" has such meaning as may be prescribed; and

"registered housing association" has the same meaning as in the Housing Association Act 1985.

Power to prescribe matters by regulations

5.—(1) The Secretary of State may by regulations prescribe anything requiring to be prescribed for the purposes of this Schedule.

(2) The regulations may—

(*a*) make different provision for different cases or descriptions of case, including different provisions for different areas, and

(*b*) contain such incidental, supplementary or transitional provisions as the Secretary of State considers appropriate,

and shall be made by statutory instrument which shall be subject to annulment in pursuance of a resolution of either House of Parliament.

Interpretation

6. In this Schedule "lease" means a lease at law or in equity, and references to the grant of a lease shall be construed accordingly.]

21-70 AMENDMENT

This Schedule was inserted by the Housing and Planning Act 1986, Sched. 4, para. 6.

• • • • •

Section 40 SCHEDULE 6

THE PLACES OF WORSHIP (ENRANCHISEMENT) ACT 1920, AS AMENDED

Right of persons holding leasehold interest in place of worship or minister's house to acquire freehold

21-71 1.—(1) Where premises held under a lease to which this Act applies are held upon trust to be used for the purposes of a place of worship or, in connection with a place of worship, for the purpose of a minister's house, whether in conjunction with other purposes or not, and the premises are being used in accordance with the terms of the trust, the trustees, notwithstanding any agreement to the contrary (not being an agreement against the enlargement of the leasehold interest into a freehold contained in a lease granted or made before the passing of this Act), shall have the right as incident to their leasehold interest to enlarge that interest into a fee simple, and for that purpose to acquire the freehold and all intermediate reversions:

Provided that—

(*a*) if the premises exceed two acres in extent, the trustees shall not be entitled to exercise the right in respect of more than two acres thereof; and

(*aa*) where the person entitled to the freehold or an intermediate reversion requires that underlying minerals be excepted, the trustees shall not be entitled to acquire his interest in the minerals if proper provision is made for the support of the premises as they have been enjoyed during the lease and in accordance with the terms of the lease and of the trust; and (*b*) this Act shall not apply where the premises are used or are proposed to be used for the purposes of a place of worship in contravention of any covenant contained in the lease under which the premises are held or in any lease superior thereto; and

(*c*) this act shall not apply where the premises form part of land which has been acquired by or is vested in any municipal, local or rating authority or in the owners thereof for the purposes of a railway, dock, canal or navigation under any Act of Parliament, Provisional Order or Order having the force of an Act of Parliament and the freehold reversion in the premises is held or retained by such owners for those purposes.

(1A) Where the residence house of a benefice is held by the incumbent under a lease to which this Act applies, this Act shall have effect (with any necessary modifications) in relation to the enlargement of the incumbent's leasehold interest into a fee simple, and in relation to the estate so acquired, as it would have effect if the residence house were vested for that interest in trustees; and the powers and provisions of the Parsonages Measure 1938 (as amended by any subsequent enactment) relating to the purchase of houses for parsonages shall apply for and in relation to the acquisition under this Act of the freehold reversion.

(2) The leases to which this Act applies are leases (including underleases and agreements for leases or underleases), whether granted or made before or after the passing of this Act, for lives or a life or for a term of years where the term as originally created was a term of not less than twenty-one years, whether determinable on a life or lives or not.

Procedure for acquisition of reversionary interests

2. For the purpose of acquiring such reversionary interests as aforesaid, Part I of the Compulsory Purchase Act 1965 shall apply as if the trustees were an authority authorised to acquire the premises by virtue of a compulsory purchase order, made under the Acquisition of Land (Authorisation Procedure) Act 1946; but in relation to any acquisition under this Act the following provisions shall have effect:—

(*a*) in Part I of the Compulsory Purchase Act 1965 section 4 (time limit for acquisition) shall not apply, and for purposes of the said Part I "land" shall include easements in or relating to land;

(*b*) the consideration payable in respect of any intermediate reversion may, at the option of the person entitled to that reversion be an annual rentcharge for a term corresponding to the unexpired residue of the term of the reversion;

(*c*) in determining the amount of any compensation the value of any buildings erected, or improvements made by the trustees, shall be excluded;

(*d*) no allowance shall be made on account of the acquisition being compulsory;

(*e*) in determining the amount of compensation in any case where the rent reserved under the lease is less than the full annual value of the land the compensation, so far as it is payable in respect of the interest of the lessor expectant on the expiration of the term of the lease, shall not be ascertained on the basis of the rent so reserved, but, subject always to the foregoing provisions of this section, on the estimated full value of the land at the expiration of the term of the lease.

Effect of enfranchisement on covenants

3. The estate in fee simple acquired by the trustees shall be held by them upon the same trusts as those upon which the leasehold interest would have been held by them if it had not been enlarged into a fee simple, and shall be subject to all the same covenants and provisions relating to user and enjoyment and to all the same obligations of every kind other than the payment of rent as those to which the leasehold interest would have been subject if it had not been so enlarged, and all such covenants, provisions, and obligations shall be enforceable against the trustees and their successors in title by the persons who, but for the enlargement of the leasehold interest under this Act, would for the time being have been entitled to enforce such covenants, provisions, or obligations:

Provided that any covenant to insure against fire, whether in any particular office or not, and to reinstate and apply the insurance money in reinstating the premises in case of damage by fire, and any other covenant to do any act which may or will be beneficial to the demised premises alone, shall continue in force only where the consideration is payable in the form of a rentcharge, and so long as that rentcharge is payable.

Definitions

5. In this Act, unless the context otherwise requires—

The expression "place of worship" means any church, chapel, or other building used for public religious worship, and includes a burial ground, Sunday or Sabbath school or caretaker's house attached to or used in connection with and held upon the same trusts as a place of worship;

The expression "freehold reversion" means the estate of fee simple in the premises subject to the lease held by the trustees and any lease superior thereto;

The expression "intermediate reversion" means any leasehold interest in the land (whether under a lease or underlease or under an agreement for a lease or underlease) superior to the lease held by the trustees;

The expression "trustees" means the persons in whom the leasehold premises are for the time being vested for the purposes of a place of worship or minister's house under any trust whether express or implied and includes their predecessors in title.

Short title and extent

6.—(1) This Act may be cited as the Places of Worship (Enfranchisement) Act 1920.

(2) This Act shall not extend to Scotland or Northern Ireland.

21–72 **Sections 40 and 41**

SCHEDULE 7

REPEALS

• • • • • •

PART II

Repeals arising out of section 40 *of this Act*

Chapter	Short Title	Extent of Repeal
10 & 11 Geo. 5, c. 56.	The Places of Worship (Enfranchisement) Act 1920.	Section 4. In section 5, in the definition of "freehold reversion" the words from "and, where" onwards, and the definition of "the county court". The Schedule.

The repeals in this Part of this Schedule are made subject to the provisions of section 40 (8) of this Act.

Housing Act 1974

(1974 c. 44)

• • • • • •

Raising of rateable value limits for enfranchisement or extension under Leasehold Reform Act 1967 21–72/1

118.—(1) In section 1 of the Leasehold Reform Act 1967, in subsection (1) (*a*) (certain tenants entitled to enfranchisement or extension of their leaseholds where rateable value is within certain limits on a particular day) after the words "rent and" there shall be inserted the words "subject to subsection (5) and (6) below" and after subsection (4) there shall be added the following subsections:—

"(5) If, in relation to any house and premises, the appropriate day for the purposes of subsection (1) (*a*) above falls on or after 1st April 1973 that subsection shall have effect in relation to the house and premises,—

(*a*) in a case where the tenancy was created on or before 18th February 1966, as if for the sums of £200 and £400 specified in that subsection there were substituted respectively the sums of £750 and £1,5000; and

(*b*) in a case where the tenancy was created after 18th February 1966, as if for those sums of £200 and £400 there were substituted respectively the sums of £500 and £1,000.

(6) If, in relation to any house and premises,—

(*a*) the appropriate day for the purposes of subsection (1) (*a*) above falls before 1st April 1973, and

(*b*) the rateable value of the house and premises on the appropriate day was more than £200 or, if it was then in Greater London, £400, and

(*c*) the tenancy was created on or before 18th Februqry 1966.

subsection (1) (*a*) above shall have effect in relation to the house and premises as if for the reference to the appropriate day there were substituted a reference to 1st April 1973 and as if the sums of £200 and £400 specified in that subsection there were substituted respectively the sums of £750 and £1,500."

(2) In any case where, by virtue of the amendments of section 1 of the Leasehold Reform Act 1967 effected by subsection (1) above, the right specified in subsection (1) of that section is conferred on a tenant, section 19 of that Act (retention of management powers for a general benefit of neighbourhood) shall have effect in relation to the house and premises to which the tenant's right applies as if for the reference in subsection (1) of that section to an application made within two years beginning with the commencement of Part I of that Act there were substituted a reference to an application made within two years beginning with the date on which this Act is passed.

(3) After subsection (4) of section 1 of the Leasehold Reform Act 1967 there shall be inserted—

"(4A) At any time the tenant may take the action provided in Schedule 8 to the Housing Act 1974 for his rateable value to be adjusted and in all such cases the agreed rateable value or that determined by the Court or District Valuer shall be the rateable value for the purposes of that Act."

(4) In section 9 of the Leasehold Reform Act 1967 (purchase price of enftanchisement) there shall be inserted after subsection (1):—

"(1A) Notwithstanding, the foregoing subsection, the price payable for a house and premises, the rateable value of which is above £1,000 in Greater London and £500 elsewhere, on a conveyance under section 8 above, shall the the amount which at the relevant time the house and premises, if solf in the open market by a willing seller, might be expected to realise on the following assumptions:—

(*a*) on the assumption that the vendor was selling for an estate in fee simple, subject to the tenancy, but on the assumption that this Part of this Act conferred no right to axcquire the freehold;

(*b*) on the assumption that at the end of the tenancy the tenant has the right to remain in possession of the house and premises under the provisions of Part I of the Landlord and Tenant Act 1954;

(*c*) on the assumption that the tenant has no liability to carry out any repairs, maintenance or redecoration under the terms of the tenancy or Part I of the Landlord and Tenant Act 1954;

(*d*) on the assumption that the price be diminished by the extent to which the value of the house and premises has been increased by any improvement carried out by the tenant or his precedessors in title at their own expense;

(*e*) on the assumption that (subject to paragraph (*a*) above) the vendor was selling subject, in respect of rentcharges and other rents to which section 11 (2) below applies, to the same annual charge as the coveyance to the tenant is to be subject to, but the purchaser would otherwise be effectively exonerated until the termination of the tenancy from any liability or charge in respect of tenant's incumbrances; and

(*f*) on the assumption that (subject to paragraphs (*a*) and (*b*) above) the vendor was selling with and subject to the rights and burdens with and subject to which the conveyance to the tenant is to be made, and in particular with and subject to such permanent or extended rights and burdens as are to be created in order to give effect to section 10 below.

(1B) For the purpose of determining whether the rateable value of the house and premises is above £1,000 in Greater London, or £500 elsewhere, the rateable value shall be adjusted to take into account any tenant's improvements in accordance with Schedule 8 to the Housing Act 1974."

(5) This section shall come into force on the passing of the Act.

• • • • • •

Section 118 SCHEDULE 8

REDUCTION OF RATEABLE VALUE IN CASE OF CERTAIN IMPROVEMENTS

1.—(1) Where the tenant, or any previous tenant, has made or contributed to the cost of an improvement on the premises comprised in the tenancy and the improvement is one to which this Schedule applies, then, if the tenant serves on the landlord a notice in the prescribed form requiring him to agree to a reduction under this Schedule, their rateable value as ascertained for the purposes of [section 1 of the Leasehold Reform Act 1967] shall be reduced by such amount, if any, as may be agreed or determined in accordance with the following provisions of this Schedule. **21–73**

(2) This Schedule applies to any improvement made by the execution of works amounting to structural alteration, extension or addition.

2.—(1) The amount of any such reduction may at any time be agreed in writing between the landlord and the tenant.

(2) Where, at the expiration of a period of six weeks from the service of a notice under paragraph 1 of this Schedule any of the following matters has not been agreed in writing between the landlord and the tenant, that is to say,—

(*a*) whether the improvement specified in the notice is an improvement to which this Schedule applies:

(*b*) what works were involved in it;

(*c*) whether the tenant or a previous tenant under the tenancy has made it or contributed to its cost; and

(*d*) what proportion his contribution, if any, bears to the whole cost;

the county court may on the application of the tenant determine that matter [. . .].

(3) An application under the last foregoing sub-paragraph must be made within six weeks from the expiration of the period mentioned therein or such longer time as the court may allow.

3.—(1) Where, after the service of a notice under paragraph 1 of this Schedule, it is agreed in writing between the landlord and tenant or determined by the county court—

(*a*) that the improvement specified in the notice is one to which this Schedule applies, and what works were involved in it, and

(*b*) that the tenant or a previous tenant under the tenancy has made it or contributed to its cost, and, in the latter case, what proportion his contribution bears to the whole cost, then if, at the expiration of a period of two weeks from the agreement or determination, it has not been agreed in writing between the landlord and the tenant whether any or what reduction is to be made under this Schedule, and the tenant, within four weeks from the expiration of that period, makes an application to the valuation officer for a certificate under the next following sub-paragraph, that question shall be determined in accordance with the certificate unless the landlord and the tenant otherwise agree in writing.

(2) On any such application the valuation officer shall certify—

(*a*) whether or not the improvement has affected the rateable value on the 1st

April, 1973 (as ascertained for the purposes of [section 1 of the Leasehold Reform Act 1967]), of the hereditament of which the premises consist or, as the case may be, in which they are wholly or partly comprised, and

(*b*) if it has, the amount by which the rateable value would have been less if the improvement had not been made.

(3) An application for such a certificate shall be in the prescribed form and shall state the name and address of the landlord, and the Valuation Officer shall send a copy of the certificate to the landlord.

(4) Where the amount of the reduction under this Schedule falls to be determined in accordance with such a certificate, it shall be equal to the amount specified in pursuance of head (*b*) and sub-paragraph (2) of this paragraph, but proportionately reduced in any case where a proportion only of the cost was contributed by the tenant or a previous tenant under the tenancy.

(5) Where at the time of an application for a certificate under this paragraph a proposal for an alteration in the valuation list relating to the hereditament is pending and the alteration would have effect from a date earlier than the 2nd April, 1973, the Valuation Officer shall not issue the certificate until the proposal is settled.

[4. Where a notice under paragraph 1 of this Schedule is served on or after 21st December 1979, the tenant shall bear the reasonable costs incurred by the landlord in investigating any matter specified in it.]

FORM . . .

Leasehold Reform Act 1967

21–74 Notice by Tenant to Landlord of Tenant's Improvements affecting Rateable Value

Date ....

To ....landlord of ....

1. [I] [A previous tenant of the above mentioned premises under the tenancy] [made] [contributed to the costs of] the improvements[s] to the above mentioned premises particulars of which are set out in the First Schedule hereto (Note 1).

2. I hereby require you to agree to a reduction in the rateable value of the premises for the purposes of the Leasehold Reform Act 1967.

3. I propose that the rateable value shall be reduced to £ .... (Note 2).

If you do not agree to this reduction (Note 3), do you agree that—

(*a*) the improvements[s] [is] [are] [an] improvement[s] made by the execution of works amounting to the structural alteration or extension of the premises or a structural addition thereto;

(*b*) the works set out in the Second Schedule hereto were involved in the making of the improvements[s];

(*c*) [I] [A previous tenant under the tenancy] [made the improvement[s]] [contributed to the cost of the improvement[s]];

(*d*) the proportion of the cost borne by me or a previous tenant is ....

Signature of tenant ....

First Schedule

Description of Improvement(s)

Second Schedule

Description of Works

Strike out words in square brackets if inapplicable.

Note 1

The improvement must be one made by the execution of works amounting to the structural alteration or extension of the premises or a structural addition thereto, *e.g.* the erection of a garage in the grounds.

Note 2

If the amount of the reduction is agreed in writing between the landlord and the tenant, the amount of the reduced rateable value as so agreed will be substituted for the purposes of the Leasehold Reform Act 1967 for the rateable value on 1st April 1973.

Note 3

If the amount of the reduction is not agreed in writing between the landlord and the tenant, the Valuation Officer will have to decide whether the improvement has affected the rateable value of the premises, and if so, what the value would have been had the improvement not been made. The name and address of the Valuation Officer can be obtained from the local authority. Before, however, an application is made to the Valuation Officer, the landlord and the tenant must try to agree in writing on the items mentioned at (*a*) to (*d*) of this paragraph, or such of those items as are material. If at the end of a period of six weeks after the service of this notice any of these items have not been agreed, the tenant may, within a further six weeks or so much longer time as the court may allow, apply to the county court to settle the matter.
If it has either been agreed or determined by the county court that there has been an improvement of the kind described in Note 1 involving specified works, and that the improvement was carried out by the tenant or a previous tenant, or that the tenant or a previous tenant contributed to its cost, and in the latter case what proportion the contribution bears to the whole cost of the works, then, if within a period of two weeks after the agreement or determination of the county court the landlord and the tenant have still not agreed in writing whether any or what reduction is to be made, the tenant has a further four weeks in which to make an application in the statutory form to the Valuation Officer for a certificate as to whether or not the improvement has affected the rateable value, and if so, the amount by which the value would have been less if the improvement had not been made.

FORM . . .

Leasehold Reform Act 1967 21–75

Application by Tenant to Valuation Officer for Certificate as to Reduction for the purposes of the Leasehold Reform Act 1967, in the Rateable Value of premises on account of Tenant's Improvements

Date ....

To the Valuation Officer.

1. I am the tenant of , and my landlord is of
2. It has been [agreed in writing between me and my landlord] [determined by the county court] that the improvement[s] specified in the First Schedule hereto [is an improvement] [are improvements] to which [Schedule 8 to the Housing Act 1974] applies, and that I or a previous tenant under the tenancy made the improvement[s] or contributed to [its] [their] cost, and that the works specified in the Second Schedule hereto were involved in the improvement[s].
3. It has not been agreed between me and my landlord whether any or what reduction is to be made under said Schedule [Eight] in the rateable value of the premises for the purposes of the Leasehold Reform Act 1967, and I hereby make application to you for a certificate under paragraph 3(2) of the said Schedule [Eight] (Note 4).

Signature of tenant ....

First Schedule

Description of Improvement(s)

Second Schedule

Description of Works

Strike out words in square brackets if inapplicable.

Note 4

If the Valuation Officer certifies that the rateable value would have been less but for the improvement by the amounts mentioned in the certificate, the rateable value will be reduced by those amounts for the purposes of the Leasehold Reform Act 1967 except in the case where a proportion only of the cost was contributed by the tenant, in which case the amounts of the reductions will be proportionately reduced accordingly.

AMENDMENTS

The words in square brackets were substituted, and those in para. 2 omitted, by the Housing Act 1980, Sched. 21, para. 8.

• • • • • •

Leasehold Reform Act 1979

(1979 C.44)

An Act to provide further protection, for a tenant in possession claiming to acquire the freehold under the Leasehold Reform Act 1967, against artificial inflation of the price he has to pay.

[4th April 1979]

Price to tenant on enfranchisement

21–76 **1.**—(1) As against a tenant in possession claiming under section 8 of the Leasehold Reform Act 1967, the price payable on a conveyance for giving effect to that section cannot be made less favourable by reference to a transaction since 15th February 1979 involving the creation or transfer of an interest superior to (whether or not preceding) his own, or an alteration since that date of the terms on which such an interest is held.

(2) References in this section to a tenant claiming are to his giving notice under section 8 of his desire to have freehold.

(3) Subsection (1) applies to any claim made on or after the commencement date (which means the date of this Act), and also to a claim made before that date unless by then the price has been determined by agreement or otherwise.

Citation and extent

2.—(1) This Act may be cited as the Leasehold Reform Act 1979; and the 1967 Act and this Act may be cited together as the Leasehold Reform Acts 1967 and 1979. 21–77

(2) This Act extends to England and Wales only.

Housing Act 1980

(1980 c.51)

Exclusion of shared ownership tenancies from Leasehold Reform Act 1967

140.—(1) Where, after the commencement of the section, a tenancy of a house is created by the grant of a lease at a premium and either— 21–78

(*a*) the lease is granted by a body mentioned in subsection (2) below and complies with the conditions set out in subsection (3) below; or

(*b*) the lease is granted by a registered housing association and complies with the conditions set out in subsection (4) below;

the tenancy shall not be treated for the purposes of Part I of the Leasehold Reform Act 1967 (enfranchisement and extension of long leaseholds) as being a long tenancy at a low rent at any time when the interest of the landlord belongs to such a body or, as the case may be, to a registered association.

(2) The bodies referred to in subsection (1) (*a*) above are—

(*a*) the council of a district, the Greater London Council, the council of a London borough, the Common Council of the City of London or the Council of the Isles of Scilly;

(*b*) a development corporation established by an order made, or having effect as if made, under the [New Towns Act 1981];

(*c*) the Commission for the New Towns;

(*d*) the Development Board for Rural Wales.

(3) The conditions mentioned in subsection (1) (*a*) above are—

(*a*) that the lease provides for the tenant to acquire the freehold, whether under an option to purchase or otherwise, for a consideration which is to be calculated in accordance with the terms of the lease and which is reasonable, having regard to the premium or premiums paid by the tenant under the lease; and

[(*aa*) the Inner London Education Authority;

(*ab*) a joint authority established by Part IV of the Local Government Act 1985;]

(*b*) that it states the landlord's opinion that by virtue of this section the tenancy will not be a long tenancy at a low rent for the purposes of the Leasehold Reform Act 1967 at any time when the interest of the landlord belongs to a body mentioned in subsection (2) above.

(4) The conditions mentioned in subsection (1) (*b*) above are—

(*a*) that the lease is granted at a premium which is calculated by reference to a percentage of the value of the house or of the cost of providing it;

(*b*) that at the time when it is granted it complies with the requirements of regulations made by the Secretary of State for the purposes of this section; and

(*c*) that it states the landlord's opinion that by virtue of this section the tenancy will not be long tenancy at a low rent for the purposes of the Leasehold Reform Act 1967 at any time when the interest of the landlord belongs to a registered housing association.

(5) If, in any proceedings in which it falls to be determined whether a lease complies with the condition in subsection (3) (*a*) above, the question arises whether the consideration payable by the tenant on acquiring the freehold is reasonable, it is for the landlord to show that it is.

(6) In this section "registered housing association" means an association registered under [Housing Associations Act 1985].

AMENDMENT

21–79 The words in square brackets in subs. (2) (*b*) were substituted by New Towns Act 1981, Sched. 12, para. 27. Paras. (*aa*) and (*ab*) in subs. (2) were added by the Local Government Act 1985, Sched. 14, para. 58. The words in square brackets in subs. (6) were substituted by the Housing (Consequential) Provisions Act 1985, Sched. 2, para. 44.

The section was repealed by the Housing and Planning Act 1986, Sched. 4, para. 7, but the repeal does not affect the operation of the section in relation to leases granted before the commencement of that Schedule: *ibid.* para. 11.

Leasehold valuation tribunals

21–80 **142.**—(1) Any matter which under section 21 (1), (2) or (3) of the Leasehold Reform Act 1967 is to be determined by the Lands Tribunal shall instead be determined by a rent assessment committee constituted under Schedule 10 to the 1977 Act.

(2) A rent assessment committee shall, when constituted to make any such determination, be known as a leasehold valuation tribunal.

(3) Part I of Schedule 22 to this Act has effect with respect to leasehold valuation tribunals, and the 1967 Act is amended in accordance with Part II of that Schedule.

• • • • • •

Section 142 SCHEDULE 22 21–81

LEASEHOLD VALUATION TRIBUNALS

PART I

SUPPLEMENTARY PROVISIONS

Constitution of tribunals

1. The president of a panel drawn up under Schedule 10 to the 1977 Act shall, when constituting a leasehold valuation tribunal, ensure that at least one of its members is a person who has experience in the valuation of land.

Appeals

2. No appeal shall lie from a decision of a leasehold valuation tribunal to the High Court by virtue of section 13(1) of the Tribunals and Inquiries Act 1971 and no case may be stated for the opinion of the High Court in respect of such a decision, but any person who—

(*a*) appears before a tribunal in proceedings to which he was a party; and

(*b*) is dissatisfied with its decision,

may, within such time as rules under section 3(6) of the Lands Tribunal Act 1949 may specify, appeal to the Lands Tribunal.

3. A leasehold valuation tribunal shall not be treated as a person aggrieved for the purposes of section 3(4) of the Lands Tribunal Act 1949 (which enables a person aggrieved by a decision of the Tribunal on a point of law to require the Tribunal to state a case for decision of the Court of Appeal).

4. For the purposes of Part I of the Leasehold Reform Act 1967 a matter is to be treated as determined by a leasehold valuation tribunal—

(*a*) if the tribunal's decision is not appealed against, on the expiration of the time for bringing an appeal; or

(*b*) if the decision is appealed against, and not set aside in consequence of the appeal, at the time when the appeal and any further appeal is disposed of by the determination of it and the expiration of the time for bringing a further appeal (if any) or by its being abandoned or otherwise ceasing to have effect.

Costs

5. The costs which a person may be required to bear under section 9(4) or 14(2) of the 1967 Act (matters the cost of which are to be borne by person giving notice of his desire to have the freehold or an extended lease) do not include costs incurred by landlord in connection with a reference to a leasehold valuation tribunal.

6. Where the county court gives any such certificate as is authorised by section 20(4) of or paragraph 8(1) of Schedule 2 to the 1967 Act (certificate of unreasonably delay or default by landlord or tenant) the Lands Tribunal may make the like order as to costs of proceedings on an appeal before the Tribunal in relation to the matter in question as the county court is authorised to make by section 20(4) or paragraph 8(1).

Provision of information

7.—(1) Where a matter is referred to a leasehold valuation tribunal for determination, the tribunal may by notice in writing served on the tenant or landlord or on a superior landlord requires him to give to the tribunal, within such period but not less than 14 days from the service of the notice as may be specified in the notice, such information as the tribunal may reasonably require.

(2) If any person fails without reasonable cause to comply with any notice served on him

under this paragraph he shall be liable, on summary conviction, to a fine not exceeding [level 3 on the standard scale].

PART II

21–82 AMENDMENTS OF 1967 ACT

8.—(1) In section 21(1) (jurisdiction of Lands Tribunal) for "the Lands Tribunal" substitute "a leasehold valuation tribunal."

(2) After section 21(1) insert—

"(1A) An application to a leasehold valuation tribunal under subsection (1) above must be in the prescribed form and contain the prescribed particulars.

"(1B) No application may be made to a leasehold valuation tribunal under subsection (1) above to determine the price for a house and premises unless either—

(*a*) the landlord has informed the tenant of the price he is asking; or

(*b*) two months have elapsed without his doing so since the tenant gave notice of his desire to have the freehold under this Part of this Act."

(3) In section 21(2), for "the Lands Tribunal" substitute "a leasehold valuation tribunal" and for "the Tribunal" substitute "a tribunal."

(4) In section 21(3) for "the Lands Tribunal" (twice) substitute "a leasehold valuation tribunal" and for "the Tribunal" substitute "a tribunal."

(5) For section 21(4) substitute—

"(4) Without prejudice to the generality of section 102 of the County Courts Act 1959 or section 74 of the Rent Act 1977, the powers thereby conferred to make rules of procedure shall extend to prescribing the procedure consequent to any such transfer.".

(6) After section 21(4) insert—

"(4A) The Secretary of State may make regulations prescribing—

(*a*) the form of any application under subsection (1) above; and

(*b*) the particulars which it must contain;

and any such regulations shall be made by statutory instrument subject to annulment in pursuance of a resolution of either House of Parliament."

(7) Section 21(5) (costs of proceedings before Lands Tribunal) is repealed.

9. In section 31(2)(*a*) (consent of Church Commissioners required to provisions of conveyance) after "the court" insert "a leasehold valuation tribunal."

10. In paragraph 5(3) of Schedule 1 (price for intermediate leasehold interests) for "the Lands Tribunal" (twice) substitute "a leasehold valuation tribunal."

11. In paragraph 2(2) of Schedule 2 (compensation payable to tenant for loss of house and premises) for "the Lands Tribunal" substitute "a leasehold valuation tribunal."

12. Paragraph 8(2) of Schedule 2 (costs of proceedings before Lands Tribunal) is hereby repealed.

21–83 AMENDMENT

Para. 7 is printed as amended by the Criminal Justice Act 1982, s.46.

Housing Act 1985

(1985 c. 68)

• • • • • •

Modifications of Leasehold Reform Act 1967 *in relation to leases gained under this Part*

Exclusion of leases where landlord is housing association and freeholder is a charity

172.—(1) Part I of the Leasehold Reform Act 1967 (enfranchisement and extension of long leasholds) does not apply where, in the case of a tenancy or sub-tenancy to which this section applies, the landlord is a housing association and the freehold is owned by a body of persons or trust established for charitable purposes only. **21–84**

(2) This section applies to a tenancy created by the grant of a lease in pursuance to this Part of a dwelling-house which is a house.

(3) Where Part I of the 1967 Act applies as if there had been a single tenancy granted for a term beginning at the same time as the term under a tenancy falling within subsection (2) and expiring at the same time as the term under a later tenancy, this section also applies to that later tenancy.

(4) This section applies to any sub-tenancy directly or indirectly derived out of a tenancy falling within subsection (2) or (3).

Exclusion of shared ownership leases granted under this Part

173.—(1) Where a tenancy of a dwelling-house which is a house is created by the grant of a lease in pursuance of the right to be granted a shared ownership lease, then, so long as the rent payable under the lease exceeds £10 per annum, neither the tenant nor the tenant under a sub-tenancy directly or indirectly derived out of the tenancy shall be entitled to acquire the freehold or an extended lease of the dwelling-house under Part I of the Leasehold Reform Act 1967. **21–85**

(2) Subsection (1) applies notwithstanding the provisions of section 174 (leases granted under this Part to be treated as long leases at a low rent).

Leases granted under this Part to be treated as long leases at a low rent

174. For the purposes of Part I of the Leasehold Reform Act 1967 (enfranchisement and extension of long leasehold)— **21–86**

(*a*) a tenancy created by the grant of a lease in pursuance of this Part of a dwelling-house which is a house shall be treated as being a long tenancy notwithstanding that is it granted for a term of 21 years or less, and

(*b*) a tenancy created by the grant of such a lease in pursuance of the right to be granted a shared ownership lease shall be treated as being a tenancy at a low rent notwithstanding that rent is payable under the tenancy at a yearly rate equal to or more than two-thirds of the rateable value of the dwelling-house on the first day of the term.

Determination of price payable

21–87 **175.**—(1) Where, in the case of a tenancy or sub-tenancy to which this section applies, the tenant exercises his right to acquire the freehold under Part I of the Leasehold Reform Act 1967, the price payable for the dwelling-house shall be determined in accordance with section 9(1A) of that Act notwithstanding that the rateable value of the dwelling-house does not exceed £1,000 in Greater London or £500 elsewhere.

(2) This sections applies to a tenancy created by the grant of a lease in pursuance of this Part of a dwelling-house which is a house.

(3) Where Part I of the 1967 Act applies as if there had been a single tenancy granted for a term beginning at the same time as the term under a tenancy falling with subsection (2) and expiring at the same time as the term under a later tenancy, this section also applies to that later tenancy.

(4) This section applies to any sub-tenancy directly or indirectly derived out of a tenancy falling within subsection (2) or (3).

(5) This section also applies to a tenancy granted in substitution for a tenancy or sub-tenancy within subsections (2) to (4) in pursuance of Part I of the 1967 Act.

• • • • • •

Housing and Planning Act 1986

(1986 c. 63)

Further provisions with respect to shared ownership leases

21–88 **18.** The provisions of Schedule 4 have effect to exclude certain shared ownership leases from the operation of the provisions of—

(*a*) the Rent Act 1977 and the Rent (Agriculture) Act 1976, and
(*b*) Part I of the Leasehold Reform Act 1967 (right of long leaseholder to enfranchisement or extension of lease).

• • • • • •

Determination of price for leasehold enfranchisement

21–89 **23.**—(1) In section 9(1A) of the Leasehold Reform Act 1967 (determination of price payable for enfranchisement of higher value houses), in paragraph (*a*) (assumption that vendor is selling subject to existing tenancy) after "no right to acquire the freehold" insert "or an extended lease and, where the tenancy has been extended under this Part of this Act, that the tenancy will terminate on the original term date.".

(2) In section 23(5) of the Leasehold Reform Act 1967 (provisions as to tenancy granted in satisfaction of tenant's rights under Part I), in

paragraph (*b*) (provisions which apply as if the insert "section 9(1) and (1A) above,".

(3) The above amendments do not apply—

(*a*) where the price for enfranchisement has been determined, by agreement or otherwise, before the commencement of this section; or

(*b*) where the notice under section 8 of the Leasehold Reform Act 1967 (notice of desire to have the freehold) was given before the passing of this Act; or

(*c*) where notice under section 14 of that Act (notice of desire to have extended lease) was given before 5th March 1986.

• • • • • •

Section 18 SCHEDULE 4 **21–90**

• • • • • •

Part I of the Leasehold Reform Act 1967 (c.88)

3. In section 1 of the Leasehold Reform Act 1967 (tenants entitled to enfranchisement or extension), after subsection (1) insert—

"(1A) The references in subsection (1)(*a*) and (*b*) to a long tenancy at a low rent do not include a tenancy excluded from the operation of this Part by section 33A of and Schedule 4A to this Act.".

4. In section 3(2) of the Leasehold Reform Act 1967 after "long tenancy at a low rent" insert "(other than a lease excluded from the operation of this Part by section 33A of and Schedule 4A to this Act)".

5. After section 33 of the Leasehold Reform Act 1967 insert—

"Exclusion of certain shared ownership leases.

33A. The provisions of Schedule 4A to this Act shall have effect to exclude certain shared ownership leases from the operation of this Part of this Act.".

6. [*This para. inserted a new Schedule 4A into the 1967 Act; see ante para. 21–69,*]

• • • • • •

Consequential amendments and repeals

7. In the Housing Act 1980, omit section 140.

• • • • • •

Transitional provisions and savings

11.—(1) The amendments made by this Schedule apply only in relation to leases granted after the commencement of this Schedule.

(2) This Schedule does not affect the operation of section 140 of the Housing Act 1980, the enactments applying that section and regulations made under it, in relation to leases granted before the commencement of this Schedule.

• • • • • •

APPENDIX C

STATUTORY INSTRUMENTS

Leasehold Reform (Notices) Regulations 1967

(S.I. 1967 No. 1768)

Dated November 27, 1967, and made by the Lord High Chancellor of Great Britain, in exercise of the powers conferred on him by section 66 of the Landlord and Tenant Act 1954 as applied by section 22(5) of the Leasehold Reform Act 1967.

1. These Regulations may be cited as the Leasehold Reform (Notices) Regulations 1967 and shall come into operation on 1st January 1968. **22–01**

2. The Interpretation Act 1889 shall apply to the interpretation of these Regulations as it applies to the interpretation of an Act of Parliament.

3. In these Regulations, unless the context otherwise requires—

"the Act" means the Leasehold Reform Act 1967;

a Form referred to by number means the Form so numbered in the Appendix to these Regulations.

4. The Forms in the Appendix to these Regulations or Forms substantially to the like effect shall be used for the following purposes:—

(i) a tenant's notice of his desire to have the freehold or an extended lease of a house and premises given under Part I of the Act shall be in Form 1;

(ii) a landlord's notice in reply to a tenant's notice of his desire to have the freehold or an extended lease of a house and premises, or in reply to a tenant's notice claiming to be entitled to acquire the freehold or an extended lease, given under Part I of the Act shall be in Form 2;

(iii) a tenant's notice claiming to be entitled to acquire the freehold or an extended lease given under section 28(1) of the Act to a landlord who is a body to which that section applies shall be in Form 3.

22-02

APPENDIX

Form 1

Leasehold Reform Act 1967

Notice of Leaseholder's Claim

Notes 1, 2 & 3. To [*Name and Address of landlord*] and all others on whom a copy of this notice may be served.

*Delete whichever is inapplicable. [[1. Take notice that I, as tenant of the house and premises described in the Schedule hereto, desire to have the freehold of the said house and premises.] *or* [1. Take notice that I, as tenant of the house and premises described in the Schedule hereto, desire to have an extended lease of the said house and premises.] I am making this claim in the exercise of my rights under the Leasehold Reform Act 1967. The particulars on which I rely are set out in the Schedule to this notice.]

Note 4. 2. You are required, if you are both my immediate landlord and the freeholder, to give me, within two months of the service of this notice, a notice in reply in the prescribed form stating whether or not you admit my right to have *[the freehold *or* an extended lease] (subject to any question as to the correctness of the particulars of the house and premises given in this notice) and, if you do not admit my right, stating the grounds upon which you do not admit it.

*Delete whichever is inapplicable.

(*The remaining paragraphs of this form should be deleted where the claimant's immediate landlord is known to be the freeholder of the house and premises.*)

Note 5. 3. If you are not my immediate landlord, or if you are my immediate landlord but not the freeholder, you must comply with the requirements of paragraphs 5 and 6 below, but you need only give me the notice in reply mentioned above if you are the person designated as "the reversioner" in accordance with paragraph 2 of Schedule 1 to the Act. If you are the reversioner, you must give the notice in reply within 2 months of the first service of this notice on any landlord.

4. I have served a copy of this notice on the following other person[s] known or believed by me to have an interest in the house and premises superior to my tenancy, namely—

(*The names and addressed of the persons on whom copies of this notice have been served should be stated here.*)

5. You are required to serve a copy of this notice forthwith on any person who is known or believed by you to have such an interest, but is not stated in this notice to have been served with a copy or known by you to have received a copy. If you serve a copy on any person you are required to add his name to the list of persons receiving copies as set out in paragraph 4 of this notice, and to notify me.

6. If you know who is, or you believe yourself to be, the person designated as the reversioner in accordance with paragraph 2 of Schedule 1 to the Act, you are required to give written notice to me stating whom you know or believe to be the reversioner, and to serve copies of it on all persons known or believed by you to have an interest superior to my tenancy. Note 5.

7. Anyone who receives a copy of this notice is required forthwith to serve a copy on any person who is known or believed by him to have such an interest but is not stated in the copy or known by him to have received a copy. If he serves such a further copy on any person he is required to add that person's name to the list of persons receiving copies set out in paragraph 4 of this notice and to notify me.

8. If anyone who receives a copy of this notice knows who is or believes himself to be the person designated as the reversioner he is required to give written notice to me stating whom he knows or believes to be the reversioner and to serve copies of it on all persons known or believed by him to have an interest superior to my tenancy. Note 5.

Dated this day of 19 .

Signed .... (Tenant)
.... (Address)

[The name and address of my solicitor or agent, to whom further communications may be sent it ....
....]

THE SCHEDULE

1. *The address of the house.*
2. *Particulars of the house and premises sufficient to identify the property to which the claim extends.* Note 6.
3. *The rateable value of the house and premises on 23rd March 1965* (*or on the date such a value was first shown in the valuation list, if this date is after 23rd March 1965*).
4. *Particulars of the tenancy of the house and premises sufficient to identify the instrument creating the tenancy and to show that the tenancy is and has at the material times been a long tenancy at a low rent.* Note 7.
5. *The date on which the claimant acquired the tenancy.*
6. *The periods for which in the last ten years and since acquiring the tenancy, the claimant*

has and has not occupied the house as his residence; and the following particulars about any such periods during which the claimant has occupied the house as his residence—

(i) *what parts (if any) of the house have not been in his own occupation and for what periods;*

(ii) *what other residence (if any) he has had and for what periods, and which was his main residence.*

Note 8 7. *Additional particulars where claimant relies on section 6 or 7 of the Act.*

Notes

1. Where the tenant's immediate landlord is not the freeholder, the claim may in accordance with the provisions of the Leasehold Reform Act 1967 be served on him or any superior landlord, and copies of the notice must be served by the tenant on anyone else known or believed by him to have an interest superior to his own. (Schedule 3, paragraph 8(1))

2. Where the landlord's interest is subject to a mortgage or other charge and the mortgagee or person entitled to the benefit of the charge is in possession of that interest, or a receiver appointed by him or by the court is in receipt of the rents and profits, the notice may be served either on the landlord or on the person in possession or the receiver. (Schedule 3, paragraph 9(1))

3. Any landlord whose interest is subject to a mortgage or other charge (not being a rent-charge) to secure the payment of money must (subject to special provisions applicable to debenture-holders' charges) on receipt of the claim inform the mortgagee or person entitled to the benefit of the charge. (Schedule 3, paragraph 9(2))

4. The landlord must (unless note 5 applies) serve a notice in reply in Form 2 prescribed in the Leasehold Reform (Notices) Regulations 1967 within two months of service on him of this notice. If he does not admit the tenant's right to have the freehold or an extended lease the notice in reply must state the grounds on which it is not admitted. If the landlord intends to apply to the court for possession of the house and premises in order to redevelop it (section 17) or to occupy it (section 18), his notice must say so. If he does not so intend, but he objects under subsections (4) or (5) of section 2 of the Act to the inclusion in the claim of a part of the house and premises which projects into other property, or to the exclusion from the claim of property let with the house and premises but not occupied with and used for the purposes of the house by any occupant thereof, he must give notice of his objection with or before his notice in reply; unless in his notice in reply he reserves the right to give it later, in which case it must still be given within two months of the service on him of the tenant's notice. if the landlord admits the claim, the admission is binding on him, unless he shows that he was misled by misrepresentation or concealment of material facts, but it does not conclude any question of

the correctness of the particulars of the house and premises as set out in the claim. (Schedule 3, paragraph 7)

5. Where the tenant's immediate landlord is not the freeholder any proceedings arising out of the tenant's notice, whether for resisting or for giving effect to the claim, must be conducted by the person who is designated "the reversioner" in accordance with paragraph 2 of Schedule 1 to the Act and he must give the notice in reply. The reversioner means the landlord whose tenancy carries an expectation of possession of the house and premises of 30 years or more after the expiration of all inferior tenancies, and if there is more than one such landlord, it means the landlord whose tenancy is nearest to that of the tenant; if there is no such landlord, it means the owner of the freehold. The tenant will be informed in the notice in reply if it is given by a landlord acting as the reversioner.

6. "Premises" to be included with the house in the claim are any garage, outhouse, garden, yard and appurtenances which at the time of the notice are let to the tenant with the house and are occupied with and used for the purposes of the house or any part of it by him or by another occupant.

7. Where there have been successive tenancies particulars should be given of each tenancy. In the case of a lease already extended under the Act, the date of the extension and the original term date should be given.

8. Where the claimant is giving the notice by virtue of section 6 (rights of trustees and beneficiaries under trusts) or section 7 (rights of members of family succeeding to tenancy on death) he is required (by paragraph 6(2) of Schedule 3) to adapt the notice and show under paragraph 7 of the Schedule to this notice the additional particulars bringing the claim within section 6 or 7. Where the tenancy is or was vested in trustees the claimant should, for the purposes of a claim made in reliance on section 6 of the Act, state the date when the tenancy was acquired by the trustees, the date when the beneficiary occupied the house by virtue of his interest under the trust, and particulars of any periods of occupation by the beneficiary which are relied upon as bringing the case within section 6 of the Act. Where the claimant was a member of the previous tenant's family and became tenant on the latter's death, then, for the purposes of a claim made in reliance on section 7 of the Act, the claimant should state the date on which the previous tenant acquired the tenancy, particulars of his relationship to the previous tenant and his succession to the tenancy, and particulars in respect of any period of occupation by the previous tenant and by himself on which the claimant relies as bringing the case within section 7 of the Act.

AMENDMENT

Para. 1 of Form 1 was substituted by S.I. 1969 No. 1481.

Form 2

Leasehold Reform Act 1967

Notice in Reply to Leaseholder's Claim

Note 1.

To [*Name and address of the claimant*

**Delete any words or paragraphs in square brackets which are inapplicable.*

1. I have received *[a copy of] your notice dated .... claiming the right to have *[the freehold *or* an extended lease] of the house and premises described in your notice in accordance with the provisions of the Leasehold Reform Act 1967.

Note 2.

2. *[I admit your right (subject to any question as to the correctness of the particulars given in your notice of the house and premises), *or* I do not admit your right, on the following grounds—
(*State grounds on which the tenant's right is not admitted*)

....
....
....]

Note 3.

*[3. I intend *[*or* intends] to apply to the court for possession of the house and premises under *[section 17 *or* section 18] of the Act.]

Note 4.

*[4. I reserve the right to give notice under section 2 of the Act of my objection to the exclusion from the house and premises claimed by you of premises let to you with the house and premises but not at present occupied by you, or to the continued inclusion in the house and premises of parts lying above or below other premises in which I have an interest.]

Note 5.

†Delete if you are the claimant's immediate landlord and also the freeholder.

†[5. This notice is given by me as the person designated by paragraph 2 of Schedule 1 to the Act as the revisioner of the house and premises].

Signed ....
Date ....

[The name and address of my solicitor or agent to whom all further communications may be sent is ....
....]

Notes

1. This notice must be given within two months of the service of Notice of Leaseholder's Claim. Where there is a chain of landlords the time limit

will run from the date of the first service of the claimant's notice on any landlord. (Schedule 3, paragraph 7(1))

2. If the landlord admits the claim he will not thereafter be able to dispute the claimant's right to have the freehold or an extended lease, unless he shows that he was misled by misrepresentation or concealment of material facts, but the admission does not conclude any question as to the correctness of the particulars of the house and premises as set out in the claim. (Schedule 3, paragraph 7(4))

3. If the landlord (on the assumption, where this is not admitted, that the claimant has the right claimed) intends to apply to the court for an order for possession of the premises for use as a residence under section 18 or for redevelopment under section 17 of the Act, the notice must say so. (Schedule 3, paragraph 7(3)) (Where the claim is to have the freehold, only certain public authorities or bodies can resist it on the ground of an intention to redevelop the property.)

4. If the landlord intends to object (under subsections (4) or (5) of section 2 of the Act) to the exclusion from the claim of property let with the house and premises but not occupied and used for the purposes of the house by any occupant thereof, or to the inclusion of part of the house and premises which projects into other property of the landlord's, notice of his objection must be given before or with this notice, unless the right to give it later is reserved by this notice. (Schedule 3, paragraph 7(2)) In any case notice of the objection must be given within two months of the service of the claimant's notice.

5. Where there is a chain of landlords this notice must be given by the landlord who is designated "the reversioner" in accordance with paragraph 2 of Schedule 1 to the Act. The reversioner means the landlord whose tenancy carries an expectation of possession of the house and premises of 30 years or more after the expiration of all inferior tenancies, and if there is more than one such landlord it means the landlord whose tenancy is nearest to that of the tenant; if there is no such landlord, it means the owner of the freehold.

Form 3 22–03

Leasehold Reform Act 1967

Notice of Leaseholder's Claim under section 28(1)(b)(ii)

To [*Name and address of the landlord*]

1. Take notice that I, as tenant of the house and premises described in the Schedule hereto, claim to be entitled to acquire the freehold or an extended lease of the said house and premises. The particulars on which I rely are set out in the Schedule to this notice.

Note 1. 2. On   you served on my a copy of a certificate given under *[section 28 of the Leasehold Reform Act 1967, certifying that the house and premises will in ten years or less be required for relevant development, *or* section 57 of the Landlord and Tenant Act 1954, certifying that it is requisite that the use or occupation of the house and premises or a part thereof should be changed,] and I am making this claim in the exercise of my rights under section 28 of the Leasehold Reform Act 1967.

**Delete whichever alternative is innaplicable.*

Notes 2 & 3. 3. You are required to give me, within two months of the service of this notice, a notice in reply in the prescribed form stating whether or not you admit my claim (subject to any question as to the correctness of the particulars of the house and premises given in this notice) and, if you do not admit my claim, stating the grounds upon which you do not admit it.

Dated this   day of   19 .

Signed .... (Tenant)

.... (Address)

[The name and address of my solicitor or agent, to whom all further communications may be sent is ....
....]

THE SCHEDULE

1. *The address of the house.*

Note 4. 2. *Particulars of the house and premises sufficient to identify the property to which the claim extends.*

3. *The rateable value of the house and premises on 23rd March 1965 (or on the date such a value was first shown in the valuation list, if this date is after 23rd March 1965).*

Note 5. 4. *Particulars of the tenancy of the house and premises sufficient to identify the instrument creating the tenancy and to show that the tenancy is and has at the material times been a long tenancy at a low rent.*

5. *The date on which the claimant acquired the tenancy.*

6. *The periods for which in the last ten years and since acquiring the tenancy, the claimant has and has not occupied the house as his residence; and the following particulars about any such periods during which the claimant has occupied the house as his residence—*

(i) *what parts (if any) of the house have not been in his own occupation and for what periods;*

(ii) *what other residence (if any) he has had and for what periods, and which was his main residence.*

Note 6. 7. *Additional particulars where the claimant relies on section 6 or 7 of the Act.*

Notes

1. In accordance with the provisions of the Leasehold Reform Act 1967 this notice may not be served later than two months after a copy of the certificate has been served on the tenant.

2. The landlord must serve a notice in reply in Form 2 prescribed in the Leasehold Reform (Notices) Regulations 1967 within two months of service on him of this notice. If he does not admit the tenant's claim to be entitled to acquire the freehold or an extended lease the notice in reply must state the grounds on which it is not admitted. If the landlord admits the claim, the admission is binding on him, unless he shows that he was misled by misrepresentation or concealment of material facts, but it does not conclude any question of the correctness of the particulars of the house and premises as set out in the claim. (Schedule 3, paragraph 7)

3. If the landlord admits the claim the tenant will not be entitled to a grant of the freehold or a new tenancy of the house and premises, but, if the landlord obtains an order of the court under section 17 of the Act for possession of the house and premises in order to redevelop it, the tenant will become entitled to be paid compensation for the loss of the house and premises in accordance with Schedule 2 to the Act.

4. "Premises" to be included with the house in the claim are any garage, outhouse, garden, yard and appurtenances which at the time of the notice are let to the tenant with the house and are occupied with and used for the purposes of the house or any part of it by him or by another occupant.

5. Where there have been successive tenancies particulars should be given of each tenancy. In the case of a lease already extended under the Act, the date of the extension and the original term date should be given.

6. Where the claimant is giving the notice by virtue of section 6 (rights of trustees and beneficiaries under trusts) or section 7 (rights of members of family succeeding to tenancy on death) he is required (by paragraph 6(2) of Schedule 3) to adapt the notice and show under paragraph 7 of the Schedule to this notice the additional particulars bringing the claim within section 6 or 7. Where the tenancy is or was vested in trustees the claimant should, for the purposes of a claim made in reliance on section 6 of the Act, state the date when the tenancy was acquired by the trustees, the date when the beneficiary occupied the house by virtue of his interest under the trust, and particulars of any periods of occupation by the beneficiary which are relied upon as bringing the case within section 6 of the Act. Where the claimant was a member of the previous tenant's family and became tenant on the latter's death, then, for the purposes of a claim made in reliance on section 7 of the Act, the claimant should state the date on which the previous tenant acquired the tenancy, particulars of his relationship to the previous tenant and his succession to the tenancy, and particulars in respect of any period of occupation by the previous tenant and by himself on which the claimant relies as bringing the case within section 7 of the Act.

Leasehold Reform (Enfranchisement and Extension) Regulations 1967

(S.I. 1967 No. 1879)

Dated December 15, 1967, *made by the Lord High Chancellor of Great Britain, in exercise of the powers conferred on him by section* 22 (2) *of the Leasehold Reform Act* 1967.

22–04 **1.**—(1) These Regulations may be cited as the Leasehold Reform (Enfranchisement and Extension) Regulations 1967 and shall come into operation on 1st January 1968.

(2) In these Regulations and the conditions set out in the Schedule to them, unless the context otherwise requires:—

"the Act" means the Leasehold Reform Act 1967;

"conveyance" includes any conveyance, assignment, transfer or other assurance for giving effect to section 8 of the Act;

"landlord" means the estate owner in respect of the fee simple of the property to which the tenant's notice relates, or the reversioner within the meaning of Schedule 1 to the Act, or any other person who is conducting the proceedings arising out of the notice in accordance with the provisions of the Act or an order of the court;

"lease" means a lease to be granted to give effect to a tenant's notice;

"property" means the house and premises which are required to be granted to the tenant for an estate in fee simple, pursuant to section 8, or for a term of years pursuant to section 14 of the Act;

"tenant" means a tenant of a house who has given notice under Part I of the Act of his desire to have the freehold or an extended lease and includes his executors, administrators and assigns;

"tenant's notice" means in relation to Part I of the Schedule a notice given by a tenant under Part I of the Act of his desire to have a freehold, and in relation to Part 2 of the Schedule a notice given by a tenant under Part I of the Act of his desire to have an extended lease.

(3) The Interpretation Act 1889 shall apply to the interpretation of these Regulations as it applies to the interpretation of an Act of Parliament.

2. In any transactions undertaken to give effect to a tenant's notice of his desire to have a freehold the landlord and the tenant shall, unless they otherwise agree, be bound by the conditions laid down in Part I of the Schedule to these Regulations as if the conditions formed part of a contract between them.

3. In any transactions undertaken to give effect to a tenant's notice of his desire to have an extended lease the landlord and the tenant shall, unless they otherwise agree, be bound by the conditions laid down in Part

2 of the Schedule to these Regulations as if the conditions formed part of a contract between them

4. Where as a result of non-compliance with the conditions laid down in the Schedule to these Regulations, the landlord and the tenant are discharged from the performance of the obligations arising in giving effect to the tenant's notice, such obligations arising between the tenant and persons other than the landlord having an interest superior to the tenancy shall likewise be discharged.

SCHEDULE **22–05**

PART I

Enfranchisement

Payment of deposit

1. At any time after receipt of tenant's notice the landlord may, by notice in writing given to the tenant, require a sum equal to three times the annual rent for the property payable under his tenancy (or, in the case of a notice given under section 34 of the Act, the former long tenancy) or £25, whichever is the greater, to be deposited with the landlord, or a person nominated by him in the notice as his agent or as stakeholder, on account of the price payable for the property and any other sums payable by a tenant in accordance with the provisions of the Act; and the tenant shall, within 14 days of the giving of the notice, pay the sum demanded to the landlord or person nominated by him.

Evidence of tenant's right to enfranchise

2. At any time after receipt of the tenant's notice the landlord may, by notice in writing given to the tenant, require him to deduce his title to the tenancy and to furnish a statutory declaration as to the particulars of occupation of the property on which the tenant relies in the tenant's notice; and the tenant shall within 21 days of the giving of the landlord's notice comply with the requirement.

Delivery of proof of landlord's title

3.—(1) Where—

- (i) a tenant has received no notice in reply to his tenant's notice within 2 months of giving it, or
- (ii) a tenant has
  - (*a*) received a notice in reply stating that his right to have the freehold is admitted, or
  - (*b*) has received a notice in reply that his right is disputed but has established that right by agreement or an order of the court,

  and, in either case, the property to be conveyed has been established by agreement or an order of the court,

the tenant may by notice in writing given to the landlord require him to deduce his title delivering:—

- (*a*) in the case of land registered in the register of title kept at Her Majesty's Land Registry an authority to inspect the register together with all the particulars and information which pursuant to section 110 of the Land Registration Act 1925 have or may be required to be furnished on a sale of registered land,
- (*b*) in the case of any other land, an abstract of his title to the property,

and the landlord shall not later than 4 weeks after receipt of the notice, comply with the requirement contained therein.

(2) Where any landlord or the tenant has served notice under paragraph 5 (2) of Schedule 1 to the Act, "landlord" in this condition includes a landlord who served the notice or upon whom such a notice has been served.

Requisitions

4.—(1) The tenant shall within 14 days after delivery of the abstract or of the authority to inspect the register together with particulars and information (whether or not delivered within the time required) send to the landlord a statement in writing of all objections and requisitions (if any) to or on the title or the evidence of the title, and the abstract or the particulars and information.

(2) All objections and requisitions, other than those going to the root of the title, not included in any statement sent within the aforesaid period shall be deemed waived, and any matters which could have been raised in such objections or requisitions, other than matters going to the root of the title, shall be deemed not to form a defect in the title for the purposes of section 9 (2) of the Act.

(3) The landlord shall give a written answer to any objections or requisitions within 14 days of their receipt, and any observations on the answer shall be made within 7 days of the receipt of the answer, and if they are not so made, the answer shall be considered satisfactory.

(4) Any objections not included in any observations so made shall be deemed waived and any matter which could have been raised in any observations so made shall be deemed not to form a defect in the title for the purposes of section 9 (2) of the Act.

Particulars of rights of way and restrictions

5.—(1) When or at any time after giving his notice in reply to the tenant's notice the landlord may by notice in writing given to the tenant require him within 4 weeks to state what rights of way and provisions concerning restrictive covenants he requires to be included in the conveyance in accordance with section 10 of the Act.

(2) At any time when under condition 3 the tenant would be entitled to require the landlord to deduce his title he may by notice in writing given to the landlord require him within 4 weeks to state what rights of way over the property and provisions concerning restrictive covenants he requires to be included in the conveyance in accordance with the provisions of the Act.

(3) A notice given under this condition shall contain a statement as to the rights of way and provisions concerning restrictive covenants by the person giving the notice to be included in the conveyance.

(4) If the tenant does not comply with a notice given under this condition within the time specified or, where no such notice has been given, does not communicate to the landlord a statement of the rights and provisions he requires to be included in the conveyance when or before serving a notice on the landlord under condition 3, the tenant shall be deemed to require no rights of way or provisions concerning restrictive covenants to be included in the conveyance.

(5) If the landlord does not comply with a notice given under this condition within the time specified, or, where no such notice is given, does not communicate to the tenant a statement of the rights and provisions he requires to be included in the conveyance at or before the time fixed for compliance with a notice served on him under condition 3, the landlord shall be deemed to require no rights of way or provisions concerning restrictive covenants to be included in the conveyance.

Completion

6.—(1) After the expiration of one month after the price payable for the property under section 9 of the Act has been determined by agreement or otherwise, either the tenant or the landlord may give the other notice in writing requiring him to complete the conveyance of the property to the tenant, and thereupon the completion date shall be the first working day after the expiration of 4 weeks from giving of the notice.

(2) Completion shall take place at the office of the landlord's solicitor or, if he so requires, at the office of the solicitor of his mortgagee.

Apportionment of rent and outgoings

7. The tenant shall (subject to the next following condition) pay rent up to date when the conveyance is completed (whether on the completion date or subsequently) and shall as from that date pay all outgoings; and any current rent and all rates and other outgoings shall, if

necessary, be apportioned as on that date (the date itself being apportioned to the landlord) and the balance be paid by or allowed to the tenant.

Election for interest in lieu of rent

8.—(1) If from any cause whatsoever (save as hereinafter mentioned) completion is delayed beyond the completion date, the rent shall continue to be payable under the tenancy until actual completion unless the landlord by notice in writing given to the tenant elects to receive interest on the price payable for the property in lieu of rent, in which event in lieu of the rent payable under the tenancy, the price payable (or if a deposit has been paid the balance thereof) shall bear interest at a rate per annum of 2 per cent. above the bank rate from time to time in force as from the giving of the notice to the tenant until actual completion.

Provided that, unless the delay in completion is attributable solely to the tenant's own act or default, the tenant may—

(*a*) at his own risk, deposit the price payable or, where a deposit has been paid, the balance thereof, at any bank in England or Wales, and

(*b*) forthwith give to the landlord or his solicitor notice in writing of the deposit,

and in that case the landlord shall (unless and until there is further delay in completion which is attributable solely to the tenant's own act or default) be bound to accept the interest, if any, allowed thereon, as from the date of such deposit, instead of the interest accruing after such date which would otherwise be payable to him under the foregoing provisions of this condition.

(2) No interest under paragraph (1) of this condition shall become payable by a tenant if, and so long as, delay in completion is attributable to any act or default of the landlord or his mortgagee or Settled Land Act trustees.

Preparation of conveyance

9.—(1) The conveyance shall be prepared by the tenant.

(2) A draft of the conveyance shall be delivered at the office of the landlord's solicitor at least 14 days before the date fixed for completion in accordance with condition 6 and the engrossment of the conveyance for execution by the landlord and other parties, if any, shall be delivered at that office a reasonable time before the date of completion.

(3) Where the conveyance is to contain restrictive covenants and the tenant intends contemporaneously with the conveyance to execute a mortgage or convey any interest in the property to a third party, he shall inform the landlord of his intention and, if necessary, allow the landlord time to give a priority notice for the registration of the amended covenants at least 14 days before the conveyance is completed.

(4) Where a conveyance is to contain any covenant by the tenant or any grant or reservation of rights affecting other property of the landlord, the tenant shall, if the landlord so requires, execute and hand over to the landlord on completion as many duplicates of the conveyance as the landlord may reasonably require and the duplicates shall be prepared and engrossed by the tenant, and where any duplicate is executed the tenant shall, if so required by the landlord, produce the original duly stamped so as to enable the stamp on the duplicate to be denoted.

Failure to comply with obligations

10.—(1) If either the landlord or the tenant shall neglect or fail to perform any of his obligations arising from the tenant's notice or arising out of any of these conditions, then the other party may give to the party in default at least 2 months' notice in writing referring to this condition, specifying the default and requiring him to make it good before the expiration of the notice.

(2) If the tenant does not comply with such a notice given by the landlord then, without prejudice to any other rights or remedies available to the landlord under the Act or otherwise,

(*a*) the landlord and tenant shall thereupon be discharged from the further performance of their obligations, other than the tenant's obligation to pay the landlord's costs, and

(*b*) the deposit money, if any, shall be forfeited to the landlord,

but if the landlord recovers any sums in the exercise of any remedy he shall give credit for the deposit against any sums so recovered.

(3) If the landlord does not comply with such a notice given by the tenant, then the tenant may require the deposit money, if any, to be returned to him forthwith and shall be discharged from the obligation to pay the landlord's reasonable costs imposed by section 9 of the Act, and thereupon the landlord and the tenant shall be discharged from the further performance of their obligations, but without prejudice to any other rights or remedies available to the tenant under the Act or otherwise.

Cancellation of land charges etc.

11. Where under section 5(5) of the Act a tenant's notice has been registered as a land charge or a notice or caution in respect thereof has been registered and either the tenant gives notice of withdrawal under section 9(3) or section 19(4) of the Act or the landlord is otherwise discharged from the obligations arising out of the notice, the tenant shall at the request of the landlord forthwith at his own cost procure the cancellation of the registration.

Notices

12. Any notice to be given to any person in accordance with these conditions shall be deemed to be effectively given if served personally on that person, or left at his last known place of residence, or sent by post to him or his solicitor or other duly authorised agent at his last known address.

Extension of time limits

13.—(1) These conditions shall have effect as if any period of time for the performance of any act or compliance with any notice (except a notice given under condition 10) by the landlord were twice the length of the period thereby laid down, where a person acting as reversioner under the provisions of Schedule 1 to the Act so requires by notice in writing given to the tenant at any time before the expiration of that period.

(2) Any period when proceedings are pending in any court or tribunal with reference to any matter arising in giving effect to a tenant's notice shall be disregarded in computing any period of time laid down by these conditions or any notice served thereunder.

(3) Any period of time laid down by these conditions or any notice served thereunder shall be extended for such further period as may be reasonable in all the circumstances if any party required to do any act within that period dies or becomes incapable of managing his affairs before the expiration of that period.

22–06

Part 2

Extension

Evidence of tenant's right to have an extended lease

1. At any time after receipt of the tenant's notice the landlord may, by notice in writing given to the tenant, require him to deduce his title to the tenancy and to furnish a statutory declaration as to the particulars of occupation of the property on which the tenant relies in the tenant's notice; and the tenant shall within 21 days of the giving of the landlord's notice comply with the requirement.

Terms of new tenancy

2.—(1) Where—

(*a*) a tenant has received no notice in reply to his tenant's notice within 2 months of giving it, or

(*b*) a tenant has

(i) received a notice in reply stating that his right to have an extended lease is admitted, or

(ii) has received a notice in reply that his right is disputed but has established that right by agreement or an order of the court,

and, in either case, the property to be leased has been established by agreement or an order of the court,

then the tenant may, by notice in writing given to the landlord, require him within 4 weeks to state what modifications in the terms of the existing tenancy, and what further provisions, other than as to payment of rent, are to be made by the terms of the new tenancy in accordance with section 15 of the Act.

(2) Where the requirements of paragraph (1)(*b*) of this condition are satisfied the landlord may, by notice in writing given to the tenant, require him within four weeks to state what modifications in the terms of the existing tenancy and what further provisions other than as to payment of rent are to be made by the terms of the new tenancy, in accordance with section 15 of the Act.

(3) A notice given under this condition shall contain a statement as to the modifications in the terms of the existing tenancy and the further provisions to be made by the terms of the new tenancy, required by the person giving the notice.

(4) If either party does not comply with a notice given under this condition within the time specified or, where no such notice has been given, does not communicate to the other a statement of the modifications and provisions he requires to be made when or before serving a notice under this condition, he shall be deemed to require the new tenancy to be on the same terms as the existing tenancy and not to require any further provisions (other than as to payment of rent) to be made by the terms of the new tenancy in accordance with section 15 of the Act.

Preparation of lease

3.—(1) Within eight weeks after the giving of a notice by either party under condition 2, a draft of the lease shall be submitted by the landlord to the tenant for approval, and the tenant shall approve the draft in writing with or without amendments within 21 days thereafter.

(2) If the tenant does not approve the draft with any amendment required by him within the time laid down by this condition, he shall be deemed to have approved it in the form submitted by the landlord.

(3) The lease and as many counterparts as the landlord may reasonably require shall be prepared by the landlord and the counterpart or counterparts shall be delivered to the tenant for execution a reasonable time before the completion date, and on completion (whether on the completion date or subsequently) the tenant shall deliver the counterpart or counterparts of the lease, duly executed, to the landlord and the landlord shall deliver the lease, duly executed, to the tenant.

Completion

4.—(1) After the expiration of the time for approval of the draft lease by the tenant either the landlord or the tenant may give the other notice in writing requiring him to complete the grant of the lease, and thereupon the completion date shall be the first working day after the expiration of 4 weeks from the giving of the notice.

(2) Completion shall take place at the office of the landlord's solicitor.

Failure to comply with obligations

5.—(1) If either the landlord or the tenant shall neglect or fail to perform any of his obligations arising from the tenant's notice or arising out of any of these conditions, then the other party may give to the party in default at least 2 months' notice in writing referring to this condition, specifying the default and requiring him to make it good before the expiration of the notice.

(2) If the tenant does not comply with such a notice given by the landlord, the landlord and the tenant shall be discharged from the further performance of their obligations, other than the tenant's obligation to pay the landlord's costs, but without prejudice to any other rights or remedies available to the landlord under the Act or otherwise.

(3) If the landlord does not comply with such a notice given by the tenant, the tenant shall be discharged from the obligation to pay the landlord's reasonable costs imposed by section 14 of the Act, and thereupon the landlord and the tenant shall be discharged from the further performance of their obligations, but without prejudice to any other rights or remedies available to the tenant under the Act or otherwise.

Cancellation of land charges etc.

6. Where under section 5(5) of the Act a tenant's notice has been registered as a land charge or a notice or caution in respect thereof has been registered and the landlord is discharged

from the obligations arising out of the notice, the tenant shall at the request of the landlord forthwith at his own cost procure the cancellation of the registration.

Notices

7. Any notice to be given to any person in accordance with these conditions shall be deemed to be effectively given if served personally on that person, or left at his last known place of residence, or sent by post to him or his solicitor or other duly authorised agent at his last known address.

Extension of time limits

8.—(1) These conditions shall have effect as if any period of time for the performance of any act or compliance with any notice (except a notice given under condition 5) by the landlord were twice the length of the period thereby laid down, where a person acting as reversioner under the provisions of Schedule 1 to the Act so requires by notice in writing to the tenant at any time before the expiration of that period.

(2) Any period when proceedings are pending in any court or tribunal with reference to any matter arising in giving effect to a tenant's notice shall be disregarded in computing any period of time laid down by these conditions or any notice served thereunder.

(3) Any period of time laid down by these conditions or any notice served thereunder shall be extended for such further period as may be reasonable in all the circumstances if any party required to do any act within that period dies or becomes incapable of managing his affairs before the expiration of that period.

Lands Tribunal Rules 1975

(S.I. 1975 No. 299)

Dated February 28, 1975, made by the Lord Chancellor, in exercise of the powers conferred on him by section 3 of the Lands Tribunal Act 1949 and section 28(6) of the Law of Property Act 1969, after consultation with the Council on Tribunals in accordance with section 10 of the Tribunals and Inquiries Act 1971, and with the approval of the Treasury in regard to fees.

Preliminary

Citation and commencement

22–07 **1.** These Rules may be cited as the Lands Tribunal Rules 1975 and shall come into operation on 1st April 1975.

Interpretation

2.—(1) The Interpretation Act 1889 shall apply to the interpretation of these Rules as it applies to the interpretation of an Act of Parliament.

(2) In these Rules, unless the context otherwise requires—

"the Act" means the Lands Tribunal Act 1949;

"the Act of 1961" means the Land Compensation Act 1961;

"appeal against a determination" means an appeal against a

determination of any question by any government department, authority or person from whom an appeal to which the determining authority is the respondent lies to the Lands Tribunal;

["date of decision" means the date endorsed on the document issued by the court, tribunal, authority or person which records the decision against which the appeal is lodged;]

"drainage rates appeal" means an appeal from the decision of a local valuation court in relation to the value of land for the purpose of drainage rates;

"hereditament" includes a hereditament for the purpose of drainage rates;

"net annual value" means the net annual value of the hereditament to which an appeal relates as shown in the valuation list, or, if that value is not shown in the valuation list, the rateable value so shown;

"the office" means the office for the time being of the Lands Tribunal;

"the President" means the President of the Lands Tribunal, or the member appointed under section 2(3) of the Act to act for the time being as deputy for the President;

"proceedings" means proceedings before the Lands Tribunal;

"rating appeal" means an appeal from the decision of a local valuation court in relation to the general rate;

"reference" has the meaning assigned to it by rule 15;

"the registrar" means the registrar of the Lands Tribunal or, as respects any powers or functions of the registrar, any officer of the Lands Tribunal authorised by the Lord Chancellor to exercise those powers or functions;

"the Tribunal" means the member or members of the Lands Tribunal selected under section 3(2) of the Act to deal with a case;

"valuation officer" has the meaning assigned to it by section 115(1) of the General Rate Act 1967;

"valuation proceedings" means proceedings before a local valuation court.

[(2A) In these Rules any reference to the hearing of any proceedings includes, unless the context otherwise requires, the determination of proceedings without an oral hearing.]

AMENDMENT

The words in square brackets in para. (2) were inserted by S.I. 1981 No. 600. **22–08**
Rule 2A was added by S.I. 1977 No. 1820.

• • • • • •

Statement of case and exchange of valuations

11.—(1) Where notice of intention to appear has been given and the **22–09**

appeal is on a point of law or the net annual value of the hereditament to which the appeal relates exceeds £1,250—

(i) within 28 days after the time limited by rule 10 for giving the notice, the appellant shall send to the registrar and to each party by whom notice has been given a statement of his case, including the facts to be proved and any points of law on which he intends to rely at the hearing;

(ii) within 28 days after receiving the appellant's statement, every party who intends to appear in opposition to the appeal shall send to the registrar, the appellant and every other party to the appeal a reply stating his case, including the facts to be proved and any points of law upon which he intends to rely at the hearing:

Provided that nothing in this paragraph shall preclude any party from sending a statement of his case to the registrar.

(2) Every statement or reply sent to the registrar in accordance with paragraph (1) above shall be accompanied by—

(i) every valuation of the hereditament which it is proposed to put in evidence (including particulars and computations in support of the valuation), or a statement of the value or values which the parties have agreed to attribute to the hereditament in the event of the Tribunal allowing or dismissing the appeal, as the case may be, and

(ii) a description of any comparable hereditaments to which the party intends to refer at the hearing in support of his case,

together with sufficient copies of the documents for service upon every other party to the appeal; and the registrar shall, within 7 days after receiving all the documents required to be supplied under this paragraph, send to each party a copy of the documents supplied by the other parties.

(3) If at the hearing of the appeal any party seeks to rely upon any valuation or other document which appears to the Tribunal not to have been sent to the registrar in accordance with this rule [the Tribunal may] adjourn the hearing on such terms as to costs or otherwise as it thinks fit.

AMENDMENT

22–10 The words in square brackets in para. (3) were substituted by S.I. 1981 No. 105.

• • • • • •

Part III

Other Appeals

Notice of appeal

12. [(1) Any appeal to the Lands Tribunal other than one to which Part I or Part II applies may be instituted within 28 days from the date of the decision appealed against by sending to the registrar a written notice of appeal in Form 3 or 3A as may be appropriate together with a copy of the decision. The appellant shall at the same time inform the registrar of the names and addresses of the parties to the dispute in respect of which the decision was given and shall supply the registrar with sufficient copies of the notice of appeal for service upon each of those parties and upon the court, tribunal, authority or person from whose decision the appeal is brought.] **22–11**

(2) Upon receiving a notice of appeal, the registrar shall—

(i) enter particulars of the appeal in the Register of Appeals;

(ii) serve a copy of the notice upon every party to the dispute (other than the appellant) and upon the court, authority or person from whose decision the appeal is brought;

(iii) inform the appellant and every person upon whom a copy of the notice of appeal has been served of the number of the appeal entered in the Register, which shall thereafter constitute the title of the appeal;

(iv) inform the appellant of the date on which copies of the notice of appeal were served.

Amendment

Para. (1) was substituted by S.I. 1981 No. 600. **22–12**

Notice of intention to appear

13.—(1) Every party other than the appellant shall, if he intends to appear on the hearing of the appeal, give written notice of his intention, stating— **22–13**

(i) whether he intends to appear separately or jointly with some other person;

(ii) the grounds on which he intends to rely;

(iii) an address for service of notices and other documents upon him.

[(iv) Whether he does or does not propose to call an expert witness to give evidence.]

(2) The notice shall be given to the registrar and to the appellant within 21 days from the date of service of the copy of the notice of appeal.

AMENDMENT

22–14 Subpara. (1)(iv) was inserted by S.I. 1981 No. 600.

• • • • • •

PART VII

GENERAL PROCEDURE

Selection of members of Tribunal

22–15 **31.**—(1) The President may at any time substitute another member of the Lands Tribunal for a member previously selected by him as the Tribunal, or as a member of the Tribunal, to hear a case, and where members of the Lands Tribunal have been selected for a class or group of cases under the provisions of section 3(2) of the Act, the President may from time to time vary the members so selected.

(2) Where the President has appointed any member of the Lands Tribunal to be the chairman of any members selected as aforesaid, the chairman may exercise the like power of substituting one member for another previously selected as the Tribunal, or as a member of the Tribunal, to hear a case in that class or group of cases.

Sittings of Tribunal

22–16 **32.**—(1) The Tribunal shall sit at such places in England and Wales as the President may from time to time determine.

(2) The registrar shall send to each party to proceedings before the Tribunal a notice informing him of the place and date of the hearing which, unless the parties otherwise agree, shall not be earlier than 14 days after the date on which the notice is sent.

(3) Upon receiving notice of intention to appear from a person who is not already a party to the proceedings, the registrar shall send to that person a notice informing him of the place and date of the hearing.

(4) Any person to whom notice has been sent under paragraph (2) or (3) above may apply to the registrar in accordance with the provisions of rule 45 for an alteration of the place or date of the hearing.

[*Sittings of Tribunal*

22–17 **33.** The Tribunal shall sit in public unless it is determining an appeal, reference or application without a hearing in accordance with the provisions of Rule 33A or it is acting as an arbitrator under a reference by consent.

Contested proceedings without hearing

33A.—(1) Notwithstanding the provisions of rule 39 as to oral evidence and of rule 44, but subject to the provisions of paragraph (2) below, the Tribunal shall have power to determine any appeal, reference or application without an oral hearing and any party to any proceedings instituted under these Rules may apply to the registrar in accordance with the provisions of rule 45 for a direction that the Tribunal shall exercise this power. **22–18**

(2) An order shall not be made on an application under this rule in respect of any proceedings relating to the amount of compensation—

(i) which is payable in respect of the compulsory acquisition of land; or

(ii) which depends directly or indirectly on the value of any land

without the consent signed by or on behalf of the person who is claiming such compensation.

(3) After an order has been made that the Tribunal will determine certain proceedings without an oral hearing, the Tribunal may, of its own motion or on the application of any party to those proceedings require any party to the proceedings to furnish to the Tribunal such statements of case, or reply thereto, or further and better particulars thereof, as the Tribunal may specify.

(4) After an order has been made that the Tribunal will determine certain proceedings without an oral hearing, any party to those proceedings may submit in writing to the Tribunal any representations which he wishes the Tribunal to take into consideration.

(5) Any statements, replies or particulars required by virtue of paragraph (3) above, and any representations made by any party, and any document or other information required to be delivered by any party to any proceedings to which this rule applies in accordance with the provisions of rule 40, shall be sent to the registrar, together with sufficient copies of the same for all the other parties to the proceedings, within 28 days of the order or requirement (as the case may be).

(6) The registrar shall, within 7 days of receiving by virtue of this rule any statements, replies, particulars, representations, document or other information, send to every other party to the proceedings a copy of the same.

(7) If, after having received a copy of any statement, replies, particulars, representations, document or information under paragraph (6) above, any party to any proceedings wishes to make any representations to the Tribunal he may submit the same in writing to the registrar within 28 days of the receipt by him of the said copy and the provisions of paragraph (5) and (6) above shall apply to such representations; but no party to any proceedings shall make any representations on more than

one occasion in those proceedings except by the leave of the Tribunal or the registrar.

(8) If any party to any proceedings to which this rule applies intends to rely upon the evidence of an expert witness, then the provisions of rule 42 shall apply as if references in that rule to the calling of witnesses and the hearing of evidence were references to representations.

(9) The Tribunal may at any time and for any reason order that proceedings which it was in the process of deciding without an oral hearing shall be heard and may thereupon give directions for the disposal of those proceedings in accordance with these rules.

(10)(*a*)(i) If an application under paragraph (1) above is made in any proceedings before a notice of intention to appear has been given in accordance with rule 6, 10 or 13 or, such notice having been given in accordance with rule 10 before any statement of case or reply has been sent to the registrar in accordance with rule 11, then the time limits specified in rules 10 and 11 respectively shall run from the date upon which an order is made in accordance with this rule that those proceedings shall be heard.

(ii) Where notice of intention to appear is given in accordance with rule 6, 10 or 13 in any proceedings in respect of which an application is made under paragraph (1) above, whether such notice is given before or after such application is made, that notice shall be of no effect as regards appearance unless an order is made in accordance with this rule that the proceedings shall be heard, but the notice shall otherwise be effective according to its tenor subject, however, to the provisions of this rule; and save as aforesaid rule 10 shall not apply to any proceedings to which this rule applies.

(iii) Where any of these provisions of rule 11 have been complied with in proceedings in respect of which an order is made under this rule that those proceedings will be determined without an oral hearing and before that order is made, the statement of case or reply and accompanying documents shall be treated as representations made in accordance with the provisions of this rule; and save as aforesaid rule 11 shall not apply to any proceedings to which this rule applies.

(*b*) Rules 52 and 53 shall not apply to any proceedings to which this rule applies.]

AMENDMENT

22–19 Rules 33 and 33A were substituted and inserted by S.I. 1977 No. 1820.

View of land

22–20 **34.**—(1) Subject to the provisions of paragraph (2) below, the Tribunal may inspect the land or hereditament which is the subject of the proceedings and may, if it thinks fit, enter on the land or hereditament for that purpose.

(2) When the Tribunal intends to enter on any premises in pursuance of paragraph (1) above, it shall give notice to the parties of that intention and the parties shall be entitled to attend the inspection.

(3) The provisions of this rule shall apply, so far as practicable, to any comparable land or hereditament to which the attention of the Tribunal is directed as they apply to the land or hereditament which is the subject of the proceedings.

Assessors

35.—(1) If it appears to the President that any case coming before the 22–21
Tribunal calls for special knowledge and that it would be desirable for the Tribunal to [be assisted by] assessors, he may direct that the Tribunal shall hear [or determine] the case with the aid of an assessor or assessors appointed by him after any consultations he may think fit.

(2) The remuneration to be paid to any assessor appointed under this rule shall be such as the President may, with the approval of the Minister for the Civil Service, determine.

AMENDMENTS

The words in square brackets in para. (1) were substituted by S.I. 1977 No. 1820. 22–22

Proceedings to be consolidated or heard together

36.—(1) Where more than one notice of appeal has been given in 22–23
respect of the same land or hereditament, an application to the registrar in accordance with the provisions of rule 45 for an order that the appeals be consolidated may be made by any party to the appeals.

(2) Where two or more notices of appeal have been given in respect of different lands or hereditaments raising the same issues or where two or more notices of reference have been given in respect of several interests in the same subject in dispute, an application may be made by any party to the proceedings that the appeals, or as the case may be the references, be heard together.

(3) Where any such notices of appeal or notices of reference as are referred to in paragraph (1) or (2) above have been given, the President or the Tribunal may, without any application in that behalf, order that the appeals or references be consolidated or heard together.

(4) An order may be made with respect to some only of the matters to which the notices of appeal or notices of reference relate.

Power to select test case in appeals from local valuation courts

37. Where two or more appeals against the decision of a local valuation 22–24 court appear to the President to involve the same issues, he may, with the written consent of all parties to the appeals, direct that one appeal, to be selected by him, shall be heard in the first instance as a test case and that the parties to each appeal shall, without prejudice to their right to require the Tribunal to state a case for the decision of the Court of Appeal, be bound by the decision of the Tribunal on the appeal so selected.

Application of Arbitration Act 1950

22–25 **38.** Sections 12, 14, 17, 18(5), 20 (subject to any enactment which prescribes a rate of interest) and 26 of the Arbitration Act 1950 shall apply to all proceedings as they apply to an arbitration unless a contrary intention is expressed in the arbitration agreement, and, where the Tribunal is acting as arbitrator under a reference by consent, sections 1, 2, 3, 4(1), 5, 18(3) and (4), 24(2) and (3) and 27 of the Arbitration Act 1950 shall also apply.

Evidence

22–26 **39.**—(1) Evidence before the Tribunal may be given orally or, if the parties to the proceedings consent or the President or the Tribunal so orders, by affidavit, but the Tribunal may at any stage of the proceedings make an order requiring the personal attendance of any deponent for examination and cross-examination.

(2) The provisions of paragraphs (2) to (6) of rule 45 shall apply to an application to the President for leave to give evidence by affidavit, with the substitution of references to the President for references to the registrar.

(3) Nothing in the Civil Evidence Act 1972, or in rules of court made under it, shall prevent expert evidence from being adduced before the Tribunal by any party notwithstanding that no application has been made to the Tribunal for a direction as to the disclosure of that evidence to any other party to the proceedings.

[*Power to order discovery, etc.*

22–27 **40.**—(1) The Tribunal or, subject to any direction given by the Tribunal, the registrar may on the application of any party to the proceedings or of its or his own motion order any party:

(*a*) to deliver to the registrar any document or other information which the Tribunal may require and which it is in the power of the party to deliver;

(*b*) to afford to every other party to the proceedings an opportunity to inspect those documents (or copies of them) and to take copies;

(*c*) to deliver to the registrar an affidavit or make a list stating whether any document or class of document specified or described in the order or application is, or has at any time been in his possession, custody or power, and stating when he parted with it;

(*d*) to deliver to the registrar a statement in the form of a pleading setting out further and better particulars of the grounds on which he intends to rely and any relevant facts or contentions;

(*e*) to answer interrogatories on affidavit relating to any matter at issue between the applicant and the other party; or

(*f*) to deliver to the registrar a statement of agreed facts, facts in dispute and the issue or issues to be tried by the Tribunal:

Provided that nothing in this rule shall be deemed to require any information to be disclosed contrary to the public interest.

(2) Where an order is made under paragraph (1) above, in the case of proceedings, other than those to which rule 33A(5) applies, the Tribunal or the registrar, as the case may be, may give directions, as to the time within which any document is to be sent to the registrar (being at least 14 days from the date of the direction) and the parties to whom copies of the document are to be sent.

(3) The provisions of rule 45 shall apply to this rule as appropriate to applications and in relation to cases where the registrar acts of his own motion.]

AMENDMENT

This rule was substituted by S.I. 1981 No. 105. **22–28**

Failure to supply documents

41. If it appears to the Tribunal that any party to proceedings has failed **22–29**
to send a copy of any document required under these Rules to be sent to any other party or to the registrar, the Tribunal may direct that a copy of the document shall be sent as may be necessary and that the further hearing of the proceedings be adjourned, and may in any such case require the party at fault to pay any additional costs occasioned thereby.

Expert witnesses

42.—(1) This rule applies to any proceedings except appeals from **22–30**
decisions of local valuation courts under Part II and applications for certificates under Part VI.

(2) Not more than one expert witness on either side shall be heard unless otherwise ordered:

Provided that, where the proceedings include a claim for compensation in respect of minerals or disturbance of business, as well as in respect of land, one additional expert witness on either side on the value of the minerals or, as the case may be, on the damage suffered by reason of the disturbance may be heard.

(3) An application for leave to call more than one, or more than one additional, expert witness may be made to the registrar in accordance with the provisions of rule 45 or to the Tribunal at the hearing.

(4) Where more than one party intends to call an expert witness, every such party shall, within 28 days after being so requested by the registrar, send to the registrar a copy of each of the following documents relating to the evidence to be given by the expert witness, together with sufficient copies for service upon the other parties—

(i) every plan and valuation of the land or hereditament which is the subject of the proceedings (including particulars and computations in support of the valuation) which it is proposed to put in evidence;

(ii) either a statement of any prices, costs or other particulars and any plans relating to a property or properties other than that land or hereditament which are proposed to be given in evidence in support of the valuation, or a statement that no such prices, costs, particulars or plans will be relied upon.

(5) The registrar shall, within 7 days after receiving all the documents required to be supplied by the parties under paragraph (4) above, send to each party copies of the documents supplied by the other party.

(6) If an application for leave to call more than one, or more than one additional, expert witness is made at the hearing and is granted by the Tribunal, or if at the hearing any party seeks to rely upon any plans, valuations or particulars which appear to the Tribunal not to have been sent to the registrar in accordance with this rule, [the Tribunal may] adjourn the hearing on such terms as to costs or otherwise as it thinks fit.

AMENDMENT

22–31 The words in square brackets in para. (6) were substituted by S.I. 1981 No. 105.

Appellant limited to grounds of appeal

22–32 **43.** On the hearing of an appeal under Part I, II or III or of an application under Part V, the appellant or applicant shall not be entitled to rely upon any grounds not stated in his notice of appeal, statement of case or application unless the Tribunal thinks it just in all the circumstances, and on such terms as to costs or adjournment or otherwise as it may think fit, to allow such additional grounds to be put forward as may appear to the Tribunal to be material.

Right of audience

22–33 **44.** In any proceedings, a party may appear and be heard in person, by counsel or solicitor, or, on obtaining leave of the Tribunal (or of the President or the registrar in the case of an interlocutory application), by any other person.

Interlocutory applications

45.—(1) Except where these Rules otherwise provide, an application for directions of an interlocutory nature in connection with any proceedings shall, unless otherwise ordered by the President, be made to the registrar. **22–34**

(2) The application shall be made in writing and shall state the title of the proceedings and the grounds upon which the application is made.

(3) If the application is made with the consent of all parties it shall be accompanied by consents signed by or on behalf of the parties.

(4) If the application is not made with the consent of every party, then, before it is made, a copy shall be served on every other party and the application shall state that this has been done.

(5) A party who objects to the application may, within 7 days after service of a copy on him, send written notice of objection to the registrar and to the applicant, and before making an order on the application the registrar shall consider all the objections which he has received and, if any party wishes to appear before him, the registrar shall give him and every other party an opportunity to do so.

(6) In dealing with an application under this rule, the registrar shall have regard to the convenience of the parties and the desirability of limiting so far as practicable the costs of the proceedings and shall communicate his decision in writing to every party.

(7) The registrar may, and shall if so required by the applicant or by a party objecting to an application under this rule, refer the application to the President for decision.

(8) A party aggrieved by a decision of the registrar on an application under this rule may appeal to the President by giving notice in writing to the registrar and to every other party within 7 days after service on him of notice of the decision or within such further time as may be allowed by the registrar, but an appeal from a decision of the registrar shall not act as a stay of proceedings unless so ordered by the President.

(9) Where an application under this rule is made—

(i) as respects a case which has been included by the President in a class or group of cases under the provisions of section 3(2) of the Act, or

(ii) as respects a case for which a member or members of the Lands Tribunal has or have been selected,

the powers and duties of the President under this rule may be exercised and discharged in relation to the application by any member or members of the Lands Tribunal authorised by the President in that behalf.

[*Pre-trial review*

22–35 **45A.**—(1) The Tribunal and, subject to any direction given by the Tribunal, the registrar, may on the application of a party to the proceedings or of its or his own motion order a pre-trial review to be held on a day being not less than 14 days after the making of the order unless the parties to the proceedings agree otherwise and the registrar shall send to each party to the proceedings a notice informing him of the place and date of the pre-trial review.

(2) On the pre-trial review the Tribunal or the registrar shall give all such directions as appear necessary or desirable for securing the just, expeditious and economical disposal of the proceedings.

(3) The Tribunal or the registrar shall endeavour on the pre-trial review to secure that the parties make all such admissions and agreements as ought reasonably to be made by them in relation to the proceedings and may record in the order made on the review any admission or agreement so made or any refusal to make any admission or agreement.

(4) Where any party seeks a specific direction, he shall, so far as practicable, apply for such direction on the pre-trial review and shall give to the registrar and every other party notice of his intention to do so, and if an application which might have been made on the review is made subsequently the applicant shall pay the costs of and occasioned by the application, unless the Tribunal is of the opinion that there was sufficient reason for the application not having been made on the review.

(5) The provisions of rule 45 relating to interlocutory applications shall have effect as if the pre-trial review were the hearing of an interlocutory application and accordingly the Tribunal or the registrar may, on the review, exercise any of the powers exercisable on an interlocutory application and may do so of its or his own motion.

(6) If any party does not appear on the pre-trial review the Tribunal or the registrar, after giving the parties an opportunity to be heard, may make such order as may be appropriate for the purpose of expediting or disposing of the proceedings.]

AMENDMENT

22–36 This rule was inserted by S.I. 1981 No. 105.

Certificates of value

22–37 **46.** An application for a certificate of value under section 35 of the Act of 1961 shall be made in writing to the registrar, and the party by whom the application is made shall provide the registrar on his request with such information as may be required to enable the certificate to be given.

Administration of oaths

47. The registrar shall have power to administer oaths and take **22–38** affirmations for the purpose of affidavits to be used in proceedings.

Extension of time

48.—(1) Subject to the provisions of paragraph (2) below, the time **22–39** appointed by or under these Rules for doing any act or taking any steps in connection with any proceedings [. . .] may be extended, on an application to the registrar in accordance with the provisions of rule 45, upon such terms (if any) as the justice of the case may require and an extension may be ordered although the application is not made until after the expiration of the time appointed.

(2) The times appointed by rule 11(1) for sending a statement of case and reply and the time appointed by rule 42(4) for sending copies of documents to the registrar may, by consent of the parties and on written notification sent to the registrar and received by him before the expiration of the time appointed by these Rules or fixed by a previous extension by consent, be extended for a period not exceeding 2 months on each notification and 4 months in the aggregate.

AMENDMENT

The words omitted from para. (1) were repealed by S.I. 1981 No. 105. **22–40**

Preliminary point of law

49.—(1) The President may, on the application of any party to **22–41** proceedings, order any point of law which appears to be in issue in the proceedings to be disposed of at a preliminary hearing before a member or members of the Lands Tribunal selected by the President for that purpose and; if, in the opinion of the member or members, the decision on the point of law substantially disposes of the proceedings, he or they may order that the argument shall be treated as the hearing of the case or may make such other order as may be just.

(2) The provisions of paragraphs (2) to (6) of rule 45 shall apply to an application under this rule with the substitution of references to the President for references to the registrar.

Sealed offers

50.—(1) An unconditional offer of any sum, or of readiness to accept **22–42** any sum, as compensation shall not be disclosed to the Tribunal until it has decided the amount of compensation to be awarded to the party to or by whom the offer was made, but a copy of the offer enclosed in a sealed cover may be sent to the registrar or delivered to the Tribunal at the hearing by the party who made the offer and shall be opened by the Tribunal after it has decided the amount of the compensation.

(2) Where the proceedings relate to the price payable on the acquisition of a freehold property or the rent to be paid under an extended lease in accordance with the provisions of the Leasehold Reform Act 1967 and that price or rent is or has become the only issue in the proceedings, the provisions of paragraph (1) above shall apply to an unconditional offer of readiness to agree to a specified price or rent.

Withdrawal of appeal, dismissal of appeal etc., before hearing

22-43 **51.**—(1) An appeal, reference or application may be withdrawn by sending to the registrar a written notice of withdrawal signed by all parties to the proceedings or by their solicitors or agents.

(2) An appellant or applicant may, at any time before the hearing of the proceedings, apply to the President for an order to dismiss the proceedings, and the President may thereupon make such order as may be just.

(3) The provisions of paragraphs (2), (4), (5) and (6) of rule 45 shall apply to an application under paragraph (2) above with the substitution of references to the President for references to the registrar.

(4) Where any party has failed to pursue any proceedings with due diligence or has failed to comply with any of these Rules, the registrar may, after giving the parties an opportunity to be heard, make an order that the proceedings be heard by the Tribunal or make such other order as may be appropriate for the purpose of expediting or disposing of the proceedings.

(5) The provisions of rule 45(8) shall apply to any order made by the registrar under paragraph (4) above.

Procedure at hearing

22-44 **52.**—(1) Unless the Tribunal otherwise directs—

(i) of an appeal under Part I, II or III, the appellant shall begin;

(ii) on a reference under Part IV, a party claiming compensation or a party to whom any rent or rentcharge requiring to be apportioned is payable shall begin and, in any other case, the party by whom the proceedings were instituted shall begin;

(iii) on an application under Part V or VI, the applicant shall begin.

(2) Subject to the provisions of these Rules and to any direction given

by the President, the procedure at the hearing of any proceedings shall be such as the Tribunal may direct.

Default of appearance at hearing

53. If on an appeal under Part I, II or III or on an application under Part V the appellant or applicant does not appear at the time and place appointed for the hearing, the Tribunal may dismiss the appeal or application and, if any other party to those proceedings or any party to a reference under Part IV does not appear at the time and place appointed, the Tribunal may hear and determine the appeal, application or reference in his absence and may make such order as to costs as it thinks fit: **22–45**

Provided that, where proceedings have been dismissed or determined under this rule in the absence of a party, the Tribunal may, on an application made by that party within 7 days of the dismissal or determination, if it is satisfied that he had sufficient reason for his absence, set aside the dismissal or determination on such terms as to costs or otherwise as he thinks fit.

Decision of Tribunal

54.—(1) The decision of the Tribunal on an appeal, reference or application shall be given in writing, together with a statement of the Tribunal's reasons for its decision: **22–46**

Provided that the Tribunal may give its decision and its reasons orally in cases where it is satisfied that no injustice or inconvenience to the parties would be occasioned by its doing so.

(2) On an appeal against the decision of a local valuation court, the Tribunal shall—

(i) if the appeal is a rating appeal, give such directions with respect to the manner in which the hereditament in question is to be treated in the valuation list as appear to the Tribunal to be necessary to give effect to the contention of the appellant, if and so far as that contention appears to the Tribunal to be well founded;

(ii) if the appeal is a drainage rates appeal, quash the determination to which the appeal relates, alter the determination in such manner as the Tribunal thinks just or dismiss the appeal.

(3) Where an amount awarded or value determined by the Tribunal is dependent upon the decision of the Tribunal on a question of law which is in dispute in the proceedings, the Tribunal shall ascertain, and shall state in its decision, the alternative amount or value (if any) which it would have awarded or determined if it had decided otherwise on the question of law.

(4) The registrar shall send a copy of the decision (or, where the

decision was given orally, a statement of its effect) to every party who has appeared before the Tribunal, and—

(i) in the case of an appeal against the decision of a local valuation court, to the clerk of the local valuation panel from which that court was constituted and, if the appeal is a rating appeal, to the valuation officer;

(ii) in the case of an appeal under Part III, to the court, authority or person from whose decision the appeal was brought.

(5) If any directions are given by the Court of Appeal for the amendment of any decision of the Tribunal on which a case has been stated for the decision of the Court of Appeal, the amendments shall be made by the Tribunal accordingly and the registrar shall send copies of the amended decision to every person who was notified of the original decision in accordance with paragraph (4) above.

Consent orders

22–47 **55.** Where the parties to any proceedings have agreed upon the terms of any order to be made by the Tribunal, particulars of the terms, signed by all the parties or by their solicitors or agents, shall be sent to the registrar, and an order may be made by the Tribunal in accordance with those terms in the absence of the parties.

Costs

22–48 **56.**—(1) Except in cases to which the provisions of subsection (1), (2) or (3) of section 4 of the Act of 1961 apply, the costs of and incidental to any proceedings shall be in the discretion of the Tribunal.

[(1A) Without prejudice to paragraph (1) above, the registrar may make a recommendation to the Tribunal as to the award of costs in respect of any application or proceedings heard by him.

(1B) Any party dissatisfied with a recommendation of the registrar under paragraph (1A) above may, within 10 days of the recommendation, appeal to the Tribunal or, where no member of the same has been selected as respects the proceedings, to the President against the recommendation and the Tribunal or, as the case may be, the President may thereupon make such order as to the payment of costs as it or he thinks just, including an order as to the payment of the costs of the appeal.]

(2) If the Tribunal directs that the costs of a party to the proceedings shall be paid by any other party, the Tribunal may settle the amount of the costs by fixing a lump sum, or it may direct that the costs shall be taxed by the registrar on a scale specified by the Tribunal, being a scale of costs prescribed by the Rules of the Supreme Court or by the County Court Rules.

(3) Any party dissatisfied with a taxation of costs directed by the

Tribunal may, within 7 days of the taxation, serve on any other interested party and on the registrar objection in writing specifying the items objected to and the grounds of objection and applying for the taxation to be reviewed in respect of those items.

(4) Upon such application, the registrar shall review the taxation of the items objected to and shall state in writing the reasons for his decision thereon.

(5) Any party dissatisfied with a decision of the registrar under paragraph (4) above may, within 10 days of the decision, apply to the President to review the taxation, and the President may thereupon make such order as he thinks just, including an order as to the payment of the costs of the review, but otherwise the taxation shall be final in respect of all matters to which objection has not been taken.

AMENDMENTS

Paras. (1A) and (1B) were inserted by S.I. 1981 No. 105. **22–49**

Service of notices

57.—(1) Any notice or other document required or authorised to be served on any person for the purpose of these Rules shall be deemed to have been duly served by pre-paid post to that person at his ordinary address or to his address for service specified in any notice given under these Rules; and any notice or other document required or authorised to be sent to the registrar shall be sent to him at the office. **22–50**

(2) Any application or communication to be made to the President or to any member of the Lands Tribunal in respect of any case shall be addressed to the registrar at the office.

Change of address

58. A party to any proceedings may at any time by notice in writing to the registrar and to every other party to those proceedings change his address for service under these Rules. **22–51**

Substituted service

59. If any person to whom any notice or other document is required to be sent for the purpose of these Rules cannot be found, or has died and has no personal representative, or is out of the United Kingdom, or if for any other reason service upon him cannot be readily effected in accordance with these Rules, the President or the Tribunal may dispense with service upon that person or may make an order for substituted service upon such other person or in such other form (whether by advertisement in a newspaper or otherwise) as the President or the Tribunal may think fit. **22–52**

Failure to comply with Rules

22–53 **60.** Any failure on the part of any person to comply with the provisions of these Rules shall not render the proceedings or anything done in pursuance thereof invalid, unless the President or the Tribunal so directs.

Fees

22–54 **61.**—(1) The fees to be taken in respect of proceedings shall be those specified in Schedule 2.

(2) Fees shall be paid by cheque or postal order, drawn in favour of Her Majesty's Paymaster-General, or otherwise in cash, and in accordance with the directions contained in Schedule 2.

(3) The hearing fee shall, unless the Tribunal otherwise directs, be payable by the party by whom the proceedings were instituted (without prejudice to his right to recover the amount of the fee from any other party by virtue of any order as to costs) on receipt of notification from the registrar.

Transitional provisions, repeals, etc.

22–55 **62.**—(1) These Rules shall apply to proceedings commenced before the date on which they come into operation as well as to proceedings commenced on or after that date.

(2) The Lands Tribunal Rules 1963, the Lands Tribunal (Amendment) Rules 1968, the Lands Tribunal (Amendment) Rules 1970 and the Lands Tribunal (Amendment No. 2) Rules 1970 are hereby revoked.

Rule 2(4)

SCHEDULE 1

22–56

FORMS

. . . . . .

[FORM 3A

Rule 12(1)

Notice of Appeal Against Decision of Leasehold Valuation Tribunal

To:—The Registrar,
Lands Tribunal

Type of hereditament and address to be copied from decision of Leasehold Valuation Tribunal.

Description ....
....
....
....
....
....

I/We ....
of .... Here state usual address.
hereby give notice of appeal against the decision in respect of the property described above as a leasehold valuation tribunal which sat at ....

....on the .... Here insert places and date of decision.
....19....

The grounds of appeal are that .... Here state briefly the grounds of appeal and the amount of the price or revised rent or compansation claimed to be appropriate.
....
....
....
....

I/We do not propose to call an expert witness to give evidence in support of the valuations on which I/we shall rely at the hearing of the appeal. Strike out words not applicable.

All communications regarding the appeal should be addressed to me/us at the address above [*or* to my/our solicitor/agent .... Strike out words not applicable.

....

of ....

....

Signed ....

Dated ....

Note:— The following documents **must** *be sent to the registrar with the notice of appeal—*

(*1*) a copy of the decision of the leasehold valuation tribunal appealed against;

(*2*) a list of the names and addresses of every party to the leasehold valuation tribunal proceedings; and

(*3*) sufficient copies of the notice of appeal for service by the registrar on the leasehold valuation tribunal and every party referred to in paragraph (2) above.]

AMENDMENT

This form was inserted by S.I. 1981 No. 600. 22–57

• • • • • •

Rent Assessment Committee (England and Wales) (Leasehold Valuation Tribunal) Regulations 1981

(S.I. 1981 No. 271)

Dated February 24, 1981, *made by the Secretary of State for the Environment, as respects England, and the Secretary of State for Wales, as respects Wales in exercise of their powers under section* 74 *of the Rent Act* 1977 *and under section* 21(4A) *of the Leasehold Reform Act* 1967 *and of all other powers enabling them in that behalf, and after consultation with the Council on Tribunals, hereby make the following regulations:*

Citation and commencement

22–58 **1.** These regulations may be cited as the Rent Assessment Committee (England and Wales) (Leasehold Valuation Tribunal) Regulations 1981 and shall come into operation on 31st March 1981.

Interpretation

22–59 **2.** In these regulations, unless the context otherwise requires—

"application" means an application to a leasehold valuation tribunal under section 21(1) of the Leasehold Reform Act 1967, and

"tribunal" means a leasehold valuation tribunal.

Applications

22–60 **3.** The form of application prescribed under section 21(4A) of the Leasehold Reform Act 1967 is as follows:

(*a*) in the case of application under section 21(1)(*a*) of the 1967 Act, form number 1 in the Schedule hereto,

(*b*) in the case of an application under section 21(1)(*b*) of the 1967 Act, form number 2 in the Schedule hereto, and

(*c*) in the case of an application under section 21(1)(*c*) of the 1967 Act, form number 3 in the Schedule hereto,

or, in each case, a form substantially to the like effect.

22–61 **4.** On receipt of an application, the tribunal shall send a copy of the application and of each of the documents which accompanied it to each person named in it as a respondent.

Hearings

5.—(1) A hearing shall be on such date, and at such time and place as the tribunal shall appoint. **22–62**

(2) Notice of such date, time and place shall be given by the tribunal to the parties to the proceedings not less than 14 days before the said date, and a copy of the notice shall be sent to any other person who is not already a party to the proceedings and gives notice to the tribunal of his intention to appear at the hearing.

(3) The notice referred to in paragraph (2) above shall contain a statement to the effect that an appeal to the Lands Tribunal from a decision of a tribunal may only be made by a person who appeared before the tribunal in proceedings to which he was a party.

(4) The tribunal may, where they consider it appropriate, arrange that a hearing in respect of one application shall be held together with the hearings in respect of one or more other applications.

(5) A hearing shall be in public unless, for special reasons, the tribunal decide otherwise, but nothing in these regulations shall prevent a member of the Council on Tribunals in that capacity from attending any hearing.

6. At a hearing— **22–63**

(*a*) the parties shall be heard in such order and, subject to the provisions of these regulations, the procedure shall be such as the tribunal shall determine;

(*b*) a party may call witnesses, give evidence on his own behalf and cross-examine any witnesses called by any other party; and

(*c*) a party may appear either in person or by a person authorised by him in that behalf whether or not that person is of counsel or a solicitor.

Non-appearance

7. If a party does not appear at a hearing, the tribunal, on being satisfied that the requirements of these regulations regarding the giving of notice of a hearing have been duly complied with, may proceed to deal with the application. **22–64**

Adjournment

8.—(1) The tribunal at their discretion may of their own motion, or at the request of the parties, or one of them, at any time and from time to time, postpone or adjourn a hearing, but they shall not do so at the request of one party only unless, having regard to the grounds on which and the time at which such request is made and to the convenience of the parties, they deem it reasonable to do so. **22–65**

(2) The tribunal shall give to the parties such notice of any postponed or adjourned hearing as is reasonable in the circumstances.

Documents

22–66 **9.**—(1) Before the date of a hearing, the tribunal shall take all reasonable steps to ensure that there is supplied to each of the parties—

(*a*) a copy of, or sufficient extracts from or particulars of, any document relevant to the application which has been received from a party (other than a document which is in the possession of such a party or of which he has previously been supplied with a copy); and

(*b*) a copy of any document which embodies the results of any enquiries made by or for the tribunal for the purposes of the application.

(2) Where at a hearing—

(i) any document relevant to the application is not in the possession of a party present at that hearing; and

(ii) that party has not been supplied with a copy of, or sufficient extracts from or particulars of, that document;

then unless—

(*a*) that party consents to the continuation of the hearing; or

(*b*) the tribunal consider that that party has sufficient opportunity to deal with that document without any adjournment of the hearing;

the tribunal shall adjourn the hearing for a period which they consider will afford that party a sufficient opportunity for dealing with that document.

Inspections

22–67 **10.**—(1) The tribunal may, and shall at the request of any of the parties (subject in either case to any necessary consent being obtained), inspect the house and premises which are the subject of the application.

(2) An inspection may be made before, during or after the close of a hearing, as the tribunal may decide, and the tribunal shall give to the parties and their representatives an opportunity to attend.

(3) Notice of an inspection shall be given as though it were notice of a hearing, but the requirements for such notice may be dispensed with or relaxed in so far as the tribunal are satisfied that the parties have received sufficient notice.

(4) The provisions of this regulation shall apply, so far as is reasonable and practicable, to any comparable house or premises to which the attention of the tribunal is directed as they apply to the house and premises which are the subject of the application.

(5) Where an inspection is made after the close of a hearing, the

tribunal shall, if they consider it expedient to do so on account of any matter arising from the inspection, reopen the hearing; and if the hearing is to be reopened paragraph (2) of regulation 5 of these regulations shall apply as it applied to the original hearing, save in so far as its requirements may be dispensed with or relaxed with the consent of the parties.

Decisions

11.—(1) The decision of a tribunal shall be recorded in a document signed by the chairman of the tribunal (or in the event of his absence or incapacity, by another member of the tribunal) which shall contain the reasons for the decision but shall contain no reference to the decision being by a majority (if that be the case) or to any opinion of a minority. **22–68**

(2) The chairman (or in the event of his absence or incapacity, another member of the tribunal) shall have power, by certificate under his hand, to correct any clerical mistakes in the said document or any errors arising in it from an accidental slip or omission.

(3) A copy of the said document and of any such correction shall be sent by the tribunal to each party.

Provision of information

12. Where, under paragraph 7 of Schedule 22 to the Housing Act 1980 a tribunal by notice in writing require the giving of such information as the tribunal may reasonably require, the notice shall contain a statement to the effect that any person who fails without reasonable cause to comply with the notice is liable on summary conviction to a fine not exceeding £200. **22–69**

Giving of notice

13. Where any notice or other written matter is required under the provisions of these regulations to be given or supplied by the tribunal it shall be sufficient compliance with these regulations if such notice or other matter is sent by post in pre-paid letter and addressed to the party for whom it is intended at his usual or last known address, or if that party has appointed an agent to act on his behalf, to that agent at the address of the agent supplied to the tribunal. **22–70**

22–71

SCHEDULE

FORM NO. 1

LEASEHOLD REFORM ACT 1967

APPLICATION FOR DETERMINATION BY LEASEHOLD VALUATION TRIBUNAL ON ACQUISITION OF FREEHOLD

I/We apply for the determination by a Leasehold Valuation Tribunal of the price payable under section 9 of the Leasehold Reform Act 1967 for the house and premises named in paragraph 1 below and submit the following particulars. The respondents to this application are the persons (other than myself/ourselves) named in paragraphs 2 to 5 of those particulars.

*[I/We also apply to the Leasehold Valuation Tribunal for the determination under section 21(2) of the 1967 Act of the matters described in paragraph 12 below rating to the house and premises.]

* Cross out this paragraph if it does not apply.

THE PARTICULARS

1. Address of house and premises ....

2. Name and address of landlord to whom rent is payable by the tenant ....

3. Name of tenant (and address if different from 1 above) ....

4. Is the landlord mentioned in (2) above the freehold owner of the premises Yes ☐ No ☐
   If NO, give the names and addresses of
   (*a*) the freeholder ....
   (*b*) any additional, intermediate landlords standing between the landlord mentioned in paragraph 2 and the freeholder ....

5. Is anyone, to the applicant's knowledge, entitled to the benefit of a charge on the freeholder's, or any other landlord's interest in the house and premises, such as a mortgagee (e.g. a building society?) Yes ☐ No ☐
   If YES, give names and addresses, if known ....

6. State the date on which notice was given by the tenant of his desire to acquire the freehold ....
   and enclose a copy of the notice.

7. Has the landlord given notice stating whether or not he admits the tenant's right to have the freehold? Yes ☐ No ☐
   If YES, give the date of the notice .... and enclose a copy of it.

8. Has the landlord informed the tenant of the price he is asking? Yes ☐ No ☐
   If YES, enclose a copy of the letter or notice from the landlord giving details of it.

9. Have any other formal notices been given following the notice by the tenant of his desire to have the freehold? Yes ☐ No ☐
   If YES, enclose copies of all the notices.

10. State the price which the applicant considers to be appropriate £.................................

11. Have the terms of the conveyance (other than the price) been agreed? Yes ☐ No ☐
   If YES, enclose details or a copy of a draft conveyance.

12. Is this also an application under section 21 (2) of the Leasehold Reform Act 1967:—
(*a*) to determine what provisions ought to be contained in the conveyance? Yes ☐ No ☐
If YES, give details on a separate sheet and enclose a copy of the existing lease.
(*b*) to apportion between the house and premises (or part of them) and other property, the rent payable under any tenancy? Yes ☐ No ☐
If YES, give details on a separate sheet.

---

13. (*a*) Has any application been made to a Court to determine any question relating to this matter? Yes ☐ No ☐
(*b*) If YES, has the Court made an Order? Yes ☐ No ☐
If YES, enclose a copy of the Order.

---

14. Is the applicant
(*a*) the owner of the freehold? Yes ☐ No ☐
(*b*) a landlord? Yes ☐ No ☐
(*c*) the tenant? Yes ☐ No ☐

Signed ....
[On behalf of ....]
If signed by an agent, given name and address of agent ....
....
Date ....

FORM NO. 2

LEASEHOLD REFORM ACT 1967

APPLICATION FOR DETERMINATION BY LEASEHOLD VALUATION TRIBUNAL OF THE RENT TO BE PAYABLE

I/We apply for the determination by a Leasehold Valuation Tribunal of the amount of the rent to be payable under section 15 (2) of the Leasehold Reform Act 1967 for the house and premises named in paragraph 1 below and submit the following particulars. The respondents to this application are the persons (other than myself/ourselves) named in paragraphs 2 to 5 of those particulars. 22–72

*[I/We also apply to the Leasehold Valuation Tribunal for the determination under section 21 (2) of the 1967 Act of the matters described in paragraph 11 below relating to the house and premises.]

* Cross out this paragraph if it does not apply.

THE PARTICULARS

---

1. Address of house and premises ....

---

2. Name and address of landlord to whom rent is payable by the tenant ....

---

3. Name of tenant (and address if different from 1 above) ....

---

4. Has a new tenancy, expiring 50 years after the original tenancy, already been granted for the house and premises? Yes ☐ No ☐

If YES, give the name and addresses of—
(*a*) the landlord named in the new lease ....
(*b*) any additional, intermediate landlords standing between the landlord named in the new lease and the tenant ....
Enclose a copy of the new lease and then GO TO QUESTION 10.

---

5. If a new tenancy has *not* yet been granted give the name and address of—
(*a*) the person who will grant the new lease ....
(*b*) any additional, intermediate landlords standing between that person and the tenant ....
and enclose a copy of the existing lease.

---

6. Have the terms (other than rent) for the new tenancy been agreed? Yes ☐ No ☐
If YES, enclose a copy.

---

7. Give the date of the notice by the tenant of his desire to have an extended lease ....
and enclose a copy of the notice.

---

8. Has the landlord given notice stating whether or not he admits the tenant's right to have an extended lease? Yes ☐ No ☐
If YES, give the date of the notice .... and enclose a copy of it.

---

9. Have any other formal notices been given following the notice by the tenant of his desire to have an extended lease? Yes ☐ No ☐
If YES, enclose copies of all the notices.

---

10. State the amount of rent the applicant considers appropriate—£..................................

---

11. Is this also an application under section 21 (2) of the Leasehold Reform Act 1967:—
(*a*) to determine what provisions ought to be contained in the lease granting the new tenancy? Yes ☐ No ☐
If YES, give details on a separate sheet.
(*b*) to apportion between the house premises (or part of them) and other property, the rent payable under any tenancy? Yes ☐ No ☐
If YES, give details on a separate sheet.

---

12. (*a*) Has any application been made to a Court to determine any question relating to this matter? Yes ☐ No ☐
(*b*) If YES, has the Court made an Order Yes ☐ No ☐
If YES, enclose a copy of the Order.

---

13. Is the applicant—
(*a*) the owner of the freehold? Yes ☐ No ☐
(*b*) a landlord? Yes ☐ No ☐
(*c*) the tenant? Yes ☐ No ☐

Signed ....
[On behalf of ....
If signed by an agent, give name and address of agent ....
....
Date ....

FORM NO. 3

LEASEHOLD REFORM ACT 1967

APPLICATION FOR DETERMINATION BY LEASEHOLD VALUATION TRIBUNAL OF COMPENSATION PAYABLE TO A TENANT

I/We apply for the determination by a Leasehold Valuation Tribunal of the amount of the compensation payable under section 17 or 18 of the Leasehold Reform Act 1967 for the loss of the house and premises named in paragraph 1 below and submit the following particulars. The respondents to this application are the persons (other than myself/ourselves) named in paragraphs 2 to 4 of those particulars. 22–73

*[I/We also apply to the Leasehold Valuation Tribunal for the determination under section 21 (2) of the 1967 Act of the amount of a sub-tenant's share under Schedule 2 to the Act of the compensation payable to the tenant.]

* Cross out this paragraph if it does not apply.

THE PARTICULARS

1. Address of house and premises ....

2. Name and address of landlord by whom compensation is payable ....

3. Name of tenant (and address of different from 1 above) ....

4. It is also an application under section 21 (2) of the Leasehold Reform Act 1967 to determine the amount of a sub-tenant's share under Schedule 2 to the Act of the compensation payable to the tenant? Yes ☐ No ☐

If YES, give the name and address of the sub-tenant ....

5. Give details on a separate sheet of the circumstances under which the claim for compensation arises and enclose copies of—

(*a*) the lease and of any agreements for sub-tenancies, and

(*b*) all other relevant documents, applications to the Court and Court Orders, or notices.

6. State the amount of compensation which the applicant considers appropriate £..................

7. Is the applicant—

(*a*) the landlord? Yes ☐ No ☐

(*b*) the tenant? Yes ☐ No ☐

Signed ....

[On behalf of ....]

[If signed by an agent, give name and address of agent ....

Date ....

County Court Rules 1981

(S.I. 1981 No. 1687)

. . . . . .

Order 3, rule 4

Originating applications

22–74 **4.**—(1) Any proceedings authorised to be brought in a county court and not required by any Act or rule to be commenced otherwise shall be brought by originating application.

(2) An originating application shall be in writing and shall state—

(a) the order applied for and sufficient particulars to show the grounds on which the applicant claims to be entitled to the order;

(b) the names and addresses of the persons (if any) intended to be served (in this rule called "respondents") or that no person is intended to be served, and

(c) the applicant's address for service.

(3) The applicant shall file—

(a) the originating application together with as many copies as there are respondents; and

(b) a request for the issue of the originating application.

(4) On the filing of the documents mentioned in paragraph (1) the proper officer shall—

(a) enter the originating application in the records of the court and fix the return day;

(b) prepare a notice to each respondent of the return day and annex to each such notice a copy of the application, and

(c) deliver a plaint note to the applicant.

(5) The return day shall be a day fixed for the hearing of the originating application or, if the court so directs, a day fixed for a pre-trial review.

(6) Rule 3(2)(d)(ii) of this Order and the provisions of Order 7 shall apply, with the necessary modifications, to the service of an originating application as if the notice of the return day were a fixed date summons.

. . . . . .

Order 49, rule 8

Leasehold Reform Act 1967

8.—(1) In this rule a section referred to by number means the section so numbered in the Leasehold Reform Act 1967 and "Schedule 2" means Schedule 2 to that Act. **22–75**

(2) Where a tenant of a house and premises desires to pay money into court pursuant to section 11(4) or section 13(1) or (3)—

(a) he shall file in the office of the appropriate court an affidavit stating—

(i) the reasons for the payment into court,

(ii) the house and premises to which the payment relates and the name and address of the landlord, and

(iii) so far as they are known to the tenant, the name and address of every person who is or may be interested in or entitled to the money;

(b) on the filing of the affidavit the tenant shall pay the money into court and the proper officer shall enter the matter in the records of the court and send notice of the payment to the landlord and to every person whose name and address are given in the affidavit pursuant to sub-paragraph (a)(iii);

(c) any subsequent payment into court by the landlord pursuant to section 11(4) shall be made to the credit of the same account as the payment into court by the tenant and sub-paragraphs (a) and (b) shall apply as if for the references to the tenant and the landlord there were substituted references to the landlord and the tenant respectively;

(d) the appropriate court for the purposes of sub-paragraph (a) shall be the court for the district in which the property is situated or, if the payment into court is made by reason of a notice under section 13(3), any other county court specified in the notice.

(3) Where the proceedings on an application are ordered to be transferred to a leasehold valuation tribunal under section 21(3), the proper officer shall—

(a) send notice of the transfer to all parties to the application and

(b) send to the leasehold valuation tribunal copies certified by the registrar of all entries in the records of the court relating to the application, together with the order of transfer and all documents filed in the proceedings.

(4) Where an application is made under section 17 or 18 for an order for possession of a house and premises the respondent shall—

(a) forthwith after being served with the application, serve on every person in occupation of the property or part of it under an immediate or derivative sub-tenancy, a notice informing him of the proceedings and of his right under paragraph 3(4) of Schedule 2 to appear and be heard in the proceedings with the leave of the court, and

(b) within 14 days after being served with the application, file an answer stating the grounds, if any, on which he intends to oppose the application and giving particulars of every such sub-tenancy.

• • • • • •

Housing (Exclusion of Shared Ownership Tenancies from the Leasehold Reform Act 1967) Regulations 1982

(S.I. 1982 No. 62)

Dated January 20, 1982, *the Secretary of State for the Environment, in relation to England, and the Secretary of State for Wales, in relation to Wales, in exercise of the powers conferred by section* 140 *of the Housing Act* 1980 *and of all other powers enabling them in that behalf, hereby make the following regulations:—*

Citation and commencement

22–76 **1.** These regulations may be cited as the Housing (Exclusion of Shared Ownership Tenancies from the Leasehold Reform Act 1967) Regulations 1982, and shall come into operation on 22nd February 1982.

Requirement for exclusion of tenancies from Leasehold Reform Act 1967

2. A lease granted by a registered housing association complies with these regulations for the purposes of section 140(4)(*b*) of the Housing Act 1980 if—

(i) it provides for the tenant to acquire the landlord's interest in the property, whether under an option to purchase or otherwise, for a consideration which is to be calculated in accordance with the terms of the lease and which is reasonable, having regard to the premium or premiums paid by the tenant under the lease; or

(ii) it is a lease for the elderly, as defined in regulation 3 below.

Interpretation

3. In regulation 2 above, "lease for the elderly" means a lease which—

(i) is a lease of one of a group of dwelling-houses which it is the practice of a registered housing association to let for occupation by persons of pensionable age, where a social service or special facilities are provided in close proximity to the group of dwelling-houses for the only or main purpose of assisting those persons;

(ii) does not provide for the tenant to acquire the interest of the landlord under an option to purchase;

(iii) provides for an absolute covenant by the tenant not to under let or part with possession of the property or any part thereof, nor to assign the same except—

(*a*) to the tenant's spouse if he is residing at the property at the date of the tenant's death, or

(*b*) to a member of the tenant's family or household, who was residing with him at the time of his death, where the grant of a tenancy in the property to that person would not infringe the objects of the landlord;

(iv) provides that, if during the term the tenant's affairs are made subject to the jurisdiction of the Court of Protection or if the tenant shall die, then the landlord shall be entitled to determine the term by giving to the tenant not less than six months' notice in writing; and

(v) provides that the tenant shall at any time be entitled to surrender the term by giving to the landlord not less than six months' notice in writing.

INDEX